Myth and Tragedy

in Ancient Greece

Myth and Tragedy

in Ancient Greece

Jean-Pierre Vernant

Pierre Vidal-Naquet

ZONE BOOKS · NEW YORK

1990

© 1988 Urzone, Inc.
ZONE BOOKS
1226 Prospect Avenue
Brooklyn, NY 11218

First Paperback Edition, Revised
Sixth Printing 2006

Chapters 1-7 originally published in France as *Mythe et
Tragédie en Grèce Ancienne* © 1972 by Librarie François
Maspero. Chapters 1-7 and 13 first published in the English
language by The Harvester Press Limited, Brighton,
England © 1981 by The Harvester Press Limited.

Chapters 8-17 originally published in France as *Mythe et
Tragédie en Grèce Ancienne Deux* © 1986 by Editions
La Découverte.

Printed in the United States of America.

Distributed by The MIT Press,
Cambridge, Massachusetts, and London, England

Library of Congress Cataloging-in-Publication Data

Vernant, Jean-Pierre.
   [Mythe et tragédie en Grèce ancienne. English]
   Myth and tragedy / Jean-Pierre Vernant and Pierre
Vidal Naquet; translated by Janet Lloyd.
     p.   cm.
   Translation of: Mythe et tragédie en Grèce ancienne
   Bibliography: p.
   Includes index.
   ISBN 978-0-942299-19-9 (0-942299-19-1)
   1. Greek drama (Tragedy) – History and criticism.
2. Mythology, Greek, in literature. I. Vidal-Naquet,
Pierre, 1930–. II. Title.
PA3131.V413   1988   87-34050
882'01–dc19   CIP

Contents

Preface to Volume I   7

Preface to Volume II   13

I   *The Historical Moment of Tragedy in Greece: Some of the Social and Psychological Conditions*   23

II   *Tensions and Ambiguities in Greek Tragedy*   29

III   *Intimations of the Will in Greek Tragedy*   49

IV   *Oedipus Without the Complex*   85

V   *Ambiguity and Reversal: On the Enigmatic Structure of* Oedipus Rex   113

VI   *Hunting and Sacrifice in Aeschylus'* Oresteia   141

VII   *Sophocles'* Philoctetes *and the Ephebeia*   161

VIII   *The God of Tragic Fiction*   181

IX   *Features of the Mask in Ancient Greece*   189

X   *The Lame Tyrant: From Oedipus to Periander*   2 0 7

XI   *The Tragic Subject: Historicity and Transhistoricity*   2 3 7

XII   *Aeschylus, the Past and the Present*   2 4 9

XIII   *The Shields of the Heroes*   2 7 3

XIV   *Oedipus in Athens*   3 0 1

XV   *Oedipus Between Two Cities: An Essay on* Oedipus at Colonus   3 2 9

XVI   *Oedipus in Vicenza and in Paris*   3 6 1

XVII   *The Masked Dionysus of Euripides'* Bacchae   3 8 1

Notes   4 1 5

Subject Index   5 0 7

Index of Textual References   5 2 3

Preface to Volume I*

This volume contains seven studies published in France and else-where. We have collected them together because they all belong to a research project on which we have been collaborating over the years and that owes its inspiration to the teaching of Louis Gernet.[1]

What exactly do we mean by *Myth and Tragedy*? Tragedies are not, of course, myths. It can on the contrary be claimed that the tragic genre only emerges at the end of the sixth century, at the moment when the language of myth ceases to have a hold on the political realities of the city. The tragic universe lies between two worlds, for at this date myth was seen as belonging both to a past age — but one still present in men's minds — and to the new values developed so rapidly by the city-state of Pisistratos, Cleisthenes, Themistocles, and Pericles. One of the original features of trag-edy, indeed the very mainspring of its action, is this dual relation-ship with myth. In the tragic conflict the hero, the king, and the tyrant certainly still appear committed to the heroic and mythical tradition, but the solution to the drama escapes them. It is never provided by the hero on his own; it always expresses the triumph of the collective values imposed by the new democratic city-state.

In these circumstances, what does the task of the analyst

Myth and Tragedy in Ancient Greece was originally published in France as two volumes. The first volume was comprised of chapters 1-7, and the second volume of chapters 8-17.

involve? Most of the studies collected in this book are the product of what is generally known as structural analysis. However, it would be quite mistaken to confuse this type of reading with the decoding of myths in the strict sense of that term. The methods of interpretation may be related but the purpose of the study is quite different. To be sure, the decoding of a myth first traces the articulations of the discourse — whether it be oral or written — but its fundamental purpose is to break down the mythological account so as to pick out the primary elements in it and then set these beside those to be found in other versions of the same myth or in different collections of legends. The story initially considered, far from being complete in itself or constituting a single whole, instead, in each of its episodes, opens out on to all the other texts that employ the same code system. And it is the keys to this system that must be discovered. In this way, for the student of myth, all myths, whether rich or poor, belong to the same level and are of equal value from a heuristic point of view. No single one has the right to be given preference over the others and the only reason for the interpreter to single it out is that, for reasons of convenience, he has chosen it as the model or reference point to be used in his inquiry.

Greek tragedies such as we have undertaken to study in these articles are quite different. They are written works, literary productions that were created at a particular time and in a particular place, and there is, strictly speaking, no parallel for any one of them. Sophocles' *Oedipus Rex* is not one version among others of the myth of Oedipus. The inquiry can only be fruitful if it takes into consideration, first and foremost, the meaning and intention of the drama that was acted in Athens in about 420 B.C. But what do we mean by meaning and intention? It goes without saying that our aim is not to discover what was going on in Sophocles' head as he wrote his play. The playwright left us no personal reflections nor any diary; had he done so they would have represented no more than supplementary sources of evidence that we should have had to submit to critical appraisal like any others. The *intention* we refer to is expressed through the work itself, in its structure, its internal organization, and we have no way of reaching back from the work to its author. Similarly, although fully aware of the profoundly historical character of the Greek tragedies, we do not seek to explore the historical background, in the narrow sense of the word, of each play. An admirable book has been written, retracing the history of Athens through the work of Euripides,[2] but it is extremely doubtful whether a similar undertaking could be justified for Aeschylus and Sophocles; such attempts that have been made in this direction do not seem to us to be convincing. It is certainly legitimate to believe that the epidemic described at the beginning of *Oedipus Rex* owes something to the plague Athens suffered in 430, but at the same time one may point out that Sophocles had read the *Iliad*, which also contains a description of an epidemic that threatened an entire community. All things considered, the illumination that such a method can shed upon a work does not amount to very much.

In fact, our analyses operate at very different levels. They stem both from the sociology of literature and from what one might call a historical anthropology. We do not claim to explain tragedy by reducing it to a number of social conditions. We attempt to grasp it in all its dimensions, as a phenomenon that is indissolubly social, aesthetic, and psychological. The problem does not consist in reducing one of these aspects to another but in understanding how they hinge together and combine to constitute a unique human achievement, a single invention to which there are three historical aspects: From the point of view of the institution of tragic competitions it can be seen as a social phenomenon; in that it represents a new literary genre it is an aesthetic creation; and in that it introduced the concepts of the tragic consciousness and tragic man it represents a psychological mutation. These are the three aspects that constitute a single phenomenon and they demand the same mode of explanation.

Our studies presuppose a constant tension between our modern concepts and the categories used in ancient tragedies. Can

Oedipus Rex be illuminated by psychoanalysis? How does tragedy elaborate the meaning of responsibility, the agent's commitment in his actions and what today we would call the psychological functions of the will? In posing such problems it is necessary to set up a clear-headed and strictly historical dialogue between the *intention* of the work and the mental habits of the interpreter. This should help to reveal the (usually unconscious) presuppositions of the modern reader and compel him to re-examine himself as regards the assumed objectivity of his interpretation.

But this is no more than a starting point. The Greek tragedies, like any other literary work, are permeated with preconceptions, presuppositions that compose as it were the framework of everyday life in the civilization for which they are *one* form of expression. For example, the opposition between hunting and sacrifice, which we have thought ourselves justified in using to further our analysis of the *Oresteia*, is not a feature peculiar to tragedy. We find it reflected in many texts through several centuries of Greek history. If it is to be correctly interpreted one must inquire into the very nature of sacrifice as the central procedure of the Greek religion, and into the place of hunting both in the life of the city and in mythical thought. It must further be remembered that the issue here is not the opposition between hunting and sacrifice *as such* but the way in which this opposition shapes a specifically literary work. Similarly, we have attempted to compare tragedies with contemporary religious practices or social institutions. For instance, we have thought it possible to illuminate *Oedipus Rex* by making a double comparison: first, with a ritual procedure, the *pharmakos*, and second with a political institution, namely ostracism, which is strictly limited to a specific period since it does not make its appearance in Athens before Cleisthenes' reform of 508 and disappears shortly before classical tragedy itself.[3] And again, we have attempted to shed some light on an unfamiliar aspect of the *Philoctetes* by referring to the procedure by which a young Athenian acceded to the full rights of citizenship, namely the ephebeia. We should perhaps again emphasize an important point. We are not attempting to uncover any secrets by means of these analyses. Was Sophocles thinking of ostracism or the ephebeia when he wrote his plays or was he not? We do not, nor shall we ever, know. We are not even sure that the question is a meaningful one. What we should like to show is that where communication between the poet and his public was concerned, ostracism or the ephebeia constituted a communal framework of reference, the background that made the very structures of the play intelligible.

Finally, quite apart from these juxtapositions, there is the tragic work's own specific nature. Oedipus is neither an expiatory victim nor is he ostracized. He is a character in a tragedy, placed by the poet at the crossroads of a decision, confronted with a choice that is ever present and ever renewed. How is the hero's choice expressed in the course of the play, in what manner do the speeches counter and correspond to one another, how is the tragic figure integrated into the tragic action? Or, to put it another way, how does the temporality of each character fit into the progress of the mechanisms set up by the gods? These are some of the questions that we have considered. Of course the reader will appreciate that there are many others to be asked and that the answers we offer are no more than suggestions. This book is only a beginning. We hope to carry it further but meanwhile we are convinced that, if this type of research has any future, other scholars than ourselves will be sure to pursue it independently.[4]

J.-P. V. and P. V.-N.

Preface to Volume II

In 1972 François Maspero published seven studies of ours under the title *Mythe et Tragédie*. At that time we, somewhat imprudently, suggested that that volume would be "followed as quickly as possible by a second." Without explicitly saying so at the time, we even believed a third volume not beyond the bounds of possibility.

It took us fourteen whole years to keep our promise and for *Myth et Tragédie II* to be published. Who knows if we shall be granted a further thirteen years to produce Volume III? But time has really nothing to do with it. The book, as it stands, not as it ought to be or might have been, is what we are presenting to a public that greeted the work of our earlier collaboration with an altogether unexpected enthusiasm both in France and abroad.

In the intervening fourteen years we have each been working and publishing either on our own or with other friends. Despite our close relations and friendship, our fields of research have not necessarily coincided. Greek tragedy nevertheless remained a common interest even if, confident of our agreement on the fundamentals in this field, we were approaching it each in our own way; and the hope of one day producing the present volume never deserted us. Like *Myth and Tragedy I*, the present work may at first sight look like an amalgam of disparate studies: ten studies (instead of seven), all of which have already appeared in one form or another in France or elsewhere,[1] either in "scholarly" journals or in publications aimed at what is known as the "general educated public." As we pointed out in *Myth and Tragedy I*, the studies all stem from a common inspiration, namely the teaching of Louis Gernet and his efforts to understand the moment of tragedy, a moment that occurred in between law as it was about to be born and law as it was already constituted.

The present volume differs from *Myth and Tragedy I* in a number of ways. The first book was entirely devoted to fifth-century tragedy in general and to systematic analyses of several individual plays: Aeschylus' *Oresteia* and Sophocles' *Oedipus Rex* and *Philoctetes*. In each case the purpose was to understand both the driving mechanisms of the works and the relationship or dialogue set up between them and the political and social institutions of their day. We pursued our quest for understanding by passing to and fro between the inside and the outside of the plays, but the field remained strictly limited to tragedy in the fifth century. Using perhaps slightly more subtle techniques, the present volume in part explores much the same area: Aeschylus' *Seven against Thebes*, Sophocles' *Oedipus at Colonus*, and Euripides' last work, the *Bacchae* are the subjects of detailed studies that, without scorning the resources of philology of the most traditional kind, also call upon techniques of what is conventionally known as structural analysis. But the rest of the essays are of a more general nature: reflections on the subject of tragedy itself or on the masked god of tragic fiction, and overall views of Aeschylus and Sophocles.

The studies centered on Dionysus and his mask, or rather masks, are a new departure. We have not studied Dionysus at the origins of tragedy but have sought to show how Dionysus, the god of appearances, could be made manifest in and through the pluralism of tragedy. Present though Dionysus may be in tragedy, he extends far beyond it on every side and consequently we have not hesitated to step outside the theater in our pursuit of him.

In our earlier volume, the word "and" in *Myth and Tragedy* was emphatic: We were explicitly determined not to regard tragedy simply as an ordinary form of mythical narrative and stressed our view that myth was both *in* tragedy and at the same time rejected by it. Sophocles presents Oedipus as a figure from the most distant times, from an age long before the democratic city; and he destroys him, just as Aeschylus destroys the Atreidai. While not rejecting that model, we have also tried out another idea: Is there perhaps a link between tyranny, parricide, and incest to be found outside the tragic form? That is the question to which the third of the studies in this work addresses itself, in the hope that it might then shed some light on *Oedipus Rex*. Finally, we have looked beyond classical tragedy to consider the question of what became of it in the subsequent history of our culture, a history not always continuous, indeed fraught with discontinuities. In our first volume we were already considering the relations between fifth-century tragedy and both its ancient and its more or less modern interpreters. We examined not only the legitimacy of the interpretation of Aristotle's *Poetics* but also that of Freud in *The Interpretation of Dreams*. What we have attempted here, in particular in connection with *Oedipus Rex* is, however, rather different: How was this tragedy understood in Vicenza in the late sixteenth century, when it was decided to put it on for the first time since antiquity in a theater that claimed to have derived its inspiration from the buildings of antiquity? How was this same tragedy subsequently transformed and many times recreated in Paris between the time of Louis XIV and the French Revolution? All this will no doubt help us to understand the intellectual history of the sixteenth and eighteenth centuries; but we should also be able through these points of reference to gain a better understanding of how our own reading of ancient tragedy has been formed.

But perhaps there is more to be said. Today, in 1986, neither the authors of this book nor scholarly thinking on Greek tragedy are quite the same as they were when our first volume appeared in 1972. We then wrote, "This book is only a beginning. We hope to carry it further but meanwhile we are convinced that, if this type of research has any future, other scholars than ourselves will be sure to pursue it independently." Even in 1972 we were not alone, nor did we ever claim to be, in introducing an interpretative approach that since then has undergone considerable development. It is enough to cite a few names to make the point: in America, Charles Segal and Froma Zeitlin; in England, Richard Buxton and Simon Goldhill; in Italy, Maria Grazia Ciani and Diego Lanza, among many others; in Rumania, Liana Lupas and Zoe Petre; in France, Florence Dupont, Suzanne Saïd, and above all, Nicole Loraux. This list, which on close inspection will be found to be quite diverse, is not designed simply as a list of honor, nor do we seek to define ourselves as some sectarian group set up in opposition to orthodoxy or to other sectarian groups. In our efforts to understand Greek tragedy, we may use one particular model that we are constantly striving to refine, but at the same time, so far as we can, we continue to derive our inspiration from wherever we can find it, from classical philology no less than from anthropology.

That being so, it is necessary to draw attention to a number of points, if only because our first volume became the object of a number of attacks either because it was misunderstood or, on the contrary, because it was understood all too well.

One theme is central to many of the studies devoted over the past few years to the Greek city, that is to say the city of the anthropologists rather than that of the historians of events and institutions.[2] It is the theme of blood sacrifice, for this defines the civic community in relation both to the gods and to the wild world surrounding it.[3] Sacrifice is certainly not foreign to tragedy but it is doubly distorted there as compared to the social practices of the Greek city: In the first place, it is simply a representation; secondly, it is human rather than animal and so is a corrupt sacrifice.[4]

René Girard, the vast scope of whose work seems to us to stem from a kind of gnosticism, has presented sacrifice, and more particularly the expulsion of the scapegoat, as the basis of a theory which, for want of a better expression, we shall describe as one of redemption and salvation.[5] In relation to the sacrifice of the tragic scapegoat, be it Oedipus or Antigone, the sacrifice of Christ represents at once an advance, from obscurity to clarity, and a reversal: "Everything is there in black and white, in four texts simultaneously. For the basis of violence to be effective, it must remain hidden; here it is completely revealed."[6] It would be possible to write an epilogue to this mythical ordering of history, seeking its origins in the epistle to the Hebrews or patristic literature[7] or, closer to home, in Joseph de Maistre, but we will pass over that subject now. As René Girard has made quite plain, it is Greek tragedy that provided him with the model of what he calls the "sacrificial crisis." Yet in the fifth-century Greek city, tragic sacrifice was by no means a theoretically acceptable social practice. Such representations were, on the contrary, condemned. If that is so, how can the tragedies be regarded as sacrificial crises, as they are by many of René Girard's disciples, or rather, how could they possibly *not* be, given that, thanks to a major distortion, the very idea of a sacrificial crisis is taken from Greek tragedy? Why censure us for calling Oedipus a *pharmakos* rather than a "scapegoat"? Was it really so as "not to incur the blame of those of [our] colleagues who are impervious to the odour of the victim which emanates from the myth"?[8] Was it because we did not agree that Oedipus obscurely prefigured Christ in the same way as the heroes of Euripides' *Bacchae* did in the eyes of the Christian author of *Christus patiens*?[9] After all, Oedipus is *not* a *pharmakos*, that figure who was ritually expelled from the city of Athens during the Thargelia festival. *Pharmakos* is one of those extreme terms that make it easier to understand the tragic hero, but the two are by no means one and the same thing.[10] Oedipus does not belong to a prehistory of salvation, in the guise of a victim. If tragedy was a direct expression of the "sacrificial crisis," how is it that it is historically confined not simply to the Greek city but specifically to fifth-century Athens?

Several of the analyses developed in these two volumes revolve around the notion of ambiguity. According to one Italian critic, the use of that word and the emphasis laid upon that idea in the study of Greek tragedy points not to a piece of scholarly research but to the unease that characterizes "certain of today's intellectuals who are perpetually in a state of crisis or, rather, constantly in quest of new models and new contemporary fashions."[11] It is with that acute sociological observation that V. Di Benedetto brings one analytical study to a close and introduces a number of others in which he seeks to demonstrate a radical incompatibility between our methods and Marxist orthodoxy. The truth is that we are no more concerned by that particular orthodoxy than by any others, and it would be easy enough for us, in our turn, to wax ironical at the expense of the radical ambiguity of those critical comments themselves. They come from an author who is himself most ambiguous since he appears as a "Marxist" only in his polemical writing; his own work on Greek tragedy stems from the most colorless of nineteenth-century philological traditions.[12] V. Di Benedetto is by no means averse to dualism or even Manichaeanism. He distinguishes between two Vernants: a "good" one, the pupil of Louis Gernet, who duly accepts that Greek tragedy reflects the encounter of two models of thought, one from before the *polis*, the other contemporary with the triumphant city; and a "bad" one, a disciple of the psychologist Ignace Meyerson, perverted by his master and a number of other influences.[13] Yet by what miracle is it that two different centuries, two juridical models, two political models, two religious models, on the one hand "reaction" and on the other "progress," coexist within a single literary genre and within the work of three great poets, just as Eteocles coexists with Polynices? Must we not inevitably appeal to what Nicole Loraux has called "tragic interference"?[14] As we see it, tragic ambiguity is more than just a subject for elegant scholarly discussion; it is to be found deep within the very language of tragedy, in what has by now for a long time been known as the "ambiguous discourse" of Ajax, in words that are themselves subject to several interpretations in the interplay explored by the poets between the heroes and the chorus, the actors and the spectators, the gods and human beings. There is ambiguity between the human way of proceeding in the drama and the plan decided by the gods, between what the tragic characters

18

say and what the spectators understand; ambiguity too within the heroes themselves — for example in the character of Eteocles, between the values of the *polis* and those of the *oikos*. If anyone is incapable of seeing that, all we can do is recall and adapt the advice given to Jean-Jacques Rousseau by the little Venetian courtesan and suggest: "*lascia le tragedie greche e studia la matematica.*"

It is a quite different debate, with different repercussions, that brings us into occasional conflict with Jean Bollack and his followers past and present. As others have returned to Marx or to Freud, Jean Bollack has both practiced a return to the Text and made this the basis of a theory aimed at turning philology into a total science of the Text.[15] But are the rules that he draws up valid for each and every text?

> Two complementary methods serve to reconstitute the meaning. The first method takes as its starting point one's understanding of the terms in their current, typical use and leads to what may be called a calculus of probabilities. It can be applied to works such as Lysias' speeches and Menander's comedies, in which speech does not dominate language. An external coherence is assumed on the basis of a statistical analysis of vocabulary and grammar. The other method leads to the decoding of expressions that are exceptional and individual. It depends upon the clarity of autonomous structures and may be applied to works in which speech incorporates many pre-existant elements in the language and other words, as do the odes of Pindar and the tragedies of Sophocles.... In a text which stems from common language, it is legitimate to seek the predominant common factor, whatever corresponds to good sense as determined by the majority view. But an ode by Pindar immediately places the interpeter in a completely different situation, analogous to that of Pindar himself, faced as he was with the "good sense" of his own age.[16]

However, if it is true that, unlike the prose speeches of the orators, poetic texts invariably play upon several levels of meaning, it follows that these texts, even more than others, are at the mercy of the "good sense" of the copyists through whom they have come down to us. Meanwhile, a systematic return to the manuscripts, though possibly of propaedeutic value, inevitably involves an element of illusion, for it can never, of itself, provide access to a "transparency of meaning,"[17] since such a transparency is itself the polar opposite of poetic language. One of the virtues of Bollack's best translations is that they protest against the very idea of a "transparency of meaning." But there is more to the problem: If it is also true that "the total empathy required by the most powerful works excludes the neutrality of judgment made from outside and, in many cases, from the vantage point of a limited understanding,"[18] the interpreter is liable to find himself caught between two solitudes, the text's and his own, clinging to the (possibly to some extent illusory) hope that, precisely through such an empathy, the gap between them may be bridged and the meaning defined and illuminated. The danger is that the very preconceptions and prejudices that stand between the modern interpreter and the ancient text, which Bollack sought precisely to eliminate, may thus be reintroduced.

In his review of our first volume of *Myth and Tragedy*,[19] Jean Bollack was prepared to recognize that we did not underestimate the tragic author's originality, but he went on to declare: "That originality is ultimately subject to the greater or lesser domination of pre-established codes" and "the basis of the work, that is to say the terms of its conflicts and their causes, is still imposed from outside. Paradoxical though it may seem, the tragedian is no more than an interpreter or a virtuoso." In the last analysis, "we must turn to the state of the society to provide the principle for understanding the work."[20] In fact, what we had written was: "But although tragedy, more than any other genre of literature, thus appears rooted in social reality, that does not mean that it is a reflection of it. It does not reflect that reality but calls it into question. By depicting it rent and divided against itself, it turns it into a problem."[21]

But let us move on from this debate over the "principle for understanding" the work — for in its way, it is as pointless a debate as that of the chicken and the egg. The real problem posed by Jean Bollack is that of the legitimacy of appealing to historical and sociological explanations to provide not the immediate context of each tragedy, but the horizon without which the meaning could not emerge. As we try to explain what happens to Sophocles' hero in *Oedipus at Colonus* when he is installed in Athens, we are careful to point out[22] that the juridical categories cannot fully account for what Oedipus becomes in Athens. However, without precise knowledge of those juridical categories, we could not even pose the question, we could not even — with or without empathy — attempt to enter into dialogue with the ancient poet. A single example will serve to show how easy it is for the most treacherous anachronisms to slip in. In Sophocles' *Oedipus Rex*, Laius' servant realizes that the man before him, the new sovereign of Thebes, is that self-same child with pierced feet whom he handed over to the shepherd of the king of Corinth. In the French translation by Jean and Mayotte Bollack, what he says to Oedipus at that point is: "*Si tu es cet homme que lui* [*le berger de Corinth*], *il dit que tu es, sache que tu es né damné* [If you are the man whom he (the shepherd from Corinth) says you are, know that you were born damned]."[23] What the Greek text says is: "ἴσθι δύσποτμος γεγώς [know that you were born for a fatal destiny]." What does the use of the word "damned,"[24] with all its Christian overtones, contribute? Nothing, apart from an immediacy that is "disturbing," not because it transmits a tragic anxiety, but because it replaces that with the idea of Augustinian or Calvinistic predestination. The dialogue with the ancient poet is shattered. To resume it, we must follow the advice of a poet of our own times:

Le bonheur jaillit de mon cri,
pour la recherche la plus haute,

21

un cri dont le mien soit l'écho.
[Happiness gushes from my cry,
in the highest quest:
for a cry of which mine is an echo.]

— Paul Éluard

We take the greatest pleasure in thanking all those who have made this book possible: our audiences and correspondents both in France and abroad, the staff of the Éditions de la Découverte who, by taking over the promises and project of François Maspero, have made possible the survival of the series to which this work belongs, François Lissarrague who provided the cover illustration for the French edition and whose friendship and skill have so often been of value to us, Françoise Frontisi-Ducroux who is the co-author of one of the present work's chapters that she has, with her customary generosity, allowed us to include. We also thank our friend Janet Lloyd for her cooperation and her careful and faithful translation. Hélène Monsacré, aided by Agathe Sauvageot took on the difficult task of rereading the assembled texts as a whole, eliminating many imperfections and standardizing their presentation. We would like to assure them all — and many others whom we have not named — that this book is not only ours but theirs too.

J.-P. V. and P. V.-N.

CHAPTER I

The Historical Moment[1] of

Tragedy in Greece: Some of the

Social and Psychological Conditions

Over the last half-century the inquiries of Greek scholars have centered above all on the origins of tragedy.[2] Even if they had produced a conclusive answer to that question the problem of tragedy would not thereby have been resolved. We should still have to grasp what is essential to it, namely how to account for the innovations introduced by Attic tragedy by reason of which it must, from the point of view of art, social institutions, and human psychology, be regarded as an invention. As a literary genre with its own rules and characteristics tragedy introduces a new type of spectacle into the system of the city-state's public festivals. Furthermore, as a specific form of expression it conveys hitherto unrecognized aspects of human experience; it marks a new stage in the development of the inner man and of the responsible agent. Whether seen from the point of view of a tragic genre, of a tragic representation, or of tragic man, the phenomenon appears to have certain irreducible characteristics.

Thus the problem of origins is, in a sense, a false one. It would be better to speak of antecedents. Even then it should be pointed out that they lie at quite a different level from the phenomenon to be explained. They are not commensurable with it; they cannot account for tragedy as such. To take one example, the mask would seem to underline the relation of tragedy to ritual masquerades. But by its very nature and function the tragic mask is something quite other than a religious costume. It is a human mask, not an animal disguise. Its role is not a ritual but an aesthetic one. The mask may be one way, among others, of emphasizing the distance, the difference between the two elements on the tragic stage, elements that are opposed but at the same time integrally linked. On the one hand there is the chorus, which in principle, without masks would seem merely disguised, a collective figure played by an association of citizens; on the other the tragic character, played by a professional actor whose individualized mask sets him apart from the anonymous group of the chorus. This individualization in no way makes the figure wearing the mask a psychological subject, an individual "person." On the contrary, the mask integrates the tragic figure into a strictly defined social and religious category, that of the heroes. Through it he becomes the incarnation of one of those exceptional beings whose legendary exploits, recorded in the heroic tradition of the poets, constitute for the fifth-century Greeks one dimension of their past. It is a distant past of an age gone by which stands in contrast to the order of the city, but it nevertheless remains alive in the civic religion in which the cult of the heroes, of which Homer and Hesiod knew nothing, holds a place of the first importance. Thus the tragic technique exploits a polarity between two of its elements: on the one hand the chorus, an anonymous and collective being whose role is to express, through its fears, hopes, and judgments, the feelings of the spectators who make up the civic community; on the other the individualized figure whose action forms the center of the drama and who is seen as a hero from another age, always more or less alien to the ordinary condition of a citizen.

This duality between the tragic chorus and the tragic hero is matched, in the very language of the tragedy, by another duality: choral lyric as opposed to the dialogue form used by the protagonists of the drama, where the meter is more akin to prose. The heroic figures brought closer by the language of ordinary men not only come to life before the eyes of the spectators but furthermore, through their discussions with the chorus or with one another, they become the subjects of a debate. They are, in a way, under examination before the public. In its songs, the chorus for its part, is less concerned to glorify the exemplary virtues of the hero, as in the tradition of lyric in Simonides or Pindar, than to express anxiety and uncertainties about him. In the new framework of tragic interplay, then, the hero has ceased to be a model. He has become, both for himself and for others, a problem.

We think these preliminary remarks will make it easier to focus upon the terms in which the problem of tragedy is to be posed. Greek tragedy appears as a historical turning point precisely limited and dated. It is born, flourishes, and degenerates in Athens, and all almost within the space of a hundred years. Why? It is not enough to note that tragedy is an expression of a torn consciousness, an awareness of the contradictions that divide a man against himself. We must seek to discover on what levels, in Greece, these tragic oppositions lie, of what they are composed and in what conditions they emerged.

This is what Louis Gernet set out to do in an analysis of the vocabulary and structures of each tragedy.[3] It enabled him to show that the true material of tragedy is the social thought peculiar to the city-state, in particular the legal thought that was then in the process of being evolved. The tragic writers' use of a technical legal vocabulary underlines the affinities between the most favored tragic themes and certain cases that fell within the competence of the courts. The institution of these courts was sufficiently recent for the novelty of the values determining their establishment and governing their activity still to be fully appreciated. The tragic poets make use of this legal vocabulary, deliberately exploiting its ambiguities, its fluctuations, and its incompleteness. We find an imprecision in the terms used, shifts of meaning, incoherences and contradictions, all of which reveal the disagreements within legal thought itself and also betray its conflicts with a religious tradition and moral thought from which the law is already distinct but whose domains are still not clearly differentiated from its own.

The fact is that law is not a logical construction. It developed historically, out of "prelegal" procedures. It disengaged itself from and stands in opposition to these but is still to some extent integrally linked with them. The Greeks do not have an idea of absolute law, founded upon certain principles and organized into a coherent system. For them there are, as it were, differing degrees of law. At one pole law rests upon the authority of accomplished fact, upon compulsion; at the other it brings into play sacred powers such as the order of the world or the justice of Zeus. It also poses moral problems regarding man's responsibility. From this point of view divine *Dikē* herself may appear opaque and incomprehensible, in that for human beings she includes an irrational element of brute force. Thus, in the *Suppliants*, we see the concept of *kratos* oscillating between two contrary meanings. Sometimes it denotes legitimate authority, legally based control, sometimes brute force in its aspect of violence, completely opposed to the law and to justice. Similarly, in *Antigone*, the word *nómos* may be used with precisely opposed connotations by different protagonists. What tragedy depicts is one *dikē* in conflict with another, a law that is not fixed, shifting and changing into its opposite. To be sure, tragedy is something quite different from a legal debate. It takes as its subject the man actually living out this debate, forced to make a decisive choice, to orient his activity in a universe of ambiguous values where nothing is ever stable or unequivocal.

This is the first aspect of conflict in tragedy. The second is closely linked with it. As we have seen, as long as it remains alive tragedy derives its themes from the legends of the heroes. The fact that it is rooted in a tradition of myths explains why it is that in many respects one finds more religious archaism in the great tragedians than in Homer. At the same time, tragedy establishes a distance between itself and the myths of the heroes that inspire it and that it transposes with great freedom. It scrutinizes them. It confronts heroic values and ancient religious representations with the new modes of thought that characterize the advent of law within the city-state. The legends of the heroes are connected with royal lineages, noble *genē* that in terms of values, social practices, forms of religion, and types of human behavior, represent

26

for the city-state the very things that it has had to condemn and reject and against which it has had to fight in order to establish itself. At the same time, however, they are what it developed from and it remains integrally linked with them.

The tragic turning point thus occurs when a gap develops at the heart of the social experience. It is wide enough for the oppositions between legal and political thought on the one hand and the mythical and heroic traditions on the other to stand out quite clearly. Yet it is narrow enough for the conflict in values still to be a painful one and for the clash to continue to take place. A similar situation obtains with regard to the problems of human responsibility that arise as a hesitant progress is made toward the establishment of law. The tragic consciousness of responsibility appears when the human and divine levels are sufficiently distinct for them to be opposed while still appearing to be inseparable. The tragic sense of responsibility emerges when human action becomes the object of reflection and debate while still not being regarded as sufficiently autonomous to be fully self-sufficient. The particular domain of tragedy lies in this border zone where human actions hinge on divine powers and where their true meaning, unsuspected by even those who initiated them and take responsibility for them, is only revealed when it becomes a part of an order that is beyond man and escapes him.

It is now easier to see that tragedy involves a particular *moment* and that the period when it flourished can be pinned down between two dates, each of which represents a different attitude toward the tragic spectacle. The earlier date is marked by the anger of Solon, who left one of the first dramatic representations in disgust, even before the institution of tragic competitions. Plutarch tells us that when Thespis pointed out that it was, after all, only for fun, the old law-giver, perturbed by the growing ambitions of Pisistratos, replied that the consequences of such fictions on the relations between citizens would soon be clear for all to see. For the sage, moralist, and statesman who had undertaken the task of founding the order of the city-state upon moderation and contract, who had had to break the arrogance of the nobles and was trying to spare his country the *hubris* of a tyrant, the "heroic" past seemed too near and too alive for it to be reproduced without risk as a spectacle in the theater. At the end of this period we may consider Aristotle's remarks concerning Agathon, the young contemporary of Euripides who wrote tragedies with plots closely modeled on the latter's. The link with legendary tradition is now so stretched that it is no longer felt necessary to engage in a debate with the "heroic" past. The dramatist can continue to write plays in which he invents the plot himself, following a model that he believes to be in conformity with the works of his great predecessors, but for him, his public, and the whole of Greek culture, the mainspring of tragedy has snapped.

Jean-Pierre Vernant

CHAPTER II

Tensions and Ambiguities in

Greek Tragedy[1]

What can sociology and psychology contribute toward the interpretation of Greek tragedy? They cannot, to be sure, replace the traditional philological and historical methods of analysis. On the contrary, they must draw upon the scholarly research in which specialists have been engaged for so long. Nevertheless, they bring a new dimension to Greek studies. By attempting to situate the tragic phenomenon exactly within the social life of the Greeks and by indicating its place in the psychological history of Western man, they bring into the open problems that Greek scholars have hitherto only come upon incidently and tackled indirectly.

We should like to consider some of these problems. Tragedy emerged in Greece at the end of the sixth century. Within a hundred years the tragic seam had already been exhausted and when Aristotle in the fourth century set out, in his *Poetics*, to establish the theory of tragedy, he no longer understood tragic man who had, so to speak, become a stranger. Tragedy succeeded epic and lyric and faded away as philosophy experienced its moment of triumph.[2] As a literary genre, tragedy seems to give expression to a particular type of human experience, one that is linked with specific social and psychological conditions. Seeing it in this way, as a phenomenon with its own historical moment precisely defined in space and time, imposes certain methodological rules for interpreting the tragic works. Each play constitutes a message, enclosed within a text and inscribed within the structures of a discourse that must be analyzed at every level from the appropriate philological, stylistic, and literary points of view. But it is a text that can only be fully understood when account is taken of its particular context. It was the context that made it possible for the author to communicate with his fifth-century public, and that same context makes it possible for the work to rediscover its full authenticity and to convey its full significance to the reader of today.

But what do we mean by context? To what level of reality does it belong? How does it relate to the text? It is a mental context, in our view, a human world of meanings and consequently homologous with the text in question. It comprises verbal and intellectual equipment, categories of thought, types of reasoning, the system of representations, beliefs and values, forms of sensibility, and the modalities of action and of agent. We might describe it as a mental world peculiar to the Greeks of the fifth century were it not that such a formula runs a severe risk of being misunderstood. It might suggest that a mental domain already existed somewhere, fully established, and that all tragedy had to do was reflect it in its own particular way. But no mental universe exists as such, over and above the collection of diverse practices that man follows and constantly renews within the field of social life and cultural creation. Each type of institution, each category of work has its own mental universe that it has had to elaborate so as to constitute an autonomous discipline, a specialized activity corresponding to a particular domain of human experience.

Thus the entire mental universe of religion is present in the rituals, myths, and graphic representations of the divine. When law becomes established in the Greek world, there are a number of different aspects to it: social institutions, human practices, and mental categories, and it is these that define legal thought as opposed to other forms of thought, in particular religious ones. Similarly, with the advent of the city there developed a whole system of strictly political institutions, modes of behavior, and thought. Here again there is a striking contrast with the old mystical forms of power and social action that, together with the practices and mentality that went with them, are now replaced by the regime of the *polis*. And it is the same with tragedy. It would not be possible for it to reflect a reality in any way foreign to it. It elaborates its own mental world for itself. The vision and the object of plastic art only exist in and through painting. In the same way, the tragic consciousness is born and develops along with tragedy. It is by being expressed in the form of an original literary genre that tragic thought, the tragic world, and tragic man are created.

To put it in spatial terms then, we could say that the context, in the sense that we are using the word, is not something that exists side by side with the works, on the periphery of tragedy. It is not so much juxtaposed to as underlying the text. It is not really so much a *con*text as an under-text, which a scholarly reading must decode within the very fabric of the work, proceeding in two ways, now making a detour around the text and now going back over it. First the work must be situated by extending the field of inquiry to cover the complex of social and mental conditions that prompted the appearance of the tragic consciousness. But after that the inquiry must be concentrated exclusively on tragedy's distinguishing features: its forms, its object, and its own specific problems. No reference to other domains of social life — religion, law, politics, ethics — can be pertinent unless we can also show how tragedy assimilates into its own perspective the elements it borrows, thereby quite transmuting them. To take one example: The almost obsessive use of a technical legal terminology in the language of the tragic writers, their preference for themes connected with crimes of bloodshed that fall within the competence of one court or another, the very form that some of the plays take, namely that of a judgment, make it imperative that, to understand the exact meanings of the terms and all the implications of the drama, the historian of literature step outside his own specialized field and make himself a historian of Greek law. However, legal thought will not shed any light directly upon the tragic text as if the latter were no more than a transfer from it.

The detour by way of the law is merely a necessary preliminary for the interpreter. In the end it brings him back to tragedy itself and the world that goes with it, and he can then explore certain dimensions of this world that, without that detour, would have remained concealed within the fabric of the text. The fact is that no tragedy is a legal debate any more than the law, in itself, comprises any elements of tragedy. Words, ideas, and schemata of thought are used by the poets quite differently from the way they are used in a court of justice or by the orators. Once they are taken out of their technical context, their function to some extent changes. In the hands of the tragic writers, intermingled with and opposed to other terms, they become elements in a general clash of values and in a reappraisal of all norms that are part of an inquiry that is no longer concerned with the law but is focused upon man himself: What is this being that tragedy describes as a *deinos*, an incomprehensible and baffling monster, both an agent and one acted upon, guilty and innocent, lucid and blind, whose industrious mind can dominate the whole of nature yet who is incapable of governing himself? What is the relationship of this man to the actions upon which we see him deliberate on the stage and for which he takes the initiative and responsibility but whose real meaning is beyond him and escapes him so that it is not so much the agent who explains the action but rather the action that, revealing its true significance after the event, recoils upon the agent and discloses what he is and what he has really, unwittingly, done? Finally, what is this man's place in a world that is at once social, natural, divine, and ambiguous, rent by contradictions, in which no rule appears definitively established, one god fights against another, one law against another and in which, even in the course of the play's action, justice itself shifts, twists, and is transformed into its contrary?

Tragedy is not only an art form; it is also a social institution that the city, by establishing competitions in tragedies, set up alongside its political and legal institutions. The city established under the authority of the eponymous archon, in the same urban space and in accordance with the same institutional norms as the popular assemblies or courts, a spectacle open to all the citizens, directed, acted, and judged by the qualified representatives of the various tribes.[3] In this way it turned itself into a theater. Its subject, in a sense, was itself and it acted itself out before its public. But although tragedy, more than any other genre of literature, thus appears rooted in social reality, that does not mean that it is a reflection of it. It does not reflect that reality but calls it into question. By depicting it rent and divided against itself, it turns it into a problem. The drama brings to the stage an ancient heroic legend. For the city this legendary world constitutes the past — a past sufficiently distant for the contrasts, between the mythical traditions that it embodies and the new forms of legal and political thought, to be clearly visible; yet a past still close enough for the clash of values still to be a painful one and for this clash still to be currently taking place. As Walter Nestle correctly points out, tragedy is born when myth starts to be considered from the point of view of a citizen. But it is not only the world of myth that loses its consistency and dissolves in this focus. By the same token the world of the city is called into question and its fundamental values are challenged in the ensuing debate. When exalting the civic ideal and affirming its victory over all forces from the past, even Aeschylus, the most optimistic of the tragic writers, seems not to be making a positive declaration with tranquil conviction but rather to be expressing a hope, making an appeal that remains full of anxiety even amid the joy of the final apotheosis.[4] The questions are posed but the tragic consciousness can find no fully satisfactory answers to them and so they remain open.

This debate with a past that is still alive creates at the very heart of each tragic work a fundamental distance that the interpreter needs to take into account. It is expressed, in the very form of the drama, by the tension between the two elements that occupy the tragic stage. One is the chorus, the collective and

33

anonymous presence embodied by an official college of citizens. Its role is to express through its fears, hopes, questions, and judgments the feelings of the spectators who make up the civic community. The other, played by a professional actor, is the individualized character whose actions form the core of the drama and who appears as a hero from an age gone by, always more or less estranged from the ordinary condition of the citizen.[5] This dichotomy between chorus and tragic hero is matched by a duality in the language of tragedy. But here already there is an aspect of ambiguity that seems to us to characterize the tragic genre. It is the language of the chorus, in the chanted passages, that carries on the lyrical tradition of a poetry celebrating the exemplary virtues of the hero of ancient times. For the protagonists of the drama the meter of the passages of dialogue is, on the contrary, close to that of prose. Even as the setting and the mask confer upon the tragic protagonist the magnified dimensions of one of the exceptional beings that are the object of a cult in the city, the language used brings him closer to the ordinary man.[6] And even as he lives his legendary adventure this closeness makes him, as it were, the contemporary of the public, so that the tension that we have noted between past and present, between the world of myth and that of the city, is to be found again within each protagonist. At one moment the same tragic character appears projected into a far distant mythical past, the hero of another age, imbued with a daunting religious power and embodying all the excesses of the ancient king of legend. At the next, he seems to speak, think, live in the very same age as the city, like a "bourgeois citizen" of Athens amid his fellows.

So it is misguided to inquire into the greater or lesser unity of character of the tragic protagonists, as some modern critics do. According to Wilamowitz, the character of Eteocles in the *Seven against Thebes* does not seem drawn with a firm hand; his behavior at the end of the play is not really compatible with the portrait indicated earlier on. For Mazon, on the contrary, this same Eteocles is one of the finest figures in the Greek theater; he embodies the very type of the doomed hero with perfect coherence.

Such a debate would only make sense given a drama of the modern type, constructed around the psychological unity of its protagonists. But Aeschylus' tragedy is not centered upon one particular character, in all the complexity of his inner life. The real protagonist of the *Seven* is the city, that is to say the values, modes of thought, and attitudes that it commands and that Eteocles, at the head of Thebes, represents so long as the name of his brother, Polynices, is not pronounced before him. For as soon as he hears Polynices mentioned he is given over to another world rejected by that of the *polis*: He becomes once again the Labdacid of legend, the man of the noble *genē*, the great royal families of the past that are weighed down by ancestral defilement and curses. Faced with the emotive religious fervor of the women of Thebes and the warrior impiety of the men of Argos, he embodies all the virtues of moderation, reflection, and self-control that go to make up the statesman. But when he abandons himself to a hatred for his brother that altogether "possesses" him he suddenly flings himself toward catastrophe. The murderous madness that henceforth characterizes his *ēthos* is not simply a human emotion; it is a daemonic power in every way beyond him. It envelops him in the dark cloud of *atē*, penetrating him as a god takes possession of whomever he has decided to bring low, from within, in a form of *mania*, a *lussa*, a delirium that breeds criminal acts of *hubris*. The madness of Eteocles is present within him, but that does not prevent it also appearing as extraneous and exterior to him. It is identified with the malignant power of defilement that, once engendered by ancient crimes, is transmitted from one generation to the next right down the Labdacid line.

The destructive frenzy that grips the leader of Thebes is none other than the *miasma* that is never purified, the Erinyes of the race, now lodged within him as a result of the *ara* or curse that Oedipus lays upon his sons. *Mania, lussa, atē, ara, miasma, Erinys* — all these nouns refer in the last analysis to one and the same mythical factor, a sinister *numen* that manifests itself in many guises, at

35

different moments, both within a man's soul and outside him. It is a power of misfortune that encompasses not only the criminal but the crime itself, its most distant antecedents, its psychological motivations, its consequences, the defilement it brings in its wake and the punishment that it lays in store for the guilty one and all his descendents. In Greek there is a word for this type of divine power, which is not usually individualized and which takes action at the very heart of men's lives, usually to ill-fated effect and in a wide variety of forms: It is *daimōn*. Euripides is faithful to the tragic spirit of Aeschylus when he uses the word *daimonan* to describe the psychological state of the sons of Oedipus, bent on fratricide through the curse of their father; they are indeed, in the true sense of the word, possessed by a *daimōn*, an evil spirit.[7]

One can see to what extent and in what sense it is justifiable to speak of a transformation in the character of Eteocles. It has nothing to do with unity or discontinuity in the personality, in the sense that we use such expressions today. As Aristotle notes, the tragic action does not unfold in conformity with the demands of a particular character; on the contrary, it is the character that must yield to the demands of the action, that is to say the *muthos*, the story, of which the tragedy is, in a strict sense, an imitation.[8] At the beginning of the play the *ēthos* of Eteocles corresponds to a particular psychological model, that of the *homo politicus*, as conceived by the Greeks of the fifth century. What we would call a transformation *in the character* of Eteocles ought, more correctly, to be described as a switch to a different psychological model, a shift *in the tragedy* from a political psychology to the mythical one implied in the Labdacid legend by the episode of the mutual murder of the two brothers. One could even go on to say that it is this reference first to one model and then to another and this clash within a single character of two opposed types of behavior, two forms of psychology that imply different categories for action and agent, that are the essential constituents of the tragic effect in the *Seven*. So long as tragedy remains alive there is no weakening of this duality, or rather tension, in the psychology of the protagonists. All that the hero feels, says and does springs from his character, his *ēthos*, which the poets analyze just as subtly and interpret just as positively as might, for example, the orators or a historian such as Thucydides.[9] But at the same time these feelings, pronouncements, and actions also appear as the expression of a religious power, a *daimōn* operating through them. Eventually the great art of tragedy even came to consist in conveying simultaneously what in Aeschylus' Eteocles is still expressed successively. Thus every moment in the life of the hero unfolds as if on two levels. Each would, by itself, adequately account for the peripeteiai of the drama, but the purpose of the tragedy is precisely to present them as inseparable. Each action appears to be in keeping with the logic of a particular character or *ēthos* even at the very moment when it is revealed to be the manifestation of a power from the beyond, or a *daimōn*.

Tragic man is constituted within the space encompassed by this pair, *ēthos* and *daimōn*. If one of the two is eliminated he vanishes. To paraphrase a pertinent remark of R.P. Winnington-Ingram,[10] it could be said that tragedy rests on a double reading of Heraclitus' famous dictum, ἦθος ἀνθρώπῳ δαίμων. The minute it becomes impossible to read it equally well in the two different senses (as the syntactical symmetry allows) the formula loses its enigmatic character, its ambiguity, and the tragic consciousness is gone. For there to be tragedy it must be possible for the text simultaneously to imply two things: It is his character, in man, that one calls *daimōn* and, conversely, what one calls character, in man, is in reality a *daimōn*.

For our mentality today (and even, to a large extent, already for Aristotle's), the two interpretations are mutually exclusive. But the logic of tragedy consists in "operating on both planes," in shifting from one meaning to the other, always — to be sure — conscious of the opposition between them but never rejecting either. An ambiguous logic, it might be objected. However, this is no longer the naive ambiguity of myth, which does not yet question itself. On the contrary, tragedy, at the very moment when it passes from one level to the other, carefully emphasizes the distance between them and underlines the contradictions. Yet, even in Aeschylus, it never provides a solution that could eliminate the conflicts either by reconciling them or by stepping beyond the oppositions. And this tension that is never totally accepted nor entirely obliterated makes tragedy into a questioning to which there can be no answers. In a tragic perspective man and human action are seen, not as things that can be defined or described, but as problems. They are presented as riddles whose double meanings can never be pinned down or exhausted.

There is another domain, apart from that of the individual character, in which the interpreter must seek to grasp the aspects of tension and ambiguity. We have already mentioned the fact that the tragic writers are prone to the use of technical legal terms. But when they use this terminology it is almost always to play on its ambiguities, its vagueness, and its incompleteness. We find terms used imprecisely, shifts of meaning, incoherences and contradictions, which betray internal clashes and tensions at the very heart of a system of legal thought that lacks the elaborated form of that of the Romans. The legal terminology is also used to convey the conflicts that exist between legal values and a more ancient religious tradition, the beginnings of a system of moral thought already distinct from the law although the boundaries between their respective domains are not yet clearly drawn. The fact is that the Greeks have no idea of absolute law, founded upon definite principles and organized into a coherent whole. For them there are, as it were, degrees and separate layers of law, some of which overlap or are superimposed upon one another. At one extreme the law consecrates *de facto* authority and is based on constraint of which it is, in a way, simply an extension. At the other it borders on the religious: It brings into play sacred powers, the order of the world, the justice of Zeus. It also poses moral problems regarding the greater or lesser responsibility of human agents. From this point of view divine justice, which often visits the crimes of fathers upon their sons, may frequently appear as opaque and arbitrary as violence done by a tyrant.

Thus in the *Suppliants* the idea of *kratos* can be seen to oscillate between two contrary accepted meanings, unable to settle for the one rather than the other. On the lips of King Pelasgus *kratos*, associated with *kurios*, refers to a legitimate authority, the control rightfully exercised by the guardian over whoever is legally dependent upon his power. On the lips of the Danaids the same word, drawn into the semantic field of *bia*, refers to brute force, constraint imposed by violence, in its aspect that is most opposed to justice and right.[11] This tension between two contrary senses is expressed in a particularly striking manner in line 315, whose ambiguity has been demonstrated by E.W. Whittle.[12] The word *rhusios*, which also belongs to legal parlance and is here applied to the effect of Zeus' touch upon Io, has two simultaneous and contradictory meanings: One is the brutal violence of rape, the other the gentle sweetness of a deliverance. The effect of ambiguity is not gratuitous. It is deliberate on the part of the poet and introduces us into the heart of a work one of whose major themes consists precisely of an inquiry into the true nature of *kratos*. What is authority, the authority of the man over the woman, of husband over wife, of the head of the State over all his fellow citizens, of the city over the foreigner and the metic, of the gods over mortal men? Does it depend on right, that is to say mutual agreement, gentle persuasion, *peithō*? Or, on the contrary, upon domination, pure force, brute violence, *bia*? The word play to which a vocabulary as precise in principle as that of the law lends itself makes it possible to express as an enigma the problematic character of the bases of power exercised over others.

What is true for the legal language is no less so for the forms of expression used by religious thought. The tragic writers are not content simply to oppose one god to another, Zeus to Prometheus, Artemis to Aphrodite, Apollo and Athena to the Erinyes. The divine universe as a whole is presented, at a deeper level, as being in a state of conflict. The powers it comprises are presented grouped into violently contrasted categories between which concord is difficult or impossible to achieve because they belong to different levels. The ancient deities belong to a different religious world from the "new" gods, just as the Olympians are alien to the Chthonic powers. The same duality may exist at the heart of a single divine figure. The Zeus from above whom the Danaids at first beg to *persuade* Pelasgus to respect his duties toward suppliants is opposed to another Zeus, the Zeus below to whom they turn as a last resort, seeking that he should *compel* the king to give in.[13] Similarly, the *dikē* of the dead is opposed to celestial *dikē*: Antigone comes into violent conflict with the throne of the latter because she has wished to recognize only the former.[14]

But the oppositions stand out clearly above all in the context of man's experience of the divine. In tragedy we find not just one category of the religious but various forms of religious life that appear to be opposed or mutually exclusive. In the *Seven*, the chorus of Theban women appeals to a divine presence in an anguished manner, with frantic impulses, tumultuous cries, and a fervor that directs them and keeps them attached to the most ancient idols, the *archia bretē*, not in the temples consecrated to the gods but even in the center of the town, in the public square. This chorus embodies a religion of women that is categorically condemned by Eteocles in the name of another type of religion that is both virile and civic. For the Head of State, the emotive frenzy of the women not only stands for disorder, cowardice,[15] "wildness,"[16] but also contains an element of impiety. True impiety presupposes wisdom and discipline, *sōphrosunē*[17] and *peitharchia*;[18] it is addressed to gods whose distance from humans it recognizes instead of seeking, as does the women's religion, to overcome it. The only contribution Eteocles will allow the women to make toward a public and political religion that knows how to respect the distant character of the gods without trying to mix the divine with the human, is the *ololugē*, the wail, which is described as *hieros*[19] because the city has integrated it into its own religion, recognizing it as the ritual cry to accompany the fall of the victim in the great blood sacrifice.

The conflict between Antigone and Creon reflects a similar antinomy. It is not an opposition between pure religion, represented by the girl, and total irreligion, represented by Creon, or between a religious spirit and a political one. Rather, it is between two different types of religious feeling: One is a family religion, purely private and confined to the small circle of close relatives, the *philoi*, centered around the domestic hearth and the cult of the dead; the other is a public religion in which the tutelary gods of the city eventually become confused with the supreme values of the State. Between these two domains of religious life there is a constant tension that, in certain cases (for instance, those depicted in the tragedy), can lead to insoluble conflict. As the leader of the chorus points out,[20] it is pious to honor the gods in all piety but the supreme magistrate at the head of the city is duty-bound to enforce respect for his *kratos* and the law he has promulgated. After all, as Socrates in the *Crito* was to assert, piety, like justice, commands that you obey the laws of your country, even if they are unjust, and even if this injustice recoils against you, condemning you to death. For the city, that is to say its *nomoi*, is more venerable, more *sacred* than a mother, a father, or all one's ancestors put together.[21] Neither of the two religious attitudes set in conflict in the *Antigone* can by itself be the right one unless it grants to the other the place that is its due, unless it recognizes the very thing that limits and competes with it. It is significant in this respect that the only deities referred to by the chorus are Dionysus and Eros. As mysterious nocturnal gods that elude human comprehension and are close to women and foreign to politics, they condemn first and foremost the pseudo-religion of Creon, the Head of State who reduces the divine to the dimensions of his own poor common sense so as to saddle it with his own personal hatred and ambitions. But the two deities also turn against Antigone, enclosed within her family *philia* and of her own free will sworn to Hades, for even through their link with death, Dionysus and Eros express the powers of life and renewal. Antigone has been deaf to the call to detach herself from "her kin" and from family *philia* in order to embrace another *philia*, to accept Eros and, in her union with a stranger, to become in her own turn a transmitter of life.

In the language of the tragic writers there is a multiplicity of different levels more or less distant from one another. This allows the same word to belong to a number of different semantic fields depending on whether it is a part of religious, legal, political, or common vocabulary or of a particular sector of one of these. This imparts a singular depth to the text and makes it possible for it to be read on a number of levels at the same time. The dialogue exchanged and lived through by the heroes of the drama undergoes shifts in meaning as it is interpreted and commented upon by the chorus and taken in and understood by the spectators, and this constitutes one of the essential elements of the tragic effect. On the stage the various heroes of the drama employ the same words in their debates but these words take on opposed meanings depending on who utters them.[22] The term *nómos* as used by Antigone means the opposite to what Creon, in all confidence, calls *nómos* and one could, with Charles Paul Segal detect the same ambiguity in the other terms whose place in the texture of the work is of major importance: *philos* and *philia, kerdos, timē, sebas, tolma, orgē, deinos.*[23] So the function of the words used on stage is not so much to establish communication between the various characters as to indicate the blockages and barriers between them and the impermeability of their minds, to locate the points of conflict. For each protagonist, locked into his own particular world, the vocabulary that is used remains for the most part opaque. For him it has one, and only one, meaning. This one-sidedness comes into violent collision with another. The tragic irony may well consist in showing how, in the course of the drama, the hero is literally taken "at his word," a word that recoils against him, subjecting him to the bitter experience of the meaning that he has persisted in refusing to recognize. The chorus, more often than not, hesitates and oscillates, rebounding from one meaning to the other, or sometimes dimly suspecting a meaning as yet unrevealed, or actually unconsciously formulating in a play on words an expression with a twofold meaning.[24]

It is only for the spectator that the language of the text can be transparent at every level in all its polyvalence and with all its ambiguities. Between the author and the spectator the language thus recuperates the full function of communication that it has lost on the stage between the protagonists in the drama. But the tragic message, when understood, is precisely that there are zones of opacity and incommunicability in the words that men exchange. Even as he sees the protagonists clinging exclusively to one meaning and, thus blinded, tearing themselves apart or destroying themselves, the spectator must understand that there are really two or more possible meanings. The language becomes transparent and the tragic message gets across to him only provided he makes the discovery that words, values, men themselves, are ambiguous, that the universe is one of conflict, only if he relinquishes his earlier convictions, accepts a problematic vision of the world and, through the dramatic spectacle, himself acquires a tragic consciousness.

Greek tragedy is strongly marked by a number of characteristics: tension between myth and the forms of thought peculiar to the city, conflict within man, within the domain of values, the world of the gods, and the ambiguous and equivocal character of language. But perhaps the essential feature that defines it is that the drama brought to the stage unfolds both at the level of everyday existence, in a human, opaque time made up of successive and limited present moments, and also beyond this earthly life, in a divine, omnipresent time that at every instant encompasses the totality of events, sometimes to conceal them and sometimes to make them plain but always so that nothing escapes it or is lost in oblivion. Through this constant union and confrontation between the time of men and the time of the gods, throughout the drama, the play startlingly reveals that the divine intervenes even in the course of human actions.

Aristotle notes that tragedy is the imitation of an action, *mimēsis praxeōs*. It presents characters engaged in action, *prattontes*. And the word "drama" comes from the Doric *dran* that corresponds to the Attic *prattein*, to act. In effect, in contrast to epic and lyric, where the category of action is not represented since man is never envisaged as an agent, tragedy presents individuals engaged in action. It places them at the crossroads of a choice in which they are totally committed; it shows them on the threshold of a decision, asking themselves what is the best course to take. "Pylades, what shall I do [Πυλάδη, τί δράσω]?" cries Orestes in the *Choephori*[25] and Pelasgus, at the beginning of the *Suppliants*[26] reflects: "I do not know what to do; my heart is gripped in anguish; should I take action or not?" But the king immediately goes on to say something that, taken in conjunction with the preceding lines, underlines the polarity of tragic action: "To act or not to act and tempt fate [τε καὶ τύχην ἑλεῖν]?" To tempt fate: In the tragic writers, human action is not, of itself, strong enough to do without the power of the gods, not autonomous enough to be fully conceived without them. Without their presence and their support it is nothing — either abortive or producing results quite other than those initially envisaged. So it is a kind of wager — on the future, on fate and on oneself, ultimately a wager on the gods for whose support one hopes. In this game, where he is not in control, man always risks being trapped by his own decisions. The gods are incomprehensible to him. When, as a precaution before taking action, he consults them and they deign to answer, their reply is as equivocal and ambiguous as the situation on which he asked for their advice.

44

From a tragic point of view then, there are two aspects to action. It involves on the one hand reflection, weighing up the pros and cons, foreseeing as accurately as possible the means and the ends; on the other, placing one's stake on what is unknown and incomprehensible, risking oneself on a terrain that remains impenetrable, entering into a game with supernatural forces, not knowing whether, as they join with one, they will bring success or doom. Even for the most foreseeing of men, the most carefully thought out action is still a chancy appeal to the gods and only by their reply, and usually to one's cost, will one learn what it really involved and meant. It is only when the drama is over that actions take on their true significance and agents, through what they have in reality accomplished without realizing it, discover their true identity. So long as there has been no complete consummation, human affairs remain enigmas that are the more obscure the more the actors believe themselves sure of what they are doing and what they are. Installed in his role of solver of riddles and king dispensing justice, convinced that the gods inspire him, and proclaiming himself the son of *Tuchē*, Good Luck, how could Oedipus possibly understand that he is a riddle to himself to which he will only guess the meaning when he discovers himself to be the opposite to what he thinks he is: not *Tuchē*'s son at all but his victim, not the dispenser of justice but the criminal, not the king saving his city but the abominable defilement by which it is being destroyed? So it is that, at the moment when he realizes that he is responsible for having forged his misfortune with his own hands, he accuses the deity of having plotted and contrived everything in advance, of having delighted in tricking him from start to finish of the drama, the better to destroy him.[27]

Just as the tragic character comes into being within the space between *daimōn* and *ēthos*, so tragic culpability is positioned in between on the one hand the ancient religious concept of crime-defilement, *hamartia*, sickness of the mind, the delirium sent by the gods that necessarily engenders crime, and on the other the new concept in which the guilty one, *hamartōn* and, above all, *adikōn*, is defined as one who, under no compulsion, has deliberately chosen to commit a crime.[28] In its attempts at distinguishing the different categories of crime that fall within the competence of different courts, the *phonos dikaios, akousios, hekousios*, the law — even if still in a clumsy and hesitant manner — lays emphasis on the ideas of intention and responsibility. It raises the problem of the agent's different degrees of commitment in his actions. At the same time, within the city framework where all the citizens, following public discussions of a secular nature, themselves direct the affairs of the State, man himself is beginning to experiment as an agent who is more or less autonomous in relation to the religious forces that govern the universe, more or less master of his own actions and, through his *gnōmē*, his *phronēsis*, more or less in control of his own political and personal destiny. This experimentation, still wavering and indecisive, of what was subsequently in the psychological history of Western man to become the category of the will — as is well known, in ancient Greece there was no true vocabulary to cover willing — is expressed in tragedy in the form of an anxious questioning concerning the relation of the agent to his actions: To what extent is man really the source of his actions? Even while he deliberates concerning them deep within himself, taking the initiative and responsibility for them, does not their true origin lie somewhere outside him? Does not their significance remain opaque to the one who commits them, since actions acquire their reality not through the intentions of the agent but through the general order of the world over which the gods preside?

For there to be tragic action it is necessary that a concept of human nature with its own characteristics should have already emerged and that the human and divine spheres should have become sufficiently distinct from each other for them to stand in opposition; yet at the same time they must continue to appear as inseparable. The tragic sense of responsibility makes its appear-

46

ance at the point when, in human action, a place is given to internal debate on the part of the subject, to intention and premeditation, but when this human action has still not acquired enough consistency and autonomy to be entirely self-sufficient. The true domain of tragedy lies in that border zone where human actions are hinged together with the divine powers, where — unknown to the agent — they derive their true meaning by becoming an integral part of an order that is beyond man and that eludes him. In Thucydides, human nature, *anthrōpinē phusis*, is defined in absolute contrast to religious power as represented by *Tuchē*. The two are radically heterogeneous orders of reality. In tragedy they appear rather as two opposed but complementary aspects, the two poles of a single ambiguous reality. Thus all tragedy must necessarily be played out on two levels. In its aspect of an inquiry into man as a responsible agent, it only has value as a counterpoint to the central theme. It would therefore be mistaken to focus exclusively upon the psychological element. In the famous carpet scene of the *Agamemnon*, the sovereign's fatal decision no doubt depends partly upon his wretched human vanity and also perhaps upon the guilty conscience of a husband who is the more ready to accede to the requests of his wife given that he is returning home to her with Cassandra as his concubine. But that is not the essential point. The strictly tragic effect comes from the intimate relation yet at the same time extraordinary distance between the banal action of stepping on a purple carpet with the all too human motivations this involves, and the religious forces that this action inexorably sets in motion.

The moment Agamemnon sets foot on the carpet the drama reaches its consummation. And even if the play is not quite over, it can introduce nothing that is not already accomplished once and for all. The past, the present, and the future have fused together with a single meaning that is revealed and encapsulated in the symbolism of this action of impious *hubris*. Now we know what the sacrifice of Iphigenia really was: not so much obedience to the orders of Artemis, not so much the painful duty of a king not wishing to be in the wrong where his allies were concerned,[29] rather the guilty weakness of an ambitious man who, his passion conspiring with divine *Tuchē*,[30] made the decision to sacrifice his own daughter. And we know now what the capture of Troy was: not so much a triumph of justice and punishment of the guilty, rather, a sacrilegious destruction of an entire city with its temples. And in this twofold impiety all the ancient crimes of the Atreidae live again and all those that are to follow are encompassed: the blow that is to strike down Agamemnon and that, through Orestes, will eventually reach Clytemnestra too. At this culminating point of the tragedy, where all the threads are tied together, the time of the gods invades the stage and becomes manifest within the time of men.

Jean-Pierre Vernant

Chapter III

Intimations of the Will in

Greek Tragedy

For those who belong to Western contemporary societies, the will constitutes one essential dimension of the person.[1] The will can be described as the person seen as an agent, the self seen as the source of actions for which it is held responsible before others and to which it furthermore feels inwardly committed. The modern insistence on the uniqueness and originality of the individual person is matched by the feeling that we fulfill ourselves in what we do, we express ourselves in works which are manifestations of our authentic being. The continuity of the subject seeking himself in his own past, recognizing himself in his memories, is matched by the permanence of the agent who is responsible today for what he did yesterday and whose awareness of his own internal existence and coherence is all the stronger in that the sequence of his actions forms a chain, is contained within a single framework and constitutes a single, continuous career.

For modern man, the category of the will presupposes that the person is oriented toward action and that this and practical accomplishments in their diverse forms are highly valued. But much more than this: In action the agent is recognized as preeminent; the human subject is assumed to be the origin and efficient cause of all the actions that stem from him. In his relations with others and with nature, the agent apprehends himself as a kind of center of decision, holding a power that springs neither from the emotions nor from pure intelligence: It is a power *sui generis* that

Descartes goes so far as to describe as infinite, "the same in us as it is in God," because in contrast with understanding which in created beings is bound to be limited, the power of the will knows no degree: Like free will, of which it is, for Descartes, the psychological aspect, if one possesses it at all one possesses it entirely. The will can, in effect be seen as the power — the indivisible power — to say yes or no, to acquiesce or refuse. This power manifests itself in particular in the act of decision. By committing himself by making a choice, by coming to a decision, whatever its context, an individual makes himself an agent, that is to say a responsible and autonomous subject who manifests himself in and through actions that are imputable to him.

There can thus be no action without an individual agent who is its center and source; there can be no agent without this power that links the action to the subject who decides upon it and who thereby assumes full responsibility for it. Such statements have come to seem so natural to us that they no longer appear to present any problems. We are inclined to believe that it is as natural for man to make decisions and act "as he wills" as it is for him to have arms and legs. And even where a civilization such as that of archaic and classical Greece has in its language no word that corresponds to our own term, we still have no compunction in endowing the men of that time, as it were despite themselves, with this function of the will that they themselves never named.

The whole of Meyerson's work sets us on our guard against the assumptions of these would-be psychological "truths." And the inquiries that he pursued both in his writing and in his lectures into the history of the person destroys the myth of a universal, permanent, psychological function of the will. The will is not a datum of human nature. It is a complex construction whose history appears to be as difficult, multiple, and incomplete as that of the self, of which it is to a great extent an integral part. We must therefore beware of projecting onto the ancient Greeks our own contemporary system for the organization of modes of behavior involving the will, the structures of our own processes of decision and our own models of the commitment of the self in action. We must examine, without *a priori* assumptions, the forms taken in Greek civilization by the respective categories of action and of the agent. We must try to see how, through various forms of social practice (religious, political, legal, aesthetic, and technical), certain relations between the human subject and his actions came to be established.

In recent years Greek scholars have come up against this problem in connection with tragedy and tragic man. A recent article by André Rivier gives a precise account of the debate.[2] He notes that as early as 1928, Bruno Snell identified in Aeschylus' dramatic technique elements of a tragic image of man centered on the themes of action and the agent. In contrast to Homer and the lyric poets, Aeschylus places his heroes on the threshold of action, faced with the need to act. One repeatedly observes the same dramatic schema: He presents them in a situation that leads to an *aporia*, an impasse. At the crossroads of a decision on which their entire fate depends, they find themselves up against a difficult but unavoidable choice. However, if it is a matter of necessity that they should opt for one or the other of two solutions, their decision in itself remains a contingent one. It is in effect taken after an internal debate, a considered deliberation as a result of which the final decision takes root in the soul of the protagonist. According to Snell this "personal," "free" decision constitutes the central theme in Aeschylean drama that, seen in this light, appears as a creation devised to isolate a pure, almost abstract "model" of human action. This human action is conceived as the initiative of an independent agent who faces up to his responsibilities and finds the motives and impulses for his committed action deep within himself.[3] Drawing psychological conclusions from this interpretation, Zevedei Barbu was later to propose that the elaboration of the will as a fully constituted function manifests itself in and through the development of tragedy, in Athens, during the fifth century B.C.: "One can regard (Aeschylean) drama as full proof of the emergence within Greek civilization of the individual as a free agent."[4]

This is the analysis that Rivier's study sets out to demolish on a number of essential points. The emphasis Snell places on the decision made by the subject, with all the more or less implicit associated notions of autonomy, responsibility, and liberty tends to belittle the role — which was nevertheless a decisive one — of the superhuman forces that are at work in the drama and that give it its truly tragic dimension. These religious powers are not only present outside the subject; they also intervene at the heart of his decision, subjecting him to constraint even in what were claimed to be his "choices." Indeed, according to Rivier, a precise analysis of the texts shows that, seen from the point of view of the subject or agent, all that the deliberation does is make him aware of the *aporia*; it has no power to motivate one option rather than the other. In the end it is always an *anankē* imposed by the gods that generates the decision. At a particular moment in the drama "necessity" comes down altogether on one side of the scales, terminating the earlier situation of equilibrium just as it had initiated it. So tragic man does not have to "choose" between two possibilities; rather, he "recognizes" that there is only one way open before him. This involvement reflects not the free choice of the subject but his recognition of this religious necessity that he cannot elude and that makes him someone internally "compelled," *biastheis*, even while he is making his "decision." If there is any scope for the will, it is certainly not autonomous will in the Kantian, or even simply the Thomist, sense of the term. It is a will bound by the reverential fear of the divine, if not actually coerced by the sacred powers that inform man from within.

As well as attacking Snell's thesis, André Rivier's critical analysis is aimed at those interpretations that, while recognizing the determining role of the supernatural powers in the action of the tragic hero, nevertheless seek to salvage the autonomy of the human subject by still claiming a place for the will in his decision. Such is the theory of the double motivation proposed by Albin Lesky and adopted, with various nuances, by most contemporary Greek scholars.[5] We know that in Homer there is sometimes a double explanation for the actions of the heroes of the epic: Their behavior may be interpreted equally well as the effect of divine inspiration or stimulus or as the result of a strictly human motivation and these two possibilities are nearly always too closely interconnected for it to be possible to dissociate one from the other. According to Lesky, in Aeschylus this schema of a double motivation becomes a constitutive element of the tragic image of man. The hero of the drama is certainly faced with a superior necessity that is imposed upon him and that directs him, but the impulse of his own character prompts him to appropriate this necessity, to make it his own to the point of willing, even of passionately desiring what, in another sense, he is forced to do. In this way the margin of free choice, without which it would seem that the subject cannot be held responsible for his actions, is reintroduced at the heart of the "necessary" decision. For how could one accept that the characters in the drama should so cruelly have to expiate actions for which they are not responsible and that are therefore not really theirs? How could these actions be theirs if they have not personally willed them and how could they will them except through a free and autonomous choice? And yet, Rivier asks, "is it really inconceivable, seen from a different point of view from our own, that man should will what he has not chosen, that he may be held responsible for his actions quite independently from his intentions? (And is this not precisely the case where the ancient Greeks are concerned?)"

The problem is thus not contained by the limits of a discussion of the dramatic technique of Aeschylus and the meaning of tragic action. In a Greek context, the whole conceptual system involved in our own representation of what is willed is brought into question. From this point of view, Rivier's own thesis is perhaps not unassailable to a psychologist. We must no doubt dismiss the model of the autonomous decision that modern interpreters are tempted to project, more or less consciously, upon the ancient texts. But by the very same token do we, in our turn, have the right to use the term "will," even with the qualification that it is a bound will and that the decision involved has a different structure from ours since it excludes choice? The will is not a simple category; its dimensions and implications are complex. Quite apart from autonomy and free choice whose validity Rivier legitimately challenges in the case of the Greeks, it presupposes a whole series of conditions: (1) that within the mass of events as a whole it should be possible to distinguish ordered sequences of actions felt to be purely human and sufficiently interconnected and circumscribed within space and time to constitute a unified line of behavior with a particular beginning, course, and end; (2) that the individual should be recognized as such and grasped in his role of agent; (3) that there should be a corresponding development of the concepts of personal merit and culpability so that subjective responsibility takes the place of what has been called the objective crime; and (4) that there should be the beginnings of some analysis of the different levels of on the one hand intentions, and, on the other, the deeds brought to accomplishment. These are all elements that have developed in the course of a long history involving the internal organization of the category of action, the status of the agent, the place and role of the individual in his action, the relations of the agent to different types of action, and the degrees to which he is committed in what he does.

Rivier tells us that the reason for his using the term "will" is to make it clear that the Aeschylean hero, even if deprived of choice in his decisions, is nevertheless very far from passive. Man's dependence in relation to the divine does not subjugate him in a mechanical way as an effect to its cause. According to Rivier, it is a dependence that liberates, that can in no way be described as inhibiting man's will or rendering his decisions sterile since, on the contrary, it promotes his moral energy and deepens his powers of action. However, an absence of passivity, energy, and powers of actions are features that are too general to characterize those elements of the will that, from the psychologist's point of view, constitute it as a specific category linked to that of the person.

Decision without choice, responsibility divorced from intention are, we are told, the forms that the will takes among the Greeks. The whole problem lies in knowing what the Greeks themselves understood by choice and the absence of choice and by responsibility, with or without intention. Our ideas of choice and free choice, of responsibility and intention, are not directly applicable to the ancient mentality any more than our idea of the will is, for in antiquity these notions appear with meanings and forms that are often disconcerting to a modern mind. Aristotle is a particularly significant example in this respect. It is well known that, in his moral philosophy, Aristotle is concerned to refute doctrines according to which the wicked man does not act fully of his own volition but commits his misdeed despite himself. This seems to him in some respects to be the "tragic" concept, represented in particular, in Aristotle's view, by Euripides whose characters sometimes openly declare that they are not guilty of their crimes since, they claim, they acted despite themselves, under constraint, *bia*, dominated, violently compelled by the force of passions all the more irresistible in that they are incarnations within the heroes themselves of divine powers such as Eros or Aphrodite.[6]

Socrates' point of view, on another level, is similar. For him, since all wickedness is ignorance, nobody ever does evil "willingly" (to follow the usual translation). In order to justify the principle of the personal culpability of the wicked man and to provide a theoretical basis for the declaration of man's responsibility, Aristotle elaborates a doctrine of moral action. This represents the most systematic attempt in classical Greek philosophy to distinguish according to their internal conditions all the different modalities of action,[7] from the action performed despite oneself, under external constraint or in ignorance of what one is doing (as when one administers poison, believing it to be a medicine), down to the action performed not only of one's own volition but in full knowledge of what one is doing, after due deliberation and decision. To convey the highest degree of consciousness and commitment in an action on the part of the subject, Aristotle forges a new concept. He uses the term *proairesis* – a rare term and one of hitherto indefinite meaning – giving it a precise technical sense within the framework of his moral system. *Proairesis* is action taking the form of a decision; it is the exclusive prerogative of man to the extent that he is a being endowed with reason, as opposed to children and animals, which are without it. *Proairesis* is more than *hekousion*, a word that is usually translated in French by *volontaire* (intentional or willed),[8] but that cannot really have so strong a meaning. The usual opposition in Greek, in both common speech and legal terminology, between *hekōn, hekousios* on the one hand and *akōn, akousios* on the other in no way corresponds to our own categories of "what is willed" (*volontaire*) and "what is not willed" (*involontaire*). These contrasting expressions should rather be translated as "of one's own volition" and "despite oneself." This is the sense given them by Gauthier and Jolif in their commentary on the *Nicomachean Ethics*, when they use the French terms "de plein gré" and "malgré soi."[9] To see that *hekon* cannot mean willed, intentional (*volontaire*) we have only to note that, when declaring that an act of passion is performed *hekōn* and not *akōn*, Aristotle substantiates this by pointing out that otherwise we should have to say that neither would animals be *hekontes* in their action, an expression that patently cannot have the sense of "intentionally."[10] The animal acts *hekōn*, as do men, when it follows its own inclination, under no constraint from any external power. So while any decision (*proairesis*) is an action carried out of one's own volition (*hekōn*), in contrast "what one does of one's own volition is not always the result of a decision." Thus when one acts through desire (*epithumia*) that is to say lured on by pleasure, or passionately, through *thumos*, without taking the time to reflect, one certainly does it of one's own volition (*hekōn*) but not as a result of a decision (*proairesis*). To be sure, *proairesis* also rests upon a desire, but a rational desire, a wish (*boulēsis*) informed by intelligence and directed, not toward pleasure, but toward a practical objective that thought has already presented to the soul as a good. *Proairesis* implies a previous process of deliberation (*bouleusis*). At the end of this process of reasoned calculation it sets up a choice — as the word indicates (*hairesis*=choice) — that is expressed in a decision that leads directly to the action. This aspect of choice in a practical domain, which commits the subject to action the very moment he has come to a decision, distinguishes *proairesis* firstly from *boulēsis*, the movement of which may come to nothing and remain in the pure form of a "wish" (for one may wish for the impossible), and secondly from a purely theoretical judgment that is concerned with the truth but in no way with the domain of action.[11] On the contrary, deliberation and decision only take place with regard to things that "lie within our power," that "depend on us" (*ta eph' hēmin*) and that can be effected in action not just in one single way, but in several. Here, Aristotle opposes to the *dunameis alogoi*, the irrational powers that can only produce one single effect (for example, heat can only act by heating), the powers that are accompanied by reason, *meta logou*, that are capable of producing opposite effects, *dunameis tōn enantiōn*.[12]

This doctrine presents aspects at first sight so modern that certain interpreters have seen *proairesis* as a free power to choose for the subject as he takes his decision. Some have attributed this power to reason that they understand to be the sovereign determinant of the ultimate ends of the action. Others, on the other hand, rightly stressing the anti-intellectualist reaction against Socrates and, to a large extent, also against Plato that Aristotle's analysis of action represents, have elevated *proairesis* to be a true capacity to will. They have seen it as the active faculty of determining oneself, a power that remains to the very last above the appetites directed, in the case of *epithumia*, toward what is pleasant and, in the case of *boulēsis*, to what is good, and that to some extent quite independently from the pressure desire exerts upon him, impels the subject to take action.

None of these interpretations can be upheld.[13] Without entering in detail into the Aristotelian psychology of action, we may state that *proairesis* does not constitute a power independent from the two types of faculty that, according to Aristotle, alone are at work in moral action: on the one hand the desiring part of the soul (*to orektikon*), on the other the intellect or *nous* in its practical function.[14] *Boulēsis*, desire informed by reason, is directed toward the end of the action: It is what moves the soul toward the good, but, like envy and anger, it is a part of the order of desire, *orexis*.[15] Now the function of desire is entirely passive. So the wish (*boulēsis*) is what directs the soul toward a reasonable end, but it is an end that is imposed upon it and that it has not chosen. Deliberation (*bouleusis*) on the other hand belongs to the faculty that directs, that is to say the practical intellect. In contrast to the wish, however, this has no connection with the end; it is concerned with the means.[16] *Proairesis* does not opt between good and evil, between which it would have a free choice. Once an end has been decided upon — health, for instance — the deliberation consists in the chain of judgments by which reason reaches the conclusion that certain practical means can or cannot lead to health.[17] The last judgment, made at the end of the deliberation, concerns the last means in the chain; it presents it as not only possible on the same grounds as all the others but furthermore as immediately realizable. From this moment on the wish, instead of aiming at health in a general and abstract manner, includes within its desire for the end the concrete conditions by which it can be realized. It concentrates on the last condition that, in the particular situation in which the subject finds himself, effectively brings health within his grasp at that particular moment. Once the desire of *boulēsis* has thus fixed upon the immediately realizable means, action follows and does so necessarily.

This necessity immanent in every phase of wishing, deliberating, and deciding is what justifies the model of the practical syllogism that Aristotle employs to explain the workings of the mind in the process of making a decision. It is as the commentators of the *Ethics* put it: "Just as the syllogism is nothing other than the conjunction of the major and minor, the decision is nothing other than the point of junction or fusion of the desire that the wish represents and the thought that the judgment represents."[18]

Thus: "The wish is *necessarily* what it is and the judgment *necessarily* what it is and action *necessarily* follows upon their conjunction which is the decision."[19] David J. Furley for his part points out that the movement of volition is described by Aristotle in terms of mechanistic physiology; to use the expression employed by Aristotle in the *De motu animalium*, everything comes about necessarily (*ex anankēs*) without there ever being any question of a free movement, in between the stimulus and the response, or of a power of making any choice other than the one the subject does make.[20] Donald James Allan also expresses surprise: The whole of Aristotle's theory of action seems to imply a psychological determinism that appears to us incompatible with its declared purpose of laying a moral and legal basis for responsibility. However, the same author also makes the pertinent observation that it is only from our point of view that Aristotle's psychology is "determinist," and that the adjective is not really appropriate as it presupposes an alternative, namely the "indeterminist" solution.[21] Now, from Aristotle's own point of view, such an antinomy is not pertinent. In his theory of moral action he is not concerned either to demonstrate or to refute the existence of psychological liberty. He never even refers to such a thing. Neither in his work nor in the language of his times can one find any word to refer to what we call free will.[22] The idea of a free power of decision remains alien to his thought. It has no place in his inquiry into the problem of responsible action either in connection with his notion of a choice made with deliberation or of an action accomplished of one's own volition.

This lacuna is an indication of the distance that separates the ancient Greeks' concept of the agent from the modern one. There are other "gaps" that are characteristic of the morality of the ancient world: no word that corresponds to our concept of duty, the tenuous place in the system of values held by the notion of responsibility, the vague and indecisive nature of the idea of obligation.[23] Taken all together, they underline the different orientation of Greek ethics and contemporary moral consciousness. Also, however, and even more profoundly, they reflect the absence, on a psychological level, of an elaborated category of the will, an absence already betrayed linguistically by the lack of any terminology to describe actions stemming from it.[24] As we have already noted, Greek has no term that corresponds with our idea of will. The meaning of *hekōn* is both wider and has a less precise psychological sense: wider, since it is possible to include within the category of *hekousion*, as Aristotle does, any action not imposed through external compulsion, actions carried out through desire and impulse as well as actions that are the result of reflection and deliberation; and it has a less precise psychological meaning since the levels and modalities of intention ranging from a simple inclination to a plan deliberately decided upon remain confused as the term is employed in common usage. There is no distinction between the intentional and the premeditated: *hekōn* has both meanings.[25] As for *akōn*, as Louis Gernet pointed out, it associates all kinds of ideas that, from the point of view of psychology, should be carefully distinguished right from the start. The single expression of *phonos akousios*, referring to the murder committed despite oneself, can mean now a total absence of guilt, now mere negligence, now a positive lack of prudence, now even a more or less fleeting impulse or the quite different case of homicide committed in legitimate self-defense.[26] The fact is that the *hekōn–akōn* opposition is not the fruit of disinterested reflection on the subjective conditions that make an individual the cause responsible for his actions. It is rather a matter of legal categories that, at the time of the city-state, were imposed by the law as norms for common thought. Now the law did not proceed on the basis of a psychological analysis of the varying degrees of the responsibility of the agent. It followed criteria designed to regulate, in the name of the State, the exercise of private vengeance, by drawing distinctions, in accordance with the varying intensity of emotional reaction aroused in the group in question, between the various forms of murder calling for different legal sentences. Dracon is believed to have given Athens, at the beginning of the seventh century, an organized system of courts competent to judge crimes of bloodshed. They covered a number of grades of gravity arranged in descending order according to the strength of collective feeling regarding the excusability of the crime. In this system the *phonos hekousios* included within a single category all murders calling for the full penalty and these fell within the competence of the Areopagus. The *phonos akousios* included excusable murders, which were the province of the Palladion, while the *phonos dikaios* covered justifiable murders, which were the concern of the Delphinion. This third category, even more than the other two, associates together actions that, from the point of view of the psychology of the agent, are extremely heterogeneous. In effect it applies to all cases of murder that custom, for various reasons, fully exculpates and considers unquestionably legitimate. These range from the execution of the adulterer to homicide committed accidentally in the course of public games or in warfare. It is clear then that the distinction made in law by the semantic opposition between *hekōn* and *akōn* is not, in the first instance, founded upon a distinction between what is willed and what is not willed. Rather, it rests upon the differentiation that, in particular historical conditions, the social conscience establishes between actions that are altogether reprehensible and those that are excusable. The two groups are set alongside that of legitimate actions and are seen as representing two antithetical values.

We must furthermore bear in mind the basically intellectualist character of the entire Greek terminology for action, whether it be a matter of the action performed of one's own volition or the one performed despite oneself, the action for which the subject is responsible or the one for which he is not, the action that is reprehensible or the one that is excusable. In the language and mentality of the ancient Greeks, the concepts of knowledge and of action appear to be integrally connected. Where a modern reader expects to find a formula expressing will he instead finds one expressing knowledge. In this sense Socrates' declaration, repeated by Plato, that wrongdoing is ignorance, a lack of understanding, was not so paradoxical as it seems to us today. It is in effect a very clear extension of the most ancient ideas about misdeeds attested in the pre-legal (*préjuridique*) state of society, before the advent of the city-state. In this context a misdeed, *hamartēma*, is seen at the same time as a "mistake" made by the mind, as a religious defilement, and as a moral weakness.[27] *Hamartanein* means to make a mistake in the strongest sense of an error of the intelligence, a blindness that entails failure. *Hamartia* is a mental sickness, the criminal who is prey to madness, a man who has lost his senses, a *demens*, *hamartinoos*. This madness in committing a misdeed or, to give it its Greek names, this *atē* or *Erinus*, takes over the individual from within. It penetrates him like an evil religious force. But even while to some extent it becomes identified with him, it at the same time remains separate, beyond him. The defilement of crime is contiguous and attaches itself, over and beyond the individual to his whole lineage, the whole circle of his relatives. It may affect an entire town, pollute a whole territory. A single power of evil may embody the crime and its most distant beginnings in the criminal and outside him too, together with its ultimate consequences and the punishment for which it rebounds from one generation to the next. As Louis Gernet points out, in such circumstances the individual as such is not the main factor in the crime: "The crime exists outside him, it is objective."[28] In the context of religious thought such as this in which the action of the criminal is seen, in the outside world, as a daemonic power of defilement and, within himself, as an error of the mind, the entire category of action appears to be organized in a different way from our own. Error, felt to be an assault

on the religious order, contains a malignant power far greater than
the human agent. The individual who commits it (or, to be more
precise, who is its victim) is himself caught up in the sinister force
that he has unleashed (or that exerts itself through him). The
action does not emanate from the agent as from its source; rather,
it envelops him and carries him away, swallowing him up in a
power that must perforce be beyond him since it extends, both
spatially and temporally, far beyond his own person. The agent is
caught in the action. He is not its author; he remains included
in it. Within such a framework there can clearly be no question
of individual will. The distinction between what is intentional
and what is enforced in the action of the subject does not even
make sense here. How could one of one's own volition be misled by error? And once it has been committed how could the
hamartia possibly not carry its punishment within itself, quite independent of the intentions of the subject?

With the advent of law and the institution of the city courts, the
ancient religious conception of the misdeed fades away. A new
idea of crime emerges.[29] The role of the individual becomes more
clearly defined. Intention now appears as a constitutive element
of the criminal action, especially in the case of homicide. The
divide between the two broad categories of *hekōn* and *akōn* in
human behavior is now considered a norm. But it is quite clear
that this way of thinking of the offender is also developed within
the framework of a purely intellectualist terminology. The action
performed fully of one's own volition and that which is performed despite oneself are defined as reciprocal opposites in terms
of knowledge and ignorance. The word *hekōn*, of one's own volition, comes to include the idea, in its pure and simple form,
of intention conceived in general terms and without analysis.
This intention is expressed by the word *pronoia*. In the fragments
of the Draconian code that have come down to us the expression
ek pronoias replaces *hekōn*, standing in opposition to *akōn*. In fact

the expressions *ek pronoias* and *hekōn ek pronoias* are exactly syn-
onymous. *Pronoia* is a mode of knowledge, an act of the intellect
made before the action, a premeditation. The culpable intention that makes the act a crime is seen not as a will to do evil
but rather as a full knowledge of the situation. In a decree from
the Hecatompedon, which is the most ancient legal text to have
come down to us in its original form, the understanding of the
new requirements for subjective responsibility is expressed by the
word *eidōs*; to be at fault it is necessary for the offender to have
acted "knowingly."[30] Conversely, *agnoia*, ignorance, which previously constituted the very essence of the misdeed, now stands
in opposition to *hekousion* and comes to define the category of
crimes committed despite oneself, *akōn*, without criminal intention. Xenophon writes: "Misdeeds that men commit through
agnoia I hold all to be *akousia*."[31] Plato himself was obliged to recognize alongside "ignorance," which for him was the general cause
of crime, a second form of *agnoia* that was more strictly defined
and became the basis for the misdeed performed without criminal intention.[32] The paradox of an *agnoia* that is both the constitutive principle of the misdeed and at the same time excuses it
by expunging it is also to be found in the semantic evolution of
the words related to *hamartia*. The evolution is twofold.[33] On the
one hand the terms come to carry the notion of intention: One
is only guilty, *hamartōn*, if one has committed the criminal action
intentionally; anyone who has acted despite himself, *akōn*, is not
guilty, *ouk hamartōn*. The verb *hamartanein* can designate the same
thing as *adikein*: the intentional crime that is prosecuted by the
city. On the other hand, the concept of the intentional that is
implied in the primitive idea of a mistake made through a man's
blindness also bears fruit as early as the fifth century. *Hamartanein*
comes to apply to the excusable misdeed where the subject was
not fully aware of what he was doing. As early as the end of the
fourth century *hamartēma* comes to be used to express the almost
technical idea of the unintentional crime, the *akousion*. Thus Aristotle sets it in opposition to the *adikēma*, the intentional crime,

and to the *atuchēma*, the unforeseeable accident that has nothing to do with the intentions and knowledge of the agent.[34] Thus this intellectualist psychology of the intention makes it possible, over several centuries, for two contradictory meanings to coexist within the same family of terms: to commit a misdeed intentionally and to commit it unintentionally. The reason for this is that the notion of ignorance operated at two quite different levels of thought in quite different ways. On the one hand it retained the earlier association of sinister religious forces that can overtake a man's mind and render him blind to evil. On the other, it had already acquired the positivist sense of an absence of knowledge regarding the concrete conditions in which an action is perpetrated. The ancient kernel of myth remains sufficiently alive in the collective imagination to provide the schema necessary for what is excusable to be represented in a way in which, precisely, it is possible for "ignorance" to assume the most modern of meanings. But on neither of the two levels of meaning for this term, which is, as it were, balanced between the idea of ignorance that causes the misdeed and that of ignorance that excuses it, is the category of will implied.

Another type of ambiguity appears in the compound forms of the *boul-* family, which are also employed to express different modalities of the intentional.[35] The verb *boulomai*, which is sometimes translated as "to will" (*vouloir*), is used in Homer less frequently than *thelō* and *ethelō*. It has the meaning of "to desire," "to prefer." In Attic prose it tends to supplant *ethelō* and means the subject's own inclination, his intimate wish, his personal preference, while *ethelō* takes on the specialized meaning of "to consent to" and is often used with an object that is the opposite of that which is the subject's own inclination. Three nouns connected with action were derived from *boulomai*: *boulēsis*, desire, wish; *boulēma*, intention; and *boulē*, decision, plan, council (in the sense of the ancient political institution).[36] It is clear that the group of terms lies somewhere between the level of desire or spontaneous inclination and that of reflection, intelligent calculation.[37]

65

The meaning of the verbs *bouleuō* and *bouleuomai* is less equivocal: to sit in council, to deliberate. We have seen that in Aristotle *boulēsis* is a kind of desire; so, insofar as *boulēsis* means inclination or wish, its meaning is not so strong as actual intention. On the other hand the meaning of *bouleuō* and its derivatives *boulēma, epiboulē, proboulē*, is stronger. They indicate premeditation or, to translate the Aristotelian term *proairesis* more precisely, the pre-decision that, as Aristotle stresses, implies two associated ideas: on the one hand that of deliberation (*bouleuomai*) through calculation (*logos*) and reflection (*dianoia*) and, on the other, the idea that this has taken place at some previous point in time.[38] The notion of the intentional thus oscillates between the spontaneous tendency of a desire and intelligent premeditated calculation. In their analyses the philosophers distinguish and sometimes oppose these two poles but the way the words are used makes it possible to move from one to the other or to shift between them. Thus, in the *Cratylus*, Plato connects *boulē* with *bolē*, a throw. His reason for doing so is that *boulesthai* (to wish) means *ephiesthai* (to incline toward) and he adds that *bouleuesthai* (to deliberate) also does. In contrast, *aboulia* (lack of reflection) consists in missing the target, in not achieving "what one desired [ἐβούλετο], that on which one has deliberated [ἐβουλεύετο], that toward which one was inclined [ἐφίετο]."[39] Thus not only wishing but also deliberating implies a movement, a tension, a spurt of the soul toward the object. This is because, in the case of inclination (*boulomai*) as in that of reasoned deliberation (*bouleuō*) the truest cause for the subject's action is not to be found in the subject himself. He is always set in movement by an "end" that directs his behavior as it were from outside him, namely either the object toward which his desire spontaneously reaches out or that which reflection presents to his thought as something desirable.[40] In the former case the intention of the agent appears to be linked with and subject to the desire; in the latter, it is impelled by his intellectual knowledge of what is best. But between the spontaneous movement of desire and the intellect's vision of the good, there seems to be no area where the will could find its own particular field of application and where the subject, in and through his own action of willing, could become the autonomous center for his decision, the true source of his actions.

If this is true how should we understand Aristotle's declarations to the effect that our actions lie within our power (*eph' hēmin*), that we are the responsible causes for them (*aitioi*), that man is the origin and father (*archē kai gennētēs*) of his actions as of his children?[41] They certainly indicate a desire to root actions deep within the subject, to present the individual as the efficient cause of his action so that wicked men or those who lack self-control may be held responsible for their misdeeds and may not invoke as an excuse some external constraint of which they claim to be the victims. Nevertheless, we must interpret the expressions used by Aristotle correctly. He writes on several occasions that a man's actions "depend upon himself." The exact meaning of this "*autos*" becomes clearer if it is compared to the expression in which he defines living creatures as being endowed with the power "of moving themselves." In this context *autos* does not have the meaning of a personal self nor of a special faculty possessed by the subject to control the interplay of the causes that operate within him.[42] *Autos* refers to the human individual taken as a whole, conceived as the sum total of the dispositions that make up his particular character or *ēthos*. Discussing the Socratic theory that wickedness is ignorance, Aristotle points out that men are responsible for this ignorance; it depends upon them, lies within their power (*ep' autois*), for they are free (*kurioi*, literally "masters") to do something about it. He then dismisses the objection that the wicked man is, precisely by reason of his wicked state, incapable of doing such a thing. He declares that the wicked man is himself, by reason of his dissolute life, the responsible cause (*aitios*) for finding himself in this state. "For in every domain, actions of a certain type produce a corresponding type of man."[43] The character or *ēthos* that belongs to every kind of man depends upon the sum total of dispositions (*hexeis*) that are developed by practice and fixed by force of habit.[44] Once the character is formed the subject acts in conformity with these dispositions and would be unable to act in any other way. But, Aristotle says, prior to this he was free (*kurios*) to act in various ways.[45] In this sense, if the way in which each of us conceives the end of his action necessarily depends on his character, his character also depends on himself since it has been formed by his own actions. At no moment, however, does Aristotle seek to found upon psychological analysis the capacity possessed by the subject to decide to do one thing rather than another while his dispositions were not yet fixed, and thus to assume responsibility for what he would do later on. It is difficult to see how the young child, without *proairesis*, could have any more power than the grown man to determine himself freely and to forge his own character. Aristotle does not inquire into the various forces that are at work in the formation of an individual temperament, although he is not unaware of the role of nature or of that of education or legislation. "It is therefore of no meager importance that we should have been brought up with such-or-such habits; on the contrary this is of sovereign importance, or rather everything depends on this."[46] If everything depends on this, the autonomy of the subject fades away in the face of the weight of social constraints. But Aristotle is unconcerned: His point was essentially a moral one, so it is enough for him to establish between the character and the individual seen in the round the intimate and reciprocal link that is the basis for the subjective responsibility of the agent. The man is "father" of his actions when their origin, *archē*, and their efficient cause, *aitia*, are to be found "in him." But this inner causality is only defined in a purely negative fashion: Whenever an action can be assigned no external source of constraint, it is because the cause is to be found "in the man" because he has acted "voluntarily," "of his own volition," so that his action can legitimately be imputed to him.

In the last analysis Aristotle does not refer the causality of the subject, any more than his responsibility, to any kind of will power. For him it depends upon an assimilation of the internal, the spontaneous, and what is strictly autonomous. The confusion of these different levels of action shows that even if the subject has already taken on his own individuality and is accepting responsibility for all the actions that he performs of his own volition, he remains too much bound by the determining factors upon his character and too closely welded to the internal dispositions of his nature – which control the practice of vice and virtue – for him to emerge fully as the seat of personal decision and to assume, as *autos*, his full stature as agent.

This long digression by way of Aristotle will not have been unprofitable if it enables us to shed some light upon the model of action peculiar to tragedy, by setting it into a wider historical perspective. The development of subjective responsibility, the distinction made between an action carried out of one's own volition and one performed despite oneself, and the account taken of the agent's personal intentions are all innovations of which the tragedians were aware; and through the advances made in law, they had a profound effect upon the Greek concept of the agent and also altered the individual's relation to his own actions. So the far-reaching effects of these changes that occurred from Homeric man to Aristotle, via tragedy, should not be underestimated. Yet they are changes that take place within limits so circumscribed that, even for the philosopher anxious to base individual responsibility upon the purely internal conditions of action, they remain set within a psychological framework in which the category of the will has no place.

Let us now return to the general questions regarding tragic man posed by Rivier. Do we have to admit that in the case of the Greeks we find will without choice and responsibility independent of intention? It is not possible to answer yes or no to this partly because of the transformations we have just mentioned but also, and more importantly, because it would seem that the question should not be formulated in these terms at all. In Aristotle, a decision is conceived to be a choice (*hairesis*) and intention appears a constitutive element of responsibility. At the same time, neither the choice of *proairesis* nor the intention, even when the result of deliberation, refer to any internal power of auto-decision on the part of the agent. Reversing Rivier's formula, we might say that one does indeed find choice and responsibility based on intention in a Greek such as Aristotle but what is lacking, precisely, is will. Furthermore, in Aristotle's analyses stress is laid on the contrast between what is accomplished under constraint and what is performed by the subject of his own volition. For the latter — and for it alone — he is responsible, whether he took action in a spontaneous manner or whether he decided upon it following calculation and reflection. But what is the significance of this antinomy that tragedy should, it would seem, be unaware of if it is true that, as Rivier claims, the "decisions," for which Aeschylus' works provide a model, always appear as subjection of the hero to a constraint imposed upon him by the gods? Aristotle's distinction between the two categories of action does not oppose *constraint* to *free will* but rather a constraint imposed from outside to a determination that operates from within. And even if this internal determination is different from external constraint, it is nevertheless something that is necessary. When the subject follows the disposition of his own character or *ēthos* he is reacting necessarily, *ex anankēs*, but his action nevertheless emanates from himself. Far from being constrained to make the decision that he does, he shows himself to be the father and cause of what he is doing and so bears full responsibility for it.

Thus the problem is to determine whether the *anankē* that Rivier has shown to be, in Aeschylus, the mainspring of the tragic decision, always — as he believes — takes the form of an external pressure exerted upon man by the gods. May it not also be presented as being immanent in the hero's own character or appear in both these aspects at the same time, so that, from the tragic point of view, the power that engenders the actions appears in two opposed but inseparable guises?

Here we must certainly take account of the tendency that developed between Aeschylus and Euripides to make tragedy more "psychological," to lay increasing emphasis upon the personal feelings of the protagonists. J. de Romilly goes so far as to write that in Aeschylus the tragic action "involves forces that are superior to man; and in the face of these forces the characters of the individuals fade away and appear secondary. In Euripides, in contrast, all the attention is upon the characters of the individuals."[47]

It is quite right to note such differences of emphasis. It nevertheless seems to us that throughout the fifth century Attic tragedy presents one particular model of human action that is peculiar to it and defines it as a specific literary genre. It is a model that retains the same essential characteristics for as long as tragedy remains alive. In this sense tragedy can be seen as a particular stage in the development of the categories of action and of the agent. It marks a particular moment and, as it were, turning point in the history of the ancient Greeks' approach to the notion of the will. We shall now attempt to define this tragic status of the agent more closely and to understand its psychological implications.

Our task is made easier by the recent publication of two articles, one by Albin Lesky, the other by R.P. Winnington-Ingram, the conclusions of which are in many respects similar. In 1966 Lesky returned to his idea of the double motivation, giving a closer definition of its significance as regards decision and responsibility in Aeschylus.[48] Where he writes of free volition, of will, of freedom of choice, the terminology he uses is open to the full weight of Rivier's criticisms. Nevertheless, his analyses clearly show how much the dramatist ascribes to the hero himself in the taking of his decision. Let us take the case of Agamemnon as an example. When he resolves to sacrifice his daughter Iphigenia it is, according to Rivier, only under a double constraint imposed upon him like an objective necessity: It is impossible for him to escape from the order of Artemis communicated to him by Chalcas the diviner; it is also impossible to desert an alliance of war whose goal – the destruction of Troy – is in accordance with the demands of Zeus Xenios. The expression used in line 218, "when the harness of necessity was yoked to his neck," sums up and illustrates the state of total subjection that, according to Rivier, leaves the king no margin for initiative and at the same time undermines all the claims of contemporary interpreters who seek to explain his behavior by personal motivation.

This aspect of submission to superior powers is undeniably present in the work. But for Lesky it is only one aspect of the dramatic action. There is another that may — to our modern way of looking at it — appear incompatible with the first but that, as the text makes quite clear, is an essential element in the tragic decision. The sacrifice of Iphigenia is certainly necessary by reason of the situation that presses upon the king like fatality, but, at the same time, this murder is not only accepted but passionately desired by Agamemnon who is therefore responsible for it. What Agamemnon is constrained to do under the yoke of *Ananke* is also what he desires to do with all his heart and soul if it is only at this price that he can be victorious. From the point of view of the human decision that controls its execution, the sacrifice ordered by the gods assumes the form of a monstrous crime for which the price will have to be paid. "If this sacrifice, this virginal blood is what binds the winds, it is permitted to desire it fervently, most fervently," declares the son of Atreus.[49] What Agamemnon declares to be religiously permissible is not an action he is compelled despite himself to commit; rather, it is his own intimate desire to do anything and everything that might open up the way before his army. And the repetition of the same words (ὀργᾷ περιοργῶς ἐπιθυμεῖν) with the emphasis they lay on the violence of this passion, underlines the fact that it is Agamemnon himself, for reasons personal to him that must clearly be condemned, who rushes headlong into the path that the gods, for other reasons, have chosen. The chorus declares that the king "has had a change of heart that is impure, sacrilegious: He is prepared to dare anything, his mind is made up. . . . He dares to become the sacrificer of his own daughter in order to help an army to recapture a woman

and to open up the sea to his ships."[50] Another passage, to which
the commentators have not perhaps devoted enough attention,
seems to us to confirm this interpretation of the text. The chorus says that at that time the leader of the Achaean fleet "made
himself the accomplice of a capricious destiny rather than criticize a diviner."[51] The oracle of Artemis that Chalcas transmits is
not imposed upon the king as a categorical imperative. It does
not say, "Sacrifice your daughter," but simply "if you want the
winds they must be paid for with the blood of your child." By
submitting to this, without in any way questioning (*psegein*, to
blame) the monstrosity of it, the king shows that the life and love
of his daughter cease to count for him the moment that they
become an obstacle to the warlike expedition of which he has
assumed command. It may be objected that this war is willed by
Zeus, that the Trojans must be made to expiate Paris' crime against
hospitality. But here too the tragic facts are ambiguous. Their significance and meaning change as one passes from the one point
of view to the other, that is the divine and the human, that the
tragedy both unites and opposes. From the point of view of the
gods the war is indeed fully justified. But by becoming themselves
the instrument of Zeus' *Dikē*, the Greeks in their turn enter the
world of crime and impiety. They are led not so much by respect
for the gods as by their own *hubris*. In the course of the drama
the destruction of Troy, like the killing of Iphigenia and the slaughter of the pregnant hare that foreshadows both, is described from
two, contrasting, points of view: It is the sacrifice of a victim
piously offered to the gods to satisfy their vengeance but it is also
quite the opposite, a horrible sacrilege perpetrated by warriors
thirsting for murder and blood, veritable wild beasts like the two
eagles that have devoured not only the tender, defenseless female
but also the little ones she carried in her womb.[52] When the
justice of Zeus recoils against Agamemnon it does so through
Clytemnestra. And the origin of the king's retribution is to be
found even beyond these two protagonists, in the curse that has
lain on the entire line of the Atreidae ever since the criminal feast-

73

ing of Thyestes. Demanded by the Erinyes of this race and willed by Zeus, the murder of the king of the Greeks is nevertheless prepared, decided, and executed by his wife for reasons very much her own and very much in line with her own character. However much she may invoke Zeus or the Erinyes, it is really her own hatred for her husband, her guilty passion for Aegisthus and her virile lust for power that decide her to action. She attempts, in the presence of Agamemnon's corpse, to justify herself before the old men of the chorus: "You say that this is my work. Don't you believe it. Don't even believe that I am the wife of Agamemnon. Taking the form of the wife of this dead man, it is really the ancient, bitter, vengeful spirit (*alastōr*) of Atreus who has payed with this victim."[53] What is here expressed with such force is the ancient religious concept of crime and punishment. Clytemnestra, the individual responsible for the crime she has just committed, tries to efface herself and disappear behind a daemonic presence that is far beyond her. She claims that it is really the Erinyes of the race who are using her who should be incriminated, the *atē* or spirit of criminal waywardness that belongs to the line of the Atreidae that has once again manifested its sinister power; it is the ancient defilement that has, of itself, occasioned this new defilement. But it is significant that the chorus dismisses this interpretation and that it does so using legal terminology: "Who will come forward to bear witness that you are innocent of this murder?"[54] Clytemnestra is not *anaitios*, nonculpable, nonresponsible. And yet the chorus is not sure. Mingled with the evidence of this altogether human responsibility of criminals such as Clytemnestra and Aegisthus (and Aegisthus boasts that he has acted of his own volition as the instigator of the crime), is the feeling that supernatural forces may have had a hand in the events. Through failing to criticize the oracle Agamemnon made himself the accomplice of destiny; perhaps, the chorus now admits, the *alastōr* or vengeful spirit was indeed the "auxiliary" (*sullēptōr*) of Clytemnestra. In this way the designs of the gods and the plans or passions of men are both at work in the tragic decision. This "complicity" finds expression in the use of legal terms: *metaitios*, co-responsible, *xunaitia*, common responsibility, *paraitias*, partial responsibility.[55] In the *Persiae* Darius declares: "When a mortal himself (*autos*) works for his own downfall, a god comes to abet (*sunaptetai*) him."[56] The nature of tragic action appears to us to be defined by the simultaneous presence of a "self" and something greater that is divine at work at the core of the decision and creating a constant tension between the two opposed poles.

To be sure, the subject's own part in his decision does not belong to the category of the will. It is all very well for André Rivier to make ironic remarks on this point, noting that, short of holding that the Greeks placed the will on the same level as the feelings and passions, the very vocabulary of Aeschylus (*orgē*, passion; *epithumein*, to desire) rules out speaking of personal will where Agamemnon is concerned. Nevertheless it is our view that the text equally excludes the interpretation of constraint pure and simple. It is only for our modern selves that the problem is posed in terms of a choice between free will on the one hand and constraint in various forms on the other. If we think in the categories of the ancient Greeks we shall say that when Agamemnon was carried away by his desire he was acting if not in a willed manner (*volontairement*) at least voluntarily (*volontiers*), of his own volition (*hekōn*) and that, in this sense, he does indeed appear to be *aitios*, the responsible cause of his own actions. Furthermore, in the case of Clytemnestra and Aegisthus, Aeschylus does not simply insist on the passions — hatred, resentment, ambition — that motivated their criminal action; he also emphasizes that the murder, already long premeditated, has been painstakingly prepared, devised in every detail so that the victim shall not escape.[57] Terminology connected with the passions is thus overlaid with the intellectual terminology of premeditation. Clytemnestra boasts of not having acted in a thoughtless way (οὐκ ἀφρόντιστος) and of having employed lies and cunning to catch her husband the more surely in the trap.[58] And Aegisthus, in his turn, is complacent at having been behind the queen, the one who hatched the plot in

75

the shadows, drawing together all the threads of the conspiracy so that his *dusboulia*, his plot of murder, should be realized.[59] Thus the chorus is simply repeating his own words when it accuses him of having killed the king deliberately, *hekōn*, with premeditation (βουλεῦσαι, 1.1614; ἐβούλευσας, 1.1627 and 1634). But whether it is a case of impulsion and desire, as with Agamemnon, or of reflection and premeditation, as with Clytemnestra and Aegisthus, the ambiguity of the tragic decision remains unaffected. In both cases the resolution arrived at by the hero emanates from himself, is in keeping with his own personal character. At the same time in both cases it is a manifestation, at the heart of human life, of the intervention of supernatural powers. No sooner has the chorus referred to the impious change of mind that gives the king of the Greeks the audacity to sacrifice his daughter than it describes the source of men's misfortunes as "fatal frenzy that inspires mortals with audacity."[60] As Rivier points out, this rush of frenzy, *parakopa*, which obscures the intelligence of the king, belongs to the same divine aspect of decision taking as *atē*, the religious power sent by the gods to mislead men and bring them to their doom. Equally, the gods are just as much present in Agamemnon's emotional impulse as in Clytemnestra's cold resolution or Aegisthus' lucid premeditation. Even while the queen is exulting in the splendid piece of work that she has accomplished "with her own hand," she at the same time attributes its authorship to *Dikē*, to the Erinyes, and to *Atē*, claiming to have been merely their instrument.[61] And the chorus, even while laying direct responsibility for the crime at her door and pouring its scorn and hatred upon her,[62] also recognizes in the death of the king a manifestation of *Atē*, the work of *Dikē*, the hand of a *daimōn* who has made use of two women (Helen and Clytemnestra) with equally evil souls (*psuchē*) in order to bring down the accursed descendence of Tantalus.[63] As for Aegisthus, in exactly the same way he too claims the credit for having drawn together all the threads of the plot and at the same time praises the Erinyes for having woven the net that caught Agamemnon in the trap.[64] Lamenting over the corpse of the king, in the presence of Clytemnestra, before her accomplice has appeared, the chorus recognizes in the misfortune that has struck the son of Atreus the great law of justice established by Zeus: that punishment shall fall upon the guilty. Agamemnon was bound, when the time came, to pay the price for the bloodshed of his child. The chorus concludes that nothing happens to men that is not the work of Zeus.[65] However, as soon as Aegisthus appears and speaks, the only *dikē* invoked by the chorus is that which, in stoning him, the people intend to mete out to the criminal now revealed by his crime in his true character of cowardly seducer, unscrupulous man of ambition, and arrogant cynic.[66]

Thus in Aeschylus the tragic decision is rooted in two types of reality, on the one hand *ēthos*, character, and on the other *daimōn*, divine power. Since the origin of action lies both in man himself and outside him, the same character appears now as an agent, the cause and source of his actions, and now as acted upon, engulfed in a force that is beyond him and sweeps him away. Yet although human and divine causality are intermingled in tragedy, they are not confused. The two levels are quite distinct, sometimes opposed to each other. But even where the contrast seems most deliberately stressed by the poet, it is not that these are two mutually exclusive categories and that, depending on the degree of initiative on the part of the subject, his actions may fall into either the one or the other; rather, depending on the point of view, these same actions present two contrary yet indissociable aspects. R.P. Winnington-Ingram's remarks on Sophocles' *Oedipus* prove the point conclusively.[67] When Oedipus kills his father and marries his mother without knowing or wishing it, he is the plaything of a destiny imposed upon him by the gods even before his birth. "What man," wonders the king of Thebes, "could be more hated by the gods than I [ἐχθροδαίμων]? . . . Would it not be correct to conclude that my misfortunes are the work of a cruel *daimōn*?"[68] And a little further on his thoughts are echoed by the chorus: "Taking your personal destiny [δαίμων] as an example, yes, your destiny, unhappy Oedipus, I would say that no human life is a

happy one."[69] Expressed by the word *daimōn*, Oedipus' destiny is
seen as a supernatural power attached to his person, which directs
the course of his whole life. That is why the chorus exclaims:
"Despite yourself [ἄκοντα] it has revealed Time, which sees all
things, to you."[70] This misfortune to which Oedipus is subjected
(*akōn*) appears to be opposed in every way to the new misfortune
that he imposes upon himself deliberately when he puts out his
eyes. The servant who announces it to the public describes it as
an evil this time committed of his own volition, not undergone
despite himself (κακὰ ἑκόντα κοὐκ ἄκοντα); and he goes on to say
that the most agonizing sufferings are those chosen by oneself
(αὐθαίρετοι).[71] The opposition *akōn-hekōn*, twice stressed in the text
and reinforced by the parallel contrast between that which is
caused by a *daimōn* and that which is a personal choice, could not,
it seems, be more strict or more rigorous. One might be tempted
to believe that it draws a clear line of demarcation in the drama
between that which is imposed upon Oedipus as a result of the
fatality of the oracle and that which stems from his own personal
decision. On the one hand there are the ancient trials announced
in advance by Apollo, for which the causes are divine; on the other,
the hero's self-inflicted mutilation for which the cause is human.
Yet when the doors of the palace open and the king comes forward onto the stage, blind and bleeding, the very first words of
the chorus suffice to dispel this apparent dichotomy: "Oh, suffering dreadful to behold [δεινὸν πάθος]...what madness [μανία]
has struck you...what *daimōn* has crowned your destiny that was
the work of an evil *daimōn* [δυσδαίμονι μοίρᾳ]?"[72] Oedipus is no
longer presented as an agent responsible for his misfortune but
as a victim undergoing the ordeal that is imposed upon him. And
this is the hero's own opinion too: "Oh, *daimōn*, to what lengths
have you gone!"[73] The two contrary aspects of the action he has
accomplished by blinding himself are both united and opposed
in the very same expressions that the chorus and himself both use.
When the chorus says to him: "What a dreadful thing you have
done [δράσας].... What *daimōn* impelled you to do it?"[74], he

replies: "It is Apollo who is the author [τελῶν] of my atrocious sufferings [κακὰ πάθεα] but nobody but my unfortunate self [ἐγὼ τλάμων] with his own hand [αὐτόχειρ] struck the blow."[75] The divine causality and the human initiative that just now appeared to be so clearly opposed to each other have now come together and, at the very heart of the decision "chosen" by Oedipus, a subtle play of language produces a shift from the aspect of action (*drasas, autocheir*) to that of passivity (*pathea*).

What is the significance, in a psychological history of the will, of this tension that the tragedians constantly maintain between the active and the passive, intention and constraint, the internal spontaneity of the hero and the destiny that is fixed for him in advance by the gods? Why this ambiguity in precisely the literary genre that, for the very first time in Western history, seeks to portray man in his condition as an agent? Placed at the crossroads of a decisive choice, with before him an option that will settle the way the whole drama is to unfold, the tragic hero is presented as actively committed, facing up to the consequences of his actions. We have elsewhere already stressed that the rise, flowering, and decline of tragedy – all within the space of less than a hundred years – mark a particular historical moment of strictly limited duration, a period of crisis in which transformation and abrupt change are sufficiently interwoven with elements of continuity for there to be a clash, sometimes a painful one, between the ancient forms of religious thought that lived on in legendary traditions and the new ideas connected with the development of law and new political practices.[76] This debate between the mythical past and the present of the city-state finds expression in particular in tragedy, which brings into question the position of man as an agent, and pursues an anxious inquiry into the relationship between man and his own actions. To what extent is the protagonist of the drama, seen as a model by virtue both of his exploits and his ordeals and endowed with a "heroic" temperament that

79

totally commits him to all that he undertakes, to what extent is he truly the source of his own actions? We see him on the stage deliberating upon the options open to him, weighing the advantages and disadvantages, assuming the initiative in what he does, taking action that is in line with his own character and advancing further and further along the path he has chosen, bearing the consequences and accepting responsibility for his decisions; yet all the while does not the basis and origin of his actions lie elsewhere than within himself? Does not their true significance remain beyond him right up to the end, because they depend not so much upon his own intentions and plans as upon the general order of the world, presided over by the gods, which alone can give human enterprises their authentic meaning? Only right at the end of the drama does it all become clear to the agent. As he undergoes what he believed he himself had decided, he understands the real meaning of what has in fact been accomplished without his either desiring or knowing it. In his purely human dimensions the agent is not the sufficient cause and reason for his actions: On the contrary, it is his action, recoiling upon him as the gods have, in their sovereignty, ordered, that reveals him to himself, showing him the true nature of what he is and what he does. So it is that, on completion of the inquiry that he, in his passion for justice, has led for the good of the city, and without having done anything of his own volition for which he can personally be held responsible from the point of view of the law, Oedipus finds himself to be a criminal, an outlaw, afflicted by the gods with the most horrible defilement. But the very weight of this crime that he must assume without having committed it intentionally, the harshness of a punishment that he bears with fortitude without having deserved it, raise him above the human condition at the same time as they cut him off from the society of other men. From a religious point of view he is characterized by excess, by the gratuitous nature of his misfortune: His death will come to be regarded as an apotheosis and the presence of his tomb will guarantee the salvation of those who agreed to give him asylum. In contrast, at the end of Aeschylus' trilogy, Orestes, who is guilty of a monstrous crime, the premeditated murder of his mother, is acquitted by the first human court ever instituted in Athens. Those taking up his defense plead that, there being no criminal intention on his part, given that he acted upon the imperious order of Apollo that he could not elude, his action must be classified as *dikaios phonos*, justifiable murder. Yet here too an ambiguity remains; we detect a hesitation. The fact is that the human judgment is indecisive. The acquittal is obtained only thanks to a procedural artifice, after Athena has, by casting her vote, restored the equality of votes for and against Orestes. The young man is thus legally absolved thanks to Athena, that is to say thanks to the tribunal of Athens, although from the point of view of human morality he is not fully exonerated.

Tragic guilt thus takes shape in the constant clash between the ancient religious conception of the misdeed as a defilement attached to an entire race and inexorably transmitted from one generation to the next in the form of an *atē* or madness sent by the gods, and the new concept adopted in law according to which the guilty one is defined as a private individual who, acting under no constraint, has deliberately chosen to commit a crime. To the modern mind these two concepts appear radically to exclude one another. But tragedy, even as it opposes them, has them counterbalance each other to various degrees so that, since neither of the two terms of the antinomy ever quite disappears, tension is never entirely absent. Decision and responsibility are understood on two different levels in tragedy and thus have an ambiguous, enigmatic character; they are seen as questions that, in default of any fixed and unequivocal answers, always remain open.

The tragic agent also appears to be tugged in two opposite directions. Sometimes he is *aitios*, the responsible cause of his actions to the extent that they are an expression of his character as a man; sometimes a plaything in the hands of the gods, the victim of a destiny that can attach itself to him like a *daimōn*. The action of a tragedy presupposes that a notion of human nature with its own distinctive characteristics should already have emerged so that the human and divine levels are distinct enough to be set in opposition. But if it is to be tragic it is also necessary that these two levels should continue to be seen as inseparable. In that it presents man as committed to his actions tragedy bears witness to the progress made in the psychological elaboration of the agent. But at the same time it is also evidence of the extent to which, for the Greeks, this category is still limited, indecisive, and vaguely defined. The agent is no longer included in his actions, swallowed up by them. But he is still not in himself truly the center and the productive cause. Because his actions take place within a temporal order over which he has no control and to which he must submit passively, his actions elude him; they are beyond his understanding. We know that the Greeks did not consider the artist or artisan producing their works through their *poiēsis* to be their true authors. *They* create nothing. Their role is simply to embody in matter some preexistent *form* that is independent from and superior to their *technē*. The work itself is more perfect than the worker; the man is less than his task.[77] And equally, in practical action, his *praxis*, man does not measure up to what he does.

In fifth-century Athens the individual, with his own particular character, emerged as subject to the law. The intention of the agent was recognized as a fundamental element in responsibility. Through his participation in political life in which decisions were taken following open, positivist, and secular debate, each citizen began to be aware of himself as an agent responsible for the conduct of affairs, more or less master, more or less in a position to direct the uncertain course of events by reason of his *gnōmē*, his powers of judgment, his *phronēsis*, his intelligence. But neither the individual nor his internal life had acquired enough consistency and autonomy to make the subject the center of the decision from which his actions were believed to emanate. Cut off from his familial, civic, and religious roots the individual was nothing; he did not find himself alone, he ceased to exist. As we have seen, even in law the idea of intention remained vague and equivocal.[78] In making a decision a subject did not exercise a power of auto-determination truly his own. The grip individuals or groups held on the future was so limited and the prospect of ordering the future remained so alien to the Greek category of action that the perfection of practical actions appeared greater to the extent that they were less committed to time, less directed toward an objective projected and prepared for in advance. The ideal for action was to abolish the temporal distance between the agent and his action, to have them fully coincide in a pure present.[79] For the Greeks of the classical period, to act meant not so much to organize and dominate time as to exclude oneself from it, to bypass it. Swept along in the current of human life, action turned out to be illusory, vain, and impotent without the help of the gods. What it lacked was the power of realization, the efficacy that was the exclusive privilege of the divine. Tragedy expresses this weakness inherent in action, this internal inadequacy of the agent, by showing the gods working behind men's backs from beginning to end of the drama, to bring everything to its conclusion. Even when, by exercising choice, he makes a decision, the hero almost always does the opposite of what he thinks he is doing.

The very way that tragedy developed bears witness to the relative inconsistency of the Greek category of the agent and its lack of internal organization. In the plays of Euripides the divine background is toned down or, at any rate, distanced from the vicissitudes of human life. Here, in the last of the great tragic writers, the spotlight is in preference directed onto the individual characters of the protagonists and their mutual relationships. But left in this way to his own devices, to a large extent disentangled from the supernatural and restored to his own human dimensions, the agent is still no more vigorously portrayed. On the contrary, instead of action being depicted as it was in Aeschylus and Sophocles, in Euripides tragedy shifts toward the expression of the pathetic. As J. de Romilly notes, "By no longer being concerned with the divine significance, one is no longer concerned with action: one's attention turns to the sufferings and tricks of human life."[80] In the work of Euripides human life, cut off from the general order of the world governed by the gods, appears so indeterminate and confused "that it leaves no room for responsible action."[81]

Jean-Pierre Vernant

CHAPTER IV

Oedipus Without the Complex[1]

In 1900 Freud published *Die Traumdeutung*. It was in this work that he referred for the first time to the Greek legend of Oedipus. His experience as a doctor led him to see in the child's love for one of his parents and his hatred for the other the root of the psychic impulses that determine the later appearance of neuroses. Childhood attraction and hostility toward mother and father occur in normal subjects as in neuropaths, although not to the same degree. This discovery, which seemed to have a general application, was, according to him, confirmed by a myth that had come down to us from the mists of classical antiquity. This was the Oedipus myth that Sophocles used as his theme in his tragedy entitled *Oidipous Turannos* or *Oedipus Rex*.

But in what respects is it possible that a literary work belonging to the culture of fifth-century Athens, itself a very free transposition of a much more ancient Theban legend dating from before the institution of the city-state, should confirm the observations of a doctor on the patients who throng his consulting rooms at the beginning of the twentieth century? From Freud's point of view the question needs no answer because it is one that there is no point in asking. As he sees it the interpretation of the Greek myth and drama poses no problems of any kind. It is not necessary to decode them using the appropriate analytical methods. To the psychiatrist they are immediately comprehensible, perfectly transparent, and at once yield up a meaning that guarantees uni-

85

versal validity to the doctor's psychological theories. But where is this "meaning" to be found — the meaning that is supposed to be immediately revealed in this way to Freud, and after him to all psychoanalysts as if they were latter-day Tiresiases with a gift of second sight enabling them to reach beyond mythical or literary forms of expression to grasp a truth invisible to the profane? It is not the meaning sought by the Greek scholar or the historian, the meaning present within the work, contained in its structures, a meaning that must be painstakingly reconstructed through a study at every level of the message that a legendary tale or a tragic fiction constitutes.

For Freud, the meaning becomes apparent through the immediate reactions of the public, through the emotions that the play arouses. He is quite clear on this point: It is the constant and universal success of the tragedy of Oedipus that proves that, equally universally, there exists in the child's psyche a whole set of tendencies similar to those that lead the hero to his doom. If *Oedipus Rex* moves us, just as it affected the citizens of Athens, it is not — as was hitherto believed — because he is the embodiment of a tragedy of destiny in which the omnipotence of the gods is opposed to the pitiful will of men; it is because Oedipus' destiny is in a way our own, because we carry within us the same curse that the oracle pronounced against him. By killing his father and marrying his mother he is fulfilling a childhood desire of our own that we strive to forget. The tragedy is thus in every respect comparable to a psychoanalysis: By lifting the veil that conceals from Oedipus the face of the incestuous parricide that he is, it reveals us to ourselves. The material of the tragedy consists of the dreams that each of us has dreamed: Its meaning bursts shatteringly upon us with the horror and guilt that overwhelm us when, through the inexorable progression of the drama, our early desires for the death of our father and union with our mother rise to the surface of our consciousness that has been pretending never to have experienced them.

This demonstration has all the semblance of the rigor of an argument based on a vicious circle. The procedure is as follows: A theory elaborated on the basis of clinical cases and contemporary dreams is "confirmed" by a dramatic text from another age. But the text can only provide this confirmation provided that it is itself interpreted by reference to the framework of the modern spectator's dream — as conceived at least by the theory in question. For it not to be a vicious circle it would be necessary for the Freudian theory not to present itself from the outset as a self-evident interpretation but rather to emerge, on completion of a painstaking analysis, as a necessity imposed by the work itself, a condition for the understanding of its dramatic organization, the tool for the whole decoding of the text.

Here we seize upon the difference in method and orientation between the Freudian approach on the one hand and historical psychology on the other. Freud's point of departure is an intimate experience undergone by the public, which is historically unlocated. The meaning attributed to this experience is then projected onto the work in question regardless of its own sociocultural context. Historical psychology proceeds in the opposite manner. It takes as its starting point the work itself as it comes to us, in its own particular form. This is then studied from every point of view possible in an analysis appropriate to the particular type of creation. Where a tragedy such as *Oedipus Rex* is concerned, the analysis — linguistic, thematic, and dramatic — at every level leads on to a problem of greater magnitude, namely that of the historical, social, and mental context that gives the meaning of the text its full force. It is only by referring to this general context that we can get some picture of the problems with which the Greek tragedy was concerned. They presuppose a definite ideological field, modalities of thought, forms of collective sensitivity — in short human experience of a particular kind — all of which are linked with a particular society. And it is only within the frame-

87

work of these problems that communication was established between the author and his fifth-century public. For the modern interpreter it is only if account is taken of this context and framework that all the significant meanings and pertinent features of the text can be revealed. Only once the task of deciphering the meaning is completed is one in a position to tackle the questions of psychological content and the reactions of the Athenian spectators to the drama and to understand what the "tragic effect" was for them. So not until this study is completed is it possible to reconstruct the intimate experience that, with its supposedly transparent significance, constituted for Freud both the point of departure and the key to the decipherment.

Thus the material of the tragedy is not the dream, postulated as a human reality outside history, but the social thought peculiar to the fifth-century city, with all the tensions and contradictions that appear in it when the advent of law and the institutions of political life place in question the old religious and moral traditional values. These are the very values extolled in heroic legend from which tragedy draws its themes and characters — although not now to glorify them as lyric poetry continued to do, but rather to bring them publicly into question in the name of the new civic ideal, in the presence of an audience who, in a Greek theater, constituted a kind of popular assembly or tribunal. These internal conflicts within social thought are expressed in tragedy by being transposed in accordance with the demands of a new literary genre with its own rules and field of problems. The sudden rise of the tragic genre at the end of the sixth century, at the very moment when law is beginning to elaborate the concept of responsibility by differentiating, albeit still in a clumsy and hesitant manner, the "intentional" from the "excusable" crime, marks an important turning point in the history of the inner man. Within the framework of the city, man begins to try himself out as an agent who is more or less autonomous in relation to the religious powers that dominate the universe, more or less master of his own actions and more or less in control of his political and personal destiny. This still hesitant and uncertain experimentation in what was to become, in the psychological history of the Western world, the category of the will is portrayed in tragedy as an anxious questioning concerning the relationship of man to his actions: To what extent is man really the source of his actions? Even when he seems to be taking the initiative and bearing the responsibility for them does not their true origin lie elsewhere? Does not their significance remain to a large extent hidden even from the one who performs them so that it is not so much the agent that explains the action, rather the action that, by revealing its real meaning after the event, reflects light upon the agent's nature, revealing what he is and what in actual fact he has unwittingly done. There is an intimate connection between the social context in which the conflict of values appears insoluble and practical human behavior that is now seen as altogether "problematic" since it no longer has an exact place within the religious order of the world. This explains how it is that tragedy represents a historical turning point very precisely defined in terms of time and space. It is born, flourishes, and disappears in Athens within the space of a hundred years. By the time Aristotle writes his *Poetics* the mainspring of tragedy is already broken for both the public and those writing for the theater. The need is no longer felt for a debate with the "heroic" past nor for a confrontation between the ways of the past and those of the present. Elaborating a rational theory of action by attempting to distinguish more clearly between the varying degrees to which the agent is committed to his action, Aristotle can no longer know what the tragic consciousness or tragic man really are. These things are part of an age now passed away.

In the Freudian interpretation this historical aspect of tragedy remains totally incomprehensible. If tragedy draws its material from a type of dream that has universal significance, if the impact of tragedy depends upon stimulating an emotional complex that we all carry within us, then why was tragedy born in the Greek world at the turn of the fifth and sixth centuries? Why did other civilizations know nothing of tragedy? And why was the tragic seam so rapidly exhausted in Greece itself and its place taken by a philosophical type of thought that did away with the contradictions upon which tragedy constructed its dramatic universe, by accounting for them rationally?

But let us take our critical analysis further. For Freud, the impact of tragedy is connected with the particular nature of the material that Sophocles uses in *Oedipus Rex*, that is to say, in the last analysis, the dreams of making love with one's mother and murdering one's father. These, he writes, are the key to tragedy: "The legend of Oedipus is the reaction of our imagination to these two typical dreams and as, in the adult, the dreams are accompanied by feelings of revulsion, the legend has to include horror and self-punishment in its contents." It would be easy to add some qualification to this "has to," pointing out for example that in the earliest versions of the myth there is, in the legendary material, not the slightest suggestion of any self-punishment: Oedipus passes peacefully away still installed upon the throne of Thebes without there being any question of his having put his eyes out. It is only Sophocles himself who, to satisfy the needs of the genre, gives the myth its truly tragic version – the only version that Freud, not himself a scholar of myth, can have known and for that reason the only one that we shall be discussing in this study. In support of his thesis Freud writes that when attempts have been made, in dramas of destiny similar to *Oedipus Rex*, to reproduce a tragic effect using material other than Oedipal dreams the result has been total failure. And he cites as examples a number of bad modern dramas. At this point one is speechless with amazement. How can Freud forget that there are plenty of other Greek tragedies besides *Oedipus Rex* and that, of those of Aeschylus, Sophocles and Euripides that have come down to us, there is virtually not a single one that has anything to do with Oedipal dreams? Does this mean that they are bad plays, producing no tragic effect? If the ancient Greeks admired them and the modern public are as moved by some of them as much as by *Oedipus Rex*, this is because tragedy is not connected with a particular type of dream and the tragic effect is not determined by the subject matter, be this dreams or otherwise, but by the form that that subject matter is given. It is a form that must convey a sense of the contradictions that rend the divine universe, the social and political world, and the whole domain of values, and that thus presents man himself as a *thauma*, a *deinon*, some kind of an incomprehensible, baffling monster, both an agent and one acted upon, guilty and innocent, dominating the whole of nature with his industrious mind yet incapable of controlling himself, lucid and yet blinded by a frenzy sent to him by the gods. In contrast to epic and lyric poetry where man is never presented as an agent, tragedy at the outset positions the individual at the crossroads of action, facing a decision in which he becomes totally committed. But his ineluctable choice takes place in a world full of obscure and ambiguous forces, a divided world in which "one justice is in conflict with another," one god with another god, in which right is never fixed but shifts even within the course of the dramatic action, is "twisted" and transformed into its contrary. Man believes he is choosing for the best; he commits himself heart and soul; and it turns out to be a choice for evil that, through the defilement attached to the crime committed, reveals him to be a criminal.

It is this complex interplay of conflicts, reversals, and ambiguities that we must grasp as they are conveyed through a series of tragic discrepancies or tensions: tensions in the vocabulary, where the same words take on opposite senses for different speakers who use them, according to the different meanings that they have in religious, legal, political, and popular vocabulary; tensions within the tragic character himself who now appears to be projected into a distant, mythical past, the hero of another age, embodying all

91

the excessive features of the ancient kings of legend, and now seems to live in the age of the city itself, a citizen of Athens surrounded by his fellows; and tensions within each dramatic theme since every action, as if double, unfolds on two levels, on the one hand that of men's ordinary lives, on the other that of the religious forces that are obscurely at work the world over. For the tragic consciousness to operate the human and divine levels must in effect be sufficiently distinct to stand in opposition (in other words some concept of human nature must have emerged), but on the other hand they must still appear as inseparable. The tragic sense of responsibility emerges when human action has already become an object of reflection, of internal debate, but has not yet acquired sufficient autonomy to be fully self-sufficient. Tragedy's true domain is that border zone where human actions are intermeshed with divine powers and reveal their true meaning, unsuspected even by those who initiated them and bear responsibility for them, when they fall into place in an order which is beyond man himself and eludes him. Every tragedy thus necessarily operates on two levels. Its role as an inquiry into man considered as a responsible agent takes on significance only in counterpoint to the central theme. It would therefore be mistaken to concentrate exclusively upon the psychological element. In the famous carpet scene of the *Agamemnon*, the king's fatal decision does indeed to some extent depend upon his pathetic vanity as a man all the more inclined to accede to his wife's pleas given that he brings Cassandra home with him as a concubine. But this is not the essential point. The specific tragic effect is produced by the fact that there is an intimate relationship and at the same time an extraordinary distance between on the one hand the unexceptional action of walking on a purple carpet together with the all too human motivations that lie behind it, and on the other the religious forces that this action inexorably unleashes.

In the analysis of any tragic work all these different levels of tragedy must be respected together with all the links and oppositions between them. If one proceeds, on the contrary, as Freud does, by successive simplification and reduction — of all Greek mythology to one particular legendary schema, of the whole of tragedy to one particular play, of this one play to one particular aspect of the story and of this aspect to a dream — one might just as well substitute, for example, Aeschylus' *Agamemnon* for Sophocles' *Oedipus Rex* and maintain that the tragic effect is produced because, given that every woman at some time dreams of murdering her husband, it is distress at her own guilt that is revealed and that overwhelms her, in her horror at Clytemnestra's crime.

Freud's interpretation of tragedy in general and *Oedipus Rex* in particular has had no influence on the work of Greek scholars. They have continued their research just as if Freud had not spoken. Wrestling with the works themselves, no doubt they felt that Freud's suggestions were "beside the point," that he had not tackled the real questions — those that the text itself imposes as soon as one seeks to understand it fully and accurately. True, a psychoanalyst might suggest a different explanation for this lack of recognition or rejection of Freudian views. He might well see it as the proof of a psychological barrier, a refusal to admit to the role of the Oedipus complex both in one's personal life and in human development as a whole. Debate on this point has been reopened by the article in which Didier Anzieu sets out to repeat the work undertaken by Freud at the beginning of the century, this time on the basis of the new data available in 1966.[2] If, armed only with the insight afforded by psychoanalysis, Anzieu can venture into the field of classical antiquity and there discover what the specialists continue not to see, does it not prove that the latter are blind or rather that they want to be and make themselves blind because they refuse to recognize their own image in the figure of Oedipus?

So we must examine the value of the universal Oedipal key, the secret of which is known only to the psychoanalyst and that is supposed to enable him to decipher all human works without any further preparation. Is it really the key to the doors of the mental world of the ancient Greeks? Or does it simply force the locks?

We shall concentrate upon two aspects of Anzieu's long study only. They are essential to his thesis and will suffice for the purposes of the present discussion. As a first stage Anzieu reread the whole of Greek mythology from beginning to end. As he did so he believed he could discern the Oedipal fantasy reflected on almost every page. So, if he is right, we shall have been wrong in reproaching Freud for having concentrated exclusively upon one particular legendary schema — that of Oedipus, taking no notice of the rest. According to Anzieu almost all Greek myths reproduce, in the form of an infinite number of variants, the theme of incestuous union with the mother and murder of the father. If this is the case, Oedipus simply sets the seal on the whole of mythology by giving clear formulation to what it had always been expressing in a more or less partial, camouflaged, or transposed manner.

However, in this mythology as presented by Anzieu, reinterpreted and forced into an Oedipal mold, it is impossible for the Greek specialist to recognize the legends with which he is familiar. They have lost their distinctive features and character and their own specific field of application and no longer look the same. One of the scholars who has studied them most assiduously has suggested as a guiding rule that one never comes across two myths with exactly the same meaning. If, on the contrary, they are all repetitions of one another, if synonymy is the rule, then mythology in all its diversity can no longer be regarded as a system with meaning. If all it can say is Oedipus, Oedipus, and nothing but Oedipus, it no longer means anything at all.

But let us see how the psychoanalyst forces the legendary material to fit in with the demands of the model that, even before embarking on his study, he carried in his mind as a magus carries the truth. Let us start at the beginning, as Anzieu does, that is with the myth of origins told by Hesiod in the *Theogony*. Greek scholars have linked Hesiod's text with a long tradition of Eastern theogonies. They have also shown what Hesiod's own original contributions were and how his overall concept, the details of his account and even his vocabulary prefigured the set of philosophical problems that were later to emerge. He treated not only the origins of things and how order gradually emerged from chaos but also, though not yet explicitly formalized, the relations between the one and the many and between the indeterminate and that which is defined, the conflict and union of opposites, the possible mixture and balance between them, and the contrast between the permanence of the divine order and the transience of earthly life. This is the ground in which the myth is rooted and where it must be situated if it is to be understood. Authors as diversely oriented as Cornford, Vlastos, and Fraenkel have been in agreement in the commentaries in which they explore these different levels of meaning. It is true, however, that if one takes the myth of the mutilation of Ouranos out of its context and reduces it to a simple schema — that is to say if, instead of reading it in Hesiod one reads it instead in a handbook of mythology aimed at the general public — one could be tempted to say, as Anzieu does, that given that the mother (Gaia, Earth) twice commits incest with her sons (first with Ouranos and later, indirectly, with Kronos) and that furthermore Kronos castrates his father in order to chase him from his mother's bed, the story does have a "startlingly proto-Oedipal character" ("*un caractère proto-oedipien éclatant*"). But let us examine the matter more closely. At the beginning of the world there is *Chaos*, an undifferentiated void, a bottomless, directionless yawning gap where there is nothing to stop the wandering of a falling body. Opposed to *Chaos* is Gaia who stands for stability. Once Gaia has appeared, something has taken shape. Space has found the beginnings of orientation. Gaia is not only stability, she is also the universal Mother who engenders everything that exists, all that has form. Gaia starts off by creating from her own self, without the help of *Erōs* — that is, without sexual union — her male opposite: Ouranos, the male sky. With Ouranos, issued directly from herself, Gaia then has union, this time in the proper sexual sense of the word, and from this produces a lineage of children who, being a mixture of the two opposite principles, already have an individuality, a particular identity although they remain primordial beings, cosmic powers. The fact is that the union of earth and sky, these two opposites one of which is the issue of the other, takes place in a disordered fashion, without any rules, in a state of quasi-confusion of the two contrary principles. The sky still lies upon the earth entirely covering it; and because there is no distance at all between their cosmic parents the offspring are unable to develop in the light of day. The children thus remain "hidden" instead of revealing their true form. Now Gaia grows angry with Ouranos; she encourages one of her sons, Kronos, to lie in wait for his father and mutilate him while he sprawls on top of her, in the night. Kronos obeys. The great Ouranos, castrated by the swipe of a sickle, withdraws from his position on top of Gaia, cursing his sons. Now earth and sky are separate and each remains immobile in its proper place. There opens up between them the great empty space in which the succession of *Day* and *Night* alternately reveals and conceals every form. Earth and Sky will never again be united in permanent confusion similar to that which reigned before Gaia made her appearance, when nothing but *Chaos* existed in the world. Henceforth only once a year, at the beginning of autumn, will the sky make the earth fruitful with its seed raining down and the earth bring forth life in the form of vegetation. And once a year, too, men must celebrate the sacred marriage between the two cosmic powers, their union that takes place *at a distance* in the open and orderly world in which contraries are united but remain distinct from one another. However, this tearing apart in which being will be able to flourish has been obtained at the cost of a crime that will have to be paid for. From now on there will be no concord without conflict. It will no longer be possible to hold the forces of conflict and those of union apart in the tissue of existence. The bleeding testicles of Ouranos have fallen partly on the land and partly in the sea; on land they give birth to the Erinyes, the Melian nymphs and the Giants — that is to all the powers of "blood vengeance" and war that preside over fighting and conflict; in the sea they give birth to Aphrodite, who presides over sexual union and marriage, and the forces of concord and harmony. The separation of sky and earth inaugurates a world in which beings are engendered through union between contraries, a world governed by the law of complementarity between opposites that both clash and at the same time agree.

This simple, but rather more accurate, summary of the significant elements in the myth makes a comparison with Oedipus already look more suspect. We are told that Gaia commits direct incest with her son Ouranos. But Ouranos is her son in a very particular way since she engendered him without recourse to sexual union, without a father, and produces him from herself as if he were her double as well as her opposite. There is therefore no triangular Oedipal situation — mother, father, and son — but instead a schema of duplication from a basis of one. In the case of Kronos it is indeed true that he is the son of Gaia in the true sense. But in point of fact Gaia is not united with Kronos at all. Kronos does not take his father's place in the maternal bed; he marries Rhea. Gaia encourages Kronos, not to kill his father, but to castrate him, in other words to relegate him to his place in the cosmic sky where he must remain in order to allow the world to grow in the space thereby created and the whole diversity of creatures to be engendered in accordance with the regular order of birth that takes the place of sexual confusion.

Once the myth of origins has been edged into a different mold in this way, the psychoanalyst can give free rein to his imagination. We are told that Ouranos is castrated "just as the old man of the primitive hoard, whose myth Freud developed in *Totem and Taboo*, is supposed *really* to be killed and devoured by his sons." The truth is that nowhere else in the Greek myths do we find any god or any hero emasculated by his sons, or indeed emascu-

97

lated at all. But what of it? "Symbolical substitutes for castration can be found: hurling from a great height, cutting, gouging out, usurping someone's place and power." Furthermore, the devouring of his children by the father or by the wild beasts to which he has exposed them is supposed to constitute a "primal and radical form of castration." Thus the myths of succession, of the struggle for sovereignty – whose significance, in the Indo-European world, has been emphasized by Georges Dumézil – the heroic legends of children being exposed, the various themes of falling or being hurled from a height and those of swallowing and engulfing, all of them can be telescoped together and amalgamated into a universal castration (either of the father by the son, or vice versa).

Let us take the case of Hephaestus, a figure declared by Anzieu to "possess an Oedipus complex." Why? "He responds to his mother's desire that he should be her phallus and supplant his father; he follows her suggestion and is punished by his father, the punishment being a symbolical substitute for castration." To this evidence Anzieu adds one other suggestion, namely that initially the object of Hephaestus' desire is a maternal substitute, Aphrodite. But what is the truth of the matter? In some versions Hephaestus is conceived without a father by Hera alone, who desires in this way to get her own back against Zeus for the birth of Athena who was conceived and born without her, or to pay him back for all his infidelities. But there is nothing to suggest that the goddess yearns for another phallus nor that she wants to install her son in the place of Zeus. Does Hephaestus' lameness really stand for castration? In effect it is not so much lameness as a divergence in the direction of his feet, a gait oriented in two directions at once, forward and backward, connected with his powers as a magician. Zeus hurls Hephaestus down from the heights of the heavens: Is this really the vengeance of a father threatened by a son in love with his own mother? There are other versions in which it is Hera who in anger casts her offspring down to earth. And finally, Hephaestus' ardent desire is directed not so much toward Aphrodite as toward Charis; and the links between

98

the power of "charm" embodied by Charis and the special magic gifts that Hephaestus uses to give life to his works of art and to dead materials have already been established. But even if we accept the versions in which Aphrodite is the wife of the blacksmith god, in what way can she be said especially to play the role of a substitute mother? Short of becoming a pederast, Hephaestus could hardly avoid taking a female goddess as his wife and whatever the identity of this goddess, the theme of the maternal substitute would be more or less true — in other words equally false. Elsewhere Hephaestus pursues Athena. Once again the cry of incest goes up. But given that the gods of Olympos are all members of one and the same family, they hardly have a choice except that between misalliance or endogamy. Besides, in the present case Athena is not Hephaestus' sister since she is the daughter of Metis and Zeus while he is the child of Hera. At all events Hephaestus' plans of seduction come to nothing. As is well known, Athena remains a virgin. We are told that in this way she satisfies "Zeus' unconscious desire for her." The father wants to keep his daughter for himself alone, "as the imaginary object of his desire." Not only is this explanation completely gratuitous but it explains nothing at all. Of all the female deities only three remain virgins: Athena, Artemis, and Hestia. Why these and not the others? We need, then, to explain this virginity as a differentiating feature marking these three goddesses out from the others who, despite also being the daughters of their father, nevertheless make quite normal marriages. In an earlier study we have attempted such an analysis in the case of Hestia.[3] As for Athena, her virginity has nothing to do with a supposed unconscious desire on the part of Zeus, but is connected with her status as a warrior goddess. In the rites of adolescence, marriage and warfare appear as two complementary institutions. Marriage is for the girl what warfare is for the boy. For the young girl emerging from childhood it represents the normal goal of her sex, access to full femininity. This is why a girl who devotes herself to warfare — whether she be an Amazon or the goddess Athena — must remain in the state of *parthenos*, in other words refuse to take the pathway that leads toward the full femininity that marriage represents for every adolescent girl crossing the threshold of puberty.

Another way of "oedipalizing" the most diverse legendary themes is to label as incestuous unions that the Greeks themselves considered to be perfectly legitimate and that are therefore not incestuous at all. Thus, a girl's marriage with an uncle or with a paternal cousin is regularly interpreted as a "substitute" for incest with the father. But in the context of ancient civilizations this substitution is quite impossible. For if union with a father constitutes an abominable crime and defilement for the ancient Greeks, marriage with an uncle or with a paternal cousin is, in contrast, in some cases — as in that of the epiclerate — if not obligatory at least preferred. What right has one to identify two types of union one of which is formally prohibited, the other recommended, and that therefore stand in opposition on every count so far as incest — which is precisely where they are assimilated — is concerned?

No less arbitrary is the way family attachments are identified with incestuous desires. For the Greeks, family bonds defined an area of human relations in which personal feelings and religious attitudes were indissociable. The reciprocal affection between parents and children on the one hand and brothers and sisters on the other represents the model of what the Greeks called *philia*. The word *philos*, which has a possessive force corresponding to the Latin *suus*, denotes first and foremost that which is one's own, that is, for the relative, another relative close to him. Aristotle on several occasions and in particular when writing about tragedy tells us that this *philia* is based on a kind of identity felt between all the members of an immediate family. Each member of the family is an *alter ego*, a sort of double or multiplied self, for each of his relatives. In this sense *philia* is opposed to *erōs*, loving desire, which is focused upon one "other" than oneself, other in sex and other in family connections. For the Greeks who remain faithful to the tradition of Hesiod on this point, sexual union takes place between opposites, not between those who are similar. Thus, to identify family attachment and incestuous desire *a priori* — on the basis of no special indication in the text — is to confuse two types of feelings that the Greeks themselves were extremely careful to distinguish and even oppose. As is to be expected, such a misinterpretation does not make it any easier to understand the ancient works. Let us take an example from the lineage of the Labdacids, to which Oedipus himself belongs. According to Anzieu, the daughters of Oedipus are incestuous as is their father: "They dream of becoming his companions." If by "companions" one understands that they assist and support their father in misfortune in accordance with their filial duty, this is no dream but the very truth. If by "companions" one means that they desire sexual union with Oedipus, it is Anzieu who is dreaming. If one rereads all the tragedies and sifts through every word in *Oedipus at Colonus*, one still finds nothing to justify such an interpretation. Anzieu goes on to say: "The virgin Antigone, despite Creon's formal order, fulfills her funereal duties to her condemned brother Polynices who attacked his own country. Her incestuous attachment to her brother is a displaced incestuous attachment to her father." At this point we are no longer faced with silence on the part of the texts. They are most explicit. Following the deaths of Oedipus and his two sons there is no male descendant to carry on the Labdacid line. When she scatters dust over the corpse of Polynices Antigone is not prompted by an incestuous affection for the brother she is forbidden to bury; she is proclaiming that she has an equal religious duty to all her dead brothers, whatever their lives may have been. For Antigone, all of whose *philoi* have descended to Hades, fidelity to the family *philia* involves fidelity to the cult of the dead, for this alone can now perpetuate the religious existence of the *genos*. The fact that this attitude condemns her to death simply strengthens the girl's determination. What she is saying is that, in her situation, the domain of family *philia* and the domain of death are one and the same and form a separate world, enclosed on itself and with its own laws, its own infernal *Dikē* that is different from that of Creon, of men and of cities, different perhaps also from that other *Dikē* enthroned in the sky at Zeus' side. Thus, for Antigone, refusing to renege on *philia* means, to borrow Creon's phrase, refusing to honor any god but Hades. This is why, at the end of the tragedy, the girl too is condemned to death. It is not only because of the single-minded, uncompromising, "uncooked" element in her character but even more because, entirely absorbed in *philia* and death, she refuses to recognize anything in the world that is not encompassed by these two, in particular anything to do with life and love. The two deities invoked by the chorus, Dionysus and Eros, do not just condemn Creon. Although they are on Antigone's side as nocturnal, mysterious gods, close to women and alien to politics, they turn against the girl because, even in their links with death, they express the powers of life and renewal. Antigone would not heed their appeal to detach herself from her "own" and from *philia* and to become accessible to "an other," that is to recognize Eros and, by entering into union with a "stranger," herself to transmit life in her turn. Thus the opposition between *philia* and *erōs*, family attachment and sexual desire, holds a place of major importance in the structure of the drama. When the two are confused together and one called a "substitute" for the other, the text is not made clearer; on the contrary, the play is ruined.

But let us come to the second aspect of Anzieu's article that we should like to consider. It concerns Oedipus in person. In the interests of clarity we must define the problem precisely. We shall not here be concerned with the entire Oedipean mythology, that is to say all the legendary versions that can be studied within the context of the history of religions. We shall be considering only the Oedipus of *Oedipus Rex*, the tragic character as presented by

Sophocles. Is a psychological interpretation relevant in this particular instance? We have already expressed our deep skepticism
with respect to a Hephaestus with an Oedipus complex. But is
Oedipus himself intelligible as a character, an *ēthos*, without the
complex that bears his name? Does the tragic action, the *drama*,
have any meaning if one does not recognize, with Anzieu, that
the oracle that reveals his destiny of parricide and incest to Laius'
son is simply "the formulation of a fantasy of which he is unconscious and that determines how he behaves?"

Let us see how, guided so to speak by Ariadne's thread, Anzieu
follows Oedipus' progress:

> The first act takes place on the road from Delphi to Thebes.
> Oedipus is returning to consult the oracle that revealed to him
> his destiny of parricide and incest. He has decided, in order
> to escape this destiny, not to go back to Corinth. (It is a remark-
> able mistake if he knows that those in Corinth are his adop-
> tive parents. It is precisely by returning to them that he would
> have nothing to fear. And similarly, if Oedipus had decided to
> marry a young girl he would have guarded against committing
> incest with his mother.) In contrast, by setting out to seek his
> fortune (and giving himself over to free associations) Oedipus
> is going to fulfill his destiny (that is to say his fantasy).

So everything would appear to suggest that, if he wishes to avoid
fulfilling the prophecy, Oedipus should return to Corinth where
he is not at risk. His "remarkable mistake" is a symptomatic action
betraying the fact that he is unconsciously obeying his desire for
incest and parricide. But for there to be any basis at all for this
reading it is necessary to suppose – as Anzieu does – that Oedipus
is well aware that Merope and Polybus, the rulers of Corinth who
have brought him up as their own son, are not his true mother
and father but simply adoptive parents. Now, all through the play,
up to the point when the truth bursts upon him, Oedipus appears
to be convinced of the contrary. Not just once but on several occa-

sions Oedipus declares without any shadow of doubt that he is the son of Merope and Polybus.[4] Far from his having left Corinth despite the security that his remaining there would have offered, it is on the contrary to attempt to escape his destiny that Oedipus has fled the town where he believes his parents are living: "Loxias once said that I should have to make love with my own mother and, with my own hands, shed the blood of my father. That is why for many years I have been living far from Corinth. I was right to do so. Yet it is a sweet thing to see the faces of those who gave birth to us."[5]

What is Anzieu's justification for making the text say the opposite to what it spells out so clearly? If we restrict ourselves to the letter of his study, we shall find no answer at all to this question. However, by playing devil's advocate, we could base an argument on one passage that, when interpreted in terms of depth psychology, might support his thesis and call into question the sincerity of Oedipus' declarations regarding his origins. We refer to lines 774-793. Oedipus explains to Iocasta that his father is Polybus of Corinth and his mother Merope, a Dorian woman. He was considered in his home town as the first among citizens and the heir to the throne occupied by his father. But one day, in the course of a feast, a drunkard insults him, calling him "a supposititious son." Filled with indignation, Oedipus seeks out his parents who freely express their anger against the perpetrator of this outrage. Their anger soothes Oedipus but the words continue to obsess him. Unknown to Polybus and Merope, he goes to Delphi to question the oracle regarding his origins. But instead of replying to his question, the oracle announces that he will sleep with his mother and kill his father. It is then that Oedipus decides to leave Corinth.

Why did Sophocles introduce this episode, it could be asked. Is it not so as to suggest that deep within himself Oedipus already knows that his real parents are not those supposed to be such, but refuses to admit this to himself the better to indulge in his fantasy of incest and parricide? We believe, on the contrary, that

Sophocles' reasons have nothing to do with depth psychology. They are a response to other kinds of requirement. First, an aesthetic requirement. The discovery of the true origins of Oedipus cannot come as a completely unexpected revelation, a totally unpredictable twist in the situation. It must be prepared for, both psychologically and dramatically. Oedipus' allusion to this incident of his youth, the first crack in the edifice of his supposed genealogy, is indispensable to this preparation.

Next, a religious requirement. In tragedy, the oracle is always enigmatic but never lies. It does not deceive man but allows him the opportunity to err. If the god of Delphi had made his prediction to Oedipus without him having any cause to wonder about his origins, the oracle would have been guilty of deliberately leading him astray; it alone would have caused him to flee from Corinth and cast him upon the road to Thebes leading to incest and murder. But to Oedipus' question: Are Polybus and Merope my parents? Apollo makes no answer. He simply offers a prediction; you will sleep with your mother and kill your father – and this prediction, in all its horror, leaves the question he had asked unanswered. So it is Oedipus who is in the wrong not to bother about the god's silence and to interpret his words as if they provided the answer to the question of his origins. Oedipus' mistake stems from two features in his character: In the first place he is too sure of himself, too self-confident in his *gnōmē* or judgment[6] and not inclined to question his own interpretation of the facts.[7] And secondly, being proud by nature, he invariably, no matter where he is, wants to be the master, number one.[8] These are the more truly psychological reasons that influenced Sophocles. Oedipus describes himself, with haughty self-confidence, as "the one who solves riddles." And the entire drama is, in a way, a detective story that Oedipus takes it upon himself to disentangle. Who killed Laius? The investigator discovers the murderer to be himself, but he is all the more determined to pursue the inquiry because his suspicions from the start fall upon his brother-in-law, Creon, whom he considers as a rival jealous of his own power and popularity.

Judging Creon by his own desire for power, he convinces himself at one fell swoop that, prompted by *phthonos*, envy of the great, his brother-in-law seeks to usurp his place on the throne of Thebes and that, at some point in the past, he may well have guided the hands of the former king's murderers. It is this *hubris* characteristic of a tyrant — to use the chorus' name for him[9] — that causes Oedipus' downfall and is one of the mainsprings of the tragedy. For the inquiry concerns not only the murder of Laius but also the question of Oedipus himself, Oedipus the clairvoyant, the solver of riddles, who is a riddle to himself that, in his blindness as king, he cannot solve. Oedipus is "double" just as the oracle's pronouncement is: He is a "savior" king who, at the beginning of the play, is the object of the prayers of an entire people as if he were a god holding the city's destiny in his hands; but he is also an abominable defilement, a monster of impurity concentrating within himself all the evil and sacrilege in the world, who must be ejected as a *pharmakos*, a scapegoat, so that the city can become pure once again and be saved.

Established as he is as a divine king, convinced that he is inspired by the gods and that *Tuchē* stands guard at his side, how could Oedipus possibly suspect that, as one and the same person, he will also be a shameful thing for all to shun? He will have to pay for his second sight with his own eyes and through suffering he will learn that in the eyes of the gods he who rises the highest is also the lowest.[10] A sadder but a wiser man, in *Oedipus at Colonus*, he subsequently climbs the opposite path: At the extreme zenith of misfortune and deprivation the very excess of his defilement qualifies him to be the tutelary hero of Athens. But in *Oedipus Rex* all that path has yet to be trodden. Oedipus is unaware of the part of himself that is a shadow that he carries within him as the sinister reflection of his glory. That is why he cannot "hear" the ambiguous silence of the oracle. For the question he poses to the god of Delphi is the very riddle that he is himself unable to solve: Who am I? "The son of Polybus and Merope" means to Oedipus that he is the son of a king, born to a great destiny. And

the reason why being called a "supposititious" son is a torment-
ing insult that hurts him more than is reasonable is that, above
all, he is fearful of a humble birth and blood of which he would
be ashamed. The oracle with its horrible threat at least reassures
him on this point. So he leaves Corinth without further considering the question of whether this "native land" that the god forbids him to set foot on is indeed the city whose rulers are those
who say they are his parents. When, in the course of the drama,
a messenger from Corinth informs him that he was a foundling
his reaction is no different. Iocasta, who at this point understands
everything, implores him to let the matter rest and to drop the
inquiry. Oedipus refuses. The dismayed queen leaves him with
her last words: "Wretch, may you never know *who you are!*" Who
is Oedipus? That is the very question he asked the oracle, the riddle he comes up against time and time again throughout the play.
But once again, as at Delphi, Oedipus misunderstands the true
meaning of the words. And his "misunderstanding" has nothing
to do with depth psychology. He thinks that Iocasta warns him
against the inquiry because it might reveal his lowly origins and
make her queenly marriage seem a misalliance with a nobody, the
son of a slave. "Let her continue to take pride in her opulent
family.... Proud woman that she is, she is no doubt ashamed of
my lowly birth." But the quality of "being" that Iocasta has just
discovered in Oedipus and that freezes her with horror is not her
husband's servile or common extraction nor the distance that
might in that case separate them; on the contrary, it is his exalted
lineage, the identical royal blood that runs in the veins of both
of them, linking them too closely, making of their marriage not
a misalliance but incest and of Oedipus a living defilement.

Why is it that, right from the outset, Anzieu distorts the meaning of the drama by supposing, against all the evidence in the text,
that Oedipus knows full well that his parents are not those who
pass as such? It is no chance "misunderstanding" but an absolute

necessity for the psychoanalytic interpretation. The fact is that, if the drama rests on Oedipus' ignorance regarding his true origins, if he truly believes — as he so often declares — that he is the beloved and loving son of the rulers of Corinth, then clearly the hero of *Oedipus Rex* has no trace of an Oedipus complex. At birth Oedipus was handed over to a shepherd ordered to have him exposed to death on Cithaeron. But he was instead placed in the care of the childless Merope and Polybus and brought up by them, treated and loved as their own child. So the maternal figure in Oedipus' sentimental life can only be Merope. It cannot possibly be Iocasta whom he has never seen until his arrival at Thebes. She is in no way a mother to him. He marries her through no choice of his own but because she is given to him, without his asking for her, as is the royal power that, by solving the Sphinx's riddle, he wins but can only assume if he shares the bed of the rightful, titular queen.[11] Anzieu writes: "One thing is certain, that Oedipus finds happiness in his mother's bed. In repossessing his mother he rediscovers that first happiness that he lost when he was so early separated from her and exposed on Cithaeron." If Oedipus finds happiness at Iocasta's side it is because psychologically her bed is not that of a mother; it is not the μητρὸς λέχος he mentions in line 976, referring to the bed of Merope. And when Iocasta's bed does become the bed of his mother it is for both him and her the very symbol of their misfortune. The marriage with their queen that the Thebans offer Oedipus cannot represent repossession of his mother to him as to him Iocasta is a stranger, a *xenē*, since he believes himself to be a foreigner resident in Thebes, a ξένος μέτοικος, to use Tiresias' words.[12] And for him separation from his "mother" happened not at his birth when he was left on Cithaeron but on the day that, in leaving Corinth, he had also to leave behind "the sweet face of his parents."[13] Perhaps it will be suggested that Iocasta is a "substitute" for Merope and that Oedipus enjoys his conjugal relations with the queen of Thebes *as if* this were a union with his mother. Nothing rings true in such an interpretation. If Sophocles had wanted to, he could

easily have suggested it. But instead he wiped out everything in
the personal relations between the husband and wife that, before
the final revelation, might hint at the links between a son and a
mother. Iocasta remained childless for many years; Oedipus was
born to her late. So she is considerably older than her son. But
there is nothing in the tragedy to suggest the difference in age
between the two who become husband and wife. If Sophocles
has effaced this detail it is not only because it would have struck
the Greeks as strange (as a wife was always much younger than
her husband) but also because it would have suggested if not an
inferiority on the part of Oedipus in the marital relationship at
least, on Iocasta's side, a "maternal" attitude that would not have
fitted in well with the dominating, authoritarian, and tyrannical
character of the hero.[14] Relations of an "Oedipal" type, in the
modern sense of the expression, between Iocasta and Oedipus
would have been directly in conflict with the tragic intention of
the play that is centered on the theme of Oedipus' absolute power
and the *hubris* that necessarily stems from it.

At the end of his analysis of the tragedy and to cap his interpretation, Anzieu proposes to attribute to Creon too, in his turn, an
incestuous attachment for his sister, Iocasta. He suggests that the
two brothers-in-law are rivals not only for the throne but also for
the same woman. "The incestuous attachment between Creon and
Iocasta and Oedipus' jealousy toward the brother of his wife and
mother is a hypothesis necessary for the drama to become completely comprehensible." No doubt the hypothesis is indeed necessary, but not for an understanding of the drama, rather to force
it into the framework set up by a pre-established interpretation.
There is not a scrap of evidence for an incestuous attachment
between the brother and sister. Oedipus is not at all jealous of
their affection for each other. If he were, Iocasta's intervention
on behalf of Creon would be ineffective for it could only increase
the anger of the jealous Oedipus. Oedipus is convinced only that

Creon is jealous of him — not in an erotic sense but in the social sense indicated by the Greek word that is used: *phthonos*, which denotes envy felt for one who is richer, more powerful, cleverer.[15] The rivalry between the two men (or rather the phantom rivalry that the suspicious mind of the tyrant dreams up, for in reality Creon is not his rival at all and seeks no other power than that which is already his by reason of his status) — this rivalry is concerned only with the competition for power.[16] As Oedipus sees it, Creon cannot tolerate his victory over the Sphinx, his popularity,[17] and his sovereign power. He suspects him of having plotted against him from the very first day;[18] he accuses him of now wishing to assassinate him and openly seize his power. Convinced as he is that Creon seeks to kill him because he is king, he by the same token suspects him from the very beginning of the play and accuses him in terms that are less and less veiled of having been the real instigator of Laius' murder.[19] Here again an "Oedipal" view of the characters and their relationships does not illuminate the text at all: It distorts it.

Nevertheless, there is in *Oedipus Rex* one speech that Freud himself noted and that has often been put forward as evidence to support the psychoanalytic interpretation. When Oedipus mentions his anxiety over the oracle to her, Iocasta replies that "plenty of people have already shared their mother's bed in their dreams" and that there is nothing to worry about. The discussion between the king and queen is concerned with the question of how much credence should be given to oracles. The Delphic oracle has predicted that Oedipus will share his mother's bed, but is there really any cause to be upset by this? Among the Greeks, dreams too are often considered to be oracular. So Oedipus is not the only one to have received such a "sign" from the gods. Now, according to Iocasta, either this sign has no meaning that men can possibly interpret in advance[20] and so should not be given too much importance or, if it does indeed predict something, it is more likely to be a favorable event. Sophocles, who knows his Herodotus as does the Athenian public he is addressing, is here thinking of the episode of Hippias as told by the historian.[21] The apprentice tyrant marching on Athens to regain power there with the help of the Persian army dreams that he is united with his mother. He immediately concludes with delight that "he is going to re-enter Athens, restore his power and die there of old age." The fact is that, for the Greeks, as Anzieu himself points out, following Marie Delcourt, to dream of union with one's mother — that is with the earth from which everything is born and to which everything returns — means sometimes death, sometimes taking possession of the land, winning power. There is no trace in this symbolism of the anxiety and guilt that are peculiar to the Oedipus complex. So it is impossible that dreams, seen as a reality outside history, should contain and yield up the meaning of works of culture. The meanings of dreams themselves, inasmuch as they are symbolic, appear as a cultural fact that can be discovered by means of a study of historical psychology. In this connection one might suggest that psychoanalysts should themselves adopt more historical methods and use the various *Keys to Dreams* that through the ages have appeared in the Western world, to search for the constant elements and the possible transformations within the symbolism of dreams.

Jean-Pierre Vernant

CHAPTER V

Ambiguity and Reversal:

On the Enigmatic Structure

of *Oedipus Rex*[1]

In his study of ambiguity in Greek literature written in 1939 W.B. Stanford noted that, from the point of view of ambiguity, *Oedipus Rex* is quite exceptional.[2] This work can be taken as a model. No literary genre of antiquity made such full use of the double entendre as did tragedy and *Oedipus Rex* contains more than twice as many ambiguous expressions as Sophocles' other plays (fifty, according to the count made by Hug in 1872[3]). However, the problem is not so much one of quantity as of nature and function. All the Greek tragedians have recourse to ambiguity as a means of expression and as a modality of thought. But the double meaning takes on a quite different role depending on its place in the organization of the tragedy and the level of language at which the tragic poet is using it.

It may be a matter of an ambiguity in the vocabulary corresponding to what Aristotle calls *homōnumia* (lexical ambiguity); such an ambiguity is made possible by the shifts or contradictions in the language.[4] The dramatist plays on this to transmit his tragic vision of a world divided against itself and rent with contradictions. On the lips of different characters the same words take on different or opposed meanings because their semantic significance is not the same in religious, legal, political, and common parlance.[5] Thus for Antigone, *nómos* denotes the opposite to what Creon, in the particular position in which he is placed, also calls *nómos*.[6] For the girl the word means "religious rule"; for Creon it means "an edict promulgated by the head of state." And, in truth, the semantic field of *nómos* is broad enough to cover, among others, both these meanings.[7] In these circumstances the ambiguity conveys the tension between certain meanings felt to be irreconcilable despite their homonymy. Instead of establishing communication and agreement between the characters, the words they exchange on the stage on the contrary underline the impermeability of their minds, the barrier between them. They emphasize the obstacles that separate them and mark out the lines along which conflict will develop. For each hero, enclosed within his own particular world, the word has one and only one meaning. One unilateral position comes into violent conflict with another. The irony of the tragedy may consist in showing how, in the course of the action, the hero finds himself literally "taken at his word," a word that recoils against him, bringing him bitter experience of the meaning he was determined not to recognize.[8] It is only over the heads of the protagonists that, between the author and the spectator, another dialogue is set up in which language regains its ability to establish communication and, as it were, its transparency. But what the tragic message, when understood, conveys is precisely that within the words men exchange there exist areas of opacity and incommunicability. By seeing the protagonists on the stage clinging exclusively to one meaning and thus, in their blindness, bringing about their own destruction or tearing each other to pieces, the spectator is brought to realize that in reality there are two or even more possible meanings. The tragic message becomes intelligible to him to the extent that, abandoning his former certainty and limitations, he becomes aware of the ambiguity of words, of meanings, and of the human condition. Recognizing that it is the nature of the universe to be in conflict, and accepting a problematical view of the world, the spectator himself, through the spectacle, acquires a tragic consciousness.

Aeschylus' *Agamemnon* provides excellent examples of another type of tragic ambiguity: veiled implications consciously employed by certain characters in the drama who in this way mask within the speech they address to their interlocutor another speech, the opposite of the first, whose meaning is perceptible only to those on the stage and in the audience who possess the necessary information.[9] When greeting Agamemnon on the threshold of his palace, Clytemnestra makes use of this language with a double register. In the ears of the husband it has the pleasant ring of a pledge of love and conjugal fidelity; for the chorus it is already equivocal and they sense some threat within it, while the spectator can see its full sinister quality because he can decode in it the death plot that she has hatched against her husband.[10] Here the ambiguity conveys not a conflict of meanings but the duplicity of a particular character. It is a duplicity of almost demoniacal proportions. The same speech, the very words that draw Agamemnon into the trap, disguising the danger from him, at the same time announce the crime about to be perpetrated to the world in general. And because the queen, in her hatred for her husband, becomes in the course of the drama the instrument of divine justice, the secret speech concealed within her words of welcome takes on an oracular significance. By pronouncing the death of the king she makes it inevitable, like a prophet. So it is in fact the truth that Agamemnon fails to understand in Clytemnestra's words. Once spoken, the speech acquires all the practical force of a curse: What it pronounces it registers in existence, in advance and forever. The ambiguity of the queen's speech is exactly matched by the ambiguity of the symbolic values attached to the purple carpet she has had spread before the king and on which she persuades him to step. When he enters his palace, as Clytemnestra bids him, in terms that at the same time suggest quite another dwelling place, it is indeed the threshold to Hades that Agamemnon, without knowing it, crosses. When he places his bare foot upon the sumptuous cloths with which the ground has been spread, the "purple path" created beneath his steps is not, as he imagines, an almost excessive consecration of his glory but instead a way to deliver him over to the powers of the underworld, to condemn him without remission to death, to the "red" death that comes to him in the same "sumptuous cloths" that Clytemnestra has prepared in advance to trap him, as in a net.[11]

The ambiguity one finds in *Oedipus Rex* is quite different. It is concerned neither with a conflict in meanings nor with the duplicity of the character controlling the action and taking pleasure in playing with his or her victim. In the drama in which he is the victim, it is Oedipus and only Oedipus who pulls the strings. Except for his own obstinate determination to unmask the guilty party, the lofty idea he had of his duty, his capacities, his judgment (his *gnōmē*), and his passionate desire to learn the truth at all costs, there is nothing to oblige him to pursue the inquiry to its end. One after another Tiresias, Iocasta, and the shepherd all try to deter him. But in vain. He is not a man to content himself with half-measures or settle for a compromise. Oedipus goes all the way. And at the end of the road that he, despite and against everyone, has followed, he finds that even while it was from start to finish he who pulled the strings it is he who from start to finish has been duped. Thus, at the very moment when he recognizes his own responsibility in forging his misfortunes with his own hands, he accuses the gods of having prepared and done it all.[12] The equivocal character of Oedipus' words reflects the ambiguous status that the drama confers upon him and on which the entire tragedy rests. When Oedipus speaks he sometimes says something other than or even the opposite of what he thinks he is saying. The ambiguity of what he says does not reflect a duplicity in his character, which is perfectly consistent, but, more profoundly, the duality of his being. Oedipus is double. He is in himself a riddle whose meaning he can only guess when he discovers himself to be in every respect the opposite of what he thought he was and appeared to be. Oedipus himself does not understand the secret speech that, without his realizing, lurks at the heart of what he says. And, except for Tiresias, no witness to the drama on stage is capable of perceiving it either. It is the gods who send Oedipus' own speech back at him, deformed or twisted around, like an echo to some of his own words.[13] And this inverted echo, which has the ring of a sinister burst of laughter, in reality sets the record straight. The only authentic truth in Oedipus' words is what he says without meaning to and without understanding it. In this way the twofold dimension of Oedipus' speech is an inverted reflection of the language of the gods as expressed in the enigmatic pronouncement of the oracle. The gods know and speak the truth but they make it manifest by formulating it in words that appear to men to be saying something quite different. Oedipus neither knows nor speaks the truth but the words he uses to say something other than the truth make it startlingly obvious – although Oedipus does not realize this – for whoever has the gift of double hearing in the same way as the diviner has second sight. Oedipus' language thus seems the point at which, within the very same words, two different types of discourse, a human and a divine one, are interwoven and come into conflict. At the beginning they are quite distinct and separate from each other; by the end of the drama, when all is revealed, the human discourse is stood on its head and transformed into its own opposite: The two types of discourse become as one and the riddle is solved. Seated on the stepped slopes of the theater, the spectators occupy a privileged position that enables them, like the gods, to hear and understand the two opposed types of discourse at the same time, following the conflict between them right through from start to finish.

So it is easy to see how it is that, from the point of view of ambiguity, *Oedipus Rex* has the force of a model. Aristotle, noting that the two fundamental elements of a tragic tale, apart from the "pathetic," are recognition (ἀναγνώρισις) and the peripeteia (περιπέτεια), that is to say the reversal of the action into its contrary (εἰς τὸ ἐναντίον τῶν πραττομένων μεταβολή), points out that in *Oedipus Rex* the recognition is finest because it coincides with the peripeteia.[14] Oedipus' recognition in effect has bearing upon none other than himself. And the hero's final self-identification constitutes a complete reversal of the action in both the senses that can be given

117

to Aristotle's words (words that are themselves not devoid of ambiguity): First, Oedipus' situation, from the very fact of recognition, turns out to be the contrary of what it was before; second, Oedipus' action ultimately brings about a result that is the opposite of that intended. At the beginning of the drama the stranger from Corinth, the solver of riddles and savior of Thebes, installed at the head of the city and revered like a god by the people for his knowledge and devotion to public affairs, is confronted with another riddle, the death of the former king. Who killed Laius? At the end of the inquiry the purveyor of justice discovers himself to be also the assassin. Developing behind the gradual unfolding of the detective story that provides the material of the drama is Oedipus' recognition of his own identity. When he appears for the first time at the beginning of the play, telling the suppliants of his determination to discover the criminal at all costs and of his confidence of success, he expresses himself in terms whose ambiguity emphasizes the fact that behind the question that he thinks he is answering (who killed Laius?) can be detected the outlines of another problem (who is Oedipus?). The king proudly declares: "By going right back, in my turn, to the beginning [of the events that have remained unknown] I am the one who will bring them to light [ἐγὼ φανῶ]."[15] The scholiast does not fail to point out that something lies hidden in the *egō phanō*, something that Oedipus did not mean but that the spectator understands "since everything will be discovered in Oedipus himself [ἐπεὶ τὸ πᾶν ἐν αὐτῷ φανήσεται]." *Egō phanō* means "It is I who will bring the criminal to light" but also "I shall discover myself to be the criminal."

What then is Oedipus? Like his own discourse, like the pronouncement of the oracle, Oedipus is double, enigmatic. Psychologically and morally he remains the same from beginning to end in the drama: a man of action and decision, unfailing courage and domineering intelligence who can be accused of no moral fault and no deliberate failing where justice is concerned. But, without his knowing it, without having wished or deserved it, the figure of Oedipus proves to be in every aspect — social, religious, and human – the opposite of what, as leader of the city, he seems to be. The Corinthian stranger is in reality a native of Thebes; the solver of riddles is a riddle he himself cannot solve; the dispenser of justice is a criminal; the clairvoyant, a blind man; the savior of the town, its doom.. Oedipus, he who is renowned to all,[16] the first among men,[17] the best of mortals,[18] the man of power, intelligence, honors, and wealth discovers himself to be the last, the most unfortunate,[19] and the worst of men,[20] a criminal,[21] a defilement[22] an object of horror to his fellows,[23] abhorred by the gods,[24] reduced to a life of beggary and exile.[25]

Two features emphasize the significance of this "reversal" in Oedipus' condition. In his very first words to him, the priest of Zeus refers to Oedipus as though he were in some way the equal of the gods: δεοῖσι ἰσούμενον.[26] When the riddle is solved the chorus recognizes in Oedipus the model of a human life that, through this paradigm, it sees as the equal of nothing at all (ἴσα καὶ τὸ μηδέν).[27] To start with Oedipus is the mind with second sight, the lucid intelligence that, without anybody's aid, helped by neither god nor man, was able, by virtue of his own gnōmē alone, to guess the riddle of the Sphinx. He has nothing but scorn for the blind gaze of the diviner whose eyes are closed to the light of the sun and who, in his own words, "lives by the shadows alone."[28] But when the shadows have been dispersed and all has become clear,[29] when light has been shed on Oedipus, precisely then is it that he sees the daylight for the last time. As soon as Oedipus has been "elucidated," uncovered,[30] presented as a spectacle of horror for all to see,[31] it is no longer possible for him either to see or to be seen. The Thebans turn their eyes away from him,[32] unable to contemplate full in the face this evil "so frightful to behold,"[33] this distress the description and sight of which is too much to bear.[34] And if Oedipus blinds his eyes it is, as he explains,[35] because it has become impossible for him to bear the look of any human creature among either the living or the dead. If it had been possible he would also have stopped up his ears so as to immure himself in a solitude that would cut him off from the society of men.

The light that the gods have cast upon Oedipus is too dazzling for any mortal eye to withstand. It casts Oedipus out of this world that is made for the light of the sun, the human gaze and social contact, and restores him to the solitary world of night in which Tiresias lives: Tiresias with the gift of second sight, who has also paid with his eyes for having acceded to the other light, the blinding, terrible light of the divine.

Seen from a human point of view, Oedipus is the leader with second sight, the equal of the gods; considered from the point of view of the gods he is blind, equal to nothing. Both the reversal of the action and the ambiguity of the language reflect the duality of the human condition that, just like a riddle, lends itself to two opposite interpretations. Human language is reversed when the gods express themselves through it. The human condition is reversed — however great, just, and fortunate one may be — as soon as it is scrutinized in relation to the gods. Oedipus had "shot his arrow further than other men, he had won the most fortunate happiness."[36] But in the sight of the Immortals he who rises highest is also the lowest. Oedipus the fortunate reaches the depths of misfortune. As the chorus puts it, "What man has known any but an illusory happiness from which he later falls into disillusion? Taking your destiny as an example, yes yours, unhappy Oedipus, I cannot believe any human life to be a happy one."[37]

If this is indeed the meaning of the tragedy, as Greek scholars believe it to be,[38] it will be recognized that *Oedipus Rex* is not only centered on the theme of the riddle but that in its presentation, development, and resolution the play is itself constructed as a riddle. The ambiguity, recognition, and peripeteia all parallel one another and are all equally integral to the enigmatic structure of the work. The keystone of the tragic structure, the model that serves as matrix for its dramatic construction and language, is reversal. By this we mean the formal schema in which positive becomes negative when one passes from the one to the other of the two levels, human and divine, that tragedy unites and opposes in the same way as, in Aristotle's definition, riddles join together terms that are irreconcilable.[39]

This logical schema of reversal, corresponding with the ambiguous type of thought that is characteristic of tragedy, offers the spectators a particular kind of lesson: Man is not a being that can be described or defined; he is a problem, a riddle the double meanings of which are inexhaustible. The significance of the work is neither psychological nor moral; it is specifically tragic.[40] Parricide and incest correspond neither with Oedipus' character, his *ēthos*, nor with any moral fault, *adikia*, that he has committed. If he kills his father and sleeps with his mother it is not because, in some obscure way, he hates the former and is in love with the latter. Oedipus' feelings for those whom he believes to be his real and only parents, Merope and Polybus, are those of tender filial affection. When he kills Laius it is in legitimate defense against a stranger who struck him first; when he marries Iocasta it is not a love-match but marriage with a stranger that the city of Thebes imposes upon him so that, as reward for his exploit, he can ascend the throne: "The city bound me to a fateful marriage, an accursed union, without my knowing.... I received this gift that I should never have received from Thebes, after serving her so well."[41] As Oedipus himself declares, in committing parricide and incest neither his person ($\sigma\tilde{\omega}\mu\alpha$) nor his actions ($\acute{\epsilon}\rho\gamma\alpha$) were to blame. In reality he himself has done nothing ($o\mathring{\upsilon}\kappa\ \acute{\epsilon}\rho\epsilon\xi\alpha$).[42] Or rather, while he was committing an action, its meaning became reversed without his knowledge and through no fault of his. Legitimate defense turned into parricide; marriage, the consecration of his honor, turned into incest. Although innocent and pure from the point of view of human law, he is guilty and defiled from the point of view of religion. What he has done without knowing it and with no evil intent or criminal volition is, notwithstanding, the most terrible crime against the sacred order that governs human life. Like birds that eat the flesh of birds, to borrow Aeschylus' expression,[43] he has twice satiated himself with his own flesh, first by shedding the blood of his father and then by becoming united with the blood of his mother. Through a divine curse as gratuitous as the divine choice that singles out other heroes of legend and from which they benefit, Oedipus thus finds himself cut off from society, rejected by humanity. Henceforth, he is *apolis*, the embodiment of the outsider. In his solitude he seems both lower than humanity — a wild beast or savage monster — and higher than it, stamped as he is, like a *daimōn*, with a religious quality to be feared. His defilement, his *agos* is simply the reverse side to the supernatural power that has concentrated itself in him to bring him to his doom: Defiled as he is, he is also consecrated and holy, he is *hieros* and *eusebēs*.[44] To the city that takes him in and to the land that receives his corpse he guarantees the greatest of blessings.

This network of reversals makes its impact through stylistic and dramatic devices as well as through ambiguous expressions — in particular through what Bernard Knox[45] calls an inversion in the use of the same terms in the course of the tragic action. We can only refer the reader here to his fine study from which we will take no more than a few examples. One way of effecting this reversal is by describing Oedipus' condition in terms whose meanings are systematically inverted as one passes from an active to a passive construction. Oedipus is described as a hunter on the trail, tracking down and flushing out the wild beast[46] at large in the mountains, pursuing and putting it to flight,[47] relegating it to a place far from human beings.[48] But in this hunt the hunter ultimately finds himself the quarry: Pursued by the terrible curse of his parents,[49] Oedipus wanders away, howling like a wild animal,[50] before putting out his eyes and fleeing into the wild mountains of Cithaeron.[51] Oedipus heads an investigation that is both legal and scientific, as is stressed by the repeated use of the verb *zētein*.[52] But the investigator is also the object of the investigation, the *zētōn* is also the *zētoumenon*[53] just as the examiner or questioner[54] is also the answer to the question.[55] Oedipus is both the one who discovers[56] and the object of the discovery,[57] the very one who is discovered.[58] He is the doctor who speaks of the evil from which the city is suffering in medical terms, but he is also the one who is diseased[59] and the disease itself.[60]

Another form of reversal is the following: The terms used to describe Oedipus at the height of his glory one by one become detached from him and applied instead to the figures of the gods. The greatness of Oedipus shrinks to nothing as the greatness of the gods, in contrast with his, becomes increasingly evident. In line 14 the priest of Zeus with his first words addresses Oedipus as sovereign: κρατύνων; in line 903 the chorus prays to Zeus as sovereign: ὦ κρατύνων. In line 48 the Thebans call Oedipus their savior: σωτήρ; in line 150 it is Apollo who is invoked as savior, to put an end (παυστήριος) to the evil, as Oedipus earlier "put an end" to the Sphinx.[61] At 237 Oedipus gives orders in his capacity as master of power and of the throne (ἐγὼ κράτη τε καὶ θρόνους νέμω); at 200 the chorus prays to Zeus as "master of power and of the thunderbolt [ἀστραπᾶν κράτη νέμων]." At 441, Oedipus recalls the exploit that made him great (μέγαν); at 871, the chorus recalls that amid the heavenly laws there lives a great (μέγας) god who never ages. The dominion (ἀρχάς) that Oedipus flatters himself he wields[62] is recognized by the chorus to lie, forever immortal, between the hands of Zeus.[63] The help (ἀλκήν) that the priest begs from Oedipus at line 42 is sought by the chorus from Athena at 189. In the first line of the tragedy Oedipus addresses the suppliants as a father to his children; but at 201 the chorus gives the title of father to Zeus, imploring him to rid the city of its pestilence: ὦ Ζεῦ πάτηρ.

The very name of Oedipus lends itself to such effects of reversal. He himself is ambiguous, stamped with the enigmatic character that is the mark of the entire tragedy. Oedipus is the man with the swollen foot (*oidos*), an infirmity that recalls the accursed child rejected by its parents and exposed to savage nature to die. But Oedipus is also the man who knows (*oida*) the riddle of the foot and who succeeds in deciphering, without twisting its meaning,[64] the oracle of the Sphinx,[65] the sinister prophetess, her of the obscure song.[66] This is the knowledge that sets the foreign

hero on the throne of Thebes in the place of its legitimate heirs.
The double meaning of Oedipus is to be found in the name itself
in the opposition between the first two syllables and the third.
Oīda: I know; this is one of the key words on the lips of Oedipus
triumphant, of Oedipus the tyrant.[67] *Pous*: foot; the mark stamped
at birth on one whose destiny is to end up as he began, as one
excluded like the wild beast whose *foot* makes it flee,[68] whose
foot isolates him from other men, who hopes in vain to escape
the oracles,[69] pursued by the curse of the terrible *foot*[70] for having infringed the sacred laws with a *foot* raised high[71] and unable
henceforth to free his *foot* from the misfortunes into which he
has cast himself by raising himself to the highest position of
power.[72] The whole of the tragedy of Oedipus seems to be contained in the play to which the riddle of his name lends itself.
The eminently knowledgeable master of Thebes, protected by
Tuchē (Good Luck), seems to be opposed on every point by the
accursed child, the *Swollen Foot* rejected by his native land. But
before Oedipus can know who he really is, the first of his two
personalities, the one he first assumes, must be so thoroughly
inverted that it becomes as one with the second.

When Oedipus solves the Sphinx's riddle the solution his wisdom discovers is, in a way, already relevant to himself. The bale-
ful songstress' question is: Who is the being that is at the same
time *dipous*, *tripous*, and *tetrapous*? For *oi-dipous* the mystery is an
apparent, not a real one: Of course the answer is himself, man.
But his reply is only apparent, not real knowledge: The true problem that is still masked is: What then is man, what is Oedipus?
Oedipus' pseudo-reply makes Thebes open wide her gates to him.
But by installing him at the head of the State, it is also the instrument that, while misleading him as to his true identity, brings
about his parricide and incest. For Oedipus, resolving his own mystery involves recognizing in the stranger who is the ruler of Thebes
the child who was native to that country and formerly rejected
by it. However, this identification does not integrate Oedipus
definitively into the country that is his own and establish him on

the throne he occupies as the legitimate son of the king rather than as a foreign tyrant. Instead, it turns him into a monster that must be expelled forever from the town and cut off from the world of human beings.

The figure of Oedipus the Sage, placed far above other men, is revered like a god as the unchallenged master of justice who holds in his hands the salvation of the entire city. But at the end of the drama this figure is inverted into its opposite: Reduced to the lowest degree of degradation, we find Oedipus the Swollen Foot, the abominable defilement in whom all the world's impurity is concentrated. The divine king, the purifier and savior of his people becomes one with the defiled criminal who must be expelled like a *pharmakos* or scapegoat so that the town can regain its purity and be saved.

It is this axis on which the divine king occupies the highest point and the *pharmakos* the lowest that governs the whole series of reversals that affect the figure of Oedipus and turn the hero into a "paradigm" of ambiguous, tragic man.

The quasi-divine character of the majestic figure advancing to the threshold of his palace at the beginning of the tragedy has not failed to strike the commentators. Even the ancient scholiast noted, in his commentary to line 16, that the suppliants approach the altars of the royal house as if these were the altars of some god. The expression used by Zeus' priest: "You behold us assembled close to *your* altars" seems all the more loaded with significance in that Oedipus himself asks: "Why do you thus kneel in a posture of ritual supplication before me, with your wreaths crowned with bands?" This veneration for a man who is placed higher than other men because he has saved the town "with the help of a god,"[73] because he has, by some supernatural favor, revealed himself to be *Tuchē*, the city's Good Luck,[74] persists unabated from beginning to end of the play. Even after the revelation of Oedipus' double defilement the chorus still praises as its savior the one whom it calls "my king" who "stood like a tower in the face of death."[75] Even as it describes the inexpiable crimes of the unfortunate Oedipus, the chorus concludes by saying: "And yet, to tell the truth, it is thanks to you that I have been able to draw breath again and find rest."[76]

But it is at the most crucial point in the drama, when the fate of Oedipus rests on a razor's edge, that the polarity between the status of demi-god and that of scapegoat is the most clearly apparent. The situation at this point is as follows: It is already known that Oedipus may be the murderer of Laius; the agreement in the oracles pronounced on the one hand to Oedipus and on the other to Laius and Iocasta increases the dread that oppresses the hearts of the protagonists and Theban notables. Then the messenger from Corinth arrives; he announces that Oedipus is not the son of those whom he believes to be his parents; he is a foundling; the messenger himself received him from the hands of a shepherd on Mount Cithaeron. Iocasta, for whom everything has now become clear, entreats Oedipus not to pursue the inquiry any further. Oedipus refuses. The queen then warns him for the last time: "Wretch, may you never know who you are!" But yet again the tyrant of Thebes misunderstands the meaning of what it is to be Oedipus. He thinks that the queen is afraid to hear that the foundling's birth was a lowly one and that her marriage turns out to be a misalliance with a nobody, a slave, a son of slaves to the third generation.[77] It is precisely at this point that Oedipus finds new heart. The messenger's account arouses in his dejected spirits the wild hope that the chorus shares with him and proceeds to express with joy. Oedipus declares himself to be the son of *Tuchē*, who in the course of the years has reversed the situation, changing him from "small" to "great,"[78] who, in other words, has transformed the misshapen foundling into the wise master of Thebes. The words are full of irony: Oedipus is no son of *Tuchē* but, as Tiresias predicted,[79] her victim; and the "reversal" is the opposite one, reducing the great Oedipus to the smallest stature possible, bringing the equal of the gods down to the equal of nothing at all.

Yet the false impression that Oedipus and the chorus share is an understandable one. The exposed child may be a reject to be got rid of, a misshapen monster or a humble slave. But he may also be a hero with an exceptional destiny. Saved from death and victor in the trial imposed upon him at his birth, the exile reveals himself to be a chosen one invested with supernatural powers.[80] Now that he has returned in triumph to the country that expelled him, he will live there not as an ordinary citizen but as its absolute master, reigning over his subjects like a god set down in the midst of men. This is why the theme of the exposed child appears in almost all of the Greek legends about heroes. If Oedipus was at birth rejected in this way, cut off from his human lineage, it is no doubt — the chorus imagines — because he is the son of some god, of the nymphs of Cithaeron, of Pan or Apollo, Hermes or Dionysus.[81]

This mythical image of the hero exposed and saved, rejected and returning in triumph, is continued in the fifth century in a transposed form, in one particular representation of the *turannos*. Like the hero, the tyrant accedes to royalty via an indirect route, bypassing the legitimate line; like him, his qualifications for power are his actions and his exploits. He reigns by virtue not of his blood but of his own qualities; he is the son of his works and also of *Tuchē*. The supreme power that he has succeeded in winning outside the ordinary norms places him, for better or for worse, above other men and above the law.[82] As Bernard Knox rightly observes, the comparison of tyranny to the power of the gods — and the Greeks defined these as "the most strong," "the most powerful" — is a commonplace in the literature of the fifth and fourth centuries. Euripides[83] and Plato[84] both speak of the *turannos isotheos*, tyranny that is the equal of a god in that it is the absolute power to do as one wishes, to do anything one wants.[85]

The other, complementary and opposed side to Oedipus, his role as a scapegoat, has not been so clearly noted by the commentators. It was certainly noticed that, at the end of the tragedy, Oedipus is hounded from Thebes just as the *homo piacularis* is expelled so as to "remove the defilement [τὸ ἄγος ἐλαύνειν]."[86] But it was Louis Gernet who first made a precise link between the theme of the tragedy and the Athenian ritual of the *pharmakos*.[87]

Thebes suffers from a *loimos* that manifests itself, in the traditional way, by the failure of all sources of fertility: Earth, flocks, and women are no longer productive while at the same time plague decimates the living. Sterility, disease, and death are all felt to be the power of the same defilement, a *miasma* that has disrupted the whole of life's normal course. What must be done is find the criminal who is the city's defilement or *agos*, and eliminate the ill by eliminating him. As is well known, this is what was done at Athens, in the seventh century, to expiate the impious murder of Kylon, when the Alcmeonids were declared impure and sacrilegious and expelled, *enageis kai alitērioi*.[88]

But in Athens, as in other Greek cities, there was also an annual ritual aimed at the periodical expulsion of all the defilement accumulated over the past year. Helladius of Byzantium reports as follows: "It is the custom in Athens to parade two *pharmakoi*, with the object of purification, one for the men, the other for the women...!"[89] According to legend the origin of the ritual was the Athenians' impious murder of Androgaeus the Cretan. To remove the *loimos* released by the crime, the custom of repeated purification by means of *pharmakoi* was introduced. The ceremony took place on the first day of the festival of the *Thargelia*, on the sixth day of the month of *Thargeliōn*.[90] The *pharmakoi*, wearing necklaces of dried figs (black or green, according to which sex they represented), were paraded through the town; they were beaten about their sexual organs with scilla bulbs, figs, and other wild plants,[91] and then expelled. In the earliest days at least, they were possibly stoned to death, their corpses burnt and their ashes strewn to the winds.[92] How were these *pharmakoi* selected? They were most likely recruited from the dregs of the population, from among the *kakourgoi*, gibbet fodder whose crimes, physical ugliness, lowly condition, and base and repugnant occupations marked them out as inferior, degraded beings, *phauloi*, the refuse of society. In the *Frogs*, Aristophanes contrasts the well-born citizens who are wise, just, good, and honest, resembling the sound city currency, with the false coins of copper, "the foreigners, rascals, knaves, sons of knaves, and newcomers whom the city would not easily have chosen at random, even for *pharmakoi*."[93] Tzetzes, citing fragments from the poet Hipponax, notes that when a *loimos* afflicted the city, they chose the most ugly person of all (*amorphoteron*) as the *katharmos* and *pharmakos* of the stricken town.[94] At Leukas, a criminal under sentence of death was used for the purification. At Marseilles, some poor wretch came forward, offering himself for the salvation of all. He won a year's grace during which he was supported at the expense of the public. When the year had elapsed he was paraded around the town and solemnly cursed so that all the faults of the community should fall upon his head.[95] So it was quite natural that the image of the *pharmakos* should come to Lysias' mind when he was denouncing to the judges the repugnant villainy of a character such as Andocides, impious, sacrilegious, a denouncer and traitor, hounded from one town to another and, in his misfortunes, seemingly marked by the finger of god. To condemn Andocides "is to purify the town to free it from defilement, to expel the *pharmakos*."[96]

There was another aspect to the Athenian Thargelia. They combined with the expulsion of the *pharmakos* another ritual that took place on the seventh of the month, the day dedicated to Apollo. The first fruits of the land were consecrated to the god in the form of the *thargēlos*, a pastry and a pot containing seeds of all kinds.[97] But the central feature of the festival consisted in parading the *eiresiōnē*, an olive or laurel branch garlanded with wool and decorated with fruits, cakes, and little phials of oil and wine.[98] Young boys carried these "May trees" through the town, depositing some at the threshold of the temple of Apollo and hanging others outside the doors of private dwellings, *pros apotropēn limou*, to ward off famine.[99] The *eiresiōnē* in Attica, Samos, Delos, and Rhodes and the *kōpō* in Thebes represented the rebirth of springtime. To the accompaniment of songs and a collection of gifts,

these processions consecrated the end of the old season and ush-
ered in the young new year under the sign of donations, abun-
dance, and health.[100] The Athenian ritual clearly indicates the need
for the social group to reinvigorate the forces of fertility on which
its life depends, by dismissing those that have, as it were, with-
ered away during the year. The *eiresiōnē* remained hanging outside
the doors of the houses, fading and withering, until it was replaced
on this day of the Thargelia by another that the new year had
made to flourish.[101]

But this renewal symbolized by the *eiresiōnē* could only take
place if every defilement had been banished from the group and
from the land and men made pure once again. As Plutarch notes,[102]
the first fruits of all kinds that adorn the *eiresiōnē* commemorate
the end of the *aphoria*, the sterility that afflicted the land of Attica
in punishment for the murder of Androgaeus, the very murder
that the expulsion of the *pharmakos* is intended to expiate. The
major role played by the *eiresiōnē* in the Thargelia explains why
Hesychius glosses Θάργηλος by *hē hiketeria* (ή ικετηρία), for in form
and in function the *eiresiōnē* is exactly like the branch carried
by a suppliant.[103]

These *hiketeriai*, these suppliants' branches festooned with wool,
are precisely what, at the beginning of Sophocles' drama, the representatives of Theban youth, children and very young people
divided into age groups, carry in procession to the doors of the
royal palace and deposit before the altars of Apollo to conjure away
the *loimos* that afflicts the town. Another detail makes it possible
to define more precisely the ritual procedure depicted in the first
scene of the tragedy. We are twice told that the town is loud with
"paeans mingled with tears and lamentation."[104] Normally the
paean is a joyful song for victory and for actions of magnanimity.
It stands in contrast to the threnody, the chant of mourning of
plaintive dirge. But we know through a scholiast to the *Iliad* that
there is also another kind of paean that is "sung to bring about
the end of evils or to avert them."[105] According to the scholiast,
this cathartic paean, the memory of which was perpetuated in par-

ticular by the Pythagoreans, might equally well appear as a threnody. This is the paean mingled with sobs mentioned in the tragedy. This purificatory song is sung at a very precise moment in the religious calendar, at the turning point of the year represented by the season of spring that, at the threshold of summer, marks the start of the period of human activities that include harvesting, navigation, and warfare.[106] The Thargelia, which take place in May, before the start of the harvesting, belong to this complex of spring festivals.

These details must have driven home the connection with the Athenian ritual all the more forcefully to the spectators of the tragedy given that Oedipus is explicitly presented as the *agos*, the defilement that must be expelled.[107] In his very first words he describes himself, without meaning to, in terms that evoke the figure of the scapegoat: Addressing the suppliants, he says "I know very well that you are all suffering; and as you thus suffer, there is not one of you who suffers as much as I. For your pain only affects each one of you as an individual and nobody else, but my soul [ψυχή] laments over the town, myself and you, all at once."[108] And a little further on he says, "I suffer the misfortune of all these men even more than if it were my own."[109] Oedipus is mistaken; this evil that Creon immediately calls by its correct name, *miasma*,[110] *is* in fact his own. But even while under this misapprehension, he speaks truly without realizing it: It is because, as the *miasma*, he is himself the *agos* of the city that Oedipus does indeed carry the whole weight of all the misfortune that afflicts his fellow citizens.

Divine king and *pharmakos*: These are the two sides to Oedipus that make a riddle of him by combining within him two figures, the one the reverse of the other, as in a formula with a double meaning. Sophocles lends general significance to this inversion in Oedipus' nature by presenting the hero as a model of the human condition. But the polarity between king and scapegoat (a polarity that the tragedy situates at the very heart of the figure of Oedipus) is something that Sophocles did not need to invent. It was already part of the religious practice and social thought of the Greeks. The poet simply gave it new significance by having it symbolize man and his fundamental ambiguity. If Sophocles chooses the pair *turannos-pharmakos* to illustrate what we have called the theme of reversal, it is because the two figures appear symmetrical and in some respects interchangeable in their opposition. Both are presented as *individuals* responsible for the *collective* salvation of the group. In Homer and Hesiod the fertility of the land, herds, and women depends upon the person of the king, the descendant of Zeus. If he shows himself to be *amumōn*, beyond reproach, in his justice as monarch, then everything in his city prospers;[111] but if he goes astray *the entire town* pays for the fault of *the one individual*. The son of Kronos brings down misfortune, *limos* and *loimos*, both famine and pestilence, upon the whole community. Men die, women no longer bring forth children, the land remains sterile and the herds do not reproduce.[112] So when a divine scourge afflicts a people the normal solution is to sacrifice the king. If he is the master of fertility and this fails it is because his power as sovereign has somehow been turned upside down; his justice has become criminal, his virtue a defilement, the best man (*aristos*) has become the worst (*kakistos*). Thus the legends of Lycurgus, Athamas, and Oinoclos involve getting rid of the *loimos* by stoning the king, by his ritual killing or, failing this, by the sacrifice of his son. But it may also happen that a member of the community is delegated to assume the role of the unworthy sovereign, the role of the king turned inside out. The king unburdens his responsibilities upon an individual who is a kind of inverted image of all that is negative in his own character. This is indeed what the *pharmakos* is; the king's double, but reversed like the carnival kings crowned for the duration of the festival, when order is turned upside down and the social hierarchies reversed: Sexual taboos are lifted, theft becomes lawful, slaves take the place of their masters, women exchange their clothes with men — and in these circumstances the one who sits upon the throne must be the lowest, the most ugly, the most ridiculous, the most criminal. But when the festival is over the counter-king is expelled or put to death, carrying away with him all the disorder that he embodied and of which he thereby purges the community.

In the ritual of the Thargelia, in classical Athens, certain features that evoke the sovereign, the master of fertility are still detectable in the figure of the *pharmakos*.[113] The revolting figure who has to embody the defilement lives at the expense of the State, feeding on dishes of exceptional purity: fruit, cheese, and sacred cakes of *maza*;[114] he is adorned in the procession, like the *eiresiōnē*, with necklaces of figs and with branches and he is beaten on his sexual organs with scilla bulbs; and the reason for this is that he possesses the beneficent virtue of fertility. His defilement is a religious qualification that can be used to good effect. His *agos*, like that of Oedipus, turns him into a *katharmos*, a *katharsios*, a purifier. Furthermore, the ambiguity of this figure even comes through in the etiological accounts that are supposed to explain the origins of the ritual. The version of Helladius of Byzantium that we have cited is contradicted by that given by Diogenes Laertius and Athenaeus,[115] which runs as follows: When Epimenides was purifying Athens from the *loimos* caused by the murder of Kylon, two young men, one of whom was called Cratinos, voluntarily offered themselves to purify the land that had nourished them. These two young men are presented not as the rejects of society but as the very flower of Athenian youth. According to Tzetzes, as we have seen, a particularly ugly person (*amorphoteros*) was chosen to be *pharmakos*: According to Athenaeus, Cratinos was on the contrary *meirakioneumorphon*, an exceptionally handsome lad.

This symmetry between the *pharmakos* and the king of legend in which the former, at the bottom of the scale, took on a role analogous to that which the latter played at the top, may throw some light upon the institution of ostracism whose many bizarre features have been noted by J. Carcopino.[116] As we know, there is no longer a place within the framework of the city for the figure of the king, the master of fertility. When ostracism became an institution in Athens at the end of the sixth century it was the figure of the tyrant that took over, in a transposed form, certain religious characteristics of the ancient sovereign. The main purpose of ostracism was to remove any citizen who, by rising too high, might accede to the tyranny. But in this positivist form the explanation fails to account for certain archaic features of the institution. It came into operation every year, probably between the sixth and the eighth prytanies, in accordance with rules quite unlike those that governed the ordinary procedures of law and political life. Ostracism was a sentence aimed at "removing a citizen from the city" by imposing a temporary exile lasting ten years.[117] It was not passed by the tribunals but by the assembly, without anybody having been publicly denounced or even accused. At a preliminary hearing it was decided, by a show of hands, whether or not there was any occasion to use the procedure of ostracism that year. No name was mentioned and no debate took place. If the vote was positive the assembly regathered at a meeting called specially, some time later. It was held in the agora not, as was usual, on the Pnux. The vote itself was taken by each participant writing the name of his choice on a potsherd. Again no debate took place; no name was proposed; there was no accusation and no defense. The vote was passed without any appeal being made to reasons of a political or legal nature. It was all organized so as to make it possible for the popular feeling that the Greeks called *phthonos* (a mixture of envy and religious distrust of anyone who rose too high or was too successful) to manifest itself in the most spontaneous and unanimous fashion (there had to be at least 6,000 voters) regardless of any rule of law or rational justification.[118] The only things held against the ostracized man were the very superior qualities that had raised him above the common herd, and his exaggerated good luck that might call down the wrath of the gods upon the town. The fear of tyranny was confused with a more deep-seated religious apprehension directed against one who put the entire group in peril. As Solon wrote, "a city can perish from its too great men [ἀνδρῶν δ'ἐκ μεγάλων πόλις ὄλλυται]."[119]

Aristotle's development of the idea of ostracism is characteristic in this respect.[120] He says that if a man oversteps the common level in virtue and in political skill, he cannot be accepted
on an equal footing with the rest of the citizens: "Such a being
will in effect naturally be as a god among men." And Aristotle
goes on to say that this is why the democratic states introduced
the institution of ostracism. In doing so they were following the
example of myth: The Argonauts abandoned Heracles for a similar reason. The ship Argo refused to carry him like the other pas-
sengers, on account of his excessive weight. Aristotle concludes
by remarking that the situation is similar in the arts and sciences:
"A choir master would not accept among his singers anyone with
a voice whose beauty would surpass the whole of the rest of the
chorus put together."

How could the city possibly take to its bosom one who, like
Oedipus, "has shot his arrow further than anyone else" and has
become *isotheos*? In ostracism it creates an institution whose role
is symmetrical to and the reverse of the ritual of the Thargelia.
In the person of the ostracized one the city expels whatever it is
in it that is too high and that embodies the evil that can fall on
it from above. In that of the *pharmakos*, it expels whatever is most
vile and embodies the evil that threatens it from below.[121] Through
this double and complementary rejection it sets its own limits
in relation to what is above and what is below. It takes the true
measure of man as opposed on the one hand to the divine and
the heroic and, on the other, to the bestial and the monstrous.

In his political theory, Aristotle gives explicit and deliberate
expression to what the city thus spontaneously brings about
through the interplay of its institutions. He declares that man is
by nature a political animal; so whoever is found to be by nature
ἄπολις is either φαῦλος, a degraded being, less than a man or else
κρείττων ἢ ἄνθρωπος, above humanity, more powerful than man. He
goes on to say that such a man is "like an isolated piece at draughts
[ἅτε ὢν ὥσπερ ἄζυξ ἐν πεττοῖς]" and a little later he returns to this
idea when he notes that whoever cannot live in the community

"forms no part of the state and so is either a brutish beast or a god [ἢ θηρίον ἢ θεός]."[122]

This is an exact definition of the double and contradictory nature of Oedipus' status; he is above and also below human beings, a hero more powerful than man, the equal of the gods, and at the same time a brutish beast spurned and relegated to the wild solitude of the mountains.

But Aristotle's remark goes even further. It allows us to understand the role of the parricide and perpetrator of incest through the reversal that combines within Oedipus' person one who is both the equal of the gods and the equal of nothing at all. These two crimes in effect constitute an infringement of the basic rules of a game of draughts in which each piece occupies in relation to the others a precise place on the checker board of the city.[123] By being guilty of these crimes Oedipus has shuffled the cards, mixed up the positions and pieces: He is now disqualified. Through his parricide followed by incest he installs himself in the place formerly occupied by his father; he makes Iocasta assume the roles of both mother and wife; he identifies himself both with Laius (as the husband of Iocasta) and with his own children (to whom he is both father and brother) and in this way he mixes up the three generations of the lineage. Sophocles underlines this confusion, this identification of what ought to remain distinct and separate, with an emphasis that has sometimes shocked modern readers but that the interpreter must take into full account. He does so by means of a play on words centered on *homos* and *isos*, similar and equal, together with their compound forms. Even before he knows anything of his true origins Oedipus describes himself, from the point of view of his relationship to Laius, as sharing the same bed and having a *homosporon* wife.[124] On his lips the word means that he is impregnating with his seed the same woman that Laius has impregnated before him; but in line 460 Tiresias gives the word its true meaning: He tells Oedipus that he will discover himself to be both the murderer of his father and his *homosporos*, his co-impregnator.[125] *Homosporos* usually has a different meaning, namely: born of the same seed, blood relative. And indeed, without knowing it, Oedipus is of the same blood as both Laius and Iocasta. The fact that Oedipus and his own sons are equal is expressed in a series of brutally forceful images: The father has sowed the seed for his sons in the very spot where he himself was sown; Iocasta is a wife, is not a wife but a mother whose furrow has produced in a double harvest both the father and the children; Oedipus has sown his seed in the woman who gave him birth, in whom he himself was seeded and from these same furrows, the "equal" furrows, he has obtained his own children.[126] But it is Tiresias who lends the full weight to this terminology expressing equality when he addresses Oedipus as follows: Misfortunes will come that "will make you the equal of yourself by making you the equal of your children."[127] The identification of Oedipus with his own father and his own children, the assimilation of mother and wife in the person of Iocasta make Oedipus the equal of himself, that is turn him into an *agos*, an *apolis* being incommensurable and without equality with other men, who believing himself to be the equal of a god in the end finds himself to be the equal of nothing at all.[128] For no more than does the wild beast, does the *isotheos* tyrant recognize the rules of the game on which the human city is based.[129] Among the gods, who make up a single family, incest is not forbidden. Kronos and Zeus each attacked and dethroned their own father. Like them, the tyrant may believe that all is permitted to him; Plato calls him a "parricide"[130] and compares him to a man who, by virtue of a magic ring, is free to infringe the most sacred of laws with impunity: He may kill whomever he pleases, be united with whomever he likes; he is "the master who may do anything, like a god among men."[131] Similarly, wild beasts are not obliged, either, to respect the prohibitions upon which human society rests. They are not, as the gods are, above the laws by virtue of their greater powers, but below them through default of *logos*.[132] Dio Chrysostomus records Diogenes' ironic remark on the subject of Oedipus: "Oedipus bewails the fact that he is both father and brother to his children and husband and son to his wife; but that is something that neither cocks nor dogs nor birds complain about";[133] for among these creatures there are no such things as brothers, fathers, husbands, sons, or wives. Like isolated pieces in a game of draughts, they live without rules, knowing neither difference nor equality,[134] in the confusion of *anomia*.[135]

Disqualified from the game, excluded from the city and rejected by the human race because of his parricide and incest, Oedipus is discovered, at the end of the tragedy, to be identical to the monstrous creature referred to in the riddle that he, in his pride of "wise man" believed he had solved. The Sphinx's question was: What is the creature with one voice that has two, three, and four legs? Confusing and mixing them up, it referred to the three successive ages of man that he can only know one after another: He is a child when he crawls on four legs, an adult when he stands firmly on his two feet, and an old man leaning on his stick. By identifying himself simultaneously with his young children and his old father, Oedipus, the man standing on his two feet, obliterates the barriers that ought to keep the father strictly separate from the sons and the grandfather so that each human generation occupies its appointed place both in the sequence of time and in the order of the city. Here is the last tragic reversal: It is his victory over the Sphinx that turns Oedipus into, not the solution that he guessed, but the very question posed, not a man like other men but a creature of confusion and chaos, the only creature (we are told) of all those that live upon earth, in the air or in the water who has "changed his nature" instead of keeping it clear and distinct.[136] As formulated by the Sphinx then, the riddle of man does have a solution but it is one that recoils against the monster's victor, the solver of riddles, and reveals him to be himself a kind of monster, a man in the shape of a riddle — and this time a riddle to which there is no solution.

A number of conclusions may be drawn from our analysis of *Oedipus Rex*. First, there is one model that is at work in the tragedy on every level at which it operates: in the language, in a number of stylistic features; in the structure of the drama where recognition and peripeteia coincide; in the theme of the destiny of Oedipus; and in the person of the hero himself. The model is not set out anywhere as a particular image, idea, or complex of feelings. It takes the form of a purely operational schema of reversal, a rule of ambiguous logic. But the tragedy gives content to this form. For instance, in the case of the face presented by Oedipus, the paradigm of the double man, the reversed man, the rule is embodied in the reversal that transforms the divine king into the scapegoat.

Second, if the complementary opposition between the *turannos* and the *pharmakos* on which Sophocles plays is indeed, as we believe, present in the institutions and political theory of the ancient Greeks, is the tragedy doing any more than simply reflecting a structure that already exists in the society and thought of the community? Our own belief is, on the contrary, that far from reflecting this it challenges it, brings it into question. For in social practice and theory, the polar structure of the superhuman and the subhuman is aimed at giving a more precise picture of the specific features of the field of human life as defined by the body of *nomoi* that characterize it. The relationship between the above and the below is merely that between the two lines that clearly define the boundaries within which man is contained. In contrast, in Sophocles, the superhuman and the subhuman meet and become confused within the same figure. And, given that this figure is the model of man, the boundaries that contained human life and made it possible to establish its status without ambiguity are obliterated. When man decides, like Oedipus, to carry the inquiry into what he is as far as it can go, he discovers himself to be enigmatic, without consistency, without any domain of his own or any fixed point of attachment, with no defined essence, oscillating between being the equal of the gods and the equal of nothing at all. His real greatness consists in the very thing that expresses his enigmatic nature: his questioning.

And finally, perhaps the most difficult thing is not, as we have attempted, restoring to tragedy its true meaning, the meaning it had for the Greeks of the fifth century, but rather understanding the misunderstandings to which it has given rise or rather how it is that it has given rise to so many. What is the source of the work of art's relative malleability that accounts for both its fresh and its perennial qualities? If in the last analysis the true mainspring of the tragedy is this kind of reversal that operates as a logical schema, it is understandable that the drama remains open to a number of different interpretations. We can also understand how it is that *Oedipus Rex* has acquired new meanings as, in the course of the history of Western thought, the problem of the ambiguity of man has shifted and changed its ground while the enigma of human existence has come to be formulated in different terms from those used by the ancient Greek tragedians.

Jean-Pierre Vernant

CHAPTER VI

Hunting and Sacrifice in

Aeschylus' *Oresteia*[1]

The *Oresteia* begins with the appearance of a beacon that has been carried from the destroyed city of Troy to Mycenae, to bring about "light in the darkness" and "the return of summer in mid-winter,"[2] but which in fact heralds events that are the opposite to what they seem. The trilogy ends with a nocturnal procession "by the light of dazzling torches [φέγγει λαμπάδων σελασφόρων]"[3] whose brilliance, this time, is not deceptive but sheds light upon a reconciled universe – though this does not mean, of course, a universe free from all tensions. As a result of the tragic action disorder gives way to order among the gods both young and old whose quarrels are mentioned at the outset of the *Agamemnon* in the shape of the conflict between the Ouranidai[4] and who confront each other both before the tribunal of Athens and before men in general. However, from beginning to end two themes appear to run right through the trilogy, the theme of sacrifice and that of hunting. The *Eumenides* ends with the procession uttering the ritual cry women make when a sacrificial animal is slain, the *ololugē*:[5] "And now give forth the ritual cry in response to our song [ὀλολύξατε νῦν ἐπὶ μολπαῖς]." But the first sacrificial image appears as early as line 65 of the *Agamemnon*, where the entry into battle is compared to the sacrifice that introduces the marriage ceremony, the *proteleia*, and immediately after this there appears the theme of the sacrifice that is unacceptable to the gods or, as it is sometimes called, the "corrupt sacrifice": "Feed your fire with wood from beneath and with oil from above, but nothing will appease the inflexible wrath that falls upon offerings that the flames refuse to consume."[6]

The image of hunting is no less in evidence. The omen that underlines the entire *Agamemnon* and not just this play but the entire past, present, and future of the Atreidae, is a scene of animal hunting in which two eagles devour a hare with young. As for the *Eumenides*, this play suggests a man-hunt in which Orestes is the quarry and the Erinyes the hounds. These hunting "images" have been collected in a useful monograph, although the scope of its analysis does not rise above a very banal literal level.[7] The importance of the theme of the sacrifice was totally missed even by a scholar such as Eduard Fraenkel, who simply speaks of a "travesty of ritual language to enhance a gruesome effect."[8] However, during recent years it has been the subject of considerably more serious studies. In some, such as that of Froma Zeitlin, it has been a matter of pinpointing its various meanings in the course of the trilogy.[9] In others, which are more ambitious and more controversial, attempts have been made to link the study of sacrifice to the whole of Greek tragedy, as in the work of W. Burkert and J.-P. Guépin.[10]

Nevertheless, until now nobody appears to have noticed that there is a link between hunting and sacrifice and that, in the *Oresteia*, the two themes are not only interwoven but also superimposed the one upon the other, and that it would therefore be profitable to study the two themes in conjunction.[11] And yet, after all, it is the very same characters, Agamemnon and Orestes, who play the role first of hunters and then of hunted, first of the sacrificers and subsequently of the sacrificed (or those threatened with this fate). In the omen of the hare with young devoured by the eagles the hunt is an image of a monstrous sacrifice, that of Iphigenia.

Greek hunting is a subject that has been relatively little explored. Yet it has a wide range of representational meanings. In the first place, it is a social activity that is differentiated according to the various stages of a man's life: Thus I have been able to make a distinction and contrast between the hunt of the ephebe and the hunt of the hoplite, between the cunning and the heroic hunt.[12] But it is also something more: In a large number of texts from tragedy, philosophy, or mythography, hunting is an expression of the transition between nature and culture. In this respect it is, surely, similar to war. To give but one example, when, in the myth of the *Protagoras* of Plato,[13] the Sophist describes the human world before the invention of politics, he says: "First, men lived apart from each other and no city existed. Because of this they were destroyed by animals that were always and everywhere stronger than they, and their industry that sufficed to feed them was yet inadequate to fight against the wild animals [πρὸς δὲ τὸν τῶν θηρίων πόλεμον ἐνδεής]. For they did not yet possess the art of politics, of which warfare is a part."[14]

Equally close are the links between hunting and sacrifice, that is, between the two methods open to the Greeks of acquiring meat to eat. Does the one derive from the other, as Karl Meuli suggests, that is, do the sacrificial rites derive ultimately from rites of the prehistoric huntsmen such as are still practiced, particularly in Siberia?[15] In order to prove his thesis on a historical basis, Karl Meuli is forced to admit that the rites of the huntsmen passed through two stages before they became the rites of the sacrificers — that the agricultural civilization of the Greeks took the place of a pastoral civilization that, in its turn, had derived from a civilization based on hunting.[16] Even if we were to accept these as proven facts, it is hard to see what they could tell us about the relationship between hunting and sacrifice in the case of the Greeks of the classical age, that is, in the case of a people who were not essentially a hunting community but who still did go hunting[17] and for whom the hunt continued to provide many myths and social representations. In the circumstances even the historian — particularly one who is not simply an antiquarian — must engage in a synchronic study.

According to the myth reported by Hesiod, on either side of the altar upon which the Olympian sacrifice was carried out[18] when the quarrel between the gods and mortal men was being resolved at Mecone, there were, on the one side, the inhabitants of heaven and, on the other, the dwellers upon earth. The gods received the bones and the smoke, the men the cooked flesh. The myth of Prometheus is closely linked to that of Pandora: possession of fire, which is necessary to the sacrificial meal, that is, at the level of the myth, simply to the meal, has as its counterpart, coming from Zeus, "the accursed breed and race of women"[19] and consuming sexuality. This is the destiny of the Iron Age man, a laborer whose only salvation lies in working the fields.

The function of the hunt both complements and stands in contrast to that of sacrifice. In a word, it determines the relationship between man and nature in the wild. The hunter is first the predatory animal such as the lion or the eagle, second the cunning animal such as the snake or the wolf (in Homer, most of the hunting images are of animals[20]), and third, he who possesses a skill (*techne*) that is precisely what neither the lion nor the wolf do possess. This is what is expressed in, among numerous other texts, the myth of Prometheus as described in Plato's *Protagoras*.

The act of sacrifice involves cooking; the sacrificed beast is, *par excellence*, the ox used for the plough. This sacrifice that in an extreme case, is a crime and that is forbidden in certain texts[21] is dramatized in the ceremony of the *Bouphonia* held in honor of Zeus Polieus, in Athens. Here the sacrificed beast, stuffed with straw, is harnessed to a plough while each of its "murderers" − from the priest down to the sacrificial knife − is "judged."[22] But the link between the sacrifice and the agricultural world is actually far more fundamental than might be suggested by this festival that one might suppose to be of marginal importance. There is a fine archaic illustration of this: When, having exhausted their supplies, the followers of Odysseus decide to sacrifice the oxen of the Sun, what they lack are the necessary agricultural products. Instead of toasting barleycorn, they use oak leaves and, for the libations, water instead of wine. The result is a disaster: "The cooked and the uncooked flesh lowed as the spits turned."[23] And yet there was an alternative to this impious sacrifice and Odysseus himself pointed it out: hunting and fishing.[24]

In general, it is true to say that the hunt is the opposite to the classical Olympian sacrifice. We know that the sacrifice of hunted animals is a rare phenomenon (and this is all the easier to understand as the animal to be sacrificed must be alive). In general, hunting is linked with gods who are hostile to the city, the gods of nature in the wild like Artemis and Dionysus.[25] Frequently, as in the Iphigenia myth, the sacrifice of a hunted animal appears as a substitute for human sacrifice, the savage nature of the victim to some extent mitigating the savage nature of the act.

Between these opposite extremes there are, however, intermediary zones that are used to good effect in tragedy. Euripides' *Bacchae* gives a striking description of the Dionysiac omophagy (the tearing up of raw meat), an action in which hunting and sacrifice are confused. Pentheus is the victim of just such a sacrificial hunt.

I do not propose to list the passages of the *Oresteia* where sacrifice, hunting, and occasionally fishing are mentioned but rather to emphasize the main themes in the three plays that we shall find to be contrasted with one another in some measure, item for item.

Let us start off with the chorus immediately following the *parados* of the *Agamemnon*[26] and the account of the omen that appeared to the Achaeans at Aulis. Even more than in Cassandra's great scene, the poet here "joins together distant memories and future prophecies"[27] but, for the very reason that this is still early on in the play, all the hints here are far more veiled.[28]

"Two kings of birds appear before the kings of the fleets, one entirely black [κελαινός], the other white of tail. They appeared close to the palace on the side of the hand that bears the lance, perched in full view, devouring a hare with brood unborn deprived of the chance of a last run, together with all its litter." Calchas immediately deduces that the eagles are the Atreidae, that they will capture Troy, that Artemis, being insulted by the murder of the doe hare is liable to insist upon an even heavier ransom (Iphigenia), which will in its turn entail other catastrophes: "For a treacherous keeper guards the home, ready to assert herself one dreadful day – Anger who remembers all and seeks vengeance for a child [μίμνει γὰρ φοβερὰ παλίνορτος οἰκονόμος δολία μνάμων μῆνις τεκνόποινος]."[29] It is thus that the cunning vengeance to be taken by Clytemnestra is predicted, in terms that can hardly be described as indirect.

Hunting terms and terms linked with sacrifice are here closely intermingled. The doe hare is "deprived of the chance of a last run [λοισθίων δρόμων],"[30] and this is a technical expression to be found elsewhere.[31] It is hardly necessary to dwell upon the fact that this doe is a hare, the prototype of the hunted animal and, according to Herodotus, the only species of which the female can conceive even while pregnant, such is the extent to which nature demands them as victims.[32] The hare, then, is the antithesis of the lion and the eagle. Homer describes Achilles as follows: "He has the vigor of the black eagle, the hunting eagle that is both the strongest and swiftest of the birds [αἰετοῦ οἴματ' ἔχων μέλανος τοῦ θηρητῆρος ὅς θ' ἅμα κάρτιστός τε καὶ ὤκιστος πετεηνῶν]"; he is like "the high flying eagle making for the plain through the dark clouds to snatch a tender lamb or a hare from its form [πτῶκα λαγωόν]," "the eagle, surest of all birds, the dark hunter called the Black One [μόρφνον θηρητῆρ', ὅν καὶ περκνὸν καλέουσιν]."[33] But it is not simply a question of any hunt. As has been pointed out,[34] a hunting rule mentioned by Xenophon recommends that "sportsmen" should leave newborn animals to the goddess: τὰ μὲν οὖν λίαν νεογνὰ οἱ φιλοκυνηγέται ἀφιᾶσι τῇ θεᾷ.[35] The eagles' hunt is a hunt both royal and at the same time impious, for it trespasses upon Artemis' domain.

However, this hunt is also a sacrifice, as Calchas says quite plainly, fearing lest Artemis should insist upon "another monstrous sacrifice whose victim would be hers alone [θυσίαν ἑτέραν ἄνομόν τιν' ἄδαιτον],"[36] and the sacrificial element is emphasized in the extraordinary line 136, a masterpiece of Aeschylean ambiguity, which expresses Artemis' anger against "her father's winged hounds [αὐτότοκον πρὸ λόχου μογερὰν πτάκα θυομένοισιν]" and which means both "slaying a trembling hare and its young before their birth" and also "sacrificing a trembling, cowering woman, his own child, on behalf of the army."[37]

Could one express the meaning of the portent more precisely than Calchas does? The prophet himself emphasizes the underlying ambivalence. The favorable elements are clearly indicated. The eagles appear "on the side of the arm that bears the lance,"[38] that is, from the right; one of them has a white back and white is a color held to be favorable in religion.[39] The eagles' hunt is successful. In one sense the hare with young is Troy,[40] which will be caught in a net from which neither child nor grown man will be able to escape:[41] Troy's capture will be a hunt.[42] On the other hand the doe hare is also, as we have seen, Iphigenia sacrificed by her father. Artemis, the most beautiful one, the kind one ($εὔφρων ἁ καλά$ of line 140) extends her dangerous protection "to the feeble whelps of the ravening lions as much as to the tender young of all beasts of the fields."[43] Agamemnon is also a lion;[44] Iphigenia is inevitably the victim of her father, whether as the pregnant hare, the eagles' victim, or as the daughter of the lion, Artemis' victim. Artemis, the goddess of nature in the wild, whose name is invoked by Calchas when he proposes the sacrifice of Iphigenia,[45] only intervenes because Agamemnon, in the shape of the eagle, has already entered the world of wild nature.[46] Moreover, well before the scene at Aulis, other litters of young creatures besides those of the doe hare had been sacrificed and devoured during the impious feast described in Cassandra's great scene. Later on, Clytemnestra says that it is "the bitter, vengeful spirit of Atreus" that has "struck down this full-grown victim to avenge the babes [$τόνδ' ἀπέτεισεν, τέλεον νεαροῖς ἐπιθύσας$]."[47] The doe hare can also be identified with the young children who were massacred.

The eagles are the Atreidae, but the first of them to be mentioned, the black eagle, the dark hunter definitively devoted to misfortune,[48] can be none other than the hero of the drama, Agamemnon. Is he not further on compared to a "black-horned bull?"[49] The color white, which is thus implicitly attributed to

Menelaus, no doubt reminds us that the whole affair was to have a happy ending for him. Menelaus is the hero who survives in the satirical drama with which the play ends, the *Proteus*.[50] However, to make the interpreter's task still more complicated, these eagles (*aetoi*) are also vultures (*aigupioi*), which the chorus leader at the opening of the play describes wheeling above their deserted aerie, claiming — and obtaining — justice for the theft of their little ones or, in other words, for the theft of the stolen Helen.[51] Is this contrast entirely without importance? Did Aeschylus use two different words to refer to the same bird? This is what has generally been argued[52] and it is true that the two birds are sometimes confused.[53] Even so, it is strange that it should be the noble, royal creature, the eagle of the heights, which is presented as committing a horrible action and the ignoble creature, the carrion eater, which is seeking justice.[54] Is not the vulture an animal that, quite unlike the eagle, is attracted by whatever is rotting, by the stench of corpses, and that dies when confronted by sweet-smelling perfumes?[55] Is not this "contradiction" on the contrary one of the mainsprings of the play? The theme of decay is, after all, very much present. In Cassandra's great scene, the prophetess cries out: "This palace stinks of murder and of bloodshed. *Chorus* — Say rather that it smells of burnt offerings upon the hearth. *Cassandra* — It is like the waft that rises from the grave. *Chorus* — You ascribe to it a smell that has nothing in common with incense."[56]

In one sense the whole play is going to show us how this corrupt sacrifice, namely the murder of Iphigenia, follows upon others and brings others in its wake just as that monstrous hunt, the feasting of the eagles, is preceded and followed by others.

The Trojan war itself is a hunt, and the chorus describes "these countless hunters armed with shields [*πολύανδροί τε φεράσπιδες κυναγοί*]" who "rush in pursuit of the vanished trace of [Helen's] ship."[57] These hunters are not "strangers";[58] they are simply identical to all those hunters dressed as hoplites or bearing a shield that are at the very least to be seen on Attic vases, contrasted there to the ephebe hunters who are naked[59] (see Figures 1 and 2). How-

Figure 1. The hoplite, partly hidden by his shield, which is decorated with a triskele, and accompanied by his dog, sets out for the hunt. He is flanked by two Scythian archers. Black figure Amphora (end of the sixth century), *The Louvre*, F (260); *C.V.A.*, Louvre, fasc. 5, France, fasc. 8, III He. 54, 4; M.F. Vos, *Scythian Archers*, n. 166. Photo Chuzeville (Louvre).

ever, as is suggested immediately afterward by the parable of the lion cub, these hoplite hunters do not behave like hoplites. We are about to pass from the world of battle (*machē*) to that of the animal hunt that is wild and impious. The herald says as much at the end of the speech he makes upon arriving back in Argos: "Priam's sons have paid twice over for their sins."[60]

Clytemnestra had already suggested, cynically, that a war that did not respect the gods of the vanquished would be a dangerous war for the victors.[61] Agamemnon later spells it out even more clearly when he describes the capture of Troy: The vengeance was ὑπερκότως,[62] quite out of proportion to the rape of Helen. The hoplites, an ἀσπιδηστρόφος λεώς, an army of agile shields,[63] are indeed the victors but these hoplites fight during the night [64] and this is contrary to the Greek code of battle. The army, issue from the horse's womb, is the "consuming beast of Argos"[65] that leaps forward and "like a cruel lion, has lapped up the royal blood till it has drunk its fill."[66] The war, then, is a repetition of the hare's murder with the lion, another royal animal, taking the place of the eagles. Cassandra's great scene and the murder of Agamemnon in their turn repeat not only the sacrifice of Iphigenia but also the war and the death of Thyestes' children. It is hardly necessary to point out that here too the terms used are constantly those of the sacrifice[67] and of hunting. Cassandra is a hound;[68] Agamemnon is both a man struck down in a sacrifice that is all the more monstrous for being accompanied by oaths and the ritual cry of the family Erinyes,[69] and at the same time an animal caught in a net, which is hunted down before being killed.[70] He is victim both to Clytemnestra, the she-lion, and to Aegisthus, the cowardly lion that is also a wolf (a creature both cruel and cunning in the eyes of the Greeks).[71] He is also the sacrificer who is sacrificed[72] and this hunt-cum-sacrifice is in its turn a repetition of the original murder that took the horrible form of a human sacrifice accompanied by oath swearing[73] and that was worse than a human sacrifice since it was an οἰκεία βορά, a family feasting, the result of cannibalism in the home.[74] The raw and the cooked,[75] the hunt

Figure 2. Calydon's wild boar hunt; the hunters are named but the fact that the youths are completely naked and the symmetry of their positions emphasize the collective aspect of the hunt. (Are these ephebes in the process of being integrated?) The other side shows a typical ephebe exploit: Theseus killing the minotaur. This is not the only example of such a juxtaposition. The paradox is that in Figure 1, the hoplite hunter is all alone and here the group of young men is naked. The Munich cup, signed by Glaukites and Archicles (about 540), *Museum Antiken Kleinkunst*, n.2443; Beazley *A.B.V.*, Glaukites n.2, p. 163; cf. G. Daltrop, *Die Kalydonische Jagd in der Antike*, Hamburg-Berlin 1968, p. 18 and pl. 7. Photo M. Hirmer, from P.E. Arias and M. Hirmer's book, *Le Vase Grec*, Paris 1960, p. 50. Printed here by permission of Hirmer Fotoarchiv., Munich.

and the sacrifice – these meet each other at the precise point where man has become no more than an animal. The *oikeia bora* is, in short, the equivalent of incest.

There is one remarkable fact that I believe confirms the above analysis: While, in the *Agamemnon*, the capture of the human being who is to be sacrificed is described in metaphors relating to hunting, the execution itself is usually described in metaphors relating to stock-raising. Iphigenia is first a goat, then a lamb;[76] Agamemnon, whom Clytemnestra had described as a farmyard dog,[77] just as she is the bitch,[78] is caught in a net but slaughtered like a bull.[79] This is another way of conveying the sacrilege since domestic animals that are, in effect, the normal victims for sacrifice, must give some sign to indicate their assent,[80] and this is the exact opposite to death in a trap. Perhaps Euripides' *Bacchae* can provide us with an interesting point of comparison. When Agave returns from her hunting expedition, carrying the head of her son, Pentheus,[81] she at first imagines that she has brought back from the mountain Dionysus' ivy wreath, "the blessed quarry [μακάριον θήραν]," then that it is a young lion cub caught without a net, which is a real feat of hunting, and lastly, before discovering the truth, she imagines that it is a young calf, νέος μόσχος, which is however as hairy as a wild beast, ὥστε θὴρ ἄγραυλος.[82] And so Agave praises Bacchus, the skillful hunter, the great huntsman, ἄναξ ἀγρεύς.[83] Where Dionysus has been so clever is in making Agave *hunt* her son even though she subsequently treats him as a domestic animal, without knowing how close he was to being this. What Agave does unconsciously is done in full consciousness by the hunter-sacrificers of Agamemnon. This wild beast that they slaughter as if it were a domestic animal is actually their closest kin, their daughter, or their husband.

Thus the *Agamemnon* ends in a total reversal, an inversion of values: The female has killed her male,[84] disorder takes over in the city, the sacrifice turned out to be an anti-sacrifice, a perverted hunt. True enough, the last line, spoken by the queen, suggests the re-establishment of order but this is a deceptive and inverted order and is to be overthrown in the *Choephori*.

In a recent study of the first stasimon of the *Choephori*, Ann Lebeck has shown that the second play in the trilogy has not only the same fundamental structure as the *Agamemnon*[85] but that it is its exact counterpart.[86] Where, in the one, a victim is received by his murderer, in the other a murderer is received by his victim. In the first case the welcoming woman deceives the returning man while in the second it is the returning man who deceives the welcoming woman. This applies down to the last detail. The *Choephori* is indeed a true mirror image of the *Agamemnon*. However, as has been pointed out,[87] there is a fundamental difference between the two plays. The theme of the "corrupt sacrifice" has virtually disappeared. Orestes does not make a monstrous sacrifice of his mother; he simply carries out the oracle's orders. Yet the theme has not disappeared altogether and the chorus of captives exclaims: "Let me at last utter alone the sacramental cry over the man struck down and his slaughtered wife [Ἐφυμνῆσαι γένοιτό μοι πυκάεντ' ὀλολυγμὸν ἀνδρὸς θεινομένου γυναικός τ' ὀλλυμένας]."[88] In the speech of Orestes, the blood of Aegisthus, but not that of Clytemnestra, forms a libation to the Erinys, the deity of the underworld, and this is no sacrilege. In retrospect too we can see changes. Agamemnon is no longer the warrior caught in a trap and struck down by a sword avenging both the mistakes made in the Trojan war and the sacrifice of Iphigenia. The war is totally justified: "Justice has come at last; it has at last struck down the sons of Priam, and with heavy retribution";[89] and of the sacrifice of Iphigenia no mention is made, even by the queen.[90] Agamemnon here becomes a pure sacrificer and his tomb becomes an altar (βωμός) like that which is raised to the gods of heaven;[91] he has been a θυτήρ,[92] a sacrificer to Zeus.[93] Zeus will have no more hecatombs unless Agamemnon is avenged.[94] In anticipation, the reign of Orestes is associated with banquets and sacrifices. The murder of Agamemnon has become hardly anything more than an abominable trap. Orestes deplores the fact that he was not killed as befits a warrior, in battle.[95] When Electra and her brother invoke their dead father, Electra says: "Remember the snares of their new-fangled plots" and Orestes refers to "chains not made of bronze by which you were captured, my father."[96] The poet mentions these "chains not made of bronze" several times — when Orestes describes the machination (μεχάνημα)[97] to which his father fell victim and when he defines his mother herself as a trap for wild beasts, ἄγρευμα δηρός.[98] No more than a fleeting mention is made of the sword of Aegisthus that stains with Agamemnon's blood the net which snared the king and it is the actual net itself that is described as the murderer, πατροκτόνον δ' ὕφασμα.[99]

These remarks lead me to consider the central character of the *Choephori*, Orestes, who, although he is not strictly speaking a sacrificer, is a hunter and a warrior. What strikes us immediately with Orestes is his twofold nature: I do not refer here simply to the fact that he is both guilty and innocent, a fact that allows us to foresee the ambiguity of his acquittal in the *Eumenides*. The chorus, at the end of the *Choephori*, does not know whether he represents salvation or destruction: σωτῆρ, ἢ μόρον εἴπω.[100] But more fundamental is the fact that from the outset of the play Orestes is seen to have that ambivalence that, as I have attempted to show elsewhere,[101] is the characteristic of the pre-hoplite, the ephebe, the apprentice-adult and apprentice-warrior who must use guile before adopting the hoplite code of battle.

Orestes' first act is to offer a lock of hair at his father's tomb, as a sign of bereavement. This offering of mourning (πενθητήριον)[102] is, as the hero himself declares,[103] a repetition of the offering made in thanksgiving for his δρεπτήριον which, as an adolescent, Orestes made to the river Inachos.[104] The lock is discovered by Electra and her companions and it leaves the leader of the chorus in some doubt as to whether it belongs to a man or a girl. The truth is that it is quite possible to mistake Orestes for Electra who is his double.[105] The sign of recognition between brother and sister is a piece of tapestry embroidered by Electra in years gone by and that represents a scene of wild animals, δήρειον γραφήν.[106] And it is, precisely, a kind of hunt that they are about to embark upon together:

154

an ephebe hunt in which guile has its, in this case, legitimate place.

There are many striking examples of Orestes' ambivalence in matters of warrior-like behavior. Thus, foretelling Aegisthus' murder, Orestes pictures himself "enmeshing (his adversary) in supple bronze [ποδώκει περιβαλὼν χαλκεύματι]."[107] A net can be used for enmeshing but bronze is used for fighting. In one sense this hunt is really a *machē*: Ares pitted against Ares as *Dikē* is against *Dikē*.[108] However, the guileful nature of this battle is also striking. Orestes says: "Having killed a revered hero by treachery, they [Clytemnestra and Aegisthus] must be caught and must perish in the self-same snare,"[109] and Clytemnestra echoes his words: "We killed by craft; by craft we are now to die [δόλοις ὀλούμεθ', ὥσπερ οὖν ἐκτείναμεν]."[110] Orestes depends upon "cheating Persuasion," πειθὼ δολία,[111] and once the murder is accomplished the chorus declares in triumph: "He has come at last, he who, fighting in the darkness, knows how to exact the punishment through guile [ἔμολε δ' ᾧ μέλει κρυπταδίου μάχας δολιόφρων ποινά]."[112] However, the very use of the word *machē* alerts us to the fact that this is no ordinary kind of guile; the chorus goes on to say: "Zeus' daughter, she whom men rightly call Justice, guided his arm as he struck [ἔθιγε δ' ἐν μάχᾳ χερὸς ἐτήτυμως]."[113] When, at the beginning of the play, the chorus is picturing the ideal avenger, it tells of a warrior armed both with a Scythian *palintonos* bow that must be drawn back to be strung[114] and also with a sword "whose blade and hilt are all of a piece, for fighting at closer quarters."[115] Orestes is to be both hoplite and bowman.[116] Later on, when summing up, the chorus proclaims that Orestes' victory — or rather that of the oracle — has been accomplished (ἀδόλοις δόλοις) "by treachery that is not treacherous."[117]

It is the animal metaphors that must complete our study. It is said of Electra that she has the heart of a wolf[118] and this places her on the side of guile and deceit. As for Orestes, he is a serpent, not only in his mother's famous dream where she sees him hanging like a snake from her breast,[119] but also according to the definition that he applies to himself: "It is I who, becoming a snake, shall kill her [ἐκδρακοντωθεὶς δ' ἐγὼ κτείνω νιν]."[120] However, this

relationship with his mother is reversible, for Clytemnestra is herself a snake.[121] She is the viper that has taken the young of the
eagle;[122] she is "a sting-ray or viper";[123] she it is who is the real
serpent while the serpent Orestes is also one of the eagle's abandoned young complaining of their hunger "for they are not old
enough to bring back food to the nest as their father did."[124]
Together with Electra he is seen as one of these. So it is that the
image with which the *Agamemnon* begins reappears but now it is
inverted. It is no longer the *vultures* that cry out for vengeance
for the theft of their little ones but the young eaglets that are
deprived of their parents.[125] Yet Orestes is also the adult royal creature: In reply to Clytemnestra who calls her son a serpent,[126] the
chorus declares: "He has entered the house of Agamemnon as
the double lion and the double Ares,"[127] he is the very one who
"with a fortunate blow cuts off the heads of the two serpents,"[128]
Clytemnestra and Aegisthus. The serpents do, it is true, also make
a reappearance upon the heads of the Erinyes.[129] Thus the destiny
of Orestes is not clear-cut: He is a double character, both hunter
and warrior, serpent and lion. And in the *Eumenides* Orestes is to
be found as the quarry in danger of being sacrificed.

I have attempted to show how, with varying degrees of ambiguity, the opposition between nature in the wild and civilization
is constantly present in the first two plays of the trilogy. In the
Eumenides this opposition emerges quite clearly and even en-
croaches on the world of politics. The fact that we leave the world
of men to see the gods come face to face with one another is only
a matter of appearances. In the last analysis the play is about
man and the city.

The speech of the Pythian priestess, in the prologue, gives an
account of the origins of Delphi that is original to Aeschylus. It
is a story of a "non-violent" succession (οὐδὲ πρὸς βίαν)[130] in which
there is no reference to the murder of Python. The deities that
control the site fall into two interlocked groups: On one side is
Earth and her daughter Phoebe; on the other Themis (Order) and
Phoebus. Nature in the wild and civilization alternate in the suc-

cession. The last incumbent, Phoebus, is supported by Zeus but he is accompanied from Delos to Parnassus by the Athenians: "The children of Hephaestus open up the way for him, taming for him soil hitherto untamed [χθόνα ἀνήμερον τιθέντες ἡμερωμένην]."[131] Similarly, the invocation addressed by the Pythian priestess to the gods that ends, as is befitting, with an appeal to Zeus who guarantees the new order, clearly divides the gods into two categories. On the one hand is Pallas Pronoia, who opens the list at the end of which Zeus comes and, on the other, the "nymphs of the Corycian cave, the sanctuary of birds"[132] which is also the lair of Dionysus "Bromios," the noisy one – "Let me not forget him [οὐδ' ἀμνημονῶ]"[133] — the river Pleistos and Poseidon, the earth shaker.

The Dionysus invoked at this point is important to my thesis. He is a hunter[134] who "led the Bacchae forth to combat [ἐστρατήγησεν] and prepared the death of a hare for Pentheus."[135] This is the very death that the Erinyes are preparing for Orestes. In this way we are alerted to the issue at the outset of the play: The wildness of the world may be integrated and dominated by Zeus and this transition may take place without violence (as it does in the lawsuit of Athens) but nonetheless it meanwhile exists. To deny its existence would be to deny a part of reality.

So Orestes, the hunter in the *Choephori*, has now become the quarry. He is a fawn that escapes the net,[136] a cowering fawn (καταπτακών),[137] a hare whose sacrifice will pay for the death of Clytemnestra.[138] Once again Aeschylus uses the technical vocabulary of the hunt.[139] The Erinyes are the huntresses[140] but they are huntresses that are purely animal. The wildness that was one side of the personalities of Agamemnon, Clytemnestra, and of Orestes himself is unmitigated in their case. They are serpents[141] and they are also bitches.[142] Their purely animal nature is very strongly emphasized, by Apollo it is true, in line 193 and following: "You should make your dwelling in the cave of some blood-gorged lion [λέοντος αἱματορρόφου] instead of coming to defile others by inflicting your foulness in this temple of prophecy." At the capture of Troy, Agamemnon's army was also the bloodthirsty lion.[143] The Erinyes

157

even transgress the bounds of wild and animal nature; they are the "accursed virgins, the ancient hags from some bygone age whose presence neither god nor man nor beast can bear [οὐδὲ ϑήρ]."[144]

Color symbolism naturally plays its part in expressing all this. These "children of the night"[145] who wear only black robes,[146] whose hatred is equally black[147] are threatened by the winged serpent, by the white arrows of Apollo.[148] These deities also receive sacrifices that define their character equally clearly. The ghost of Clytemnestra reminds them of her offerings: "Have you not often lapped up[149] my offerings, wineless libations, sober, soothing draughts [νηφάλια μειλίγματα]? Have I not offered up more than one victim at night, at your sacred banquets, upon the ritual hearth [ἐπ' ἐσχάρᾳ πυρός] at an hour given to no other god?"[150] The composition of the sacrifice is significant: It consists only of "natural" products, of nothing that depends upon agriculture, and in the sacrifice the offerings are totally consumed.[151] The Erinyes can claim the two extremes: What is "pure" and "natural" is also what is raw. They do not drink wine but they do eat men. Except with regard to the wine[152] they resemble Euripides' Bacchae who feed upon milk and honey that well up from the ground and who eat the raw flesh of the he-goat before tearing Pentheus to pieces. The goddesses of the night also address Orestes with the following words: "There is no need for knife and altar, for my feasting shall be upon your living flesh, you, the victim fattened ready for my sacrifice."[153] Here the anti-sacrifice is described for what it is, without the parody that was suggested by the murder of Agamemnon. But the most striking expression of all comes in lines 264-6: "In return you shall, while yet alive, quench my thirst with a red offering taken from your very limbs." A red offering, ἐρυθρὸν πελανόν. The *pelanos* is a purely vegetable offering made into a cake or liquid. It is a *pelanos* that Electra offers up on the tomb of Agamemnon.[154] A red *pelanos* is indeed a striking image of all that is monstrous.

The nature of the Erinyes is not altered when they become the Eumenides. As the goddesses of the night, they are the focus of the nocturnal festival with which the trilogy ends. They usually receive their victims, their sacrificial offerings, the σφάγια[155] and θυσίαι,[156] with their throats cut. Henceforth however, being the protectresses of growing things, they are entitled to the first fruits, "the sacrifices for birth and for marriage."[157]

Far from being the deities of blood and of wild nature, they become the protectresses of vegetation, of agriculture, and of stock-breeding and this includes both animals and men: "Let the rich fertility of the soil and of the flocks never cease from bringing prosperity to my city! Let the offerings of men find protection there also."[158] There is a quite startling change in vocabulary from that of the hunt to that of agriculture and husbandry. The huntresses have a throne, *hedra*.[159] Athena requests the Eumenides to bear themselves as the *phitupoimēn*,[160] the man who tends plants, the gardener who forks the earth in order to get rid of the weeds, the impure grasses: τῶν εὐσεβούντων δ' ἐκφορωτέρα πέλοις.[161] Wild nature still has its share both within the city, since Athena herself takes over the "policy" of the Erinyes: "no anarchy or despotism"[162] and since fear (φόβος) remains in its place there together with respect (σέβας),[163] and also outside the city, insofar as it forms a barrier: "the fire that lays waste the young buds shall not creep across your frontiers."[164] Fury, "the bloody needles that tear at young guts [αἱματηρὰς θηγάνας σπλάγχνων βλάβας νέων]"[165] and the world of animality must be reserved for war against foreigners: "I do not call it battle when birds of the same aviary fight against each other [ἐνοικίου δ' ὄρνιθος οὐ λέγω μάχην]."[166] The shares of each kind in the different types of sacrifice has been determined.

Pierre Vidal-Naquet

CHAPTER VII

Sophocles' *Philoctetes*

and the Ephebeia[1]

This chapter is intended to complement and illustrate an earlier piece of research. In my earlier study I tired to focus on what could be called the paradox of the Athenian ephebeia.[2] When he takes his famous oath, the ephebe swears to conform with the collective code of the hoplites, that of the fight of phalanx against phalanx — a fight characterized by loyalty and solidarity: "I shall not abandon my companion in the ranks." Now, with the etiological account of the festival of the Apatouria during which, within the phratry, the ephebes made a sacrifice of their hair, we are in quite a different world: a world of cunning, of *apatē*. In the single face-to-face combat between the "black" (Melanthos) and the "fair" (Xanthos), the former won the day and thereupon acceded to the throne of Athens, but only thanks to some divine or human trick. The paradox was in effect that of the entire ephebeia and indeed not only of that Athenian institution but also of the whole corpus of rituals and procedures that symbolized the passage of the Greek youth from the state of childhood to that of adulthood that is to say of the warrior.[3] The ephebe is opposed to the hoplite both by the location of his warrior activities and by the nature of the fighting in which he takes part. The ephebe (or the Lacedaemonian *kruptēs*) is associated with the frontier zone. He is the *peripolos*, the one who circles around the city without entering it, just as the ephebe of Plato's *Laws*, the *agronomos*, does in a literal sense. As part of the institution, he stays in the frontier forts (the Cretan *oureia*). His normal mode of fighting is not an open clash in the hoplite manner, itself in a way a legacy from the Homeric way of fighting; rather it consists in ambush, nocturnal or otherwise, and cunning. These characteristics suggest that it fitted into a fairly classical schema of initiation, similar to the "trial in the bush" familiar to so many "primitive" societies, particularly in Africa. Furthermore, a study of Greek mythology indicates that very often this trial was given dramatic form as a hunt carried out either by individuals or small groups, in which the young participants were entitled to use cunning or *apatē*.[4] However, this right to use cunning was naturally restricted in terms of both space and time. Unless he got lost in the bush, as happens, in the song in the *Lysistrata*, to Melanion,[5] the "black hunter" after whom I entitled my earlier study, the young man had perforce to return. It would be interesting to know at what precise point in their training the ephebes took their oath, at the beginning or the end of the two years of "military service" that the fourth-century ephebeia consisted in.[6] In it there is no mention either of cunning or of frontier zones. Quite the contrary. It is in effect a hoplite oath. The famous invocation with which it ends is particularly significant: "The boundary stones of the country, the wheat, barley, vines, olive trees, and fig trees." The future hoplite's field of activity is to be not the indeterminate open spaces of the frontiers but the cultivated space of the fields. We should not be misled by the mention of "boundary marks of the country." We are not concerned here with *eschatia*, the disputed zones where Melanthos and Xanthos — and plenty of other heroes or groups of heroes from Greek fables and history too — fought one another. These are the boundary posts that physically mark out the *chōra* in the strict sense of the word, that is, the cultivated land.[7] To be sure, this ideal schema was considerably modified in the course of history. The forms of combat that had for a long time remained the prerogative of the young men, the prehoplites, the night fighters, were gradually adopted generally during the Peloponnesian war and became even more popular in the fourth century as the mercenary gradually took over from the soldier-citizen.[8]

The schema as thus summarized seems to me to be able to illuminate certain aspects of the *Philoctetes*, the last but one extant tragedy of Sophocles. It was presented in 409 B.C. at a time when the Peloponnesian war had taken a tragic turn for Athens. I need hardly say that my intention is not to unveil some "secret" in the *Philoctetes* that may have escaped the play's commentators. It is highly doubtful that there are any such secrets. But comparing a literary work, as deeply rooted in the civic liturgy as a Greek tragedy is, with an institutional schema is a method that has already proved rewarding on other occasions and that might suggest a new historical — and at the same time structural — reading of the work.

The legend of Philoctetes[9] is mentioned briefly in the *Iliad* (2, 718-25), discussed in the *Little Iliad* and in the *Cypria*[10] and was, even before Sophocles, the subject of lost tragedies by Aeschylus and Euripides.[11] It provided Sophocles with a very simple plot: After being wounded by a poisonous snake, Philoctetes has been abandoned on the island of Lemnos, crippled and giving off a revolting smell but the possessor of the infallible bow of Heracles. He remains in exile there for ten years until the day when a Greek expeditionary force brings him back to Troy where he is to be cured. Having been captured by Odysseus, the diviner Helenus reveals to him that only the presence of Philoctetes and his bow can ensure the capture of Troy.[12] In Aeschylus' play — as in that of Euripides that was presented at the same time as *Medea*, in 431 — the essential role in returning Philoctetes to the soldiers of the Greek army was played by Odysseus; but whereas Aeschylus' Odysseus initially tried to obtain Philoctetes' bow through cunning, Euripides' character succeeded through persuasion (*peithō*) in the course of a great debate with the Trojan envoys: It is difficult to imagine a more directly political theme.[13]

From the point of view simply of the dramatic plot, Sophocles is doubly original in comparison with his predecessors. Both Aeschylus and Euripides had Philoctetes in dialogue with the inhabitants of Lemnos, who formed the chorus. One of Euripides' characters, Actor, Philoctetes' confidant, is himself a Lemnian. In Sophocles, in contrast, the hero is totally isolated. He lives on "a land without anchorage and without inhabitants [οὔτ' εὔορμον οὔτ' οἰκουμένην]."[14] The Lemnians have no role to play and their existence is not even mentioned.[15] The chorus is composed of the crew of the Greek ship. Furthermore, whereas Pindar in the first *Pythian* has Philoctetes sought out by anonymous "god-like heroes,"[16] in Euripides Odysseus, a figure taken over from Aeschylus, is accompanied by Diomedes,[17] otherwise only present in the summary in the *Little Iliad*. Sophocles in his turn makes an innovation by giving a crucial role to the young Neoptolemus, the son of Achilles. He it is whom Odysseus entrusts with seizing both the bow and the hero himself by means of cunning. The greater part of the play takes the form of dialogues between Philoctetes, the old hero, wounded and in exile for the past ten years, and the adolescent whose youth is constantly emphasized.

Sophocles' play as it stands has considerably intrigued the commentators who have stressed its supposed or real "anomalies" (mention has often been made of the "baroque element" in this play of Sophocles) and have either brought into question or, on the contrary, confirmed its "orthodoxy" in relation to the rest of Sophocles' work.[18] There are plenty of reasons to account for their high degree of interest. The *Philoctetes* is the only extant tragedy from a Greek author in which there is no female role and also the only one in which the problem posed is resolved *ex machina* by a deity.[19] The relations between men and gods in this play have seemed so unusual that commentators have wondered whether, as in Sophocles' other plays, the emphasis lay on the coherence of the world of the gods as compared to the ignorance and blindness of men or whether, on the contrary, Sophocles has not, following the example of Euripides, introduced the opacity of the human condition into the world of the gods.[20]

I shall dwell here on only one point in this controversy, but it is one of capital importance. In the *Philoctetes* we have an example, unique in Sophocles' work, of a tragic hero who undergoes a transformation. At first, despite the repugnance that he, as a king's son faithful to his original nature (*phusis*), feels, the young Neoptolemus agrees to fool Philoctetes with lying words dictated by Odysseus, in order to gain possession of his bow. Then he changes his mind,[21] deciding first to tell the truth,[22] then to return the bow,[23] and finally to quit both Lemnos and the field of battle at Troy and return home with Philoctetes.[24] This presents a striking contrast with the usual behavior of Sophoclean heroes who clash head on with both the world of the city and that of the gods and who are broken in the end by the machination of the gods.[25] It is clearly very tempting to explain this mutation on "psychological" grounds or at least on grounds that tragic commentators would so describe and such temptations have inevitably seduced some scholars.[26] But this "psychologizing" has also provoked a reaction, most forcefully expressed by Tycho von Wilamowitz.[27] His explanation for the difficulties of the *Philoctetes* and for the mutation of its heroes was based purely on the laws of "dramatic technique" and the theatrical point of view. But while it may have accounted for a number of details[28] it could provide no overall explanation and ran the risk of losing sight of Sophocles' characters inasmuch as they represent not just dramatic roles but tragic *heroes*.[29]

As the reader no doubt realizes, the purpose of this study is to advance the discussion by making a detour by way of a comparison between the "mutation" of the young Neoptolemus and the institution mentioned at the beginning of this paper: namely the initiation for the ephebeia.

One of the most characteristic features of Sophocles' last plays, the *Philoctetes* and *Oedipus at Colonus*, is the ever increasing importance of the problem of localization, what J. Jones has called "a kind of interdependence of man and place."[30] The place of the action is described as an *eschatia*,[31] a sort of world's end. There can, in the whole of Greek literature, be few such striking descriptions of nature in the wild and man abandoned to a state of wild-

ness. The term used to describe the solitude of Philoctetes is *erēmos*
and it recurs no less than six times.[32] Even more significant,
Philoctetes has been *exposed* in the technical sense of the term:
Odysseus reminds us, "It is I who, years ago exposed the son of
Poias [Ποίαντος υἱὸν ἐξέθηκ' ἐγὼ ποτε]."[33] The meaning of "exposed"
is: left in a place that is the opposite of the household enclosure
or the cultivated land in the neighborhood, and is instead the wild
and distant countryside. In some cases it can be the sea or a river
in that these can be symbols of the other world. But above all it
is the uncultivated land where the flocks and herds live, far from
houses, gardens, and fields — the alien and hostile space of the
agros.[34] As J. Jones, again, points out, this solitude is not that of
Robinson Crusoe.[35] Nor, as the chorus explicitly states, is it a pastoral world: "He does not play one of Pan's flutes like a shepherd
in the fields [οὐ μολπὰν σύριγγος ἔχων ὡς ποιμὴν ἀγροβάτας]."[36] The
wildness of this world is strongly emphasized by the setting itself.
Whereas the scene is usually set at the palace doors, here we are
presented with the opening to a cave.[37]

This wild world is carefully opposed to two others, the three
together forming what has been called the spatial triangle of the
Philoctetes.[38] The first is the Trojan field of battle, that is to say
the world of the city as represented by the citizens under arms,
the hoplites. The second is the world of the *oikos*, the family world
of Philoctetes and Neoptolemus. It is between these two that the
heroes have to choose.

Philoctetes is presented as entirely alien to the world of cultivated fields: "For his food he harvested neither the grain that
comes to us from the sacred earth nor any of those other fruits
that we cultivate, we mortals who eat bread.... Ah! what a pitiful existence is that of a man who for ten years has not experienced the joy of having a glass of wine poured out for him!"[39]
The hero in exile has no family and no companion (μηδὲ ξύντροφον
ὄμμ' ἔχων), "can meet no fraternal glance,"[40] even believes his father
to be dead.[41] Odysseus sees him as one who, socially, is dead: "A
man without friends, without city, a corpse among the living

[ἄφιλον, ἔρημον, ἄπολιν, ἐν ζῶσιν νεκρόν]."⁴² Odysseus justifies the sentence of exile passed upon him on the grounds that, on account of his cries, the army "was unable to proceed peacefully with either libation or sacrifice,"⁴³ in other words his presence made it impossible to carry out the civic cult. Philoctetes himself falls back on this explanation when he is contemplating the possibility of embarking: "Once you embark in my company, how will it still be possible to burn the offerings for the gods and to offer libations to them?"⁴⁴ The word that best describes his condition is *agrios*, wild. Philoctetes has, in the strictest sense, been made "wild."⁴⁵ The vocabulary by which he is described is that used of the wildness of animals.⁴⁶ As has been well said,⁴⁷ he has a "close connection — almost kinship — with animals." The ill that tortures him, itself described as *agrios*, is the share of wildness that is in him.⁴⁸

Philoctetes thus finds himself situated on the borderline between humanity and animal wildness. There are still a few indications that he belongs to the human race in the cave in which he lives: "a roughly hewn wooden cup — the product of a really clumsy workman. And, there too, the means for making fire."⁴⁹ This is the fire for cooking that is the hero's constant salvation, *ὅ καὶ σώζει μ' ἀεί*.⁵⁰ This extreme position is quite naturally symbolized by hunting, the only activity that makes it possible for Philoctetes to live outside the *chōra*, outside the city and cultivated fields: "In this way he is fated to spend his life shooting at game with his winged arrows, wretched and wretchedly."⁵¹ But Philoctetes' relations with the animals that are his companions and victims are reversible. When, through the trick devised by Odysseus, he is deprived of his bow, the hunter is in danger of being hunted: "My bow will no longer bring down the winged bird nor the wild beast of the mountains and it is I, woe is me, who as I die will provide a meal for the game which formerly nourished me.⁵² The beasts that I used to hunt will in their turn hunt me."⁵³ The instrument used for this hunting is precisely the bow that Heracles bequeathed to Philoctetes, the bow that, as Odysseus reminds Neoptolemus at the beginning of the play, has "infallible, death-dealing shafts."[54] As has often been pointed out, the bow is the counterpart to the wound: infallibility and incurability are inextricably linked.[55] But there are more important points to make: The bow is what guarantees Philoctetes' *life*. Sophocles, following Heraclitus, plays on the word βιός (bow) and βίος (life)[56]: "You have taken my life by taking my bow [ἀπεστέρηκας τὸν Βίον τὰ τόξ' ἑλών]"[57] But the bow is also what isolates Philoctetes from the world of human beings. In one version of the myth it is precisely with one of the arrows from Heracles' bow that Philoctetes wounds himself.[58] This is not the version followed by Sophocles. His Philoctetes is more directly at fault since he has violated the sanctuary of Chryses.[59] But a bowman cannot be a hoplite and, as will be seen, when Philoctetes is cured he is no longer, strictly speaking, a bowman. In the famous dialogue on the respective virtues of bowmen and hoplites, in Euripides' *Heracles*,[60] the spokesman for the hoplites is doing no more than voice the moral rule of his time when he declares: "The bow is not proof of a man's courage [ἀνδρὸς δ' ἔλεγχος οὐχὶ τόξ' εὐψυχίας]."[61] This *eupsuchia* consists in "remaining at one's post unflinching in the ranks and, without averting or dropping one's eyes, watching a whole field of brandished lances approaching."[62] The bow makes it possible for Philoctetes to survive but it also turns him into an accursed hunter, always on the borderline between life and death just as he is on the borderline between humanity and savagery. He has been bitten by a "viper that kills men"[63] and yet it has not killed him. "He seems to be a victim consecrated to the god of the dead";[64] he speaks of dying, he proclaims his death and yet cannot achieve it.[65] He is, as we have already pointed out, "a corpse among the living,"[66] "a corpse, the shadow of a wisp of smoke, a vain phantom";[67] although he is never actually called it, politically he is the epitome of an *atimos*, a man civically dead.[68]

Disembarking from their ship, Odysseus, a mature man and Neoptolemus, an adolescent, still almost a child, enter this desolate world and approach this wild man. To Philoctetes, Neoptolemus is not just a child but even a son. H.C. Avery has calculated that Neoptolemus is called *pai* (child) or *teknon* (my son) sixty-eight times altogether and on fifty-two of these sixty-eight occasions it is Philoctetes who uses these words.[69] Now this child is also twice called a man, *anēr*, first at line 910 when he has started to admit the trick by which he was trapping Philoctetes and a second and final time by Heracles, right at the end of the play when he invites Philoctetes to fight "with this man [σὺν τῷδ' ἀνδρί]."[70] This simple comparison seems to me to establish that Neoptolemus does in effect change status, that in the course of the play he passes through the ephebe initiation.[71]

In *Couroi et Courétes* Henri Jeanmaire has shown that the mythical accounts of the childhood of royal figures had the value of models for the ephebe adolescents. In the *Philoctetes* it is clear that we are presented with the making of a king's son. Odysseus reminds us of this right at the start of the play: "The child of the most valiant of the Greeks, the son of Achilles [ὦ κρατίστου πατρὸς Ἑλλήνων τραφεὶς Ἀχιλλέως παῖ]"[72] and the first time the chorus speaks it is to remind Neoptolemus that he is the heir to power:[73] "It is in your hands, my son, that from the depths of the ages the supreme power has come to rest." Now let us reread the first dialogue between Odysseus and Neoptolemus. It presents on stage an officer and a soldier who is a beginner. Odysseus invokes the order he received in years gone by to explain and justify the "exposing" of Philoctetes on Lemnos.[74] He reminds Neoptolemus that he is a serving soldier and owes him obedience.[75] As Bernard Knox saw clearly, this is Neoptolemus' "first exploit."[76] There is no evidence that Neoptolemus has ever borne arms. True, when Odysseus persuades the young man to tell Philoctetes that the arms of Achilles have been refused to the hero's son and instead allotted to himself, Odysseus,[77] he is encouraging him to tell a lie, but it is a lie of a quite singular kind. Philoctetes for his part reverts to it at the end of the play when Neoptolemus has revealed the whole trick.[78] At that point his companion does not contradict him and anyway the author of the *Ajax* knew perfectly well that Odysseus had indeed inherited the arms of Achilles for a short period. We can understand all this only if we accept that Neoptolemus is indeed right at the beginning of his career as a soldier.

One detail even suggests that Sophocles is perhaps alluding to the oath that turned an ephebe into a hoplite: "You have not taken the oath [σὺ μὲν... οὔτ᾽ ἔνορκος],"[79] says Odysseus to Neoptolemus. Technically, he is alluding to the oath sworn by Helen's suitors but is legitimate to see this as an allusion to the ephebe oath and when Neoptolemus swears to remain on the spot, ἐμβάλλω μενεῖν,[80] the allusion becomes even clearer. This first exploit carried out by Neoptolemus takes place, as we have seen, outside civic space, in the surroundings normal for the initiations of ephebes or *kruptai* and, like the model provided by the etiological myth of the Apatouria, it is a trick, an *apatē*.[81] Odysseus employs the vocabulary of reconnaissance and military espionage right from the start of the play.[82] This ambush is also a hunt. When Odysseus has managed to persuade Neoptolemus to gain possession of Philoctetes' bow by cunning, the young man replies "We must hunt it to capture it, if that is how it is [θηρατέ᾽ οὖν γίγνοιτ᾽ ἄν, εἴπερ ὧδ᾽ἔχει]."[83] When Philoctetes faints, Neoptolemus pronounces the following hexameters that have an oracular character: "What I can see is that we shall have captured this bow [θήραν τήνδ᾽... ἔχομεν τόξων] in vain if we depart without the man."[84] And Philoctetes refers to his hands as game (συνθηρώμεναι) for the man who has captured him.[85]

To be sure, this terminology of hunting and war is metaphorical. The *Philoctetes* is no *Red Badge of Courage*. The hunt in which Neoptolemus is engaged is a linguistic one: "It is with your language that you must steal away the soul of Philoctetes [τὴν Φιλοκτήτου σε δεῖ ψυχὴν ὅπως λόγοισι ἐκκλέψεις λέγων]."[86] It is the language of deceit; Odysseus rejects both the use of force and the use of persuasion.[87] It is ambiguous language like that which will be used by the pseudo-merchant.[88]

Let us now return to the military metaphor. One thing needs to be clearly understood: Given that the situation of the ephebe is by definition a transitory one, Neoptolemus is incapable of justifying his action in any other way than by invoking obedience to the established power.[89] The ephebes may adopt a practice and mythology of *apatē* but it is certainly not an ethic. Odysseus, the "master of the novices,"[90] sums the situation up in his own way when he says to Neoptolemus: "We will make a show of our honesty later on. For the time being, lend yourself to me for a short moment — a day at the most — of knavishness. After that, for the rest of your life you can have yourself called the most scrupulous of moral men."[91] The whole point of the ephebe's exploit ends once it is completed: There is no way of prolonging it. So while Neoptolemus is tricking Philoctetes he voices their common admiration for the hoplite ideal — in its aristocratic form, needless to say. Was not Neoptolemus-Pyrrhus the father of the Pyrrhic warrior dance, a hoplite dance if ever there was one?[92] Odysseus himself, while attempting in the name of Zeus to convince Philoctetes to accompany him to Troy, suggests that he should be a ὅμοιος τοῖς ἀριστεῦσιν,[93] a member of the warrior elite that seizes Troy. The fact remains, however, that Odysseus is hardly in a position to make such a proposal given that throughout the play he chooses the part of *technē* not of *aretē*. Despite the fact that the oracle transmitted by Helenus declared that not only the bow but also Philoctetes' own *voluntary* presence was necessary if Troy was to be taken,[94] either Odysseus is concerned only with the bow or else he proposes to carry Philoctetes off to Troy by force.[95] He behaves and speaks as though the bow could be separated from the man. He says that there are other bowmen besides Philoctetes and that his bow can be entrusted to Teucer.[96] If we examine the three scenes where he is present we notice that the military terminology is combined with the vocabulary used to characterize the Sophists.[97] Is Odysseus a politician pure and simple? No doubt he is, in the sense that Thucydides' Cleon or the Athenians in the Melian dialogue are pure politicians. Sophocles has even made an Athenian politician of him.[98] He ends his admonition to Neoptolemus with an appeal not only to Hermes and Nikē but also to Athena Polias.[99] The pseudo-merchant explains, at his behest, that the sons of Theseus, King of Athens, have set off in pursuit of Neoptolemus.[100]

171

His last declaration is that he is going to give an account "to the entire army [τῷ δὲ σύμπαντι στρατῷ],"[101] that is to say, in political terms, that he is going to convene the people's assembly. Having said which we should nevertheless point out that we are here in the world of tragedy, not that of history or of political philosophy. The pure politician, Odysseus, places himself outside the *polis* through being excessively political. He is the exact antithesis to Philoctetes, the man who is hypercivilized as opposed to the one who has become wild. He is another version of the figure represented by Creon and, to borrow the words that a well-known chorus of *Antigone* applies to the man who is armed with nothing but *technē*, he is, far from being *hupsipolis*, an *apolis* like Philoctetes himself – but for opposite reasons.[102] So it is that although in one sense he accomplishes his mission, he is also the loser in the adventure related in the *Philoctetes*. At the beginning of the play Neoptolemus is described as *his* son[103] but subsequently the young man becomes first the son and then the comrade of Philoctetes.[104] Neoptolemus, whose very name moreover suggests youth, acts as a necessary mediator between Odysseus and Philoctetes. It is impossible for Odysseus and the wounded hero, each isolated in their own obsessions, to communicate. As an ephebe, the son of Achilles is connected with nature in the wild and it is this that makes it possible for him to establish a relationship with Philoctetes; as a soldier and future citizen he owes obedience to Odysseus who is a holder of office. However, the presence of Odysseus ceases to be necessary once the other two men are reintegrated into "normal" life. So by the time Heracles arrives to resolve the problem, Odysseus has disappeared. He is not present at the final scene in which Heracles resolves the situation and ensures the return of Philoctetes and Neoptolemus to the bosom of the city.

But there is indeed a problem that has to be resolved, and a strictly tragic one. For Neoptolemus to pass through the stage that separates the ephebe from the hoplite it is not enough that he should become himself again, as Philoctetes urges him to do,[105] and return to his original *phusis*.[106] The hoplite code to which they

172

both subscribe presupposes their participation in the war. When Philoctetes poses the question to be found in every Greek tragedy — τί δράσω "What shall I do?"[107] — after Neoptolemus has for the last time entreated him to return to the field of battle, he — like Antigone — chooses the values of the family: "Take us back home [πέμψον πρὸς οἴκους] and then remain at Skyros."[108] He promises that Neoptolemus shall win his father's gratitude. Thus Philoctetes chooses both his suffering and the bow that is linked with it. When Neoptolemus is anxious about what to do if the Achaeans come to lay waste his lands, he replies that he will help him with the arrows of Heracles. All he will really be doing is changing to another Lemnos. Neoptolemus makes the same choice. In military terms *that* is called desertion and Tycho von Wilamowitz, writing during the First World War was in no doubt about it![109]

The fact that he chooses the values of the family as opposed to those of the city is all the more remarkable in that there is another figure in reality present throughout the tragedy although he only makes his appearance at the end. Philoctetes, who is the king of Malia as Sophocles is well aware,[110] is on several occasions described as a man of Oeta,[111] a mountain that, to be sure, is not far from his kingdom but is better known as the location of the funeral pyre of Heracles. This is where Philoctetes received the bow from the hero turned god. But the point is that the Heracles referred to here, this Heracles who is, so to speak, the father of Philoctetes,[112] is not Heracles the bowman, hunter, and killer of wild animals; rather, he is "the warrior with the bronze shield [ὁ χάλκασπις ἀνήρ],"[113] that is to say a hoplite Heracles. As in all of Sophocles' plays, the gods' plan is accomplished without the actors realizing it.[114] The reintegration of Philoctetes into the world of men, which is the object of Neoptolemus' ephebe exploit, is in reality already on foot from the moment that Philoctetes for the first time in ten years hears Greek being spoken, that is to say re-establishes contact with language.[115] The proposition put to him is that he should be cared for and cured at Troy and this is indeed what eventually comes to pass.[116] But perhaps the most remarkable thing is the way that Heracles sets himself up as spokesman for this hoplite ideal that is constantly present in the play. I say remarkable because the myth here is of crucial importance. Every Greek knew that Philoctetes killed Paris in *single combat*[117] with the arrows of Heracles and it is not easy to interpret this exploit in hoplite terms. But note Heracles' words at the end of the play: "Departing with this man [Neoptolemus] for the city of Troy... with my arrows you will bring down Paris, the author of all your ills."[118] And, immediately, the god goes on to introduce a distinction between what will be gained by the bow and what by Philoctetes through his personal warrior valor, through the merit that will be his as a result of fighting beside the other Greeks: "You will take Troy and the share of the booty that will then be yours as a prize for your courage among all our other warriors.[119] You will send it to your palace, to your father Poias, on the plateau of the Oeta, your country. But as for that which you will receive from the army in memory of my arrows,[120] carry that to my funeral pyre."[121] So what comes from the bow is to return to the funeral pyre of Heracles. In effect a distinction is made between Philoctetes the bowman and Philoctetes the hoplite. As for Neoptolemus, his position is also going to change. His transformation into a full-fledged warrior is completed. When, as a man who believes himself destined to take the town, he wondered what role the bow was to play in the downfall of Troy, Odysseus had replied to him, "You cannot do it without the bow, the bow cannot do it without you [οὔτ' ἂν σὺ κείνων χωρὶς οὔτ' ἐκεῖνα σοῦ]."[122] Heracles, this time addressing the son of Achilles, uses a similar expression but now it refers to Philoctetes, not the weapon: "You cannot conquer the plain of Troy without him and he cannot do it without you."[123] The partnership of man and bow has become the partnership of two men, two fighters. Heracles goes on to say: "Like two lions sharing the same lot,[124] watch over each other, he over you, you over him [ἀλλ' ὡς λέοντε συννόμω φυλάσσετον οὗτος σὲ καὶ σὺ τόνδε]."[125] It is the oath that the ephebe swears, never to abandon his comrade in the ranks.

Thus the wild man has been reintegrated into the city; the ephebe has become a hoplite. But there is still one more mutation to take place, that of nature itself. Right up to the end of the play Lemnos is a land deserted by men, a country of wild and cruel nature, of predatory creatures and wild beasts. Philoctetes' cave was described as "a dwelling that is not one."[126] But the land to which Philoctetes bids farewell is a pastoral one, even if he remembers that he has suffered there. It is not that it has become "civilized" but the wildness has, so to speak, changed its sign rather in the way that the island in Shakespeare's *Tempest* is at one moment that of Caliban and at another that of Ariel. The animals are replaced by nymphs. A whole world of water materializes:[127] "Well, now that I am leaving, at least let me salute this land. Farewell, home[128] that has kept me for so long; and you, nymphs of the damp fields, and you, the male tumult of the waves.... The hour has come to leave you, fountain and water of Lycian Apollo."[129] And as for the sea, it no longer isolates but now reunites him with other men: "Farewell, soil of Lemnos surrounded by the waves, may a happy crossing carry me away without disaster."[130] The play ends with a prayer of *euploia*,[131] for a fortunate sea voyage, under the sign of Zeus and the nymphs of the sea. It is the divine order that makes it possible for men to become the masters of wild nature. And that is the ultimate reversal in the *Philoctetes*.

APPENDIX

On a Vase in the Museum of Syracuse

Ever since its discovery in 1915 in the necropolis of Fusco, near Syracuse, the vase whose principal side is reproduced here, in Figure 3 (the other side represents a maenad seated between two satyrs), has frequently been the subject of discussion and comment. The commentaries have not proved fruitless. A.D. Trendall has conclusively established its author as one of the most ancient of the "painters of Paestum," the "painter of Dirce," all of whose work appears to provide a commentary on scenes from tragedy (although in a spirit that has more in common with satyrical drama than with tragedy in the strict sense of the word, as is shown by the very frequent presence of young satyrs). He has also established its date as approximately between 380 and 360 B.C.[132]

The central figure was identified immediately.[133] It is Philoctetes, bearded and with unkempt hair. He is seated on a leopard skin in the middle of a cave outlined by a red archway underscored by irregular black lines, while large white patches indicate the unevenness of the rocks.[134] His wounded left foot rests on the rock. In his right hand he holds a feather, no doubt to alleviate his pain, and his left hand grasps his bow. Above him are birds, the catch from his last hunt. I say "his last" because his quiver, hanging at his left side, is *empty*. Under his left arm is an amphora embedded in the ground. The two figures visible above the cave pose no problems either. On the left, standing on a rock, is Athena, wearing a helmet and carrying a hoplite shield. On the right is Odysseus, recognizable from his *pilos* (sailor's cap) and his beard. He is holding a *closed* quiver (containing the arrows of Philoctetes?) Further to the left, leaning against a tree, is a scantily clad ephebe whose embroidered chlamys is thrown back and whose detached cross-belt seems to merge with the tree. He may either represent Diomedes, who is Odysseus' companion in Euripides' play, or Sophocles' Neoptolemus.[135] The question of his identity is a relatively minor problem as it is quite clear that what we have here is an ephebe apparently receiving instructions from the warriorlike Athena.[136] The problem begins when we come to identify the young, richly clad and adorned woman standing on the right with her hand resting on the rock, who appears to be talking with Odysseus. As Pierre Wuilleumier has correctly noted, she is "foreign . . . to all literary and artistic representations of this scene."[137] None of the interpretations that have been suggested is convincing[138] and, to date, the secondary literature mentions no parallel for it. It is, in any case, by no means certain that the figure represents a goddess. She bears no distinctive mark indicating her

Figure 3. Cloche-shaped crater with red figures from the Syracuse Museum (36319); *C.V.A.* Italia (*Museo Archeologico di Siracusa*) XVII, fasc. 1, IV, E, 8; A.D. Trendall, *The Red-figured Vases of Lucania, Campania and Sicily*, Oxford 1967, Campanian, I, n.32, p. 204 (Museum Photograph).

to be divine and she is not raised up as Athena is. At all events, we need hardly remind the reader that in none of the interpretations of the myth of Philoctetes known to us is there any mention of any woman. So it is impossible, for the moment, to decide on the identity of this figure.

The remarks that follow are of a tentative and provisional nature, since new evidence may always turn up. They attempt to throw some light on the vase by taking a different approach. It is difficult not to notice the relations of symmetry and inversion between the two sides that flank the cave and the wild man inside it. Let us attempt to analyze these oppositions and symmetries.

The opposition between the two male and the two female figures is obvious. The two women are wearing bracelets and necklaces and are both clothed while the male figures are naked or scantily clad in accordance with classical convention. But the figures of the same sex are also opposed to each other, as youth to maturity. The ephebe is naturally beardless and has a graceful body and his hair is covered by his headgear. In contrast Odysseus' *pilos* is pushed back, revealing his abundant locks. His beard, unlike that of Philoctetes, is carefully groomed, as is his hair. Furthermore, the upper part of the vase is opposed to the lower by the presence or absence of weapons. (Here the loosened cross-belt of the ephebe takes on its full importance.) But the female figure on the left, Athena, carries the weapons that characterize male maturity – those of the hoplite. Her arm is strong and her bosom understated. In contrast, Odysseus carries a quiver, the symbol of cunning. If we accept that this quiver contains the arrows of Philoctetes, the cunning is furthermore twofold: cunning of the weapon and cunning of Odysseus' action. The two young people are opposed to each other not only by their respective sexes (the femininity of the figure on the right is strongly emphasized both by the richness of the apparel, the *chiton* and the *himation*, and by the contour of the breasts). The ephebe stands at some distance from the cave and the world of wild nature whereas the young woman is touching the outside wall with her right hand. The opposition between them is emphasized further by details in their dress. The chlamys of the ephebe is decorated with the same design as the tunic of Philoctetes, which perhaps suggests a spiritual relationship of the kind described by Sophocles, while the woman's belt displays a pattern very similar to that on the quiver held by Odysseus. This provides a discreet counterpoint to the more obvious symmetrical relationships between the nudity of the men and the ornaments of the women.[139] So it might be said that the scene on the left appears to be centered on the virtues of the hoplite, that is the traditional warrior values, while the right hand side represents the techniques of cunning and of female seduction and that Philoctetes is positioned at the center of this contest (*agon*). However, to a certain extent the male-female polarity inverts the opposition for on the left it is the woman who is armed as a hoplite and on the right the adult man who represents cunning. Perhaps this is a pictorial representation of the drama of the ephebe who becomes a hoplite via the devious route of the world of wild nature and "female"[140] cunning.

Pierre Vidal-Naquet

CHAPTER VIII

The God of Tragic Fiction*

The Greeks had a famous saying about tragedy: "What has it to do with Dionysus?" or, put more categorically, "There is nothing there that has anything to do with Dionysus." Those words, which reflected the astonishment of the public and were to become proverbial, were, according to Plutarch,[1] first pronounced in the early decades of the fifth century when the theater audience beheld Phrynicus and Aeschylus developing on stage, with all due weight and majesty, the very elements that give tragedy its specific character, namely — to use Plutarch's own terms — *muthos* (that is to say a coherent plot relating a legendary story such as that of Heracles, the Atreidai, or Oedipus) and *pathos*.

The shock felt by the ancient Greeks is understandable. As they saw it, the connection between Dionysus and tragedy ought to have been plain to see. We know that tragedies were first performed around 534 under Pisistratus, on the occasion and within the framework of the god's most important festival, the Great Dionysia, celebrated in the early spring — at the end of March — in the middle of the city, on the slopes of the Acropolis. These celebrations were known as the "city Dionysia," to distinguish them from the so-called "rural Dionysia" whose joyful processions, choruses, and competitions of singing and dancing enlivened the hamlets and villages of the Attic countryside in the depths of winter, in December.

The three days of dramatic performances were a part of the

major festival held in honor of Dionysus, and they were closely connected with other ceremonies: dithyrambic competitions, processions of young people, blood sacrifices, and the parading and exhibiting of the god's idol. They were thus allotted a particular place in the cult ceremonial and constituted an essential element in the whole complex ritual. Furthermore, the theater building consecrated to Dionysus incorporated within its precinct a temple to the god, where his image was housed; at the center of the *orchestra*, where the chorus performed, was a stone altar, the *thymelē*; and on the tiered steps a fine carved seat, in the place of honor, was reserved by right for the priest of Dionysus.

The Quest for Divine Madness

In view of all this, there naturally arises the question of the internal link that it would be normal to expect to find between the tragic drama presented on the stage and the religious world of the Dionysiac cult to which the theater was so manifestly attached. It does seem surprising that, whether one thinks of themes or the texture of the work or the unfolding of the spectacle, tragedy in its true form — that is to say in fifth-century Athens — reflects nothing that particularly relates to this god who stands somewhat apart in the Greek pantheon. Dionysus embodies not self-control, moderation, the recognition of one's limits, but the quest for divine madness and ecstatic possession, nostalgia for a fulfillment from elsewhere; not stability and order, but the exceptional benefits of a kind of magic, escape toward a different horizon. He is a god whose elusive countenance, though close at hand, leads his devotees along the paths of otherness, opening up the way to a type of religious experience that is virtually unique in paganism, radical self-disorientation. Yet it was not to the mythical tradition relating to this unusual god — his passion, his wanderings, his mysteries, and his triumph — that the tragic poets turned for their inspiration. With very few exceptions, one being Euripides' *Bacchae*, all the tragedies take as their subject heroic legends with which epic had made every Greek familiar and that, strictly speaking, had nothing to do with Dionysus.

On this point, modern scholarship takes as its starting point the perplexities that the ancient Greeks themselves manifested. Attempts have been made to understand Greek tragedy by re-establishing its links with its religious origins; scholars have sought to seize upon its real impact by revealing the ancient Dionysiac basis from which it is supposed to have emerged and that, they believe, can reveal the secret of the tragic spirit in all its purity. The undertaking is risky so far as the facts are concerned, and it is vain and illusory in principle. Let us take the facts first: The documents to which appeal is made in order to root tragedy in the sacred rituals of the past are uncertain, equivocal, and often contradictory. Consider the example of the actors' masks, which are immediately likened to the animal disguises to be found in figurative representations where they are worn by the troupes of satyrs and sileni who joyfully escort Dionysus with their burlesque dances. But the tragic mask — that Thespis, the creator of tragedy, is believed to have come to use only after at first covering the face with white lead — is a human mask, not an animal disguise. Its function is aesthetic: It meets the precise requirements of the dramatic spectacle, not a religious need to translate states of possession or aspects of monstrosity by means of a masquerade.

Aristotle made two remarks about the antecedents of tragedy, from which we can glean little more than what he tells us directly. He states that tragedy "came from the prelude to the dithyramb,"[2] that is to say from those who led the cyclical chorus in songs and dancing, usually — but not always — for Dionysus. That is all very well. But, in establishing this connection, Aristotle was chiefly concerned with indicating the series of transformations that, at every level, led tragedy, if not to turn its back upon, at least to break with its "dithyrambic" origins in order to become something else and, as he put it, find "its own natural form."[3] Aristotle's second remark concerns the "comic diction" from which tragedy moved away when it abandoned the tetrameter peculiar to a type of poetry that "suited the Satyrs and was better for dancing" and instead adopted the iambic meter.[4] In Aristotle's view, this was the only meter suitable for dialogue, the direct verbal exchange that, for the first time in literature, the dramatist presented before the public just as if his characters were there on the stage, conversing together in flesh and blood. Should we conclude that the dithyrambic round was originally danced, sung, and mimed in honor of Dionysus by men disguised as satyrs, impersonating goats or dressed up in goatskins, and that the evolution of the tragic chorus, stationed around the *thymelē*, as it were echoed this? Nothing could be more uncertain. The participants in the dithyrambic contests that took place alongside the tragic competitions on the occasion of the Great Dionysia did not wear masks. And it was not tragedy but satyrical drama that, in the fifth century, carried on the tradition of phallic songs incorporating elements of disguise, buffoonery, and licentiousness. As a spectacle, tragedy stands at the opposite pole to such representations.

Scholars have accordingly turned elsewhere in their search for the umbilical cord linking tragedy with its religious matrix. Investigating the very name of tragedy (*trag-oidia*, the song of the he-goat), they have supposed the tragedian (*tragoidos*) to be either one who sang to win the goat as a prize or one who sang at the ritual sacrifice of the goat. From there, it was but a short step to suggesting that, at the center of the *orchestra* (the altar around which the chorus moved) was the place where the sacrifice of the goat originally took place and that the goat in question must have been regarded as an expiatory victim whose religious function was, each year, to purify the city from its defilement and completely absolve it from its wrongdoing. The scholars who took that step cleared the way for an interpretation of drama that is close to that suggested by René Girard,[5] who assimilates the tragic spectacle to the ritual ceremony of sacrificing a scapegoat. In his view, the "purification" of passions that tragedy produces in the public's soul is effected through the same mechanisms as those deployed by the social group in order to free itself from the tensions within it, by focusing all its aggression upon a single victim that the group as a whole puts to death, as the incarnation of evil.

Unfortunately though, this goat, the *tragos*, is nowhere to be found. No goat — male or female — was sacrificed either in the theater or during the Great Dionysia. Furthermore, when, in other contexts, Dionysus is given a religious epithet suggesting some kind of goat, it is the term *aix* (she-goat) that is used, never *tragos*.

Tragedy: An Invention

However, to tell the truth, all these difficulties, real though they may be, are of secondary importance. The decisive fact is that both the evidence that allows us to trace the development of tragedy in the late sixth and early fifth centuries and the analysis of the great works that have come down to us from Aeschylus, Sophocles, and Euripides demonstrate clearly that tragedy was, in the strongest sense of the term, an invention. To understand it, we should evoke its origins — with all due prudence — only in order the better to gauge its innovatory aspects, the discontinuities and breaks with both religious practices and more ancient poetic forms. The "truth" of tragedy is not to be found in an obscure, more or less "primitive" or "mystical" past secretly haunting the theater stage. Rather, it can be discovered in all the new and original elements that tragedy introduced on the three levels where it shifted the horizon of Greek culture. First, at the level of social institutions: Prompted, no doubt, by the tyrants, those early representatives of popular tendencies, the civic community introduced tragic competitions, placed under the authority of the chief magistrate, the archon, and subject, down to the slightest organizational details, to the same rules as those that applied to democratic assemblies and courts. From this point of view, tragedy could be said to be a manifestation of the city turning itself into theater, presenting itself on stage before its assembled citizens. Next, at the level of literary forms: Here we find the elaboration of a poetic genre designed to be played out or mimed on a stage, written to be seen as well as heard, planned as a spectacle and, for those reasons, fundamentally different from all pre-existing genres. Finally, at the level of human experience, we find that, with the development of what may be called a tragic conscious- ness, man and his actions were presented, in tragedy's own pecu- liar perspective, not as stable realities that could be placed, defined, and judged, but as problems, unanswerable questions, riddles whose double meanings remain enigmatic however often decoded. Epic, which provided drama with its themes, charac- ters, and the framework for its plots, had presented the great fig- ures of the heroes of former times as models. It had exalted the heroic values, virtues, and high deeds. Through the interplay of dialogue and the clash between the major protagonists and the chorus, and through the reversals of fortune that occur in the course of the drama, the legendary hero, extolled in epic, becomes a subject of debate now that he is transferred to the theatrical stage. And when the hero is thus publicly brought into question, in fifth-century Athens, it is the individual Greek in the audience who discovers himself to be a problem, in and through the pre- sentation of the tragic drama.

Following or together with other Greek scholars, we have already expressed ourselves fully enough on all these points, and need not dwell on them.

Nevertheless, at the end of this brief discussion, the reader will no doubt return to the question that, in the wake of the Greeks themselves, we posed at the beginning of this study. He or she will want to know what, in our opinion, all this has to do with Dionysus. Our reply is twofold. It is clear beyond doubt that there is a religious dimension to Greek theater. But religion did not have the same meaning nor did it occupy the same place in antiquity as it does for us. It was not really sepa- rated from either the social or the political spheres. Every nota- ble collective manifestation within the framework of either city or family, whether in the public or in the private sphere, incor- porated aspects of a religious festival. This applies to the install- ment of a magistrate, an assembly meeting, or a peace treaty, just as it does to a birth, a meal shared with friends, or setting out on a voyage. It also, *a fortiori*, applies to the theater.

But the question remains: Within that religious context, why Dionysus? If the collection of strictly historical causes, which are difficult to disentangle, needs to be complemented or rather replaced by reasons of a different order, reasons that concern not the origins of tragedy, but the meaning that a modern reader is tempted to give it, I would be inclined to suggest the following: Tragedy's connection with Dionysus lies, not so much in roots that, for the most part, elude us, but rather in whatever was new in what tragedy introduced, in whatever constituted its modernity for fifth-century Greece and, even more, for us. Tragedy depicted on stage characters and events that, in the actual manifestation of the drama, took on every appearance of real existence. Yet, even as the audience beheld them with their own eyes, they knew that the tragic heroes were not really there nor could be since, attached as they were to a completely bygone age, they by definition belonged to a world that no longer existed, an inaccessible elsewhere. Thus, the "presence" embodied by the actor in the theater was always the sign, or mask, of an *absence*, in the day-to-day reality of the public. Caught up by the action and moved by what he beheld, the spectator was still aware that these figures were not what they seemed but illusory simulations — in short, that this was *mimēsis*. Tragedy thus opened up a new space in Greek culture, the space of the imaginary, experienced and understood as such, that is to say as a human production stemming from pure artifice. I have elsewhere written: "A consciousness of the fiction is essential to the dramatic spectacle; it seems to be both its condition and its product."[6] A fiction, an illusion, the imaginary: Yet, according to Aristotle, this shadow play that the illusionist art of the poet brings to life on the stage is more important and true for the philosopher than are the accounts of authentic history engaged in recalling how events really occurred in the past. If we are right in believing that one of Dionysus' major characteristics is constantly to confuse the boundaries between illusion and reality, to conjure up the beyond in the here and now, to make us lose our sense of self-assurance and identity, then the enigmatic and ambiguous face of the god certainly does smile out at us in the interplay of the theatrical illusion that tragedy introduced for the first time onto the Greek stage.

Jean-Pierre Vernant

CHAPTER IX

Features of the Mask in

Ancient Greece*

Ancient Greece was familiar not only with the comic or tragic masks worn on stage by actors, but with other masks too — sculpted in marble, modelled from clay, or carved in wood – masks designed to represent a deity or to cover the face of one of his devotees for the duration of the ritual.

These were religious masks, then, different from theatrical ones. Such a distinction may at first sight seem surprising since, in Athens, as in other ancient cities, the dramatic competitions were indissociable from the religious ceremonies held in honor of Dionysus. The competitions took place on the occasion of festivals held to celebrate the god, during a city's Great Dionysia, and right down to the end of antiquity they retained their sacred character. Furthermore, the theater building itself incorporated a temple to Dionysus; at the center of the *orchestra* a stone altar to the god, the *thymelē*, was located while on the tiered steps of the auditorium, in the place of honor, the finest seat of all was reserved for the priest of Dionysus.

But there is a difference between on the one hand the theatrical mask, an accessory whose function, like that of other items of costume, was to resolve certain problems of tragic expressivity and, on the other, two different types of mask: first, those donned in ritual masquerades in which the faithful disguised themselves for strictly religious purposes; second, the mask of the god himself that, simply through its countenance with its strange eyes, expressed certain characteristics peculiar to Dionysus, the divine power whose presence seemed ineluctably marked by his absence.

The fact that there were religious masks for certain deities in ancient Greece poses a problem that we must approach from a more general angle, that of the diverse ways of depicting the gods. The Greeks made use of more or less every symbolic means of representing the gods: They were to be found in rough stone, on beams, pillars, in the likenesses of animals or monsters, as human beings and as masks. As is well known, during the classical period, the canonical form accepted for religious statues was that of an anthropomorphic image. But in the case of certain divine powers who are exceptions to the rule in this respect and constitute a special group, the mask continued to be used, retaining all its symbolic potency. Who are these gods for whose presentation the mask was specially used? What is it that they share in common and that connects them with this particular area of the supernatural better evoked by the mask than by any other form of representation?

Let us consider three major divine powers that may be regarded as constituting this special group.

The first is a power who is nothing but a mask, and who operates in and through it: Gorgo, the gorgon. The second is a goddess who is never herself represented by a mask but in whose cult masks and disguises are particularly important: Artemis. The third is the deity whose relationship with the mask is so close that in the Greek pantheon he is known as the god of the mask: Dionysus. There are differences and contrasts between these three figures from the beyond, but also collusions and overlaps that make it possible to pose the problem of the mask in the religious world of the Greeks in general terms.

Gorgo

The visual model of the gorgon takes two forms: One is a female figure with a monstrous visage, Medusa, the only gorgon of the three who was mortal. Perseus cut off her head, taking care to avoid its petrifying gaze, then presented it to Athena, who mounted it at the center of her aegis, thereafter known as the *Gorgoneion*. But first and foremost, Gorgo is a mask, used in many ways: Displayed on a temple pediment, as a bas-relief, on an acroterium or an antefix, her role appears to have been apotropaic as well as decorative. Hung in artisan workshops, she watched over the potters' kilns and protected the forges from harmful demons. In private households, the Gorgo mask was part of the domestic scene, appearing over and over again on bowls and amphoras. It was also to be found in the form of an emblem on warriors' shields.

Whether seen standing or as a disembodied mask, from her first appearance in the seventh century onward, in all the various forms to be found in Corinthian, Attic, and Laconian imagery, one constant feature dominates all her representations: the frontal view of her face.

Even when her body and legs are depicted in profile, as was customary, Gorgo's round, distended, staring countenance is always presented full face to the beholder.

Like Dionysus who, as we shall see, is the only Olympian god to be represented facing front, Gorgo is a power whom human beings cannot approach without falling beneath her gaze. In some vase paintings, Gorgo's dominating gaze is emphasized by the two great prophylactic eyes that flank her mask (Figure 4).[1] The mask of Dionysus and those of satyrs are sometimes similarly framed (Figure 5). In a variant to this motif Gorgo's face is lodged in the depths of each eye, in the position of the pupil, which the Greeks called *Korē* or "young girl."[2]

In the texts, particularly in epic, the gaze of the Gorgon, which sometimes gleams from the eyes of the frenzied warrior, provokes horror: unreasoning, pointless panic, naked fear, terror of supernatural dimensions. The Gorgonian eye of the irresistible fighter, his face distorted in a grimace resembling the hideous countenance on Athena's aegis, foretells impending, inevitable death, paralyzing and petrifying the victim's heart.[3] For that reason, the Gorgoneion is the most common emblem displayed on the heroic shields found in vase paintings.⁴ Its visual impact is reinforced by the sound that it evokes. Gorgo's distended mouth conjures up the great cry of Athena resounding through the Trojan camp and the dreadful bellow of Achilles returning to battle, but it also suggests the sound of the flute that Athena invented to imitate the shrill voices of the gorgons.⁵ While playing the flute, the goddess caught sight of her reflection in the water of a spring. Repulsed at seeing her puffed-out cheeks, as distended and ugly as a gorgon's mask, she flung her new toy away. Marsyas, the satyr, seized it.⁶ The warrior's flute, the flute used in initiatory rites of possession, is the instrument of a delirium that may prove fatal.⁷

Thus exposed to the Gorgon's gaze, man faces the powers of the beyond in their most radically alien form, that of death, night, nothingness. Odysseus, the heroic model of endurance, turns aside at the entrance to the underworld, saying: "Sheer panic turned me pale, gripped by the sudden fear that dread Persephone might send me up from Hades' Halls some ghastly monster like the Gorgon's head."⁸ Gorgo marks out the boundary of the world of the dead. To pass that frontier is to become, oneself, beneath her gaze and in her image, what the dead are — empty heads without strength, heads shrouded in night.⁹

The Greek artists gave formal expression to that radical otherness, depicting it as a monstrosity so as to make it manifest for all to see. The monstrosity stemmed from a systematic blurring of all the categories that are kept distinct in the organized world but are confused and intermingled in this face. In the Gorgo's countenance the bestial is superimposed upon the human: Her strangely broad, round head evokes a leonine mask; her hair is rendered either as a mane or, more often, as a seething mass of snakes. Her huge ears are bovine. The skull-like grin slashed across her face reveals the pointed teeth of a wild beast or the tusks of a wild boar. Her gigantic tongue lolls out over her chin. She froths at the mouth like an unpredictable, terrifying horse, an animal from the beyond that is often portrayed cradled in her arms, or whose body she may assume, becoming a female centaur.¹⁰

Figure 4. Mask of Gorgo, flanked by two prophylactic eyes (Naples Museum).

Figure 5. Mask of Dionysus, flanked by two prophylactic eyes (Madrid Museum).

Part human, part animal, she is also a fusion of genders. Her
chin is bearded or bristly and, when portrayed in a standing position, she is frequently given male sexual organs. But in other representations this female creature, sexually united with Poseidon,
is shown in the process of giving birth. Usually however, she brings
forth her two offspring, Pegasus the horse and Chrysaor the giant,
from her severed neck.[11]

Like the Graiae sisters, ancient girls born with white hair and
wrinkled as the skin that forms on milk, Gorgo's cheeks and brow
are scored with lines. Like them, she is at once young and old.

Although repulsively ugly, she is also attractive, as Poseidon's
desire for her testifies. In one tradition she is a ravishing girl who
competes in beauty with a goddess and is punished for her pre-
sumption.[12] In later times, Medusa was represented as a woman of
great beauty, as fascinating as the death that she carries in her eyes.

Gorgo is young-old, beautiful-ugly, masculine-feminine, human-
bestial; and she is also mortal-immortal. Her two sisters are immortal. Only she is dead, but her severed head is still alive and
death-dealing. Born in the realm of night, in the subterranean
regions close to the world of the dead, the three gorgons are
winged and their magic powers of flight enable them to move upon
and below the earth and also to soar high into the air. Medusa's
son, Pegasus, the original (and origin of the) horse, sprung from
her severed neck, henceforth establishes the link between heaven
and earth as he carries the thunderbolt between the two.

This disorganized countenance, where contraries meet and normally distinct categories are confused, provokes horror and evokes
death but can also express frenzied possession. Frenetic delirium,
which the Greeks called *Lussa*, or the Rabid One, claps Gorgo's
mask onto the face of whoever is possessed. His eyes roll, his features are convulsed, his tongue lolls out and his teeth grind. As
depicted in tragedy, the frenzied Heracles, massacring his own children, is just such a demented one: the very incarnation of Gorgo.[13]

In literary texts, it is the disturbing strangeness of this convulsed face that is emphasized; but the figurative representations

often stress the opposite aspect of monstrosity, the grotesque. While not totally evacuating the latent horror, most depictions of Gorgo are comical, humorous, burlesque. They resemble *mormolukeia*, bogeymen or scarecrows invented to frighten little children. The horror can be exorcized through this process of inversion: The threat becomes a kind of protection; the danger, now directed against the enemy, becomes a means of defense.

In some cases, the grotesque aspect arises from an association that is imposed between the face and the sexual organs. Like the satyr, that equivocal being whose erect phallus is designed to provoke laughter, Gorgo is clearly associated with the display of sexual organs, in her case female ones. This is demonstrated most clearly by Baubo, another figure that some texts assimilate to the ogresses of children's tales or to the ghosts of the night, and who plays an important role in the etiological accounts of the rites of Eleusis. It is she who, through her comical foolery, succeeds in dispelling Demeter's grief and making the goddess laugh. According to accounts given by the Church Fathers, Baubo, at her wits' end, had the idea of pulling up her skirt to exhibit her abdomen.[14] The sexual parts that she revealed resembled the face of a child. By manipulating them, Baubo made it look as though the face was laughing, and Demeter burst out laughing too. In other contexts, in particular where initiatory rituals are involved, the exhibition of sexual organs provokes a sacred terror; but here, it provokes hilarity and the anguish of mourning is brought to an end. Similar faces-cum-sexual organs, or sexual organs-cum-masks, the sight of which has a liberating effect, are also to be found on the curious statuettes of Priene, where the face is superimposed upon the abdomen and merges with it.[15]

Artemis

Artemis is never depicted as a masked figure. Her typical appearance, as sculpted or rendered in vase paintings, is well known: She is the beautiful and athletic virgin huntress, clad in a short tunic and grasping her bow. In many cases, she is accompanied by her hounds or surrounded by animals. To the extent that, in the Greek world, this goddess takes on certain features of a pre-hellenic deity, the *Potnia thērōn* or "Mistress of wild animals," it is certainly possible to detect resemblances between the way she is depicted and the most archaic of the figurative representations of Gorgo.[16] But that is not a line that we intend to pursue. The reason why Artemis may be regarded as a goddess of masks is that in her cult, and particularly in the initiatory rites for young people over which she presides, masks and masquerades play an exceptionally important part. In order to determine their meaning and attempt to understand what it is that links Apollo's twin sister to the supernatural zone that the mask is specifically designed to express, we must examine the figure of Artemis, situate her position in the pantheon as a whole, and mark out more clearly the place assigned to her in the organization of the supernatural powers.[17]

The space over which Artemis presides is that of the frontier regions: the mountains that bound and separate the states, places far away from the towns, where the great sanctuaries of the goddess often fall under threat from neighboring peoples and enemies. These are marginal areas where, in thick forests and on arid hill-tops, the goddess leads her pack of hounds, hunting down the wild beasts that are her property and that she also protects. She also reigns over beaches and seashores, the limits of land and sea where, in some legends, she first arrived in the form of a strange and disquieting statue washed in from some barbarian country. Her place is also in the plains of the interior, on the shores of lakes, in marshlands and on the banks of certain rivers where stagnant waters and the threat of flooding create an area that is half water, half earth, where the dividing line between the dry and the wet, what is liquid and what is solid, remains vague.

What are the features that such diverse spaces share in common? The world of Artemis is not a completely wide space, representing a radical otherness in relation to the cultivated land of the city territory. Rather, it is a place of margins, border zones where what is "other" becomes manifest in the contacts made with it, where the wild and the civilized live side by side, coming into opposition certainly, but thereby mutually infiltrating one another.

Artemis is a *kourotrophē* goddess, who presides over the delivery, birth, and upbringing of children. Positioned as she is, at the intersection of the wild and the tame, her role is to take charge of the offspring of human beings, who belong to her as do the offspring of animals, both wild and domesticated. She raises these children from their unformed state of newborn babes to maturity, taming and calming them, shaping them so that they may cross the decisive thresholds represented for girls by marriage, and for boys by the acquisition of citizenship. In the course of a series of trials completed in the context of the wild, on the margins of the city, the young must have the power to break the ties that have bound them to this different world ever since their childhood. First and foremost, here, at the ambiguous stage in which the separation between the sexes remains uncertain, a clear dividing line must once and for all be drawn between the boys and the girls.

Artemis ripens the girls, makes them nubile and prepares them for marriage in which sexual union will take place in the most civilized fashion. Artemis herself rejects marriage, turning away from the violence of the sexual act, a bogey that terrifies the young wife; and the haunting fear of violation and rape, actions which, instead of integrating femininity with culture, divert both sexes into wildness, can be detected in many mythical accounts of *parthenoi* devoted to Artemis. The violence is male, to be sure, but danger also threatens from the female side when a young girl, too eager to imitate her goddess, rejects marriage and swings over to total animality, becoming a fierce huntress who pursues and massacres the male she ought to marry.

The Brauronia ritual in Attica provides a model of the way in which Artemis prepares for the correct integration of sexuality into culture. The little girls of Athena could not be married — that is, live with a man — unless, between the ages of five and

ten, they had acted out the part of a bear. The miming of a bear
did not indicate a return to the wild, as in the case of Callisto
who was changed into a bear as a punishment for having failed to
remain faithful to the virginal world of the goddess and, through
an act of violence, for having known sexual union and childbirth.
In the case of the little Athenian girls, it was a matter of reliving
the part of a she-bear who, in times past, came to live, tame,
among human beings, growing up in their company, in the sanctuary of Artemis. One little girl was naughty or cheeky – certainly
imprudent – enough to tease the animal excessively: She got her
face scratched, and her brother, in a rage, killed the bear. Ever
since, by way of reparation, the daughters of the citizens of Athens had imitated the bear, gradually becoming tame, as she had,
overcoming their latent wildness so that they could eventually
go and live with a husband, without danger to either partner.

Perhaps masks were used during these ceremonies. We cannot
be sure, despite a vase fragment that shows a female figure, possibly a priestess, wearing a bear's mask.[18] However, the imitation
of animal models was very much a part of symbolic masquerades.

As for the boys, before graduating to citizenship they had to
acquire the physical and moral qualities essential to a soldier-citizen. This process was particularly institutionalized in Sparta where
the male population was, moreover, from infancy right through
to old age, divided into strictly organized age groups. As early as
the age of seven, a boy destined one day to become one of the
"Peers" was introduced into the framework of communal education, where he was subjected to a rigorous training involving compulsory duties and a series of tests, and in which the passage from
childhood to adolescence was strongly marked.

In the course of this *paideia*, *mimēsis* played an important role,
both in the pattern of compulsory daily behavior and also during
the occasional masquerades.

For example, the young boys had to practice a virtue known
as *sōphrosunē*: This involved walking in silence in the streets, hands
hidden beneath their cloaks, never glancing to right or left but

keeping their eyes fixed on the ground. They were never to answer back, never to raise their voices. They were expected to show that, even where modesty was concerned, the male sex was superior to the female. Xenophon reports that they could be truly taken for girls.[19] But in conjunction with this chaste, reserved, as it were hyper-feminine demeanor, they had to do things that were normally forbidden: steal from the adults' tables, plot and scheme, sneak in and filch food without getting caught. In fierce collective fights in which no holds were barred — biting, scratching, kicking all allowed — they were expected to demonstrate the most violent brutality, behave as total savages, attaining the extreme limits of the specifically male virtue known as *andreia*: the frenzy of the warrior bent on victory at all costs, prepared to devour the enemy's very heart and brain, his face assuming the frightful mask of Gorgo: here, hyper-virility, swinging over into animality, the savagery of the wild beast.

On other occasions these young models of modesty and reserve gave themselves up to buffoonery, verbal clowning, insults, and obscenities.

It is probably to this context that we should connect the masks discovered during the archaeological excavations in the sanctuary of Artemis Orthia.[20] They are ex-voto, terra cotta masks, mostly too small to fit even a child's face; and they are believed to be reproductions of the wooden masks worn during religious ceremonies held in honor of Artemis.

Some represent old, wrinkled, toothless women who put one in mind of the Graiae, the distant sisters of the Gorgons (Figure 6). Then there are grimacing satyrs, large numbers of representations of Gorgo, grotesque faces, more or less bestial, sometimes only partly formed. Discovered among them were also a few impassive visages of young, helmeted warriors.

All this suggests that during these masquerades and ritual games, the young Spartans were expected to mime out the most diverse and contrary of attitudes with gestures and the use of disguises and masks: feminine reserve and animal ferocity, modesty

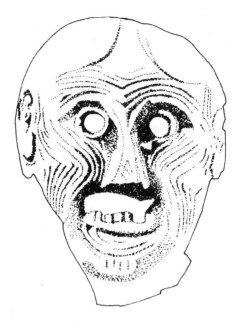

Figure 6. Mask of an old woman, found in the sanctuary of Artemis Orthia (Museum of Sparta).

and obscenity, the degradation of old age and the vigor of the young warrior, successively exploring every aspect of marginality and strangeness, assuming every possible form of otherness, learning how to break rules so as the better to internalize rules that they would thereafter have to keep.

In a similar fashion — and in many other societies — order, to be affirmed, needs periodically to be contested and turned upside down during the few days of Carnival when role reversal reigns supreme: Women are dressed as men, men as women or animals, slaves take the place of their masters, the carnival king symbolically ejects the city leader. During these days, every negation of the established values — obscenity, animality, buffoonery, the grotesque, and the terrifying are all unleashed upon the civilized world.

200

Just so, under the vigilant protection of Artemis, the goddess of marginal places and transitions, Greek children underwent an apprenticeship, learning their social identity. The little girls acted out the slow process leading from the fundamental wildness of their sex to the civilized behavior of the good wife, while boys learned to know every kind of excess in order to recognize and embrace the norms of citizenship, without fear of regression or revolt.

Dionysus

With Dionysus the process seems to take place the other way around. He is in fact complementary to Artemis. It is upon the fully socialized adult, the integrated citizen, the mother of a family sheltered in the conjugal home, that this god exerts his powers, introducing the unpredictable dimension of the "elsewhere" into the very heart of daily life.

We possess very little documentation on the cult devoted to the god of masks. In the descriptions of the Dionysiac festivals there is nothing to tell us whether the ritual is addressed to the god represented simply as a mask or to a religious, anthropomorphic statue similar to those of the rest of the group of great Olympians to which he belongs. This is the first aspect of his ambivalence. Although an authentically Greek god of just as impeccable origin and just as great antiquity as the others — he is already present in Mycenae — he is nevertheless the "stranger," "other," the one perpetually arriving from across the sea, sometimes — like Artemis — in the form of a strange-looking idol washed ashore by the waves, at other times turning up in person from barbarian Asia, followed by his throng of Bacchants whom he unleashes upon a terror-struck Greece.

However, we are provided with two types of documentation to help us to distinguish the specific characteristics of the god of the mask.

First, there is the archaeological documentation: on the one hand, marble masks of various dimensions with nonperforated orifices, which were not worn but hung up, as the holes used in their suspension indicate;[21] on the other, vase paintings showing a mask-idol fixed to a pillar.

Second, the dramatic literary text of Euripides' *Bacchae*, which represents on the theater stage, the all-powerful force of Dionysiac *mania* in a particularly ambiguous manner. Hidden by his tragic mask, an actor embodies the god, who is the protagonist of the drama. But this god, himself masked, conceals himself beneath a human appearance that, in its turn, is also equivocal. As a man-woman wearing an Asiatic robe, with his painted face framed by long plaits and his strange gaze, Dionysus passes himself off as one of his own prophets, come to reveal to the eyes of all the epiphany of the god whose essential forms of manifestation are metamorphosis, disguise, and the mask.[22]

The tragic text and the figurative representations underline one of the fundamental characteristics of this particular deity: He is always seen full face. Like Gorgo, Dionysus is a god with whom man can only make contact face to face: It is impossible to look at him without falling beneath the fascination of his gaze, a gaze that drives a man out of his own mind.

That is what the Dionysus of the *Bacchae* explains to the impious Pentheus, when Dionysus pretends to be one of his own followers who has been initiated in the course of a decisive confrontation with the god: "I saw him see me."[23]

That is also the message conveyed by the vase paintings. On the François vase,[24] the gods are seen passing in procession, all in profile. Suddenly the countenance of Dionysus, presented facing front, strikingly breaks the regularity of the parade. With his staring eyes, he fixes the spectator who is thus placed in the position of an initiate to the mysteries. And as depicted on drinking cups, the god, his body seen in profile, whether standing or reclining on a bed, with a *canthare* or a drinking horn in his lifted hand, or drunkenly staggering, still gazes straight into the eyes of whoever looks at him.

But the fascination of his unavoidable eyes is best expressed by

Figure 7. Religious mask of Dionysus (Museum of the Villa Giulia, Rome).

the representations of his masked idol (Figure 7). A bearded mask
with tumbling locks crowned with an ivy wreath is hung on a pillar. Below stream the folds of some gauzy material. Around this a
religious ceremony is being organized. Having emerged from their
ecstatic trance, women are solemnly handling the wine receptacles. Beneath the gaze of the god, toward whom their own eyes are
turned, drawing those of the spectator, they serve out the dangerous beverage that is harmful if not consumed in accordance with
the ritual precautions. For Dionysus has taught human beings how
to use wine properly, the way to dilute and tame the fierce liquid that can drive a man out of his mind. There, before the mask,
the women, who do not drink the wine, ladle it out with pious
dignity and distribute it to be quaffed by the men and the gods.[25]

On another vase, the huge mask is flanked by writhing maenads and gesticulating satyrs. The latter are themselves masks, mixed creatures, half men, half beasts, as alarming as the horse whose ears and tail they have and as grotesque as the donkey or the he-goat whose lust they imitate. Their gambols and leaping give animated expression to another aspect of Dionysism, the joyful, liberating delirium that seizes whoever does not reject the god, whoever is ready to join him in calling the established categories into question, in wiping out the frontiers that separate animals from men and men from gods, in forgetting social roles, sexes, and ages, and in dancing without fear of ridicule, as do the two white-haired old men in the *Bacchae*, Tiresias and Cadmus, wise enough to recognize and accept the divine madness.

When the mask is represented in profile, either singly or doubly, at the center of an image, the dance of the maenads around the pillar seems to express a different aspect of the ritual: the human attempt to evoke and fix this divine presence whose elusive quality and irremediable otherness is emphasized by the hollow, empty-eyed mask; the aim of the encircling group of worshipers is to pin it down to a particular spot on earth, here, in the midst of the world of nature, not in the sacred space of a temple.[26]

All these empty accessories, the bearded mask, the ivy crown, and the billowing garment, that represent the god with whom man can merge in a face-to-face encounter of fascination, are props that man himself can don, assuming the marks of the god upon himself, the better to become possessed by him. The whole point of Dionysism, which brings man into immediate contact with the otherness of the divine, is to become other oneself, swinging into the gaze of the god or becoming assimilated to him through mimetic contagion.

A parallel phenomenon was produced in fifth-century drama, in which the Greeks set up a theatrical space to contain a spectacle of characters and actions that, instead of being incorporated into reality by being thus presented, were thereby relegated to the quite separate world of fiction. When the spectators beheld Agamemnon, Heracles, or Oedipus before their very eyes, in the guise of their masks, they knew that those heroes were forever absent, could never be there where they saw them, belonged to a bygone age of legends and myths. What Dionysus brought about, and what the mask also rendered possible through what was brought to life when the actor donned it, was an eruption into the heart of public life of a dimension of existence totally alien to the quotidian world.

The invention of theater, a literary genre that presented fiction on stage as if it were real, could only make its impact within the framework of the cult of Dionysus, the god of illusions, confusion, and the constant muddling of reality and appearances, truth and fiction.

This brief survey of the religious uses of the mask in the Greek world makes it possible to distinguish a number of features common to all three of the divine powers who occupy the sector of the supernatural that is characterized by the mask. Alongside those positive similarities, we can also shed some light upon the oppositions that govern the respective relations between these three figures.

By bringing masks into play, the Greeks found it possible to face up to a number of diverse forms of otherness: the radical otherness of death in the case of Gorgo, whose petrifying gaze plunged whomever it dominated into terror and chaos; a radical otherness in the case of those possessed by Dionysus too, but an opposite kind: For those who accepted it, Dionysiac possession afforded access to a world of joy where the confining limitations of the human condition disappeared. In contrast to these two types of vertical otherness, so to speak, which drew human beings in the one case downward, in the other upward, either to the confusion of chaos or to fusion with the divine, the otherness explored by the young Greeks under the patronage of Artemis seems situated on a horizontal axis, in terms of both space and time: within the chronology of human existence punctuated by a series of stages and passages from one to the next; and within the concentric space of civilized society that stretches from the city to the distant zones of the mountains and the sea, from the heart of culture to the borders of wild nature. The wildness might seem to bring Artemis close to Gorgo, but Artemis marks it out and delimits it simply the better to reject it and keep it at a distance, by relegating it to the surrounding horizon. As the young move slowly through their apprenticeship, learning of these differences, the goddess leads them toward a correct integration into civic life. The function of Dionysus appears to be to burst asunder the very patterns that she establishes in measured fashion in the course of her rituals of transgression. Wiping out prohibitions, confusing categories, and disintegrating social frameworks, Dionysus introduces into the heart of human life an otherness so complete that it has the power, as does Gorgo, to propel its enemies toward horror, chaos, and death, just as it can also raise its devotees to a state of ecstasy, a full and joyous communion with the divine.

Dionysus' gaze and that of Gorgo share a fascinating power. But, like the cult of Artemis, the cult of Dionysus also involves unbridled masquerades. In each of these three cases, the mask serves to express tensions between contrary terms, the terrifying and the grotesque, wild nature and culture, reality and illusion. In all three cases, hilarity is associated with the use of the mask and relieves those tensions; laughter liberates man from terror and death, from the anguish of mourning, the shackles of prohibitions and respectability; laughter frees human beings from their heavy social constraints.

The Lacedaemonians consecrated a sanctuary to this. Laughter — *Gelos*, in Greek — next to those occupied by its two dark acolytes: Terror (*Phobos*) and Death (*Thanatos*). And in austere Sparta, Lycurgus, the legislator, set up a statue to it at the very heart of the city.[27]

Jean-Pierre Vernant and Françoise Frontisi-Ducroux

CHAPTER X

The Lame Tyrant:

From Oedipus to Periander*

In his *Structural Anthropology*, Claude Lévi-Strauss, by way of a demonstration of his method, set out an analysis of the myth of Oedipus that has become a classic.[1] There are two points to note about his interpretation. First, to Greek scholars it seemed, to put it mildly, debatable. Second, it brought about such a radical change in the study of myth that reflection — on the part of Lévi-Strauss himself as well as other scholars — on the Oedipus legend has, ever since, been diverted into new and, I believe, productive channels.

I shall mention only one aspect of these new lines of thought. So far as I know, Lévi-Strauss is the first to have noticed the importance of a characteristic feature of all three generations of the Labdacid lineage: a lopsided gait, a lack of symmetry between the two sides of the body, a defect in one foot. Labdacus is the lame one, whose legs do not match, being neither of equal length nor equally strong; Laius is the asymmetrical, clumsy one, the left-hander; *Oidipous* is the one with a swollen foot. At first, Lévi-Strauss believed he could interpret these Greek characters' names, all of which indicate a defect in their gait or a deformed foot, in the light of the Amerindian myths in which autochthonous men, born from the earth, remain bound to the earth from which they have incompletely emerged, through some anomaly in the manner of their locomotion, in their way of moving as they walk on the ground. It was an interpretation that was difficult to maintain as the application of the Greek facts to the American models proved gratuitous and arbitrary.[2]

But Lévi-Strauss himself, as if obsessed by the myth, to which, either directly or indirectly, he has since repeatedly returned, dropped that early hypothesis and proceeded to expand and modify his interpretation on a number of essential points. I will mention two. First, in his inaugural lecture to the Collège de France,[3] he connected the theme of the riddle, curiously omitted from his first analysis, to that of Oedipus' gait. He suggested that the riddle should be understood as a question isolated from its answer, that is to say formulated in such a way that it is beyond reach; the answer cannot be connected with it. The riddle thus represents a defect or impossibility of communication in a verbal exchange between the two interlocutors: The first asks a question to which the second can only respond with silence. Later, in a more recent study,[4] he placed himself at an extreme level of abstraction, attempting to distinguish the formal framework of the mythical structure. The hypothesis that he evolved was as follows: Lameness, which makes a man walk crookedly, stammering, which makes anyone with a tongue – rather than a foot – that is lame slur his speech and fail to convey his meaning directly to the listener, or thirdly, forgetfulness, which makes it impossible to thread one's memories together in one's mind, are all comparable marks that the myth uses, in conjunction with the themes of indiscretion and misunderstanding, to express defects, distortions, or blocked channels of communication at various levels of social life: sexual communication, the transmission of life (normal childbirth stands in opposition to sterility or monstrosity); communication between successive generations (fathers pass on their status and functions to their sons); verbal exchanges and coherence within oneself (alertness of mind and understanding of oneself as opposed to forgetfulness, division, or splits within one's personality, as found in Oedipus).[5]

This new approach – closer to the reading of the myth proposed by Terence Turner and to my own reading in an earlier analysis of Sophocles' tragedy – is what I should like to test out, insofar as it relates to lameness. (I shall, at least for the time being, leave aside the matter of stuttering, that is to say – from a classical scholar's point of view – all the stories concerning the origins of Cyrene, the foundation of which was postponed and deviated through "forgetfulness" on the part of the Argonauts, but was eventually achieved, despite blocked communications with the god of Delphi and after many false moves and detours, by Battus, the "Stutterer," the eponymous founder of the royal dynasty of the Battiads, the last representative of which was a Battus who, as Herodotus notes, was "lame and infirm on his feet [χωλός τε ἐὼν καὶ οὐκ ἀρτίπους]."）[6]

I propose to examine to what extent an interpretative framework of this kind will allow us to pick out the features that are common to two very different kinds of accounts: on the one hand a myth, the legend of the Labdacids, on the other Herodotus' "historical" account of the dynasty of the tyrants of Corinth, the Cypselids, descended from the lame Labda.

Such an endeavor presupposes one condition – namely that among the Greeks themselves, the category of "lameness" should not be limited strictly to defects of foot, leg, or gait, but should symbolically extend to take in more than just the domain of spatial locomotion, and metaphorically express any form of behavior that may be seen as unbalanced, deviant, impeded, or blocked. In *Cunning Intelligence in Greek Culture and Society*, Marcel Detienne and myself expanded upon the subject of the significance of lameness in myth at quite sufficient length, so I need not dwell upon the point here.[7] Allow me simply to remind the reader of an equivocal aspect of lameness: its ambivalence.[8] Compared with normal gait, it constitutes a defect. A person who is lame is deficient in some way: One leg lacks something (length, strength, or straightness). But this departure from the rule may also confer upon the cripple the privilege of a status beyond the common run, or some exceptional qualification: not a defect, but the sign or promise of a unique destiny. Seen from this angle, the asymmetry between the two legs acquires a quite different aspect that is positive instead of negative. It endows, so to speak, the ordinary way of walking with a new dimension, liberating the walker from the normal need to move straight forward in a single direction. This point needs to be explained in greater detail. Because the cripple's two feet are not on the same plane, the limping gait produces a zig-zagging, oscillating, unbalanced progress that weaves from one side to the other. Seen in relation to normal movement, where one foot follows the other, proceeding regularly along the same path, this limping gait is, of course, defective. But taken to extremes, pushed to the limit, the kind of dislocation involved in this lurching progress of the cripple coincides with another form of locomotion. It is a superior and superhuman type of movement that swings right around upon itself, describing a full circle, a type of movement that the Greeks believed to be peculiar to a number of exceptional categories of beings: Instead of forging ahead in strides, one foot after another, these all progressed in a circular fashion, like a wheel, with every spatial direction confused in a revolving motion that abolishes the opposition between front and back which, by imparting a direction to the progress of a normal human being, at the same time subjects him to strict limitations. The movement of Hephaestus, the lame god, "rolling" around his bellows in his workshop, was circular in this fashion;[9] so was that of the primordial men, those beings described by Aristophanes in the Symposium[10] who were "complete" in comparison to the men of the present, cleft as they are in two (down an axis separating front from back). Thanks to the separate movements of each of their four legs in relation to the other three (not to mention the four arms that complemented their lower limbs), these primordial lame creatures – lame, par excellence, so to speak – moved forward or backward equally well, like wheels.[11] Their circular mode of locomotion resembled that of the wheeled tripods constructed by the magic of Hephaestus, the god, in his own image, in such a way that the animated automata could move forward and backward with equal ease.[12] Also similar were the animals of the island of the sun, whose revolving progress, described by Iambulus, was but one of the marvels that testified to the Island dwellers' superiority over ordinary mortals.[13]

But one text in particular, the seventh book of Plato's *Republic*,[14] shows that, for the Greeks, lameness was not just a matter of feet; those lame in spirit were opposed to those who were agile, quick, steady on their two legs, *bebaioi*, and those who went straight, *euthus, orthos*. Plato makes a distinction between well-born souls, made for philosophy, and souls that are "deformed and lame." In so doing, he assimilates, as if it were self-evident, intellectual lameness and bastardy of soul, for the *cholos* is a *nothos*, a bastard, not a *gnesios* of direct and legitimate descent[15] like the son who "resembles the father" who has engendered him in a regular fashion, without deviation or deformity since he is born in a direct, unhalting line. Two texts carry decisive weight on the relations between lameness and descent: Xenophon, *Hellenica*, III, 3, 1-3, and Plutarch, *Agesilaus*, III, 1-9. When Agis, the king of Sparta died, it was necessary to choose a successor. Agis left one son, Leotychidas, and a brother, Agesilaus. Normally, succession would pass to the son, not the brother of the deceased king. Furthermore, Agesilaus was physically lame. But Leotychidas was suspected to be in truth the son of Alcibiades, well-known to have been the lover of Agis' wife, Timaia, during his visit to Sparta. To support the cause of Leotychidas, the diviner Diopeithes came up with an "ancient oracle" running more or less as follows: "Bethink thee now, O Sparta, though thou art very glorious, lest from thee, sound of foot (*artipous*) there spring a maimed royalty (*chole basileia*), for long will unexpected toils oppress thee."[16] The choice of a royal successor to Agis was between his lame brother and his son, presumed a bastard. Which was the lamer of the two, the *cholos* or the *nothos*? Lysander's — and the Lacedaemonians' — answer left no doubt. According to Xenophon (Hellenica II, 3, 3): "He did not suppose the god was bidding them beware lest a king of theirs should get a sprain and become lame, but rather lest one who was not of the royal stock become king [μὴ οὐκ ὤν τοῦ γένους]." And Plutarch writes as follows: "It mattered not to the god that one who halted in his gait should be king, but if one who was not lawfully begotten, nor even a descendant of Heracles, should be king, this was what the god meant by the 'maimed royalty.' "[17]

In this perspective, let us now examine the series that comprises Labdacus, Laius, Oedipus, and his two sons, Eteocles and Polynices.

Labdacus, the lame one, dies when his son is still a baby, only one year old. The legitimate lineage is broken as the normal link between father and son is cut. The throne is occupied by a stranger, Lucus. Young Laius is not only pushed aside from the throne but is sent away, expelled from Thebes. He takes refuge with Pelops.

When Laius, the left-hander, grows up, he proves to be unbalanced and one-sided both in his sexual relations and his relations with his host. His erotic behavior is rendered deviant by his excessive homosexuality and by the violence to which he subjects the young Chrysippus, Pelops' son, thereby breaking the rules of symmetry and reciprocity that should obtain both between lovers and between guest and host. Chrysippus kills himself. Pelops pronounces a curse against Laius, condemning his race to infertility: The *genos* of the Labdacids is not to be perpetuated.

Laius returns to Thebes, is re-established on the throne and marries Iocasta (or Epicasta). Then he receives a warning from an oracle. He must not have a child. His lineage is condemned to sterility and his race bound to disappear. If he disobeys and engenders a son, this "legitimate" son, instead of resembling his father and carrying on the direct line, will destroy it and sleep with his mother. The *gnēsios*, the well-born son, will turn out to be worse than a *nothos*, beyond even bastardy: He will be a monster.

Laius' sexual relations with his wife are deviant, in the homosexual manner, to avoid producing children. But on one evening of drunkenness, he forgets to take care: He plants a child in the furrow of his wife. This son, at once legitimate yet cursed, is expelled at birth from Thebes, left out on the open slopes of Mount Cithaeron, to die of exposure. But in fact he goes both

less far and further. He escapes death, so remains in the land of
the living; but he is carried away, removed from his proper place,
diverted along a path that marks his foot with the sign of both
his origins and his rejection.[18] He finds himself in Corinth, living with strangers whose son he believes himself to be and bearing a name that at once reflects and conceals the lineage to which
he really belongs and from which he was excluded at birth.

The story of Oedipus concerns his return to his place of origin, his reintegration into the lineage in which he is both a legitimate son and an accursed child. This return takes place, in the
manner of a boomerang, not at the right time, in the correct conditions of a rightful succession that respects the regular order of
the generations, but in all the violence of overidentification: Oedipus does not come duly in his turn to take the place that his father
has vacated and left to him; instead, he takes that place through
parricide and maternal incest. He goes back too far and now finds
himself, as a husband, in the belly that nurtured him as a son, and
from which he should never have emerged.

Two sequences in the story powerfully illuminate these aspects
of the myth. Having emerged from adolescence, the now adult
Oedipus leaves Corinth to escape from those he believes to be
his parents. At the very moment when he begins travelling, by
way of Delphi, to his native Thebes, Laius, moving in the opposite direction, sets out from Thebes for Delphi, to consult the
oracle about the calamity that afflicts his city, to wit, the Sphinx.
The two men meet at a junction of three roads but judge the path
too narrow for them both to pass at once. Instead of proceeding
along the same way, which would have led them each in turn to
occupy the same position – without clash or confusion – father
and son meet, after being forcibly separated, on a path where they
are bound to collide. The two generations of the lame clash instead
of the one succeeding the other. Oedipus kills his father who,
from up in his chariot, falls to the same level as him.

The second sequence relates to the riddle of the Sphinx. First,
let us read one of the versions that Pausanias brought back from

Thebes. It is most valuable from our point of view, since in it the Sphinx is a bastard daughter of Laius, and her role is to test all the monarch's sons in order to distinguish the *nothoi* from the *gnēsioi*[19]:

> There is another version of the story that makes [the Sphinx] the natural daughter of Laius who, because he was fond of her, told her the oracle that was delivered to Cadmus from Delphi. No one, they say, except the kings, knew the oracle. Now Laius (the story goes on to say) had sons by concubines, and the oracle delivered from Delphi applied only to Epicasta and her sons. So when any of her brothers came in order to claim the throne from the Sphinx, she resorted to trickery in dealing with them, saying that if they were the sons of Laius they should know the oracle that came to Cadmus. When they could not answer, she would punish them with death, on the ground that they had no valid claim to the kingdom or to relationship. But Oedipus came because it appears he had been told the oracle in a dream.

Next, we come to the riddle itself. A connection certainly exists between the riddle and ways of walking but, in Oedipus' case, there is even more to it than Lévi-Strauss imagined. In the Sphinx's riddle, man is defined by the way that he moves about, by his gait. The riddle defines him in opposition to all other living creatures, all the animals that move forward and about on land, in the sky, and in the water, that is to say all those that walk, fly, or swim (with four feet, two feet, or no feet).[20] All these creatures are born, grow up, live, and die with a single modality of locomotion. Man is the one to change the way that he moves about, assuming in succession three different gaits: four-footed, two-footed, then three-footed. Man is a being who both remains the same throughout (he has a single voice, *phonē*, a single essence) and also becomes other: Unlike the rest of the animal species, he goes through three different statuses in existence, three "ages": childhood, adulthood, and old age. He must pass through them in succession, each at the appointed time, since each implies a particular social status, a change in his position and role within the group. The human condition is committed to a temporal order because the succession of ages in the life of each individual must be structured in accordance with the sequence of the generations, respecting it and keeping in step with it, so as to avoid a return to chaos.

Oedipus, *Oidipous*, guesses the riddle; he himself is the *dipous*, the man with two feet. But his error, or rather the effect of the curse that affects his lame lineage, is that, through solving the riddle, supplying the question with its answer, he also returns to his place of origin, to his father's throne and his mother's bed. Instead of rendering him like a man who walks straight in life, following on directly in his lineage, his success identifies him with the monster evoked by the Sphinx's words: the being who at one and the same time has two feet, three feet, and four feet, the man who, in his progression through life, does not respect the social and cosmic order of the generations but instead blurs and confuses them. Oedipus, the adult with two feet, is the same as his father, the old man who walks with a stick, the "three-footed" one whose place he has taken as the leader of Thebes and even in Iocasta's bed; he is also the same as his children who crawl on all fours and who are not only his sons but also his brothers.[21]

The two sons he has fathered, Eteocles and Polynices, will not communicate normally either with him or with each other. Oedipus will curse them, just as Pelops cursed Laius. They will clash, just as Oedipus and Laius did, to be united only in the death that each deals the other. Thus, at the end of this long detour marked by the sign of lameness, the Labdacid lineage, instead of proceeding forward in a straight line, returns to its point of departure and is abolished. Laius, the clumsy left-hander, the son of a lame father, can produce no direct, rightful descendants to continue his lineage.

Before moving on to Herodotus, to compare "history" with legend, I should like, in the wake of many others, to formulate a number of questions that this myth tests out in its account of the misfortunes that beset a limping gait, problems that, so to speak, underlie the ground explored by the story.

How can man be a part of what is the same, be firmly rooted in it, if he becomes "other" three times in the course of his existence? How can the permanence of an order be maintained among creatures subjected, at each age of life, to a complete change of status? How can the attributes and functions of king, father, husband, grandfather, and son remain intact, unchanging, when they are successively assumed by other persons and when a single person must become in turn son, father, husband, grandfather, young prince, and old king?

Then again, what are the necessary conditions for a son to follow straight in the wake of his father so as to take his place, sufficiently like his procreator for that place to remain somehow the same, yet sufficiently distinct from him for the replacement of the one by the other not to lead to chaotic confusion?

Now let us see whether this approach can illuminate the way that Herodotus' story is put together at V, 92 and III, 50-4, or shed any light upon the fifth-century Greek image of the figure of the tyrant.

If we are to believe Herodotus, it was to warn the Lacedaemonians and their allies against tyranny, "a thing as unrighteous and bloodthirsty as aught on this earth," that the Corinthian Socles decided to recount an adventure that he was well placed to know about, the story of the Cypselids, the tyrants of his own city. As told by Herodotus, this piece of "history" combines elements of an old wives' tale, a story of marvels, and a tragedy. In the course of an extraordinary sequence of episodes and surprising twists, an inexorable necessity is revealed to be at work. Herodotus states: "It was written that Eetiōn's offspring should be the source of ills for Corinth,"[22] as if the misfortune that the gods had decided was to preside at the heart of the city had to be embodied in this marginal family, both accursed and elect, a lineage of individuals predestined, even before birth, through their deviant origins, to play the role of tyrant.

Up to this point Corinth had been ruled by an oligarchy, the Bacchiads, as the members of the small group that monopolized power were known. In order to keep for themselves the privileges of the royalty that they thus assumed in common, the Bacchiads always intermarried, reserving their daughters for each other and exchanging them within the group, as wives. The Bacchiads thus not only exercised royal power collectively; together, established at the heart of the city, they also represented the, so to speak, collective Father of the royal lineage. Now, one of them had a lame daughter called Labda. None of the Bacchiads were willing to marry her. Labda's infirmity relegated her to the margins of the family to which she belonged. The lame girl was pushed out of the straight line of descent, turned aside from the direct lineage that she should, in normal circumstances, have prolonged. Or perhaps, as Louis Gernet suggested, the terms of the relationship between marriage and lameness should be reversed: "Having married outside her rank, the girl came to be called 'the lame one.' "[23] At all events, whether her lameness prevented her from marrying in accordance with the rules, or her marriage against the rules caused her to be called lame, Labda was disqualified from bearing an authentic Bacchiad, a legitimate son who resembled the father who engendered him and whose true copy he should rightfully have been. In relation to the group of King-Fathers, Labda's son was to inherit a lame birth from his mother.

Rejected by those who would normally have presented their suit, Labda found a Corinthian willing to be her husband, a Lapith by origin, descended from Kaineus. This Kaineus was believed to have been androgynous, both man and woman, like Tiresias. Through his deviant nature, his strangeness, and his ambivalence (an androgynous being might be either effeminate or alternatively a superman), the hermaphrodite could be associated with a kind of lameness in sexual status (an androgynous being was not male on both sides alike, but half man, half woman). This is supported

217

by a fragment of Hesiod that, in relation to another figure, establishes a total equivalence between bisexuality and lameness: According to this text, Pleisthenes, whom Hesiod represents as father of both Agamemnon and Menelaos, was "either hermaphrodite *or* lame."[24]

Like Laius, also in his own way a man who was sexually lame, Labda's husband repaired to Delphi, to consult the oracle on the subject of his line of descent, *peri gonou*, for he had had no children from either Labda or any other woman. Also like Laius, he wanted to find out from the god's own lips whether he would ever be able to have any. Apollo's reply to Laius took the form of a prohibition and threat: You should not have a son; if you do produce one, he will kill you and sleep with his mother. To Labda's husband, Ēetiōn, the god immediately pronounced as follows:

Labda conceiveth anon; and a rolling stone she shall bear thee,
Fated on princes to fall, and execute justice on Corinth.[25]

The lame woman pushed out of the direct lineage gave birth to a child who, rolling and spinning like a stone crashing down a mountainside, eventually reached the place from which, through his mother, he had been removed.[26] And, like a ball bowled in a game of skittles, the return of the one formerly excluded was, unhappily for Corinth, to bring down the *andres mounarchoi*, the grown men, the adults standing on their own two feet (the collective Father), who were also the legitimate masters of power (the Royal Ones).

The analogies with the schema that we have detected in the story of Oedipus are all the more striking in that they are even reinforced by the very differences between the situations of the respective protagonists. In the one case we find a legitimate son, rejected *after his birth* by his true parents and excluded from the royal (and lame) lineage of the Labdacids to which he belongs. When he returns to Thebes, it is in the hope that, by fleeing Corinth, he can save the lives of his false parents who have adopted him as a son and whose legitimate child he believes himself to be, although he is really their adopted son. Those he destroys by returning to Thebes and installing himself in the place and position of his father are his legitimate parents, whom he fails to recognize and so treats as strangers. In the second case, it all happens *before* the child's birth; it is through his mother that the son is excluded, reduced to a lineage that is lame, inferior, and illegitimate, compared to what it should have been. It is with the full agreement of his true, lame parents, whose legitimate son he is, that he later rolls like a stone onto the Fathers who represent the direct lineage in Corinth and who, by relegating him in advance to a lame birth, made of him not their own authentic son but a stranger to that Bacchiad lineage that his return is to destroy.

These initial divergences in the family statuses of the protagonists account for the different treatments of the theme of exposure which, in the historical account and the myth alike, occupies a position of central importance. Oedipus is exposed by his legitimate father and mother, who entrust him to their shepherd, telling him to make sure he dies. The shepherd cannot bring himself to kill the child and hands him on to another shepherd who, in turn, presents him to his masters, the sovereigns of Corinth. The death by exposure, from which he was unexpectedly delivered, is the source of Oedipus' name, a name that is, so to speak, the sign of his destiny since it refers to an infirmity that could be said to be both the mark left upon his body by his rejection and also the mark of his full membership in the lame family of the Labdacids.[27]

No sooner is Labda's child born than he, too, is subjected to a trial that puts one in mind of the exposure of little Oedipus, but does so as it were the other way around, by reversing the terms. The lame mother conceals her child for as long as necessary by hiding him inside an earthenware jar, used as a hive.[28] The purpose of this apparent rejection, this fictitious disappearance of the baby whom it is suddenly impossible to find anywhere in the domestic space, is not the same as that of exposure. The aim is not to send the child far away to be devoured by savage beasts on a wild, deserted mountainside, but on the contrary to preserve him, to save his life by hiding him so that he escapes detection, inside the very house. It is the Bacchiads, the *andres mounarchoi*, the masters of power and of the legitimate lineage, who wish the child dead. Once they have understood the meaning of the oracle delivered to Ēetiōn, they secretly decide to bring about the death of the newborn infant. As soon as Labda has given birth, the collective Father delegates ten of its members to do away with her baby. As they make their way toward the house of the unsuspecting lame mother, the group decides that whoever is first handed the newborn child by the trusting mother must dash it to the ground, on the threshold of the house. But "it had to be" that the lame lineage should bring Corinth its penalty of tears. As luck would have it, "by heaven's providence," as Herodotus puts it,[29] no sooner was the baby placed in the arms of one of the Bacchiads than he smiled and, overcome with pity, the man hurriedly passed him on to the next, who promptly followed suit. The child was thus passed from hand to hand around the whole group of would-be assassins, eventually ending up where he started, back in his mother's arms. The Bacchiads left, but on the doorstep fell to quarrelling, each one blaming all the rest. They decided to return to Labda and complete the murder all together, as a group. But she had heard them through the closed door and had time to hide the child where nobody would think of looking for him, in a *kupselē*, an empty beehive.[30] The Bacchiads ransacked the house but the child could not be found. It was as if he had indeed vanished from the family home.

Thus, the lame woman's son escaped, as Oedipus did, from the death to which he seemed destined. Like Oedipus, he acquired his name from this episode, a name that suggests both the extreme peril surrounding his birth and also his unhoped-for salvation. He was called Cypselus, the child of the *kupselē*.[31] The episode reveals a whole series of convergences between Oedipus and Cypselus. The newborn child escapes death by being passed from hand to hand, from one shepherd to another and on to the king of Corinth, or from one Bacchiad on to all the rest. In both cases, those charged with executing the murder are careful not to reveal what really happened. Like Laius' shepherd, the ten Bacchiads decide not to mention the matter and, claiming their mission to be accomplished, allow it to be believed that the harmful child has been destroyed.

As soon as he has emerged from adolescence and become an adult standing on his own two feet, Oedipus betakes himself to Delphi, questions the oracle regarding his birth and, appalled by its reply, instead of returning to Corinth, travels in the direction of Thebes, whose tyrant he is to become.

At the same stage in his life, as soon as he has reached man's estate, Labda's son also goes to consult the oracle at Delphi. Hailing him as "King of Corinth," the god unequivocally urges him to march on the town and take it. So it is that Cypselus, who is installed as tyrant of Corinth, puts to death a fair number of the *andres mounarchoi.*

But it falls to his son, Periander, to embody the tyrant in his full dimensions. It is fair to say that, in succeeding Cypselus, Periander also fulfills him. It is he who fully accomplishes the tyrannical vocation of his father. Herodotus writes: "Whatever act of slaughter or banishment Cypselus had left undone, that did Periander bring to accomplishment."[32] First he tackles the men. All those who stand the slightest bit taller than the rest are cut down and laid low on the ground, just as Oedipus strikes Laius with his staff, knocking him from his chariot to the ground, at his feet. Next, the women. The Greek tradition represents Periander, the model tyrant, as another Oedipus: He is said to have secretly consummated sexual union with his mother, Crateia.[33] Once the royal fathers are slaughtered, all that remains for the lame woman's descendant to do is sleep in the bed of a mother whose name so clearly proclaims what she represents: sovereignty over a city that the tyrant proceeds to make completely his own.

In Herodotus' account, which does not mention the episode of maternal incest, there is a curious sequence that perhaps occupies an analogous position to it in relation to the murder of the collective Father. Immediately after recalling the fate suffered by the males of the city and the group of Fathers as a whole, remarking that "whatever act of slaughter or banishment Cypselus had left undone, that did Periander bring to accomplishment," Herodotus passes onto the women: "And in a single day, he stripped all the women of Corinth naked, by reason of his own wife, Melissa."[34] By assembling in the temple of Hera the entire female population of the town, free women and servants alike, to strip them of the festive clothes and ornaments that they had donned, the tyrant was undressing the whole of Corinthian womanhood as one, stripping it naked in one fell swoop, in honor of his own deceased wife, as if the entire race of Corinthian women were destined to take the place that the death of his spouse had left vacant at his side.

But tyranny, a lame royalty, cannot succeed for long. The oracle that had given the go-ahead to Cypselus, opening up the path to power before him, had right from the start fixed the limit that could no more be passed by the lineage descended from Labda than by that descended from Laius. The god had proclaimed "Cypselus, son of Ēetiōn, great king of Corinth renowned," but had immediately added: "Happy himself and his sons; yet his sons' sons shall not be happy."[35] By the third generation, the "shock effect" of the "rolling stone" that emerged from Labda's womb could no longer be felt. For the lineage of the lame ones installed on the throne of Corinth, the moment had arrived for their destiny to waver, tip, and plunge into misfortune and death.

This is the reversal of fortune that Herodotus recounts in detail in Book III, in the long excursus that he devotes to the theme of the hostility between Corinth and its colony, Corcyra.[36] I have briefly referred to the disappearance of the lineage of the Labdacids, foretold at the start to Laius and eventually brought about, after Oedipus' temporary promotion, by the tragic deaths of both his sons, each one opposed not only to his father but also to his brother, to be reunited only in death, as they killed each other. Let us now, along with Herodotus, take a closer look at the end of the Cypselids, the descendants of Labda. By his wife Melissa,

Periander too had two sons, of almost the same age. But the two youths had nothing in common.[37] Periander's misfortunes may be summarized as follows: His elder son was close and devoted to him, but was his opposite in that he was slow-witted and thoughtless, lacking concentration, and unable to communicate with himself in his own mind, for he had no memory. His younger brother was just like Periander in that he was intelligent, determined, and possessed a precise and reliable memory, but he refused to communicate with his father; he would not address a word to him, never even answer him. On the one hand, a blank memory, on the other silence. In both cases the channels of communication were blocked for Labda's descendants.

The drama began with the death of Melissa whom Periander beat to death in a rage. The boys' maternal grandfather, Procles, the tyrant of Epidaurus, sent for them and treated them with the greatest affection. Before returning them to Corinth, he asked: "Know you, boys, him who slew your mother?" The elder paid no heed to the words; not understanding them, he put them out of his mind and forgot them.[38] The younger, Lycophron, was so horrified by the revelation that, back in Corinth, where he regarded his father as his mother's murderer, he refused to say another word to him: "nor would he answer him when addressed or make any reply to his questions."[39] Periander was so angry that he drove the boy from the palace.

By persistently questioning the son who was incapable of "understanding" and remembering, Periander at last himself managed to "understand" what was bothering his younger child.[40] He thereupon forbade anyone to give this son shelter in their homes. Everybody was to drive him away. Lycophron's refusal to communicate with his father turned him into an outlaw within his own city, ejected wherever he turned, a being with neither hearth nor home, a child spurned by his own family. But Lycophron's status was ambiguous. Although Periander's orders placed him in the position of one who was *apolis*, forced into solitude, cut off from all social connections, his legitimate birth neverthe-

223

less marked him out as his father's successor as tyrant. It pointed him toward the leadership of the city, a position as high above the common run as his condition as one excluded was below it. So, "though they were afraid," people "did yet receive him, as being Periander's son."[41]

To eject Lycophron from his refuges, Periander had his herald proclaim that whoever gave him a welcome or even conversed with him would be liable to a heavy fine. Nobody would even speak to the young man now. Stubborn as he was, Lycophron accepted this state of total isolation and noncommunication. Through having refused to follow his father along the straight path toward a succession that would lead him to his proper place, in the palace, he wandered about, reeling from one side to another, to "lie untended in porches."[42] The grandson of Cypselus, the rolling stone whose momentum crushed the royal Fathers in its path, was now himself a rolling stone, but in his case one like the subject of our own proverb about the misfortunes of anyone who cannot remain still, the "rolling stone that gathers no moss."

Lycophron was by now starving to death. One day Periander encountered him, filthy and at his last gasp. His anger cooled and he asked his son which of the two was preferable, tyranny or the life of a vagrant (ἀλήτην βίον): "You are my son," he told him, "and a prince of wealthy Corinth, ...come away to my house."[43] But the boy's only reply was that his father must now pay the fine for having spoken to him.

As one expells a *pharmakos*, Periander then sent his son away to Corcyra, out of sight (ἐξ ὀφθαλμῶν μιν ἀποπέμπεται).[44] In this story, the tyrant does not put his eyes out so as not to see, as Oedipus did; he expells his son so as not to have to look upon him.

But times change, as men do. As the years passed (Ἐπεὶ δὲ τοῦ χρόνου προβαίνοντος),[45] Periander grew old. Now, the two-footed man was three-footed: He no longer felt strong enough to carry the responsibilities of power. The time had come to make way for his son. The elder son would not do; his limping mind could not move fast enough; he was too slow (νωθέστερος)[46] to follow in his father's footsteps. So Periander dispatched to his younger son first a messenger, then his sister, to persuade him to return to Corinth and there assume his rightful place. His sister told him: "Despotism is a thing hard to hold [unstable: χρῆμα σφαλερόν]; many covet it and our father is now old and past his prime; give not what is your estate to others."[47] But Lycophron was adamant: He would not return to Corinth so long as he knew his father was still living there. His decision resembles that taken by Oedipus at Delphi, when he swore never to set foot again in Corinth so long as his father remained alive: similar decisions, with the difference that the father whose presence Oedipus shunned — out of affection, not hatred — was in reality a stranger and, in avoiding that false parent, Oedipus crossed the path of another stranger with whom he clashed violently, a stranger who was in fact his true father.

To overcome his son's resistance, Periander then suggested a solution that should have resolved this difficult problem of succession between two individuals linked by the closest ties of kinship but set totally apart by both their feelings and their places of residence, and that should also have avoided the misfortunes encountered by the Labdacid lineage. Through a third messenger, the tyrant proposed that he and his son should exchange positions, with no danger of meeting. Without ever finding themselves on the same spot, Lycophron should return to Corinth, there to take over the tyranny, while Periander would move to Corcyra and settle there forever. Lycophron agreed to this deal. Everything was now apparently resolved, through this switch-over: The legitimate son would, at the appointed time be restored to his rightful place, on his father's throne; and the young man and the old man, always radically set apart from each other, would have no occasion to meet in confrontation, clashing, as Oedipus, on his way back to his native land, clashed with Laius travelling the same path in the opposite direction.[48]

Everything seemed to be satisfactorily, "logically" arranged. But an oracle remains an oracle: The Pythia had decreed: "Cypselus

Eētides, great King of Corinth renowned, Happy himself and his sons; yet his sons' sons shall not be happy." At the last moment, the people of Corcyra, who had got wind of the plan, killed the son so as not to have to receive his father in his place. Labda's lineage, like that of Labdacus, was obliterated instead of carrying on the direct line through successive generations.

What conclusion should we draw from this strange parallelism between the destiny of the Labdacids of legendary Thebes and that of the Cypselids of historical Corinth? In his "Mariages de tyrans" Louis Gernet pointed out that, innovator though he may have been, a tyrant was a "natural" product of the past: "His excesses had their models in legends."[49] Those are the models that orient Herodotus' narrative from start to finish. When the father of history reports, as facts, the events that established a lineage of tyrants as the leaders of Corinth, he "naturally" mythologizes and his account accordingly lends itself to a type of analysis similar to that which may be applied to the legend of Oedipus. Gernet goes on to remark, precisely in connection with Corinth: "From the perspective of the legend, tyranny could only be the result of a disruptive marriage."[50] There is a reason to explain why Herodotus should use and so closely connect the themes that we have detected in the saga of the Labdacids: lameness, tyranny, power won and lost, the continued or blocked sequence of generations, direct or deviated succession, the correct or deviant nature of sexual relations, agreement or misunderstanding in communications between fathers and sons and between one son and another, alertness of mind or lack of recall. The reason is that in the way that the Greeks imagined the figure of the tyrant, as projected in the fifth and fourth centuries, he took on the features of the hero of legend, an individual at once elect yet accursed. By rejecting all the rules that the Greeks regarded as the basis for communal life, the tyrant placed himself beyond the social pale. He was outside the network of relations that, in accordance with a series of strict norms, connected one citizen with another, a husband with a wife, a father with a son. For better or worse, he withdrew from the channels through which individuals establish communications with one another and establish themselves as ordered communities. The wayward, solitary path along which the tyrant, rejecting the beaten track and the posted route, ventures, exiles him far from the city of men, with its regulated forms of exchange and reciprocal contacts, relegating him to an isolation comparable both to that of a god, who is too far above men to come down to their level, and to that of a wild beast, so dominated by its appetites that it can brook no restraint.[51] The tyrant despises the rules that control the ordering of the social fabric and, through its regularly woven mesh, determine the position of each individual in relation to all the rest, in other words — to put it more crudely, as Plato does — he is perfectly prepared to kill his father, sleep with his mother, and devour the flesh of his own children.[52] Like both a god[53] and a wild beast, he is, in his ambivalence, the very incarnation of the mythical representation of lameness with its two contrary aspects: Because his progress is superior to human gait in that, as it rolls, it encompasses every direction at once more quickly and with more agility, he overcomes the limitations that affect a straight way of walking, but at the same time his gait falls short of the normal modalities of locomotion in that, mutilated, unbalanced, and wavering as it is, he stumbles along in his own particular fashion only to fall the more definitively in the end.

Postscript

I. *A Rumanian Oedipus*

In an attempt to shed light upon the relations that ancient Greek myth establishes between lameness, parricide, and incest, we have compared Oedipus, the tyrant of Attic tragedy, and Periander, a tyrant from the history of Corinth. Now we should like to add to this "classical" dossier a new and quite different piece of evidence. It is popular in nature, drawn from Rumanian folklore. We owe our discovery of it to the friendship of Dr. Paul Galmiche, a great expert on podology, whose interests and expertise are by no means limited to the field of medicine. He kindly brought to our notice the text of a cantilena, published in Bucharest in 1967 in the volume of *Chants d'autrefois* collected and edited by Cristea Sandra Timoc. An English version based on the French translation by Mme C. Lemaire, whom we most warmly thank, is given at the end of this study.

At first sight, the Rumanian tale may appear quite unrelated to the Greek legend: The general tone, setting, actors, circumstances, and changes of fortune are different, as is its happy ending. But one does not have to be very learned to recognize it immediately as a derived version of the myth of Oedipus. The essential elements of the adventure – what one might call the hard kernel of the fable, which provides the mainspring of the plot – remain intact, perfectly preserved. We find ourselves not in Thebes or Corinth, but in a country hamlet so tiny that it is invisible, nestling unnamed among the greenery. There is no princely lineage, no royal palace: just the cottage of a peasant who possesses a vineyard. No Apollo, no Delphic oracle; instead, three fairies, who take over from the midwives and watch over the child's birth. It is they who, on the third day, appear to the mother in a dream, to warn her of the destiny that awaits the newborn child: Without knowing it or wishing to do so, this son will kill his father, sleep with his mother and "thunder" in the house, ruling there as a sovereign lord.

Being thus warned of the misfortunes that threaten them, the parents, rather than kill the child, shut him in a barrel that the father then kicks over, sending it "rolling" away to the Danube. Exposed in this fashion, in his round, floating prison of wood, like so many Greek heroes delivered over to the mercy of the waves at birth, inside a *larnax* (a wooden chest, serving as an ark), the child is washed down the river. Boatmen notice him, take him in and rear him. On reaching manhood, he takes to the road. As he passes through his native village, he meets a stranger – his father – who asks him why he is on the move in this way. He says he is looking for somewhere to settle down. The man gives him work on his land, employing him to guard his vineyard. The boy's job is to keep watch each night, with a rifle, and to fire at anyone who approaches without light before cock-crow. For a month, all goes well. But one fine night, the master inadvertently approaches without brandishing a light. Obeying his instructions to the letter, the son takes aim, fires, and lays him low with the first shot. The dead victim is buried. Two weeks pass, with no male in the house or conjugal bed. When this period has elapsed, the widow invites the young man to come and take her husband's place. He accepts at once, only too happy to put down roots and find a home after all his wanderings. On the wedding night, mother and son thus find themselves in bed together, about to be united physically as man and wife. Fortunately, however, just before making love they exchange a few words and begin to talk. Immediately, they recognize their true relationship to each other: She is his mother, he her son. Although the parricide came to pass, maternal incest is thus narrowly avoided. Despite being married, the couple never physically consummate the forbidden union. The two generations find one another again, they are reunited and live together, but without thereby being sinfully defiled. The son-husband can honorably take care of his mother for the rest of her life and "reign" unchallenged over all the household wealth.

So this is an "optimistic" version, respecting the force of the censure applied to sexual union with one's mother that the Greek myth disregarded. But the euphemistic nature of the story makes no difference to the fundamental structure of the legend. The entire plot, from the rejection of the newborn child up to his return to his family as a man, revolves around the closely overlapping themes of the father's murder, maternal incest, and the conquest of power – even though, in this peasant context, the power is domestic rather than royal and political.

The Rumanian tale also preserves one other feature. This takes on all the more significance given that, in the new version, it is so unexpected that one might be tempted to dismiss it as an inauthentic addition or a gratuitous detail were it not for the fact that the combined stories of Oedipus and Periander have already underlined its place in the organization of the myth. The barrel is introduced in the very first sequence. Its presence in the house of a grower of vines is, to be sure, perfectly normal. But as it rolls down the slopes to the waters of the Danube, taking the child from the house of his birth as it spins away, removing him from the home where, in normal circumstances, he would have grown up to follow in his father's footsteps, this barrel, which foretells and prepares for a sudden and dangerous return, surely puts one in mind of the "rolling stone" to which Labda, the lame one, gives birth, the rolling stone that will return without warning, like a boomerang, to knock down the royal Fathers of Corinth. At the end of the narrative, the analogy is explicitly confirmed. As they talk together, lying in the same bed, the mother recognizes her son from his bowed, hoop-shaped legs. How did the young man acquire this deformation of the limbs that determines his way of walking, limbs which, in his case, are bowed instead of straight? The answer is made quite clear in the text. It is because, instead of being swaddled – that is to say kept closely wrapped at the heart of the family space, entirely dependent upon his procreators whom he should succeed at the appointed time – the child was immediately placed inside a circular barrel. His first means of locomotion was "rolling" around in the barrel, adopting the revolving movement that at the start of his life carried him away from the house where, to become rooted there, he should have remained swaddled in his cradle. Having rolled away in this barrel, which tore him at birth from his home and parents, to return to them he would have to limp along a winding way, turning, at the crossroads, into paths that led to parricide and incest.

II. *The Song of the Fairies*[54]
 In the spinach green that blankets
 The banks of the Talıgrad,
 Lies a tiny village,
 So small it can't be seen.
 But there in the tiny village
 There once lived a young bride.
 After her winter marriage,
 Her happy moment came:
 She gave birth to a child.
 She sent off for the midwives
 To come and tend the infant,
 As usually happens.
 Three days after the birth,
 She beheld the fairies.[55]
 But what happened that night?
 Behold, the woman dreamed,
 As if it were the truth,
 That three women came to her
 And the eldest of them said:
 "If this child grows up,
 May he die from a rifle shot
 And crumple into two."
 But the youngest told her:
 "When this child grows up,
 He will take his mother
 To be a wife to him
 And will thunder in his house."
 But hearing this, the woman
 When the morning came,
 Told her husband of the dream
 And the mystery before them.
 Hearing her, the husband
 Seized his gun and aimed,
 Ready to shoot, by God!

To kill the child, my brother!
But realizing this, the wife,
With open mouth, cried out:
"Hey, my man, not like that.
Do you know what we must do?
We'll put him in a barrel
And then we'll kick it over
And dispatch it to the Danube
With no more cause to worry."
At these words, the husband
Climbed up to the loft
And there he chose a barrel,
Big as about two buckets.
He just knocked out the bottom,
Took hold of the child,
Did not even swaddle him,
And laid him in the barrel.
Then he put the bottom back
And kicked it to the Danube.
Off floated the barrel,
Down the stream it went
For three whole days and nights
Till close to a little village,
There it was by chance
That some barges lay at rest.
But then the boatmen saw it
And they leaped into a boat
And soon they caught the barrel
And put it on a barge
And when they removed the bottom,
Good God, what did they see?
The child in there was living still
And the boatmen took him out
And brought him up on milk.
He grew one day, he grew the next

And at last was seventeen.
Then the boatmen said to him:
"Now boy, now listen well.
Look, this is how it happened:
You must know that we found you
In an abandoned barrel
Tossed into the Danube.
Until this day, we raised you
As well as we could manage
But the time has come to leave:
Go off and find new paths to tread
And look for work somewhere.
You must find work on your own
In this world, if you're to live."
But when he heard the words they spake
The boy began to cry, for he had no one of his own
In the whole wide world.
He walked from village to village,
And at last he reached his own
And there he met his father.
But the father did not know his son
And the boy knew not his father.
His father put this question, then:
"My good lad, my friend,
Why is it that you're walking thus?"
And the boy made answer to him:
"Well, I'll tell you, uncle,
I want to find a place,
A place where I can be of use
In this world, so that I can live
And earn, to clothe myself."
On hearing this, the father said:
"If that is your concern,
Then come along now to my house
And we will do a deal,

All set up fair and square.
I will pay you what you ask
If you but guard my vines.
If anybody comes along
Before the cock's first crow
And looms up in my vineyard,
You at once must shoot him;
I leave it all to you."
He put a rifle in his hand
And led him to the vineyard.
He watched one day, he watched the next,
He watched for one whole month,
And when his master brought him food,
He always brought a lantern.
But one day he was later,
Detained by all his tasks.
At last he took the supper,
Before the cock's first crow.
As soon as the boy saw him come,
Mindful of his task,
He aimed his rifle at him
And fired a single shot
Which laid his father low.
At the break of day,
He saw it was his master.
He hurried to the village,
Running down the valley
And said there to his mother:
"My mistress, in the night
I fired upon my master.
He did not signal me
When he came among the vines!"
On hearing this, the wife
Fetched her husband's corpse
And buried it in style.

Two weeks passed away,
Then said the wife to him:
"You, my boy, till now
Have served as my farmhand
But now you'll be my husband."
On hearing this, the boy
Was very pleased indeed
For he was very poor
And had no one in the world.
Now he was to stay.
And when the evening came,
He leaped promptly into bed.
The Good God really urged them on.
Yet his wife spoke to him:
"Now wait, my boy, let's see,
And find out who we are
For we are too alike."
The boy replied to her:
"Ah, wife, wife! What am I?
Some boatman fished me out
As I floated down the Danube
In an old abandoned barrel.
That was where they found me
And they kindly brought me up."
But when the mother heard him,
She opened her mouth and said:
"Alas for me! What sin!
For you have wed your mother!
Your legs have grown so curved
Because mama never wrapped you
But put you in a barrel."
"Never mind, my mother,
For now we are together.
The good God has protected us
And we have done no sin!"

235

And so he lived on there
And took care of his mother
And reigned there over all the wealth,
Unstained in heaven's sight.
Ah, Good God, let this tale be told
As long as the sun shines down.

Jean-Pierre Vernant

CHAPTER XI

The Tragic Subject:

Historicity and Transhistoricity*

Of all the literary genres that Greece bequeathed us, tragedy is surely the one that best illustrates the paradox that Marx, in the Introduction to his *Critique of Political Economy*,[1] formulated on the subject of Greek art in general and the epic in particular. If it is true that works of art, like any other social products, are connected with a specific historical context and that their genesis, structures, and meaning can only be understood within and through that context, how is it that they remain alive and continue to communicate with us when the forms of that social life have been transformed at every level and the conditions necessary for their production have disappeared? To put it another way, how can one claim that the tragic works and genre are historical if one also recognizes their transhistoricity, the fact that they have survived across the centuries?

Let us recall the much-quoted terms in which Marx put it: "But the difficulty is not in grasping that Greek art and epos are bound up with certain forms of social development. It rather lies in understanding why they still constitute with us a source of aesthetic enjoyment and in certain respects prevail as the standard and model beyond attainment."[2]

Marx posed the problem in passing. He was not really concerned with art. It was not central to his thought. Marx made no attempt to found a system of Marxist aesthetics. In this passage, he was simply out to make the point that an "unequal rela-

237

tion"[3] exists among the general development of a society, the expansion of material production, and art. The highest, and most exemplary, forms of art may arise in relatively undeveloped or even the least developed societies.

In relation to the ideology of his own times, Marx's suggested solution to the problem was neither original nor particularly Marxist. For Marx, as for all educated individuals of his generation in Germany, Greece was the cradle of humanity. Marx was well aware that, outside Greece and even earlier than it, there had been other civilizations, other cradles. But as he saw it, none of those beginnings, none of those first steps so typically represented the infancy of humanity, which was bound in the course of its normal development to pass through a series of successive ages. Marx observed that there are some children who are badly brought up, others who are precocious, and that many peoples belonged to those two categories. But the Greeks were "normal" children.[4] And Marx suggested that their art's attraction for us stems from the naivety and spontaneity peculiar to the nature of healthy youth and from the charm of a well-balanced child, which attracts and delights the adult because in it he detects the promise of what he himself has become in his maturity, a phase of his own life now all the more precious to him because it has gone forever.

Today, nobody could accept Marx's solution to the problem. Why should the Greeks represent the childhood of humanity? Why should that childhood be any more healthy or "normal" than that of the Chinese, the Egyptians, the Babylonians, or the Africans? Besides, is it really its childlike quality, the naivety and naturalness, that attracts us in Greek tragedy, in Euripides' *Bacchae*, for example? Can we possibly claim that it is a normal, childlike quality that attracts us in Plato's *Symposium, Timaeus, Parmenides*, or *Republic*? If so, we are bound to recognize that this was a singularly advanced and sophisticated childhood.

All the same, some of Marx's remarks should help us to tackle this problem of the extent to which art is historical and the extent to which it is transhistorical. In another of his works,[5] he notes that man is the only animal in which the senses (sight, hearing, smell, etc.) result not only from the biological evolution of the species but also from its social and cultural history, in particular the history of each of the various arts in all their specificity, as they operate within their own particular fields. Painting creates objects with plastic shape and form, the products of, as it were, an exploration of the visual domain: a world of forms, colors, tones, expressing light and movement. Music creates a world organized by sounds, harmonies, dissonances, rhythms. Similarly, the linguistic arts, each one in its own sector, attempt to express certain levels of human reality in a literary form.

Marx writes: "The *forming* of the five senses is a labor of the entire history of the world down to the present."[6] "The eye has become a human eye, just as its *object* has become a social, *human* object — an object made by man for man."[7] In other words, the eye became human when products were created for members of the social group to look at, objects to be seen. This means that, quite apart from their practical interest, their "use value," there was an aesthetic dimension to them or, as Marx puts it, they were beautiful to behold. Marx goes on to say: "The senses have therefore become directly in their practice *theoreticians*."[8] His way of putting it is astonishingly modern. Applying this to the field of painting, we may say that the eye of the painter, in conjunction with his hand, sets up an architecture of forms, a language of figurative and colored geometry that, while totally different from the language of mathematics, nevertheless, in its own way and within its own register, explores the visual field with all its possibilities and rules of compatibility and incompatibility; in short, it constitutes a body of knowledge, a kind of experimentation within the domain of optics. To go back to Marx's formula, just as man's musical sense is only aroused by music, his sense of shape and form develops and changes in and through the practice of picture-making. The richness of vision and the specific forms that it takes within the framework of a particular civilization go hand in hand with the way that the figurative arts have developed there, and depend upon their orientation.

Marx also states: "Only through the objectively unfolded richness of man's essential being is the richness of subjective *human* sensibility (a musical ear, an eye for beauty of form — in short, senses capable of human gratification, senses affirming themselves as essential powers of man) either cultivated or brought into being."[9] Then come the following essential lines: "For not only the five senses but also the so-called mental senses — the practical senses (will, love, etc.) — in a word, *human* sense — the human nature of the senses — comes to be by virtue of its object [Marx means an object "made by man for man"], by virtue of humanized nature."[10] Humanized nature means this world of products, particularly works of art, that at each moment of history constitute the framework for every type of human activity.

All that Marx says of the relation between the hand and the work, namely that the hand creates the work but the work also creates the hand, since the hand is both the organ and the product of the work, he more or less repeats in connection with art and its works: "The object of art, as well as any other product, creates an artistic and beauty-enjoying public."[11] In art, production produces not only an "object for the subject" but also "a subject for the object"[12] — for the new object just created.

The invention of Greek tragedy, in fifth-century Athens, amounted to more than just the production of the literary works themselves, objects for spiritual consumption designed for the citizens and adapted to them; through the spectacle, reading, imitation, and establishment of a literary tradition, it also involved the creation of a "subject," a tragic consciousness, the introduction of tragic man. Similarly, the works of the Athenian dramatists express and elaborate a tragic vision, a new way for man to understand himself and take up his position in relation to the world, the gods, other people, himself, and his own actions. Just as there can be no musical art without music and its historical development, there is no tragic vision outside tragedy and the tradition of the literary genre that it founded.

In this respect, the status of Greek tragedy would seem to be comparable to that of a science such as Euclidian geometry or an intellectual discipline such as philosophy as established by Plato and Aristotle, when they founded their schools. Euclid's oeuvre consists of texts, conditioned and marked by the date when they were produced; but it also comprises a field of studies that starts somewhere and ends somewhere, the constitution of a new object, to wit, space seen as an idealized abstraction — together with a mode of demonstration and reasoning, that is to say a specifically mathematical language: in short, a realm of reality, a new type of mental operation, intellectual tools hitherto undiscovered. Plato and Aristotle, the Academy and the Lyceum, introduced a new practice of philosophy and a whole horizon of new problems to go with it: what is being, what is knowing, what is the relation between the two? They also established a new vocabulary, a type of discourse, a mode of argument, philosophical thought. Even today, to philosophize presupposes becoming a part of that tradition, placing oneself within the bounds of the intellectual horizon revealed by the development of philosophy, no doubt to expand, modify, or question it, but always by entering its tradition, taking up problems at the point to which they have been elaborated by earlier philosophers. Just as painters look at, not "nature," but the works of art of the Old Masters and those of their contemporaries, so philosophers respond to those who have gone before them; their thinking is done in relation to them, to counter them or in an attempt to solve difficulties that earlier reflection has revealed in the field of philosophical research.

In similar fashion, if it is legitimate to refer to the plays of Shakespeare and Racine and certain contemporary works as tragedies, that is because, despite the displacements and changes in perspective that are connected with their historical contexts, they are rooted in the tradition of ancient Greek theater. There, already sketched in, they found the human and aesthetic framework peculiar to the type of drama that introduced and gave full expression to the tragic consciousness.

What can be said of this "tragic man," born in Athens on the theater stage in the fifth century B.C.? By what features should we characterize him, both in his historicity and his transhistoricity? For that brief moment in which he emerged and established himself with the great Attic dramatists sufficed to mark out within Western culture a domain in which it was henceforth possible for anyone to come through the tragic experience, understanding it and living it within himself.

Following that lengthy introduction, I shall limit myself to two points. I need do no more than mention the first, as I have dwelt upon it at length elsewhere.[13] Tragedy takes heroic legend as its material. It invents neither the characters nor the plots of its plays. It finds them in the Greeks' shared knowledge concerning what they believe to be their past, the far horizon of the men of former times. But within the space of the stage and the framework of tragic representation, the hero is no longer put forward as a model, as he used to be in epic and in lyric poetry. Now he has become a problem. Now, as the action unfolds and through the interplay of the dialogue, what used to be praised as an ideal, the touchstone of excellence, is brought into question before the public. The hero becomes the subject of a debate and interrogation that, through his person, implicates the fifth-century spectator, the citizen of democratic Athens. From the point of view of tragedy, human beings and human action are seen, not as realities to be pinned down and defined in their essential qualities, in the manner of the philosophers of the succeeding century, but as problems that defy resolution, riddles with double meanings that are never fully decoded.

The second point is the following: Tragedy played a decisive role in man's apprehension of "fiction," in the strictest sense of the term. It was this that made it possible for a Greek poet, at the turn of the fifth to fourth centuries, to see himself purely as an imitator, the creator of a world of reflections, illusions, pretences, and fables, all of which constituted a world of fiction, alongside the world of reality. By elaborating a theory of *mimēsis*,[14] or imitation, that was closely linked with the new experience afforded by the tragic spectacle, Plato and Aristotle set out to determine the status, place, and function of what we today refer to as art, or "the imaginary." In the epic tradition, the poet, inspired by the muses and acting as their prophet, did not imitate reality; he unveiled it, in the manner of a diviner declaring "what is, was, and is to be." His words did not represent being but rendered it present. What of tragedy? It sets before the public's eyes legendary figures from the heroic age, making them speak and act as the spectators look on. As I have pointed out, neither the characters nor their destinies are fictitious to the Greek audience. They really have existed, but in other times, in an age now gone forever. They are men of the past belonging to a sphere of existence quite different from that of the audience. By being set on stage, they are made to seem present, characters truly there, although at the same time they are portrayed as figures who cannot possibly be there since they belong to somewhere else, to an invisible beyond. What the public sees before it in the theater is not a poet recounting the trials withstood in ancient times by men now gone whose absence is, so to speak, implied by the very narration. Instead, those trials take place before its very eyes, adopting the form of real existence in the immediacy of the performance. The tragic poet becomes totally invisible behind the characters on stage, acting and speaking for themselves as if alive. In Plato's analysis, it is this directness of speech and action that constitutes the essence of *mimēsis*: Instead of speaking in his own name and recounting events indirectly, the author disappears inside the protagonists and apes them by taking on their appearance, manners, feelings, and words. The precise meaning of *mimeisthai*, to imitate, is to simulate the presence of one who is absent. Faced with such a representation, there are only two possible responses. The first puts one in mind of the earliest cinema spectators, when the seventh art was in its infancy. Totally unaccustomed to it, as they were, and not having had time to develop what might be called a consciousness of fiction or a way of reacting to the imaginary, they would boo the villains and cheer on and applaud the good guys on the screen, as if the shadows flickering there were living beings of flesh and blood; they mistook the spectacle for reality. The second response is to enter into the game, understanding that what can be seen on the stage belongs not to the plane of reality, but to what must be defined as the plane of theatrical illusion. A consciousness of the fiction is essential to the dramatic spectacle; it seems to be both its condition and its product.

That being so, it becomes easier to understand the significance and implications of a singular feature of Greek tragedy. Throughout the fifth century, it confined itself to the field that it had, to some extent, made its own: that of heroic legend. It might have happened otherwise, as is proved by the fact that in 494 one of the very first plays in the tragic repertory, *The Fall of Miletus*, by the poet Phrynicus, staged a disaster that the Persians had inflicted upon the Ionian city of Miletus only two years earlier. This was not a legendary but a historic tragedy, one might even say a tragedy of contemporary events. Consider Herodotus' account of its reception: "The whole theater broke into weeping; and they fined Phrynicus a thousand drachmae for bringing to mind national calamities [οἰκήια κακά], their own that touched them so nearly, and forbade forever the acting of that play."[15] At the dawn of the fifth century, when tragedy was taking its first steps, the great events of the time, the dramas of collective life, the misfortunes that affected each and every citizen were not considered suitable for the theater stage. They were too close, did not allow for the distancing, the transposition that made it possible for feelings of pity and terror to be displaced into a different register, no longer experienced in the same way as in real life, but immediately apprehended and understood as fiction.

But what of *The Persians*? It is true that in 472 Aeschylus put on a tragedy that presented the defeat the barbarians had suffered at Salamis, eight years earlier. Aeschylus had taken part in the battle in person, as had some of the audience, and the *choregos* in charge of the production was none other than Pericles. But the point is that what strikes one in *The Persians* is, in the first place, that the misfortunes that constitute the kernel of the plot could not be seen as their own by the Greek public. It is others, foreigners, who are affected by these strange misfortunes. Second, by placing himself among the Persians and adopting their point of view, the tragic poet made up for the absence of the customary gap set between the audience and the happenings of a long-gone legendary age by introducing a distance of a different kind, spatial this time, a cultural separation that made it possible to assimilate the Persian kings and their court to the world of the heroes of the past. The "historic" events evoked by the chorus, recounted by the messenger and interpreted by Darius' ghost are presented on stage in a legendary atmosphere. The light that the tragedy sheds upon them is not that in which the political happenings of the day are normally seen; it reaches the Athenian theater refracted from a distant world of elsewhere, making what is absent seem present and visible on the stage.

What the Greeks called history, the inquiry into conflicts between cities, within cities, or between Greeks and barbarians was a matter for Herodotus or Thucydides. Tragedy found its material elsewhere, in the legends of the past. By refusing to place itself on the level of contemporary events and current political life, it acquired in Aristotle's eyes not less but more value, more truth than history.[16] To present current events on stage would amount to no more than recounting what was happening. Producing a tragedy was a completely different undertaking. It was not a matter of inventing imaginary characters or devising a plot that took one's fancy. It meant using the names and destinies of universally known figures regarded as models, to construct a scenario, an arrangement of selected scenes in such a way as to show how and why such-and-such a character, being what he was, was likely, or even bound to take such-and-such an action that would lead to such-and-such a result. Out of all the events that might have happened, history recounts those that actually did take place. By dint of reorganizing its legendary subject matter according to its own criteria and organizing the development of the plot in accordance with the logic of probability or necessity, tragedy, in contrast, shows how, in the strict course of things, human events may or must come about. In the mind of the philosopher comparing it to history, tragedy thus appeared as a more serious and philosophical creation. Thanks to the freedom afforded it by the fiction of the *muthos*, it could acquire a general significance, whereas history, through the nature of its subject matter, was limited to the particular. This general significance of tragedy stemmed from the fact that in the logic of the action, the kind of man whose particular destiny the poet chose to submit to the test of the tragic process appeared as being obliged "in all probability or necessity" to behave as he did.

Because the subject dramatized by the tragedy is a fiction, the effect produced by the painful or terrifying events that it presents on stage is quite different from what it would be if those events were real. They touch and concern us, but only from a distance. They are happening somewhere else, not in real life. Because they only exist on an imaginary level, they are set at a distance even as they are represented. Their effect upon the public, which remains uninvolved, is to "purify"[17] the feelings of fear and pity that they would arouse in real life. The events are conveyed through a drama that has a beginning and an end, sequences linked in an organized fashion, episodes arranged as a coherent whole, and an overall formal unity. Because of that, instead of simply arousing the emotions of pity and fear, they confer upon them an intelligibility that would be lacking in real life. Once the opacity that belongs to particular, accidental incidents is dispelled by the logic of a scenario that purifies by dint of simplifying, condensing, and systematizing, human sufferings normally either simply deplored or undergone are now seen in the mirror of tragic fiction and become comprehensible. Although they are connected with individual characters and events and with the particular historical and social framework that surrounds them, they acquire a much wider resonance and significance.

Ancient drama explores the mechanisms through which an individual, however excellent he may be, is brought to his downfall, not as the result of external constraints or his own perversity or vices, but because of an error, a mistake such as anyone might make. In this way, it lays bare the network of contradictory forces that assail all human beings, given that, not only in Greek society but in all societies and cultures, tensions and conflicts are inevitable. By these means, tragedy prompts the spectator to submit the human condition, limited and necessarily finite as it is, to a general interrogation. The scope of tragedy is such that it carries within itself a kind of knowledge or a theory concerning the illogical logic that governs the order of human activities. Tragedy is created through the production of a scenario, that is to say the representation and dramatized development of an imaginary experience or – as Aristotle puts it[18] – through a *mimēsis praxeōs*, the simulation of a coherent sequence of actions leading to disaster. Through this, human beings accede to an inspired yet lucid realization of the irreplaceable value of their existence and also its extreme vanity.

Jean-Pierre Vernant

CHAPTER XII

Aeschylus, the Past and the Present*

Sets: Of Tragic Poets and Others

In 405 B.C., shortly after the deaths of Euripides and Sophocles, Aristophanes represented Dionysus visiting the underworld in the company of a chorus of frogs, to bring back the foremost of the tragic poets. The competition or *agōn* is played out between Aeschylus and Euripides; Sophocles remains in the background, but takes second place. The competition is more complex than it seems: Aristophanes pronounces Aeschylus the victor and pours scorn upon Euripides, yet it is Euripides who is present in almost every line of Aristophanes' verse, and the latter's literary preference was to be shared by the fourth century and the Hellenistic-Roman period.

Aeschylus, Sophocles, and Euripides. That is the canonical sequence, in order of age: The ancient Greeks, slightly forcing the dates, liked to say that when the battle of Salamis (480) was taking place, Aeschylus (born in about 525) was fighting, Sophocles (born in 496 or 495) was singing the paeon, and Euripides (born about 485) was being born. So the canonical order is no modern creation and Aristophanes' judgment made its mark. In the next century, Lycurgus had a law passed that "laid down that bronze effigies be made of the poets Aeschylus, Sophocles, and Euripides and that their tragedies be transcribed and copies kept in the archives so that the city secretary could have actors read them, forbidding them to alter the text when they performed the play."[1] These are honors comparable to those that the city granted, for the most part during the classical and Hellenistic periods, to its benefactors (*euergetai*). But this does not mean that the tragic poets are always represented by that triad of names. For example, surprisingly enough, it is not, strictly speaking, to be found in Aristotle's *Poetics*, a work that was to remain influential for centuries. The only chapter in which those three tragic writers are mentioned together also refers to Agathon (the late fifth-century writer well known from his appearance in Plato's *Symposium*). Euripides is far and away the most often cited author, while Aeschylus receives no more mentions than Agathon; and Aristotle also refers to many other tragic poets whose works have completely disappeared.

In 264 B.C., in the city of Paros in the Cyclades, a chronicle of Greek — essentially Athenian — history was engraved on marble. It covered the period stretching from the reign of Cecrops, placed at 1581, down to the archontate of Diognetes in Athens (264) and it included many dates that might be described as "cultural." Apart from Thespis, the creator of tragedy, the only tragedians mentioned are the three major poets. Euripides' first victory in the tragic competition (442) is mentioned immediately after the death of Aeschylus (456) and Sophocles' death (405) comes right after that of Euripides (406), which is clearly less surprising. So far as cultural diffusion goes, the statistics from literary papyri show that, while Euripides is far and away ahead, the three great tragic poets were more or less the only ones who were really widely known.

The grouping of these three as a set has thus been forced upon us. But to what extent is it a natural one? Sophocles competed with Aeschylus and Euripides with Sophocles, but they were not the only competitors involved. Imitation, *mimēsis*, between poets is one of the laws of Greek literature. It would, for example, be impossible to read the *Electra*s of Euripides and Sophocles without referring the one to the other and comparing them with Aeschylus' *The Libation Bearers*. Euripides' *The Phoenician Women* constitutes, so to speak, a first "reading" of the *Seven against Thebes*. But quite apart from the memory of the more or less legendary figure of Thespis, even Aeschylus does not mark an absolute beginning. The first line of *The Persians* (472) refers back to the first line of Phrynicus' *Phoenician Women* (476), of which little more than the opening is known to us but whose "old Sidonian airs, sweet as honey"[2] remained famous throughout the fifth century, as Aristophanes, once again, informs us. A set comprising not three but four names would have been by no means unthinkable.

However that may be, one way or another, these three tragic poets became the classics, if it is true that becoming a classic involves the possibility, or indeed the necessity, of one's works being revived. The three poets were turned into classics at the end of their own century. In the case of Aeschylus the process may have been under way even earlier. The anonymous author of the *Life of Aeschylus* (11), a mediocre work that has come down to us in a section of the manuscript tradition, informs us that the Athenians "were so fond of Aeschylus that after his death they decided that whoever was prepared to put on his works would obtain a chorus from the city." This was a way of having the dead writer compete and of giving him a considerable advantage. We also know that *The Persians* was revived in Sicily one year after it was presented in Athens.

Right down the ages, the set of three has for the most part been respected, although every period has had its particular preferences;[3] and there is no denying that it is marvelously suited to all sorts of constructions — to Hegelian dialectic for example, where the arts are represented as evolving from the "symbolic" and where "content predominates over form"; or to the "romantic" where "form predominates over content," taking in a "classic balance between the two along the way." Who better than Aeschylus, Sophocles, and Euripides could illustrate such a schema (although, as it happened, Hegel failed to notice this)?

But perhaps we, for our part, should not limit our attention to these three tragic poets. Confining ourselves still to the dra-

251

matic sphere, we might at least broaden the range of our discussion to include comedy. Aristophanes is not only an ironic reader and commentator on the three tragic poets; he also reminds us that their "trilogies" (of which only one, Aeschylus' *Oresteia*, has survived) were rounded off by a "satyr play." This was an intermediary genre quite close to comedy and we know from a few rare fragments that Aeschylus was adept as Aristophanes himself at handling phallic ribaldry.

But that set too might be discarded, for we could suggest others, either within antiquity or extending beyond it. Aeschylus may be read — and probably hoped to be — in relation to Homer and Hesiod. Alternatively, he may be read in contrast to his lyric contemporaries Pindar and Bacchylides, or to the fifth-century philosophers, Heraclitus, Empedocles, and Parmenides. Another way to read the tragic poets is in association with the historians: The Aeschylus-Herodotus parallel is bound to arise in any reading of *The Persians* and attempts have sometimes been made to explain Thucydides with the help of Aeschylus.

Here is a cross-referenced reading of this kind. In *The Frogs*, Dionysus consults Aeschylus and Euripides on the desirability of recalling to Athens that famous and at times popular adventurer, Alcibiades. Euripides is against the idea. "And what say you?" the god asks Aeschylus, who replies: " 'Twere best to rear no lion in the State:/But having reared, 'tis best to humor him" (1430-2). It is clearly an allusion to the famous chorus from *Agamemnon*:

> A man reared in his house a lion's whelp, robbed of its mother's milk yet desiring still the breast. Gentle it was in the prelude of its life, kindly to children and a delight to the old. Much did it get, held in arms like a nursling child, with its bright eye turned toward his hand and fawning under compulsion of its belly's need. But brought to full growth by time, it showed forth the nature that it had from its parents. (717-28)

In the early years of this century, Francis Cornford tried, in a famous work,[4] to show that history according to Thucydides remained trapped in a tragic mold. He laid considerable emphasis on the figure of Alcibiades, entitling the chapter devoted to him "The Lion Cub." It might be objected that, even if correct, his analysis throws no light at all upon Aeschylus. But can we be so sure? Aristophanes was a better reader of Aeschylus than many of our twentieth-century critics. What is the meaning of the metaphor of the lion cub? Who is this "priest of Atē [the god of vengeance] by ordinance of heaven...reared in the house" (735-6)? This strophe is situated in between an evocation of "Paris, 'evil-wed,'" who was made welcome in Sparta only to violate Menelaos' hospitality, and another that describes Helen as "Love's flower that stingeth the heart." Both brought misfortune to Troy. But, as has conclusively been shown,[5] the lion is also one who was raised there in the city and who has become not a king but a tyrant, that is to say Agamemnon himself. And that is a way of posing the whole problem of the status of the tragic hero in relation to the city that projects him into the limelight and at the same time rejects him. Can we be so sure that Aristophanes and Thucydides have not helped us to understand that?

We might even move outside the arts of speech and writing, although that would be to venture onto treacherous terrain. There are, for example, vase painters who may have been influenced by the representation of the *Oresteia*, although that does not authorize us to transpose the language of tragedy into painting. The two art forms were not necessarily in step. One's instinct would be to relate the first tragic poet to the greatest painter of black figure vases, Exekias, but the painter was in action a full half-century earlier than the poet. However, it is sometimes worth bearing in mind coincidences that may be meaningful. It is not necessarily absurd to relate the central scene of the *Seven against Thebes* to a sculpted pediment.[6] Aeschylus himself refers to works produced by artisans and sculptors working in bronze and marble, not only in that scene but elsewhere too.

Indeed, why even remain inside the Greek world?

In 1864, Victor Hugo devoted an entire book to introducing a new translation of Shakespeare by his son François-Victor. In it, he briefly listed the geniuses who had preceded and foreshadowed Shakespeare, the implication being that Shakespeare had himself preceded and foreshadowed Victor Hugo. The list ran as follows: Homer, Job, Aeschylus, Isaiah, Ezekiel, Lucretius, Juvenal, Tacitus, Saint John, Saint Paul, Dante, Rabelais, and Cervantes. The Hebrew world (although Job is taken to be an Arab), the Greek world and the Latins — who are better represented — early Christianity, the Middle Ages, and the Renaissance. On a world scale, the sector represented is certainly limited. Victor Hugo explains why. In some parts of the world — the Far East and the Germanic countries, for example — "vast collective oeuvres" exist that are not the work of individual geniuses. "The poems of India, in particular, have the ominous fullness of the possible imagined by insanity or related by dreams." Aeschylus is set up as a parallel and a contrast to Job: "Aeschylus, enlightened by the unconscious divination of genius, without suspecting that he has behind him, in the East, the resignation of Job, completes it, unwittingly, by the revolt of Prometheus; so that the lesson may be complete and so that the human race, to whom Job has taught but duty, shall feel in Prometheus Right dawning."[7] This is total nonsense, written at a time when even orientalists did not realize that the book of Job, which dates from after the exile, is roughly contemporary with the work of Aeschylus. Nevertheless, here is what a great contemporary historian has recently written:

Confucius, Buddha, Zoroaster, Isaiah, Heraclitus — Aeschylus! The list would probably have puzzled my grandfather and his generation. It makes sense now...; it symbolizes the change in our historical perspective.... These men did not know one another...yet we feel that we have now discovered a common denominator that makes all of them..."relevant" to us.[8]

That "common denominator" is a common preoccupation with

the relations between the justice of men and that of the gods. To establish Aeschylus within a set such as this is beyond the scope of the present work. All the same, it seemed only fair to mention the possibility.

Tragic Democracy

Aeschylus, who was born around 525, was about eighteen years old at the time of Cleisthenes' great reforms that led to democracy. He was present at Marathon (490) and at Salamis (480) and thus lived through the troubled years that followed the Persian Wars. These were marked by clashes between on the one hand the democrats, led first by Ephialtes, assassinated in 461, then by Pericles, and on the other their opponents whose representative leader was Cimon, the son of Miltiades. At the time of Aeschylus' death, at Gela, Sicily in 456, Cimon, who had been ostracized in 461, may have recently been authorized to return to Athens, then at war with Sparta. But the fundamental conflict was by no means resolved. One important step had been Ephialtes' reform of 462, which had annulled the Areopagus' role as a council of "guardians of the laws," limiting it to functions of a judiciary nature. Now the Boulē, the council appointed by lottery, was, alongside the popular assembly, the only deliberative organ with a political function.

We do not know what Aeschylus' position was, how he voted in the Assembly, or to which side he belonged during this time of change. Or, to be more precise, we have only two clues at our disposal, outside his dramatic works. In 472 Pericles, then aged 20, acted as his chorēgos, that is to say, was the wealthy Athenian who financed the tetralogy of plays of which the second, the only one preserved, was The Persians. In 476, Themistocles had acted as chorēgos for Phrynicus. That choice might indicate that the poet belonged to the democratic camp. On the other hand, Pausanias writes (I, 14, 5): "Aeschylus, who had won such renown for his poetry and for his share in the naval battles before Artemisium and at Salamis, recorded at the prospect of death nothing else, and merely wrote his name, his father's name, and the name of his city, and added that he had witnesses to his valor, in the bay at Marathon and in the Persians who landed there." We do indeed possess the text of an epitaph that may be the one dictated by Aeschylus, then in Sicily, and engraved on his tomb by the people of Gela: "This memorial holds Aeschylus, son of Euphorion, an Athenian who died in Gela, rich in wheat. The long-haired Persians and the famous bay of Marathon know his worth."[9] To mention Marathon and omit Salamis might be seen as an ideological choice, a preference for the republic of the hoplites rather than that of the much more numerous sailors. But even if that was Aeschylus' personal choice at the end of his life, it tells us very little about what he said in his works, which anyway would not necessarily coincide with the times when his personal political choices were taken. The passage at the end of the *Oresteia* that praises the judiciary role of the Areopagus has been variously interpreted: sometimes as extolling Ephialtes, sometimes as criticizing him.

Euripides' political choices can be traced virtually year by year. Sophocles was a strategist alongside Pericles and toward the end of his life sat on a committee that paved the way for the coup d'etat of 411, but the city of which he writes is neither that of the democrats nor that of the oligarchs. His extant works were written over a period of several dozen years. The case of Aeschylus is quite different. It used to be thought that *The Suppliants* was almost contemporary with the advent of democracy. However, through the discovery of a papyrus we now know that this play should be dated to 464.[10] His seven tragedies, all that remain from a vast corpus of works (ninety tragedies and twenty or so satyr plays) appeared within a very short space of time: 472, *The Persians*; 467, the *Seven*; 458, the *Oresteia* trilogy. Only *Prometheus* is undated, but it is believed to be later than the *Seven*, some say even later than the *Oresteia*; others, mistakenly, question its authenticity.

It is impossible, then, to forget the background operations of an important, largely shadowy figure: the reformer Ephialtes, definitely one of the creators of Athenian democracy. However, there is no evidence for placing Aeschylus in his camp. In truth, the problem needs to be posed in different terms.

Tragedy was one of the forms through which the new democratic city established its identity: Setting the actor in opposition to the chorus (it was Aeschylus who introduced a second actor), it took its prince-turned-tyrant from distant myth, set him on stage and assessed him, representing his errors and the mistaken choices that led him to catastrophe. In *The Persians*, the hero is not a long-gone Greek prince but a contemporary Persian king. But the other plays in that trilogy also presented on stage the blindness of kings. Barbarian space fulfilled the same function as Greek time, as Racine was to remember when he wrote his preface to *Bajazet*.

Tragedy was "one of the forms": There were others that were very different, such as the funeral speech, which in contrast to tragedy presents a city of model unity.[11]

But if the king, without actually being a tyrant, is nevertheless father to the tyrant,[12] the chorus cannot be said to present the people, most certainly not the soldier-citizens. Composed, as it is, of goddesses (*Prometheus*), the Furies (the *Eumenides*), women or even captive women (the *Seven*, *The Suppliants*, *The Libation Bearers*), old men (*The Persians*, *Agamemnon*), the chorus is not qualified to embody the city whether in arms or at peace. The political dialogue between Eteocles, the sole, sovereign leader, and the women of Thebes is an impossible one. "Listen to women, though you like it not," the women tell the hero who has chosen the seventh gate and with it a duel to the death with his brother (712). In a democratic city, the council put forward proposals, the assembly voted decisions, and the magistrates executed those decisions. Furthermore, both the magistrates and the members of the council were also members of the assembly. In tragedy, the *decision* is made by the hero and it is a repetition of an earlier decision that may have been made long before: as in the cases of the Atreidae or the Labdacids. Does Agamemnon's error date from his decision to step on to the carpet reserved for the gods that Clytemnestra spreads before him, from the sacrifice of Iphigenia, from the crime of Atreus, or from the bloodthirsty sacking of Troy? Eteocles' mistake repeats the mistakes of Oedipus and Laius.[13] So the temporal framework within which their choices are made is not that of the city. The chorus, for its part, makes no decisions. Only in *The Suppliants* does it to some extent take part in the action. Before the play opens, it has collectively decided to reject marriage. The women of this chorus are *in* the tragedy. In *Agamemnon*, the old men of the chorus act as members of the *boulē*, it is true, but the impotence of the chorus as a whole, when faced with the murder, is displayed almost in caricature. One after another, each member states his opinion, after which their leader concludes by saying: "I am supported on all sides [by the majority] to approve this course: that first we have clear assurance how it stands with Atreus' son" (1370-1). At the end of the *Seven* (which may not be entirely by the hand of Aeschylus himself), the city splits into two camps and it is two women, Antigone and Ismene, who place themselves at the head of the two factions.

The people are not present on the stage. Their place is on the tiered seats of the theater. Are they even represented? At the beginning of the *Seven*, they are, by a silent group to whom Eteocles' very first words are addressed (1-2): "Citizens of Cadmus [more precisely, 'of the city of Cadmus'], to say what the hour demands is the part of him who guards the fortunes of the State, guiding the helm upon the stern, his eyes not closed in sleep." The Danaids, who make up the chorus of *The Suppliants* insist that the king of Argos should himself make the decision to receive them. The democratic Pelasgus refuses to do so and instead takes the matter to the people's assembly (365-75). The assembly passes a decree granting the girls metic status. In fact, it is in connection with this vote that we find the first mention (in the texts available to us) of the word *dēmos* (people) used in association with *kratein* (to rule). But we know of this assembly only by report: It is not represented on the stage or on the *orchestra*.

In the *Eumenides*, the judges who are to decide Orestes' fate and who eventually do vote upon it are also represented by silent players. Only Athena speaks as well as voting; and it is her vote that leads to Orestes' absolution (734-53). Here, the city is represented by its eponymous goddess. Such are the displacements of tragic democracy.

Gods and Men

In a tragedy such as Euripides' *Bacchae* (406), it is the introduction of a god in disguise, Dionysus, into the world of men and his disturbing presence there that triggers the tragic course of events. In Sophocles' plays, the time of the gods and the time of men are kept separate but, in the last analysis, the former makes sense of the latter. Little by little, the meaning of the oracles is modified, until it becomes crystal clear. Appearances of gods on stage are rare: only Athena, at the beginning of *Ajax* and the deified Heracles at the end of *Philoctetes*.

In Aeschylus, we find constant interference between the divine and the human worlds. Each reflects the other. Every human conflict reflects a conflict between the divine forces. Every human tragedy is also a divine one.

That is not because Aeschylus was writing at such an early date. One should not imagine that he lived in some primitive world as yet incapable of conceptualizing man's relationship to the gods or to nature. The domination, transcendence, and final triumph of Zeus provide the framework for every work of Aeschylus, just as they do for the works of Sophocles. But whereas Sophocles' Zeus is outside history, in Aeschylus Zeus has a history, just as he does in Hesiod, a history that Aeschylus brings to its conclusion.

> He who aforetime was mighty, swelling with insolence for every fray, he shall not even be named as having ever been; and he who arose thereafter, he hath met his overthrower and is past and gone. But whosoe'er, heartily taking thought beforehand, giveth the title of victory in triumphant shout to "Zeus," he shall gain wisdom altogether.

That is how the lineage of the children of Ouranos is described in the *Agamemnon* (167-75): Ouranos, Kronos, then Zeus. But a different history might have been possible. *Prometheus* is a tragedy set in the world of the gods. Zeus is a tyrant and Prometheus a slave, but a slave who is master of time, able to subject Zeus to a repetition of crimes in a sequence such as afflicted the Atreidae and the Labdacids: yesterday Kronos against Ouranos, next Zeus against Kronos, tomorrow the son of Zeus against his father. In this astonishing tragedy, *Kratos*, Domination or Power, makes an appearance on stage, with *Bia*, Violence or Force, at his side.

The *Oresteia* trilogy is punctuated by the clash of the young political gods against the old deities of kindred blood, just as it is by the struggles of the lineage of Agamemnon and Clytemnestra. Many modern scholars have been misled by the historical illusion created by Aeschylus. They have believed that this clash truly represented a mutation, that Aeschylus was dramatizing a progression from a religion of the earth and nature to a civic religion, a switch from matriarchy to patriarchy, from clan to city.[14] However, Aeschylus was out to dramatize not history, but the present.

Human beings seek for signs. The relative world in which they live is a world of Persuasion, *Peithō*.[15] But what kind of *Peithō*: the "holy Persuasion" of which Athena speaks at the end of the *Eumenides*, which gives her voice "sweet beguilement" and which transforms the Erinyes into the Eumenides, or the "treacherous persuasion" mentioned by the chorus leader in *The Libation Bearers*, which leads Clytemnestra to her death, just as it drew Agamemnon on to his? Eteocles is concerned with signs too, as he strives to decode and reverse them, listening to the messenger as he describes the shields of the *Seven against Thebes*, one by one. They are signs that gradually create for us a picture that it is possible for *us* to interpret much better than Eteocles; in the last analysis, what they portend is triumph for Zeus, salvation for the city, and death for both the brother-kings.

Signs may take other forms such as dreams, never transparent, or omens. Thus at the beginning of *Agamemnon*, we are reminded of the omen that marked the departure for Troy: "... the inspiriting omen appearing to the kings of the ships — the kingly birds, one black, one white of tail, hard by the palace, on the spear hand, in a station full conspicuous, devouring a hare with a brood unborn, checked in the last effort to escape" (114-20). Calchas, the diviner, makes a try at an interpretation: The two eagles are the Atreidae and they will take possession of Troy; but by violating the rules of hunting and killing innocent animals, against the rules laid down by Artemis who rules over wild nature, they will unleash a storm. What does the pregnant hare represent? Both Troy and Iphigenia, sacrificed by her father, and also the innocent children offered as a feast to Thyestes by Atreus. All this multiplicity of meanings and the overdetermination of omens are characteristic of Aeschylus. Then the network of omens is complemented by a network of images and metaphors. The Atreidae are represented by eagles, creatures of the heavens and are also compared to vultures, birds from the depths that gorge greedily on corpses: "Loud rang the battle cry they uttered in their rage, even as vultures scream that, in lonely grief for their brood, driven by the oarage of their pinions, wheel high over their aeries, for that they have lost their toil of guarding the nurselings' nest" (47-54). We should not attempt to separate poetry from tragic meaning in Aeschylus' works, for within the text they constitute a single dimension. There is no break between metaphors and omens, between images and the signs sent by the gods: The lions and eagles from these omens and comparisons seem to leap suddenly onto the stage. This continuity is perhaps the most astonishing aspect of all of Aeschylus' art.

Dreams, omens, and images are not the only things that establish connections between the obscurities in the human world and the opaque world of the gods. Diviners and prophets constitute further intermediaries. Equally, no break separates the status of the interpreter of a metaphorical dream from that of a diviner. At the beginning of *The Libation Bearers*, it is the memory of Clytemnestra's crime, or perhaps her remorse, that is described as prophetic or, to be precise, "a power who divines...in dreams":

> For with thrilling voice that set each hair on end, the inspir-
> ing power who divines for the house in dreams, with breath
> of wrath in sleep, at dead of night uttered a cry for terror from
> the inmost chamber, falling heavily upon the women's bower.
> And the readers of dreams like these, interpreting heaven's will
> under pledge, declared that those beneath the earth complain
> in bitter anger and are wroth against their slayers. (32-42)

Aeschylus' tragedies are full of manifestations of the divine and
of the mantic art. Calchas, for example, strives to interpret the
omen of the pregnant hare. Amphiarus is described as "the man of
the double curse," just as Polynices is called "the man of a thousand quarrels." Such word play is a constant feature in Aeschylus'
dramas and helps to confer meaning on the text. Amphiarus does
not appear physically on stage but is referred to by name. He is
one of the Seven, he curses both Tydaeus, the first of the heroes,
and Polynices, the last. Of all the shields described at such length,
his is the only one that bears no emblem at all for "his resolve is
not to seem the bravest, but to be it" (592). For the diviner, the
one who can tell the meaning of things, it is a way of sweeping
the shields of his companions from the world of being and relegating them to the world of seeming; he invites us to regard them
as so many misleading appearances.

Sophocles' diviners – Tiresias, for example, in *Antigone* and *Oedipus Rex* – are diviners pure and simple: They anticipate the tragedy but remain peripheral to it, as do the messengers, heralds,
and servants who appear in both his works and those of Aeschylus.

The Pythia of Delphi appears at the beginning of the *Eumenides*.
She tells of the past of that holy place, a past that prefigures what
Athens will become at the end of the trilogy, that is to say a place
where the divine powers act in concert rather than in opposition:
However, she does not foretell the future but instead appeals to
Apollo, the doctor, healer, and interpreter of dreams.

262

The only intermediary between the past, the present, and the future whose destiny is not at stake in the tragedy is Darius' ghost, the deceased model of an old, lucid king, that is to say an impossible king. He appears on stage solely to condemn the young, foolish king (*The Persians*, 719 ff.).

Apollo is both an oracular and an interpreter god. His oracle has led Orestes to murder his mother. But in the trial that is held in Athens and that introduces law where none had until then existed, he is both a witness and a litigant, just as the Erinyes are. In two of Aeschylus' characters, the diviner and the tragic hero/heroine are totally fused. One is a woman: Cassandra; the other a god: Prometheus.

Prometheus is a diviner-god and doctor-god (though unable to heal himself), who mediates between the immortals and human beings, whom he has taught the technical and social skills, and he tells the only human character in the tragedy, Io, what her destiny is to be. At the same time, Prometheus is both the victim and the master of the secret upon which Zeus' future depends. His past concerned man; his future concerns the salvation of Zeus; but it is by virtue of his present suffering, the fact that he is torn between the past and the present, that he becomes a tragic character. Cassandra, who is Apollo's victim and the beneficiary of his gifts, enters the palace with knowledge of both the past (the murder of Thyestes' children) and the future (Agememnon's murder and her own): "And now the prophet, having undone me, his prophetess, hath brought me to this deadly pass." This is not to mention that she also knows what lies in the more distant future, namely the vengeance of Orestes. She does not speak in riddles; here, it is her character that is an enigma, not her words.

The normal mode of communication between the gods and men is sacrifice, the invention of Prometheus. But there are, precisely, no regular sacrifices in Aeschylus' tragic world: on the contrary, every sacrifice is "corrupt,"[16] and this goes for the *Oresteia* as well as for the *Seven against Thebes*. Every attempt to sacrifice is brought to a halt, as when the queen of the Persians tries to sacrifice to the gods. Conversely, every murder, whether of a brother, a daughter, a spouse, or a father, is depicted as a sacrifice. The suicide planned in *The Suppliants* also takes the form of an offering to the gods of Argos. In Greek tragedy, the norm is presented only to be transgressed or because it has already been transgressed. It is in this respect that Greek tragedy derives from Dionysus, the god of confusion and transgression.

Men and the City

Many kinds of order are comprehended by the Greek city. It is a space located on cultivated land, bordered by the mountains or the "desert," where Bacchants wander, shepherds graze their flocks, and ephebes undergo their training; a time based on the permanence of magistracies and constant relays of magistrates; a sexual order founded on the political dominion of males and the temporary exclusion of the young; a political order in which the family order is more or less included; a Greek order that excludes barbarians and restricts the presence of even Greek foreigners; a military order in which hoplites are more important then bowmen, light-armed troops, and even cavalry; a social order based upon the exploitation of slaves and the relegation of artisan trades, if not individual artisans, to a marginal role. The civic order is the product of the combination and reciprocal effects of all these inclusions and exclusions.

In tragedy, the city must both recognize itself and bring itself into question. In other words, tragedy involves both order and disorder. The tragic author displaces the political order, turns it upside down, sometimes does away with it altogether. The presentation or staging (in the literal sense) of the evidence depends upon these shifts. Only in *Prometheus* does the action take place in a distant desert where Power (*Kratos*) and Violence (*Bia*) take direct action. In most plays the scene is set in front of the royal palace or some temple, as in Delphi at the beginning of the *Eumenides*. But in the case of *The Suppliants*, the action takes place before a holy place that is situated on the city boundary, near the river bank: What is at stake is whether these strangers who claim to be women of Argos may be admitted inside the city. It is a theme that was to recur, for example, in Sophocles' *Oedipus at Colonus*, but this is the earliest instance of its use that has come down to us. Wild nature serves as a constant reference point, as does the bestiary connected with it: lions and wolves, animal predators at once hunting and hunted, hunting that interacts with both sacrifice and war: one should not kill an enemy as one hunts a wild beast; one should sacrifice to the gods not hunted animals but domesticated beasts, man's companions in the dominion that he imposes over cultivated land.[17] The wild world and the barbarian world may overlap to some degree, as in the case of Egypt referred to in *The Suppliants*, but the two should not necessarily be identified. Xerxes represents the wild to the extent that it is his *hubris*, his arrogant folly, that has led him on across the seas to Greece, while Darius' widow, woman though she is, together with the chorus of faithful old men, represents the world of culture.

In one tragedy only, the second part of the *Eumenides*, the scene is set in the heart of the city, at "the hearth of Athena," on the Acropolis, before a group of citizens destined to be renewed generation after generation not far away, on the hill of Ares, known as the Areopagus. The silent figures represent the beginnings of civic time. Both the Erinyes and Orestes are foreigners in the eyes of Athena and their judges, foreigners whose relationship to the city has yet to be defined. Orestes is eventually acquitted but does not become a citizen. The Eumenides, like the suppliants at Argos, are granted the status of metics, divine metics in their case. It is they who set out the political program of the budding Athenian democracy: "neither anarchy nor despotism" — a program reiterated by Athena: "Ye shall surely be preeminent guiding your land and your city in the straight path of righteousness" (992-4).

Agamemnon fears "the anger of his people" but disregards it and thereby establishes himself as a tyrant. The only Aeschylean character who is explicitly democratic is a king: Pelasgus in *The Suppliants*. The daughters of Danaus appeal to him in the name of kinship. His reply shows them that more is in fact at stake: the fate of the entire city.

Eteocles is at once a political leader who appears to tackle the quasi-barbarian threat to the Greek city of Thebes with lucid acumen, and at the same time a scion of the accursed lineage of the Labdacids. The tragic action separates things that appear to be inextricably intermingled. Politically speaking, Polynices is an enemy and traitor to Thebes; from the point of view of his lineage, he is Eteocles' double. Does the death of the two brothers bring the city salvation arising from the ruination of the lineage? Yes and no: The chorus splits into two and the two sisters, Antigone and Ismene, take their places at the head of two factions that, if we are to believe the manuscripts at our disposal, will, in their turn, continue to destroy each other. The tragedy goes on: one right against another.

The paradox constituted by a couple of women taking over the city prompts the following reflection: While the Greek city is certainly not the only civilized system to exclude women from political life, it is particularly unusual in that it dramatizes that exclusion, making it one of the driving forces of the tragic action. Once again, it is the exceptions that prove the rule. Clytemnestra, a woman who, we are told, speaks with as much sense as a wise man, usurps both political power and family sovereignty. Her crime is the murder of a husband; but in *The Libation Bearers*, where the chorus describes all the things that a criminal woman may do, the list of crimes that it envisages runs as follows: the murder of a father, a son, a husband, but not of a daughter. And the couple formed by Clytemnestra and her daughter Electra (whose name some scholars read as *Alectra*, meaning "without marriage") is indeed a strange one, for Electra is the virgin daughter of a polygamous mother. Her will is as virile as her mother's, but whereas her mother was bent upon destroying Agamemnon, Electra is determined to avenge her father.[18]

If "the dream of a purely paternal heredity never ceased to haunt the Greek imagination," the same could be said of the dream of a world without women. Apollo voices the former when he takes the witness stand at Orestes' trial; Eteocles expresses the latter at the beginning of the *Seven*. Meanwhile, the Danaids, characters created — or rather, recreated — by Aeschylus, for their part dream of a world without men.[19] That dream clearly lacks the force of the first two which could, to some extent, be sustained by the current political and social realities. But only to some extent: For Apollo is but one element in the tragedy; and whatever a tragic character such as Eteocles says reflects his own *hubris*, his total lack of moderation. In the *Oresteia*, Athena, that is to say the city, declares as she acquits Orestes: "In all things save wedlock I am for the male with all my soul, and am entirely on the father's side" (737-8). All the same, she tries hard, and with success, to persuade the female Erinyes, the divine avengers of bloodshed, to settle in Athens and politically promote the values that they protect: "For ye have not been vanquished. Nay, the trial resulted fairly in ballots equally divided, without disgrace to thee" (795-6). Even feminine values may stem from *timē*, or civic honor.[20]

Man-woman, adult-youth: The complementarity is perfectly natural. A young man is feminine until such time as he becomes adult by passing through the trial of initiation. At the beginning of *The Libation Bearers*, Orestes and his sister appear almost as twins. The subject of age groups in Greek tragedy is unfortunately one that has not yet been tackled. Aeschylus' Orestes is perhaps the only character in Greek tragedy who can be followed from his infancy right through to adulthood, taking in the adventure of his fictitious death. In the testimony of his nurse, in *The Libation Bearers*, when he is believed dead, we discover him as an infant; later he appears as an adult, alive and transformed by time, when he is brought to trial in Athens: "Long since, at other houses, have I been thus purified both by victims and by flowing streams" (451-2). Between those two points, we see him as he is in *The Libation Bearers*: a double character, at once male and female, valorous and cunning, a daytime warrior who also fights by night, a hoplite yet also a bowman.[21] He is a tragic ephebe. Eteocles, for his part, is also a hoplite, but a hoplite on his own is a contradiction in terms (for a hoplite only functions in the battle line) and it is precisely this contradiction that constitutes one aspect of the split in his personality.

The theme of hoplite values and the collective discipline of the phalanx certainly receives strange treatment in Aeschylean tragedy. Constantly proclaimed, even triumphant in the epilogue to the *Eumenides*, they are values that are, at the same time, constantly denied not only by the heroes but also by the collective groups in his plays. In *Agamemnon*, Clytemnestra explains how a courageous army that is respectful of its enemy's gods should behave. But the capture of Troy is the work not of hoplites but of the "fierce Argive beast" (824) that pounced and "like the ravening lion, lapped his fill of princely blood" (827-8). Eteocles, the hoplite, dies in single combat. But the most curious problem of all is posed by the tragedy of *The Persians*. The tragic characters are Persians, chief amongst them the king, Xerxes, and the play is clearly written by an Athenian to the glory of his own people and Greeks in general. But the techniques deployed in the narrative are amazing. The Persian army, described at the beginning of the play, is composed mainly of cavalry, bowmen, and chariot-borne fighters. When the chorus leader ponders on the outcome of the war, what he says is: "Is it the drawing of the bow that hath triumphed, or is it the might of the spear-headed lance that hath prevailed?" (146-8). The spear is the weapon of the hoplite, associated with the values of open combat, where phalanx clashes against phalanx; the bow is a weapon of cunning and of the night. But, still at the beginning of the play, the Greeks and the Persians also come to grips symbolically, in the forms of hawk and eagle. Both are birds of prey, but it is the eagle that is associated with the values of sovereignty and the soaring heights; yet it is the Persian eagle that flees to "the low altar [ἐσχάρα] of Phoebus" (205-6), while the hawk drops upon it from above. As for the war itself, it is above all represented by the naval battle of Salamis, provoked thanks to the cunning of Themistocles, and its end is described using an image from fishing with nets: The Greeks lay low the Persians as fishermen do tuna fish (424) in the "chamber of death." Thermopylae, the first hoplite battle of the Second Persian War is never mentioned. Moreover, Darius' ghost does no more than hint at the great hoplite, and largely Lacedaemonian, battle at Plataea in 479: "So great shall be the mass of clotted gore spilled by the Dorian lance upon Plataean soil" (816-7). Should we account for these surprises by pointing out that in this instance hoplite values clashed not only with Aeschylus' patriotism, which led him to minimize the exploits of the hoplites of Sparta, but equally with facts that were well known to the spectators (such as the role of cunning in warfare and the importance of the naval battle)?

One episode indicates a difficulty that would still remain unresolved. Herodotus was writing forty years after Aeschylus, but was not a tragic poet. According to him, even as the battle of Salamis was raging, Aristides — who emerges from Athenian historiography as a moderate — landed on the little island of Psyttaleia with a party of hoplites and massacred the Persians whom he found there (VIII, 95). Now, at the end of the messenger's speech, Aeschylus gives a different account of the episode, which he sets after the battle and, although the action of cuirasse-clad soldiers is certainly mentioned, the massacre starts off with a barrage of projectiles: "Oft-time they [the Persians] were struck by stones slung from their hands, and arrows sped from the bowstring kept ever falling upon them and working them destruction" (459-61). Only after deploying these weapons did the Greeks finish off their enemies by putting them to the sword. Is this a case of Aeschylus recording the truth and Herodotus telling one of his lies? Some scholars have supposed so,[22] while others have argued against such a thesis. Or is it an effect of the constraints of the tragic narrative, which persists to the end in having the warriors of the Persian empire wiped out by the least formidable of fighters, who are of course heroic but are also protected and guided by the gods. Over and above Themistocles' cunning messenger there is "some destructive power or evil spirit that appeared I know not whence"

(353-4); "some power divine destroyed our army and swayed the scale of fortune with unequal weight" (345-6). Herodotus, in contrast, reports Miltiades as telling the polemarch Callimachus, on the eve of Marathon: "If we join battle before some at Athens be infected by corruption, then, *if the gods are impartial*, we may well win in this fight" (VI, 109). Can that really be described as a historical, as opposed to tragic, account?

The mention of bowmen, those "poor devils" of the classical city, draws us away from the center of the city to its marginal and inferior categories. What part do slaves and artisans play in Aeschylus' works, and what is the significance of their presence?

Some of the servants and slaves who appear in Aeschylus' tragedies are simply there to say their piece; they themselves are transparent and their words are unaffected by their status. We are not told whether the messengers in *The Persians* and the *Seven* are slaves. Their function is purely dramatic, as is that of the heralds in *The Suppliants* and *Agamemnon*. In the watchman's prologue at the beginning of the latter play, the fact that he is a slave is conveyed by an animal metaphor: Crouched on the terrace, awaiting the signal that will announce the capture of Troy, the watchman compares himself to a dog, but a dog that has "learned to know aright the conclave of the stars of night." He refers to his twofold dependence: He belongs by law to Agamemnon, in fact to the female tyrant Clytemnestra. In *The Libation Bearers*, Aegisthus' servant cries out in despair when his master is assassinated.

Actually, there are two kinds of slaves in Aeschylus' works: those born to be slaves, and captives, the latter being Greeks or the offspring of gods or kings, victims of the rights of war. Those in the first category remain anonymous, with one exception: Orestes' nurse, in *The Libation Bearers*. Like so many other slaves in Greece, she is known by the name of her native country: Kilissa, the Cilician woman. She appears in an astonishing and famous scene. The death of Orestes has just been announced but, unlike Euryclaea in the *Odyssey*, Kilissa does not recognize the baby she has suckled. There is a note of comedy to the scene. It is indeed a fact that, in not only Aeschylus but Greek tragedy as a whole, comic scenes tend to feature slaves or other humble folk and make many references to physical bodies, alive or dead: Consider, for example, the "realistic" observations of the guard in *Antigone*. Hints of comedy such as these provide one of the means whereby tragedy establishes its connection with the present.

Kilissa has raised Orestes, not on behalf of his mother but "for his father,"[23] a fact that makes it possible to integrate her tirade into the tragic action. The text of her speech is characteristic of the representation of this type of slave. Kilissa is familiar with only the body of her infant charge and from start to finish speaks of nothing else, referring to it as if it were the body of an animal:

> For the senseless thing one must nurse like a dumb beast — of course one must — by following its humor, for while it is still a babe in swaddling clothes, it has no speech at all — whether it be that hunger moves it or thirst belike, or call of need: children's young [insides] work their own relief. These needs I would forecast; yet many a time, I vow, mistaken, having to wash the child's linen, laundress, and nurse had the same office. (753-60)

Cassandra is the very model of a person reduced to slavery by right of conquest: She is at once Agamemnon's concubine, the prophetess of Apollo, and a slave. Faced with Cassandra, Clytemnestra proclaims the Greek norms of behavior but also reserves her rights as a tyrant over the body of one reduced to slavery. The whole of Clytemnestra's speech to Cassandra is worth analyzing, including the remarkable contrast she draws between the fate of slaves who fall into the hands of the *nouveaux riches* and the slaves in the households of masters "of ancient wealth": "Thou hast from us such usage as custom warrenteth" (1046), she says. But her play on words is sinister: "In no unkindness hath Zeus appointed thee a partaker in the holy water in this palace." It is her way of predicting the human sacrifice in which Cassandra will play the role of victim, just as Agamemnon does.

A similar relationship between a tyrant and one who is a slave by accident is to be found in *Prometheus*, but here it is examined in more depth and is more complex. Two gods are involved: Zeus, the tyrant and Prometheus, the slave, a slave subjected to torture, as only slaves could be. But there are slaves and slaves, and Prometheus contrasts the willing servitude of Hermes, servant to the tyrant, and his own condition: "For thy servitude rest assured, I'd not barter my hard lot, not I" (966-7). But Hermes denies that he is a slave, describing Zeus as not his master but his father.[24]

Prometheus also introduces another social category: the artisans. The case is unique: Other plays sometimes refer to the work of artisans — for example, in the description of the shields of the *Seven* and the very condition of poet was that of an artisan in Aeschylus' day,[25] a fact that linked the poet with the world of manufacture and exchange; but as a general rule artisans, whose condition as such confers no particular status upon them in the city, do not appear on the tragic stage. The artisan who is shown at work in *Prometheus*, chaining a slave to a rock with the assistance of Power and Force is, admittedly, a god, Hephaestus, who puts a certain amount of thought into his work.[26] But he is accompanied by Power and Force...and through their presence, political values eclipse the values of craftsmanship. Prometheus is the god of the technological function, Hermes the god of exchange. *Prometheus* may be the last of Aeschylus' plays to have come down to us and our view of it is inevitably distorted since we possess neither the second drama of the trilogy to which it belonged nor the last, which told of the god's liberation from his bonds. We should try to imagine what our view of the *Oresteia* would be if we only possessed *Agamemnon*. All the same, the questions that this play (*Prometheus*) raises — questions concerning the relations between power and knowledge and between the political and the technological functions — are ones that never cease to be problematic.

Pierre Vidal-Naquet

Chapter XIII

The Shields of the Heroes:

Essay on the Central Scene of the

Seven Against Thebes[1]

> *La parole écrite s'installe dans l'avènement*
> *des jours comptés, sur une ardoise de hasard.*
> — René Char
> *Chants de la Balandrane*

This study concerns three connected questions that — in varying degrees — have baffled the interpreters of Aeschylus. My intention is to show that, in the last analysis, they make up a single problem.

The first question is, if I may put it thus, that of the "psychology" of Eteocles. It is always remarked upon: It is as if this character, who is *the* main character of Aeschylus' play, underwent, after line 653, what might be described as an abrupt mutation. Gilbert Murray, in his somewhat emotional way of dealing with such problems, gives a pretty fair representation of the general opinion. Up to line 652 Eteocles is a man who is "cool and at his ease, ready-witted and concerned for the morale of his people." He is, in sum, the ideal leader for the polis. Then comes the turning point: "In a flash, Eteocles is a changed man. His coolness and self-control are gone. He is a desperate man overmastered by the curse."[2] What has happened? In the previous scene Eteocles has decided that having stationed six Theban heroes to face the enemy leaders at the first six gates of Thebes, he will himself take up his post at the seventh.

273

ἐγὼ δέ γ᾽ ἄνδρας ἓξ ἐμοὶ σὺν ἑβδόμῳ
ἀντηρέτας ἐχθροῖσι τὸν μέγαν τρόπον
εἰς ἑπτατειχεῖς ἐξόδους τάξω μολών, (283)
(I myself, as seventh, will lead a crew of champions to face
the foe heroically at our seven gates.)[3]

Lines 285–6 suggest that he is acting in a rational manner aimed
at controlling the unforeseeable:

πρὶν ἀγγέλους σπερχνούς τε καὶ ταχυρρόθους
λόγους ἱκέσθαι καὶ φλέγειν χρείας ὕπο.
(Before panic-stricken messengers and a flurry of foaming stories comes with news to inflame us at this crisis.)

Panic-stricken messengers.... It is precisely after hearing a messenger whom he has, so to speak, discounted in advance, that
Eteocles' behavior changes abruptly. He hears out the *angelos*, the
spy he has sent behind the enemy lines, listening calmly to the
description – and it is a terrifying one – of the six first leaders
of the Argive army. He stations a Theban hero opposite each one
of them but the seventh is his brother Polynices and up goes his
famous cry:

ὦ θεομανές τε καὶ θεῶν μέγα στύγος,
ὦ πανδάκρυτον ἀμὸν Οἰδίπου γένος·
ὤμοι, πατρὸς δὴ νῦν ἀραὶ τελεσφόροι. (653)
(God-hated, hateful, beaten and trapped, O god-maddened, O
race of Oedipus ringed around with hate, my patrimony, full
of tears. The curse of my father is now fulfilled.)

Given that the transformation itself is assumed to be a fact,
the problem consists in explaining it, and one does not have to
be a great expert in historical logic to guess that there are not an
infinite number of solutions. The most simple explanation is, of
course, to account for the double character of Aeschylus' Eteocles

274

by appealing to the double nature of the sources for the poet's inspiration. Could it not be that he has combined, more or less skillfully, two irreconcilable traditions? This was the opinion expressed somewhat baldly in 1903 by Wilamowitz: "The entire drama is based on two fundamental themes (*Grundmotive*), the one totally opposed to the other. One is the *Oedipodeia*, the exemplary tale of the Oracle of Delphi, the disobedience of Laius, the curse of Oedipus, the fateful destiny of the sinful brute. This story culminates with the mutual murder of the two brothers. The other theme is that of the victorious defense of Thebes against the Argives, the fateful destiny of the Seven."[4] In other words, two different characters appear in the play, one after the other: the *second* Eteocles, the hero of the Theban epic, the savior of Thebes, is the first to appear on stage. But his place is taken, from line 653 onward, by the *first* Eteocles, the character from the Oedipal saga, the accursed son of the husband of Iocasta. Paradoxically, in 1914 Wilamowitz wrote, within the space of two pages, that Eteocles was the only character who appears as an individual in the whole of Aeschylus' drama. He suggests that his creator "did not ask himself: How am I going to depict my Eteocles? He simply took what was given (*Er nahm was ihm gegeben war*) but this was double (*Das war aber Zweierlei*).... The man who carried the hereditary curse was a different Eteocles."[5]

If I have cited Wilamowitz in this way, it was not for the purpose of showing that the greatest philologist of his time put forward an interpretation that probably not one of our own contemporaries would take seriously. It was, on the contrary, precisely in order to demonstrate that this interpretation has a history that leaves in its wake perceptions of lasting value as well as controversies now forgotten. We ourselves are part of this history and that is enough to indicate that this is not a matter of some kind of Hegelian dialectic culminating in the triumph of the Idea. Wilamowitz's explanation did have the merit of being an explanation even though today it is no more than a residual deposit of tradition.

It is generally accepted that the contemporary debate that is still evolving and to which this study aims to make its contribution was inaugurated in 1937 by Friedrich Solmsen in his article on the role of the Erinys in Aeschylus' play.[6] It is not necessary here to specify the participants in the debate or what their respective views were,[7] but it is not too difficult to outline the logical structure of the discussion.

One view is that we cannot help but put up with the contradictions of Aeschylus and the character he created. One may even believe that they are deliberate, simply one element in the "dramatic technique" of the poet, to borrow the now famous expression from Tycho von Wilamowitz's book on Sophocles. Such is the opinion of Roger Dawe, who believes that "there are . . . contradictions in Aeschylus which not even the most avant-garde interpretations can reduce to a logical system."[8] Other critics believe it to be their duty to prove that Aeschylus and Eteocles are, respectively, perfectly coherent, one as an author, the other as a character. There are, ultimately, only two ways of proceeding. Either one shows that, well *before* line 653, Eteocles was already accursed and knew it; or one attempts to prove that both *after* the crucial line, as well as before it, Eteocles remains a statesman and a general.

The first solution — which is that adopted by Solmsen himself — can for example be supported by the invocation pronounced by Eteocles at the beginning of the play:

ὦ Ζεῦ τε καὶ Γῆ καὶ πολισσοῦχοι θεοί,
Ἀρά τ' Ἐρινὺς πατρος ἡ μεγασθενής (69)
(O Zeus, Earth, and gods that guard our city, my father's curse, mighty, vengeful spirit.)

Conversely, however, it is equally true to say that Eteocles remains the military leader that he was at the beginning of the play, right up to the end. The great speech that begins at line 653 closes with a military decision:

276

φέρ' ὡς τάχος

κνημῖδας, αἰχμῆς καὶ πέτρων προβλήματα. (675)

(Come, bring me my cnemides against the lances and stones, quickly!)

Schadewaldt has shown that the ensuing dialogue between Eteocles and the chorus is punctuated on stage by the arming of Eteocles as a hoplite.[9] Eteocles loses his life but wins the war. Throughout the play he remains the good pilot, the οἰακοστρόφος of line 62, the navigator who knows how to guide the ship of the city, a prey to the unleashed elements, safely through the storm.[10] A middle course consists in a subtle elaboration of the relationship between the decision of Eteocles and that of the gods, that is, in exploring that inexhaustible double pivot of Greek tragedy. Is it Eteocles who chooses the Theban leaders who are to confront the Argive leaders? Or has the decision been taken by higher powers? It is possible to embroider endlessly upon this theme, as it is upon others.[11] Subtle as this debate has proved, one feels nevertheless tempted to agree with Dawe who writes that, in it "we are not so much learning about Aeschylus as witnessing the transactions of a private club."[12] Perhaps the most alarming thing is that many of those taking part in the discussion are less concerned to interpret the text of Aeschylus than to bestow upon Eteocles a psychological verisimilitude and depth in conformity with "our own" mental habits. They ask themselves what is happening behind the skēnē, as if there were actually anything at all happening,[13] and an extreme position is to attempt, as Leon Golden does, to make of Eteocles "at least a believable human being."[14]

But one cannot insist too often on the fact that Eteocles is not "a human being," reasonable or otherwise. He is not derived from psychoanalysis, which can only draw upon living people or fictions fairly close to us in support of this mode of interpretation; nor from a study of character in the manner of the novels of the nineteenth century. He is a figure in a Greek tragedy and it is as such that he must be studied. The values that stand in contrast to each other on either side of line 653 (if we are to retain this symbolic boundary) — that is to say the values of the *polis* and those connected with the world of the family, are not states of mind.[15] Our task is not to fill in the gaps in the text, not to turn the textual Eteocles into a living Eteocles. It is to explain the text, to make it mean something. If Eteocles is torn in two, it is not the case that this is an aspect of his character. The tear is part of the very fabric of the tragedy.

The second question is that of Eteocles and the women. It has not been much studied as such.[16] Exclamations such as that of U. Albini: "L' idea di un coro femminile trattandosi di una guerra è splendida!" ("The idea of a female chorus discoursing on war is a splendid one!")[17] hardly amount to a serious study. Eteocles is a political and military leader, a man. His first words are addressed to the citizens of Thebes or, to be more precise, to those to whom he somewhat paradoxically refers as the citizens (the co-citizens) of Cadmos:

Κάδμου πολῖται, χρὴ λέγειν τὰ καίρια
ὅστις φυλάσσει πρᾶγος ἐν πρύμνῃ πόλεως
οἴακα νωμῶν, βλέφαρα μὴ κοιμῶν ὕπνῳ. (1)
(Cadmeian citizens, right decisions must come from a city's captain, ready for action, steering with unsleeping eyes.)

But who are these citizens? There are two contrary hypotheses. Some scholars think that the only citizens addressed by the actor representing Eteocles are the citizens of Athens seated on the steps of the theater of Dionysus in the spring of the year 467.[18] They point out that, throughout the play, Thebes is simply a mask for Athens, the victor of the Persians. In point of fact Oliver Taplin seems to have proved the opposite, namely that Eteocles is in fact addressing extras in the play, extras bearing arms whom, in lines 30-5, the actor orders to man the ramparts.[19] However, this does nothing to alter the essential problem. The point is that the extras in the play are, precisely, only extras and throughout the play Eteocles' interlocutor is never a citizen, unless one counts the messenger. But he is not a tragic character, his role is a purely functional one. The *parodos*, starting at line 78, the first pronouncement of the chorus, introduces the group that is to remain Eteocles' interlocutor throughout the *Seven*, and as in other plays this chorus is composed of women. It is with the women of Thebes that Eteocles speaks. We can go even further: It is with them that he attempts an impossible civic dialogue. In the famous tirade in which Eteocles expresses his horror for the female species (lines 181-202) and his fear of female subversion, he says:

τὰ τῶν θύραθεν δ' ὡς ἄριστ' ὀφέλλεται,
αὐτοὶ δ' ὑπ' αὐτῶν ἔνδοθεν πορθούμεθα. (193)
(Thus the enemy's cause is well advanced while we are ruined from within by our own.)

The "we" of the city here refers to Eteocles and the women. We must point out straight away that the city finds itself caught between two dangers. One is an external threat, to wit, the aggression of the enemy, the other is internal, namely subversion on the part of the women. And, as we shall soon see, the situation is even more complex in that "the danger 'outside' which must not be let in, and the danger 'inside' which must not be let out," mentioned by Helen Bacon,[20] are one and the same danger. However, in the first stage in the unfolding of the tragedy, Eteocles, the military leader, also has the task of preventing the women from encroaching on the political terrain:

μέλει γὰρ ἀνδρί, μὴ γυνὴ βουλευέτω,
τἄξωθεν· ἔνδον δ' οὖσα μὴ βλάβην τίθει. (200)
(It's men's job — no place for women's plans here! — what lies outside. Stay home and cause no trouble!)

Eteocles' words can, indeed must, be set in the context of the long polemic directed against the *genos gunaikōn* that Hesiod initiated (*Theogony*, 591)[21] and that recurs so often, especially in tragedy. It is reasonable to suppose that in railing against women and telling them not to take part in the deliberations (μὴ γυνὴ Βουλευέτω), which is something that every chorus does by definition,[22] Eteocles remains within the Greek norm, at least so long as he remains the lucid leader of the city – that is to say (if we provisionally retain this dividing line), up to line 653.

But Eteocles would not be a tragic character if he did not go *beyond* the norm, that is to say if he did not overstep the boundary separating citizen from tyrant.[23] Eteocles brings into question the very existence of women:

> ὦ Ζεῦ, γυναικῶν οἷον ὤπασας γένος. (256)
> (Zeus – women! What a breed you created!)

In a striking stichomythia, it is the chorus of women that invokes the city gods while Eteocles accuses the women – these beings are, *par excellence*, apolitical – of reducing the city to slavery:

> ΧΟΡΟΣ: θεοὶ πολῖται, μή με δουλείας τυχεῖν.
> ΕΤΕΟΚΛΗΣ: αὐτὴ σὺ δουλοῖς κἀμέ πᾶσαν πόλιν. (253)
> (CHORUS: Gods of the town, keep me free from slavery!
> ETEOCLES: It is you who reduce us to slavery – myself and the entire city.)

It would be easy to extend these investigations. We shall limit ourselves to two remarks. In the famous invocation to the gods in lines 69-77, who are the female deities that Eteocles addresses alongside Zeus and the city gods? They are Ara, the Curse, the paternal Erinys, and also Gē, the earth of the fatherland. A special relationship, to which I shall be returning, links Eteocles, the other descendants of the Spartoi, and the land of Thebes. But in Greek mythology this direct relationship always implies what Lévi-Strauss would term an excess of masculinity.[24] It is the males, the issue of mother earth – and the males alone – who defend the mother earth.[25]

To the women, Eteocles has only one positive request to make:

κἀμῶν ἀκούσασ᾽ εὐγμάτων, ἔπειτα σύ
ὀλολυγμὸν ἱερὸν εὐμενῆ παιώνισον,
Ἑλληνικὸν νόμισμα θυστάδος βοῆς,
θάρσος φίλοις, λύουσα πολέμιον φόβον. (267)

(Then listen to my wishes, and with a favorable paean accompany them with the sacred cry that, in accordance with Greek custom, greets the fall of the victims. It [the cry] will give our men confidence and dissipate their fear of the enemy.)[26]

What is the meaning of this request? First, let us point out, with L. Deubner, that the paean that Eteocles expects from the women is a specifically male cry.[27] It is a war cry that women are not normally skilled at emitting. In this particular instance there can be no question of any sacrifice. No doubt Eteocles does intend to offer the gods a great sacrifice (271-8) but this *ololugmos* must be raised immediately to fulfill his wishes. In that case, it is to greet not the sacrifice or even the salvation of the fatherland,[28] but the war; not the death of an animal but the death of men. Both the poet and his public know that Eteocles is preparing to kill a man, the closest of all those close to him. The equivocation between war and human sacrifice has already been suggested in lines 230-2.[29]

ἀνδρῶν τάδ᾽ ἐστί, σφάγια καὶ χρηστήρια
θεοῖσιν ἔρδειν πολεμίων πειρωμένους·
σὸν δ᾽ αὖ τὸ σιγᾶν καὶ μένειν εἴσω δόμων. (230)

(This is men's job, to offer sacrifice and appeal to the gods when we begin to strike[30] the foe. Yours is silence, to remain home, inside)

This is, I think, a good example of what has been called "tragic interference."[31]

Now, after line 653, this relationship between Eteocles and the women is reversed. Now it is the women – the women whom the messenger, after the death of the two brothers calls "children, women, too much daughters of your mothers [παῖδες μητέρων τεθραμμένα]" (792), to adapt P. Mazon's neat French translation – it is the women who take a direct hand in politics, proffering advice to Eteocles. Here is an example that says it all.

πιθοῦ γυναιξί, καίπερ οὐ στέργων ὅμως. (712)
(Give heed to women, for all your dislike.)

Even if Eteocles, becoming entrenched in his warrior *hubris*, his ἀνὴρ ὁπλίτης (717), refuses to obey, the reversal is unaffected for it is now the women who embody the values of order, those of the city. It is a violent reversal for it was obedience, even a military discipline, that Eteocles had wanted to impose upon the women:

Πειθαρχία γάρ ἐστι τῆς Εὐπραξίας·
μήτηρ, γύνὴ σωτῆρος· (224)
(Obedience, you know, is Good Luck's mother, wife of salvation, they say.)

And note the amazing juxtaposition of μήτηρ, γυνὴ. Eteocles had proclaimed his sovereignty over the population of women and it is his right to apply the death penalty to all and sundry, "man, woman, or any other [ἀνὴρ γυνή τε χὥ τι τῶν μεταίχμιον]"[32] who bring his authority into question.

One may even wonder whether this reversal that, in the space of a single line, supplants a hypermasculine government by a gynocracy,[33] may not in its turn illuminate the much discussed ending of the *Seven*.[34] For, to judge by the texts of the manuscripts, it is indeed a political debate that sets one half of the chorus against the other half, whether or not the two groups are headed by Antigone and Ismene. It is a debate that sets in opposition on the one hand the changing law of the city and, on the other, the stable law of lineage.[35] Whether or not it is entirely from the hand of Aeschylus himself, the epilogue of the *Seven* is altogether in line with the logic of the play.

The third problem is, of course, what meaning should be attached to the famous sequence of the seven parallel speeches, the *Reden-paare* as the German critics have it, pronounced by the messenger and Eteocles, the former describing the enemy leaders, the latter turning these descriptions around and applying them to the Theban leaders. This sequence contains the description of the seven Argive shields and one Theban one – which is my particular concern in this chapter.

It is certainly not virgin territory. It is not easy to give an account of the full extent of all that has been written on this subject since 1858 when Friedrich Ritschl published his famous essay on the parallelism of the seven antithetical speeches.[36] He attempted to show that the speeches pronounced by the messenger and Eteocles were strictly parallel, with exactly the same number of lines – an endeavor that involved pruning, lopping, and cutting the text as transmitted to us until he obtained the absolute symmetry of a lyric ode. If I mention the name of Ritschl here – Ritschl whose favorite pupil was Friedrich Nietzsche – it is not because I have found what Wilamowitz called his "tyrannical dialectic"[37] convincing. It is because Ritschl's analysis, with its admittedly "terrorist"-like determination to find an absolute symmetry, shows what is in its own way an anticipation of a structuralist approach. To recall the excesses to which he was led is, for me, a way of offering up what Jakob Larsen (in totally different circumstances) called "a humble prayer to Sophrosune."[38]

Ever since Ritschl the "subject," so to speak, has been constantly reworked. But what has been the object of these studies? Has it been the same as our own – namely to account for the parallel "mutations" of Eteocles and the chorus of women by studying the principal scene in the play? Here, I am bound to note, for example, that we can learn absolutely nothing from the principal modern study, that of one of Wilamowitz's most distinguished disciples, Eduard Fraenkel, since the problem of the meaning of the scene is never even posed.[39] The fact is that what most of the modern literature on the subject has failed to do[40] is squarely attempt to show — through the network of images from which the scene is woven — how the dramatic action progresses or, to put it another way, how the Erinys of Oedipus is at work.[41] What, ideally, is the task of the interpreter? I must repeat, in the face of the positivist tradition, that it is to interpret, if only because Aeschylus' very text constantly cries out for interpretation; it demands an interpretative approach. The messenger describes, one after another, the seven warriors about to attack Thebes and, more specifically, he describes the devices that adorn their shields.[42] Seven shields are mentioned, and then an eighth is added — that of the Theban Hyperbios, but there is a total of only seven devices since the shield of Amphiaraos is blank. Of course, each device has a clear and hostile meaning with regard to Thebes. But this meaning is reversed by Eteocles in his dialogue with the messenger, upon which the chorus comments.[43] There is one thing that Eteocles — up to line 653 — does not know but Zeus and the poet who is his interpreter do: It is that the network of emblems that appears to announce the fall of Thebes foretells not only its salvation but also disaster for the house of the Labdacids and the deaths of Eteocles and Polynices.

Ideally, the task of the interpreter is a truly gigantic one. What must in effect be done is work across several different levels. First, there is what is said, directly, by the three actors on stage, the messenger, Eteocles, and the women. Then there are the characters *represented at one remove*: the Seven against Thebes and their Theban adversaries; and third, those *represented at two removes* who appear on the devices, ranging from the moon on Tydeus' shield to the would-be *Dikē* on Polynices'. Next, there is the spatial framework, again a represented one, that of the seven gates of Thebes together with the deities that guard them. And finally,

over and above Aeschylus' text and the interpretations that have
been made of it from Euripides right down to our own times,
there are the texts that Aeschylus himself used for reference, the
Homeric poems and the lost epics of the Theban cycle. That is just
a resumé of all that a detailed global study ought to bring into
play. A difficult undertaking if ever there was one, even perhaps
impossible.[44] But it is not the focus of my ambitions. I shall simply attempt to define *one* network of meanings, that of the devices,
and to relate it to the dramatic movement of the play. Later on,
of course, I may look farther afield and bring in other levels of
the text as well, but I hope I have clearly defined my initial goal.

I now propose, as a purely practical hypothesis, to offer a reading of the collection of devices with the aid of a schema borrowed
from an art form from the time of Aeschylus, that of the sculp-
tured pediment (Figure 8).[45] Not that I intend in any way to suggest that Aeschylus himself had such a schema in mind as he wrote
this tragic scene. It is just that I think that this schema will make
it possible to regroup a number of facts in a convenient fashion
so that they convey a message to *our* eyes that have read Aeschylus
and seen the pediments of Olympia. It seems to me reasonable
to suggest that these two forms of art can, after all, sometimes
be congruent. Furthermore, Aeschylus himself invites us to bring
together two forms of art. In his text he describes an imaginary
world of manufactured objects – objects that have a message, that
mean something, both as omens and as works of art. As for the
method I shall use here to describe these objects, that is the
devices, it lays no claims to originality. It is simply a matter of
applying the old scholastic rule of defining each object *per genus
proximum et differentiam specificam.*

Let us begin at the beginning: The first shield, belonging to
Tydeus, carries a ὑπέρφρον σῆμα (387), "a haughty device."

> φλέγονθ᾽ ὑπ᾽ ἄστροις οὐρανὸν τετυγμένον·
> λαμπρὰ δὲ πανσέληνος ἐν μέσῳ σάκει,
> πρέσβιστον ἄστρων, νυκτὸς ὀφθαλμός, πρέπει. (388)

(Heaven forged with flaming stars and at the center shines, most revered among the stars, the bright full moon, the eye of night.)

Eteocles ripostes by refusing to recognize any general symbolic meaning in emblems:

οὐδ' ἑλκοποιὰ γίγνεται τὰ σήματα· (398)
(No wounds are dealt by shield devices.)

But that is just his first ploy, for Eteocles, playing on the two possible meanings of the word "night" — the "physical" on the one hand and the "metaphorical"[46] one of death, on the other, declares that the symbol will recoil against its owner:

εἰ γὰρ θανόντι νὺξ ἐπ' ὀφθαλμοῖς πέσοι (403)
(For if death's darkness does fall on his eyes.)

Here, at the beginning of the series, at all events, we are in the cosmos, but a nocturnal cosmos with the moon in the center functioning as an anti-sun,[47] "a fearful black sun whence the night shines out [un affreux soleil noir d'ou rayonne la nuit]," to borrow an image of Victor Hugo's.

With the shield of Capaneus we leave the domain of the cosmos to enter that of war and warriors:

ἔχει δὲ σῆμα γυμνὸν ἄνδρα πυρφόρον,
φλέγει δὲ λαμπὰς διὰ χερῶν ὡπλισμένη·
χρυσοῖς δὲ φωνεῖ γράμμασιν "πρήσω πόλιν." (432)
(His sign is a naked man bearing fire, a flaming torch in his hands as weapon, who is crying out in golden letters, "I'll burn the town.")

We have, in effect, passed from the cosmos to the world of men, men who speak and who *write*. The shield conveys a meaning not just through the image but through its text — which is equally

Figure 8.

deceptive. The warrior is *gumnos*. The word here has its classic technical meaning. The "naked" warrior is the warrior without armor.[48] It is the lightly armed warrior who specializes in fighting by night and uses the techniques of hunting and ambush, one of the two types of soldiers of classical Greece,[49] and the text emphasizes this with its use of the verb *hoplizō*: The weapon of this warrior of the night is a torch.[50] This type of warrior stands in opposition to the heavily armed hoplite and we do not need to look far afield for him since he, in point of fact, appears in the emblem of the next warrior, Eteoclos:

> ἐσχημάτισται δ᾽ ἀσπὶς οὐ σμικρὸν τρόπον·
> ἀνὴρ δ᾽ ὁπλίτης κλίμακος προσαμβάσεις
> στείχει πρὸς ἐχϑρῶν πύργον, ἐκπέρσαι ϑέλων·

βοᾷ δὲ χοῦτος γραμμάτων ἐν ξυλλαβαῖς,
ὡς οὐδ' ἂν Ἄρης σφ' ἐκβάλοι πυργωμάτων. (465)
(His shield is arrogantly devised: A man in armor on the rungs
of a ladder attacks an enemy fortress, bent on destruction; he
bellows in lettered words that not even Ares could cast him
down from the towers.)

This is a strange hoplite indeed, fighting all on his own – not, as
is the rule, in line with other hoplites. As well as the transition
from the "naked" to the heavily armed warrior, we should note
two other shifts or, perhaps progressions from the preceding shield.
On Capaneus' shield the city was simply named: *ΠΡΗΣΩ ΠΟΛΙΝ*;
here it is represented by its most telling image, the ramparts. The
challenge issued by the naked warrior was issued to the city, that
of the hoplite is directed at the god of savage warfare: Ares.

This change of level so to speak eases in the mutation introduced by the shield of the fourth leader, Hippomedon. It is a shift
from the world of men to the primordial world of the gods and the
battle they had to wage in order to impose their sovereignty:

ὁ σηματουργὸς δ' οὔ τις εὐτελὴς ἄρ' ἦν
ὅστις τόδ' ἔργον ὤπασεν πρὸς ἀσπίδι,
Τυφῶν' ἱέντα πυρπνόον διὰ στόμα
λιγνὺν μέλαιναν, αἰόλην πυρὸς κάσιν· (491)
(The designer must have been no common one, whoever put
on the shield its emblem – Typhon shooting out from his fiery
mouth a murky smoke, sister of glittering fire.)

The written text has disappeared to return only with the last
shield, which bears a human image.[51] If one is either above the
world of men among the cosmic forces, in the company of Zeus
and his adversary Typhon, or in the monstrous world of whatever
is subhuman, in the company of the Sphinx, there is no call for
any written sign. Writing is definitely peculiar to man. With
Typhon (or Typhoeus) Aeschylus' text as it were reverts to Hesiod.

Typhoeus does not exist on his own, only in and through his battle against Zeus, described in the Theogony.[52] Depicted on a shield,
Typhon almost automatically calls forth the appearance of Zeus.
However, Zeus cannot appear on an Argive shield. To do so would
be to forecast victory for the enemy. Zeus must, *at least initially*,
appear in the Theban camp, the camp that from a military point
of view is destined to win the day:

Ὑπερβίῳ τε πρὸς λόγον τοῦ σήματος
σωτὴρ γένοιτ' ἂν Ζεὺς ἐπ' ἀσπίδος τυχών. (519)
(So Hyperbios, to match his emblem, may find a savior, Zeus,
here on his shield.)[53]

Thus Hyperbios is the only Theban whose shield is described and
must appear in our collection.[54]

At this point we must introduce a double parenthesis. First
we must point out that it is this very clash between Zeus and
Typhon that suggested to us the model of the pediment. If there
is one classic form above all others for the sculpture in the tym-
panum of the archaic and classical pediment it is that of "antithetical grouping"[55] and, in particular, of a confrontation between
the deities of order and cosmic sovereignty on the one hand and
those of primitive disorder, monsters or giants, on the other. But
furthermore, one is very conscious of the fact that Zeus is not,
cannot be, a device just like any other and this is not simply
because his place is temporarily in Eteocles' camp. His appearance
is prepared for right from the beginning of the scene. Capaneus
declares that he is "ready to act, disdaining the gods, even in defi-
ance of Zeus," and it is a point that Eteocles immediately takes
up (443). It is the thunderbolt, the weapon of Zeus, that will
strike down the aggressor; it is this, not the torch on the device,
that will in reality be πυρφόρος (444). Zeus comes first, and
last as well.

The fifth chief, Parthenopaeus, also declares that he will rav-
age the city "in spite of Zeus [Βίᾳ Διός]" (531-2), and in line 662

289

the question arises as to whether Dikē, the daughter of Zeus, is indeed on Polynices' side. It is right that Zeus, who is present throughout the scene, from start to finish, should hold his dominating position on our pediment.

We can now consider the right hand side of the pediment, starting with the device on Parthenopaeus' shield:[56]

> τὸ γὰρ πόλεως ὄνειδος ἐν χαλκηλάτῳ
> σάκει, κυκλωτῷ σώματος προβλήματι,
> Σφίγγ᾽ ὠμόσιτον προσμεμηχανημένην
> γόμφοις ἐνώμα, λαμπρὸν ἔκκρουστον δέμας,
> φέρει δ᾽ ὑφ᾽ αὑτῇ φῶτα Καδμείων ἕνα,
> ὡς πλεῖστ᾽ ἐπ᾽ ἀνδρὶ τῷδ᾽ ἰάπτεσθαι βέλη. (539)

(The city's shame is on his bronze-wrought shield, the rounded protector[57] of his body – a raw-devouring Sphinx, neatly riveted there; he wields this shield with the bright embossed shape that holds in her claws a Cadmeian, one man to take the shower of missiles hurled at him.)

The French translation of P. Mazon at this point refers to "Thebes," where the Greek text speaks of the "city." But it is true that, at the level of the emblems, we have passed from the city in a general sense to the particular city that is a plaything of destiny in the drama. It is a "Cadmeian" that the Sphinx pins down.[58] As for the presence of the monster herself, it for the first time brings us back to the intertwined legends of Thebes and the Labdacid family. "The city's shame" is also the glory and misfortune of Oedipus, king of Thebes and husband of Iocasta.

The seventh shield is that of Amphiaraos, the soothsayer, a character who – as we shall see – in a sense provides the key to the pattern as a whole.[59] We shall, for the time being, simply note the interplay of oppositions that it introduces:

> σῆμα δ᾽ οὐκ ἐπῆν κύκλῳ·
> οὐ γὰρ δοκεῖν ἄριστος, ἀλλ᾽ εἶναι θέλει (591)

(There was no device upon his round shield; he does not wish to seem but in fact to be the best.)

The whole collection of the rest of the shields is immediately shifted from the plane of being to that of seeming and the realm of ambiguous signs.

The last device appears on the shield of Polynices and it is the most complex of all. Like the second and third shields, it bears a written legend; again, like them, it depicts a human figure, a "warrior chiselled in gold." So this is not a simple hoplite like the one on the shield of Eteoclos. And next to the man is a woman *who declares* herself to be divine:

ἔχει δὲ καινοπηγὲς εὔκυκλον σάκος
διπλοῦν τε σῆμα προσμεμηχανημένον·
χρυσήλατον γὰρ ἄνδρα τευχηστὴν ἰδεῖν
ἄγει γυνή τις σωφρόνως ἡγουμένη·
Δίκη δ' ἄρ' εἶναι φησιν, ὡς τὰ γράμματα
λέγει "κατάξω δ' ἄνδρα τόνδε καὶ πόλιν
ἕξει πατρῴων δωμάτων τ' ἐπιστροφάς." (642)

(He has a newly wrought, well-rounded shield with a twofold device fashioned on it, worked in gold: a man pictured in armor, escorted by a stately woman who, as the letters read, says "I am Justice" and "I shall restore this man; he shall have his father's city and home to return to.")

With Polynices, as already with Parthenopaeus, we pass from foreign war, barbarian aggression against a city where Greek is spoken – as is indicated in lines 72-3 – to the conflict that is tearing Thebes apart. The Theban that the Sphinx holds in her power is the target of those defending Thebes. It is, by definition, the private *dike* of Polynices that is to lead him into his city, into his *oikos*.

Let us remain for a moment purely at the level of the emblems. How is the collection organized as a whole? Can we draw any provisional conclusions from this examination? In the course of our analysis we have tried to show the shifts that occur between one device and the next, as in a chromatic scale,[60] but now we can go further. The conflict between Zeus and Typhon, in which the victor is announced in advance, marks a definite break in the series. To its left is the side of the cosmos, the side of foreign war and the two fundamental forms of the warrior activity. The only female element here is the moon and it should be emphasized that its female quality is not really remarked upon by the poet. The men are male, warriors in all their violence. The "right" side is that of the legend of Oedipus, who appears on the shield of Parthenopaeus. On this side the female world predominates. Here it is indeed fitting to speak of gynocracy. On the shield of Parthenopaeus the Sphinx, which is both female and subhuman (it eats raw flesh), pins down a citizen of Thebes. It is a woman who is guide to the warrior on Polynices' shield. The left-hand side is that of the *polis* at grips with the enemy, the barbarian aggressor who wishes to destroy the city, and it sums up the first part of the play. The right-hand side reminds us of the dreadful problems of the Labdacid lineage. And, if we must come back to the "split" character of Eteocles, which was our point of departure, I would say that the left-hand side concerns Eteocles as a warrior and citizen while the right-hand side concerns Eteocles, the son of Oedipus and Iocasta and brother of Polynices. The very least that can be said is that the "break" at line 653 is carefully prepared for. As line 519 declares, the emblems do indeed have a language.

Now, if my analysis is not completely mistaken it should find confirmation of some kind in the context, that is to say, in the first instance, in the men who bear the shields and in those who are Eteocles' companions. And such is indeed the case.

It is all the more legitimate to make this shift from the devices to the men who bear them given that this is exactly what Aeschylus himself does. Thus, when "turning around" the device of Eteoclos, Eteocles speaks – in the dual – of "*two* men and the town on the shield [καί' δύ' ἄνδρε καὶ πόλισμ' ἐπ' ἀσπίδος]" (478).[61] One of the men is Eteoclos, the other the hoplite depicted on his shield. At line 544 ἐπ' ἀνδρί refers to the Cadmeian grasped by the Sphinx and his symbolic wounds stand for real wounds. And when, in line 398, Eteocles declares that emblems cannot wound, it should not be forgotten that these are the words of a tragic hero ruled by Ate ̄. The emblems will not inflict the wounds that they presage but, through them, it is truly the Erinys that is at work. The fact that its work is accomplished covertly, through cunning or *metis* – evoked throughout the scene if only by the representation of the deceptive skill of craftsmen – is one of the rules of the genre.

But let us return to the characters themselves represented on the pediment, in the order in which they appear. The left-hand side, which extends as far as Hippomedon, is truly that of male *hubris* and male savagery. Thus Tydeus:

βοᾷ παρ' ὄχθαις ποταμίαις, μάχης ἐρῶν (392)
(He yells threats by the stream, wanting battle.)

Capaneus oversteps human pride (οὐ κατ' ἄνθρωπον φρονεῖ; 425) but as Eteocles perceives, he is marked "by what for males are vain thoughts [τῶν τοι ματαίων ἀνδράσιν φρονημάτων]" (438). Eteoclos, whose shield challenges Ares, is clad in savage and barbarian equipment (βάρβαρον τρόπον; 463). Hippomedon, who carries the emblem of Typhon, is not so much man as giant (488).[62] There is nothing like this on the right-hand side – quite the contrary. Parthenopaeus is an ἀνδρόπαις ἀνήρ (533), a man who is a child who is a man, which reinforces what is already suggested by his name, a word on which the messenger plays (536). He is a metic, not a citizen, one who is marginal in relation to the city of Argos (548). His name, which stands in contrast to his wildness, is all the more feminine in character in that Parthenopaeus is not, as is the Greek rule, denoted by the name of his father, but by a reference to his mother: He is μητρὸς ἐξ ὀρεσκόου (532), the mountain-ranging

293

mother's son, in actual fact Atalanta, although she is not named.[63] Aeschylus could hardly have evoked this "matrilinear" theme better than by associating it with the "gynocratic" design of the shield.

The case of Amphiaraos is, of course, quite different. He, the diviner who, by reason of his desire "to be," has no device, gives the entire episode its significance. Two points must be made. Amphiaraos – in other words, in accordance with a kind of play on words often used by Aeschylus, "the man of the double curse"[64] – in effect curses two characters, Tydeus and Polynices, the first and the last of the series, and this is a way of giving meaning to the entire episode. He says of Tydeus that he is Ἐρινύος κλητῆρα (574), the herald, practically the usher of the Erinyes.[65] Describing Tydeus in this fashion is Aeschylus' way of alerting us, with the help of the diviner's truthful words, to what the scene is all about. What is *introduced* with Tydeus, in Amphiaraos' speech, is completed with Polynices. He is certainly cursed *politically*, as the attacker of the city of his forefathers (πόλιν πατρῷαν; 582), the land of his fatherland (585).[66] This is not simply a war against foreigners: Polynices is a Theban. However, Amphiaraos also says: "The mother-source – who can block that justly [μητρός τε πηγὴν τίς κατασβέσει δίκη]?" (584) or, to follow Paul Mazon's French translation ("Est-il donc un grief permettant de tarir la source maternelle?"), "Is there any grievance that can dry up the maternal spring?" But what spring is this? Dirke, the symbol of Thebes?[67] Perhaps, in an earlier time. But if we read μητρός as a causal genitive, it is difficult not to think also of the "maternal furrow [ματρὸς ἁγνὰν ἄρουραν]," of the chorus' speech (752-3), in which Oedipus has dared to sow his seed.[68] Polynices is to follow the opposite path. By killing his own brother and himself dying, he will in effect dry up the maternal spring. If this is the case, surely the presence of Iocasta is felt at this point.

Polynices is the last in the sequence seen, now, not by the diviner but by the messenger. He is not so much a warrior pure and simple, rather the brother of Eteocles employing the methods of legal revenge against his city. This accounts for his vocabulary in which legal and political terms are inextricably mingled. Like the figure on the shield of Eteoclos, he wants to scale the city walls (πύργοις ἐπεμβάς; 634). But he wants to be proclaimed master of the land, κἀπικηρυχθεὶς χθόνι through the herald, the κῆρυξ (634). For him Eteocles is the one who takes him prisoner, ἀτιμαστήρ (637), the one who has deprived him of his *time*. So far as his brother is concerned he wants to be the one who will exchange death or exile with him (636-8). For Polynices, external war and private justice form a single whole but, in the curse he has pronounced against him, Amphiaraos has already indicated that his *dikē* is not, as the shield proclaims, the real *Dikē*.

Now we must take a further step in our analysis and note a number of extremely strange phenomena. We must no longer pretend that we do not know what the entire play is directed toward: It is the duel between two brothers brought to catastrophe by the paternal Erinys, by those curses that Eteocles, in line 655, declares finally to be fulfilled, τελεσφόροι. Right from Tydeus, who introduced the theme, through to Polynices, it is this that we have witnessed. Everything has been a preparation for the "surprise" of the seventh gate.

But let us take a fresh look at the episode. The whole thing could, if you like, be summed up in the following lines:

τῷ τοι φέροντι σῆμ' ὑπέρκομπον τόδε
γένοιτ' ἂν ὀρθῶς ἐνδίκως τ' ἐπώνυμον (404)
(The bearer of this arrogant device will see the symbol fully justified: It does foretell violence — to himself.)

The subject is, of course, Tydeus who is to die devouring the skull of his adversary, Melanippus.[69] But at another level it is his own destiny that Eteocles repeatedly announces. The Theban leader posts the Spartos Melanippus, at the first, the Proetid gate, to confront Tydeus, and he goes on to say:

295

ἔργον δ᾽ ἐν κύβοις Ἄρης κρινεῖ·
Δίκη δ᾽ ὁμαίμων κάρτα νιν προστέλλεται
εἴργειν τεκούσῃ μητρὶ πολέμιον δόρυ.

Following Paul Mazon's French translation: "The dice of Ares may decide the outcome of the fight; but it is really the Law of blood which sends him, in its name, to fend off the enemy lances from the land to which he owes his life" (or, to put it more simply, "from the mother who gave him birth"). Very well, but what is this *Δίκη ὁμαίμων*?[70] Quite apart from the relationship between a man and the earth, the mother of the Spartoi, there are after all two characters in the play who are of the same blood and whom *Dikē* brings into conflict. In line 681 their death is described as "the death of two men of the same blood [ἀνδροῖν δ᾽ ὁμαίμοιν θάνατος]." And this is again what the chorus says in line 939. The earth has received their mingled blood: "They are well and truly of the same blood [κάρτα δ᾽ εἴσ᾽ ὅμαιμοι]," where there is a play on words on the theme of consanguinity on the one hand and the blood actually shed on the other.

In Eteocles' third speech (in a line to which I have already referred) the king vouchsafes the hope that not only the man who bears the third shield, Eteoclos, but also the hoplite who is his device, together with the town that appears on the shield, will perish under the onslaught of the Spartos, Megareus: καὶ δύ᾽ ἄνδρε καὶ πόλισμ᾽ ἐπ᾽ ἀσπίδος (478). Two remarks are prompted at this point. The first – not an original one – is that by his very name Eteo*clos* appears to be a doublet of Eteo*cles*. It has been suggested that Eteoclos is "Eteocles beyond the walls."[71] Thus the city defended by Eteocles is attacked by another Eteocles so that he is both inside and outside the city. After all, alone of the Seven, Eteoclos has an ἀνὴρ ὁπλίτης on his shield (466), which is precisely the definition that Eteocles applies to himself (717). But beyond the walls Eteocles also has another double, a much more obvious one than this quasi-homonym: to wit, his brother. When, referring to the duel, he predicts the death of two men he is telling us of his own and his brother's deaths. He, the victim of Atē, associates the city with the fate of the two warriors whereas the tragic *dénouement* dissociates precisely what the tragic *action* associates. Earlier, in lines 71-2, Eteocles foresaw his destiny with more lucidity: "At least, do not blot out my city, root and branch [μή μοι πόλιν γέ... ἐκθαμνίσητε]."[72]

But line 478 is not the last allusion to the theme of the two brothers before it becomes quite clear. Faced with the Argive enemy, Hippomedon and Parthenopaeus at this juncture, Eteocles associates two brothers, Hyperbios and Aktor (555). And when the messenger comes to the only brother who really counts, Polynices, notice that his emblem is a double one: διπλοῦν τε σῆμα (643). And perhaps this doubling is the hidden rule that governs the entire episode. Helen Bacon saw this clearly: "Each brother is subject to the law he invokes against the other. This is the inescapable knowledge which the shields express,"[73] and Aeschylus' Eteocles is, in his own way, also conscious of this:

ἄρχοντί τ' ἄρχων καὶ κασιγνήτῳ κάσις,
ἐχθρὸς σὺν ἐχθρῷ στήσομαι. (674)
(Prince against prince, brother against brother, as personal foes we'll meet!)

Right up to the political conflict in the epilogue the words henceforth used to describe Eteocles and Polynices are the same. There is a fusion between foreign and civil war, between the two sides of the pediment. Thebes is saved but its two generals, δισσὼ στρατηγώ (816) are dead.[74] Both are "quarrel-seekers," they are a couple of Polynices:

καὶ πολυνεικεῖς
ὤλοντ' ἀσεβεῖ διανοίᾳ. (832)
(And, quarrel-seekers as they were, did not both perish in a sacrilegious thought?)

It is quite clear that, despite what Eteocles says (508), it is not Hermes but Zeus who has paired off the couples in such a way as to end up with this particular one.

However, alongside this doubling, above and below it as it were, there is (as Howard Cameron correctly perceived),[75] a myth that runs right through this scene and indeed right through the entire play. It is the myth of the Spartoi, the warriors sown and harvested by Cadmos with the teeth of the dragon.[76] These warriors are autochthonous, and autochthony is a mythical procedure that eliminates the role played by women in originating the human species and that makes it possible for men to establish themselves as warrior fraternities. There is no such thing as autochthony for women.[77] But in the particular case of the Theban legend evoked by Aeschylus, these autochthonous warriors kill each other: Only five of them survive and on them Cadmos confers the status of citizens.[78]

Let us take a final glance at our schema, this time filling it out a little, for once, with data gathered from other sources. The Spartoi are explicitly mentioned as confronting Tydeus, in the shape of Melanippus (413), and Eteoclos, in the shape of Megareus (474). François Vian has noted that Polyphontus, Capaneus' adversary, is also probably a Spartos since he is the son of Autophonos, a name typical for a Spartos.[79] He is the "killer of many," the son of the "killer of himself." I can see no very compelling reasons for the rest of the Theban warriors to be Spartoi.[80]

It does seem that we can say that on the "left-hand" side of our schema, whether inside the walls or outside them, we are in an exclusively masculine world, that is to say a world in which mothers do not exist. The only mother is the earth, the earth that Eteocles invokes in line 16 when he calls on the citizens to fly to the help of the city: "the motherland, a nurse most dear [$Γῆ$ $τε$ $μητρί$, $φιλτάτῃ$ $τροφῷ$]" (17)[81] — the earth that nourished the Spartos Megareus (474). Motherhood in the true biological, rather than metaphorical, sense of the term appears for the first time in connection with Parthenopaeus who is described as "the mountain-ranging mother's son" (532), and next in connection with the crime that Polynices is about to commit (584) — that is, if my interpretation of the text is correct.[82] Now, in the very next line (585), the earth changes its gender; it becomes *patris* instead of *mētēr*.

On the shield of Polynices it is a woman who leads the hero to the dwelling of her father, a kind of inversion of the marriage rite: κατάξω δ' ἄνδρα τόνδε (647); and Eteocles breaks new ground when he refers to the childhood of his brother, the moment when he was "fleeing from the dark of the womb [φυγόντα μητρόθεν σκότον]" (664).[83] With maternity defilement reappears. Eteocles and Polynices can no longer be Spartoi or — to put it another way — they are the last of them.

One further word, before we leave Aeschylus. There was in the fifth century at least one man who read Aeschylus with care and that was Euripides.[84] In *The Phoenician Women*, Euripides mocks at Aeschylus' long description:

ὄνομα δ' ἑκάστου διατριβὴ πολλὴ λέγειν. (751)
(It is a waste of time to give every name.)

His Eteocles, far from being taken by surprise, desires to meet Polynices outside the walls (754-60). After which, of course, when the first part of the duel is over, the messenger describes the combatants. The order is not the same as it was in Aeschylus; Polynices is no longer the seventh. Equally, the devices are different, with the exception of the blank one of Amphiaraos (1110-2).[85] Parthenopaeus, the first named warrior, has not a sphinx but simply a family emblem, to wit, Atalanta hunting the boar of Calydon (1108-9). Hippomedon has Argos Panoptos for his coat of arms (1115). Tydeus protects his with a lion skin and holds in his right hand[86] "the Titan Prometheus carrying a torch as if to set fire to the town" (1112) — an obvious reference to the shield of Capaneus. Polynices carries an animated device: the mares of Potniai, devourers of human flesh, which can be made to move by means of a spindle (1123-9). Capaneus has a giant uprooting a city (1129-33) – another reference to Aeschylus. Adrastus has snakes carrying off the sons of Cadmos in their jaws (1138), clearly copied from the shield of Parthenopaeus. To uncover the pattern of this collection is a task I have not attempted. Is it any more than a systematic deconstruction of Aeschylus' schema? At all events, everything would seem to indicate that the scene of the *Seven* formed a sufficiently coherent whole for Euripides to strive to destroy it.

Pierre Vidal-Naquet

CHAPTER XIV

Oedipus in Athens*

The Poet and the City

"Fortunate Sophocles! He died after a long life, a man both lucky and talented: he wrote many fine tragedies and met with a fine end, without ever having suffered any misfortune." Those are the words with which Phrynicus, in his comedy *The Muses*, written in 405 B.C., honored Sophocles' recent death at the age of ninety (in 406). There is a clear allusion here to the opening lines of *The Women of Trachis* (1-3):

> It was long ago that someone first said:
> You cannot know a man's life before the man
> has died, then only can you call it good or bad,

as also to the lines of the end of *Oedipus Rex*:

> ...Count no mortal happy till
> he has passed the final limit of
> his life secure from pain. (1529-30)

The life of Sophocles seems to have been quite the reverse of a tragedy. It was, furthermore, conspicuously public and political, in which respect Sophocles differed both from Aeschylus, an ordinary citizen who fought at Marathon but never held any position of responsibility and from Euripides, a private man who died, shortly before Sophocles who was slightly older than him, at the court of the king of Macedon. Sophocles' life spanned the great Athenian period, ending two years before its collapse in 404. He was born in 496 or 495 — a dozen years after the reforms of Cleisthenes (508), which provided the framework for the future Athenian democracy. He was the son of Sophilus, a wealthy Athenian who owned a team of blacksmith and carpenter slaves. He came from the deme of Colonus, on the boundary with the countryside, which he was to depict in the last of his works. He gave up the idea of performing in his own tragic works on account of his weak voice. He married an Athenian and was the lover of a Sicyonian woman, which gave rise to a number of family difficulties. His legitimate son, Iophon, himself an author of tragedies, resented his alleged favoritism toward his illegitimate grandson, the poet Sophocles the Younger; but it seems unlikely that he was ever accused of senility by his children, as is claimed by an anonymous biographer. He won an unprecedented number of victories in the tragic competitions: He is supposed to have been crowned twenty-four times and never to have rated lower than second place. Aeschylus won only thirteen crowns and Euripides was winner on no more than five occasions, one of them posthumous. In 443, he served as *hēllēnotamias*, that is to say administrator for the Athenian treasury contributed by the "allies" of Athens; in 440 he was appointed *stratēgos* alongside his friend Pericles, whom he accompanied on the expedition to Samos, acting again in that capacity a few years later, in the company of the "moderate" Nicias. After the disaster of the Sicilian expedition (413), he was one of the ten "council commissioners" (*probouloi*) appointed after what amounted to a coup d'etat, which led to the short-lived oligarchic regime of 411. No doubt his long political career was furthered by his triumphs as an author of tragedies, and his political offices fell to him by election, not as the result of drawing lots. Nevertheless, none of this seems to have made a political expert of Sophocles. His contemporary, Io of Chios, declared: "In civic matters, however, he was neither wise nor efficient, but like any other individual among the better class of Athenians."[1] For "individual among the better class of Athenians," read "wealthy" and also "conformist." As a pious man and member of a group that practiced the cult of a doctor-hero, Amynus (the Helper), in 421 he provided a home for the statue of Asclepius that the Athenians had moved from Epidaurus. At his death, he was granted the supreme honor of heroization. He became Dexius, the Welcomer. The ranks of the besiegers of Athens are said to have made way for his funeral procession.

Aeschylus' *Oresteia* (458) may be regarded as testimony to the democratic reforms introduced by Ephialtes and supported by Pericles, who later succeeded him; and it is no doubt unnecessary to remind the reader that *The Persians* (472) provides our most direct "source" on the naval victory of Salamis (480). Euripides' works, seventeen of which have come down to us, make it both possible and legitimate to reconstitute the whole panorama of fifth-century Athenian history.[2] However, it is true, though paradoxical, to say that the works of the only one of the three greatest tragic poets to be involved at the highest level in Athenian political life are impossible to interpret in the light of contemporary events. Allusions to "current affairs" are few and far between and their interpretation is difficult and controversial. They illuminate neither the works nor the current events of the time. We know that Sophocles was a patriot and devoted to his native deme of Colonus, but that does not amount to much. In *Ajax*, Tecmessa bemoans the lot of bastards. Should we interpret this as an allusion to the law of 451 that restricted citizenship to men both of whose parents were Athenian?[3] Sophocles had been affected by the consequences of that law in his own family life, but then so had Pericles, who was the author of the law. Such a connection would neither illuminate nor help to date *Ajax*. The epidemic or "plague" described at the beginning of *Oedipus Rex* may be a reference to the Athenian plague of 430 but may, equally, have been suggested by Book I of the *Iliad*. Sophocles' oeuvre directly reflects nothing, or hardly anything, of the great Athenian adventure that was unfolding during the fifth century – the Persian Wars, the Athenian Empire, and the Peloponnesian Wars. A connection between Sophoclean tragedy and Athenian politics does exist though, but at a quite different level. Similarly, it is pointless to try to distinguish between the thought of Sophocles as an individual and his writing. He left no personal journal alongside *Oedipus Rex*. Admittedly, certain tragic passages can be compared with fragments from Heraclitus and Protagoras, but Sophocles does not create spokesmen for himself, as Euripides sometimes seems to. His only politics and philosophy are those of the tragedy itself and that, after all, is quite enough.

Of this vast oeuvre – comprising one hundred and twenty-three plays, according to one Byzantine lexicographer – seven tragedies have come down to us, the result of a selection of some academic of the early Roman Empire. Papyri discovered in Egypt indicate that these seven dramas were in effect those most read. The same source has also supplied lengthy fragments of a "satyr play"[4] entitled *Ichneutai*. Other fragments are known to us either through citations made by other ancient authors or through papyri. It is not beyond the bounds of possibility that an entire play might one day be discovered in Egypt. But during the Hellenistic-Roman period, Sophocles was less popular than Menander or even Euripides. Only two of his works can be dated with any accuracy: *Oedipus at Colonus*, his last play, staged in 401, after his death in 406, thanks to the efforts of his grandson, Sophocles the Younger; and *Philoctetes*, produced in 409. We know that *Antigone* was put on before Sophocles' election to the post of *stratēgos* (441). *The Women of Trachis* and *Ajax* are generally – on somewhat slender grounds – dated to 450-440, *Oedipus Rex* and *Electra* to around 430-420. In other words, we know nothing of the early years of Sophocles, whose first tragic victory came in 468. Plutarch tells us that he himself claimed that he adopted three different styles,[5] in the manner of Beethoven; however, we are in no position to verify that.

The Myth, the Hero, and the City

As Walter Nestle strikingly puts it, tragedy was born when myth began to be assessed from a citizen's point of view. The tragic poets found their subjects in the huge repertory of heroic legends left by Homer and the authors of other epic cycles, and represented in the pictures of the Athenian vase-painters. All the tragic heroes come from that repertory and it is fair to say that by the time Agathon, Euripides' younger contemporary and the representative of tragedy in Plato's *Symposium*, wrote a tragedy that for the first time featured characters from his own generation, classical tragedy was already dead (which is not to say that it did not survive as a literary genre). The only origin of tragedy is tragedy itself. The fact that a protagonist emerges from the chorus chanting a "dithyramb" in honor of Dionysus or that a second actor (in Aeschylus) or a third (in Sophocles) joins him in his confrontation with the chorus cannot be explained in terms of "origins." Nor is anything explained by the suggestion that the word "tragedy" might possibly refer to the declamation pronounced at the sacrifice of a goat (*tragos*). It is not goats that die in tragedy but men; and if a human death constitutes a sacrifice, it is certainly a distorted one.

However, Herodotus records an illuminating anecdote in this connection (V, 67). In the sixth century, the tyrant of Sicyon, Cleisthenes, the grandfather of the Cleisthenes of the Athenian revolution, apparently abolished the cult devoted to Adrastus, hero of Argos, and transferred the tragic choruses celebrated in his honor to the popular cult of Dionysus. Adrastus was a hero from the legend of the *Seven against Thebes* from which Aeschylus produced a tragedy. In religious terms, the hero is a creation of the city and does not appear to date from much further back than the eighth century. We know from archaeological studies that in the late eighth and early seventh centuries B.C., a royal tomb in Eretria, in Euboea, was surrounded by more modest ones and that they became places of worship. That is where heroes were born. They were, so to speak, recruited from all over the place, here and there, demoted gods or promoted kings. The important thing to note is that their cult was linked to their tombs, and these were situated in places that the city regarded as symbolic: in the agora, at the town gates, or on the city boundaries. The earthbound, "chthonian" hero thus stood in contrast to the celestial "ouranian" god. But another distinction was also established, as is shown by Herodotus' anecdote about the difference between a sixth-century city on the way to becoming a democracy and a full-fledged democratic city of the fifth century. Heroes and legends are connected with that world of noble families that, from every point of view — social practices, forms of religion, political behavior — represented all that the new city rejected in the course of the profound historical transformation that began in Athens with Draco and Solon (in the late seventh and early sixth centuries), to be continued by Cleisthenes, Ephialtes, and Pericles. A rift was created between heroic myth and the city, but it was not wide enough to prevent the hero from remaining an ever-present threat. Tyranny was not abolished in Athens until 510 and Oedipus is by no means the only tragic character who is a *turannos*. Justice (*dikē*) was a challenge to the noble and tyrannical tradition, but it was a justice that was as yet unestablished. Tragedy is constantly opposing one kind of *dikē* to another and shows clearly how "justice" can shift and be transferred into its opposite: Consider, for example, the dialogues between Antigone and Creon or between Creon and Haemon, or equally *Oedipus Rex*, where the hero is both the investigator acting on behalf of the city and at the same time the very subject of that inquiry.

In itself, a heroic myth is not a tragedy. It is turned into one by the tragic poet. Myths certainly incorporate any number of those *transgressions* that are the very stuff of tragedy: incest, parricide, matricide, the eating of one's children; but the myths themselves do not contain any *judgment* that evaluates those actions, such as the city was to pass and such as the tragic chorus expresses in its own particular way. Wherever it is possible for us to study the tradition in which the myth is told, we realize that it is the tragic poet who makes it come full circle in his tragedy. That is what Sophocles does. Homer's Oedipus dies on the throne of Thebes;[6] it is Aeschylus and Sophocles who turn him into a self-blinded exile. In *The Women of Trachis*, the poison that kills Heracles is not the semen of the centaur Nessus, but the blood of the hydra of Lerna. Sophocles makes that alteration, not so as "to attenuate the brutality of the primitive version" (as Paul Mazon suggests), but in order to establish the connection between on the one hand the action by which Dejanira "accidentally" but impelled by love, kills her husband Heracles and, on the other, the most useful and undeniable of his exploits, by which he rid the world of a monster. It is Sophocles, too, who sets up the opposition between Antigone and Creon, and Antigone and Ismene. Before Sophocles produced his version, Antigone and Ismene were cruelly treated not by the tyrant Creon, but by Leodamus, Eteocles' son and legitimate heir. In the legend of Philoctetes, about a warrior exiled after being wounded, then recalled to Troy and healed because his bow is indispensable to the capture of Troy, there was no suggestion of the tragic clash over the issue of cunning as opposed to honest combat that takes place between the old man excluded from the city and the young man who has not yet acceded to it. The Ajax of legend seems to have killed himself in a fit of frenzy. It is only in Sophocles' version that he regains his sanity before dying. The decision to allot the arms of Achilles to Odysseus is no longer made by the women of Troy but through a vote passed by the hero's peers.[7] Just as Antigone is set in opposition to Ismene, Electra is set in opposition to Chrysothemis, a character unknown even to Aeschylus, and that is how she becomes the intransigent guardian of the hearth of Agamemnon. And, to return yet again to *Oedipus Rex*, what did the legend of Oedipus amount to before the tragic poets took a hand? A story about a foundling child who becomes a conqueror, in which the fact that he kills his father and sleeps with his mother perhaps means no more than it would in any other of the many myths about kings acceding to their thrones.

Thus the hero is set apart from the city that judges him, and, in the last analysis, his judges are the very same who also award the prize to the winner in the tragic competition: the people assembled in the theater. Even in the cases where, with a stroke of genius, Sophocles reverses the situation and depicts not a casting out, but a return, as in *Philoctetes* and *Oedipus at Colonus*, the tragedy in which the old man exiled from Thebes becomes a hero in Athens, it is still necessary for that casting out first to have taken place: "It is only when I'm finished that I'm strong" (393).

Tragedy and History

Herodotus was Sophocles' contemporary and even his friend. He was one of the creators of historical discourse, just as Aeschylus and Sophocles were the creators of tragic discourse. Of course, Herodotus' work does not incorporate any tragedies in the strict sense of the term, for tragedy cannot be dissociated from the tragic *representation*. This involved a twofold confrontation: first, between the hero and the chorus and, second, between the chorus and the actors on the one hand and the city present on the tiered steps of the theater on the other. However, Herodotus' work does contain a number of tragic schemas. The stories of Croesus and of the Achaemenids — namely Cyrus, Cambyses, and Xerxes — all unfold following a pattern familiar to the readers of tragedy. Oracles are ambiguous and misinterpreted, invariably mistaken choices lead to a series of personal and political catastrophes. Through failing to find correct interpretation to oracles whose meaning is clear only to us, the readers, Croesus loses both his son and his empire. But who are these quasi-tragic heroes flawed by their immoderation (*hubris*) and brought low by divine vengeance (*atē*)? Virtually all of them are either Eastern despots or Greek tyrants (for example, Polycrates of Samos, among others), that is to say men who have taken over the city for their own profit. In Herodotus, the city, with its deliberative and executive organs, functions as an anti-tragic device, and that is true of "archaic" cities such as Sparta as well as of newly democratic ones such as Athens. Leonidas, king of Sparta, was killed at Thermopylae in 480, along with his three hundred warriors. Before entering the war, the Spartans consulted the Delphic oracle.[8] In this case, the oracle given had none of the ambiguity that characterizes tragic oracles and many other oracles to be found in Herodotus. It presented a straightforward political choice: Either Sparta would survive but one of its kings would die, or Sparta would be defeated but its king would live. Leonidas' choice is a political one; his is not a tragic death.

Miltiades of Athens is presented in Herodotus in two different, even opposed, guises. At Marathon (490), he is one of the ten elected *stratēgoi* of Athens, and is consequently perfectly integrated with the democratic city. But he is also the former tyrant of Chersonese, where he was a vassal of the king of the Persians and, after Marathon, his role – even in Athens – is that, not so much of a citizen, rather of a candidate for tyranny. He uses dishonest pretexts to embroil Athens in an expedition against Paros. On the eve of Marathon, the situation is the quintessential political one of a split vote. Five of the ten *stratēgoi* are in favor of attacking, five of holding back. The casting vote belongs to the nominal leader of the army, the "polemarch" Callimachus. Miltiades seeks him out, saying: "If the gods remain impartial, we may well win in this fight. Athens' freedom depends on you" (VI, 109). If the gods remain impartial.... The gods of tragedy are never impartial, even if all the decisive actions are carried out by human beings themselves. The decision at Marathon is a political one freely taken by a majority. But a few weeks later, this same Miltiades asks the Athenians to supply him with seventy ships, men and funds, "not telling them against what country he would lead them." The expedition is a failure: With a priestess of Paros for his guide, Miltiades enters the sanctuary of Demeter Thesmophoros, which is reserved for women. It is an action of immoderation. Panic-stricken, he draws back, suffering an injury from which he later dies. When consulted by the Parians, the Pythia lets it be known that the priestess was an instrument of divine vengeance: "It was not Timo, she said, that was at fault, but Miltiades was doomed to make an ill end, and an apparition had guided him in these evil courses"

(VI, 132-6). Here, the oracle makes its intervention after rather than before the event, but Miltiades is nonetheless duped by a misleading sign from the gods: Having behaved as a tyrant, he dies as a tragic victim.

The Hero and the Chorus

At the center of the circular *orchestra* stood the *thymelē*, the round altar of Dionysus. The members of the chorus moved slowly toward it when the chorus made its first entrance: This *parodos* was a solemn moment in the tragedy. The movements of the members of the chorus were dictated by the position of the *thymelē* as they turned now this way, now that, or remained still, grouped around it. Adjoining the orchestra lay the *skēnē* (hence the French *scène*, meaning "stage"), the construction where the actors took up position. Sophocles was probably the first to have it painted, which is not to suggest that an elaborate stage set was involved; it probably amounted to no more than a simple effect of perspective: in central position, a door, which could symbolize whatever was needed — the entrance to a palace, a temple, or a cave (as in *Philoctetes*). On either side, two openings allowing for entrances and exits, the one from or to the town, the other from or to the countryside. Controversy continues to rage over the question of the exact location of the actors. Archaeology can hardly afford a solution since the fifth-century theaters were built of wood and the stone-built ones that survive were reconstructed in Hellenistic or Roman times, dating at the earliest — as at Epidaurus — from the fourth century. However, to judge from the evidence provided by the texts themselves and by vase paintings, there seems little doubt that a narrow platform set in front of the *skēnē* separated the actors from the chorus. Steps constructed between the two made it possible for them to meet and speak to each other. Thus, at the beginning of *Oedipus at Colonus*, the chorus invites Oedipus to stand on the "step" formed by the rock. The Greek word used here is *bēma*, meaning both the step of a stairway and also a *tribunē* from which an orator would address an assembly of citizens. Above the *skēnē* there was a simple device for the gods to make their appearances, as Heracles does at the end of *Philoctetes*. A moveable platform could be pushed through the central door, for instance to exhibit the body of Clytemnestra at the end of *Electra*.

The major division was that established between on the one hand the three actors who took all the heroic roles and, on the other, the fifteen members of the chorus. The actors were always male: In *The Women of Trachis*, the same one would play now Dejanira, now Heracles. The chorus was collective while heroes, whether Creon or Antigone, were individuals. Both the chorus and the heroes wore costumes and masks, but the members of the chorus, like the city hoplites, were dressed in uniform. Even the chorus leader (the *coruphaios*), the essential intermediary between heroes and chorus, wore no distinctive costume. In contrast, the masks and costumes of the actors were individualized. Thus, in its own way, the chorus, confronting the hero marked by his immoderation, represented a collective truth, an average truth, the truth of the city. The hero either died or, like Creon and Philoctetes, underwent a radical transformation; the chorus lived on, unchanged. It may not have had the first word but, through its leader, it always had the last, as in *Oedipus at Colonus*: "This is where the story ends forever."

However, all that has been said above may now be reversed. First, we should note one technical but significant detail. The tragic competition was a public undertaking, as was the construction of warships; the city, which was responsible for the major task of building triremes, also provided the actors for the tragic competition. Similarly, just as a trirarch undertook as his liturgy to finance the outfitting of a ship and pay the wages of the crew, some wealthy Athenian, perhaps even a metic, under the supervision of the archon, would recruit a chorus and train it, or see that it was trained. The play as a whole was then judged by the citizens. It was the chorus, the mouthpiece of the city, which through its movements paid its respects to the altar of Dionysus, the god who, of all the Olympians, was the one most foreign to the city. Many of the chorus' words echo those of the hero, and vice versa, particularly as they enter into dialogue, modulating each other's speeches; but the fact remains that in general, when the chorus expresses itself collectively, the language and the meter that it adopts are extraordinarily complex, whereas the heroes use a simple, sometimes almost prosaic language (as, for example, in the dialogue between Creon and the guard, in *Antigone*). Furthermore, even if the chorus expresses collective and civic opinions, it is hardly ever composed of average citizens, that is to say male adults of an age to bear arms. Thirty-two tragedies have come down to us under the names of Aeschylus, Sophocles, and Euripides (although one of them, *Rhesus*, attributed to Euripides, is probably in reality a fourth-century work). Of those thirty-two, only three (*Ajax, Philoctetes,* and *Rhesus*), use a chorus composed of adult warriors (or sailors). In nine (including *Electra* and *The Women of Trachis*), the chorus is composed of women, in some cases slave women; in the twenty remaining plays (which include *Antigone, Oedipus Rex,* and *Oedipus at Colonus*), it is made up of old men. The exceptions represented by *Ajax* and *Philoctetes* are, in truth, hardly exceptions at all, since the warriors of the former and the sailors of the latter are strictly dependent upon their hero-masters, Ajax and Neoptolemus. Women, whether slaves or free, were never citizens in the Greek cities. They were beneath the city, relegated to a status of less than citizenship. As for the old men, it is tempting to describe them as super-citizens, since they were privileged in the assembly (where it was their right to speak first) and in the council (to which one could only belong after reaching a certain age — thirty, in the case of Athens). But whether less than citizens or more than citizens, women of Trachis or demesmen of Colonus, these figures were marginal to the city. In Athens, the council made proposals while the assembly made decisions; in the tragedies the chorus never makes decisions, or if it does they are derided. As a general rule, it is the hero — or the force that drives him — who commits himself to the irrevocable resolutions upon which every tragedy is based.

The Oikos *and the City*

The city was made up of individual hearths (or homes) that had to survive and perpetuate themselves in order to maintain the family religion, the seat of which was, precisely, the domestic hearth (*hestia*). On the *agora*, the *prytaneum* where the city received the guests it wished to honor, was the common hearth of the Greek *polis*, one of the places that symbolized it best. The city was made up of all these hearths. To be a *stratēgos* of Athens, it was necessary to own property in Attica and to be the father of legitimate children, and thus have a heritage to defend. But the city was not simply composed of these hearths, it engulfed them or rejected them, sometimes in violent fashion — as in Sparta, where the city-family opposition can be seen in its purest form — sometimes more subtly, as in Athens. In the fifth century, the great families, the *genē*, certainly continued to play an essential role, and a number of the city's leaders were drawn from their ranks. Pericles was a "Bouzuges" and was connected through his mother to the "Alcmeonid" *genos* that played a decisive role in the elimination of tyrants at the end of the sixth century. But the democratic city was also created in opposition to these great families. Fifth-century funerary art provides perfect testimony of a desire to stamp out the expression of family feeling, even on the occasion of deaths. The word *oikos*, which we sometimes render as "family," is itself difficult to translate. Sometimes it means family in the strict sense of the term, sometimes the family home, including all those for whom the hearth provided a focus — the parents, the children, and also the slaves.

Tragedy gives expression to this tension between the *oikos* and the city. On the deserted island that is the setting for *Philoctetes*, the two heroes are faced with the truly tragic choice between on the one hand joining the army fighting at the walls of Troy, in other words identification with the city, and, on the other, returning to the family hearth, in other words desertion. They would have chosen the latter course had they not been prevented by Heracles. Dejanira is willing to integrate Iole, the silent captive, into her home as a slave but, even if it means opposing the Panhellenic hero Heracles, she cannot divide her *oikos* and accept the presence of a second wife. In *Electra*, the tragedy sets up an opposition that leads to murder between Clytemnestra, the woman who plays a man's part, and her daughter who is determined to perpetuate the paternal hearth but whose normal "destiny" would be to leave it. In a typical play of words, both of them are described as *alektroi*, without a conjugal bed.

Antigone provides the most famous example of this tension. It is also the play that is most frequently misunderstood, despite the few illuminating lines that Hegel devoted to it in his *Aesthetics*. It is not a drama about a conflict between a "wild young girl," embodied by Antigone, and the cold reason of State, represented by Creon; that play was written by Jean Anouilh, not by Sophocles. It is in Anouilh's *Antigone* that Creon (or perhaps Pierre Laval) coolly calls a council meeting of ministers after the deaths of his entire family. Sophocles' Creon is as shattered by the catastrophe as is Antigone herself: He is a "walking corpse." The love (*philia*) that Antigone expresses in the opening lines of the play: "My sister, my Ismene...from our father sprung..." is a sentiment that relates to her *oikos*, the family that she refuses to split between the brother who is loyal to the city and the one who died attacking it (killed by that brother and killing him). But the *oikos* whose immoderate defender she becomes is the incestuous and monstrous family of Oedipus and the Labdacids.

The chorus declares:

Ancient the sorrow of Labdacus' house, I know.
Dead men's grief comes back and falls on grief.
No generation can free the next. (594-6)

Civic marriage is situated between two extremes, the very close, which is incest in which "bird eats the flesh of bird," to borrow an image from Aeschylus, and the very distant, which is marriage

to a foreigner. Oedipus committed incest and Polynices married
a princess of Argos:

> You speak of...
> ...the doom that haunts our house,
> The royal house of Thebes.
> My mother's marriage bed,
> Destruction where she lay with her husband-son,
> My father. These are my parents and I their child.
> I go to stay with them. My curse is to die unwed.
> My brother, you found your fate when you found your bride,
> Found it for me as well. Dead, you destroy my life. (862-71)

And the chorus' rejoinder is as follows: "Your self-sufficiency
has brought you down" (875). But then Creon, for his part, is
not a legitimate city magistrate. It is true that he is described,
as early as line 8, as the *stratēgos* of Thebes (the "commander,"
in the English translation by Elizabeth Wyckoff) and Ismene is
determined to obey the established powers (or, to be more precise, "those who are in charge," the technical definition for
the magistrates – and we should note this plural – in the city's
service). Creon himself does all in his power to assert his legitimacy. But it is radically denied by precisely those who, according to the city rules, are the least well placed to do so: the girl
Antigone, who declares: "The Thebans think as I do, but they
hold their tongues"; and Creon's own son Haemon, a son standing up to his father, a youth defying an adult, but also a citizen opposing a tyrant. Creon appeals to "A citizen obedient...
to (my) least command...he who accepts this teaching I can
trust, ruler or ruled, to function in my place" (668-9) – a perfect definition of ancient democracy. But in Haemon's long
speech that balances Creon's, the youth retorts: "Your presence
frightens any citizen" (690). And in the line-by-line dialogue
between father and son, the Athenian spectators were presented
with the following:

CREON: Is the town to tell me how I ought to rule?
HAEMON: Now, there you speak just like a boy yourself.
CREON: Am I to rule by other mind than mine?
HAEMON: No city is the property of a single man.
CREON: But custom gives possession to the ruler.
HAEMON: You'd rule a desert beautifully alone.
CREON: It seems the lad is firmly on the woman's side.
HAEMON: If you're a woman. It is you I care for. (734-41)

This legitimate leader, this man, this adult turns out to be a tyrant, a woman, a child. Because he is above the city (*hupsipolis*) he is also outside it (*apolis*). The chorus is unable to make a snap decision between the two opponents: "Both sides have spoken well" (725), but the logic of the tragedy, the logic of ambiguity, does come to that decision by following through to the end these two claims to legitimacy that are also two forms of immoderation.

Divine Time and Human Time
Reflections on the instability of human rights are as numerous and as commonplace in the works of the tragic writers as they are in those of their contemporary, Herodotus, or their predecessors, the lyric poets. In *Ajax*, Odysseus comments: "I see the true state of all us that live: We are dim shapes, no more, and weightless shadow" (125-6); and Athens replies: "...one short day inclines the balance of all human things to sink or rise again" (131-2). But when Oedipus perceives his misfortune, the chorus declares: "Time who sees all has found you out against your will" (1213). A contrast is thus drawn between the unstable time of human actions and the sovereign time of the gods, time that sets each individual in the place designated for him in the divine scheme of things. Divine time and human time coincide when the truth comes to light. So, after blinding himself, Oedipus can say:

It was Apollo, friends, Apollo
That brought this bitter bitterness, my sorrows to completion.

But the hand that struck me
Was none but my own. (1329-33)

The opposition between these two kinds of time is, in itself, much
more ancient than tragedy, but the point is that the tragic stage
is where these two temporalities, usually so out of step, eventually come together.

In Greek society, one of the normal means of communication
between the gods and human beings was oracular divination. In
tragedy, the one thing never questioned by the chorus is the sovereignty of the oracle. But when Iocasta perceives the truth, she
suggests the only possible way of flying in the face of the oracle:
"Best to live lightly, as one can, unthinkingly" (979). The trouble is that living "lightly" is just what the tragic heroes never do.
But there is a striking difference between the real oracles, the pronouncements known to us through the inscriptions of Delphi and
Dodona, and the tragic ones. The questions asked by the consul-
tants — individual or collective — of the real oracles envisage two
possibilities: Shall I marry or not? Should we wage war or not?
The reply given is either affirmative or negative. But with a tragic
oracle the situation is quite different. The question is a simple
one: It may be summed up in words that rise to the lips of nearly
all tragic heroes: "What shall I do?" The Delphic oracle warns
Oedipus that he will kill his father and marry his mother, but it
does not tell him that the king and queen of Corinth are not his
real parents. Creon returns from Delphi armed with the knowledge that someone is defiling the soil of Thebes, but the oracle
does not tell him who embodies the defilement. The techniques
of tragedy allow for any number of imaginable solutions to the
fundamental ambiguity. In *Philoctetes*, the prophecy of the Trojan
diviner, Helenus, is only revealed bit by bit. Is it Neoptolemus
who will take Troy? Or Neoptolemus armed with Philoctetes'
bow? Or Neoptolemus together with Philoctetes and his bow?
Only gradually do we learn the answers, and without this slow
unfolding of the revelation we could not understand the theft of

the exiled hero's bow, ordered by Odysseus and carried out by Neoptolemus. In extreme cases human behavior and the unfolding of the divine plan follow opposite courses. Like Aeschylus' *Oresteia*, Sophocles' *Electra* begins at dawn and ends at night. Dawn presents us with Orestes and the despairing Electra; night falls on the murder, in the dark depths of Aegisthus' palace. In between, a false temporality reigns, as a false tragedy is introduced into the true one with the erroneous announcement of Orestes' death in the chariot race at Delphi.

But, without doubt, it is in *Oedipus Rex* that this inclusion of human time within the time of the gods is most strikingly demonstrated. When the play begins, everything has already come to pass but as yet nobody knows it. Oedipus has already consulted the oracle, left his "parents' " home in Corinth, killed a traveller who barred his way, liberated Thebes from the Sphinx, married the city's queen and acceded to the royal throne, without regarding this sequence of events as anything other than just a sequence of events. Faced by the puzzle posed by the plague, he undertakes a judiciary inquiry, employing all the classic means of Athenian procedure: He consults the oracle, the diviners, and other witnesses too. What it shows him is himself: "All comes out clearly." The answer to the Sphinx's riddle was "man." The answer to the riddle posed by Oedipus is himself. As Aristotle noted (*Poetics*, 1452a 29 ff.), there are two elements essential to Greek tragedy, namely the *peripateia*, the reversal of the situation in which the protagonist finds himself, and *recognition*, that is to say the discovery of the truth; and in *Oedipus* the two are combined. But before the final discovery, one more hypothesis is suggested. If Oedipus is not the son of Polybus and Merope of Corinth, perhaps he is the child of Fortune (*Tuchē*) or even a wild man:

I account myself a child of Fortune,
Beneficent Fortune, and am not thereby
Dishonored. She's the mother from whom I spring;

318

> The years, my brothers, marked me, now as small
> And now again as mighty... (1080-3)

he declares, whereupon the chorus describes Mount Cithaeron, the wild frontier land that separates Thebes and Athens, as "native to him." However, in the end, there is no question of Fortune or any wild man in the tragedy. At the beginning of the play, Oedipus, the "tyrant," that is to say the one who is king by chance, is revered almost as a god by the assembled people of Thebes, young and old alike, before an altar that has every appearance of being consecrated actually to him. The moment when he discovers himself to be not merely a citizen of Thebes but indeed its legitimate king is the very point at which he is ejected from his city. That chance sequence of events now has a significance, a blinding significance, for him.

Double Speech

It was a fifth-century sophist who first composed *dissoi logoi*, "double speeches," to show that it was possible to argue first a thesis, then its antithesis. The logic of contradiction thus made its brilliant entrance into fifth-century Greece. The tragic poets — Sophocles in particular — were familiar with both the expression and the practice, but in their works the *dissos logos* is not a double speech that distinguishes between the "pros" on the one hand and the "cons" on the other; it is a speech of duplicity and ambiguity. At the level of what we would call word play, it is totally pervaded by ambiguity. Thus in *Antigone*, the poet plays on the name of Creon's son, Haemon (*Αἱμῶν* in Greek), associating it with the word for blood (*αἷμα*). Ajax's famous ambiguous speech (646-92) is understood by the chorus as an expression of the hero's resignation to the will of the gods and the command of the Atreidae: "I, though wretched, now have found my safety," he says. The audience, for its part, meanwhile realizes that Ajax has decided to kill himself. But the very structure of these plays is ambiguous and enigmatic too, as we have noticed in the cases of *Oedipus*

Rex and *Electra*. Let us try to understand why.

The political, religious, and social practice of the city instituted divisions the purpose of which was to establish everything firmly in its own domain, men in a correct relationship to each other and to the gods. The city territory thus marked out a separation between the domain of the cultivated fields that provided the citizens' livelihood and that of the wild frontier areas reserved for Dionysus and the hunters. Sacrifice, which established communication between men and gods but at the same time fixed a different status for each group (to men the meat, to the gods the aromas and the smoke), was fundamentally linked with the world of cultivated fields over which Demeter reigned. The animal sacrificed was a domestic beast, man's companion in his agricultural toil. The wild world on one side, arable land on the other: There should be no interference between hunting and sacrifice.

Warfare, also a social practice for the Greeks, exhibits a similar kind of polarity. Warfare was a collective activity, the responsibility of the body of hoplites as a whole, where each man positioned in the ranks was the companion of all his fellows and interchangeable with each of them. Battle was normally joined on the cultivated plain, which was suited to phalanxes clashing head-on and itself constituted the land that the city had to defend. All other kinds of warfare — ambushes, nocturnal fighting, frontier raids — were associated with the wild domain and limited to the wild element in the city, the young.

Through the tragic spectacle the city questioned itself. Both the heroes and the choruses successively embodied now civic, now anti-civic values. In this way, tragedy introduced an interference between things that the city itself strove to keep separate, and that interference constituted one of the fundamental forms of tragic transgression. The deified Heracles in *Philoctetes* stands for the hoplite values and it is he who eventually sends the two heroes of the tragedy off to fight side by side before the walls of Troy. The strictly human Heracles of *The Women of Trachis* is a completely different figure. As he confronts the river Acheloos "with the looks of a bull," he is described as coming from "Thebes of Bacchus, shaking his back-sprung bow [i.e., Scythian bow], his spears and club" (510-2). Those are the weapons of cunning, of classic single combat, of brutality. When Orestes makes his appearance in *Electra*, the oracle has already warned him that he must "Take not spear nor shields nor host; go yourself, and craft of hand be yours to kill, with justice but with stealth" (35-7). Before being killed by Orestes, Aegisthus has good reason to ask: "Why do you need the dark if what you do is fair?" (1493-4) and he tells Agamemnon's son, "Your father did not have the skill you boast of" (1500). *Oedipus Rex* constitutes an extreme case of ambiguity; in it, the hero is a hunter, but the quarry that he pursues is none other than himself. He ploughs the fields but the soil in which he sows his seed is none other than the maternal furrow. Ajax believes he is hunting and sacrificing warriors, human beings, but in reality the creatures that he butchers are sheep. His final action, performed not in front of the army but before the sea, on the frontiers of the wild world, is the sacrifice of a human being, himself: "The blade is firm in the ground, my slayer. And his cut...should now be deadliest" (815-6). His last farewell is specifically addressed to the soil of his own city, the plain where the army fights its battles:

> ...O my home and hallowed ground,
> Of Salamis, and my father's hearth, farewell
> ...and here all springs and streams,
> My nurses, you that wet the plains of Troy,
> Farewell! This last word Ajax gives to you. (859-63)

Knowledge, Art, Power

Athens had been determined to confirm its superiority over Sparta through its possession of the naval *technē*, an art or skill alien to the traditional Greek form of combat. In Thucydides, Pericles declares: "Seamanship, like any other skill, is a matter of art." When the Sophists set themselves up as educators of the democracy, they claimed to be teaching an art or skill. A famous chorus in *Antigone* sings the praises of the Promethean aspects of mankind and it is not simply by chance that it places seamanship at the head of human achievements:

> Many the wonders, but nothing is stranger than man.
> This thing crosses the sea in the winter's storm,
> Making his path through the roaring waves (332-7)

Here, mastery over the land and agriculture take second place. In the passage in which the chorus in *Oedipus at Colonus* sings the praises of Athens, that order is reversed; the poet passes from the wild world of "Dionysus reveller" first to the land and the olive tree, next to the horses of Poseidon and only then on to the sea. In truth, ambiguity was already present in the chorus in *Antigone*, for *deina*, the Greek word translated in English as "wonders" means both "marvelous" and "terrible." Sophocles' works present a wide range of figures who represent a humanist rationality based on *technē*, which is one aspect — but only one of many — of fifth-century Greece. At the simplest level, consider Iocasta who says, "human beings have no part in the craft of prophecy" (708-9) (the word used is again *technē*); and she tells Oedipus that the oracle ascribed to Apollo came not from the god himself "but from his servants," going on to say:

> As to your mother's bed, don't fear it.
> Before this, in dreams too, as well as oracles,
> Many a man has lain with his mother. (980-2)

It is indeed quite true that, according to Herodotus, divination sometimes gave an optimistic interpretation to such dreams of union with one's mother. In *The Women of Trachis*, Dejanira employs a different skill to win back Heracles' love: She prepares a magic potion (in reality a poison), the recipe for which she has recently obtained from the centaur Nessus.

Oedipus' position is at a different level. Through frequent word

play between his name (*Oidipous*) and the verb "I know" (*oida*),
Sophocles presents Oedipus as the one who knows. It was through
knowledge and skill that he delivered Thebes from the fearful
singer, the Sphinx. At the beginning of the play the priest, acting as spokesman for the people, appeals to Oedipus' knowledge:

> . . . Find us some strength for rescue.
> Perhaps you'll hear some wise word from some God,
> Perhaps you will learn something from a man. . . . (42-3)

When Tiresias, also speaking in riddles, declares: "The truth is
what I cherish and that's my strength," Oedipus, who rates the
diviner's skill lower than his own knowledge, retorts: "And who
has taught you truth? Not your profession, surely!" (357).

Faced with Creon, just returned from Delphi, Oedipus argues
as one skilled in the art of politics. He smells a plot hatched by
the diviner and his brother-in-law to eject him from power; and
for Oedipus knowledge and power go hand in hand.

But only one kind of knowledge is infallible: the knowledge
acquired through divination, as Oedipus knows full well since,
when faced with Tiresias, he claims that he himself possesses the
art of the diviner. The trouble is that diviners are as impotent as
they are clairvoyant.

In the century that followed the age of tragedy, Plato was to
counter Protagoras' dictum "Man is the measure of all things" with
one of his own, declaring that the measure of all things was God.
And it is fair to say that, in the tragic writers, the gods do appear
as the measure of all things but not until the *end* of the tragedy.
It is then, and only then, that the world, or rather the gods' overall plan, becomes "intelligible." Plato does not so much set the
sensible world in opposition to the intelligible world; rather, he
explains the former, which is no more than a reflection, in terms
of the latter, which it is within the powers of a philosopher to
discover. But in the tragic world, there are no philosophers capable of classifying beings in a true hierarchy; and that is why Plato

rejects tragedy. In the *Symposium*, Agathon, the tragic poet, is forced to accept the view expressed by Socrates, as is Aristophanes. There was no place in the tragic world for a hierarchy of types of knowledge or for the combination of knowledge and power envisaged by the philosopher. Power and knowledge come into constant collision in this opaque area that separates the world of the gods from that of men, and where meanings are forever a matter of guesswork. Even the chorus in *Antigone*, devoted to the praise of man, makes that point: "Clever beyond all dreams, the inventive craft that he has, which may drive him one time or another *to well or ill*" (364-6). *Oedipus at Colonus*, which shows the Theban hero acceding to eternity at the invitation of the gods and under the guidance of Theseus, the mythical founder of Athenian democracy, suggests that the first alternative was not beyond the bounds of possibility.

The Drama and the Reader

The trilogy to which *Oedipus Rex* belonged did not win the first prize in the competition in the Great Dionysia. It went to Euripides' nephew, Philocles, whose work has not come down to us (but who may have presented a drama written by his uncle). There was always the risk of losing to be faced in the tragic competition. Aristophanes' *The Frogs*, written in 406, the year of Sophocles' death, nevertheless tells us that by this date the supremacy of Aeschylus, Sophocles, and Euripides was undisputed, even if the order of merit in which they should be placed was still a matter of controversy. In the fourth-century Athens of Aristotle's contemporary, Lycurgus, bronze effigies were made of the three great tragedians and the people themselves financed new productions of their works. We are the heirs to that first burst of classicism, later modified by a series of Roman scholars.

The modern history of Sophoclean drama begins in 1585 on the third and the fifth of March, when *Edipo-Tiranno* was produced with princely pomp in Palladio's "Olympic theater" in Vicenza.[9] But just as a church designed by L.B. Alberti is no Greek temple, Palladio's theater was no ancient Greek one; in a sense it was quite the opposite. The painted sky above the stage was not the open air of the Greek theater. The stage was separated from the tiered seats in such a way as to eliminate the *orchestra* that used to mediate between the actors and the public. The patrons of the *Accademia Olimpica* were by no means representative of popular taste or opinion and the production of a *chef d'oeuvre* is not a tragic competition in which the authors, actors, and choruses of three tetralogies are all involved.

Of course, it is quite possible, today, to put on *Oedipus Rex* in the theater at Epidaurus, but an archaeological interpretation is still a modern interpretation and is bound to be so, even if each successive generation is convinced that, by delving deeper, it can discover the *real* Sophocles and the *real* Oedipus. Perhaps our own generation's only advantage is that it is in a position to claim that it is at least conscious of the deep sediment left by all these successive readings.

So we should be neither surprised nor indignant at all the contradictory grids that have been suggested as interpretative aids, one of the most recent being a psychoanalytic reading. When we attempt to understand Greek tragedy today, by systematically comparing the works themselves with the institutions, vocabulary, and forms of decision making that characterized fifth-century Athens, we do not aspire to any absolute knowledge. (There is no secret to *Oedipus Rex*; and to that extent Freud, fascinated as he was by the "famous decoder of riddles," was mistaken.) Even less do we claim to have discovered, once and for all, the meaning that the tragedy, as presented in the fifth century, held for its author and its public. All we have at our disposal are the works themselves; and there is no absolute meaning to them.

But at least that very term, "the works," should act as a caution, for the work is precisely what should be retained intact, since we can turn nowhere outside to find its meaning. Perhaps it is true that to understand the Oedipus myth we should, as Claude Lévi-Strauss somewhat paradoxically suggests, assemble all the dif-

ferent versions of the myth, those that date from before Sophocles, that of the poet himself and those of his successors, including
the inventor of the "Oedipus complex." However, a literary work
is not a myth and cannot be reduced to its basic elements. The
myth can only facilitate the reading of the work to the extent that
it differs from it, to the extent that we know — but often we do
not — what the poet has added and what he has discarded. Thus,
in *Oedipus Rex*, the Sphinx is not the female monster disgorged
by the earth and intent upon violating the young that other documents allow us to glimpse, nor is she one of Laius' daughters as
is suggested by a tradition recorded by Pausanias. She is simply
the "horrible singer" who asks the riddle.

That is not to say that we should not try to illuminate the tragedy by looking outside it. Tragedy was a spectacle that was at once
political and religious, and comparison with other political and
religious models may well prove fruitful. For instance, it has been
pointed out[10] that at the time of the production of *Oedipus*, the
play about the purifier and savior of his city, who becomes an
abominable defilement that the city rejects and expels, there
existed in Athens and elsewhere too in Greece two institutions —
the second of which seems to have been a politicized version of
the first. The *pharmakos* was a scapegoat (but a human one) whom
the city each year expelled from the town, as a symbol of all the
defilements accumulated over the past year, if necessary after
allowing him to live like some derisory king at the expense of
the public treasury for one whole year. And it is true that "Oedipus
does indeed carry the whole weight of all the misfortunes that
afflict his fellow-citizens," those very misfortunes from which
they were begging him to deliver them from at the beginning of
the play. Ostracism, the institution that Cleisthenes is said to have
introduced in Athens, and that was used between 487 and 416,
was designed to obtain a similar result by political means: The
city for a temporary period expelled those of its citizens whose
superiority was such that there was a danger of it exposing the
city to divine vengeance in the form of tyranny. As the chorus says,

in *Oedipus Rex*, "Hubris breeds the tyrant" (873), or, as Aristotle was later to put it, whoever cannot live within the community "forms no part of the city and so becomes either a beast or a god."[11] Such certainly is the fate of the character created by Sophocles.

Similarly, we know that in myth and also to a large extent in the context of the institutions of the archaic and classical periods, young citizens were stationed along the city frontiers before being integrated into the ranks of the hoplites. First, they underwent a period of military training involving ambushes or even, as in Sparta for instance, hunting and nocturnal exploits of cunning that made them into, as it were, the reverse of normal citizens. It is difficult not to draw a comparison between these facts and the situation of Neoptolemus in *Philoctetes*. He is the son of Achilles and the future conqueror of Troy, but for the time being he is an adolescent of the age of an Athenian ephebe, who lands on a desert island where he is under pressure from his leader, Odysseus, to steal Philoctetes' bow. It is an exploit that is out of keeping with both his father's past and his own future. At the end of the tragedy, the wild man whom Philoctetes had become and the young man temporarily committed to treachery are both reintegrated into the world of the city.[12]

These are no more than hypotheses, and others could be suggested in connection with other plays by Sophocles. Let me conclude with the simple observation that they are in no sense intended as substitutes for the interpretations that every reader of the Greek poet's oeuvre is bound to work out for himself.

Pierre Vidal-Naquet

CHAPTER XV

Oedipus Between Two Cities:

An Essay on *Oedipus at Colonus**

At the beginning of *Oedipus Rex* Oedipus is treated as a god. By the end of the play he is presented as a defilement by which the city of Thebes is afflicted. At the beginning of *Oedipus at Colonus*, he is a wretched, blind vagrant, the suppliant of the Eumenides and Theseus, king of Athens. By the end he has become the guest and benefactor of Sophocles' own city, the guide (ἡγεμών, 1542) who sets off toward the hero's tomb that awaits him, having resisted first Creon, who tries to force him to return to Thebes, then Polynices, who begs him to do so. In other words, he severs the connection that bound him to the *polis* of Thebes, where Creon is tyrant, and to the *oikos* of the Labdacids.

Much has been written on the subject of this model yet complex reversal,[1] and I make no claim to put forward any revolutionary views; at the most I offer certain points of clarification. This study will raise three questions between which I shall, naturally, try to establish a number of connections. First, Thebes and Athens are, of course, the two cities between which the vagrant Oedipus moves, driven from the former eventually to find asylum and death in the latter. How is the opposition between the two cities expressed and what does it signify? Second, what is the religious, juridical, and political status granted to Oedipus in Athens, not only in his lifetime but also after his death? Finally, within the dramatic space of the theater and within the wider space that is either directly or indirectly represented in it, how is the hero's transformation conveyed?

As is now generally agreed, the Greeks invented politics. But what exactly do we mean by that?[2] The human world is, in general, a world of conflicts; political action is designed to tackle those conflicts objectively, not necessarily with the hope of cancelling them. Political *decisions* are not made by a sovereign leader who speaks in the name of some deity, nor — as a rule — by a more or less unanimous consensus (although examples of the latter do exist). Usually, they are taken by a majority vote. Between the times of Solon and Cleisthenes, Athens became the breeding ground of politics *par excellence*. But, remarkably enough, Attic literature appears to have striven almost as hard to obscure that political activity as the city expended its genius on creating it. We should remember this, for example: From both historical sources and from documentary material (although these do not by any means coincide), we know of individual clashes between political leaders that the institution of ostracism made it possible to resolve, thereby restoring civic peace. We also know of important *Ecclesia* debates in which crucial decisions were made: whether or not to slaughter the Mytilenians, whether or not to undertake an expedition to Sicily. They were questions of as capital importance as those faced by modern democracies: whether to send men to the moon, whether to install Pershing missiles in Europe.... But, with the exception of the particular case of ostracism, we know nothing of the decisive factors at play that led to the decisions made.

In the light of the evidence provided by excavations in the Ceramicus, even the matter of ostracism appears quite different from the picture given by the city's ancient historians. Consider, for instance, two figures: Meno, son of Menocleides, and Callixenus, son of Aristonymus (possibly one of the Alcmeonids) to whom many of the potsherds discovered by American archaeologists refer. Both go unmentioned in the historical tradition.[3]

I must repeat: In contrast to our information on the subject of Rome, we know nothing of the electoral battles that occurred in Greece. We do not even know whether they really did take place.

The difficulties that Pericles encountered following the early setbacks in the Peloponnesian War do not really constitute an exception, for what does Thucydides actually tell us? "As regards public affairs they were won over by him [δημοσία μὲν τοῖς λόγοις ἀνεπείθοντο]"; but both the wealthy and the members of the *demos*, for different economic reasons, combined against him and "did not give over their resentment against him until they had imposed a fine upon him. But not long afterward, as is the way with the multitude, they chose him again as general and entrusted him with the whole conduct of affairs.... It was the entire city [ἡ ξύμπασα πόλις; that is to say both the wealthy and the popular classes] who judged him most worthy to fulfill this function."[4]

Elliptical as always, Thucydides does not specify whether Pericles' career as a *stratēgos* was or was not interrupted by the lawsuit brought against him and the sentence that followed. The "populus," in the general sense of the term, is not represented as politically divided. First it is against Pericles, then it rallies to his political and strategic policies. Plutarch, for his part,[5] claims to know more, but unfortunately his claims probably amount more to rhetorical show than to real information.[6] Having referred to the last speech that Thucydides (II, 60-4) claims to summarize, he goes on to say:

> The Athenians turned their ballots against him [τὰς ψήφους λαβόντας ἐπ᾽ αὐτὸν εἰς τὰς χεῖρας], became masters of his fate, stripped him of his command and punished him with a fine.... The city made trial of its other generals and counselors for the conduct of the war, but since no one appeared to have weight that was adequate or authority that was competent for such leadership, it yearned for Pericles and summoned him back to the *bēma* and the *stratēgeion*.... When the people had apologized for their thankless treatment of him and he had under-

taken again the conduct of the State and been elected general, he asked for a suspension of the law concerning children born out of wedlock . . . .

His account is certainly more detailed than Thucydides'. It is, furthermore, our only source on Pericles' loss of his post as *stratēgos*. But those apologies on the part of the people do not ring true; they seem more Roman than Greek. Besides, there is nothing here to indicate any kind of electoral campaign.

Nor do we know whether any lists of candidates of the same political color ever existed. It is by no means certain that Sophocles, who was a *stratēgos* along with Pericles at the time of the expedition to Samos (440) — as we know from the only complete list of *stratēgoi* that we possess — belonged to the same political group as Pericles; and — as is well known — to take a much later example, Aeschines and Demosthenes were both members of the same ambassadorial mission sent by Philip of Macedon.

In Athens, political debate and political conflict are usually represented not as the normal practice of the democratic city, but as the *stasis*, to use a word with a wide spectrum of meanings ranging from a simple upright position to civil war and including political faction,[7] with pejorative overtones decidedly predominant. Nicole Loraux is well aware of this:

> Division, regarded as the most absolute of dangers, establishes itself in the stricken city rent by conflicts between its own citizens. . . . To pass from divided opinions to bloody confrontation is, to be sure, no small step. However, to take that step is — at least, so people suppose — but to imitate the Greeks.[8]

But not all the Greeks, as Nicole Loraux knows better than anyone. In this connection, the various literary genres operate on different levels. Thus, to come at last to the point that I wish to make, I would suggest that history recognizes and within certain limits[9] contains political conflict, the funeral speech denies it,[10] comedy pours derision upon its very essence, and tragedy expatriates it.

What I mean is simply that when the city represented is Athens itself or an equivalent of Athens, be it the Argos of Aeschylus' *The Suppliants*, the Athens of Euripides' *The Suppliants* or his *The Heracleidae* or, finally, that of *Oedipus at Colonus*, confrontation is so to speak denied and the city is represented as Plato would wish it to be: unified.

That this is a deliberate decision is strikingly proved by a well-known passage from Aeschylus' *The Suppliants*. The decision concerning the granting of asylum to the daughters of Danaus has to be put to the vote and the chorus leader requests:

ἔνισπε δ' ἡμῖν ποῖ κεκύρωται τέλος,
δήμου κρατοῦσα χεὶρ ὅπῃ πληθύνεται;
(Tell us what end's been authorized
And where the populace, by show of hands,
Has thrown its weight.)[11] (603)

The answer given runs as follows (605): "The Argives have decreed not doubtfully [ἔδοξεν Ἀργείοισιν οὐ διχορρόπως]...." The decree that grants metic status to the Danaids is promulgated following the use of *peithō*, persuasion, in "subtle harangues of a kind to persuade the masses" (623);[12] it is voted unanimously, *pandemiai*, with no need for any intervention on the part of the herald (ἄνευ κλητῆρος, 622). The idea of any citizen of Argos failing to succor such victims is envisaged only as a future possibility (613-4).

It is true that there appears to be one exception to the rule that I am suggesting. At the end of the *Eumenides* (752), the vote is split. The silent actors who sit in judgment, on the Areopagus,[13] cast a majority vote in favor of the enemies of Orestes; it is Athena who secures his acquittal, expressing the unanimity of the city first by her personal vote, then by her casting one. Open debate was in effect limited to deities, Apollo on one side, the Erinyes on the other.

333

But if Athens is never divided in the works of the tragic poets, there is one place where *stasis* finds a special home: It is Thebes, which might also be described as an anti-city.[14] Thus, in Aeschylus' *Seven against Thebes*, the beginning stresses the *stasis* between Eteocles and the chorus of women, and the end (whether authentic or not) shows that, with the division of the chorus into the supporters of Antigone on the one hand and those of Ismene on the other, we have moved from warfare against foreigners to civil war. The same could be said for Euripides' *The Suppliants*, *The Phoenician Women*, and *Heracles*, as well as, of course, for the *Bacchae*. It would be easy to show that in this last play the *stasis* is shifted, to be found within the central character, King Pentheus, who is at once a hoplite and a woman. And, of course, the same also goes for the three Theban plays of Sophocles.

To understand to what extent Thebes, fixed in its role of the bad city, is an exception, we have only to compare it to the tragic representation of Argos-Mycenae. As I have noted, in Aeschylus' *The Suppliants* it is presented as "the united city," just as Athens is in Euripides' *The Suppliants*. In contrast, in *Agamemnon* and *The Libation Bearers*, just as in Sophocles' *Electra* and Euripides' too, it is the badly governed city, whose king is absent and that is consequently ruled by a woman. But when the evil government comes to an end, hope dawns for a better rule. The case of Euripides' *Orestes* is the most astonishing of all. Written more than half a century later than Aeschylus' *The Suppliants*, it reads like a rejoinder to it.[15] Here, the judgment passed on Orestes is quite different from that in the *Eumenides*: Orestes and his sister are brought before, not the Areopagus, where gods and men are intermingled, but an assembly of Argos which in every detail resembles that of Athens, as seen by the critics of democracy (the date being 408).[16]

A succession of orators take the stand, some adopting one view, others the opposite. The words of Thalthibius, the herald, are ambiguous; Diomedes argues in favor of exile and "the response... was mixed: some applauded, others booed" (901-2). One "Argive, but not from Argos," a metic whom the scholiast identifies as the "demagogue" Cleophon, urges death by stoning (902-16), while an anonymous peasant, one of those *autourgoi* so dear to moderate political thought in the late fifth century,[17] demands that Orestes be crowned with a wreath; and the *chrestoi*, the "better sort" of the upper classes "seemed to be convinced" (917-30). The victory eventually goes to the demagogue and the popular party. It is not *called* Athens, but there can be no doubt that it *is* Athens.

However, we should be quite clear that Thebes' relationship to Athens was quite a different matter. Thebes was more than a sounding board that could be used to express either an idealized view of Athens or, alternatively, a caricature of its less civilized aspects. Perhaps the image of Thebes that is conveyed may be accounted for by the long tradition of hostility between the two neighboring cities and, in particular, the constitution of the Boeotian League that appeared to reflect the institutions favored by Cleisthenes.[18] At all events, in tragedy Thebes functions as the paradigm of a divided city. We are dealing with an idea of Thebes, not Thebes as it really existed.[19]

Let us examine how this principle can be applied to *Oedipus at Colonus*. First, we must ask, quite simply, who is governing in Thebes at the point when Oedipus comes to Athens? Ismene sets out the problem, in her historical account of the city. At first her brothers engaged in a healthy *eris*, competing in their determination that "the throne should pass" to Creon and "that thus the city should be defiled no longer" (367-9). Then an *eris kakē* took over (372),[20] the perverse kind of rivalry that, ever since Hesiod, had been inseparable from the healthy kind. This set them first jointly against Creon, then against each other, for the younger brother Eteocles was determined to get the better of the elder, Polynices (a detail invented by Sophocles[21]), whom he managed to eject and banish. Polynices took refuge in Argos and from there engaged in hostilities against his own city (375-80). He too thus found himself between two cities, two cities at war: Thebes and — in his case — Argos. But is Eteocles really king of Thebes? Oedipus condemns the behavior of both his sons, accuses them both

335

of having deserted their father in favor of thrones, scepters and the exercise of tyranny and power (448-51, 1354-7), in short of setting *polis* above *oikos*. But Polynices tells Oedipus that Eteocles "lords it [in other words "is a tyrant"] in our house [ὁ δ' ἐν δόμοις τύραννος],"[22] a kind of domestic tyrant, the master of the *oikos*. *Political* tyranny, in contrast, is exercised by Creon, who himself proclaims his own sovereignty even as he pretends to be dependent on the city: "tyrant though I am [καὶ τύραννος ὤν]" (851). So, quite apart from Oedipus, who still has the power of saving his native city, if he agrees to die in Thebes, there are three claimants to sovereignty over Thebes: Creon, Eteocles, and Polynices, who leads an Argive army and whom Theseus regards as a man of Argos (1167) even though Oedipus' relative (*eugenēs*). "Neither anarchy nor despotism" is the Erinyes' order of the day in the *Eumenides* (525-6 and 696), an order of the day also adopted by Athena. As we have seen, Thebes is not only without leadership but at the same time subjected to a tyranny. And the city is not only tyrannical but also unjust. Oedipus accuses the city as a whole of having wed him to Iocasta and thereby being responsible for all his misfortunes (525-6). It was the city of Thebes as a whole that expelled him from the Theban territory:

πόλις βίᾳ
ἤλαυνέ μ' ἐκ γῆς χρόνιον
(Then it was that the city – in its good time –
Decided to be harsh and drove me out.) (440)

And, according to Creon, it is also Thebes as a whole that has decided that Oedipus must return (736).[23]

Not only is the city answerable for all this but, according to Creon, it is a lying city that makes use of a false *peithō*,[24] a type of persuasion that it is tempting to liken to that of modern ideological discourse. In his speech at 728-60, Creon speaks of Thebes as though it embodies the values of Athens, as though the two were interchangeable. He himself comes to Athens not as a king, but as an elder (733), on the strength of his mature years: "This is not one man's mission, but was ordered by the whole Theban people [ἀλλ' ἀστῶν ὑπὸ πάντων κελευσθείς]" (737-8).[25] He urges Oedipus, in the name of *peithō* (756) to return to his town, to the house of his ancestors, to the city that has given him sustenance. But Ismene (399-405) has already warned Oedipus that he will not be allowed to cross the frontier; he will be kept outside, on the edge, *paraulos* (785), that is to say *en agrois*, in the outside space, as the scholiast puts it. And it is not just a matter of what has happened in the past and what is supposed to happen in the future, for Creon, the representative of Thebes, transgresses the law before the very eyes of the spectators. He violates the law of Athens by carrying off Antigone and Ismene and threatening to kidnap Oedipus too, thereby increasing the booty (*rhusion*) due to his city. But, except at the superficial level of the language used, it is not really a matter of reprisals taken in accordance with an existing law: This is violence pure and simple.[26]

Are there positive aspects to balance against these negative features of Thebes? Can a distinction be drawn between Thebes on the one hand and its leaders, actual (Eteocles, Creon) or potential (Polynices)? As Oedipus predicts to Polynices, he will not take Thebes (1372). The expedition of the Seven will end in failure. On this point it would have been difficult to disregard the myth. What Theseus tells Creon is more surprising:

καίτοι σε Θῆβαι γ' οὐκ ἐπαίδευσαν κακόν·
οὐ γὰρ φιλοῦσιν ἄνδρας ἐκδίκους τρέφειν,
(I doubt that Thebes is responsible for you;
She has no propensity for breeding rascals.) (919)

These lines have provoked violent disagreement. Wilamowitz regarded them as an allusion to the party of Ismenias in Thebes, which was hostile to the city's anti-Athenian policies.[27] While he was about it he might just as well have gone all the way, as did M. Pohlenz,[28] and suggested it to be an allusion to those Thebans who, in the aftermath of the revolution of the Thirty tyrants, gave asylum to the Athenian democrats who fled to Boeotia.[29] It is suggested that these controversial lines may have been added some time between Sophocles' death in 406 and 401, when the play was first put on, for this was a troubled period when alterations may well have seemed desirable.

But there is no need to go so far. The fact that Theseus, the model sovereign of the model city should (unlike Oedipus) draw a distinction between the *city* of Thebes and its leaders is, all things considered, altogether in line with not only the logic of the tragedy as a whole but, even more, that of the character of Theseus himself.

To portray Athens as the model city,[30] standing in contrast to the anti-city, the city of unadulterated violence and *stasis*, it is enough simply to reverse the portrait of Thebes. That is borne out not solely by the famous chorus (668-719) which moves on from the subject of white Colonus to praise the Athens of the olive tree, horses, and sailors, but also by a series of remarks throughout the play. I will limit myself to a few observations. Athens is a city whose leader is never called a *turannos*. Theseus is the king (βασιλέως, 67), the leader (ἡγεμών, 289), the sovereign (ἄναξ, 1130, 1499, 1759) or the war-leader (κοίρανος, 1287),[31] a word of Indo-European origin; he is even referred to as just a man (ἀνήρ, 1486) or, more metaphorically, as the one responsible (κραίνων) for the country (862, 926). But he is never a tyrant. Even Creon, in a quite natural fashion, mentions the wise council of the Areopagus alongside the king (947). It goes without saying that Athens is a city of free men, not slaves (917), a city where the freedom of speech is respected (1287): Polynices himself is a beneficiary.[32]

Finally — and, as will be seen, this is an important point — Athens is a city in which a role of importance is played by the local elements constituted by the demes — in this case, Sophocles' own deme of Colonus, which held its head high and which provides the chorus for the play.[33] The native of Colonus who comes across Oedipus will not venture to expel him from the city "without authority from the city government [πόλεως δίχα]" (47-8). The deme is a smaller version of Athens itself and it is the *agora* of Colonus that is represented on the *orchestra*, with the chorus operating as a fraction of the political assembly, but the point is that it is but a fraction of it and Theseus, the King-cum-Ecclesia, the incarnation of popular sovereignty, is careful to make that distinction.[34] Thus, Athens is the ideal city, capable of mobilizing all its citizens, hoplites and cavalry alike, in the service of a just cause (898); it is the city that decides nothing without the sanction of the law, κἄνευ νόμου κραίνουσαν οὐδέν (913). What more is there — could there possibly be — to say?

What is Oedipus' status, positioned as he is between these two cities? With writers of tragedy it is always risky to try to express the status of the hero purely and simply in juridical terms. That is true, really, of all the tragic poets, not only because, as Louis Gernet saw, the law that tragedy expresses is still in the making, not yet definitive;[35] but also because tragedy explores extreme situations and carries solutions to extremes, which is clearly not the case with law.

Let us consider the case of Aeschylus' *The Suppliants*, the first "tragedy about foreigners."[36] The Danaids have come to Argos, declaring themselves Argives and claiming to be recognized as such by the city, despite their Egyptian appearance. They seat themselves in the sanctuary in the posture of "suppliants." The king of Argos defines their status, or rather their lack of it, for have they not ventured to Argos οὔτε κηρύκων ὕπο, ἀπρόξενοί τε, νόσφιν ἡγητῶν (238), that is, without the *foreign* heralds who should normally precede them, without the (local?) guides who should accompany them and without the Argive *proxenoi*[37] who ought to be there to welcome them? The classical sense of the word *proxenos*, as used here, seems to be a citizen of Argos who would be willing to safeguard the interests of the Danaids' city of origin, so a double difficulty arises: In the first place, these girls claim to be of Argive origin (16, 274) and, second, the city from which

they have come is one that cannot possibly enter into normal relations with Argos. As for a herald, he is present all right, but will
speak in the name of the sons of Aegyptus, the Danaids' first cousins. Finding themselves without *proxenoi*, the Danaids beg the
king to adopt this role:

> φρόντισον καὶ γενοῦ
> πανδίκως εὐσεβὴς
> πρόξενος·
> (Reflect and be
> Justly, the pious protector) (418)

Pelasgus agrees to do so and is described further on (491) as
anaidoios proxenos, the "respectful *proxenos*" of his guests and indeed
the provider of locally recruited guides for them (491-2). In
this way Pelasgus protects the daughters of Danaus and bestows
a first status upon them, *asphaleia* or safety. A second status is
granted them in more juridical circumstances, by means of a
decree passed by the popular assembly (605-24). Through this
decree, the *Ecclesia* turns the Danaids into metics who may
not be seized:[38]

> ἡμᾶς μετοικεῖν τῆσδε γῆς ἐλευθέρους
> κἀρρυσιάστους ξύν τ' ἀσυλίᾳ βροτῶν.
> (Free we are to settle here, subject
> Neither to seizure nor reprisal, claimed
> Neither by citizen nor foreigner.) (610)

Now they, like all other metics, are provided with a guarantor,
someone to answer for them, a *prostates*. But once again, the
tragic poet makes an extreme case of the situation by having the
king declare:

> προστάτης δ' ἐγώ
> ἀστοί τε πάντες, ὧνπερ ἥδε κραίνεται ψῆφος,

(Myself and all
the citizens protect you, whose voted will
Is now fulfilled) (963)

One could also point out that not all cities actually had at their disposal "many homes [δώματ'...πολλά]" (957) where they could lodge their public guests; but perhaps this exaggeration should be regarded simply as providing a model.

Aeschylus' *The Suppliants* was performed in 465. Euripides' *Heracleidae* (which dates from about 430-427), another tragedy featuring foreigners, presents a doubly interesting case.

Iolaus and the children of Heracles are ἀλώμενοι (15), "wanderers from State to State [ἄλλην ἀπ' ἄλλης ἐξορίζοντες πόλιν]" (16). As the play opens, they have just crossed the frontier to Athens (37), which like Sparta is ruled by two kings, but here they are selected by lot (36), as are the Athenian *archontes*, among the children of Pandion. Like the Danaids, the Heracleidae are suppliants who address their pleas both to their interlocutors and to the city that they represent. Eurystheus, the king of Argos, and his herald are bent upon seizing them in the name of the death sentence that has been passed on them in Argos: His attitude is similar to that adopted by Creon when he seizes the daughters of Orestes because they are Theban. Iolaus counters Eurystheus by declaring the Heracleidae to be Argives no longer. They no longer have anything in common, ἐν μέσῳ (184), with Eurystheus' representative. Following a vote (186) taken by the assembly of Argos, the Heracleidae have been legally declared foreigners in relation to their native city. The Heracleidae invoke their kinship as cousins, as did the Danaids in Argos. Aethra, the mother of Theseus and grandmother of Demophon was the grand-daughter of Pelops just as was Alcmena the mother of Heracles. The kinship confers upon them no rights in Athens, but the argument of kinship (*sungeneia*) had a certain diplomatic force in dealings between one city and another.[39] Demophon of Athens reacts as did Pelasgus of Argos. First he treats the Heracleidae as foreign guests, *xenoi*, who are led from the altar before which they are suppliants into the house; after this, the citizens may be summoned to attend a political and military assembly (335).[40]

The Heracleidae are not destined to live in Athens as metics. On the contrary, we are told they are to leave, and the words of Euripides' characters suggest that their departure and return to the Peloponnese follows immediately upon Eurystheus' defeat and death. But there is one metic who will remain in Athens, an unexpected one who is dead, a metic who becomes a hero and savior, as will the living metics who subsequently help Athens to eject its Tyrants. In the present case, the metic is Eurystheus, whose tomb at Pallene will henceforth protect the Athenians against the descendants of the Heracleidae, just as the tomb of Oedipus will protect them against the Thebans:[41]

καὶ σοὶ μὲν εὔνους καὶ πόλει σωτήριος
μέτοικος αἰεὶ κείσομαι κατὰ χθονός,
τοῖς τῶνδε δ᾽ ἐκγόνοισι πολεμιώτατος.
(. . . as the guest of Athens' soil, I'll guard
You and preserve you till the end of time.
But when these children's children march on you
In force, then I'll be their arch-enemy.) (1032)

An enemy king, once defeated and executed, after his death becomes a metic and a hero-protector. Through the accumulation of so many aspects to this character, Euripides too makes an extreme case of the situation.

And what of Sophocles' Oedipus? Is he granted more than what the living Danaids or the dead Eurystheus obtain? Does he become a citizen of Athens? It is quite clear that he is no longer a Theban. When the chorus demands that he should declare his country (206-7), Oedipus replies that he is "one without a country [ἀπόπτολις]" (208) and he later accuses Polynices of having made him into this ἄπολις (1357). Bernard Knox resolves the problem that I am tackling as follows. Setting up an opposition between

342

the destinies of Oedipus and Philoctetes, he writes: "But in this play no god appears to bring about the reintegration of Oedipus in the *polis*. He does become a citizen (ἔμπολις, 637), but a citizen of Athens, not Thebes; and his citizenship begins and ends with his mysterious death."[42] So this is a variation of the familiar Sophoclean schema of the reintegration of the hero: The dead Ajax and the living Philoctetes are reintegrated into the army that represents the *polis*. Oedipus is also reintegrated, not in his own city but in the city of Athens, in and through his death.

It is worth examining this in detail. The crucial lines, as Knox understands them, are clearly 636-7:

ἀγὼ σεβισθεὶς οὔποτ᾽ ἐκβαλῶ χάριν
τὴν τοῦδε, χώρᾳ δ᾽ ἔμπολιν κατοικιῶ.
(As I value that favor, I shall not refuse
This man's desire [to donate his body to Athens]; I declare
him a citizen.)[43]

The interpretation is not new in itself, but it has the merit of spelling out what many other scholars have taken for granted. The fact is that in the manuscript the word in question is not ἔμπολιν but ἔμπαλιν; ἔμπολιν is a posthumous emendation by S. Musgrave, published in 1800 and accepted by some editors, but not by all.[44] Musgrave and those who followed him, with the exception of Knox, were not concerned to introduce a "positive" correction in order to understand the juridical nature of Oedipus' fate in Athens. What bothered many of these interpreters was the exact meaning of ἔμπαλιν.[45] Needless to say, to parody a juridical principle that is as famous as it is neglected, every manuscript should be regarded as innocent until it is proven guilty. In this case, as it happens, ἔμπαλιν has a meaning that was recognized by the scholiast whose interpretation ran as follows: ἐκ τοῦ ἐναντίου, "on the contrary." We should thus read the passage literally, as: "Having bowed to this, I shall never expel[46] the favor of this man but shall, on the contrary, install it [his favor] in this country." Metonymically, the favor

343

or *charis* that Oedipus wishes to bestow upon Athens, that is to say the gift of his own body, is assimilated to the person of Oedipus himself, that is to say to his corpse, since Sophocles, if not Theseus, knows full well that the living Oedipus will not remain in Athens for long. Strictly speaking, I could rest my case there and declare the problem raised by Bernard Knox to be resolved, given the lack of any text to support his thesis. But we are not operating in a field of exact sciences and even if it is most unlikely that Musgrave's emendation correctly represents the Sophoclean text, it may still be worthwhile to examine the meaning that it might give to this text. *Empolis* is what grammarians describe as "a compound formed by hypostasis of a prepositional phrase." In other words, *ho empolis* is the equivalent of *ho en polei*, "one who is in the city." Similarly, in Aeschylus we find *amphiptolis*, "one who is close to the city."[47] The original meaning of *empolis* was probably one of locality, rather than of juridical status. Possibly the earliest extant example of the word is to be found in the comic author Eupolis.[48] According to Pollux, the Alexandrian grammarian, Eupolis used it with the meaning *astos*, or "local man," *enchorios*, and Pollux adds: "I think one might, equally, have said *entopios*." That is to say that the word is understood to relate to place: a town, a country, a particular spot. The juridical aspect to *polis* is not suggested but it seems only fair to note that, even in Sophocles, *astu* and *polis* are equivalent to one another.[49] Eupolis' *Diade* is dated to 412. The first and, to my knowledge, only time the word is used with a full context is in *Oedipus at Colonus* (156), a fact that appears to have encouraged Musgrave. When Theseus speaks to Oedipus of Polynices, he stresses the latter's paradoxical relationship to Oedipus:

ἄνδρα, σοὶ μὲν ἔμπολιν
οὐκ ὄντα, συγγενῆ δέ
(a man who claims to be a relative of yours,
though not of the same city) (1156)[50]

344

True enough, Polynices, a candidate for the throne of Thebes, is the leader of the Argive army, and the fact that he belonged to Argos was probably indicated by some detail in the stage set. Clearly, the word might easily take on the meaning of *politēs*. That is the definition given by Hesychius: ὁ πατρίδα ἔχων, "one who has a country," but nothing that we know of the word, even if we adopt Musgrave's emendation, justifies any assumption that Oedipus might have become a citizen in the juridical sense of the term. Another way of forming an opinion as to the significance of the word would be to examine the meanings of the derivative verb *empoliteuō*, of which several examples exist with their context in both literary texts and in inscriptions.[51]

Remarkably enough, the first extant occurrence of this verb comes in Thucydides' account of Brasidas' capture of Amphipolis (424). The account is roughly contemporary with Eupolis' *Diade* and probably earlier than *Oedipus at Colonus*.[52] Amphipolis, a city of the Athenian empire, founded in 437, comprised a mixed population. For the success of his venture, Brasidas counted upon the support of the people of Argilus, a neighboring city that was a colony set up by Andrus. Some of the inhabitants, *oiketores* (IV, 103, 3) were natives of Argilus. The Argilians in Argilus were relying upon the Argilians of Amphipolis to help them throw off the Athenian yoke so that they could rejoin the Spartan alliance. The Argilians of Amphipolis are described as *empoliteuontes* (IV, 103, 4), that is to say "residents."

A little further on (IV, 106, 1), mention is made of the small group of Athenians established in Amphipolis (βραχὺ μὲν Ἀθηναίων ἐμπολιτεῦον). These Athenians had clearly not renounced their citizenship, but they could hardly have been metics in Amphipolis. Presumably they, and others too, enjoyed double citizenship, but we know nothing, or very little, about the conditions of citizenship in Amphipolis.[53] Strangely enough, this verb again appears in the context of Amphipolis in Isocrates (*Philip*, 5). Reiterating his advice to the Athenians not to repeat the imperialistic mistakes of the past century, he urges them to eschew such colonial

345

ventures (ἀποικίας) as have previously, on four or five occasions, resulted in the deaths of those already established there (τοὺς ἐμπολιτευθέντας). It is tempting to suppose, along with M. Casevitz, that the word *empolis*, together with the verb derived from it, appeared in Athens in connection with the particular status of Amphipolis – and other places too – that were Athenian colonies with mixed populations, whose members retained their external citizenship even while belonging to the colonial city.

Our limited classical documentation can be supplemented with a slender Hellenistic contribution. Polybius (V, 9, 9) tells us that Antigonus Doson, king of Macedonia, at war with Cleomenes, the ruler of Sparta and victor of Sellasia (222), was master of the city and of the *empoliteuomenoi*. That meant not only the *homoioi* but all those who, with a variety of statuses, were *in the city*, including those whom Cleomenes himself introduced into the civic body.[54] Finally, the word appears in two inscriptions from the Peloponnese,[55] probably from the third century. The first, from Antigoneia (Mantinea) is a decree of *proxeneia* that praises an Argive for the goodwill he has always demonstrated toward not only the citizens of Antigoneia but also "those resident in Antigoneia [τῶν ἐμπολιτευόντων ἐν Ἀντιγονείᾳ]." The second also comes from Arcadia, from Tegaea and praises a citizen of Megalopolis who resided (ἐνπολίτευσας) in the city for a number of years before returning to his own (ἰδίας) city, that is to say Megalopolis. In both cases it might, at the limit, be a matter of people granted the rights of citizenship either definitively, as in Antigoneia, or temporarily, within the framework of an agreement of reciprocal citizenship, as in Tegaea.[56]

However, I do not accept that interpretation. I believe it is simply a matter of foreign residents, in other words of metics in one form or another.[57] In my view, both documents make a clear distinction between on the one hand citizens in the strict sense of the word, and on the other those who are *in* the *polis*, without *belonging* to it.

I think it was necessary to make that digression, but it still does not resolve the question of Oedipus' status in Athens. There can be no doubt that he enters the Athenian polis. But is he accepted as a citizen? That is quite another matter, whatever version of the text is adopted. What it says is that Oedipus' citizenship "begins and ends with his mysterious death." Does that mean that Oedipus only becomes an Athenian citizen through dying and becoming a part of the Athenian soil, as are the heroes? Surely not since, in Knox's view, the change of status comes about during the action of the tragedy. It takes place precisely at the point where the two girls are seized by Creon: "Oedipus is a citizen of Athens now and when, under Creon's assault, he calls for help (ἰὼ πόλις, 833),[58] it is Athens he is calling on for help against Thebes."[59] If, for the moment and for the sake of argument, we accept this line of reasoning, should we follow it through by, for example, suggesting that Theseus offers Oedipus his choice of deme? Clearly, he can either remain at Colonus or follow Theseus to Athens (638-9), and to enter the city at all implied his integration into a deme or tribe.

But as soon as one pursues Knox's line of interpretation to that point, a host of arguments arises to demolish it. In the very speech in which Theseus announces his intention of extending a welcome to Oedipus, he explains (632-3) that Oedipus is his guest on military grounds, through the comradeship that can spring up between two warriors from different cities.[60] Oedipus is treated as a foreigner after "his entrance into the city" as much as before it and the land that takes him in continues to be a foreign land.[61] And Theseus declares his intention (633) to welcome him at the κοινὴ ἑστία, that is to say the hearth that is common to *both of them* and at the *prytaneum*, the city's communal hearth that is the place where it welcomes its important guests as well as its own citizens whom it wishes or feels duty bound to honor.[62]

Let me give two specific examples that must surely make the point. As it awaits news of the kidnapped Antigone and Ismene, the chorus composed of the demesmen of Colonus invokes the gods, first Zeus and Athena, then Apollo the hunter and his sister Artemis:

στέργω διπλᾶς ἀρωγὰς
μολεῖν γᾷ τᾷδε καὶ πολίταις
(Be our protectors! Lend your grace
To both our land and its citizens) (1094)

Immediately after its mention of citizens, the chorus turns to Oedipus and addresses him (1096): "O wandering stranger [᾽Ω ξεῖν᾽ ἀλῆτα]" and when Oedipus is dead, dead and still a foreigner, the messenger begins his speech to the inhabitants of Colonus by addressing *them* as citizens: Ἄνδρες πολῖται (1579). If Sophocles had wished to imply that Oedipus had now become an Athenian, he would have said so.

But having established that point, it is still hard to say just what Oedipus does become in Athens. One of the constant features of Greek tragedy is its ambiguous play upon juridical categories in its exploration of the bounds of impossibility. That is a point that cannot be repeated too often.[63] Consider the case of Oedipus in *Oedipus Rex*. He believed himself to be autochthonous in Corinth, so Corinth, where he "was held the greatest of the citizens," is the city that he shuns after the oracle has revealed his destiny to him. Yet Tiresias has even then already explained his real situation to him:

...he [Laius' murderer] is here.
In name he is a stranger [ξένος μέτοικος: a resident foreigner]
among citizens,
(But soon he will be shown to be a citizen,
True, native Theban.) (451-5)

But how could one imagine a juridical monster such as a reigning metic, in Athens? One astonishing detail in *Oedipus at Colonus* is that Oedipus threatens to arrest Creon if the kidnapped girls

348

are not returned and to make him a metic and a resident in the country "by force and against his will [μέτοικος τῆσδε τῆς χώρας]" (934). Needless to say, that is a juridical impossibility. There are no forced metics in Athens, and Sophocles is playing upon both the word and the law.

The truth is that, to understand the point here, we must adopt a different method. I do not think that we can hope to solve the problem simply by glossing over the opposition between citizen and foreigner, an opposition that was fundamental to the ordinary life of the city. It is not possible to contain a tragic character within a *single* network of meanings. If the impasse at which we have momentarily halted has a meaning, it must be to remind us of that simple truth.

When Jean-Pierre Vernant wanted to seize upon the character of Oedipus in *Oedipus Rex*,[64] he showed that it was necessary to work on at least two different levels. On a religious level, Oedipus oscillates between the condition of divine being and that of *pharmakos*, the scapegoat that was expelled from Athens every sixth of Thargelion, in order to purify the city. On a political level, Oedipus is a powerful statesman, a potential tyrant, a threat to which the fifth-century city responded through the purely secular institution of ostracism. It is abundantly clear that the two levels could easily merge. One of our main sources of evidence of the ritual of the *pharmakos* is Lysias' speech against Andocides in which Lysias demands that the city be purified from the defilement that Andocides represents.[65] But in tragedy, precisely, there is a positive interference[66] between the two levels, not simply an ordinary confusion arising out of political rhetoric. And it is true that it is possible to argue over points of detail: In *Oedipus Rex*, the main character is not (yet) expelled from Thebes. He himself has condemned himself while the city awaits the verdict of the oracle,[67] but this incident in the narrative makes no difference to the fact that the character of Oedipus remains circumscribed within the two poles defined by Vernant. And of course, the Oedipus that is eventually revealed is not a *pharmakos* nor is he ostracized: He is something in between, and that is why he is a tragic hero.

The converse of Vernant's analysis could be applied to *Oedipus at Colonus*. Here, everything is the other way round. The potential *pharmakos* to be expelled becomes the hero who himself guides Theseus to the central spot, the tomb that will be the secret sign of his protective presence in Athens. Oedipus is a wanderer who is about to acquire a fixed abode. He is a suppliant – and we know, in particular from a recent study by J. Gould,[68] that supplication was an institution (just as was, for example, hospitality), or even a whole social factor in the sense in which Mauss defined gifts and counter-gifts – a suppliant soon to become a hero and a savior.

That is unquestionably what Oedipus becomes: a hero. It is a question that has been studied exhaustively, perhaps excessively.[69] But it is clear, despite the views of certain critics, that we should retain the idea of a heroic mutation while at the same time liberating it from any vestiges of Christian notions of personal immortality and personal rehabilitation.[70] The truth is that the very idea of the hero is bound to lead us back to the level of politics, for the hero exists not on his own account but as an essential element of the civic space.[71] The deme Colonus itself, for example, has its own eponymous hero, Colonus, a horseman:

All men of this land claim descent from him
Whose statue stands nearby: Colonus the horseman,
And bear his name in common with their own. (58-61)

Oedipus cannot possibly be a *pharmakos* who suddenly, miraculously is restored to being what he was before his defilement. Nor is he one who has been ostracized but who eventually recrosses the frontier, returning as Cimon and Aristides did to Athens, since, precisely, he never does return to Thebes and that is the fact upon which the tragedy turns. What, then, is his status in Athens?

That is the question to which we must now return. To say that he is a hero, that is to say more than a citizen, sharing that quality with other figures — such as Ajax — who have sometimes been annexed to Athens, is not enough. For it is both possible and necessary to integrate Oedipus more satisfactorily with the institutions and practices of the time of Sophocles.

During the past twenty years much work has been done on the Greek city and foreigners both in the city and outside it. Studies have concentrated particularly on the honors bestowed upon foreigners in Athens and in other cities and also upon the granting of citizenship to foreigners — "naturalization," as it has sometimes, mistakenly, been called — in Athens and elsewhere.[72]

Let me make two introductory observations. The first takes over from a point made by M.J. Osborne: What he calls "the dual aspect of a grant of citizenship"[73] needs to be underlined. The granting of citizenship was at once a mark of honor and also an eminently practical privilege, conferring rights of a most concrete nature on the beneficiary. In other words, citizenship could be either potential or very real. It was real when bestowed upon individuals or particular groups (such as the Plataeans, who were allowed to settle definitively in the city); potential when conferred as an honor upon extremely important personages, such as kings, who had no intention of settling in Athens but who were thereby assured that if ever they visited Athens they would be treated as citizens to whom special honors were due.

Let us consider two contrasting examples: Rights of citizenship, no doubt together with a wreath, were conferred upon a benefactor of Athens, King Evagoras of Cyprus, and upon his sons, probably at the beginning of 407; in 401-400 a number of foreigners, probably all metics, who had fought on the side of the Athenian democrats in the civil war, were granted citizens' rights, including the right of marriage, which they appear to have made the most of.[74] Conversely, it was also possible, though admittedly not in Athens during the classical period, to be a *proxenos* and a citizen at one and the same time. But clearly one could not be both a *proxenos* to a city, that is to say a foreigner, and also one of

its citizens in any practical sense. All the same, it should immediately be added that even in Athens one might be granted the
same honors as a "citizen" such as Evagoras, starting with the title
of *euergetes*, and the same privileges, including the right to be domiciled in Athens (*oikēsis*) and to own land there (*enktēsis*), but without receiving the title of citizen. There thus existed a range of
benefits that could be enjoyed in common by foreigners whom
the city wished to honor but who remained foreigners, secure
in the knowledge that they could, if necessary, one day enjoy the
rights of quasi-citizenship there,[75] foreigners who were honored
and granted potential citizenship, and foreigners who were honored and granted real citizenship. All were regarded as benefactors, *euergetai*, of Athens.[76]

Now let us examine the procedure for acquiring citizenship
in more detail. It varied hardly at all from one case to another
and began with an *aitēsis*, a "request accompanied by a detailed
memorandum on the candidate's qualifications, presented either
in his own name or by a third party."[77] Whoever was making the
request would naturally mention the benefits that the candidate
had or would dispense in Athens,[78] and these benefits would be
listed in the material to be considered before decreeing whether
or not citizenship was granted. *Aitēsis* may seem a neutral word,
but it was sometimes associated with *hiketeia*, "supplication," an
institution of an eminently religious nature — at least in its origins.[79] Where a new citizen was concerned, the text would in normal circumstances indicate that the beneficiary must be inscribed
as the member of a tribe or deme; but metics were also associated with the demes in which they were domiciled,[80] and in
Sophocles' day when a metic was honored without however being
granted citizenship, he was made a member of a tribe.[81]

It seems quite clear to me that this, in its essentials, is the
procedure reflected in *Oedipus at Colonus*. First there is the request.
As early as line 5, Oedipus presents himself as a man who "asks
little [σμικρὸν μὲν ἐξαιτοῦντα]."[82] But he soon makes it clear that he
is a suppliant who is also a benefactor:

ἥκω γὰρ ἱερὸς εὐσεβής τε καὶ φέρων
ὄνησιν ἀστοῖς τοῖσδ᾽·
(I come here as one endowed with grace
By those who are over nature; and I bring
Advantage to all its citizens.) (287)

He requests that Theseus meet with him, for the good of his city as well as in the interest of himself, the benefactor (308-9). The word *euergetes* may not actually be pronounced but that is unquestionably what Oedipus is — an *euergetes* of Athens who comes to present it with advantages, *kerde*, a blessing in the shape of his own body (576-8). He is patently full of good will, or *eumeneia* (631), to use a word that is also part of the epigraphical terminology.

But of course this is an *euergetes* who remains, almost to the last, marked by defilement. He is an untouchable and, as such, seeks no physical contact with Theseus (1130-6). He does not touch his hand until the very end of the play, just before he disappears forever (1632). He will be a benefactor and a blessing for Athens but — to put it bluntly now — he will never become a citizen. Theseus suggests (639-42) that Oedipus should either remain at Colonus with the demesman who first greeted him there who is, so to speak, his guarantor, his *prostates*, or that he should go with Theseus to Athens. He does not make him the member of any deme. Colonus, Sophocles' own deme, does not become Oedipus' deme, simply his place of residence, ἔνθα χρὴ ναίειν, the place where "I must live," where he will reside together (Theseus uses the word *xunousia*, 847) with the members of the deme. Even when everything, bit by bit, has been sorted out, he is not Οἰδίπους Κολώναθεν or ἐκ Κολωνοῦ, Oedipus *of* Colonus, but Οἰδίπους ἐπὶ Κολωνῷ, Oedipus *at* Colonus. Nor are his children given citizenship, although that right is granted to the descendants of *euergetai* in plenty of other decrees. To come to some kind of conclusion, I would say that what Oedipus becomes is, so to speak, a resident, a privileged metic, as do Aeschylus' Eumenides (1011), whom he meets, precisely, at Colonus.

353

Even when he becomes a hero of Athens, Oedipus remains a marginal figure.

Now let us try to situate this marginal figure in space — that is, in space as it is represented, dramatic space. As J. Jones correctly perceived and noted, the last plays of Sophocles are marked by "a kind of interdependence of man and place."[83] This is, as he says, true of *Philoctetes* and *Oedipus at Colonus*. I believe it also applies to *Electra*.

One fundamental theme recurs constantly, the theme of frontiers, whether close or distant.[84] Frontiers to the *oecoumenē*: In a speech that describes Oedipus, storm-swept and beset by old age and *stasis*, the chorus refers to the waves rolling in from all four cardinal points:

> Now from the plunging down of the sun,
> Now from the sunrise quarter,
> Now from where the noonday gleams,
> Now from Rhipaean mountains lapped in night. (1248)

The Rhipaea (*Rhipaia horē*) are mythical mountains that Sophocles clearly locates in the extreme north.[85] Then there is the frontier of Thebes: It is in the frontier region that the Thebans plan to install Oedipus, as Ismene warns him:

> σε προσθέσθαι πέλας
> χώρας θέλουσι, μηδ' ἵν' ἂν σαυτοῦ κρατοῖς.
> ([They plan] to settle you near the land of Thebes, and so have you at hand; but you may not cross the border.) (404)

Near the territory of Thebes, not *inside* it; and the same goes for Oedipus' tomb: It will not be covered by "Theban dust" (407). The shed blood of his father forbids it.[86] As I have said, in Thebes Oedipus is to live as a *paraulos*, in the space outside (785). Though received as a metic-hero in Athens, in Thebes he is to be an excluded citizen, a Philoctetes whom his city will nevertheless keep under its thumb, in a frontier no-man's land.

Then there is the frontier between Athens and Thebes. Whatever route their captors take, Ismene and Antigone, kidnapped by Creon's men, must not cross the frontier:

ἰὼ πᾶς λεώς, ἰὼ γᾶς πρόμοι,
μόλετε σὺν τάχει, μόλετ᾽, ἐπεὶ πέραν
περῶσ᾽ οἵδε δή.
(Ho, everyone! Captains, ho!
Hurry up! Come on the run!
They [the kidnappers] will be crossing the frontier by now!)
(884)

A little further on comes an allusion to the Oinoe region, the junction of the two roads leading to Thebes, the one from Eleusis and the direct north-bound route: "Where the two highways come together, the two girls must not be permitted to pass there" (902).

What seems, at first sight, much more strange is that Colonus is also described as a border zone:

ὃν δ᾽ ἐπιστείβεις τόπον,
χθονὸς καλεῖται τῆσδε χαλκόπους ὁδός,
ἔρεισμ᾽ Ἀθηνῶν.
(The spot you rest on has been called this earth's threshold of bronze[87] and buttress of great Athens.) (56)

This is the spot where the wandering Oedipus first comes to a halt, to rest (85, 99). And the oracle has told the exile that he will find shelter and hospitality "on the border of some country" or "in the last country [ἐλθόντι χώραν τερμίαν]" (89).

How should we interpret this description? Colonus is, of course, not really situated on the frontiers of Athens. When in Colonus, one *speaks* of Thebes, the anti-city, but Athens, the city *par excellence*, is actually visible:

πύργοι μὲν, οἵ

πόλιν στέφουσιν, ὡς ἀπ᾽ ὀμμάτων, πρόσω·

(the towers that crown the city still seem far away) (14)

There are two explanations for the expression "the threshold of bronze." The first is a straightforward, geographical one: Kolonos Hippios, which is a rural deme where the song of the nightingale is heard, is also one of the "frontier" demes of the town of Athens, according to the system devised by Cleisthenes. This Attic deme is situated at the northernmost point of the *astu* or town, which represents one of the three sections into which Attica is divided, the other two being the *paralia* (the coast) and the *mesogaia* (the middle section).[88]

The second explanation is mythical. Already the scholiast established a connection between the threshold of bronze of line 57 and the steep threshold, καταρράκτης ὁδός, or cleft of line 1590, the threshold where "the steps of bronze [χαλκοῖς βάθροισι]" (1591) are rooted in the soil of Athens.[89] Colonus is situated where the town and the Mesogaia meet; it is also a frontier between the gods of the underworld, visited in times past by Theseus and Pirithoos, as is vividly recalled in lines 1593-4, and the gods above. This is what makes it impossible for the messenger to tell whether the Heavens or the Underworld are responsible for Oedipus' death (1661-2) and it is why Theseus addresses his prayer to the Earth and Olympus, both at once (1654-5).

Let us return to the front of the stage and the *orchestra* facing it. Of the characters who come and go here, some – Polynices and Ismene – come from outside (Argos, Thebes), others – Theseus, the demesman of Colonus and his companions who make up the chorus – come from Athens. In this play, Colonus is a miniaturized, condensed Athens. The chorus' famous speech in praise of Athens (668-719), with its olive groves, its horses, and its oarsmen, in other words the total Athens, is inspired by Colonus and pronounced at Colonus.[90] Colonus, with its people, its gods, its hero, its sanctuaries devoted to the Eumenides, Poseidon,

Demeter, and its patron Athena, is an Athens in miniature. Was Sophocles embroidering upon what really existed there? He is, after all, the only witness to mention the existence of a sanctuary of the Eumenides in his native deme. The major sanctuary devoted to these goddesses was situated in between the Acropolis and the Areopagus and it is there, incidently, that Pausanias locates Oedipus' tomb.[91]

Right from the start of the play, space is directly represented as being divided between on the one hand the sacred wood, on the other space that is profane and accessible. Oedipus asks his daughter to find him somewhere to sit down, "in some public place or in the groves of the gods [θάκησιν...ἢ πρὸς βεβήλοις ἢ πρὸς ἄλσεσιν θεῶν]" (9-10). We are given an idea of the depths of the sacred zone when we hear of Ismene performing the lustral rituals (495-506) in a place where she will be out of earshot (489). At this spot, there is a spring, with craters for libations placed beside it (469-72).[92] Every movement Oedipus makes carries him to and fro between the sacred zone and the profane one. Upon arrival, he takes up position on a rough stone that is unhewn (ἄξεστος, 19; ἀσκέπαρνος, 101), called after one of the names of the Eumenides, the *Semnai* or Redoubtable Ones (100). Seated there, he is on the side of the sacred,[93] himself assimilated to the Eumenides. He leaves this seat to disappear "clear of the path...in the wood" (113-4).[94] Then he reappears, resuming his original position, to the horror of the chorus. At lines 166-201, the chorus issues an order and Oedipus, guided by Antigone, moves, in obedience to it, thereby rendering dialogue possible, without danger to Oedipus and without violating sacred territory. The blind man makes his way toward the demesmen of Colonus, halting when he reaches a "platform...formed of the natural rock [ἀντιπέτρου βήματος]" (192-3).[95] Here, he may not be seized: "Never, never will anyone drive you away [ἐκ τῶνδ' ἑδράνων...ἄκοντά τις ἄξει]" (176-7). Here he is at liberty to speak and to listen, τὸ μὲν εἴποιμεν, τὸ δ' ἀκούσαιμεν (190). The entire episode hinges on the possibility or impossibility of *logos* between Oedipus and the old men of Colonus:

357

ἀβάτων ἀποβάς,
ἵνα πᾶσι νόμος,
φώνει·

(If you have a mind to tell us your business, or wish to converse with our council, come down from that place: Only speak where it's proper to do so!) (167)

In this position, Oedipus is both standing on a step, *bēma*, which is described by the same term as that used for the Tribune on the Pnux and from which he may address the agora of Colonus, and at the same time he is placed under the protection of the Eumenides since here he is inviolable, on the exact frontier (yet another frontier) between the sacred and the profane.[96]

I am tempted to suggest that a similar line of separation marks Oedipus' death place, although it is not easy to give a comprehensive interpretation of every detail in this connection.[97] It is, as Ismene says, a place "away from everything [δίχα τε παντός]" (1732), but that, at least in part, reproduces the combination of woodland and a boundary to woodland. While the running water necessary for Oedipus' ablutions and libations (1599) is to be found close at hand on a hill devoted to Demeter (1600), the spot where the hero is to disappear forever is described in terms of four features: "a hollow like a crater," marked by an inscription recording the oaths exchanged by Theseus and Pirithoos; the rock of Thoricus; a stone tomb; and a hollow pear tree. Man-made artifacts (the inscription and the tomb) on the one hand, and natural ones (the rock and the pear tree) on the other, life (the pear tree, the rock of Thoricus) and death (the tomb and the descent to the Underworld). The last act in Oedipus' life is thus played out in an in-between space.

I am using theatrical terminology, for it is quite clear that this line of separation is expressed in the stage directions that Sophocles conveys for the presentation of his drama, by playing on the words used to suggest both theatrical space and the real space represented there. I do not wish to reopen the age-old controversy over whether or not a raised platform above the *orchestra* used to separate the actors from the chorus, and it is certainly not my intention to voice an opinion on the possible height of such a platform.[98] That it existed seems clear to me from Sophocles' text. Furthermore, *Oedipus at Colonus*, together with Euripides' *The Phoenician Women*,[99] probably provides the most manifest example of a separation between actors and chorus.[100] As P. Arnott has pointed out: "the idea of separation is the basis of the opening scenes."[101] The *skēnē* where Ismene disappears clearly represents the wood, but the whole business of Oedipus being led by Antigone from the unhewn stone to the step (*bēma*) where he eventually takes up his position suggests that he moves away from the *skēnē* and sinks down,[102] seating himself on one of the stairs in the flight of steps connecting the *logeion* and the *orchestra*. From a step carved in a rock, almost a platform perhaps, to the modest step of a staircase or, simpler still, the rung of a ladder: It is a good example of a certain playfulness in the way that Sophocles uses myth and the stage . . . .

Oedipus at Colonus is a tragedy about passages from one point to another. We see Oedipus, who has already crossed a number of frontiers, take up position again on a frontier; then, once exonerated by *Peithō*, holy Persuasion, pass from Athens to yet another world. In this study I have attempted to show how, right down to the details of the stage directions, this is a tragedy about frontiers, frontiers that separate people but also frontiers that enable them to come together.

Pierre Vidal-Naquet

CHAPTER XVI

Oedipus in Vicenza and in Paris:

Two Turning Points in the

History of Oedipus*

Oedipus, Sophocles' Oedipus, has by now largely outgrown Sophocles and has a long history from which I have picked out two turning points;[1] although the expression "turning point" can, strictly speaking, only be applied to the first of my two subjects, namely the performance of Sunday, March 3rd, 1585, which marked the inauguration of the "Teatro Olimpico" in Vicenza. Sophocles' *Edipo Tiranno* was presented, in a translation by Orsatto Giustiniani, on that day. The theater had been built with the sponsorship of the Accademia Olimpica of Vicenza, from the architectural designs of Andrea Palladio, himself a member of the Academy.

The second "turning point" is a long drawn-out one that lasted a whole century or more. It can be said to have started with the first French translation of Sophocles' play by André Dacier in 1692, and it encompasses a whole series of translations and adaptations of which only one, that produced by Voltaire in 1718, became famous. It may conventionally be said to have come to an end with the posthumous publication (in 1818) of the *Oedipe-Roi* by Marie-Joseph Chénier, who died in 1811.

But, quite apart from the seemingly arbitrary nature of that choice, what is the point of such a study? What light can it possibly shed on Sophocles' *Oedipus Rex*, which was first performed in Athens in about 420 B.C.?

Let us leave aside all those — more numerous than one might think — who believe themselves to possess a direct understanding of that moment in the history of Athens. I can but marvel at their confidence. There are two kinds of justification for the investigation that I shall sketch out in this chapter.

An influential group of philologists and sociologists such as Jean Bollack and his colleagues regards the work of a historian as a kind of stripping operation. Ancient commentators and modern philologists have surrounded the text with layer upon layer of successive interpretations that must be removed, as one peels an onion, so as finally to lay bare the text of Sophocles. But what text? No tape-recording was made of that first production in Athens. The history of the tradition — and with it the earliest *departures from it* — began the moment copyists started to transcribe the manuscripts. The text that is laid bare is not Sophocles' but that of a copyist or some Byzantine editor, Manuel Moschopoulos for example. Even the famous Laurentianus manuscript, a model of "transliteration" (a copy in small letters of a text written in capitals) takes us back no farther than the fifth-century A.D. codex of which it is a copy. For something earlier, we must turn to a *volumen* of the early Roman empire, which is not Sophocles' own text but an interpretation of it provided by a philologist of the time of Hadrian. And if it is true that departures from what Sophocles actually wrote started the moment the tragedy became a scholarly or literary text, in other words a "classic," we must remember that it became "literature" long before the appearance of an *interpretatio romana* in the shape of the *Oedipus* by Seneca: For the three major tragic poets were already considered "classics" by Aristophanes in *The Frogs* (406) and from the time of Lycurgus onward,[2] they were "classics" in the strict sense of the term. That was certainly a date of crucial importance in the transformation of the Greek civilization into a civilization of the written word,[3] but it came a whole century later than most of the texts concerned.

Besides, even if we had Sophocles' own manuscript and a film of the first performance, the problem would merely be shifted. To insist upon the principle of a primordial, single *meaning* that simply needs to be unearthed from the rubble of a string of successive interpretations would, I fear, be to return not to history but to blinding intuition, which I have already argued to be impossible. Who does not cherish a dream of rediscovering the spirit of the fifth century? But the only conceivable way of doing that is *through* that succession of interpretations to which our own, too, belong the moment they are formulated.

But let us pose the problem in other terms. One of the interpretations of Sophocles' play that has left its mark upon our own age is, of course, Freud's.[4] Some years ago, Jean-Pierre Vernant submitted that interpretation to a devastating critique.[5] But in truth, the strength of his critique stemmed in part from the weakness of Freud's case. Didier Anzieu had been foolhardy enough to try to show that the adventures of Oedipus himself could be explained by his "Oedipus complex."[6] According to his interpretation, every mistake that Oedipus made was symptomatic of the fact that "he was unconsciously responding to his desire to commit incest and parricide."[7] It was easy enough for Vernant to retort with a dozen or more arguments, one of them being that the person who counts most in the affections of this tragic Oedipus is not Iocasta, his natural mother, but Merope, his adoptive one; and besides, Sophocles — since it is with him that we are concerned — was at pains to avoid the slightest suggestion of sensuality in the relationship between Oedipus and Iocasta. But not all narrators of the myth were to be so cautious and, above all, the Freudians had replied in advance to Vernant and also to Anzieu, whose undertaking furthered the Freudian view itself not at all. How could Oedipus possibly have an "Oedipus complex," given that, precisely, he is himself Oedipus? To cite Jean Starobinski:

> So Oedipus has no subconscious, since he is our own subconscious, by which I mean: one of the capital roles whose form our desires take. He needs no depth since he is our own depth. However mysterious his story may be, its meaning is complete, with no gaps. Nothing is hidden: there is no need to fathom the motives and underlying thoughts of Oedipus. It would be

derisory to attribute a psychology to him: he is already a case history. Far from being a possible subject for a psychological study, he becomes one of the functional elements thanks to which a science of psychology can take shape.[8]

Very well, but what is the temporal context of these words "he" and "us" that punctuate Jean Starobinski's discussion? For us of the twentieth century, who have read Freud and may even be clients of his disciples, Oedipus is an archetype and a "case history." But can he already have been that in 420 B.C.? Or should we, perhaps, look back from Sophocles' Oedipus to another one: the Oedipus of the *Odyssey*, for example (XI, 271 ff.), who continues to reign even after all has been revealed, or to the Oedipus of the *Iliad* (XXIII, 679), who dies in battle? Or should we turn to the later work, Euripides' *The Phoenician Women* (410 B.C.), in which Iocasta lives on, with the blinded Oedipus immured in his palace, while Eteocles and Polynices clash, then kill each other? Or should we probe still later works, to examine the Oedipus of the *Roman de Thèbes* or the Judas of medieval legend who, like him, kills his father and sleeps with his mother?[9]

Or perhaps Oedipus is an abstraction whose story can be told in a few lines. But even in that case, he is an abstraction, a rationalization that we can only reach, always supposing that he exists at all, through the accounts given of him, accounts that are represented by so many texts. What I should now like to consider are two stages in the history and "re-working" of one of those texts.

Let us start with what took place on March 3rd, during the 1585 Carnival season, in Vicenza, at the Teatro Olimpico, where a performance of *Edipo Tiranno* was presented. We are relatively well informed about this event, essentially thanks to records preserved in the Biblioteca Ambrosiana in Milan and also to two studies, one by Leo Schrade, the other by Alberto Gallo, which have reconstructed what took place on the basis of that information.[10]

It was an amazing production, staged to inaugurate an amazing edifice, an "ancient theater," built between 1580 and 1585. Thanks to Filippo Pigafetta, scion of one of the great families of Vicenza, who wrote a review of the production on the very next day, addressing it to an anonymous "Illustrissimo signore e padrone asservatissimo,"[11] we are more or less well informed and we know that it was a huge success. The performance lasted three and a half hours, but the audience began to fill the theater nine and a half hours before it began. Pigafetta's report closes as follows:

> The fact is that, next after the ancient Greeks and the Romans, the people of Vicenza have composed tragic poems both earlier and better than any other nation. They made such a good job of it that they truly were not only the first, but also the best.

The people of Vicenza thus held pride of place: They had resuscitated ancient tragedy, in its original setting — an ancient theater — and they were not only the "first" in this domain (since Trissino's *Sofonisba* had been performed there half a century earlier), but also, thanks to Palladio and *Oedipus Rex*, the best.

Indeed, a historian of the ancient world *initially* feels entirely at home with this point in the history of *Oedipus Rex*. It *looks as though* this was an intensely political happening, in the full sense of the expression. In 1591, G. Marzari published his *Historia di Vicenza*, in Venice. The work was divided into two parts: The first gave a chronological account of events; the second consisted of a list, or *album*, of the city's great men. It was a list that included Palladio and others responsible for the event in which we are interested. Book I ends at 1555, with the creation of the Accademia Olimpica, the body responsible for the decision to build the *superbissimo teatro* that was such an ornament to the country and could be compared with "no other theater built for the production of plays, whether ancient or modern." A further feature takes us back to the Greco-Roman world of good works described by Paul Veyne:[12] An eighteenth-century scholar, Count Montenari, informs us on the basis of the archives of Vicenza that the building of the theater was "financed by the academicians themselves and those who wished to obtain citizenship."[13] The rights of citizenship were granted in exchange for a *private* gift given for a public monument.... All this is certainly very reminiscent of the Hellenistic world.

Orsatto Giustiniani's translation gives the same impression. The very least that can be said is that it does not underplay — indeed sometimes it underlines — the civic aspect of Sophocles' text. Take the title, for a start: Say what you like, Sophocles' *tyrannos* is not a "King" as our own translation would have it. The great dialogue that brings the royal hero up against the city, indeed that sets the two in opposition, is superbly given its full force in the Italian text. Here are a few examples. In Tiresias' speech, φανήσεται Θηβαῖος (453), Oedipus "will be shown to be a Theban" is translated as "*esser di Thebe cittadin* [to be a Theban citizen]." At the beginning of the messenger's speech (1223), "Ὦ γῆς μέγιστα τῆσδ' ἀεὶ τιμώμενοι [O you who are honored by our country]" is strikingly expanded to:

> *O Principali cittadini soli*
> *Ornamento e sostegno*
> (O you foremost citizens who alone
> Are the flower and strength
> Of the city of Thebes.)

"Πᾶσι Καδμείοισι [to all the Cadmeans]" (1288), becomes, simply, "*a tutti i cittadini* [to all the citizens]"; "ἐκ χθονός [out of the land]" (1290), is rendered as "*fuor di questa cittade* [outside this city]." And in the chorus' final speech (1523): "Ὦ πάτρας Θήβης ἔνοικοι [You that live in my ancestral Thebes]" is translated: "*O di questa mia patria incliti e degni Cittadini* [O generous and worthy citizens of this my fatherland]." There is a further difference here: Not only is the speech addressed to citizens, but to *certain* citizens in particular.

But was it really a matter of citizens? Orsatto Giustiniani, who was a patrician, senator, and politician, certainly was one of the *Principali Cittadini*, but of Venice, not of Vicenza. Vicenza had been annexed by Venice in 1404 and was part of Venice's "territory" or *chora*, as it would have been called in antiquity. It was by now no more than a ghost of a city that never appears as an autonomous political factor in the history of the sixteenth century in Italy.[14] In fact, Marzari, a historian of the town, is delighted at the support forthcoming for the Accademia Olimpica from "virtually the whole of the nobility of Lombardy and the Marches of Treviso"[15] — hardly a citizen nobility, given that it was drawn not only from the "Marches of Treviso" but also from the whole of Lombardy.[16] It is true that the municipal authority had ceded the land on which the theater was built, but it amounted to not much more than a municipal council under the close control of Venice. Pigafetta also records that the military authorities were present together with a few (Venetian) senators, but not the mayor of the town of Vicenza: "*Il clarissimo Capitano si trovo presente con alcuni Senatori e il Podestà restò fuori* [the illustrious Captain was present, together with a few Senators and the Mayor remained away]."[17]

We even possess an extremely detailed review of the performance given on March 3rd, 1585, in the shape of a letter addressed to the *podestà* (mayor) of Vicenza by Antonio Riccoboni,[18] although I confess that its political significance, if any, eludes me.

In truth, for a whole leading section of the society of Vicenza, this production and the theater itself stood for an ideal. The founders of the Accademia Olimpica, chief among them the humanist Gian Giorgio Trissino, himself a tragic author, could be described as aristocrats who had attracted the services of Palladio, the son of a humble artisan from Padua. In Vicenza, a knowledge of antiquity led not to political power itself, but perhaps to a kind of metaphor of it. Thus Filippo Pigafetta describes the Academy's leading light as follows: "The prince of the Academy is the illustrious Count Lunardo Valmarana, who has the soul of a Caesar and who came into the world to undertake magnanimous ventures."[19] The remainder of the text tells us what those "magnanimous ventures" of Count Valmarana's amounted to: receiving in his palace her most serene majesty the empress and showing passing visitors to the town around his gardens, which, needless to say, are compared to "the gardens of Sallust [*horti Sallustiani*]" in ancient Rome.

The Olympic Theater was in itself a monument to the glory of the Academicians, who are represented, in ancient costume, around the front of the stage, while the upper level displays the Labors of Hercules. James Ackerman put his finger on that particular point: "The allegorical figures proposed in Palladio's drawing were transformed by vote of the academicians in the spring of 1580 into heroic likenesses of themselves; just at the moment when Vicenza's noblemen had to abandon all hope of being heroes in fact...."[20] The theater itself is described by the same author as "an academic discourse in three dimensions, a scholarly reconstitution of an ancient Roman theater based upon long familiarity with the monuments and texts."[21] Palladio certainly was a man of great erudition, but his theater is by no means simply a dissertation in three dimensions.

Let us leave aside the difficult question of how much of the building should be attributed to Palladio himself, who designed it, and how much to V. Scamozzi, who supervised its construction. L. Magagnato[22] seems to have proven conclusively that one of the most amusing features of the theater (in our eyes), namely the depiction of a street seen in perspective dividing the stage wall into two, resulted from a misunderstanding over a passage from Vitruvius, Book 5.[23] We should also note that Palladio did away with the special seats mentioned by Vitruvius. Each aristocratic spectator was the equal of every other.

But there are more important points to make: This Greek tragedy translated into (Tuscan) Italian and chosen by virtue of being — according to Aristotle — the best, in preference to all other tragedies, ancient or modern, and also in preference to a pastoral drama,[24] was presented in a Roman theater. Palladio and Scamozzi sought no inspiration from Vitruvius' ideas about the Greek theater. Furthermore, this was a model on a reduced scale, as a contemporary, G.V. Pinelli, succinctly observed, referring to it as "il teatro troppo piccolo [the theater that is too small]."[25] It was also a roofed theater, and even if that roof (which disappeared in 1914, leaving the theater open to the sky) was a painted ceiling in 1585,[26] it was certainly not daylight that illuminated the actors and chorus, and the first performance took place at night. It is all perfectly in line with the spirit of humanism, which imitated antiquity but knew full well that it did not belong to antiquity.

Let us now consider in what respects the 1585 production referred back to the Greek drama of the fifth century B.C. We are relatively well informed on the intentions and achievements of the director Angelo Ingegneri, from Ferrara, and on the reactions that he provoked, since quite apart from a number of contemporary accounts we also possess the text of his own proposals.[27]

The staging of the play was, strictly speaking, no more "archaeological" than the theater. But for us the problem is to determine how much was supposed to be *reconstruction*, how much was deliberately changed (intended to be a transposition), and how much reflected a conscious desire for modernity.

So far as reconstruction went, it was, of course, bound to be no more than bookish and was so at the level of details. For example, at the beginning of the play, when the curtain fell: "First of all, a sweet fragrance of perfumes could be smelled; this was to make it understood that in the town of Thebes, as represented according to ancient history, sweet smells were produced on all sides in order to temper the disdain of the gods."[28] This was probably simply a response to line 4 of *Oedipus Rex*: "the town is heavy with...smells...and incense [πόλις δ' ὁμοῦ μὲν θυμιαμάτων γέμει]," as Giustiniani understood it.

It was assuredly not deliberate that the choruses, which were set to music by Angelo Gabrieli[29] and were likened by Riccoboni to the lamentations of Jeremiah,[30] were turned into interludes separating one act from the next. In many respects the handling of the relationship between the small number of chorus members (there were fifteen) and the lavish apparatus of the stage scenery constituted a striking combination of scrupulous archaeology and a semiconscious desire to be innovative.

For the great novelty of the spectacle lay in its determinedly royal lavishness. The link between chorus and city may have been more forcefully expressed in the translation than in the stage management, but the royalty of the characters was certainly made superabundantly manifest. Ingegneri described Thebes as "the famous Boeotian city and capital of an empire."[31] Oedipus had to be "of greater stature than anyone else"[32] and each time he appeared, he was accompanied by a train of twenty-eight people. Iocasta's train was twenty-five strong, while Creon, being only a prince, rated no more than six escorts.[33] In his project, Ingegneri specified that the costumes were to be Greek, not Roman, except for the priests.[34] But those costumes seem to have come not from the ancient Greek or even Byzantine East, but from an East with which the Venetians of 1585 were far more familiar, that is to say the Turkish East. It is amusing to compare the two following descriptions. Ingegneri specified: "the king's guard will be composed of men all dressed in the same color, in the Greek fashion," while Pigafetta referred to "the king, with his guard of twenty-four archers clad in the uniforms of the *Solacchi* of the Great Turk...."[35]

And despite Ingegneri's hopes, even Rome was perhaps not so far off. There can be little doubt that Seneca's Oedipus stood close behind Sophocles'. The shepherd in Laius' employ, who is unnamed in Sophocles' play, is called Forbante (Phorbas) by Ingegneri, following the Latin model.[36] All this royal pomp is more in keeping with the imperial or papal tradition[37] than with the sixteenth-century idea of ancient Greece. One contemporary critic, Sperone Speroni, writing in the name of tragedy and history, expressed disapproval of this *regal maestà* (regal majesty). The plague was raging and these were times "for supplication, not for pomp";[38] and, somewhat confusing different periods, he went on to point out that while barbarian kings wore a white fillet around their heads, the Greeks simply carried a scepter, as we learn from Homer. As for Iocasta, her costume ought to be as simple as Penelope's and two attendants would have been quite enough for her.[39]

But the essential point about this production was the keen sense of modernity that it reflected. Here Ingegneri's text is invaluable.[40] The staging of the play involved on the one hand the *apparato*: costumes, general movements on stage, and ceremonial; and on the other (apart from the music), the *action*, to which there were also two aspects: "The action consists of two things: voice and gesture."[41] Voices were addressed to the ears of the audience, gestures to their eyes. While it seemed justifiable for the actors to be dressed "as Greeks," the modern actor's art of gesture precluded the wearing of masks, for gesture was not so much a matter of arms and legs, but principally of the face and eyes: "Gesture consists in the appropriate movements of the body and its various parts: in particular the hands, even more the face and, above all, the eyes."[42] Consequently, masks were deliberately excluded from the 1585 production, although Ingegneri was perfectly well aware of their role in the ancient Greek theater.[43] It was this decision that released the production from all its more or less imaginary archaeological constraints. It turned this Greek masterpiece, chosen on the basis of the recommendations of Aristotle's *Poetics* by the Academicians of Vicenza for the inauguration of their theater, into a historical turning point lived very much in the present.

Now let us move forward rather more than a century, leaving Vicenza for Paris.

In 1692, André Dacier published a translation of Sophocles' *Electra* and *Oedipus Rex*, together with a commentary on the two plays.[44] In a number of respects this translation, which was to be followed by several others,[45] marked a turning point upon which we would do well to ponder.

1. As Marie Delcourt has pointed out,[46] this translation marks the victory of Sophocles over Seneca (of which two recent and virtually complete translations existed in Corneille's day). There were no further translations of Seneca's *Oedipus* until 1795.[47] In the adaptations of Sophocles' play, Seneca retains no more than a clandestine influence detectable in the introduction of characters such as Phorbas and "the Ghost of Laius."

2. This translation marks a departure from the "fine infidelities" of Arnaud d'Andilly and Perrot d'Ablancourt, despite the fact that it was not based on a new edition of the text. (There was no further edition until the "professors' revolution" of the late eighteenth century, when scholars took over the work of translation from educated amateurs.[48]) As René Bray has noted: "When Dacier and Mme Dacier translated Aristotle, Anacreon, Plato, Plutarch, Horace, Plautus, Terence and Sophocles, at the end of the century, they did so as scholarly philologists, not as writers seeking inspiration and a rhetorical model."[49]

3. This translation is the starting point, virtually the origin or *archē* for an astonishing number of adaptations, parodies, and studies of Sophocles' play and the Oedipus theme, a body of works that constitutes one of the lesser-known aspects of eighteenth-century literature and philosophy.

Until recently the subject had attracted little attention,[50] but it has now been treated in depth by a young research-worker, Christian Biet,[51] who has identified no less than seventeen adaptations (including two parodies and two operas), strung out between 1718 and 1811.[52]

4. Finally, remarkably enough, Dacier's translation was designed to strike a blow in the quarrel between the ancients and the moderns, an altercation in which Dacier himself vehemently took the part of the ancients. However, its effect was quite the reverse from what he had hoped, both generally and in respect of the Oedipus drama. The translations by the Daciers changed the very status of translation in French scholarly circles, where exactitude, even — within limits — literality, now became the order of the

day.[53] In 1687, Pierre Coustel had explained that aesthetic expansion was called for in the translation of secular texts: "If you simply translate literally, you make the translation weak, undistinguished and colorless; you deprive it of beauty, movement and life; the resemblance you give it to the original is almost like that of a dead man to a living one." However, he excepted the Bible from that rule: "However, the Holy Scriptures must be excepted, for they must always be translated as literally as possible: because the order of the words is often a mystery."[54] For Sophocles to be translated involved two separate phases, logically if not historically. In the first phase his writing was regarded as a text as sacred as the Bible; in the second, both were considered as profane texts. To start with, at any rate, this involved entering forbidden territory. But that is not where the matter ends for, not necessarily paradoxically, this more or less literal *translation* by Dacier was itself soon to give rise to *adaptations* that were not literal at all, with the result that the Oedipus who accompanied the ideological and political quarrels of the century became a resolutely modern figure.

Voltaire wrote the first in this series of *Oedipus* dramas and his play was immensely well received in 1718. (It was, in fact, the greatest dramatic success of eighteenth century France.) He himself sums up the situation well enough in a letter written in 1731 to the Reverend Father Porée, a Jesuit priest:

> I was full of my readings of the ancient authors and your teaching and I knew very little of the theater in Paris; I worked more or less as if I were in Athens. I consulted Monsieur Dacier, who was a native of that place. He advised me to include a chorus in every scene, as the Greeks did. It was like telling me to stroll through Paris dressed like Plato.[55]

It goes without saying that it is not my intention to make a systematic examination of these plays here, for that would amount to little more than a summary of Biet's work. I shall limit myself to a few general remarks on this corpus of plays.

The first point to make is that this is an intensely reflexive collection of works that draws upon an extensive network of references. In a study available in a French translation,[56] Hans Robert Jauss ponders on the question of why a play such as Goethe's *Iphigenia in Tauris* has now lost all impact. He suggests that it is at least in part due to the double register of references used by Goethe – references that today are meaningless – on the one hand to ancient tragedy, on the other to French classical tragedy. There can be no doubt that the works of Voltaire and his successors are also marked by this double register of references that, in their case, is complemented by many further references to political and ideological issues of their own day. As a result, these plays soon became incomprehensible and so unreadable. Of course, a historian's attitude is different: From *our point of view*, one of the interesting aspects of many of these works is the fact that they are, often explicitly, sometimes implicitly, designed as part of an ongoing aesthetic, ideological, and cultural debate. That is true of Dacier's translation, which incorporates a detailed commentary; it is also true of Voltaire's *Oedipe*, which is accompanied by a whole series of letters, the first group written by Voltaire himself and containing "a critical study of Sophocles' *Oedipus*, Corneille's, and his own."[57]

Given that it is a scholarly work, it is not particularly surprising that the 1785 edition of Father Brumoy's *Théâtre des Grecs*[58] should contain not only a translation of Sophocles' text but also the translator's reflections on the play, extracts from the versions of Seneca and Corneille, also selected by Father Brumoy, an anonymous summary of Giustiniani's *Edipo Tiranno* (still, in 1785, remembered as having been presented with much pomp and circumstance in Vicenza by the Academicians), and a detailed analysis of Voltaire's play. What could be more normal, one might think, and the same could be said of similar editions of *Electra* and *Antigone*. But it is considerably more surprising that in 1781 a gentleman such as the Comte de Lauraguais should publish a *Jocaste*, a tragedy in five acts preceded by a one hundred and eighty-three page *Disser-*

374

tation sur les Oedipe, comparing the work of Sophocles, Corneille, Voltaire, Houdar de la Motte, and his own.[59] *Oedipus* seems to be a play that cannot be published on its own. Furthermore, it constitutes an altogether exceptional pretext for aesthetic experimentation. In 1726, Houdar de la Motte, a committed champion of the "moderns" but who had also adapted the *Iliad*, produced two versions, the first in prose, the second in verse. The first was turned down by the French actors, which is why he proceeded to write the second.[60]

But the most astonishing case of all is probably that of M. de La Tournelle, a gentleman with the rank of War Commissioner, who was a friend of the Academician Boivin and a translator of Sophocles and Aristophanes. He was the author of a (lost) *Recueil* (collection) comprising no less than nine plays on the subject of Oedipus. Four of these plays, published in 1730 to 1731, are to be found in series published in Paris: they are *Oedipe ou les Trois Fils de Jocaste, Oedipe et Polybe, Oedipe ou l'ombre de Laius* and *Oedipe et toute sa Famille*. The author undertook a twofold and systematic exploration of the subject, considering it on the one hand from the point of view of the dramatic possibilities provided by Oedipus' family, both natural and adoptive,[61] on the other with a psychological perspective, concentrating on the sentiments that might be ascribed to this interesting family group. *Les Trois Fils de Jocaste* provides a remarkable enough example. The play is adapted from *Oedipus Rex*, Aeschylus' *Seven against Thebes* and Euripides' *The Phoenician Women*. In it, Polynices kills Eteocles, Iocasta kills first Polynices (a completely original idea), then herself and Oedipus together. As Christian Biet notes: "The ending leads to no new power structure; there is simply nothing left," thereby drawing attention to the political problem posed by this series of adaptations, namely the problem of power.

Up to a point, that was also the problem that the ancient tragedies expressed in the dialogue between the hero, who hailed from the depths of the age of myth, and the modern democratic city. *Oedipus Rex* is a drama played out between three parties: the tyrant,

375

the chorus representing the city, and the diviner Tiresias, who is the intermediary between the secular and the sacred domains.

All the adaptations were bound to tackle that political debate. In Corneille's *Oedipus* (1659), it had already undergone a radical transformation. In the clash between tyrannical power and legitimate power depicted in this tragedy, the *dēmos* plays no part at all.[62]

It was through these clashes, far more than through any direct treatment of the themes of incest and parricide, that the eighteenth-century *Oedipus* variations reflected the great controversies of the day. The heroes of the drama were to be the people, the priests, and the kings. In Dacier's version, there is as yet no real confrontation. Dacier made two alterations that were to provide a long-lived model: (1) he turned the priest of Zeus who addresses Oedipus at the beginning of Sophocles' play into a "high priest" in the Jewish manner; (2) while he realized that the action began "with the assembly of the people," he wasted no time in transferring the political role of the people to a chorus of "sacrificers," which he invented for his own particular purposes and which served "to inspire people with the sentiments that they ought to have."[63]

It was in Voltaire's drama that the chorus regained an autonomous political dimension, but a very limited one, as Voltaire was extremely distrustful of the chorus' political function and reduced it to a minimum. All the same, he did see that it constituted an element in the tragedy that could not be avoided. This is what he had to say about that minimum role: "The plot of an interesting play usually requires that the principal actors should have secrets to confide to each other; and also the means to confide those secrets to an entire people." And: "Today there are still some scholars who have had the courage to insist that we have no true conception of tragedy, since we have done away with the choruses. It is as if they expected us to represent Paris, London, and Madrid in a single play, just because that is what our fathers did when comedy became established in France." He concluded: "So, until such time as I am proved wrong, I shall continue to believe that one can only risk introducing a chorus into a tragedy if one takes the precaution of keeping it in its place." His final decision was twofold, its aesthetic and political aspects inextricably intermingled. On the aesthetic side, the chorus should be allowed on stage "only when it is necessary as an ornament." As for the city, both ancient and modern: "A chorus is only suitable in plays in which an entire people is involved,"[64] which it most certainly is in the case of *Oedipus Rex*, as Voltaire fully realized.

Significantly enough, Voltaire was the only one to adopt this attitude during the early years of the century. Let us divide the eighteenth-century variations chronologically, into two groups. The first dates by and large from the Regency (of Philippe d'Orleans, 1715 to 1723) and includes no less than eleven plays written between 1718 and 1731. The group of plays written at the end of the eighteenth century and the beginning of the nineteenth comprises six plays. It is noticeable that in the first group Voltaire is the only author to introduce a political chorus, while the Jesuit writer Folard, who in 1722 published a rival *Oedipus* to that of the *philosophe*, would do no more than introduce a chorus of children. Of the six plays in the second group, only one, by N.G. Léonard,[65] not published until 1798, five years after the death of its author, reduced the chorus to its simplest expression. In all the other dramas of the second group, it plays an important role and in Marie-Joseph Chénier's play it appears not only in every act, but in every scene. We must recognize that the inclusion of the chorus in these later plays was in part due to the vogue for "antiquity" that characterized the end of the century and also the Empire, but there is more to it than that. It is hard not to see this very real increase in the role of the chorus as a sign of the growing awareness of politics – in the modern, democratic sense of the term: a point that is amply confirmed by a reading of the plays themselves. Of course, we do not need all these versions of *Oedipus* to recognize that fact. All the same, it is interesting to find it confirmed, however indirectly.

377

How did the eighteenth-century theoreticians set out the problem? They passed over the fact that — whatever one might claim — it is impossible to identify the chorus totally with the city, if only because as a general rule it is composed either of people outside the city or people above it (women or old men).[66] What they deliberately focused on in ancient tragedy was the clash between the prince and the city, doing so far more emphatically than the commentators of the nineteenth century or even the twentieth. In 1730, Father Brumoy devoted a splendid page in his *Discours sur le parallèle des théâtres* to the subject of kings and tragedy. He claimed that the Greeks "want kings on stage only to revel in their fall, out of their implacable loathing for their supreme dignity." When Rochefort and Du Theil produced a second edition of this text, they added a disclaimer in the form of a note to the effect that "all this paragraph needs to be read with circumspection."[67] In 1788, Abbé Barthelemy remarked, in the chapter devoted to Greek tragedy in his *Voyage du jeune Anacharsis*: "Contemporary republicans always contemplate thrones rolling in the dust with malicious delight."[68]

On an individual level, the *political* characters of *Oedipus Rex* are the king, the queen, the high priest, and of course Creon, the modest brother-in-law/arrogant claimant to the throne. They are all taken from Sophocles except the high priest, who is a transformation or addition, sometimes confused with Tiresias, sometimes distinct from him.[69] The whole notion was parodied in 1719 by Biancolelli,[70] an actor in the employ of the Duc d'Orléans; in his play, Tiresias became a village schoolmaster. In another parody (taking off Houdar de la Motte's version of *Oedipus*), the author, Legrand, significantly enough replaced the gods and their oracle by an old rabbi and a woman with a houseful of cats.[71]

The same chronological contrast that we noted earlier in connection with the absence or presence of the chorus also operates here. In Voltaire's *Oedipus* and the plays inspired by it, all produced during a period particularly characterized by a series of religious clashes (between the Jesuits and the Jansenists, for example), it is the priests who are singled out for attack (and, through them, their God). Virtually the only couplet from Voltaire's play that is remembered today is in part inspired by the criticisms that Sophocles' Iocasta voices against diviners. Voltaire's lines run as follows:[72]

> Les prêtres ne sont pas ce qu'un vain peuple pense,
> Notre crédulité fait toute leur science.
> (Priests are not what foolish folk believe:
> Our own credulity is all that they perceive.)

The play closes with a passage openly praising the enlightened despot, to wit, Philoctetes, the "legitimate" king.

At the end of the century, the objectives of the authors' direct or indirect criticism are, quite naturally, the transgressor king and the incestuous queen. Thus, in 1786, in a play by a certain Bernard d'Héry,[73] the tragedy is about the "Great King" who clashes with the combined forces of the "High Priest" and the chorus of citizens. The subject of the Greek tragedy is interpreted as the sacrifice of the king for the sake of his people. At the end of the play, the people (the chorus) beg Oedipus to stay, whatever happens.

In 1791, Duprat de la Touloubre brought his opera to a close before Iocasta's death and Oedipus' act of self-mutilation so as to "end the spectacle with brilliance," as the author put it. This play has been interpreted (by Biet) as "a determined defense of the King-Father set on trial." Finally, in 1793, shortly before the author's death, Nicolas G. Léonard's play presented a king who became the victim of a popular rebellion. The elimination of the chorus from this play can surely not have been fortuitous. As for the republican, M.-J. Chénier, he presented an Oedipus who stood in opposition to "the right enjoyed by every inhabitant of the city to speak up and voice his opinion" (Biet).

Actually, however manifest the personal sentiments of the authors may be, they are relatively unimportant. What matters most is this progressive mutation in the figure of the king. From the debate concerning the function of kingship around which

Corneille's play and even Voltaire's revolved, we have moved to a religious and political clash between a king and his people. Considerable changes thus take place along the way between Voltaire and Chénier. A common language is used throughout, however, and that seemed a point well worth trying to make.

Today we may smile at this procession of Oedipuses from the Age of Enlightenment and, equally, at the 1585 Oedipus with his cohort of twenty-eight archers and courtiers. Nevertheless, in their own way they have contributed to the formation of the Oedipus of our own times.

Pierre Vidal-Naquet

CHAPTER XVII

The Masked Dionysus of

Euripides' *Bacchae**

Amid all the sources of evidence on Dionysus in fifth-century Athens, Euripides' *Bacchae* occupies a place of particular importance.[1] The richness and complexity of the work and the density of the text make it an incomparable document when it comes to trying to understand the particular features of the religious experience of the devotees of this god who, more than any other, assumes within the Greek pantheon the functions of the god of the mask. I have drawn upon a number of existing editions and commentaries on the play, in particular those by J.E. Sandys, E.R. Dodds, R.P. Winnington-Ingram, G.S. Kirk, Jeanne Roux, and Charles Segal[2] and am deeply indebted to all these scholars, including those with whom I disagree. But in my approach to the tragedy, I have deliberately chosen to concentrate principally on the features that might shed some light on the links connecting this god with the mask. It was, of course, important to remember that this is not a religious document but a tragedy and that it obeys all the rules, conventions, and aims peculiar to this type of literary creation. Nevertheless, the *Bacchae* was well worth studying, not least because the part played by Dionysus in this play is quite different from the usual role of the gods in tragedy. In the *Bacchae*, Dionysus takes the principal role. The poet sets him on stage as the god who himself stages his own epiphany there, in the theater, revealing himself not only to the protagonists in the drama but also to the spectators seated on the tiered steps, by manifesting his divine presence through the unfolding of the tragic drama — drama that is, moreover, specifically placed under his religious patronage. It is as if, throughout the spectacle, even as he appears on stage beside the other characters in the play, Dionysus was also operating at another level, behind the scene, putting the plot together and directing it toward its *denouement*.

The constant interaction between the Dionysus of the civic religion — the god of the official cult — and the Dionysus of the tragic representation — the god who is the master of theatrical illusion — is right from the start underlined by the duality, or double persona, of Dionysus in the theater itself. On the *theologeion* he is present as a god; on the stage he is seen as the Lydian stranger "who looks like a woman"; the two are dressed alike and wear the same mask; they are indistinguishable yet distinct from one another. The mask worn by the god and the human stranger — who is also the god — is the tragic mask of the actor, the function of which is to make the characters recognizable as what they are, to render them visually identifiable. But in the case of Dionysus, the mask disguises him as much as it proclaims his identity; it literally "masks" him; at the same time, through his misidentification and secret, this prepares the way for his authentic triumph and revelation. All the characters in the drama, including the chorus composed of his faithful female Lydian devotees, who have followed him to Thebes, see only the foreign missionary in the theatrical mask that the god wears. The spectators also see that foreigner but realize that he is a disguise for the god, a disguise through which the latter can eventually be made known for what he is: a masked god whose coming will bring the fulfillment of joy to some, but to others, those unable to recognize him, nothing but destruction. The ambiguity of the mask worn by the stranger and by the god expresses the interplay between the two, underlining both the affinities and the contrast between on the one hand the *tragic* mask that sets the seal upon the presence of a particular character, giving him a firm identity, and on the other the *religious* mask whose fascinating gaze establishes an imperious, obsessive, and overwhelming presence, the presence of a being that is not where it seems to be, a being that is also elsewhere, perhaps inside one, perhaps nowhere. It is the presence of one who is absent. It is a "smiling" mask (434, 1021), unlike the usual tragic masks, a mask that is consequently different from all the rest, a mask displaced, disconcerting, and that, seen there on the theater stage, is an echo that calls to mind the enigmatic face of some of the religious masks of the god used in the civic religion.[3]

The play is a text, then. But a text is no more innocent than an image is. In the series of pictorial representations of Dionysus, featuring the pillar with its mask,[4] the idol has, right from the start, sometimes been considered to be associated with the Lenaea, sometimes with the Anthesteria, sometimes with other ceremonies, and the overall interpretations of these scenes have varied accordingly. In similar fashion, the *Bacchae* has been, and still is, read in the light of a particular idea that we ourselves have of Dionysism. And that idea – whatever it is that we call Dionysism – is not a piece of factual evidence: It is a product of the history of religions produced, from Nietzsche onward, in our modern age. It was, to be sure, on the basis of documentary evidence that the historians of Greek religion constructed this category (of Dionysism), but they did so using conceptual tools and a framework of reference whose bases, inspiration, and implications were affected at least as much by their own religious system and spiritual horizon as by those of the Greeks of the classical period. This same text, read by excellent Greek scholars, has given rise to two radically different types of interpretation. Some scholars have read into it a categorical condemnation of Dionysism, an attack against religion in line with the skepticism displayed toward the gods for which Aristophanes criticized Euripides. Others, in contrast, have regarded it as evidence of a veritable conversion on the part of the poet who, as his life drew to a close, seems to them to have been touched by grace as it were, and to have wished to exalt a superhuman form of wisdom that, in contrast to the arrogant knowledge and reason of the sophists, stemmed from abandoning oneself to divine ecstasy, the mystic madness of the god of blessed possession.

It accordingly seemed worth examining how the category of "the Dionysiac" has been elaborated on the basis of the dichotomy established by Nietzsche between Apollo and Dionysus.[5] The key to this construction is to be found in its origin, E. Rohde's *Psyche*, published in 1893, the earliest work in a line of inquiry that started with Rohde and continued with M.P. Nilsson, J. Harrison, W. Otto, E.R. Dodds and H. Jeanmaire, to name only the major contributors. The problem that these authors faced was understanding how it was possible, within the framework of the Greek religion for which Homer provides the most important evidence, for there to arise a religion of the soul that was diametrically opposed to it, in the sense that it sought to promote something akin to the divine in each one of us: the *psuche*, which is radically alien to everything in the earthly world and aspires only to return to its heavenly origin, escaping from its earthly prison and chains, to be united with the deity.

For Rohde, the crucial point was this: Dionysism was a foreign importation into Greek culture. This historian underlines the foreignness of Dionysus by locating the god's origin beyond the frontiers of Greece, in Thrace. And he suggests that for Greek scholars, the postulate of his foreign origin must appear self-evident: Dionysus has nothing in common with truly Greek civilization and religion, the civilization and religion of the Homeric world. He is completely foreign since, instead of integrating individuals into the world in their correct place, the Dionysiac religious experience is designed to project them beyond it, into ecstasy, uniting them with the god by whom they are possessed. Rohde suggests that the practices involving trance connected with the Thracian Dionysus, which give rise to contagious and more or less pathological personality crises, must originally have been regarded by the Greeks as aberrant, wayward, and dangerous; and yet they contained the seeds of something that Greece was eventually to carry to full development: to wit, a true mysticism. It was suggested that a continuous line of development linked the collective delirium of *mania*, in a state of trance and possession, with escape from the world in order to find total self-fulfillment, the rejection of worldly existence, practices of asceticism, and a belief in the immortality of the soul. But if that is the case — if trance and possession can lead directly to spiritual techniques of purification, concentration, and separation of mind from body, if renunciation of the world, the ascetic ideal, and the quest for individual salvation stem from Dionysism — one is bound to conclude that there must be two types of Dionysism and that the boundary that separates Dionysism from Greek culture is to be found within Dionysism itself. It would follow that the whole of the side to Dionysism represented by the exaltation of joy, pleasure, wine, love, and vitality, all the unbridled exuberance directed toward laughter and masquerading, this impulse toward not ascetic purity but communion with wild nature, stemmed from Greece's "acculturation" of things non-Greek, things that were a secondary manifestation of the original, authentic Dionysism of Thrace. And that, indeed, was the solution that Rohde found himself forced to adopt. The trouble is that, in fifth-century Athens, no sign is to be found of the "real" Dionysus, that is to say Rohde's Thracian Dionysus, while his secondary, reshaped, and distorted manifestation is impossible to miss.

That is why D. Sabatucci, in his *Saggio sul misticismo greco*,[6] proceeded to suggest an interpretation that started off by reversing the terms in which the problem was expressed. Sabatucci did not regard Dionysus as the god of mysticism but considered that some of his rituals may, as a secondary development, have been re-used and given new significance with a view to promoting an experience that *could* be defined as "mystic," to the extent that it stood in opposition to the religious attitudes that were in keeping with Greek tradition. What had started out by being a purely relative means of reinforcing the conventional religious order by way of producing a reaction to a passing crisis became an end in itself. The experience lived through in the course of that crisis came to be seen as something absolute, the only absolute that could lead to the authentic revelation of "sacredness," which was now defined by its radical opposition to all the established forms of piety. The crisis of Dionysiac possession, originally considered a temporary device through which to regain a healthy condition and reintegrate oneself into the order of the world, became the only means by which to escape from the world, pass beyond the human condition, and, by becoming assimilated with the divine, accede to a state of existence that the conventional religious practices were incapable of procuring and for which, furthermore, there was no place or meaning within the system of the civic religion.

The "reversed" perspective adopted by Sabatucci no doubt seemed all the more urgently necessary given that the hypothesis of Dionysus being a foreign figure imported from Thrace or Lydia into Greece at a relatively late date was demolished when the name of Dionysus was found to be present in the Mycenaean Linear B documents. This showed that Dionysus had been a Greek god for just as long as the other gods in the pantheon. However, the problem was still not resolved. It could now be formulated as follows: Where, when, and how did these changes, these switches in the orientation of Dionysism take place? Sabatucci suggested that there existed an "Orphic complex" that took over this reinterpretation of Dionysism, associating it with various trends and forms of Orphism combined with the mysteries of Eleusis, which he considered to be an essential component of Greek mysticism. The word mysticism itself is connected with the term *mustēs, muēsis, mustikos,* and *mustērion,* which have special reference to Eleusis, where the rituals included initiation, revelation, internal transformation, and the promise of a better lot in the beyond. But the origins of words do not imply that they necessarily retained the same meanings and the same religious connotations as long as they remained in use. The first meaning of *muō* is "to shut" or "to shut itself or oneself." In the context of Eleusis, it may have referred to the shutting of one's eyes or mouth. If it referred to the eyes, the *mustai* may have been those whose eyes were still closed, that is to say those who had not "seen," who had not yet acceded to the *epopteia*; in that case *muēsis* might mean the preliminary purification, as opposed to the *telētē* or decisive and definitive accomplishment of the *epopteia*.[7] If it referred to the mouth, those who kept their mouths shut would be the initiates who were forbidden to divulge the secret revealed to them. This family of words was to retain the same meanings of secret rite, hidden revelation, *sumbola*, the significance of which is inaccessible to non-initiates, right down to the third century A.D. As used by Plotinus, they acquired further layers of meaning and eventually came to denote more than just a revelation stemming, as at Eleusis, from a vision or experienced emotion rather than from instruction.[8] Now they signified an intimate experience of the divine, a way of feeling it directly, internally, of entering into contact and communion with it within oneself. This line of development eventually led to the "ravishment in God" of which Teresa of Avila spoke, a good enough description of the forms taken by Christian mysticism. As is well known, three conditions are necessary for such ravishment: solitude, silence, and stillness. We are a far cry from Eleusis and are poles apart from Dionysism.

But let us pass on from these etymological considerations[9] and recognize, with Sabatucci, that every religious system can produce its own particular type of mystic experience and that this may be very different from that developed within the framework of Christian monotheism. Nevertheless, it is noteworthy that there is absolutely no documentation on the Dionysism of fifth-century Athens to vouch for this secondary type of Dionysism, that is to say a Dionysism systematically used to reverse the meaning of sacredness and the basic orientation of the official civic religion: no evidence of any ascetic tendencies, no rejection of the positive values of earthly life, not the slightest urge toward renunciation, no preoccupation with the soul or attempt to separate it from the body, no eschatological perspective at all. No hint of any preoccupation with salvation or immortality is to be found in the relevant rituals and pictorial representations or in the *Bacchae*. Everything is played out in the here and now. The undeniable desire to be free, to escape into an elsewhere is expressed not as a hope for another, happier life after death, but within the present life, through the experience of an extra dimension, an expansion of the human condition, which thereby accedes to a blessed otherness.

This view is confirmed by the analyses produced by anthropologists.[10] Apart from the Christian ecstasy of ravishment in solitude, silence, and stillness, they distinguish two forms of trance and possession that are, in many respects, diametrically opposed. In the first, it is the individual human being who takes the initiative, asserting his control over the situation. Thanks to the peculiar powers that he has acquired by various means, he is able to leave his body, which he abandons in a state of catalepsy to journey in another world from which he then returns to earth, remembering everything that he has seen in the beyond. Such was the status of the "magi" in Greece, strange figures with their own life discipline, spiritual exercises, ascetic techniques, and reincarnation. They are more or less legendary figures who have more in common with Apollo than with Dionysus.[11]

In the other form of trance, it is a matter not of an exceptional human being ascending to the gods, but of the gods coming down to earth of their own volition, in order to possess a mortal, to ride him, to make him dance. The one who is possessed does not leave this world; he becomes other through the power that inhabits him. On this level, a further distinction should be made. In the *Phaedrus* (265a), where Plato tackles the problem of *mania*, he makes a distinction between two kinds: on the one hand, the delirium may take the form of a human sickness from which the victim must recover; on the other, it may be a divine state with a fully positive value of its own. A similar dividing line distinguishes between practices of a corybantic type on the one hand and the cult of Dionysus on the other. In the first case, it is a matter of individuals who are sick. Their critical state of delirium or prostration is the sign of a fault, the manifestation of an impurity. They are the victims of a god whom they have offended and who punishes them by taking possession of them. So what needs to be done, in the course of ritual, is to identify the god from whose vengeance the sick person is suffering so that he can be cured through the appropriate purifications, which can liberate him from his state of possession. In a Dionysiac *thiasos* there is no god to be identified and ejected; there is no sickness: The particular pathology of the individuals involved is of no concern. The *thiasos* is an organized group of faithful devotees who, if they use trance, turn it into a form of social behavior, ritualized and controlled and for which a preliminary period of apprenticeship is probably required. Its purpose is not to cure an individual's sickness, much less to deliver him from the evil of living in a world from which he longs to escape forever; instead, it is to procure a changed state of being, through music and dancing, for a group of people, in ritual costume, in a setting of wild nature either real or simulated. The aim is for this group momentarily to undergo the experience of becoming "other," within the very framework of the city and with its agreement, if not authority: "other" not in an absolute sense, but in relation to the models, norms, and values peculiar to the particular culture of that city.[12]

Nor could it be otherwise for Dionysism. The deity that Dionysus constitutes in the Greek pantheon does not represent a domain of reality separate from the world, a domain set in opposition to the inconsistency and inconstancy of human life. His position there is ambiguous, as is his status, which is more that of a demi-god, however much he wishes to be a full god with all the privileges and attributes of one. Even on Olympus, Dionysus embodies the "other." If he had a mystical function, he would wrench men from the world of becoming and the sensible in all its multiplicity and project them over the threshold beyond which one enters into the sphere of what is unchangeable, permanent, one, and forever the same. But that is not his role. He does not detach human beings from earthly life through techniques of asceticism and renouncement. Rather, he blurs the frontiers between the divine and the human, the human and the animal, the here and the beyond. He sets up communion between things hitherto isolated, separate. His eruption into nature, the social group, and each individual human being, through trance and regulated possession, is a subversion of order. This subversion, by means of a whole range of prodigies, fantasies, and illusions, involving a disconcerting disorientation from everyday reality, projects one either upward, into an idyllic cofraternity between all beings, the blessed communion of a golden age suddenly retrieved, or, on the contrary, if one rejects and denies him, downward, into the chaotic confusion of a terrifying horror.

As I have already explained, in this analysis of the *Bacchae*, I shall concentrate solely upon such features as may illuminate the figure of the masked god and the nature of his devotees' religion.

The Dionysus of the *Bacchae* is a god intent upon imposing his imperious, demanding, overwhelming presence upon this earthly world: He is a god of "*parousia*." In every land, every city that he decides to make his own, he makes his entrance, arrives, is there. The very first word of the play is ἥκω: "Here I am, I have come." Dionysus always bursts in suddenly, as if erupting from somewhere else, somewhere foreign, a barbarian world, far away. His sudden coming is all-conquering, extending and establishing the cult of the god from city to city, from place to place. The entire tragedy, as it unfolds showing us the Dionysiac epiphany, illustrates this "coming." It shows it on stage, where Dionysus performs both as a protagonist in the midst of other actors and as the organizer of the whole spectacle, the secret manipulator of the plot that finally leads to the Thebans recognizing him as a god. But this epiphany is also addressed to the spectators whom the fiction of the drama includes, as if they were participants in the revelation of the god. Through the pity and terror that they feel for the victims, it allows them fully to perceive what is at stake and all that is implied. At the same time, thanks to the type of comprehension conveyed by the perfectly ordered tragic action, it affords them the same pleasure, the same "purification" that Dionysus grants to the cities where he chooses to appear once he is recognized, accepted, and integrated there.

This epiphany is not like that of ordinary gods, nor is it a "vision" analogous to the *epopteia* of the mysteries. Dionysus insists that he be "seen." The last words of the Prologue, which balance the "I have come" of the opening, call upon the "city of Cadmus to behold [ὡς ὁρᾷ Κάδμου πόλις]" (61). Dionysus wants to be seen to be a god, to be manifest to mortals as a god, to make himself known, to reveal himself,[13] to be known, recognized, understood.[14] This "manifestness" that must, in certain conditions, be a feature of the god's presence, is expressed forcefully in the fourth stasimon by the chorus of Lydian women devotees, who first state their desire that justice should "be manifest [φανερός]" (993), then declare what is for them a matter of principle: "My happiness depends upon pursuing that which is great and manifest [φανερά]" (1007). Next, they proceed to invoke the Dionysus of epiphanies, calling upon the god to show himself too, to make himself manifest: "Appear! [φάνηθι]" (1018). But Dionysus reveals himself by concealing himself, makes himself manifest by hiding himself from the eyes of all those who believe only in what they can see, in what is "evident before their eyes,"[15] as Pentheus himself puts it at line 501, when Dionysus is there before him, under his very nose, but invisible to him beneath his disguise. It is an epiphany alright, but of a god who is masked. To make Thebes accept his presence, to "appear" there, Dionysus has changed his "appearance," transformed his face, his external aspect, his nature.[16] He has donned the mask of a human being; he presents himself in the guise of a young Lydian stranger. Distinct from the god, yet at the same time identical to him, the stranger assumes the functions of a mask in the sense that, even as he conceals his true identity (from those who are not prepared to recognize him), he is

391

also the instrument of the god's revelation: He manifests his imperious presence before the eyes of those who, in his sight and — as
it were — face to face with him, have learned to "see what must
be seen" (924): what is most manifest under the disguise of
what is most invisible.

But how can the god and his devotee be face to face, looking
straight into each other's eyes? After all, trance is collective: It
occurs in a group, in the setting of a *thiasos*. Nevertheless, when
the band of maenads surrenders jointly to the orgiastic frenzy, each
participant acts on her own account, oblivious of any general cho-
reography, indifferent to what the others are doing (as in a *komos*).
Once the devotees have entered the dance, each as one elect is
face to face with the god, totally submissive within herself to the
power that possesses her and moves her as it will.

So although the epiphany of Dionysus can only be made manifest through the collective orgiastic behavior of a group, for each
individual concerned it takes the form of a direct confrontation, a
"fascination" in which, through the interchange of gazes and the
indissociable reciprocity of "seeing" and "being seen," all distance
is abolished between the devotee and her god, and they become
united. In trance, the human being plays the part of god while
god plays the part of human being. Momentarily, the frontiers
between them collapse, blurred by the intensity of the divine presence which, to be seen in all its immediacy before one, must first
impose its dominion over one's eyes, and having won possession
of one's gaze from within, transforms one's very mode of vision.

When Pentheus interrogates the Lydian stranger about this god
whose missionary the young man claims to be, his question draws
a clear line of demarcation between two contrary forms of vision:
that of the sleeping dreamer, which is illusory and unreal; and
that of the wide-awake, lucid man with eyes wide open, which
is authentic and irrefutable. "How did you see him? In a dream,"
he asks, "or face to face?" " Ὁρῶν ὁρῶντα," the stranger replies: "Face
to face [seeing him seeing me]" (470). "I saw him seeing me." It
is an *oblique* reply that displaces the question and stresses that the

392

god's epiphany has nothing to do with the dichotomy that shapes the convictions of Pentheus, namely his distinction between on the one hand dreams, fantasies, and illusions, and on the other true vision that provides irrefutable knowledge. The "vision" demanded by the masked god is something far beyond those two forms of knowledge, of which it makes a mockery. It is based on the meeting of two gazes in which (as in the interplay of reflecting mirrors), by the grace of Dionysus, a total reversability is established between the devotee who sees and the god who is seen, where each one is, in relation to the other, at once the one who sees and the one who makes himself seen.

In this way, Dionysus' eruption into the world and his unaccustomed presence call into question that "normal vision" that is both naive and confident and on the basis of which Pentheus judges that he can justify his rejection of the god and all the forms of behavior encouraged by him. It is a point of view that he believes to be positive and reasonable, but its secret, disturbed side is betrayed by the young man's exacerbated "voyeurism," his passionate, irrepressible (812) desire to be a spectator (θεατὴς, 829) and contemplate in the base behavior of the maenads the very things that he claims to hold in horror.[17] It is desire to see what must not be seen by a male who is a non-initiate (472, 912, 1108), to watch, to spy,[18] now openly in full daylight,[19] now seeking to see without being seen (1050), eventually to reveal himself in all his wild, bestial nature for all to see (1076),[20] showing himself clearly to those on whom he set out to spy (982, 1076, 1095). It is a supreme irony at the expense of the man whose eyes are open, whose vision is lucid: At the crisis of the drama, when his life is at stake, "The maenads saw him more clearly than he saw them" (1075).

No other text so insistently, almost obsessively, repeats such a plethora of words signifying seeing and visibility: eidos, even idea (at 471), morphē, phaneros, phainō, emphanes, horaō, eidō (and their compounds). Euripides finds it all the easier to employ this vocabulary to suggest the whole range of multiple meanings, ambiguities,

and reversals suggested by human experience confronted by Dionysus, given that the very same terms can be applied to ordinary,
normal vision, to supernatural "apparitions" engineered by the
god, to his epiphanic revelation, and to all the illusory forms of
"appearance," seeming, misleading resemblance, and hallucination.

What the vision of Dionysus does is explode from within and
shatter the "positivist" vision that claims to be the only valid one,
in which every being has a particular form, a definite place, and
a particular essence in a fixed world that ensures each his own
identity that will encompass him forever, the same and unchanging. To see Dionysus, it is necessary to enter a different world
where it is the "other," not the "same" that reigns.

Two points in the tragedy are particularly significant in this
respect. At 477, Pentheus says to the stranger: "You say you saw
the god clearly. What form did he assume?"[21] For the man who
sees things clearly, the god, like any other being or thing, must
have a definite form, a visible aspect in keeping with his nature,
an identity. The stranger replies: "Whatever form he wished" and
adds, "the choice was his, not mine." When Dionysus manifests
himself, there are no rules that he need obey regarding the mode
of his appearance because there is no pre-established form laid
down for him in which the god could be forever trapped. The
tragic text repeatedly underlines this enigmatic aspect of the
masked god, this aura of uncertainty with respect to his shape and
nature, through its use of expressions such as: this god (or stranger)
"whoever he is" or "whoever he may be."[22]

A little farther on, at line 500, the stranger, finding himself
threatened by the young king, speaks of the *daimon autos*, the god
himself, Dionysus in person, declaring: "He is here now and sees
what I endure from you."[23] Dionysus, whose vigilance never
relaxes, is invisibly present, his eyes wide open, but Pentheus' eyes
are blind to the presence of the god, who is both manifested and
disguised by the mask facing him. The king scoffs, in the manner of a man determined not to have the wool pulled over his eyes,
saying: "Where is he? I cannot see him," and the stranger's retort

is: "With me; your blasphemies have made you blind."[24]

In the second episode, Pentheus is already not quite himself. Dionysus has inspired him with a slight "distraction" (851). But although he has lost his normal senses, he has not entered the Dionysiac world. He is lost somewhere in between. When he appears in Scene 4, leaving the palace, with his hair dishevelled, dressed as a woman, in the garb of a Bacchant and holding a *thursos* — a replica or direct reflection of the stranger — he exclaims (918 ff.): "I see two suns blazing in the heavens. And now two Thebes, two cities...." Pentheus sees double, no doubt like one drunk but, more significantly, like a man torn between two different ways of seeing, oscillating with double sight between his former "lucidity," which is now disturbed, and the "visionary" Dionysiac sight, which remains beyond him. He can see two suns but still does not perceive Dionysus looking deep into his eyes. This duplication within Pentheus' personality is reinforced for the spectators in the theater by the presence on stage of two characters of the same age, the same appearance and similarly attired, who would be indistinguishable were it not for the "smile" that makes it possible to recognize the god, whose mask hides his features and conceals his presence. It is a meeting, face to face, between two beings who look exactly alike but belong to two radically opposed worlds.

The epiphany of Dionysus is that of a being who, even in proximity and intimate contact with one, remains elusive and ubiquitous, never where he seems to be, never fixed in a definitive form: a god on the *theologeion*, a smiling young man on the stage, a bull leading Pentheus to his death, a lion, a snake, a flame, or something else again. He is at once and as much on the stage, in the palace, on Cithaeron, everywhere and nowhere. When the women of the chorus exhort him to manifest himself in his full presence, they sing: "O Dionysus, reveal yourself a bull! Be manifest, a snake with darting heads that see, a lion breathing fire to be seen."[25] Bull, snake that sees, lion to be seen... and the chorus' next words are: "O Bacchus come! Come, with your [masked] smile![26] Cast your noose about his man [Pentheus]." The mask, with wide staring eyes that fix one like those of the Gorgon, expresses and epitomizes all the different forms that the terrible divine presence may assume. It is a mask whose strange stare exerts a fascination, but it is hollow, empty, indicating the absence of a god who is somewhere else but who tears one out of oneself, makes one lose one's bearings in one's everyday, familiar life, and who takes possession of one just as if this empty mask was now pressed to one's own face, covering and transforming it.

As has already been pointed out,[27] the mask is a means of expressing absence in a presence. At the crucial moment in the drama when Pentheus, perched in his tree, is up there in the sky for all to see (1073, 1076), the epiphany of the god takes the form of, not an extraordinary appearance, but a sudden disappearance. The messenger tells us, as an eyewitness, "Barely had they seen [him]...huddled at the top, when the stranger vanished":[28] He was nowhere to be seen. And from the sky, in a supernatural hush that suddenly falls on the heavens and the earth alike, there comes a voice[29] that identifies the god and urges on the maenads to attack his enemy. Dionysus is never more present in the world, never does he affect it more than at this moment when, in contrast to Pentheus, exposed to all eyes, he escapes into invisibility. When present-absent Dionysus is here on earth, he is also in the heavens among the gods; and when he is up there in heaven, he is also on this earth. He is the one who unites the normally separate heaven and earth and introduces the supernatural into the heart of nature. Here again, there is a striking contrast between Pentheus' fall and the ascension of the god (underlined by the ironic use of the same terms and expressions to refer to both). Proclaimed to be "without equal [δεινός],"[30] just as Dionysus is, Pentheus, whose fame should rise to heaven,[31] is destined to provoke his own fall[32] from the heights to which he is raised by the pine tree on which the god has perched him[33] down to the ground, where his tumble leaves him defenseless, at the mercy of the furious maenads: "From his high perch fell Pentheus, tumbling to the ground."[34]

Now, according to the words of the *parodos*, verses of happiness, exuberant Dionysiac joy, the light, aerial Dionysus, his long tresses streaming in the wind,[35] first leaps upward to the sky as he leads the *thiasos*, then immediately returns from the heights: "He drops to earth."[36] And this signals the climax of joy (*ήδύς*) on the mountainside, the delight (*χάρις*) of omophagy: It is the ultimate beatitude of a rediscovered golden age (140 ff., 695 ff.), heaven on earth. If Dionysus suddenly drops to earth, like Pentheus, it is because it is his role to use the springs (169, 446, 728), jumps (165-7), and soaring leaps[37] of the faithful, into whom he has breathed his inspiration, to project his own ubiquitous presence and, as it were, fix it at a particular spot on earth. No sooner has the pine tree bearing Pentheus sprung back "towering to heaven" (1073) and Dionysus has vanished from the visible world to become the voice that thunders from on high in the ether into the supernatural silence, than "a flash of awful fire bound earth and heaven."[38] Whether the god rises to heaven, falls to earth, or leaps and flames between the two, whether he is man, flame, or voice, visible or invisible, he is always the polar opposite to Pentheus, despite the symmetrical expressions that are used to describe them both. He brings down to earth the revelation of another dimension to existence and grants our world and our lives direct experience of the elsewhere, the beyond.

Not only does the epiphany of Dionysus elude the limitations of visible forms and shapes; it is furthermore expressed through *maya*, magic that disturbs all appearances. Dionysus is there when the stable world of familiar objects and reassuring figures veers over to become a phantasmagorical confusion in which illusions, impossibilities, and absurdities become realities. *Deina, thaumata, sophismata*, all kinds of prodigies and weirdness, all the magician's clever tricks and sleights of hand and sorceror's spells loom up in the epiphany of the masked god, just as flowers bloom as Aphrodite passes. In the *Bacchae*, we hear of one miracle in the palace and

397

others in the stables and on Mount Cithaeron, and of "fantastic things" and "awful miracles" that come to pass.[39] Dionysus opened the play declaring: "I am come." The messenger echoes that declaration at 449, saying "This stranger has come...full of many miracles." Wherever he appears on the stage of the world, the god sets up a theater of fantasies to take the place of the familiar everyday setting. Not only is he the great hunter but also the great illusionist, the master conjuror, the author and chorus leader of a sophisticated performance in which nothing and no one ever remain what they seem. Like the devil in Bulgakov's *The Master and Marguerite*, Dionysus *sphaleotas*,[40] the god who makes everything slip, start, and stumble, is the embodiment of the "other." Making the whole edifice of appearances suddenly shift, he reveals its false solidity, displaying under the baffled spectators' very noses the unfamiliar scenery of his magic and mystifications.

Dionysus cannot be pinned down in any form, he plays with appearances, confuses what is illusion and what is real. But his otherness also stems from the fact that, through his epiphany, all the cut-and-dried categories and clear oppositions that impart coherence to our vision of the world lose their distinctiveness and merge, fuse, changing from one thing into another.

Let us consider a number of them: first, male and female. Dionysus is a male god with a female appearance (*thelumorphos*, 353). His dress and his hair are those of a woman, and he transforms the virile Pentheus into a woman by making him wear the costume of his devotees. Pentheus then wants to be, and seems to be, altogether a woman and is most gratified when Dionysus tells him: "So much alike are you, I could take you for your mother or one of your aunts" (927). The spectators are the more likely to share his view given that the parts of Pentheus and Agave would both be played by the same actor.

Young and old: in the cult of Dionysus, the difference between the two states is wiped out (206-9, 694): "Did the god declare that just the young or just the old should dance? No, he desires his honor from all mankind. He wants no one excluded from his

398

worship," Tiresias declares (206-9); and the messenger reports that on Mount Cithaeron, he has seen them "all as one, the old women and the young and the unmarried girls" (694).

The far and the near, the beyond and the here and now: Dionysus does not tear one from this world, but by his presence he transfigures it.

Greek and barbarian: the Lydian stranger, from Asia, is a native of Thebes.

The one in a frenzy, the one who is mad (*mainomenos*) is also *sophos, sophistēs, sōphrōn*.

The new god (νεός, 219, 272), come to found a cult hitherto unknown, also represents "customs and traditions hallowed by age and handed down to us by our fathers" (201); "whatever long time has sanctioned, that is a law forever; the law tradition makes is the law of nature" (895 ff.).

The wild and the civilized: Dionysus makes one flee from the town, deserting one's house, abandoning children, spouse, family, leaving one's daily occupations and work. He is worshipped at night, out on the mountainside, in the valleys and woods. His servants become wild, handling snakes and suckling the young of animals as if they were their own. They discover themselves to be in communion with all beasts, both the wild and the domesticated, and establish a new and joyous familiarity with nature as a whole. Yet Dionysus is also a "civilizing" god. The chorus of his faithful Lydian maenads applauds Tiresias when he draws a parallel between Demeter and Dionysus. For the god is to what is liquid and potable all that the goddess is to what is solid and edible. The one by inventing wheat and bread, the other by inventing (279) the vine and wine, together brought to men (279) the means to pass from a wild life to a civilized one. All the same, there is a difference between wheat and wine. Wheat is entirely on the side of civilization, but wine is ambiguous. When it is neat, it conceals a force of extreme wildness, a burning fire; when diluted and consumed in accordance with the rules, it brings to civilized life an extra, as it were supernatural, dimension: joy in the feast, with evil forgotten. It is a drug (*pharmakon*) that makes pain fade away; it is the ornament, the crown, the living, happy brilliance of the banquet (380-3), the joy of the celebration.

Like wine, Dionysus is double: most terrible yet infinitely sweet.[41] His presence, which is a bewildering intrusion of otherness into the human world, may take two forms, be manifested in two different ways. On the one hand it may bring blessed union with the god, in the heart of nature, with every constraint lifted — an escape from the limitations of the everyday world and oneself. That is the experience extolled in the *parodos*: purity, holiness, joy, sweet felicity. On the other hand, it may precipitate one into chaos in the confusion of a bloodthirsty, murderous madness in which the "same" and the "other" merge and one mistakes one's nearest and dearest, one's own child, one's second self for a wild beast that one tears apart with one's bare hands: ghastly impurity, inexpiable crime, misfortune without end, without relief (1360).

Dionysus arrives in Thebes as an *archegos*, the leader of a feminine *thiasos* devoted to his cult and versed in all the rites.[42] Within this group, each member acts as bacchant by undergoing purifications (76-7), adopting a mode of life that consecrates her and unites her soul with the *thiasos*.[43] The band of faithful is thus made up of ones who know, *hoi eidotes*, and who serve the god by conforming with the ritual practices that have been revealed to them. Not only are the profane ignorant of these rites, but it is forbidden to them to know the secret. When Pentheus asks (471), "What form do they take, these mysteries [ὄργια] of yours [what is their aspect or nature, ἰδέα]," the stranger replies (472), "To whomever is not an initiate, it is forbidden to know [or to see, ἔδεναι]." And when the young king persists, saying (474), "Tell me the benefits that those who know your mysteries enjoy," he is told, "It is forbidden for you to hear." When Pentheus climbs Mount Cithaeron to spy on the maenads, his crime is that he wants to see "forbidden sights." Within the *thiasos*, the cult of the god thus

comprises an aspect of secret ritual performed within the framework of a closed and restricted group. The band of the faithful
enjoy a special relationship with the god; it is in direct contact
with him, united with him apart from and independently of the
civic community. "Dionysus, son of Zeus, not Thebes, has power
over me," sing the chorus, to justify the burst of joy with which
they greet the misfortune that falls upon the city, personified
by its leader (1037-8). Yet as soon as Dionysus appears on the
theologeion, he spells out his position clearly and precisely. It is
Thebes, the city, that must be brought to see, recognize, and
accept him. It is around Thebes that Dionysus has tied the *nebris*,
it is Thebes that he forces to rise, *thursos* in hand, after the three
women of the royal lineage have erred by rejecting him. He has
chased out "all the women of Thebes, all without exception" from
their homes, sending them off to the mountain with their minds
deranged (935-6). The *polis* must be taught the price for not having become initiated in this Bacchanalia (39-40). In the *parodos*,
when the chorus dances and sings in the square outside the palace gates and the *thiasos* praises Bromius in accordance with the
age-old rites, it does so to make the whole city come out to hear
and see. Accordingly, once it has glorified its secret rites and
exalted the ceremonies of which it has been granted knowledge, it
turns to address Thebes as a whole, to persuade it to crown itself
with garlands and don the right costume and *narthex*, in order to
consecrate itself entirely to Bacchus (109) and enter the dance as
one (πᾶσα, 114), when Bromius leads the *thiasoi* to the mountain.

Dionysus does not wish to be the patron of a sect, a restricted
group, an association closed in on itself and confined within its
secrets. He demands to be fully accepted in the ranks of the gods
of the civic community. His ambition is to see his cult officially
recognized and unanimously practiced in all the different forms
it may assume (536, 1378, 1668). The *polis*, as such, must be initiated. In this respect, the *thiasos* of the bacchants differs from
the closed groups that flourished in Athens toward the end of
the Peloponnesian War and that celebrated the mysteries of for-

401

eign gods: Cybele and Bendis, Cottyto, Attis, Adonis, and Sabazios. The religious status claimed by Dionysus is not that of a marginal, eccentric deity with a cult reserved for the brotherhood of sectarians who are conscious of being different and pleased to be so, marked out for themselves and in the eyes of all by their nonconformity to the common religion. Dionysus demands from the city official recognition for a religion that in a sense eludes the city and is beyond it. He is out to establish at the very heart and center of public life practices that, either openly or covertly, present aspects of eccentricity.

The tragedy of the *Bacchae* shows the dangers that are involved when a city retrenches within its own boundaries. If the world of the same refuses to absorb the element of otherness that every group and every human being unconsciously carry within themselves, just as Pentheus refuses to recognize that mysterious, feminine, Dionysiac element that attracts and fascinates him despite the horror that he claims to feel for it, then all that is stable, regular, and the same tips over and collapses and the other, of hideous aspect, absolute otherness and a return to chaos, come to appear as the sinister truth, the other, authentic, and terrifying face of the same. The only solution is for women to use the controlled trance, an officially recognized *thiasos* promoted to the status of a public institution, while men turn to the joy of the *komos*, wine, disguise, and carnival and for the city as a whole, in and through the theater, to make it possible for the other to become one of the dimensions of both collective life and the daily life of each individual. The victorious eruption of Dionysus is a sign that otherness is being given its place, with full honors, at the center of the social system.

To what extent can the conflict between Pentheus and Dionysus be interpreted as a dramatization of a clash between two contrasting attitudes: on the one hand the rationalism of the sophists, with their technical intelligence, their mastery of the art of argu-

ment, and their denial of all that is invisible; on the other, a religious experience that has a place for irrational impulses and leads
to intimate union with the divine?[44] There are all sorts of reasons why there is no simple answer to that question. In the first
place, Pentheus is no sophist: He is a king who is too royal, too
tyrannical (671-776), a male who is too virile (86, 796), a Greek
who is too convinced of his superiority over barbarians (483), a
man of the city who turns reasons of state into a narrowly positivistic concept. It is true that Tiresias criticizes the agility of his
tongue (268) and calls him *thrasus* (270), impudent in his use of
eloquence.[45] But, as has been demonstrated,[46] it is the diviner's
own speech that obeys a typically sophistic model. Besides, is there
such a thing as *a* sophistic way of thinking that can be described
as rationalistic? The powers that Gorgias extolls in his *Encomium
of Helen*, showing that they so bewitch the mind that no human
being can resist them, are the very ones that Dionysus puts to work
throughout the play as he casts his magic spell. To that extent,
it is the god who appears the master of sophistic marvels (a domain
in which he would indeed dominate exclusively did he not dele-
gate some portion of his powers to the tragic poet). Finally, and
above all, the tragedy does not so much establish an opposition
between reason and religion of the soul or intelligence and feeling; rather, as Charles Segal correctly perceived, it sets up two
parallel systems of values: The respective worlds of Pentheus and
Dionysus each incorporate their own forms of reason and madness, good sense and folly, wisdom and delirium.[47] Even before
Pentheus makes his entrance, scandalized at the "lack of reason"
in the talk of such wise old men as Cadmus and Tiresias (252),
his grandfather describes him as "frenetic"; and that is the very
term which he also subsequently uses to describe the state of
Agave, out of her mind in trance.[48] Tiresias certainly recognizes
the rhetorical skill of Pentheus, the *sophos aner* but, not content
to return the compliment by pointing to the young man's "lack
of reason," he goes so far as to accuse him of being delirious, a
prey to *mania*,[49] regarding him as so cruelly mad, having so com-

pletely lost his wits, that his derangement can only be explained by a drug (φάρμακον, 326-7). Right from the start, even before he encounters Dionysus, Pentheus' positivistic common sense is that of one spellbound, possessed, a μαινόμενος (which is the term that the chorus uses to refer to the enemy of the god at 399-400, 887, and 999; cf. also 915). Pentheus in his blindness is thus, like Dionysus himself, a *mainomenos*. It seems hardly necessary to point out that there is madness in human wisdom (*to sophon*) just as there is wisdom (*sophia*) in divine madness. But here too there seems more to it than meets the eye. In the third stasimon the chorus indeed calls human wisdom, τὸ σοφόν, into question (878, 897), going on to declare, in the fourth stasimon, that it has no desire for it (1005) and had already condemned it in the first stasimon, setting it in opposition to σοφία (395). In this passage, *sophia* means, not *mania*, divine madness but, on the contrary, a peaceful, measured life in keeping with the healthy thinking[50] of a mortal who does not believe himself a god and knows how to content himself with the blessings that life provides, without running after the unobtainable. This face of Dionysism is different but, as we shall see, inseparable from *mania*; it presupposes that one is constantly available to the deity, open to the presence of Dionysus; it is what accounts for the aspect of simple, popular, gnomic wisdom, *sophia*, which is what the initiates of the god claim to possess.

In the *Bacchae*, Dionysus, the mad god, plays upon the entire semantic register of "knowledge," "wisdom," "thought." He can better the most skillful sophists in the arts of cunning, trapping his adversary, misleading him to overcome him the more definitively. He endows his followers with the gift of sane thinking, together with common sense and moderation,[51] all qualities that are lacking to great minds that are blind to whatever is beyond them and whose vanity so misleads them that they lose their wits and reason.[52] As for the *mania*, the madness that the god puts to work, it takes two very different forms, one for his initiates who are united with him in the *thiasos*, another for his enemies whom the frenzy strikes as a punishment.

404

Lussa, the fit of frenetic rage, strikes only those who have not accepted Dionysism, who either oppose it openly, like Pentheus, or who, having rejected the god, are pursued by him in the mountains, spurred on by madness, as are Agave, Autonoe, Ino, and all the other women of Thebes. When the chorus calls upon the rabid bitches to lay hold of the daughters of Cadmus and hurl them against Pentheus, their invocation stresses the solidarity, the collusion between the Theban maenads, the *thiasoi* on Cithaeron and the young man they will soon tear apart for, like him, they belong to the enemy camp, hostile to the god. In the grip of trance, out of their minds, permeated by the god's spirit, they obey Dionysus, becoming the instruments of his vengeance. But they are not his faithful devotees; they do not belong to him.

The *lussa* that leads them astray (977) is matched by that of their victim-to-be. These maenads launch their "rabid attack" against a spy who is as "rabid" (λυσσώδη, 981) as they are. Indeed, one must go further. The word μαινάδες is only once formally applied to the Lydian women who make up the *thiasos* of Dionysus: at 601, when the palace miracle occurs and they throw themselves, in terror, to the ground, they address each other by that name rather than as "bacchante," the term they generally use. On the other hand, the word is used no less than fifteen times to refer to the women of Thebes. And, more importantly, the verb μαίνομαι is applied only to Pentheus (five times) and the Theban women who are also victims of the god, *never* to the women of the chorus. At the end of the drama, Cadmus says to Agave: "You were mad, the whole city was possessed by Dionysus,"[53] just as, right at the start, the god too had announced: "Every woman in Thebes...I drove from home, mad" (33). Inspired by Dionysus, who is out to punish them, the Theban women are in a state of frenzy.[54] Showing the whites of her rolling eyes and foaming at the mouth, Agave, possessed by the god "cannot reason as one ought to reason."[55] When she emerges from the trance, she eventually, painfully, recovers her reason, retaining no memory of the atrocious actions that she and her companions committed when in that other state.

The picture is quite different where the followers of Dionysus are concerned, for they are initiated into his mysteries and are close to the god. Not only are they never seen demented or seized by *mania*, but when, in the *parodos*, they recall their wanderings and dances on the mountainside, at the beck and call of the god and in his company, all is purity, peace, joy, supernatural well-being. There, even omophagy is associated with the idea of sweetness and delight.[56] Dionysus' hold over his devotees, within his *thiasos*, in accordance with all the ritual rules, is thus clearly quite different from the murderous madness and rabid derangement with which he fills his enemies, to punish their lack of piety. There is, admittedly, a slight overlap between the "converted" Lydian women and the "unbelieving" Theban ones, for the vengeance of Dionysus is timed in two stages and takes place at two levels. To punish Thebes, the god starts by chasing all the female part of the *polis*, spurring them on with *mania*, out of the town toward the mountains. There, the women live chastely and peacefully, in communion with nature, just as a true *thiasos* would.[57] Finding their city so upset in this fashion, the rest of it, the males, take action to reestablish "order" and bring the women home. Their *mania* immediately assumes the form of total mental derangement that unleashes a crazy violence.[58]

However, at no time, not even when they appear to be behaving in conformity with the model provided by the authentic *thiasos*, do the women of Thebes pursued by the vengeance of the god become fully assimilable to the faithful who celebrate his cult. Even in their *mania*, they never accede to the Dionysiac revelation. Gripped by the delirium with which Dionysus spurs them on, they have scandalized the men by throwing off their old way of thinking and abandoning their habitual lives as young girls or matrons. In the wild fastnesses of Mount Cithaeron, surrounded by prodigious happenings, they are at the mercy of the god whom they invoke, as a band, with a single voice, calling him Iacchos (725-6) or singing his praises in alternate choruses (1056-7). And yet they are denied the bliss of ecstasy, the joy of intimate communion with Dionysus. Like Pentheus, disguised as a bacchant and suffering from a "slight madness," they are lost in an "in-between" state. The young king has double vision; they suffer a personality split and find themselves as incapable as he of making the connection between what they are in their normal state and what they have become in their other state, when the god possesses them.

Denied the possibility of ever truly knowing Dionysus or "seeing" him in trance, when they come to themselves after the crisis, it is as if nothing has happened. They are incapable of making their Dionysiac religious experience their own, of appropriating it. There is a radical cleavage within them between the *mania* inspired by the god and the lucid power of reflection that characterizes their normal state. The two seem like the opposite ends of a chain that only Dionysus can join together and unite within a single *sophia*. But that can only be done if his cult is officially recognized and becomes integrated in the life of the civic community.

The case of Agave is most telling in this respect. When the young king's mother, delirious and crazy-eyed, returns from Mount Cithaeron brandishing the head of her son on the end of her *thursos*, believing it to be that of a lion cub or a young bull, she invokes Bacchus (1145), but as a "fellow huntsman, a comrade of the chase" (1146), associated with her in a hunting exploit in which she is proud to have taken the initiative by striking the first blow at her quarry (1178 ff.) and from which she would claim glory for herself and sisters (1180 ff., 1204 ff.). Her father, old Cadmus, her young son, Pentheus, together with all the inhabitants of the town, all the citizens of Thebes, must hasten to contemplate and acclaim the huntresses' prowess in a hunt accomplished with bare hands, using neither net nor javelin (1201 ff.). The victory chant into which she launches (1161) and the *komos* that she leads for the god (1167, 1172) do not proclaim the coming of Dionysus, or his presence made manifest within a *thiasos*, as does the song of the *parodos*. Instead they proclaim the great superiority of young women over the rest of the human race (1234-5): Cadmus may congratulate himself (1233; cf. 1207) on having fathered daughters whose unprecedented exploits ensure glory and happiness for him (1241-3).

The disparity between the state of mind of the god's devotees celebrating his rites and that of the women whom he is bent on destroying by driving them mad is ironically expressed through the repetition of the same terms, used in the two cases with opposite meanings. The chorus of Lydian women calls on Dionysus to "show himself," to "appear" and begs justice to make itself manifest,[59] declaring that it is "hunting for" (1006) not a vain kind of knowledge but other things that are "great and manifest" (1006-7). Agave is jubilant and declares herself happy (1197; cf. 1179; 1258) at having succeeded in hunts that are "great and manifest" (1198-9). At the beginning of the play, Dionysus declared his intention to go from town to town "to show himself."[60] What Agave has in mind to "show" to Thebes,[61] by nailing to the top of the palace the head of the lion she imagines she has brought back from the hunt, is not the god but the horrible trophy of victory of which, in her madness, she thought she could be proud. Dionysus wanted every eye in "the city of Thebes to see" (61), to contemplate his epiphany. Agave summons all the inhabitants of the town "to see" (1203) not Dionysus, but the quarry she claims credit for catching. In her "victory," "glory," and "good fortune," as in her murderous rage, Agave is blind to the god who possesses her and who dictates her actions. Though completely abandoned to Dionysus and as putty in his hands, she remains closed to his supernatural presence, alien to his epiphany. She is no longer herself but does not belong to Dionysus. Her "visions" do not stem from that "other view" with which the god favors his elect when he mingles in person in their *thiasos* and when his gaze meets theirs. They are hallucinations, a sinister caricature of authentic visions. Similarly, the good fortune of which the queen boasts in her delirium and that she is set on all her people sharing, is but a shadow, a derisory and macabre specter of the felicity that true bacchants share with their god. Agave has forfeited her former lucidity without having acquired any experience of divine ecstasy through a face-to-face encounter with Dionysus. She finds herself relegated to a world of madness that is created by the god but that his presence deserts even as he conjures it up for those whom he wishes to punish for rejecting him.

Under Cadmus' guidance, Agave will have to come slowly to her senses and recover her reason as her father gradually allows her to realize what has happened and what she has done so that, eventually — but too late — she understands[62] and recognizes the Dionysus to whom she continued to be blind even when inspired and possessed by him;[63] and this Dionysus is not the sweetly gentle god of the blessed epiphany but a terrible deity of vengeance and perdition.

So there is nothing in common between the holy beatitude or *eudaimonia* that the god bestows upon his faithful (73, 165, 902, 904) and that with which Agave believes herself blessed; the latter is entirely illusory, but she would like to show it off to an admiring Pentheus (1258). Cadmus gives a striking description of this illusory happiness that is as alien to the exaltation of Dionysiac felicity as it is to the cold consciousness of a lucid mind. He defines it, along with Agave's raving, as an in-between state of equivocacy and uncertainty in which one can hardly speak of either good fortune or bad. Faced with his daughters, exultant with joy in their delirium, the old man remarks: "If, with luck, your present madness lasts until you die, then although you could not be called happy, at least you will not be conscious of your misfortune" (1260).

The text of the *Bacchae* presents a break and a contrast between the possession-well-being of the faithful and the possession-punishment of those who are impious. At the same time, and in contrast, it establishes a continuity between the oribasic practices of the Dionysiac religion and other aspects of it which have nothing to do with *mania*. In the very first stasimon, the chorus, faced with the impious Pentheus, glorifies Piety. As it sings the praises of Dionysus, it shifts the emphasis and expresses itself in different terms. The god who leads the *thiasos* is also the joyful god whose laughter resounds to the notes of the flute, who soothes anxiety and dispenses sleep by bringing forth the grape and wine and all the brilliance (*ganos*) of festivity. Dionysus delights in feasting, peace, and opulence: "To rich and poor he gives the simple gift of wine, the gladness of the grape" (417-23). This is a popular kind of wisdom, familiar to humble folk who aspire to no more than a peaceful life governed by reason (*to phronein*). Open to the deity, conscious of the brevity of human existence, and thinking ordinary mortal thoughts, they do not pursue the inaccessible but instead devote their lives to happiness. Wise enough to shun beings who believe themselves superior, they derive their well-being from making the most of the blessings that the god makes available to them.

Scholars have pondered on this relaxing of the tension as one passes from the ardent religious fervor of the *parodos* to the somewhat pedestrian sentiments expressed in the first stasimon. As Jacqueline de Romilly writes: "From mystic ecstasy we move to a cautious kind of hedonism."[64] The modern reader cannot fail to be aware of the drop in intensity. Perhaps it was less striking to the Athenian spectators who were more familiar with the various aspects of the cult and the multiple facets presented by the figure of Dionysus in the fifth-century city. At all events, one cannot help noticing that, after delivering his account of the stupefying prodigies and incredible miracles that he has witnessed on Mount Cithaeron, the messenger — apparently quite naturally — rounds off with a conclusion to the effect that: This is a great god and he is great above all in that "he gave to mortal men the gift of lovely wine by which our suffering is stopped. And if there is no god of wine, there is no love, no Aphrodite either, nor other pleasure left for men" (773-4). Is this irony on the part of poet? In the third stasimon, which picks up the *makarismos* of the *parodos* and proceeds to celebrate the extreme well-being, indeed beatitude that the god dispenses to his devotees,[65] the tone is much the same. One should place one's faith, not in human knowledge (*to sophon*), but in the mysterious power of the deity (*to daimonion*), and in religious matters conform with the established tradition (*to nomimon*, 894-5). So what kind of felicity is the devotee of Dionysus really seeking? The chorus declares: "He who garners day by day [κατ' ἦμαρ] the good of life,[66] he is happiest. Blessed is he."

Fulfillment found in ecstasy, "enthusiasm," and possession; but also a well-being derived from wine, the joy of festivity, the pleasures of love and the felicity to be found in everyday life. All this Dionysus can bring if only men learn to welcome him and cities to recognize him, just as he can deal out misfortune and destruction if he is rejected. But in no circumstances does he ever come to announce a better fate in the beyond. He does not urge men to flee the world nor does he claim to offer a soul access to immortality achieved through a life of asceticism. On the contrary, men must accept their mortal condition, recognize that they are nothing compared with the powers that are beyond them on every side and that are able to crush them utterly. Dionysus is no exception to the rule. His devotee must submit to him as to an irrational force that is beyond his comprehension and that can dispose of him at will. The god has no need to explain himself. He is alien to our norms and customs, alien to our preoccupations, beyond good and evil, supremely sweet and supremely terrible. His pleasure is to summon up the multiple aspects of otherness around us and within us.

The Dionysus of the *Bacchae* is a god as tragic as human existence, to Euripides' way of thinking. But by showing his epiphany on stage, the poet renders both the god and life, whatever their contradictions, as intelligible as they can be.

The only way of acceding to an understanding of the masked god is to enter into his game oneself. And only a tragic poet is capable of doing that, having reflected on his art, conscious of the special skills at his command, since he is past master at casting the spells of dramatic illusion. Transposed to the stage, the

411

magic ploys of the god undergo a transmutation. They harmonize with the techniques of the dramatist and the enchantment of his poetry and thus, be they most terrible or most sweet, they contribute to the pleasure of the dramatic spectacle.

Charles Segal has correctly perceived that the deliberate "modernity" of this, Euripides' last play, devoted to Dionysus, suggests a homology between the Dionysiac experience and the tragic representation.[67]

The drama of the *Bacchae* bears witness, through the epiphany of Dionysus, to the tragic dimension of human life. But at the same time, by "purging" the terror and pity prompted by the staged imitation of the actions of the god, it brilliantly reveals to the eyes of all the spectators the *ganos*, the joyous, dazzling brilliance of art, festivity, and play: the *ganos* that it is Dionysus' privilege to dispense here on earth, the *ganos* that, like a beam of light from another world, transfigures the drab landscape of our daily life.[68]

Jean-Pierre Vernant

List of Abbreviations

(Année philologique)

ABSA *Annual of the British School at Athens*. London.

ASNP *Annali della Scuola Normale Superiore di Pisa*, Cl. di Lettere e Filosofia. Pisa.

BAGB *Bulletin de l'Association G. Budé*. Paris.

BCH *Bulletin de Correspondance Hellénique*. Athens.

BICS *Bulletin of the Institute of Classical Studies of the University of London*. London.

CPh *Classical Philology*. Chicago.

CQ *Classical Quarterly*. Oxford.

CRAI *Comptes rendus de l'Académie des Inscriptions et Belles-Lettres*. Paris.

CSCA *California Studies in Classical Antiquity*. Berkeley.

GRBS *Greek, Roman and Byzantine Studies*. Durham, N.C.

HSPh *Harvard Studies in Classical Philology*. Cambridge, Mass.

JHS *Journal of Hellenic Studies*. London.

JWI *Journal of the Warburg and Courtauld Institute*. London.

PCPhS *Proceedings of the Cambridge Philological Society*. Cambridge.

QUCC *Quaderni Urbinati di Cultura classica*. Rome.

RA *Revue Archéologique*. Paris.

RD *Revue Historique de Droit française et étranger*. Paris.

REA *Revue des Études Anciennes*. Bordeaux, Talence.

REG *Revue des Études Grecques*. Paris.

RFIC *Rivista di Filologia e di Istruzione Classica*. Turin.

RHR *Revue de l'Histoire des Religions*. Paris.

RPh *Revue de Philologie*. Paris.

SAWW *Sitzungsberichte der Österreichischen Akademie der Wissenschaft in Wien*. Vienna.

SBAW *Sitzungsberichte der Bayerischen Akademie der Wissenschaften*. Munich.

SCO *Studi Classici e Orientali*, Pisa.

SDAW *Sitzungsberichte der Deutschen Akademie der Wissenschaften zu Berlin*. Berlin.

StudClas *Studii Clasice*. Bucharest.

TAPhA *Transactions and Proceedings of the American Philological Association*. Chico, Cal.

WS *Wiener Studien. Zeitschrift für klassische Philologie und Patristik*. Vienna.

YCS *Yale Classical Studies*. New Haven.

Notes

Preface to Volume I

1. Cf. J.-P. Vernant, "La Tragédie grecque selon Louis Gernet," *Hommage à Louis Gernet*, Paris 1966, pp. 31-5.

2. R. Goossens, *Euripide et Athènes*, Brussels 1960.

3. The first ostracism carried out was in 487, the last in 417 or 416.

4. Many of the studies that are reprinted in this volume have been modified or corrected since their first appearance, or even in some cases expanded. We should like to thank Mme. J. Detienne for her valuable help in revising and correcting the text. We also thank all our friends who have been good enough to help us with their comments, in particular M. Detienne, P. Gauthier, and V. Goldschmidt.

Preface to Volume II

1. To varying degrees, they have been closely revised and in some cases reorganized and expanded, but there seems little point in enumerating these corrections and additions.

2. On this distinction, see N. Loraux, "La cité comme cuisine et comme partage," *Annales E.S.C.* (1981) pp. 614-22.

3. Among the research projects in which we have been involved either directly or indirectly, see J.-P. Vernant and M. Detienne (Eds.), *La cuisine du sacrifice en pays grec*, Paris 1979; *Le sacrifice dans l'antiquité*, Entretiens sur l'Antiquité classique (XXVII, Fondation Hardt), Vandoeuvre-Geneva 1981. P. Vidal-Naquet, *The Black Hunter*, Baltimore 1986; J.-L. Durand, *Sacrifice et labour en Grèce ancienne*, Rome and Paris 1986.

4. See *infra*, Ch. 6 and the works of F.I. Zeitlin which are cited there; see also Ch. 12, n.16 and n.19.

5. See in particular, *Violence and the Sacred*, Baltimore 1977, and more recently *The Scapegoat*, Baltimore 1986; because they are so clearly expressed, we also refer to the analyses of the positions adopted by René Girard in the "round table" devoted to him in *Esprit* (November 1973).

6. R. Girard, *Ibid.*, p. 551.

7. Cf. Frances M. Young, *The Use of Sacrificial Ideas in Greek Christian Writers from the New Testament to John Chrysostom*, Cambridge, Mass. 1979.

8. R. Girard, *The Scapegoat*, pp. 121-4.

9. The Latin title of a Greek play of the fifth century A.D., the schema and many lines of which are borrowed from Euripides, with the purpose of providing illustration for the gospels.

10. See *infra*, Ch. 5 and pp. 349-50.

11. V. Di Benedetto, in V. Di Benedetto and A. Lami, *Filologia e marxismo — Contra le mistificazioni*, Naples 1980, p. 114. As well as the two authors of *Myth and Tragedy*, the scholars attacked in this book are L. Brisson, M. Detienne and M.I. Finley.

12. See, most recently, his *Sofocle*, Florence 1983, the last chapter of which, "La buona morte," devoted to *Oedipus at Colonus*, testifies adequately enough to its Christian inspiration.

13. V. Di Benedetto and A. Lami, *op. cit.*, pp. 107-14.

14. *Critique* 317 (1973), pp. 908-26.

15. H. Wismann provides a remarkable account of that attempt and ambition in "Le métier de philologue," *Critique* (1970), pp. 462-79 and 774-81. As will be seen, *infra*, n.44, Ch. 15, we are ourselves indebted to Jean Bollack for making a number of important points.

16. H. Wismann, *loc. cit.*, p. 780.

17. *Ibid.*

18. *Ibid.*

19. And in the article, cited *supra*, by N. Loraux.

20. J. Bollack, in J. Bollack and P. Judet de la Combe, *Agamemnon I*, 1, Lille 1981, pp. LXXVI-LXXVIII. Curiously enough, at p. LXXVI n.1, J. Bollack compares our "historical perspective" with that of V. Di Benedetto: It is a surprising connection to make.

21. See *infra*, p. 33.

22. See *infra*, Ch. 14.

23. *Oedipe-Roi*, 1180-1, tr. J. and M. Bollack, Paris 1985, p. 72.

24. It reappears in this same translation, p. 52, at line 822: "*ἆρ' ἔφυν κάκος* [Am I then born to evil?]," rendered as "Suis-je donc damné de naissance? [Am I then damned from birth?]," although the poet is here echoing line 248, and Oedipus' curses pronounced against Laius' assassin. Finally, we should also note the use of the word "*damnation*" at line 828, to render the Greek *ὠμὸς δαίμων*, "a wild deity."

CHAPTER I

1. Translator's note: "moment" is here being used to define a period between two turning points.

2. This text has appeared in *Antiquitas graeco-romana ac tempora nostra*, Prague 1968, pp. 246-50.

3. In a course of lectures given at the École Pratique des Hautes Études, which have not been published.

CHAPTER II

1. Translator's note: A first version of this text has already been published in English: "Tensions and Ambiguities in Greek Tragedy," *Interpretation: Theory and Practice*, ed. Charles S. Singleton, Baltimore 1969, pp. 105-21.

2. On the fundamentally anti-tragic character of Platonic philosophy, cf. V. Goldschmidt, "Le Problème de la tragédie d'après Platon," *Questions platoniciennes*, Paris 1970, pp. 103-40. This author writes (p. 136): "The 'immorality' of the poets does not suffice to explain Plato's deep hostility towards tragedy. By virtue of the very fact that tragedy represents 'action and life,' it conflicts with the truth." That is, *philosophical* truth, to be sure. And perhaps it also conflicts with the philosophical logic according to which, given two contradictory propositions, if one is true the other must necessarily be false. Tragic man thus appears to belong to a different logic, one that does not establish such a cut-and-dry cleavage between the true and the false. This is the logic of the orators and sophists that, during the actual years when tragedy was flourishing, still reserved a place for ambiguity since, in the questions it examined, it did not seek to demonstrate the absolute validity of a single thesis but rather to con-

struct *dissoi logoi*, double arguments that, in their opposition, countered but did not destroy each other. Since, at the will of the sophist and through the power of his words, each of the two conflicting arguments could in turn be made to dominate the other. Cf. Marcel Detienne, *Les Maîtres de verité dans la Grèce archaïque*, François Maspéro, Paris 1967, pp. 119-24.

3. Only men can be qualified representatives of the city; women are alien to political life. That is why the members of the chorus (not to mention the actors) are always and exclusively male. Even when the chorus is supposed to represent a group of young girls or women, as is the case in a whole series of plays, those who represent it are men, suitably disguised and masked.

4. At the end of Aeschylus' *Oresteia*, the establishment of the human court and the integration of the Erinyes into the new order of the city do not entirely do away with the contradiction between the ancient gods and the new ones, and between the heroic past of the noble *genē* and the present of the democratic Athens of the fifth century. Certainly, a balance is achieved, but it rests upon a number of tensions. Conflict persists, in the background, between contrary forces. To this extent the tragic ambiguity is not removed; ambivalence remains. Remember, for instance, that a majority of human judges pronounced a vote against Orestes, for it was only Athena's vote that made the two sides equal. (Cf. line 735 and the scholium to line 746. The *psēphos* of 735 should be understood literally as a voting counter, a ballot cast into an urn, as is confirmed by the relation between the formula used in this line: "one more vote raises up a house once more," and by what Orestes says in line 754, once the result has been announced: "Oh, Pallas who has just saved my house...." In the same sense, cf. Euripides, *Iphigenia in Tauris*, 1469.) The parity between the votes for and those against avoids any condemnation of the man who killed his mother to avenge his father. By means of a procedural convention it absolves him legally from the crime of murder, but it does not make him innocent nor does it justify him (cf. 741 and 752: on the significance of this procedural rule, Aristotle, *Problemata*, 29, 13). It implies a kind of balance maintained between the old *dikē* of the Erinyes (cf. 476, 511, 514, 539, 550, 554-64) and the contrasting *dikē* of the new gods such as Apollo (615-9). Athena is therefore quite right when she says to the daughters of Night, "You are not beaten, it is simply that an indecisive sentence has emerged from the urn [*ἰσόψηφος δίκη*]" (794-5). Recalling their lot in the world of the gods, at the beginning of the play, the Erinyes remarked

that just because they lived underground in a darkness that the sun never penetrated, this did not mean that they did not have a *timē* of their own, their own share of honors [*οὐδ' ἀτιμίας κύρω*] (394). These are the same honors that Athena acknowledges after the verdict of the court: "You are in no way humiliated [*οὐκ ἔστ' ἄτιμοι*]" (824), the same honors that she continues, with extraordinary insistence, to proclaim right up to the end of the tragedy (796, 807, 833, 868, 884, 891, 894, 917, 1029). In fact one should note that when she establishes the Areopagus, that is to say, founds law controlled by the city, Athena is declaring the necessity of acknowledging the place of the sinister forces embodied by the Erinyes in a human society. *Philia*, mutual friendship, and *peithō*, reasoned persuasion, are not enough to unite the citizens into a harmonious community. The city presupposes the intervention of powers of another nature that act, not through gentleness and reason, but through constraint and terror. The Erinyes have already declared "there are cases where Terror [*τὸ δεινόν*] is useful and, being a vigilant guardian of hearts, should be enthroned there permanently" (516 ff.). When she institutes the council of judges on the Areopagus, Athena takes up the same theme, using those very words: "On this mountain henceforth Respect and Fear [*Φόβος*], her sister, will keep the citizens away from crime.... Let Terror [*τὸ δεινὸν*] above all not be driven away from my city, outside its walls; what mortal does what he should if he has nothing to fear?" (690-9). In line 525 the Erinyes insisted that there should be "neither anarchy nor despotism." And Athena echoes this theme: no anarchy, no despotism, when she establishes the court. By fixing upon this as the imperative rule that her town must obey, the goddess emphasizes that what is good lies between two extremes and the city rests upon the difficult reconciliation of contrary powers that must balance without destroying one another. Opposite the god of the word, *Zeus agoraios* (974) and the gentle *Peithō* who has guided the tongue of Athena, stand the severe Erinyes who command respect, fear, terror. And this power of terror that emanates from the Erinyes and that the Areopagus represents on the level of human institutions will be beneficial to the citizens whom it will prevent from committing crimes against one another. Athena is thus in a position to say, concerning the horrific appearance of the goddesses who have just agreed to dwell in Attica: "I can see great advantage for the city coming from these terrifying faces" (989-90). At the end of the tragedy it is Athena herself who celebrates the power of the ancient goddesses both among the Immortals and among the gods of the underworld (950-1) and who reminds the guardians of the city that these intractable deities have the power "to rule everything among men" (930), to give "songs to some, and tears to others" (954-5). For the rest, it seems hardly necessary to mention that, by thus associating so closely together the Erinyes-Eumenides and the founding of the Areopagus, by placing this council, whose secret and nocturnal character is twice stressed (cf. 692, 705-6) under the sign, not of the religious powers that hold sway in the agora, such as *Peithō, the persuasive word, but of those that are the inspiration for Sebas* and *Phobos,* Respect and Fear, Aeschylus is in no way being innovative. He is conforming with a mythical and cultural tradition familiar to all Athenians; cf. Pausanias, 1, 28, 5-6 (the sanctuary of the August Erinyes, *Semnai Erinyes* on the Areopagus) and compare Diogenes Laertius' information concerning Epimenides' purification of Athens: It was from the Areopagus that he dispatched his black and white ewes whose sacrifice was to efface the defilement of the city; and furthermore, he also consecrated a sanctuary to the Eumenides.

5. Cf. Aristotle, *Problemata,* 19, 48: "The characters on the stage imitate heroes, and among the ancients the leaders alone were heroes, and the people, of whom the chorus consists, were mere men" [Ross/Forster translation].

6. Aristotle, *Poetics,* 1449, 24-8: "The iambic, we know, is the most speakable of metres, as is shown by the fact that we very often fall into it in conversation, whereas we rarely talk hexameters, and only when we depart from the [conversational] tone of voice." [Ross/Ingram Bywater translation].

7. Euripides, *Phoenician Women,* 888.

8. Aristotle, *Poetics,* 1449b 24, 31, 36; 1450a 15-23; 1450a 23-5 and 38-9; 1450b 2-3.

9. On this aspect of tragedy and on the heroic nature of Sophocles' characters, cf. B. Knox, *The Heroic Temper: Studies in Sophoclean Tragedy,* Berkeley and Los Angeles 1964.

10. "Tragedy and Greek Archaic Thought," *Classical Drama and its Influence, Essays Presented to H.D.F. Kitto,* 1965, pp. 31-50.

11. At 387 ff., the king asks the Danaids if the sons of Aegyptus have, under the law of their land, any power over them, in their capacity as their closest relatives (εἴ τοι κρατοῦσι). The legal significance of such *kratos* is defined more precisely in the lines that follow. The king remarks that if such were the case nobody could oppose the claims of the sons of Aegyptus over their cousins. The latter

would accordingly have to plead the contrary case that, according to the laws of their land, their cousins do not, in reality, hold this tutelary power, *kuros*, over them. The answer of the Danaids entirely evades the question. All they see in the *kratos* is its other meaning so that, on their lips, the word takes on a sense that is quite different from that which Pelasgus lent it. For them, it no longer signifies the legitimate power of tutelage that their cousins might claim over them, but pure violence, the brutal might of the man, the male domination that woman cannot escape: "Ah! Let me never be submitted to the power of males [ὑποχείριος κράτεσιν ἀρσένων]" (392-3). On this aspect of violence cf. 820, 831, 863. The Danaids desire to oppose the *kratos* of man with the *kratos* of woman (1069). If the sons of Aegyptus are in the wrong in trying to impose marriage upon them, winning them over only by violence, not persuasion (940-941, 943), the Danaids are no less at fault, for in their hatred of the opposite sex they will go as far as murder. Thus King Pelasgus was right to reproach the sons of Aegyptus for wishing to unite themselves with girls against their will, without their father's sanction and without *peithō*. But the daughters of Danaus also fail to give due recognition to *peithō*, for they reject Aphrodite who is always accompanied by *peithō*, and allow themselves to be neither charmed nor mollified by the seduction of *peithō* (1041 and 1056).

12. "An Ambiguity in Aeschylus," *Classica et Mediaevalia*, 25, fasc. 1-2, (1964), pp. 1-7.

13. Aeschylus, *Suppliants*, 154-61 and 231.

14. Sophocles, *Antigone*, 23 and ff., 451, 538-42 on the one hand and 853 ff. on the other.

15. The *Seven* . . . , 191-2 and 236-8.

16. *Ibid.*, 280.

17. *Ibid.*, 186.

18. *Ibid.*, 224.

19. *Ibid.*, 268.

20. *Antigone*, 872-5.

21. Plato, *Crito*, 51a-c.

22. Cf. Euripides, *Phoenician Women*, 499: "Were wisdom gauged alike of all, and honour, No strife of warring words were known to men. But 'fairness,' 'equal rights' – men know them not. They name their names: no being they have as things." (Loeb trans.).

421

23. "Sophocles' Praise of Man and the Conflicts of the *Antigone*," *Arion* 3, 2 (1964), pp. 46-60.

24. On the place and role of ambiguity in the Tragic writers, cf. W.B. Stanford, *Ambiguity in Greek Literature: Studies in Theory and Practice*, Oxford 1939, Chs. x-xii.

25. *Choephori*, 899.

26. *Suppliants*, 379-80.

27. Cf. R.P. Winnington-Ingram, *op. cit.*; and as regards the same problem in Aeschylus, Albin Lesky, "Decision and Responsibility in the Tragedy of Aeschylus," *JHS* 86 (1966), pp. 78-85. As Lesky notes, "freedom and compulsion are united in a genuinely tragic way," because one of the major features of Aeschylus' tragedy is precisely "the close union of necessity imposed by the Gods and the personal decision to act."

28. In the formula that Aeschylus puts into the mouth of the leader of the Chorus (*Agamemnon*, 1337-8), the two contrary concepts are to some extent superimposed or confused within the same words. Because it is ambiguous, the phrase does indeed lend itself to a double interpretation: *νῦν δ' εἰ προτέρων αἷμ' ἀποτείσῃ* can mean: "And now, if he must pay for the blood that his ancestors have shed," but also: "And now, if he must pay for the blood he has shed in the past." In the first case, Agamemnon is the victim of an ancestral curse: He pays for crimes that he has not committed. In the second, he expiates crimes for which he is responsible.

29. Cf. *Agamemnon*, 213.

30. *Ibid.*, 187: *ἐμπαίοις τύχαισι συμπνέων*. On this line cf. the commentary of E. Fraenkel, *Aeschylus, Agamemnon*, Oxford 1950. II, p. 115, that refers back to line 219, pp. 127-8.

31. On the relations between the two orders of temporality, see P. Vidal-Naquet's study, "Temps des dieux et temps des hommes," *Revue de l'histoire des religions* 157 (1960), pp. 55-80.

CHAPTER III

1. This text has appeared in *Psychologie comparative et art, Hommage à I. Meyerson*, Paris 1972, pp. 277-306.

2. "Remarques sur le 'nécessaire' et la 'nécessité' chez Eschyle," *REG* 81 (1968), pp. 5-39.

3. Cf. Bruno Snell, *Die Entdeckung des Geistes*, Hamburg 1955, translated into English from the first edition under the title: *The Discovery of the Mind*, Oxford 1953, pp. 102-12.

4. Z. Barbu, *Problems of Historical Psychology*, London 1960, Ch. 4, "The Emergence of Personality in the Greek World," p. 86.

5. A. Lesky, *Göttliche und menschliche Motivation im homerischen Epos*, Heidelburg 1961.

6. Aristotle, *Nicomachean Ethics*, 3, 1110a 28 and the commentary by R.A. Gauthier and J.-R. Jolif, Louvain-Paris 1959, pp. 177-8.

7. *Ibid.*, "...it is our internal decisions, that is to say our intentions, rather than our exterior actions, that enable our characters to be judged," (1111b 5-6); cf. also *Eudemian Ethics*, 1228a.

8. Translator's note: This French term is stronger than the English "voluntary" or "willing," meaning rather "what is willed" or "intentional."

9. Gauthier-Jolif, II, pp. 169-70.

10. *N.E.*, 1111a 25-7 and 1111b 7-8.

11. *Ibid.*, "For choice [*proairesis*] cannot relate to impossibles and if anyone said he chose them he would be thought silly; but there may be a wish even for impossibles e.g. for immortality" (Ross translation: 1111b 20-3). "For mind as speculative never thinks what is practicable, it never says anything about an object to be avoided or pursued," *De anima*, 432b 27-8.

12. *Metaphysics*, 1046b 5-10; *N.E.*, 1103a 19-b 22.

13. Cf. Gauthier-Jolif, II, pp. 217-20.

14. Cf. *N.E.*, 1139a 17-20.

15. *Ibid.*, 1139b 2-3, "For good action is an end in the absolute sense and desire aims at this."

16. *Ibid.*, 1113b 3-5, "The end then is what we wish for, the means what we deliberate about and choose"; 1111b 26: "wish related rather to the end, choice to the means."

17. *Ibid.*, 1139a 31: "The origin...of choice is desire and reasoning with a view to an end." Cf. the commentary by Gauthier-Jolif, II, Part 2, p. 144. On the role of desire and of the *nous praktikos* in choice and decision, on the order of ends and means in the framework of an Aristotelian moral philosophy of *phronēsis*, cf. E.M. Michelakis, *Aristotle's Theory of Practical Principles*, Athens 1961, Ch. 2, pp. 22-62.

18. Cf. Gauthier-Jolif, pp. 202 and 212. Cf. *N.E.*, 1147a 29-31: "For example, let us take a universal premise: *One must taste everything that is sweet*, together with a particular case that falls within the general category: *this food before us is sweet.* Given these two propositions, if one can and is not prevented from doing so, one must necessarily [*ex anankēs*] immediately accomplish this action of tasting."

19. Gauthier-Jolif, p. 129.

20. D.J. Furley, *Two Studies in the Greek Atomists* II: *Aristotle and Epicurus on Voluntary Action*, Princeton, New Jersey 1967, pp. 161-237.

21. D.J. Allan, "The Practical Syllogism," *Autour d'Aristote*, Recueil d'études de philosophie ancienne et médiévale offert à Mgr Mansion, Louvain 1955, pp. 325-40.

22. Cf. Gauthier-Jolif, p. 217. The term *eleutheria* (*N.E.*, V, 1131a 28) "at this period refers not to psychological freedom but to the legal condition of a free man as opposed to that of a slave; the expression 'free will' only appears in the Greek language very much later when *eleutheria* acquires the sense of psychological freedom. It was to be *to autexousion* (or *hē autexousiotēs*), literally, self-control. The earliest instance occurs in Diodorus Siculus, 19, 105, 4 (1st century B.C.) but it does not have its technical sense here. The latter is already firmly established in Epictetus (1st century A.D.), who uses the word five times (*Discourses*, I, 2, 3; IV, 1, 56; 62; 68; 100); from this date onwards the word is fully accepted in Greek philosophy." The Latins later translated *to autexousion* as *liberum arbitrium*.

23. Cf. A.W.H. Adkins, *Merit and Responsibility: A Study in Greek Values*, Oxford 1960; V. Brochard, *Études de philosophie ancienne et de philosophie moderne*, Paris 1912, pp. 489-538 and the much more subtle commentary by Gauthier-Jolif, *op. cit.*, p. 182.

24. In another chapter of his work cited *supra*, B. Snell himself points out that the will "is a notion foreign to the Greeks; they do not even have a word for it," *op. cit.*, p. 182.

25. L. Gernet, *Recherches sur le développement de la pensée juridique et morale en Grèce*, Paris 1917, p. 352.

26. *Ibid.*, pp. 353-4.

27. *Ibid.*, pp. 305ff.

28. *Ibid.*, p. 305.

29. *Ibid.*, pp. 373ff.

30. Cf. G. Maddoli, "Responsibilità e sanzione nei 'decreta de Hecatom-pedo,'" *I.G.*, I², 3-4, *Museum Helveticum* (1967), pp. I-II; J. and L. Robert, Bulletin épigraphique, *REG* (1954), no. 63 and (1967), no. 176.

31. *Cyropaedia*, III, I, 38; cf. L. Gernet, *op. cit.*, p. 387.

32. *Laws*, IX, 863c.

33. Cf. L. Gernet, *op. cit.*, pp. 305, 310 and 339-48.

34. *N.E.*, 1135bff.

35. L. Gernet, *op. cit.*, p. 351; Gauthier-Jolif, *op. cit.*, pp. 192-4; P. Chantraine, *Dictionnaire étymologique de la langue grecque* I, pp. 189-90.

36. *N.E.*, 1112a 17.

37. In Aristotle, *proairesis*, as a deliberate decision of practical thought, can be defined either as a desiring intellect, *orektikos nous*, or as an intellectual desire, *orexis dianoetike*; *N.E.*, 1139b 4-5, together with the commentary by Gauthier-Jolif.

38. *N.E.*, 1112a 15-17.

39. *Cratylus*, 420c-d.

40. If Aristotle declares that man is the principle and cause (in the sense of efficient cause) of his actions, he also writes: "For the originating causes of the things that are done consist in the end at which they are aimed," *N.E.*, 1140b 16-17.

41. Cf., for example, *N.E.*, 1113b 17-19.

42. Cf. D.J. Allan, *op. cit.*, who stresses that *autos* does not have the sense of a rational self opposed to the passions and wielding its own power over the latter.

43. *N.E.*, 1114a 7-8.

44. On the correspondence of the character, *ēthos*, and the desiring part of the soul and its dispositions, cf. *N.E.*, 1103a 6-10 and 1139a 34-5.

45. *N.E.*, 1114a 3-8 and 13-21.

46. *Ibid.*, 1103b 24-5; cf. also 1179b 31ff.

47. *L'évolution du pathétique d'Eschyle à Euripide*, Paris 1961, p. 27.

48. A. Lesky, "Decision and Responsibility in the Tragedy of Aeschylus," *JHS* (1966), pp. 78-85.

49. Aeschylus, *Agamemnon*, 214-8.

50. *Ibid.*, 224-8.

51. *Ibid.*, 186-8.

52. Cf. *infra*, p. 145ff.

53. Aeschylus, *Agamemnon*, 1497-1504.

54. *Ibid.*, 1505-6.

55. Cf. the remarks of N.G.L. Hammond, "Personal Freedom and its Limitations in the *Oresteia*," *JHS* (1965), p. 53.

56. Aeschylus, *The Persians*, 742.

57. Aeschylus, *Agamemnon*, 1372ff.

58. *Ibid.*, 1377; cf. 1401.

59. *Ibid.*, 1609.

60. *Ibid.*, 1223.

61. *Ibid.*, 1431.

62. *Ibid.*, 1424-30.

63. *Ibid.*, 1468ff.

64. *Ibid.*, 1580 and 1609.

65. *Ibid.*, 1487-8.

66. *Ibid.*, 1615-6.

67. R.P. Winnington-Ingram, "Tragedy and Greek Archaic Thought," *Classical Drama and its Influence, Essays Presented to H.D.F. Kitto*, London 1965, pp. 31-50.

68. Sophocles, *Oedipus Rex*, 816 and 828.

69. *Ibid.*, 1193-6.

70. *Ibid.*, 1213.

71. *Ibid.*, 1230-1.

72. *Ibid.*, 1298-1302.

73. *Ibid.*, 1311.

74. *Ibid.*, 1327-8.

75. *Ibid.*, 1329-32.

76. Cf. *supra*, pp. 1ff.

77. Cf. J.-P. Vernant, *Myth and Thought among the Greeks*, Boston 1983, p. 274-5.

78. And even in law there is still a place for the religious idea of defilement; we have only to recall that one of the functions of the *Prytaneum* was to pass judgment on murders committed by inanimate objects or animals.

79. Cf. on this point, V. Goldschmidt, *Le Système stoicien et l'idée du temps*, Paris 1969, esp. pp. 154ff. On tragic time, cf. J. de Romilly, *Time in Greek Tragedy*, New York 1968. On the affective and emotional aspect of Euripidean time, cf. esp. pp. 130 and 141.

80. *Op. cit.*, p. 131.

81. L.A. Post, *From Homer to Menander: Forces in Greek Poetic Fiction*, Sather Classical Lectures, 1951, p. 154; cited in J. de Romilly, *op. cit.*, p. 130.

CHAPTER IV

1. This paper has previously appeared in *Raison présente*, 4 (1967), pp. 3-20.

2. *Les Temps Modernes*, (October 1966), no. 245 pp. 675-715.

3. *Myth and Thought among the Greeks*, Boston 1983, pp. 127-175.

4. At 774-5; 824-7; 966-7; 985-8; 990; 995; 1001; 1015; 1017; 1021.

5. 997 ff., and earlier at 769 ff.

6. Cf. 398.

7. Cf. 642.

8. Cf. 1522.

9. 872.

10. Cf. 873-8; 1195 ff.; 1524 ff.

11. Cf. 383-4.

12. 452.

13. 999.

14. In his *Psychopathology of Everyday Life*, London 1966, Freud writes: "The strange fact that the Oedipus legend finds nothing objectionable in Queen Iocasta's age seemed to me to fit well with the conclusion that in being in love with one's own mother one is never concerned with her as she is in the present but with her youthful mnemic image carried over from one's childhood." But the point is, precisely, that it is not possible that Oedipus should have preserved *any image* of Iocasta from his childhood days.

15. Cf. 380-1.

16. Cf. 382; 399; 535; 541; 618; 642; 658-9; 701.

17. Cf. 495 and 541.

18. Cf. 385.

19. Cf. 73 ff.; 124-5; 288-9; 401-2.

20. Cf. 709.

21. VI, 107.

CHAPTER V

1. This is the (slightly modified) text of a study published in *Echanges et com-*

munications, mélanges offerts à Claude Lévi-Strauss, Paris 1970, Vol. II, pp. 1253-79.

2. *Ambiguity in Greek Literature*, Oxford 1939, pp. 163-73.

3. A. Hug, "Der Doppelsinn in Sophokles *Oedipus König*," *Philologus*, 31 (1872), pp. 68-84.

4. "Names are finite in number whereas things are infinite in number; and so the same expression and the single name must necessarily signify a number of things," Aristotle, *De sophisticis elenchis*, I, 165a 11.

5. Cf. Euripides, *Phoenician Women*, 499 ff.: "If the same thing was equally fine and wise to all, human beings would know nothing of the conflict of quarrels. But to men nothing is the same and equal except in words: Reality is quite different."

6. The same ambiguity appears in the other terms that figure prominently in the work: *dikē, philia,* and *philos, kerdos, timē, orgē, deinos.* Cf. R.G. Goheen, *The Imagery of Sophocles'* Antigone, Princeton 1951, and C.P. Segal, "Sophocles' Praise of Man and the Conflicts of the *Antigone,*" *Arion* 3, 2 (1964), pp. 46-66.

7. Benveniste (*Noms d'agent et noms d'action en indoeuropéen*, Paris 1948, pp. 79-80) has shown that *nemein* contains the idea of a regular attribution, a share fixed by the authority of customary law. This is the meaning of the two main groups in the semantic history of the root **nem. Nómos,* meaning regular attribution, customary rule, custom, religious rite, divine or civic law, convention; *nomós,* meaning territorial attribution fixed by custom, pasturage, province. The expression *ta nomizomena* denotes all that is the gods' due; *ta nomima,* religious or political rules; *ta nomismata,* the customs or money current in a city.

8. In *Antigone,* at 481, Creon condemns the girl for transgressing "the established *nómoi.*" Toward the end of the play, at 1113, worried by the threats of Tiresias, he swears henceforth to respect the "*established nómoi.*" But the term *nómos* has changed its meaning. At 481, Creon uses it as a synonym for *kērugma,* the public edict proclaimed by the head of the city; at 1113, the word recovers, on Creon's lips, the meaning that Antigone gave it at the beginning: religious law, funerary rite.

9. As the Watchman says: "I speak for those who know; for those who do not, I deliberately hide myself (or: I forget, *λήθομαι*)" (38-9). There is a fine example of the deployment of two meanings at line 136. Practically every word is open to a double interpretation. One could understand: "Slaughtering a trembling doe with her litter before she has given birth" or equally: "Sacrificing

428

a poor trembling creature, his own daughter, at the front of the army."

10. Cf. W.B. Stanford, *op. cit.* pp. 137-62. Here are a few examples: In her first words Clytemnestra, recalling the anguish she has felt in her husband's absence, declares that if Agamemnon had received as many wounds as was rumored "his body would have more holes than a woven net" (868). There is a sinister irony to the phrase: This is exactly how the king is to die, caught in the net of death (1115), the network without opening (1382), the fishing net (1382) that she spreads over him (1110). The doors, *pulai* (604), the dwellings, *dōmata* (911), to which she on several occasions refers are not the doors of the palace, as those who are listening believe, but rather, following the religious meaning, those of Hades (1291). When she declares that the king returns to find in her γυναῖκα πιστήν...δωμάτων κύνα, she is really saying the opposite from what she seems to be: γυναῖκ' ἄπιστον, an unfaithful woman who has behaved like a bitch (606-7). As the scholiast remarks, κύων (the bitch) means a woman who has more than one man. When she refers to Zeus *Teleios*, the Zeus by whom all is accomplished so that he fulfills, τέλει, his desires (973-4), it is not the Zeus of the happy return that she has in mind as one might suppose, but the funerary Zeus, the master of death "who brings everything to its accomplishment."

11. Cf. 910, 921, 936, 946, 949 on the one hand and 960-1, 1383-1390, on the other; note the sinister play on the words εἱμάτων βαφάς (960), the dyeing of cloths, which is reminiscent of αἱμάτων βαφάς, dyeing with blood (cf. *Choephori*, 1010-23). It is well known that in Homer blood and death are called πορφύρεοι. According to Artemidorus, *Interpretation of Dreams*, I, 77 (p. 84, 2-4, Pack), "the colour purple has a certain affinity with death"; cf. L. Gernet, in *Problèmes de la couleur*, Paris 1957, pp. 321-4.

12. Cf. R.P. Winnington-Ingram, "Tragedy and Greek Archaic Thought," *Classical Drama and its Influence, Essays Presented to H.D.F. Kitto*, 1965, pp. 31-50.

13. Here again we would refer the reader to W.B. Stanford's work and to the commentaries of R. Jebb, *Oedipus Tyrannus*, 1887 and J.C. Kamerbeek, *The Plays of Sophocles*, IV, *The Oedipus Tyrannus*, 1967. We shall give a few examples only. Creon has been speaking of the brigands, in the plural, who killed Laius. Oedipus replies: How could *the murderer*, ὁ λῃστής, have committed this action without accomplices? (124). The scholiast notes: "Oedipus is thinking of his brother-in-law." But in using the singular Oedipus, without knowing it, is condemning himself. As he later recognizes (842-7), if there were *several* murder-

ers he himself is not guilty; but if there was only one man on his own, then the crime could be imputed to him. At 137-41 there are three ambiguities: (1) In getting rid of the defilement he is not doing it for distant friends, he is getting rid of it for himself; little does he know how true his words are; (2) the murderer of the king might be tempted to raise his hand against Oedipus, and indeed Oedipus later puts his own eyes out; (3) in coming to Laius' aid he is acting in his own interest — wrong, he will destroy himself. The whole of the passage at 258-65, together with its conclusion: "For these reasons, *Just as if Laius was my father*, I shall fight for him," is ambiguous. The phrase, "if his descendence had not been abortive" can equally well mean "if his descendence had not been destined to misfortune." At 551, Oedipus' threat to Creon: "If you think you can attack a relative without paying for it, you are mistaken" recoils against himself: It is he who will have to pay for the murder of his father. At 572-3 there is a double meaning: "He would not have claimed that I killed Laius," but also: "He would not have revealed that I killed Laius." At 928, the position of ἥδε, between μήτηρ and τῶν τέκνων makes a connection between *gunē* and *mētēr*: his wife, who is also his mother. At 955-6: "He announces that your father Polybus is dead," but also: "He announces that your father is not Polybus but a dead man." At 1183, Oedipus desires death and exclaims: "Oh light, would that I saw you for the last time." But *phōs* has two meanings in Greek: the light of life, and the light of day. It is the sense that Oedipus does not mean that becomes the true one.

14. *Poetics*, 1452a 32-3.
15. *Oedipus Rex*, 132.
16. *Ibid.*, 8.
17. *Ibid.*, 33.
18. *Ibid.*, 46.
19. *Ibid.*, 1204-6, 1297 ff., 1397.
20. *Ibid.*, 1433.
21. *Ibid.*, 1397.
22. *Ibid.*
23. *Ibid.*, 1306.
24. *Ibid.*, 1345.
25. *Ibid.*, 455-6, 1518.
26. *Ibid.*, 31.

27. *Ibid.*, 1187-8.

28. *Ibid.*, 374.

29. *Ibid.*, 1182.

30. *Ibid.*, 1213.

31. *Ibid.*, 1397.

32. *Ibid.*, 1303-5.

33. *Ibid.*, 1297.

34. *Ibid.*, 1312.

35. *Ibid.*, 1370 ff.

36. *Ibid.*, 1196.

37. *Ibid.*, 1189 ff. In this sense tragedy, even before Plato, takes up the opposite point of view from Protagoras and "the philosophy of enlightenment" developed by the fifth-century sophists. Far from man being the measure of all things, it is god who is the measure of man, as of everything else; cf. Knox, *op. cit.* pp. 150 ff., 184.

38. Cf., again, more recently, E.R. Dodds, "On Misunderstanding the *Oedipus Rex*," *Greece and Rome*, 2nd series, 13 (1966), pp. 37-49.

39. *Poetics*, 1458a 26. Compare this schema of reversal with that which is to be found in Heraclitus' thought, especially in fr. 88, expressed by the verb μεταπίπτειν. Cf. Clemence Ramnoux, *Héraclite ou l'homme entre les choses et les mots*, 1959, pp. 33 ff. and 392.

40. Concerning this specific nature of the tragic message cf. *supra* pp. 31-2.

41. *Oedipus at Colonus*, 525 and 539-40.

42. *Ibid.*, 265 ff., 521 ff., 539.

43. *Suppliants*, 226.

44. *Oedipus at Colonus*, 287.

45. *Oedipus at Thebes: Sophocles' Tragic Hero and his Time*, 1957, 2nd ed., 1966, p. 138.

46. *Oedipus Rex*, 109-10, 221, 354, 475 ff.

47. *Ibid.*, 469.

48. *Ibid.*, 479.

49. *Ibid.*, 419.

50. *Ibid.*, 1255, 1265.

51. *Ibid.*, 1451.

52. *Ibid.*, 278, 362, 450, 658-9, 1112.

53. Cf. Plutarch, *De curiositate*, 522c, and *Oedipus Rex*, 362, 450, 658, 659, 1112.

54. *Oedipus Rex, skopein*: 68, 291, 407, 964; *historein*: 1150.

55. *Ibid.*, 1180-1.

56. *Ibid., heurein, heuretēs*: 68, 108, 120, 440, 1050.

57. *Ibid.*, 1026, 1108, 1213.

58. *Ibid.*, 1397; *heuriskomai*.

59. *Ibid.*, 674.

60. *Ibid.*, 1293, 1387-8, 1396.

61. *Ibid.*, 397.

62. *Ibid.*, 259, 383.

63. *Ibid.*, 905.

64. Scholium to Euripides, *Phoenician Women*, 45.

65. *Oedipus Rex*, 1200.

66. *Ibid.*, 130, *Phoenician Women*, 1505-6.

67. *Oedipus Rex*, 58-9, 84, 105, 397; cf. also 43.

68. *Ibid.*, 468.

69. *Ibid.*, 479 ff.

70. *Ibid.*, 418.

71. *Ibid.*, 866.

72. *Ibid.*, 878. Cf. Knox, *op. cit.*, pp. 182-4. On his arrival, the messenger from Corinth asks: Do you know where Oedipus is? As Knox points out, the three lines 924-6 all end with the name of Oedipus together with the interrogative adverb *hopou*, giving μάθοιμ' ὅπου —, Οἰδίπου —, ὅπου. Knox writes: "These violent puns, suggesting a fantastic conjugation of a verb 'to know where' formed from the name of the hero who, as Tiresias told him, does not know where he is (413-4) – this is the ironic laughter of the gods whom Oedipus 'excludes' in his search for the truth."

73. *Oedipus Rex*, 38.

74. *Ibid.*, 52.

75. *Ibid.*, 1200-1.

76. *Ibid.*, 1219 ff.

77. *Ibid.*, 1062-3.

78. μικρὸν καὶ μέγαν, *ibid.*, 1083.

79. *Ibid.*, 442.

80. Cf. Marie Delcourt, *Oedipe ou la légende du conquérant*, Paris-Liège 1944, who fully develops this theme and draws attention to its place in the myth of Oedipus.

81. *Oedipus Rex*, 1086-1109.

82. Including the matrimonial laws that the city recognized as the norm. In "Mariages de tyrans," *Hommage à Lucien Febvre*, 1954, pp. 41-53, L. Gernet, reminding the reader that the prestige of the tyrant is in many respects derived from the past and that there are models in legend for his excessive behavior, points out that "the mythical theme of incest with one's mother has been given a new slant for Periander." This mother is called *Krateia*, which means sovereignty.

83. *Trojan Women*, 1169.

84. *Republic*, 568b.

85. Cf. *Republic*, 360b-d.

86. On Oedipus *agos*, cf. 1426; and also 1121, 656, 921; together with Kamerbeek's commentaries to these passages, *op. cit.*

87. In a lecture given at the École des Hautes Études, not yet published; now see J.P. Guépin, *The Tragic Paradox*, Amsterdam 1968, p. 89 ff. Marie Delcourt, *op. cit.*, pp. 30-7, has underlined the relationship between the ritual of exposure and that of the scapegoat.

88. Herodotus, 5, 70-1; Thucydides, I, 126-7.

89. Photius, *Bibliotheca*, p. 534 (Bekker); cf. Hesychius, s.v. φαρμακοί.

90. According to Diogenes Laertius (2, 44), the sixth of Thargelion, the birthday of Socrates, is the day when the Athenians "purify the town."

91. Photius, *op. cit.*; Hesychius, s.v. κραδίης νόμος; Tzetzes, *Chiliades*, V, 736; Hipponax, fr. 4 and 5, Bergk.

92. *Scholium to Aristophanes, Frogs*, 730; *Knights*, 1133; Suda, s.v. φαρμακούς; Harpocration, citing Istros, s.v. παρμακός; Tzetzes, *Chiliades*, V, 736.

93. Aristophanes, *Frogs*, 730-4.

94. Tzetzes, *op. cit.*; the scholiast to Aristophanes' *Knights*, 1133, writes that the Athenians supported people who were harmful and of the lowest origins to the highest degree, ἀγεννεῖς καὶ ἀχρήστους, so that they could use them for *pharmakoi*; the scholiast to *Frogs*, 703, tells us that to ward off famine they sacrificed, τοὺς φαύλους καὶ παρὰ τῆς φύσεως ἐπιβουλευομένους, degraded and disgraced creatures (literally, those who have been treated harshly by nature); cf. M. Delcourt, *op. cit.*, p. 31, n.2.

95. Leucas: Strabo, 10, 9, p. 452; Photius, s.v. *λευκάτης* –Massilia; Petronius in Servius, *ad En.*, 3, 57; Lactantius Placidus, *Comment stat. Theb.*, 10, 793.

96. *Against Andocides*, 108, 4: "*τὴν πόλιν καθαίρειν καὶ ἀποδιοπομπεῖσθαι καὶ φαρμακὸν ἀποπέμπειν.*" Lysias uses the religious terminology. On *διοπομπεῖν, ἀποδιοπομπεῖσθαι, ἀποπέμπειν* and the rites of expulsion, the *πομπαῖα*, cf. Eustathius, *ad Odys.*, 22, 481. In *O.R.*, at 696, following the quarrel between Creon and Oedipus, the chorus leader expresses the hope that the latter will remain "the city's happy guide [*εὔπομπος*]." On this point too the reversal will be perfect: the guide will be guided away, the *eupompos* will be the object of the *pompaia*, the *apopempsis*.

97. Plutarch, *Quaest. conviv*, 717d; Hesychius, s.v. *Θαργήλια*; *Schol. Aristophanes: Plutus*, 1055; *Schol. Aristophanes, Knights*, 729; Athenaeus, 114a; Eustathius, *ad Il.*, 9, 530.

98. On the *eiresīonē*, cf. Eustathius, *ad Il.*, 1283, 7; *Schol. Aristophanes, Plutus*, 1055; *Et. Magnum*, s.v. *Εἰρεσιώνη*; Hesychius, s.v. *κορυθαλια*; Suda, s.v. *Διακόνιον*; Plutarch, *Life of Theseus*, 22.

99. *Schol. Aristophanes, Plutus*, 1055; *Schol. Aristophanes, Knights*, 728: *οἱ μὲν γάρ φασιν ὅτι λιμοῦ, οἱ δὲ ὅτι καὶ λοιμοῦ*; Eustathius, *ad Il.*, 1283, 7: *ἀποτροπῆ λιμοῦ.*

The *eiresīonē* appears again, in the religious calendar, in the month of *Puanepsīon*, on the occason of the festival of the Oschophoria. The month of *Puanepsīon* marks the end of the summer season just as the month of *Thargēliōn* or the month immediately before it, the *Mounichīōn*, marks its beginning. The ritual offering of *puanion* (Athenaeus, 648b) on the seventh of the autumn month corresponds with the offering of the *thargēlos* on the seventh of the spring month: In both cases what is involved is a *panspermia*, a broth made from all the seeds of the fruits of the earth. Similarly, in myth, the springtime procession of the *eiresīonē* corresponds with the departure of Theseus (Plutarch, *Life of Theseus*, 18, 1 and 2) while the autumn procession corresponds with the return of the hero (*Ibid.*, 22, 5-7). Cf. L. Deubner, *Attische Feste*, Berlin 1932, pp. 198-201 and 224-6; H. Jeanmaire, *Couroi et Couretes*, Paris 1939, pp. 312-3 and 347 ff.; J. and L. Robert, *REG*, 62 (1949), *Bulletin épigraphique*, no. 45, p. 106.

100. The *eiresīonē*, which is a talisman of fertility, is – like the *thargēlos* – sometimes called *euetēria, hugieia*, prosperity and health. The scholiast to Aristophanes' *Knights*, 728, notes that the seasons, *ai ὦραι*, are "attached to the branches." Plato (*Symposium*, 188a-b) writes that when the seasons' composi-

tion (that is to say the relationships between the dry and the wet, and the hot and the cold) is correctly balanced, they bring *euetēria* and *hugieia* to men, animals, and plants. When, on the contrary, there is *hubris* in their mutual relations, *loimoi* occur with many diseases that also attack animals and plants. The *loimos* is a manifestation of the disordering of the seasons that is close enough to the disordering of human behavior for the latter often to be the cause of the former; the rite of the *pharmakos* represents the expulsion of human disorder; the *eiresiōnē* symbolizes the return to the rightful order of the seasons. In both cases *anomia* is removed.

101. Aristophanes, *Knights*, 728 and the scholium; *Plutus*, 1054; "the slightest spark would make it flare up like an old *eiresiōnē*," *Wasps*, 399. The drying up of the branch of spring can be compared to the drying up of the earth and of men where there is *limos* (*limos*, famine, is often associated with *auchmos*, drought). Hipponax, cursing his enemy Boupalos, the *agos* he wishes to be expelled, wants him to be *xēros limoi*, dried up by hunger, paraded like a *pharmakos* and, again like a *pharmakos*, whipped seven times on his private parts.

102. Plutarch, *Life of Theseus*, 22, 6-7. Cf. 18, 1: After the murder of Androgaeus "the deity ruined the countryside, afflicting it with sterility and disease and drying up the rivers."

103. Hesychius, s.v. Θαργήλια: "... καὶ τὴν ἱκετηρίαν ἐκάλουν Θάργηλον"; cf. also Plutarch, *Life of Theseus*, 22, 6 and 18, 1; Eustathius, *ad Il.*, 1283, 6.

104. *Oedipus Rex*, 5 and 186.

105. *Schol. Victor, ad Iliad*, 10, 391: "Paean: sung to bring evils to an end or to prevent them happening. This primitive music was connected not only with banquets and dancing but also with threnodies. It was still valued in the time of the Pythagoreans who called it a purification [κάθαρσις]." Cf. also Aeschylus, *Agamemnon*, 645; *Choephori*, 150-1; *The Seven*, 868 and 915 ff. Cf. L. Delatte, "Note sur un fragment de Stésichore," *L'Antiquité Classique*, 7, fasc. 1 (1938), p. 28-9; A. Severyns, *Recherches sur la chrestomathie de Proclus*, 1, Vol. 2, 1938, pp. 125 ff.

106. L. Delatte, *op. cit.*; Stesichorus, Fr. 37, Bergk = 14 Diehl; Iamblichus, *V.P.*, 110, Deubner; Aristoxenus of Tarentum, fr. 117, Wehrli: "The inhabitants of Locri and Rhegium, who consulted the oracle to find out how to cure the madness of their women, were told by the god that in the spring they should sing paeons for sixty days." On the significance of the spring, which is not so much a season like the others but rather a break in time, marking both the

435

renewal of the earth's produce and the exhaustion of men's reserves at this critical moment of "welding" one agricultural year to the next, cf. Alcman, Fr.
56 D = 137 Ed.: "(Zeus) made three seasons, summer, winter, and autumn
which is the third, and a fourth, the spring, when everything flourishes and grows
but when one cannot eat one's fill."

107. *Oedipus Rex*, 1426; cf. *supra*, n.86.

108. *Ibid.*, 56-64.

109. *Ibid.*, 93-4.

110. *Ibid.*, 97.

111. Homer, *Odyssey*, XIX, 109 ff.; Hesiod, *Works*, 225 ff.

112. Hesiod, *Works*, 238 ff.

113. On this double aspect of the *pharmakos*, cf. R.L. Farnell, *Cults of the Greek States*, 1907, 4, pp. 280-1.

114. Suda, s.v. φαρμακός: Hipponax, fr. 7, Bergk; Servius, *ad Aen.*, 3, 57; Lactantius Placidus, *Comment. stat. Theb.* 10, 793: "...*publicis sumptibus alebatur purioribus cibis.*..."

115. Diogenes Laertius, T, 110; Athenaeus, 602 c-d.

116. J. Carcopino, *L'ostracisme athénien*, 1935. The principal texts can be found conveniently collected together in A. Calderini's *L'ostracismo*, Como 1945. We are indebted to L. Gernet for the idea of the connection between the institution of ostracism and the ritual of the *pharmakos*.

117. μεθίστασθαι τῆς πόλεως; cf. *Et. Magnum*, s.v. ἐξοστρακισμός; Photius, s.v. ὀστρακισμός.

118. Note, in *Oedipus Rex*, the presence of the theme of *phthonos* with respect to the one who is at the head of the city, cf. 380 ff.

119. "It is from the clouds that snow and hail fall. The thunder comes from the blazing lightning. It is from men who are too great that the destruction of the city comes," Solon, fr. 9-10 (Edmonds).

120. *Politics*, 3, 1284a 3-b 13.

121. In an unpublished lecture given in February 1958 at the Centre d'études sociologiques, Louis Gernet noted that between the two opposed poles of the *pharmakos* and the man ostracized there sometimes occurred a short circuit as the institutions interacted. Such was the case in the last incident of ostracism in Athens. In 417 there were two figures of the first importance on whom the vote might have been expected to fall, Nicias and Alcibiades. The two of them

got together and managed to make the ostracism fall instead upon a third, a ruffian, Hyperbolos, a demagogue of the lower classes who was generally detested and despised. So Hyperbolos was ostracized but, as Louis Gernet notes, ostracism never recovered: Alarmed at this "mistaken choice," which emphasizes both the polarity and the symmetry of the *pharmakos* and the victim of ostracization, the Athenians were definitively disgusted by the institution.

122. *Politics* I, 1253a 2-7. In his definition of the degraded being, the subhuman, Aristotle uses the same term φαῦλος that the scholiast employs to describe the *pharmakos*. On the opposition between the brutish beast and the hero or god cf. *Nicomachean Ethics* 7, 1145a 15 ff.: "To brutishness it would be most fitting to oppose superhuman virtue, a heroic and divine kind of virtue.... Since it is rarely that a godlike man is found...so too the brutish type is rarely found amongst men."

123. In Aristotle's expression, that we have translated in the usual way "like an isolated piece at draughts," there is more than an opposition simply between *azux*, the piece on its own, and *pettoi* or *pessoi*, the normal pieces used by the players. (Cf. J. Tréheux, "Sur le sens des adjectifs περίζυξ et περίζυγος," *Revue de philologie* (1958), p. 89.) In the category of games that the Greeks referred to using the verb *pesseuein* there was one which they called by the name of *polis*. According to Suetonius, (*Peri paidiōn*, 1, 16), "πόλις is also a type of dice game in which the players took each other's pieces, positioned as in draughts [πεττευτικῶς] on squares drawn with intersecting lines. These squares were, quite wittily, called cities [πόλεις] while the pieces of the opposing player's were called dogs [κύνες]." According to Pollux (9,98), "the game in which many pieces are moved about is played on a board with squares marked by lines. The board is called πόλις, the pieces κύνες." Cf. J. Taillardat, *Suétone: Des termes injurieux. Des jeux grecs*, Paris 1957, pp. 154-5. The reason why Aristotle refers to draughts in his description of the *apolis* individual is that, in the Greek game, the checkerboard defining the respective positions and movements of the pieces may, as the name indicates, represent the layout of the *polis*.

124. *Oedipus Rex*, 260.

125. *Ibid.*, 1209-12.

126. *Ibid.*, 1256-7; 1485; 1498-1500: "κὰκ τῶν ἴσων ἐκτήσαθ' ὑμᾶς, ὧνπερ αὐτὸς ἐξέφυ."

127. *Ibid.*, 425.

128. On this "nonequality" of Oedipus in relation to the other Thebans some of whom, such as Tiresias and Creon, claim the right to a status equal to his, cf. 61, 408-9, 544, 579 and 581; 630. Oedipus also responds "not equally" to the lash of the whip Laius gives him (810). And the final wish expressed by the fallen Oedipus, concerning his children, is that Creon "does not equal their misfortunes with his own" (1507).

129. "As a brute has no vice or virtue, so neither has a god; his state is higher than virtue and that of a brute is a different kind of state from vice," Aristotle, *N.E.*, 7, 1145a 25.

130. *Republic*, 569b.

131. *Ibid.*, 360c. It is, in our opinion, in this context that we should understand the second stasimon (863-911), for which many different interpretations have been proposed. It is the only moment at which the chorus adopts a negative attitude toward Oedipus the Tyrant; but the criticisms it levels at the *hubris* of the tyrant seem quite out of place where Oedipus is concerned for he would be the last person, for example, to exploit his situation to "make dishonest gains" (889). The fact is that the words of the chorus refer not to Oedipus in person but to his "separate" status in the city. The almost religious feelings of reverence for the man who is more than a man change to horror as soon as Oedipus is shown to have been capable in the past of committing a crime and, today, not to appear to believe in the divine oracles. Now the *isotheos* no longer appears as a guide in whom one may place one's trust but as a creature knowing no control or law, a master who may be so bold as to do anything he wishes.

132. It is *logos*, word and reason, that makes man the only "political" animal. Animals only have a voice whereas "the power of speech is intended to set forth the expedient and the inexpedient and therefore likewise the just and the unjust. And it is a characteristic of man as compared with other animals that he alone has any sense of good and evil, of just and unjust and the like, and the association of living beings who have this sense makes a family and a city," Aristotle, *Politics*, I, 1253a 10-8.

133. Dio Chrysostomus, 10, 29; cf. B. Knox, *op. cit.*, p. 206; cf. also Ovid, *Metamorphoses*, 7, 386-7: "Menephron must have made love with his mother, as wild beasts do!" Cf. also 10, 324-31.

134. At the beginning of the tragedy, Oedipus tries to become a part of the lineage of the Labdacids from whom, as a stranger, he feels too distant (cf.

137-41; 258-68); as B. Knox writes, "The resounding, half-envious recital of Laius' royal genealogy emphasizes Oedipus' deep-seated feeling of inadequacy in the matter of birth.... And he tries, in his speech, to insert himself into the honorable line of Theban kings" (*op. cit.*, p. 56). But his real misfortune lies not in the too great distance separating him from the legitimate lineage, but in the fact that he belongs to this very lineage. Oedipus is also anxious about the possibility of a lowly birth that would make him unworthy of Iocasta. But here again his misfortune lies not in too great a distance but in too close a proximity, in the total lack of difference between the lineages of man and wife. His marriage is worse than a misalliance: It is incest.

135. Bestiality implies not only the absence of *logos* and *nomos*; it is defined as a state of "confusion" in which everything is haphazardly confused and mixed up; cf. Aeschylus, *Prometheus Vinctus*, 450; Euripides, *Suppliants*, 201.

136. Cf. the argument of Euripides' *Phoenician Women*: ἀλλάσσει δὲ φυὴν μόνον....

CHAPTER VI

1. This study first appeared in *Parola del Passato* 129 (1969), pp. 401-25. It takes up and develops points I made at J.-P. Vernant's seminar at the École Pratique des Hautes Études and at the conference on "Le moment d'Eschyle" organized at Bièvres in June 1969 by Gilbert Kahn. I should like to thank those who took part for their comments.

2. *Agamemnon*, 22, 522, 969.

3. *Eumenides*, 1022; cf. also πυριδάπτῳ λαμπάδι, *ibid.*, 1041-2.

4. *Agamemnon*, 169-75.

5. *Eumenides*, 1043, 1047.

6. *Agamemnon*, 68-71.

7. J. Dumortier, *Les images dans la poésie d'Eschyle*, Paris 1935; cf. pp. 71-87; 88-100; 101-11; 134-55, etc. The theme of the sacrifice, on the other hand, is very neglected; cf. pp. 217-20.

8. *Aeschylus' Agamemnon edited with a commentary*, E. Fraenkel, Oxford 1950, III, p. 653.

9. F.I. Zeitlin, "The Motif of the Corrupted Sacrifice in Aeschylus' *Oresteia*," *TAPhA* 96 (1965), pp. 463-508: "Postscript to Sacrificial Imagery in the *Oresteia*" (*Agamemnon*, 1235-7), *ibid.*, 97 (1966), pp. 645-53.

10. W. Burkert, "Greek Tragedy and Sacrificial Ritual," *GRBS* 7 (1966), pp. 87-122; J.-P. Guépin, *The Tragic Paradox: Myth and Ritual in Greek Tragedy*, Amsterdam 1968. The latter book is very rewarding indeed but J.-P. Guépin would have produced an even more useful work if he had not devoted so much effort to the impossible task of studying the ritual *origins* (especially Dionysiac) of tragedy. As it is, when he describes tragedy as a "festival of the harvest and the grape-gathering" (pp. 195-200), he omits to describe what tragedy *is* in order to attempt to explain what it comes from and he hardly makes any progress beyond the already longstanding hypotheses of J.E. Harrison and F.M. Cornford.

11. J.-P. Guépin has shown some inkling of the interest such a study would have; cf. *op. cit.*, esp. pp. 24-32; he even says (p. 26): "Of course hunting metaphors are extremely common in ancient Greek, especially in the spheres of war and love. A mere enumeration of those hunting metaphors would not help us. But sometimes one feels that something more, a ritual allusion, may be intended." He cites a number of texts that may indeed refer to a ritual hunt.

12. Cf. P. Vidal-Naquet, *The Black Hunter*, Baltimore 1986, pp. 106-128.

13. Cf. 322b.

14. Similarly Aristotle, *Politics*, I, 1256b 23; on this theme in the Greek literature concerning the "origins" of civilization, cf. T. Cole, *Democritus and the Sources of Greek Anthropology*, Ann Arbor 1967, pp. 34-6, 64-5, 83-4, 92-3, 115, 123-6.

15. K. Meuli, "Griechische Opferbräuche," *Phyllobolia für Peter von der Mühli*, Bâle 1946, pp. 185-288. However polemical this study may be, it nevertheless provides a formidable collection of facts and ideas and remains the major work on sacrifice among the Greeks. Among the recent works on this subject I have also made considerable use of J. Rudhardt, *Notions fondamentales de la pensée réligieuse et actes constitutifs du culte dans la Grèce classique*, Geneva 1958, and J. Casabona, *Recherches sur le vocabulaire des sacrifices en grec*, Aix-Gap 1966, not to mention the old and still very useful collection of P. Stengel, *Opferbräuche der Griechen*, Leipzig-Berlin 1910.

16. Cf. what he himself says on this point, *op. cit.*, pp. 223-4.

17. Besides, K. Meuli only considers the question very briefly (p. 263).

18. *Theogony*, 535-6.

19. *Ibid.*, 591.

20. See a few examples *infra*, p. 146 and for a collection bearing compari-

son with contemporary art, R. Hampe, *Die Gleichnisse Homers und die Bildkunst seiner Zeit*, Tübingen 1952, especially p. 30 ff.

21. Cf. *Schol. Arat., Phaen.*, 132; Aelian, *N.A.*, 12, 34; *Schol. Odyssey*, 12, 353; Nicholas of Damascus, fr. 103, I. Jacoby; Aelian, *Var. Hist.*, 5, 14; Varro *De re rustica*, 2, 5, 4; Columella, 6, *Praef.*; Pliny, *N.H.*, 8, 180. The scope of these texts extends far beyond the Greek world.

22. Pausanias, I, 28, 10; Aelian, *Var. hist.*, 8, 3; Porphyry, *De abstinentia*, 2, 28; for the collected works in the tradition, cf. L. Deubner, *Attische Feste*, Berlin 1932, p. 158 ff.

23. *Odyssey*, XII, 356-96.

24. *Ibid.*, 329-33; on this point see my article "Valeurs religieuses et mythiques de la terre et du sacrifice dans l'Odyssée" in M.I. Finley (ed.) *Problèmes de la Terre en grèce ancienne*, Paris and The Hague 1972, pp. 269-92.

25. An inquiry, which ought to be completed by a detailed archaeological investigation, was carried out by P. Stengel: "Über die Wild und Fischopfer der Griechen," *Hermes* (1887), pp. 94-100, reprinted in *Opferbräuche...*, pp. 197-202.

26. Cf. *Agamemnon*, 105-59.

27. J. de Romilly, *Time in Greek Tragedy*, Ithaca and New York 1968, p. 77. Cf. also *REG* (1967), p. 95.

28. Only after publication of this study did I come across the excellent article of J.J. Peradotto, "The *Omen* of the Eagles and the ἦθος of Agamemnon," *Phoenix* 23 (1969), pp. 237-63.

29. *Agamemnon*, 151-5.

30. *Ibid.*, 120.

31. Xenophon, *Cynegetica*, 5, 14 and 9, 10, and Arrian, *Cynegetica*, 17, describe the "first run" of the hunted animal. The comparison is made, in particular, by P. Mazon, p. 14 of the Budé edition.

32. Herodotus, 3, 108. On the hare in the cult of Artemis in particular at Brauron in Attica, see J.J. Peradotto, *loc. cit. supra*, p. 244.

33. *Iliad*, XIX, 252-3; 22, 310; 24, 315-6; cf. also XVII, 674-7 where it is Menelaos who is the object of the comparison, or the μελανάετος καὶ λαγωφόνος of Aristotle *H.A.*, 9, 32, 618b. For other references and for the zoological identification of these eagles (the white and the black) cf. E. Fraenkel's commentary II, pp. 67-70.

34. Mazon, p. 15 of the Budé edition.

35. *Cynegetica*, 5, 14.

36. *Agamemnon*, 151, "another sacrifice" rather than "should insist in her turn on a sacrifice" (following Mazon). The sacrifice is ἄδαιτος, that is to say there is no sacrificial meal; it is a sacrifice where everything is destroyed.

37. For a detailed demonstration I would refer to W.B. Stanford, *Ambiguity in Greek Tragedy*, Oxford 1939, p. 143. Fraenkel's commentary has nothing to say on this point.

38. *Agamemnon*, 116.

39. Cf. G. Radke, *Die Bedeutung der Weissen und der Schwarzen Farbe im Kult und Brauch der Griechen und Römern*, Berlin 1936, especially p. 27 ff.

40. Although the symbol is very different, Aeschylus' audience must have thought of the famous scene where Calchas interprets the omen of the serpent eating eight sparrows together with their mother and being turned to stone, which foretells the capture of Troy after nine years of war (*Iliad*, II, 301-29). But unlike in Aeschylus, in Homer the omen, once interpreted, is perfectly clear.

41. *Agamemnon*, 357-60.

42. Cf. *infra*, p. 148.

43. *Agamemnon*, 140-3.

44. Cf. at least *Agamemnon*, 1260 and in all probability 827-8. See B.M.W. Knox's brilliant demonstration, "The Lion in the House," *CPh* 47 (1957) pp. 17-25, which proves beyond all possible doubt that in the famous image of the growing lion-cub (*Agamemnon*, 717-36) we must see not only Paris but also the son of Atreus himself.

45. προφέρων Ἄρτεμιν, 201-2.

46. This, broadly speaking, is what we should retain from W. Whallon's study, "Why is Artemis angry?" *American Journal of Philology*, 82 (1961), pp. 78-88. On the other hand, E. Fraenkel (*op. cit.*, II, pp. 97-8) has shown how careful Aeschylus was *not to mention* the traditions according to which the Atreidae were held to have violated an enclosure reserved for Artemis or killed an animal sacred to her alone. Indeed there was no need to mention any such act since, from the tragic point of view, Agamemnon is already guilty inasmuch as he is one of the Atreidae, at the same time constantly remaining free not to be guilty. One's first impulse is to see in line 141 an allusion to the legend of the saving of Iphigenia who was carried by the goddess to Tauris, for is not Artemis "moved with pity"? But there is no text in Aeschylus that can justify this contention.

47. *Agamemnon*, 1502-3.

48. The black hunter who is an ephebe, whom I studied in the article mentioned above, is only "black" for the time being, for the duration of his ritual retreat. Here it is a question of something quite different: Agamemnon is an accursed hunter.

49. "In the snare of a net she has caught the bull with black horns; she strikes [τὸν ταῦρον· ἐν πέπλοισιν μελάγκερων λαβοῦσα μηχανήματι τύπτει]" (1126-8). I translate the lines thus despite the remarks made by Fraenkel, *op. cit.*, II, pp. 511-9, followed especially by Thomson and J.D. Denniston and D. Page in their editions of the *Agamemnon*, Oxford 1957, pp. 171-3. These authors, like Fraenkel, make μελάγκερῳ agree with μηχανήματι. J.P. Guépin, *op. cit.*, pp. 24-5, thinks it is the veil itself that is "a black-horned contrivance." However, horns go better with a bull than with a trick or a veil. I have therefore, with Mazon, kept the μελάγκερων of the Tr, F, V, and M manuscripts (before correction) and I have not adopted the correction of *M* μελαγκέρῳ. Fraenkel translates: "with black contrivance of the horned one" which is rather peculiar and he explains that μηχανήματι needs a qualifying adjective; this remark is, to say the least, open to doubt; cf. *Choephori* 980-1: "Look, you who have but heard of our afflictions, look at last at the trap, the snare which entangled my unfortunate father [ἴδεσθε δ'αὖτε τῶνδ' ἐπήκοοι κακῶν τὸ μηχάνημα, δεσμὸν ἀθλίῳ πατρί]." It is most probable that δεσμόν is in this instance not an adjective but a noun in apposition.

50. E. Fraenkel in his commentary quotes (II, p. 67) several texts which describe the eagle "with a white tail" with the word δειλία, meaning cowardice. This interpretation does not stand in contradiction to the one we are defending here. To support my interpretation may I point out that the fact that the fate of Menelaos, who disappeared in a storm on his return journey, has a happy outcome is discreetly alluded to by the herald in lines 674-9.

51. *Agamemnon*, 49-54.

52. Thus W.G. Headlam and G. Thomson, *The* Oresteia *of Aeschylus*, Cambridge 1938, p. 16; W. Whallon saw very clearly the importance of Aeschylus' bestiary for the interpretation of the work: "The repeated beast symbols of the *Oresteia* are the Aeschylean counterpart of the Sophoclean dramatic irony" (*op. cit.*, p. 81). Despite this even he concludes in the same vein: "The generic differences between the vulture and the eagle are unimportant here; the eagle might well have been the bird of vengeance, the vulture might have been the bird of

predacity" (*ibid.*, p. 80). The problem is better presented by F.I. Zeitlin, *The Motif...*, pp. 482-3.

53. Cf. D'Arcy W. Thompson, *A Glossary of Greek Birds*, Oxford 1936, pp. 5-6 and 26.

54. On the opposition – and sometimes confusion – between the vulture and the eagle, cf. the texts collected by J. Heurgon, "Vultur," *Rev. Et. Lat.* 14 (1936), pp. 109-18. All the necessary references may be found in D'Arcy Thompson, *op. cit.*

55. For this opposition compare, for example, Aesop, Fable 6; Aelian *N.A.*, 3, 7 and 18, 4; Antoninus Liberalis, 12, 5-6; Dionysus, *De aucupio*, 1, 5 (Garzya). See D'Arcy Thompson, *op. cit.*, p. 84. I should like to thank Marcel Detienne in whose book, *The Gardens of Adonis*, Hassocks 1976, this opposition plays an important part and who enlightened me on this point, and Manolis Papathomopoulos who drew my attention to the last text quoted.

56. *Agamemnon*, 1309-12.

57. *Ibid.*, 694-5.

58. As P. Mazon has it when he translates it in this way, adding an extra word to the text.

59. In his doctoral thesis on the hunting theme on Greek vases of the fifth century (1972), Alain Schnapp has collected important material that he will, I hope, one day publish.

60. *Agamemnon*, 537.

61. *Ibid.*, 338-44.

62. ὑπερκότως (822), however, is a correction made by Kayser and adopted by Mazon in the place of the impossible word ὑπερκότους that is to be found in the manuscripts. If, following Fraenkel, Thomson, and Denniston-Page, we adopt Heath's correction, ὑπερκόπους, the lines 822-3 translate as "We have obtained payment [ἐπραξάμεσθα] for the presumptuous thefts [χάρπαγάς]." χάρπαγάς is, incidentally, also a correction.

63. *Agamemnon*, 825.

64. "Toward the setting of the Pleiades [ἀμφὶ Πλειάδων δύσιν]"; ever since the Renaissance these three words have been a *Tummelplatz* of erudition. The essentials of the discussion can be found in Fraenkel, *op. cit.*, pp. 380-2 and in Thomson, *The Oresteia of Aeschylus*, Prague 1966, p. 68. Some, like the scholiast of T, take δύσις to mean the *heliacal* setting of the Pleiades (14 November) that tradi-

tionally marked the beginning of the season of bad weather. This interpretation would fit in quite well with the storm the herald mentions in lines 650 ff., and symbolically with the dangerous peripeteia that the capture of Troy and Agamemnon's return really represent. These are the general lines along which Thomson and Denniston (p. 141) argue and they even think that the information is given purely gratuitously. Others hold that δύσις simply means the nocturnal setting of the constellation and Fraenkel points out that at the time of the great Dionysia (the end of March) the Pleiades set at ten o'clock in the evening. Although it does not seem necessary to appeal to the evidence of the feeding habits of the lion with which Homer was familiar (*Iliad*, 17, 657-50), as Fraenkel does, it must be admitted that if we follow the feeling of the story it is easier to imagine a lion – even a metaphorical one – prowling about at *night* than *at the beginning of the winter season*. Tradition invariably has the capture of Troy take place during the night. Wilamowitz, followed by Mazon and Fraenkel, brought substantial support to this thesis by comparing [Sappho] fr. 52, Bergk: "the moon and the Pleiades have set, it is midnight [δέδυκε μὲν ἁ Σελάνα καὶ Πληιάδες, μέσαι δὲ νύκτες]."

65. Ἀργεῖον δάκος, ἵππου νεοσσός (823-4). Δάκος (cf. δάκνω, to bite) is used elsewhere by Aeschylus to describe the Sphinx which is portrayed upon Parthenopaeus' shield (the *Seven*, 558) and also sea monsters (*Prometheus*, 583).

66. *Agamemnon*, 827-8.

67. For the details of the text I refer the reader to the already mentioned articles by F.I. Zeitlin.

68. *Agamemnon*, 1093-4, 1184-5.

69. Cf. 1056, 1115-7 (the ritual cry), 1431 (the oaths). I do not agree with F.I. Zeitlin (*The Motif*..., p. 477) who thinks that these oaths refer to the past. Clytemnestra is fully aware of the momentous nature of the sacrilege she has just perpetrated since she even considers a supersacrilege – pouring a libation over the corpse, ἐπισπένδειν νεκρῷ (1395), which is not a part of the πρέποντα or accepted procedure, as she herself says. The expression must be understood with reference to the libations that were poured over the victim *before* its execution and also, no doubt, the libation that goes with victory: cf. D.W. Lucas, "Ἐπισπένδειν νεκρῷ, *Agamemnon*, 1393-8," *PCPhs* 195 (1969), pp. 60-8, with the essentials of whose thesis I am in agreement.

70. Images of the net and the hunting snare: for Cassandra, 1048, for Aga-

445

memnon, 1115, 1375, 1382 (fishing net), 1611. Does the theme of the net, the "garment of treachery" appear any earlier than Aeschylus? There is no literary text to provide an answer to this question. The iconographic documents are the subject of bitter controversy. E. Vermeule recently published a magnificent crater from the Boston Museum on which Clytemnestra is enveloping her husband in a sheet while Aegisthus kills him ("The Boston Oresteia Krater," *Amer. Journ. Arch.* 70 (1966), pp. 1-22; cf. H. Metzger, "Bulletin archéologique: Céramique," *REG* 81 (1968), pp. 165-6). In this article the crater is dated *after* the performance of the *Oresteia* (458), precisely on the basis of this silence on the part of the literary sources. Other authors, and in particular M.I. Davies who has just undertaken a reconsideration of the evidence ("Thoughts on the *Oresteia* before Aeschylus'," *BCH* 93 (1969), pp. 214-60), think they have found at least one earlier instance of evidence on a Gortyn pinax from the second quarter of the seventh century (figs. 9 and 10, pp. 228-9 in Davies' study). They think it represents the murder of Agamemnon. According to this interpretation Clytemnestra did the striking while Aegisthus held a net over the head of the king, but even the existence of this net appears to be in some doubt. As for the Boston crater, M.I. Davies dates it from the 470s basing his view in particular upon the fact that, unlike what happens in Aeschylus' play, here it is Aegisthus who plays the most important role (*loc. cit.*, p. 258).

71. Aegisthus, the cowardly lion: 1224; Aegisthus, the wolf companion of the lioness, 1258-9. According to the Greeks, the wolf was both treacherous and fierce, although slyness is certainly not what characterizes it in our own culture. "Überhaupt gilt er als ein schlaues Tier," as O. Keller rightly put it, *Thiere des classischen Alterthums...*, Innsbruck 1887, p. 162; cf. e.g., Aristotle, *H.A.*, I, 1, 488b where wolves are classified among animals which are at the same time "courageous, wild and sly [γενναῖα καὶ ἄγρια καὶ ἐπίβουλα]" and Aristophanes of Byzantium, *Epitome*, I, 11 (Lambros) "animals that are sly and resourceful such as the wolf [τὰ δὲ ἐπίβουλα καὶ ἐπιθετικὰ ὡς λύκος]." On the use of this cunning of the wolf in certain rites cf. L. Gernet, "Dolon le Loup," *Mélanges F. Cumont*, Brussels 1936, pp. 189-208, reprinted in *Anthropologie de la Grèce antique*, Paris 1968, pp. 154-72.

72. In Aeschylus, the famous expression "to the guilty the punishment [παθεῖν τὸν ἔρξαντα]," (*Agamemnon*, 1564) which the *Choephori* (313) uses again in the form of δράσαντι παθεῖν perhaps plays on the double meaning of ἔρδω, to accomplish and to sacrifice.

446

73. The father carries to his mouth the viscera of his children (1221): on the role of cut-up flesh and σπλάγχνα in the oath, cf. J. Rudhardt, *op. cit.*, p. 203.

74. βορά, the *nomen actionis* of βιβρώσκω (cf. P. Chantraine, *Dictionnaire Étymologique* s.v.) to devour, refers — strictly speaking — to the food of an animal. This word is only used of human food when men are reduced to the state of a savage or are compared to animals, cf. the examples collected by C.P. Segal, pp. 297-9 of his study, "Euripides, Hippolytus 108-112: Tragic Irony and Tragic Justice," *Hermes* 97 (1969), pp. 297-305. I do not know why Segal weakened his argument by writing (p. 297): "The noun βορά can be used of ordinary human food." The examples quoted in the notes certainly do not suggest this: Aeschylus, *Persians* (490) refers to the food for the Persian troops who are starving and so reduced to the state of animals; Sophocles, *Philoctetes* (274, 308), two splendid examples of the food of a man who has become a savage; Herodotus I, 119, 15, here we have a cannibal feast offered to Harpagus by Astyages. This example is parallel to that in the *Oresteia*; *ibid.*, II, 65, 15 concerns the food given to *animals* by the Egyptians; *ibid.*, III, 16, 15, fire is compared to a beast devouring its food; Euripides, *Orestes*, 189, the hero, having become mad, that is a savage, has not even any πόθον βορᾶς, which I would translate "the desire to satisfy the beast in him." There is just one example that might give rise to doubt: Sophocles, *Oedipus Rex*, 1463. This is in any case a difficult text that some scholars have suggested correcting and that has given rise to extremely varied interpretations (cf. J.C. Kamerbeek, *The Plays of Sophocles, IV, Commentary*, Leyden 1967, p. 262). Oedipus, having told Creon that his *sons*, being men, ran no risk of lacking what is necessary for life (τοῦ βίου), mentions his daughters, "for whom the table where I ate was never set without food and without my being present [αἶν οὔποθ' ἡμὴ χωρὶς ἐστάθη βορᾶς τράπεζ' ἄνευ τοῦδ' ἀνδρός]." Is not Oedipus here implicitly comparing his daughters to household animals eating the same food as himself? When, in the *Hippolytus*, 952, Theseus speaks of the ἄψυχου βορᾶς of his son, he is suggesting clearly that beneath his show of vegetarianism Hippolytus was cannibalistic and incestuous.

75. We shall bear in mind that Thyestes' children were roasted: cf. *Agamemnon* 1097.

76. *Agamemnon*, 232, 1415.

77. *Ibid.*, 896.

78. *Ibid.*, 607. The night watchman too is compared to a dog (3).

79. *Ibid.*, 1126.

80. Aristophanes, *Peace*, 960 and scholia; Porphyry, *De abstinentia* 2, 9 (Theophrastus); Plutarch, *Quaest. conviv.*, 8, 8, 279a ff.; *De defect. orac.*, 435b; *Sylloge*³, 1025, 20; cf. K. Meuli, *loc. cit.* p. 267. Of course, Agamemnon does not give his consent and he is struck three times (1384-6) whereas efforts were made to strike down the animal with a single blow and to do it painlessly (K. Meuli, *ibid.*, p. 268). J.-P. Guépin, *op. cit.*, p. 39, compares Agamemnon's murder to the sacrifice of the Bouphonia. This comparison seems indefensible to me. In the sacrifice of what was the domestic animal *par excellence* there is no suggestion at all of any preceding hunt.

81. In the messenger's speech images of hunting and those of sacrifice alternate, cf. lines 1108, 1114, 1142, 1146. I hope soon to devote a study to this double theme in the *Hippolytus* and the *Bacchae*.

82. *Bacchae*, 1188.

83. *Ibid.*, 1192.

84. *Agamemnon*, 1231.

85. Cf. A. Lesky, "Die *Orestie* des Aischylos," *Hermes* 66 (1931), pp. 190-214, esp. pp. 207-8.

86. A. Lebeck, "The first stasimon of Aeschylus' *Choephori*: Myth and Mirror Image," *CPh* 57 (1967), pp. 182-5.

87. F.I. Zeitlin, *The Motif...*, pp. 484-5.

88. *Choephori*, 385-8.

89. *Ibid.*, 935-6.

90. When the chorus sums up the dream of the Atreidae at the end of the play (1065-6) it mentions only three "storms": the murder of the children of Thyestes, the murder of Agamemnon, and the ambiguous murder of Clytemnestra.

91. *Choephori*, 106.

92. *Ibid.*, 255.

93. On the meaning of δυτήρ, more or less the equivalent of δύων, cf. J. Casabona, *op. cit.*, pp. 145-6.

94. *Choephori*, 261.

95. *Ibid.*, 345-54.

96. 492-3; Mazon translates "where you were prisoner" (*où tu fus prisonnier*) which does not render the image of the hunt; cf. *Eumenides* 460 and 627-8 where

Apollo explains that Clytemnestra did not even use the "long-range bow of the Amazonian warrior."

97. *Choephori*, 981.

98. *Ibid.*, 998.

99. *Ibid.*, 1015.

100. *Ibid.*, 1073-4.

101. Cf. my above mentioned book *The Black Hunter*, Baltimore 1986, pp. 106-128.

102. *Choephori*, 7.

103. *Ibid.*, 6.

104. On the offering of hair in general, cf. the evidence and bibliography collected by K. Meuli, *loc. cit.*, p. 205, n.1; on the way the ephebes' hair was cut, cf. J. Labarbe, "L'age correspondant au sacrifice du κούρειον et les données historiques du sixième discours d'Isée," *Bull. acad. roy. Belg.*, Cl. Lettres (1953), pp. 358-94.

105. 169 ff.; on the feminine aspects of the ephebe, cf. P. Vidal-Naquet *loc. cit.*, pp. 59-60.

106. *Choephori*, 232.

107. *Ibid.*, 576.

108. *Ibid.*, 461.

109. *Ibid.*, 556-7.

110. *Ibid.*, 888.

111. *Ibid.*, 726.

112. *Ibid.*, 946-7.

113. *Ibid.*, 948-51.

114. On the palintonos bow of the Scythians with its inverted curve, cf. A. Plassart, *REG* (1913), pp. 157-8 and A. Snodgrass, *Arms and Armours of the Greeks*, London 1967, p. 82; and the iconographic documentation collected by M.F. Vos, *Scythian Archers in Archaic Attic Vase Painting*, Gröningen 1963.

115. *Choephori*, 158-61.

116. On the opposition between the archer and the hoplite the basic text is Euripides, *Heracles*, 153-64. The evidence collected by M.F. Vos would make re-examination of the subject worthwhile. He interprets certain vases as an initiation to the hunt given to the ephebes by the Scythian archers (cf. p. 30). This interpretation would fit in well with my own ideas; see also Plate I.

117. *Choephori*, 955. On this and other similar expressions, cf. D. Fehling, "Νυκτὸς παῖδες ἄπαιδες. Eumenides 1034 und das sogennante Oxymoron in der Tragödie," *Hermes* 90, (1968-9), pp. 142-55, esp. p. 154.

118. *Choephori*, 421.

119. *Ibid.*, 527-34.

120. *Ibid.*, 549-50.

121. In the *Agamemnon* she was a lioness, a cow and, once only (1233), ἀμφίσβαινα, a serpent that can move both ways, and she is compared to Scylla. In his study, "The Serpent at the Breast," *TAPhA* 89 (1958), pp. 271-5, W.F. Whallon was well aware of this reversibility: "Clytemnestra and Orestes each assume the role of the serpent towards the other" (p. 273) but he did not draw out all the possible implications from his remark.

122. *Choephori*, 246-9.

123. *Ibid.*, 994.

124. *Ibid.*, 249-51.

125. Cf. F.I. Zeitlin, *The Motif...*, *loc. cit.*, p. 483. The fight between the eagle and the serpent where, as one hardly needs to point out, a noble animal is opposed to a creature classed with the "creatures that are not free and are sly [ἀνελεύθερα καὶ ἐπίβουλα]" (Aristotle, *H.A.*, I, 1, 488b) is a *topos* in Greek art and literature (cf. e.g., *Iliad* XII, 200-9, Aristotle, *ibid.*, IX, 1, 609a, and the facts collected by O. Keller, *op. cit.*, pp. 247-481) and it is to be found in many other cultures also; cf. the ambiguous diffusionist thesis of R. Wittkower, "Eagle and Serpent: A Study in the Migration of Symbols," *JWI* 2 (1939), pp. 293-325 (for the Greco-Roman world, see pp. 307-12); and from a different point of view, that of the "archetypes" of C.J. Jung, see M. Lurker, "Adler und Schlange," *Antaios* 5 (1963-4), pp. 344-52.

126. *Choephori*, 929.

127. *Ibid.*, 937-8.

128. *Ibid.*, 1047.

129. *Ibid.*, 1050.

130. *Eumenides*, 5.

131. *Ibid.*, 13-4.

132. *Ibid.*, 22-3.

133. *Ibid.*, 24.

134. This point was noticed by J.-P. Guépin, *op. cit.*, p. 24.

135. *Eumenides*, 25-6.

136. *Ibid.*, 111-2.

137. *Ibid.*, 252.

138. *Ibid.*, 327-8.

139. For instance ἐπιρροιζεῖν in line 424, the exact meaning of which is: to give the cry which lets the hounds loose.

140. *Eumenides*, 231.

141. *Ibid.*, 128.

142. *Ibid.*, 132.

143. Cf. F.I. Zeitlin, *The Motif...*, p. 486.

144. *Eumenides*, 68-70.

145. *Ibid.*, 416.

146. *Ibid.*, 351, 370.

147. *Ibid.*, 832.

148. *Ibid.*, 181-3.

149. ἐλείξατε (106): "lapped," rather than "sniffed at" (humé: Mazon), just as in *Agamemnon*, 828.

150. *Eumenides*, 106-9.

151. On this idea, cf. K. Meuli, *loc. cit.*, pp. 201-10.

152. But in Euripides, *Bacchae* 143, the wine flows from the ground and the long speech of the messenger emphasizes the sobriety of the three *thiasoi* on Cithaeron: "and not, as you say, drunk on wine [οὐχ ὡς σὺ φὴς ᾠνωμένας]" (686-7).

153. *Eumenides*, 304-5.

154. *Choephori*, 92.

155. *Eumenides*, 1006.

156. *Ibid.*, 1037.

157. *Ibid.*, 835.

158. *Ibid.*, 907-9; cf. also lines 937-48.

159. *Ibid.*, 855.

160. *Ibid.*, 911.

161. *Ibid.*, 910.

162. Cf. lines 525-6 and 696.

163. *Eumenides*, 691.

164. *Ibid.*, 940-1.

165. *Ibid.*, 859-60.

166. *Ibid.*, 866. P. Mazon's translation the sense of which was "fie on the fighting between birds of the same aviary [fi des combats entre oiseaux de la volière]" does not seem quite correct to me. This image can be compared with that used by Danaus in the *Suppliants* (226) to express the prohibition of incest: "Can the bird that eats the flesh of another bird remain pure [ὄρνιθος ὄρνις πῶς ἄν ἀγνεύοι φαγών]?"

CHAPTER VII

1. An earlier version of this chapter appeared in *Annales E.S.C.* (1971), pp. 623-38.

2. *The Black Hunter*, Baltimore 1986, pp. 106-128. I refer the reader to these pages for all the details of the argument and shall here do no more than summarize the principal conclusions reached.

3. Literature on the subject has for many years been dominated by H. Jeanmaire's book, *Couroi et Courètes*, Lille and Paris 1939. More recently A. Brelich has produced a synthesis, *Paides e Parthenoi*, Rome 1969; on this last work see C. Calame, "Philologie et anthropologie structurale: À propos d'un livre récent d'Angelo Brelich," *QUCC* II (1971), pp. 7-47, and C. Sourvinou, *JHS* 91 (1971), pp. 172-7.

4. On hunting in Greek initiations, see now A. Brelich, *op. cit.*, pp. 175, 198-9.

5. *Lysistrata*, 783-92.

6. The ancient sources are strictly contradictory. Lycurgus, whose testimony is clearly the most direct but is only relevant to his own time, mentions the oath taken "by all the citizens when they are inscribed on the register of the deme and become ephebes." (*Against Leocrates*, 76). A gloss on Ulpian (*Schol. ad Demosth. ambass.* 438, 17 in *Oratores Attici*, Didot. II, p. 637) does likewise. Pollux, on the other hand (8, 105, s.v. περίπολοι) locates at the *end* of the ephebe period of service both the inscription in the deme register (which is clearly incorrect) and the oath. C. Pelekidis (*Histoire de l'éphébie attique*, Paris 1962, p. 111) is inclined to follow Lycurgus. However, the word περίπολοι used to refer both to the ephebes and to soldiers belonging to the scout corps (Pelikidis, *op. cit.*, pp. 35-47) is attested at a much earlier date than the word ἔφηβοι and it is not altogether out of the question that Pollux might be depending on a more ancient source than that of Lycurgus.

7. I am indebted for my understanding of this distinction of capital importance, to the teaching of L. Robert at the École des Hautes Études (1963-4).

8. For a summary of this evolution, cf. my study, "La tradition de l'hoplite athénien," J.-P. Vernant ed., *Problèmes de la guerre en Grèce ancienne*, Paris and The Hague, 1968, pp. 161-81, esp. pp. 174-9. On the work of Xenophon as a witness of this evolution, cf. A. Schnapp's contribution to M.I. Finley's (Ed.) *Problèmes de la terre en Grèce ancienne*, 1972.

9. The fullest general study of the tradition remains that of L.A. Milani, *Il mito di Filottete nella letteratura classica e nell' arte figurativa*, Florence 1879, completed by the author under the title of "nuovi monumenti di Filottete e considerazioni generali in proposito," *Ann. Inst. Corr. Arch.* 53 (1881), pp. 249-89; see also Turk in Roscher, *Lexicon*, s.v. "Philoktet" (1898), pp. 2311-43, Fiehn, *R.E.* s.v. "Philoktetes" (1938), col. 2500-9. The iconographic evidence has increased since this work appeared but has as yet been the subject of no overall study; for a recent bibliography cf. M. Taddei, "Il mito di Filottete ed un episodio della vita del Buddha," *Archeologia Classica* (1963), p. 198-218, see p. 202, n.17. On the problems raised by a vase from the museum of Syracuse, cf. *supra* fig. 3 and the appendix.

10. Summary of the *Little Iliad* in A. Severyns, *Recherches sur la Chrestomathie de Proclus*, IV, Paris 1963, p. 83, 1.217-8: for the *Cypria*, see *ibid.*, p. 89, 1.144-6.

11. The three tragedies are summarized and compared in Dio Chrysostomus 52 and 59. Sophocles' originality, as compared both with his predecessors and with the mythical tradition is correctly analyzed by E. Schlesinger, "Die Intrige im Aufbau von Sophokles' Philoktet," *Rheinisches Museum*, N.F. 111 (1968), pp. 97-156 (esp. pp 97-109). On the trilogy of which Aeschylus' *Philoctetes* was a part, cf. F. Jouan, "Le 'Tennés' (?) d'Eschyle et la légende de Philoctète," *Les Etudes Classiques*, 32 (1964), pp. 3-9; on Euripides' *Philoctetes*, F. Jouan, *Euripide et les légendes des chants cypriens*, Paris 1966, pp. 308-17, and also T.B.L. Webster's study based, sometimes questionably, on a comparison with the pictorial evidence, *The Tragedies of Euripides*, London 1967, pp. 57-61.

12. According to the *Little Iliad*, *loc. cit.*

13. "The most political and rhetorical [Πολιτικωτάτη καὶ ῥητορικωτάτη οὖσα]" (of the three), according to Dio, 52, 11.

14. *Philoctetes*, 221. Cf. also lines 300-4 in which the island as a whole is described as a repulsive environment, and line 692: "No native approached any-

where near his wretchedness." This English translation is based on the French translation (slightly modified) by P. Mazon (collection Guillaume Budé), the text being that of A. Dain (*ibid.*); I have, however, taken note of the latest critical emendation to the manuscript tradition carried out by P.E. Easterling, "Sophocles' *Philoctetes*: Collations of the manuscripts G, R and Q," *CQ* n.s. 19 (1969), pp. 57-85.

15. With the exception of the figure of Philoctetes himself, Sophocles makes virtually no use of the extremely rich mythology linked with the island of Lemnos, in which G. Dumézil has detected a transposition of the rituals of initiation (*Le crime des Lemniennes*, Paris 1924). The only allusions are those the hero makes to the "fire of Lemnos," that is to say the fire of Hephaestos, the lame god who fell to earth on the island (800, 986-7). Marcel Detienne has suggested to me that a comparison between Sophocles' play and the "Lemnian" myths might prove fruitful; see his book *The Gardens of Adonis*, Hassocks 1977, pp. 94-7, and W. Burkert, "Jason, Hypsipyle and New Fire at Lemnos: A Study in Myth and Ritual," *CQ*, n.ś. 20 (1970), pp. 1-16.

16. *Pyth.* 1, 53.

17. Sophocles refers to this tradition in lines 591-2 in words spoken by the "merchant," that is to say the scout (σκοπός, 125) who belongs to the Greek expedition and whom Odysseus has disguised. It is not known whether or not Odysseus was accompanied in Aeschylus' play. It seems more probable that he was not.

18. The essential information on the recent bibliography can be found in H.F. Johansen, *Lustrum* 7 (1962), pp. 247-55; see also H. Musurillo, *The Light and the Darkness, Studies in the Dramatic Poetry of Sophocles*, Leyden 1967, pp. 109-29; A.E. Hinds, "The Prophecy of Helenus in Sophocles' *Philoctetes*," *CQ*, h.r. 17 (1967), pp. 169-80; E. Schlesinger, *op. cit. supra* n.11. The fullest study on the play is the dissertation by C.J. Fuqua, *The Thematic Structures of Sophocles' Philoctetes*, Cornell 1964, a microfilm of which I have been able to consult. A comic note in this bibliography is provided by I. Errandonea, *Sofocles, Investigaciones sobre la estrutura dramatica de sus siete tragedias y sobre la personalidad de sus coros*, Madrid 1958, pp. 233-302, who imagines, for example that the "merchant" and Heracles are none other than Odysseus in disguise. It was only after completing the present study that I was able to consult two recent publications, the edition with a brief commentary by T.B.L. Webster, Cambridge 1970,

which tackles hardly any of the problems considered here, and the posthumous work by R. von Scheliha, *Der* Philoktet *des Sophocles. Ein Beitrag zur Interpretation des Griechischen Ethos*, Amsterdam 1970.

19. A. Spira, *Untersuchungen zum Deus ex machina bei Sophokles und Euripides*, Frankfurt 1960, pp. 12-32, has nevertheless shown that this ending was strictly adapted to the structure of the play.

20. See the two opposed studies of, on the one hand, C.M. Bowra, *Sophoclean Tragedy*, Oxford 1944, pp. 261-306 which, in the main with reason, defends the first thesis and, on the other, H.D. Kitto, *Form and Meaning in Drama*, London 1956, pp. 87-138.

21. This change is expressed in line 1270 by the word μεταγνῶναι which ultimately comes to denote the Christian idea of repentence, thus almost inevitably giving rise to confusion.

22. *Philoctetes*, 895 ff.

23. *Ibid.*, 1286.

24. *Ibid.*, 1402.

25. The best general study is that of B.W. Knox, *The Heroic Temper, Studies in Sophoclean Tragedy*, Cambridge, Mass. 1964 (on the *Philoctetes*, see pp. 117-42); see also, by the same author, "Second Thoughts in Greek Tragedy," *GRBS* 7 (1966), pp. 213-32.

26. Thus, on 2 October 1921 Judge Holmes wrote the following revealing remarks to F. Pollock: "A propos of the rare occasions *when the Ancients seem just like us*, it always has seemed to me that a wonderful example was the *repentance* of the lad in the play of Sophocles over his deceit, and the restoration of the bow," cited by E. Wilson, *The Wound and the Bow*, London 1961, p. 246 n.1. The italics are mine. It goes without saying that, although they may express themselves rather more elaborately, plenty of modern authors, whom there seems no point in mentioning by name, are of the same opinion.

27. Tycho von Wilamowitz-Moellendorf, "Die dramatische Technik des Sophokles," *Philol. Untersuch.* 22 (1917); on the *Philoctetes* see pp. 269-312. Against "psychological" interpretations, cf. e.g., C. Garton, "Characterisation in Greek Tragedy," *JHS* (1957), pp. 247-254; K. Alt, "Schicksal und φύσις im Philoktet des Sophokles," *Hermes* 89 (1961), pp. 141-74.

28. Here is an example of the kind of explanation that a "theatrical view" can offer: in line 114, Neoptolemus appears "to be unaware" that, according to

the oracle, both the bow *and* Philoctetes in person are necessary if Troy is to be taken and this allows Odysseus to remind the audience of it; but lines 197-200 shows that Achilles' son was in reality perfectly well aware of the fact. In such a situation it is permissible to make a distinction between the "dramatic character" and the "hero," but the results of this type of inquiry are bound to be fairly limited. In any case, whatever liberties the Greek poets may have taken with the myths, they did not, for example, go so far as to imagine that the Trojan War had not taken place and I find it impossible to go along with D.B. Robinson when he tries to have us believe that the Athenian spectator might think that Philoctetes might really be abandoned at the end of the play. ("Topics in Sophocles' *Philoctetes*," *CQ*, n.s. 19 (1969), pp. 34-56; see pp. 45-51). This is to take Tycho von Wilamowitz's line of investigation much too far. The same article quite mistakenly suggests a double ending for the *Philoctetes*; cf. *contra, infra*, pp. 173-4.

29. Cf. B. Knox, *The Heroic Temper*, pp. 36-8.

30. J. Jones, *Aristotle and Greek Tragedy*, Oxford 1962, p. 219.

31. *Philoctetes*, 144.

32. *Ibid.*, 228, 265, 269, 471, 487, 1018.

33. *Ibid.*, 5. As P. Rousseau reminds me, only a father had the right to *expose* a newborn child.

34. J.-P. Vernant, *Myth and Thought among the Greeks*, Boston 1983, p. 155. The image of exposure reappears in lines 702-3 where Philoctetes is described as "a child abandoned by its nurse."

35. *Op. cit.*, p. 217. W. Schadewaldt, on the other hand, wrote in 1941: "Philoctetes lives like a Robinson Crusoe of the ancient world on the desert island of Lemnos," *Hellas und Hesperien*, p. 238.

36. *Philoctetes*, 213-4.

37. The text stresses the setting and décor: "When the terrifying wayfarer emerges from these halls [ὁπόταν δὲ μόλῃ δεινὸς ὁδίτης τῶνδ᾽ ἐκ μελάθρων]" (146-7). The comma that most editors introduce following ὁδίτης should be eliminated; cf. A.M. Dale, "Seen and Unseen in Scenic Conventions," *WS* 59 (1956), *Mélanges A. Lesky*, pp. 96-106 (see p. 105); the conclusions reached in this remarkable study seem to me in no way brought into question by the objections of D.B. Robinson, *loc. cit. supra*, n.27, pp. 45-51.

38. Cf. A. Cook, "The Patterning of Effect in Sophocles' *Philoctetes*,"

Arethusa (1968), pp. 82-93, whose psychoanalytic remarks I nevertheless am not here following.

39. *Philoctetes*, 708-15. At line 709, Sophocles uses the word ἀλφησταί that in Homer means "eaters of bread," that is to say, simply, men. On the meaning of the word, cf. my study "Valeurs religieuses de la terre et du sacrifice dans l'Odysée," *Annales E.S.C.* (1970), p. 1280 n.3.

40. *Philoctetes*, 171.

41. *Ibid.*, 497. Heracles later tells him (1430) that in reality he is alive.

42. *Ibid.*, 1018.

43. *Ibid.*, 8-9.

44. *Ibid.*, 1032-3.

45. *Ibid.*, 226. Cf. also, in line 1321, ἠγρίωσαι ("you have made a savage of me").

46. His dwelling place is an animal's lair, αὔλιον (954, 1087, 1149); his food is pasturage, βορά (274); see on this word my note *supra*, Ch. 6, n.74; he does not eat, but feeds (βόσκων, 313).

47. H.C. Avery, "Heracles, Philoctetes, Neoptolemus," *Hermes* 93 (1965), pp. 279-97; the expression cited is on p. 284. This "relationship" is confirmed by the hero himself: "Oh beasts of the mountains, my companions [ὦ ξυνουσίαι θηρῶν ὀρείων]" (936-7); cf. also lines 183-5.

48. Cf. lines 173, 265-6 (ἀγρίᾳ νόσῳ), and line 758 where, as the scholiast correctly realized, the wound is compared to a wild beast that now approaches, now moves away; Philoctetes' foot is ἔνθηρος, has become wild (697); cf. P. Biggs, "The Disease Theme in Sophocles," *CPh* (1966), pp. 223-5.

49. *Philoctetes*, 35-6.

50. *Ibid.*, 297.

51. *Ibid.*, 164-6. Cf. also lines 286-9, 710-1, 1092-4. The importance of the images and themes of hunting has been pointed out in the dissertation by C.J. Fuqua, *cit. supra.*

52. θανὼν παρέξω δαῖθ' ὑφ' ὧν ἐφερβόμην (957). The vocabulary is characteristic: The word δαίς normally means a human meal as opposed to βορά; it is only very rarely used to refer to animals' food (*Iliad*, 24, 43); the word φέρβω, on the other hand, is generally used to refer to animals. So Sophocles has reversed the meanings of the two words.

53. *Philoctetes*, 955-8. Cf. also the invocation to predatory beasts in lines 1146-57.

54. *Ibid.*, 105.

55. On this complementarity in the mythical tradition, see for example A. Brelich, *Gli Eroi Greci*, 1958, p. 244; "Les Monosandales," *Nouvelle Clio* 7-8-9 (1955-6-7), pp. 469-89; on the *Philoctetes*, cf. E. Wilson, *The Wound and the Bow*, pp. 244-64; W. Harsh, "The Role of the Bow in the *Philoctetes* of Sophocles," *American Journal of Philology* 81 (1960), pp. 408-14; P. Biggs, *loc. cit. supra*, pp. 231-5; H. Musurillo, *op. cit.*, p. 121.

56. βιός: τῶι οὖν τόξωι ὄνομα βίος ἔργον δὲ θάνατος ("The name of the bow is life, its work is death") (fr. 48, Diels). For other comparisons between the *Philoctetes* and the fragments of Heraclitus, cf. K. Reinhardt, *Sophokles*[3], Frankfurt 1947, p. 212.

57. *Philoctetes*, 931.

58. A version known by Servius, *Ad Aeneid*, 3, 402.

59. *Philoctetes*, 1327-8. So it is quite incorrect to make him totally innocent as does, for example, H. Kitto, *Form and Meaning*, p. 135; furthermore the "guilt" of Philoctetes is stressed by the chorus who compare his fate to that of Ixion, the perpetrator of an attempted rape of Hera (676-85).

60. *Heracles*, 153-64.

61. *Ibid.*, 162.

62. *Ibid.*, 162-4.

63. *Philoctetes*, 266-7. It is, in my view, quite ridiculous to try to identify exactly what species of animal bit Philoctetes, as H. Musurillo persists in doing (*op. cit.*, p. 119, n.1).

64. *Philoctetes*, 860.

65. *Ibid.*, 797-8, 1030, 1204-17.

66. *Ibid.*, 1018.

67. *Ibid.*, 946-7.

68. As has been shown by W. Schadewaldt in his well-known study, "Sophokles und das Leid," 1941, reprinted in *Hellas und Hesperien*, Zurich and Stuttgart 1960, pp. 231-47. The point is that all Sophocles' heroes are extreme cases, a remark that can be applied to many other features besides their "suffering."

69. *Loc. cit. supra*, p. 285.

70. *Philoctetes*, 1423.

71. I do not think that this suggestion has ever been made before although a number of commentators have noted the mutation of Neoptolemus without

referring to the ephebeia, e.g., M. Pohlenz, "Der Jüngling Neoptolemos reift zum Manne heran," *Die griechische Tragödie*[2], Göttingen 1964, p. 334; H. Weinstock, *Sophokles*, Leipzig and Berlin 1931, p. 79 ff.; B.W. Knox, *The Heroic Temper*, p. 141: "He has grown to manhood in the fire of his ordeal and though before he was Odysseus' subordinate, now he is to be Philoctetes' equal." The word "ephebe" has been used, but apparently accidently, by K.I. Vourveris, Σοφοκλέους Φιλοκτήτης, Athens 1963, p. 34; this author does little more than repeat Weinstock's remarks about the *Philoctetes* being a tragedy about education.

72. *Philoctetes*, 3-4.

73. *Ibid.*, 141-2.

74. *Ibid.*, 6.

75. Cf. the use of the verb ὑπηρετεῖν (to serve) in line 15 and that of the noun ὑπηρέτης (53).

76. *The Heroic Temper*, p. 122.

77. *Philoctetes*, 62-4.

78. *Ibid.*, 1364.

79. *Ibid.*, 72.

80. *Ibid.*, 813.

81. Here again the vocabulary used is characteristic: cf. the use of the words ἀπάτη (1136, 1228), δόλος, δόλιος (91, 107, 608, 1118, 1228, 1282), τέχνη, τεχνᾶσθαι (80, 88), κλέπτειν (55, 968).

82. Odysseus sends a man "to lie in ambush [εἰς κατασκοπήν]" (45).

83. *Philoctetes*, 116.

84. *Ibid.*, 839-40.

85. *Ibid.*, 1005-7.

86. *Ibid.*, 54-5.

87. *Ibid.*, 54-95.

88. *Ibid.*, 130. This theme of the role of language in the *Philoctetes* deserves to be elaborated; cf. A. Podlecki's study "The Power of the Word in Sophocles' *Philoctetes*," *GRBS* 7 (1966), pp. 233-50.

89. *Philoctetes*, 925.

90. I am indebted to F. Jouan for this expression.

91. *Philoctetes*, 82-5.

92. J. Pouilloux has shown that this tradition, attested explicitly by Lucian, *De saltatione*, 11, had already been referred to implicitly by Euripides, *Andro-*

mache, 1135: J. Pouilloux and G. Roux, *Enigmes à Delphes*, Paris 1963, p. 117.

93. *Philoctetes*, 997.

94. This is mentioned in the speech of the pseudo-Merchant (603-21) as well as in Neoptolemus' last attempt to convince Philoctetes to accompany him (1332).

95. As B.W. Knox correctly perceived: "In fact, Odysseus repeatedly and exclusively emphasizes one thing and one thing only — the bow." (*The Heroic Temper*, p. 126); cf. lines 68, 113-5, 975-83, 1055-62.

96. *Philoctetes*, 1055-62.

97. Thus σόφισμα (14), σοφισθῆναι (77), τεχνᾶσθαι (80).

98. Having said this, there seems to me to be little point in seeking for "keys" to the characters of Sophocles. It is a little game that many have indulged in ever since the eighteenth century. Alcibiades, first sent into exile and recalled, has for instance been assimilated to Philoctetes; cf. most recently, M.H. Jameson, "Politics and the *Philoctetes*," *CPh* 51 (1956), pp. 217-27.

99. *Philoctetes*, 133-4.

100. *Ibid.*, 562. Sophocles may here be alluding to his tragedy the *Skyrioi* in which, it has been suggested, the sons of Theseus set off in search of Neoptolemus on his island (cf. T. Zielinski, *Tragodumenon libri tres*, Cracow 1925, pp. 108-12, and for a representation of this same scene on a vase, C. Dugas, "L'Ambassade à Skyros," *BCH*, 1934, pp. 281-90).

101. *Ibid.*, 1257.

102. *Antigone*, 370; cf. H. Funke "Κρέων ἄπολις," *Antike und Abendland*, 12 (1966), pp. 29-50.

103. *Philoctetes*, 99-130.

104. K. Reinhardt (*op. cit. supra*, p. 176) correctly compares the relationship between Odysseus and Neoptolemus with that between Creon and his son Haemon, in the *Antigone*.

105. *Philoctetes*, 950.

106. *Ibid.*, 902.

107. *Ibid.*, 1063, 1350.

108. *Ibid.*, 1368; the expression is repeated at line 1399.

109. *Op. cit. supra*, p. 280.

110. *Philoctetes*, 725.

111. *Ibid.*, 453, 479, 490, 664, 728, 1430.

112. As has been correctly perceived by H.C. Avery in his article *op. cit. supra* in *Hermes* (1965).

113. *Philoctetes*, 726.

114. On this point Bowra is probably right as opposed to Kitto, cf. *supra* n.20.

115. *Philoctetes*, 220-31.

116. *Ibid.*, 919-20, 1376-9.

117. Μονομαχήσας Ἀλεξάνδρῳ κτείνει according to the resumé of the *Little Iliad* (*loc. cit. supra*, n.10).

118. *Philoctetes*, 1423-6.

119. *Ibid.*, 1429 (ἀριστεῖ᾽ ἐκλαβῶν στρατεύματος).

120. *Ibid.*, 1432 (τόξων ἐμῶν μνημεῖα).

121. *Ibid.*, 1428-33.

122. *Ibid.*, 115.

123. *Ibid.*, 1434-5.

124. ξύννομος may refer to a military fellowship, cf. Aeschylus, *Seven*, 354. We should also note the use of the dual that emphasizes the theme of solidarity.

125. *Philoctetes*, 1436-7.

126. *Ibid.*, 534.

127. This nuance is not altogether grasped by C. Segal who, in his otherwise excellent article ("Nature and the World of Man in Greek Literature," *Arion* 2, 1 (1963), pp. 19-57) writes: "His final words are not a welcoming of the human world but a last farewell to the wildness in which he has suffered, but there is a tie between it and the man."

128. Or rather, to be more precise, μέλαθρον, palace, but here the word does not have the same meaning (both ironic and descriptive of the décor) as in line 147; cf. *supra*, n.37.

129. *Philoctetes*, 1452-61.

130. *Ibid.*, 1464-5.

131. The wish εὔπλοια echoes the one (with a double meaning) voiced by Neoptolemus when his trick succeeded (779-81).

132. Cf. A.D. Trendall, *Paestan Pottery. A Study of the Red-Figured Vases of Paestum*, Rome 1936, pp. 7-18, no. 7.

133. Cf. B. Pace, "Filottete a Lemno, Pittura vascolare con riflessi dell' arte di Parrasio," *Ausonia* 10 (1921), pp. 150-9, and by the same author, "Vasi figurati

con riflessi della Pittura di Parrasio," *Mon. Ant. Accad. Linc.* 28 (1922), pp. 522-98 (esp. pp. 542-50). Our vase has been catalogued by F. Brommer, *Vasenlisten zur griechischen Heldensage²*, Marburg 1960, p. 329.

134. I am here drawing on P.E. Arias' commentary in the fascicle of *Corpus Vasorum Antiquorum (C.V.A.)*, Rome 1941.

135. The first hypothesis is that of B. Pace; L. Séchan (*Etudes sur la tragédie grecque dans ses rapports avec la céramique*, Paris 1926, p. 491) has pointed out that "the image, with its suggestion of youthfulness, puts one in mind, rather, of Sophocles' Neoptolemus." It is not a decisive argument as we also know of another bell-shaped crater from the same necropolis and by the same painter (Trendall, *Red-Figure Vases...*, Campanian I, no. 31, p. 204, Pl. 80-2) that indisputably represents the capture of Dolon by Odysseus and Diomedes, where the latter is depicted as a beardless, naked ephebe (cf. C. Picard, *Comptes rendus de l'Académie des inscriptions et belles-lettres*, 1942, pp. 244-6). Speaking generally, as one not an expert on such matters, I can only, once again, marvel at the audacity and conviction with which certain specialists resolve questions of the utmost delicacy arising from problems such as the connections between the theater and graphic representations. It is, for example, impossible not to be astonished when one reads in M. Beiber, *The History of the Greek and Roman Theater²*, Princeton 1961, p. 34 and fig. 119: "Vase paintings based upon stage setting for Sophocles' *Philoctetes* have only a large rock and a single tree as a setting, while those for Euripides' *Philoctetes* represent a large cave around the hero. The vases testify that Euripides had a chorus of women and used Athena as *deus ex machina* instead of Heracles who was used by Sophocles." The author forgets (1) that not only in Euripides' play but also in that of Sophocles, the hero lives in a cave; (2) that artists had other sources besides the classical theater; (3) that the young girl on the Syracuse vase in no way represents a chorus; (4) that there is no justification for making Athena the *deus ex machina* in Euripides' play unless our vase is indeed a reflection of the play, which is no more than a possibility. T.B.L. Webster does not endorse it and I am inclined to agree with him. Unfortunately, however, his argument, which runs as follows, "We should have to make the audacious supposition that the young man is Odysseus rejuvenated by Athena," is unconvincing since the point is that Odysseus was accompanied by Diomedes. Strangely enough, in a book reprinted in the same year, Webster himself does put forward this very supposition, audacious as it is, and has no hesitation in

declaring the vase to be an illustration of Euripides (*Monuments Illustrating Tragedy and Satyr Play*, London 1967, p. 162).

136. The commentary of the *C.V.A.* rightly emphasizes the oratorical nature of Athena's gesture.

137. "Questions de céramique italiote," *Revue archéologique* 33 (1931), p. 248.

138. B. Pace proposed that we should see her as a nymph, personifying the island or alternatively the goddess Bendis, but it is difficult to see what relevance such a Thracian goddess would have here. L. Séchan, dismissing both these hypotheses and also the idea that the female figure might be Peitho (Aphrodite's companion), believes rather that she represents the character of a seductress taken from a play that is unknown to us. Finally S. Setti, in a recent commentary on the vase in question ("Contributo esegetico a un vaso 'pestano,' " *Dioniso* 38 (1964), pp. 214-20), takes up Pace's first hypothesis and suggests that the girl is a nymph and that the myth, the girl and the vase all have a funerary significance. His arguments are rather weak. In particular, if we had to attribute some chthonic and funerary significance to all scenes depicted on vases discovered in tombs, as Setti appears to wish, this would entail a serious reassessment of all that we know of Greek mythology. Setti sees in this no contradiction with his general thesis and he too goes on to associate the Syracuse vase with Euripides' play, although the latter is most unlikely to have been at all funerary in character. Whatever the truth of the matter may be, it is too much to hope that the literary and iconographic traditions should coincide perfectly. For instance, a piece of evidence discovered at the time of the excavations at Castro (Etruria) associated, in connection with the island of Lemnos, Philoctetes, Palamades, and Hermes — an association for which there had been no evidence at all up until that point (cf. R. Lambrechts, "Un miroir étrusque inédit et le mythe de Philoctète," *Bulletin de l'Institut Historique de Rome* 39 (1968), pp. 1-25). The artist of this mirror fortunately provided us with some information by inscribing the name of Palamedes, without which we should have been quite unable to identify him. For my own part, I have not ventured to put forward a name for the female figure. However, I should like to note that Mlle F.H. Pairault, a member of the French School at Rome, who has herself worked on the Syracuse vase and has read a draft of this note, tells me that personally she is very much in agreement with me and would feel no hesitation in identifying the unknown figure as *Apatē*. She writes: "The vases of Magna Graecia depict many

female figures, *daimons* and *victories* who are often unidentified, and in many cases they represent personified abstractions." The figure of *Apatē* is depicted and named on a well-known vase more or less contemporaneous with the vase of Syracuse. It is the fluted crater discovered at Canusium (Apulia) which is known as the "vase of Darius" (Museum of Naples 3252; cf. M. Borda, *Ceramiche Apule*, Bergamo 1966, p. 49 and Pl. 14). Her costume and effects (a panther's skin and a torch held in each hand) are quite different from those of the female figure we are interested in but then the style (which is historico-tragic) of the painter is equally very different. See also on the vase of Darius, C. Anti, "Il vaso di Dario ed i Persiani di Frinico," *Archeologia Classica* 4, 1 (1952), pp. 23-45 (on *Apatē*, p. 27). The article *Apatē* in the *Enciclopedia dell' arte classica*, 1, p. 456 and fig. 625 by G. Bermond Montari gives only one other and very much earlier example in Attic painting.

139. I am indebted to Maud Sissung for this suggestion.

140. On the "feminine" aspects of the ephebe, cf. Ch. 6, n.105.

CHAPTER VIII

*An earlier version of this text appeared in *Comédie française* 98 (April 1981), pp. 23-8.

1. Plutarch, *Quaestionum convivalium*, I, 1, 5 (615a).

2. Aristotle, *Poetics*, 1449a 11.

3. *Ibid.*, 1449a 15.

4. *Ibid.*, 1449a 20-5.

5. René Girard, *Violence and the Sacred*, Baltimore 1977.

6. *Infra*, p. 244.

CHAPTER IX

*This study, written in collaboration with F. Frontisi-Ducroux, was first published in the *Journal de psychologie* 1/2 (1983), pp. 53-69. F. Frontisi-Ducroux has pursued her research on the mask in a thesis for a doctoral d'État submitted in Paris, on December 5, 1987. We should like to thank F. Lissarrague, who is responsible for the drawings illustrating this study.

1. Cf. E.E. Bell, "Two Krokotos Mask Cups at San Simeon," *CSCA* 10 (1977), pp. 1-15.

2. Cup FN, Cambridge GB, Fitzwilliam Museum, 61; J. Beazley, ABV 202, 2.

3. *Iliad*, V, 738; VIII, 349.

4. *Iliad*, V, 738 ff.; cf. G.H. Chase, *The Shield Devices of the Greeks*, Cambridge, Mass. 1902.

5. Pindar, *Pythian*, XII, 12-42.

6. Aristotle, *Politics*, 1342b ff.; Apollodorus, I, 4, 2; Athenaeus, XIV, 616e-f; Plutarch, *Moralia* 456b ff.

7. Plato, *Laws*, VII, 790c-791b; Iamblichus, *De mysteriis* 3, 9. Cf. the analysis by J.-P. Vernant, *La mort dans les yeux*, Paris 1985, pp. 55-63.

8. *Odyssey*, XI, 633-5.

9. *Odyssey*, X, 521, 536; XI, 29, 49.

10. Terra cotta metope from the Athenaion of Syracuse (c. 620-610); Boeotian amphora with reliefs (early seventh century; Louvre); cf. K. Schefold, *Frügriechische Sagenbilder*, Munich 1964, Pl. II and 156.

11. Hesiod, *Theogony*, 280-81.

12. Apollodorus, II, 3, 4; Ovid, *Metamorphoses*, IV, 795 ff.

13. Euripides, *Heracles*, 931 ff.

14. Clement of Alexandria, *Protrepticus*, II, 21; Arnobius of Sicca, *Adversus nationes*, V, 25, p. 196, 3 Rieff (Kern fr. 52 and 53). Maurice Olender has been working on the subject of Baubo for several years and will soon be submitting the results of his research in a thesis for a doctorat d'État.

15. Cf. J. Raeder, *Priene. Funde aus einer griechischen Stadt*, Berlin 1983, Fig. 23 a-b-c.

16. Cf. T.G. Karagiorga, *Gorgeiè Kephalé*, Athens 1970.

17. On the various aspects of Artemis mentioned here, cf. J.-P. Vernant, *Annuaire du Collège de France* (1980-1), pp. 391-405; (1981-2), pp. 408-19; (1982-3), pp. 443-57; *La mort dans les yeux*, pp. 15-24; F. Frontisi-Ducroux, "Artémis Bucolique," *RHR* CXCVIII, 1 (1981), pp. 29-56; and the collection *Recherches sur les cultes grecs et l'Occident, 2, Cahiers du Centre Jean Bérard*, Naples 1984.

18. Cf. L. Kahil, "L'Artémis de Brauron: rites et mystères," *Antike Kunst* 20 (1977), pp. 86-98.

19. Xenophon, *Constitution of the Lacedaemonians*, III, 5.

20. R.M. Dawkins, *The Sanctuary of Artemis Orthia at Sparta*, London 1929, in particular Ch. V and Pl. XLVI-LXII.

21. W. Wrede, "Der Maskengott," *Athenische Mitteilingen*, Berlin 1928, pp. 67-98, Pl. XXI-XXVII.

22. Cf. *infra*, Ch. 17.

23. Euripides, *Bacchae*, 470.

24. Florence, Mus. Arch., 4209; cf. K. Schefold, *op. cit.*, Pl. 46.

25. Cf. J.-L. Durand and F. Frontisi-Ducroux, "Idoles, figures, images: autour de Dionysos," *RA* 1 (1982), pp. 81-108.

26. Cf. "Au miroir du masque," in *La cité des images*, collective work, Paris-Lausanne 1984, p. 147 ff.

27. Plutarch, *Lycurgus*, 24, 4.

CHAPTER X

*This study was first published in *Le temps de la réflexion* II (1981), pp. 235-55.

1. *Structural Anthropology* I, London 1968, pp. 206-32.

2. In the Greek myths of autochthony, men "born from the earth" are not, as such, affected by any peculiarities of gait or in their feet. In the particular case of Thebes, the *Spartoi* – that is to say, the "sown ones," who spring directly from the soil and whose descendants intermarry with the Labdacid lineage in the royal legend of the town – certainly bear the mark of their origin on their bodies, but it has nothing to do with feet. The mark of the autochthony of the Sons of the Earth is the sign of a Lance branded upon their shoulders, to authenticate their race and testify to their warrior vocation.

3. *Structural Anthropology* II, Harmondsworth 1976, pp. 22-4.

4. "Mythe et Oubli," in *Langue, discours, société. Pour Émile Benveniste*, Paris 1975, p. 294-300.

5. Cf., in the *Annuaire de l'École pratique des hautes études*, Fifth section, "Sciences religieuses," 1973-4, the account of J.-P. Vernant's seminar devoted to these questions, pp. 161-2, and *Religions, histoires, raisons*, Paris 1979, pp. 30-1.

6. Herodotus, IV, 161, 2; the whole of this passage should be read; IV, 147-62; also Pindar, *Pyth.*, IV, 57-123 and 452-66.

7. In particular in the chapter entitled "The Feet of Hephaestus," pp. 259-73, Hassocks, Sussex 1978.

8. Cf. Elena Cassin, "Le droit et le tordu," *Ancient Near Eastern Studies in Memory of J.J. Finkelstein*, Connecticut Academy of Arts and Sciences 19 (1977), pp. 29-37, reprinted in E. Cassin, *Le semblable et le différent*, Paris 1978, pp. 50-71; and A. Brelich, "Les monosandales," *La Nouvelle Clio* 7-9 (1955-7), pp. 469-89.

9. *Iliad*, XVIII, 372: ἑλισσόμενον περὶ φύσας.

10. Plato, *Symposium*, 189e. Zeus cuts these primordial men in two so that "they shall walk erect upon two legs" (190d).

11. "...then, they had eight limbs to support and speed them swiftly around and around [κυβιστῶσι κυκλῷ...ταχύ ἐφέροντο κυκλῷ]" (190a-b).

12. *Iliad*, XVIII, 375-8.

13. Diodorus Siculus, II, 18.

14. *Republic*, VII, 535d ff.

15. *Ibid.*, 536a: χωλοῖς τε καὶ νόθοις.

16. Royalty that stands "firm on its feet" or that "limps": The formula is all the more suitable in the case of Sparta, given that the city depends on two royal lineages both of which must be intact.

17. Cf. also Plutarch, *Life of Lysander*, 22, 12: "The kingdom would be maimed if bastards and in-born men should be kings in line with the posterity of Heracles"; and Pausanias, III, 8-10.

18. In *The Frogs* (1189-95), Aristophanes paints the following picture of the misfortunes of Oedipus, in a comic vein:

"No sooner born, than they exposed the babe,
(And that in winter), in an earthen crock,
Lest he should grow a man and slay his father.
Then, with both ankles pierced and swol'n, he limped
Away to Polybus; still young, he married
An ancient crone, and her his mother too.
Then scratched out both his eyes."

To say that he dragged himself away, with swollen feet, to the home of Polybus, Aristophanes uses the verb *erro*, which is the very word used in Book XVIII of the *Iliad* to describe the way that Hephaestus comes hobbling, *choleuon*, out of his forge to greet Achilles' mother, Thetis, when she pays him a visit (lines 411, 417, 421).

It seems hardly necessary to add that this comparison is in no way meant to suggest that the Greeks really thought that Oedipus was lame, simply that his swollen foot, in conjunction with the curse laid on him at birth and his rejection from the family lineage constituted a metaphoric lameness from the point of view of lineage, marriage, power, and destiny.

19. Pausanius, IX, 26, 3-5.

20. Here is the wording of the riddle, as it appears in the argument of Euripides' *The Phoenician Women*: "There is on earth a being with two, four, and three feet and with a single voice that, alone of all those that move on the earth, in the air and in the sea, changes its nature. But when it walks supported by the most feet, that is when its limbs are the least rigorous." It is also recorded in Athenaeus, X, 456b; *Palatine Anthology*, XIV, 64; *Scholiium to Lycophron, Alexandra*, 7, I.22 Scheer, II, p. 11. There are a few variants to note: The first line, "who has one voice [φωνή]" is sometimes given as "who has one form [μορφή]"; the second line, "he changes his nature," sometimes gives φυήν, sometimes φύσιν, and, once, βοήν, his cry (which suggests a faulty spelling of όυ at the end of the first line, so that one should read "who does not have only one voice" rather than "who has one voice." Diodorus Siculus summarizes the question as follows (IV, 64): "What is it that is at the same time a biped, a triped, and a quadruped?" It is notable that in all the versions of the riddle, the normal chronological order is muddled, since the adult man (two feet) comes first, followed either by the old man (three feet) or the child (four feet). Athenaeus, XIII, 558d, records an erotic transposition in which the Sphinx is replaced by a prostitute.

21. On Oedipus' equivalence or identity both with his father and with his children, see *supra*, pp. 136-8. As Leonidas of Alexandria points out (*Palatine Anthology*, VI, 323), Oedipus "was the brother of his children, the husband of his mother."

22. V, 92, 1-2.

23. Louis Gernet, "Mariages de tyrans," in *Anthropologie de la Grèce antique*, Paris 1968, p. 350.

24. Cf. in *Nouveaux fragments d'auteurs anciens*, edited with commentary by Manolis Papathomopoulos, Jannina 1980, the text of the fragment as it appears in *Schol. ad exeg. in Iliadem*, A, 122, and the extremely pertinent commentary, p. 11-26.

25. Herodotus, V, 92, 7-13, which, on Laius, may be compared to Euripides, *The Phoenician Women*, 13-20. We accept the French translation of the wording of the oracle given in P.E. Legrand's edition. *Contra*, cf. Edouard Will, *Korinthiaka*, Paris 1955, pp. 450-1; Will understands: "which will fall upon the monarchs and do justice to Corinth," suggesting that Herodotus was using a tradition of popular stories favorable to the Cypselids and that the oracle, in the version adopted by Herodotus, had itself been given in Cypselus' reign. Will

thus draws a clear distinction between the Bacchiads, who monopolized power and deserved to be punished, and the city of Corinth, which was innocent. All the same, one of the oracles mentioned by Herodotus is addressed directly to the Corinthians, warning them of the coming of Cypselus, "a lion mighty and fierce [*ourestes*: eater of raw flesh], full many a knee shall he loosen." The outlook is not cheerful for the Corinthians and it is certainly for Corinth, the city itself, that "Ēetiōn's offspring should be the source of ills for Corinth [κακὰ ἀναβλάστειν]." For a point of comparison for the wording of the oracle, see (following N. Loraux, to whom we are indebted for this reference) Theognis, who at line 39 ff. expresses the fear that a tyrant will come and restore order in Megara. Instead of "Labda is pregnant; she will give birth to a rolling stone," Theognis has: "Our town is already pregnant and I fear that it will bring forth one who will redress our deplorable outrages."

26. On the associations of "the rolling stone," ὀλοοίτροχος, rolling down a hill, cf. *Iliad*, XIII, 136 ff.; Herodotus, VIII, 52, 10; Xenophon, *Anabasis*, IV, 2, 3.

27. Euripides is remarkably sensitive to the many ambiguous relations between the name of Oedipus, his wounded feet, his personal destiny, and the lame lineage of the Labdacids, represented by his father whose legitimate son, but also murderer, he is. In *The Phoenician Women*, he does more than simply mention the iron thongs that pierced through the heels of the infant exposed to die. The entire episode of the fatal encounter between Laius and Oedipus at the crossroads is placed under the sign of the foot. (1) The meeting of father and son, both of whose steps have brought them together at the same spot, is expressed as: "they were joined together by the same *foot* at a bifurcation of the road [ξυνάπτετον πόδα ἐς ταὐτον . . . σχιστῆς ὁδοῦ]" (37). *Xunaptein poda*, to come together, is "to be joined by foot," as *Xunaptein cheira* is "to shake hands," "to be linked by hand" (as a sign of friendship), and *sunaptein stoma* is "to be joined by mouth," to kiss. The emphasis is reinforced by the positioning of *poda* at the end of the line. (2) When the driver orders Oedipus to stand aside to let his master's chariot pass, he shouts: "Stand aside, don't get under the feet of kings [τύραννος ἔκποδον]" (40). (3) Finally, when Oedipus moves forward without hesitation, the horses, as they gallop past, "made the tendons of his feet [τένοντας πόδον] bleed with their hooves [χέλαις]" (42).

28. On the whole of this episode, cf. Georges Roux, "*Kypsele*. Où avait-on caché le petit Kypselos?" *REA* LXV (1963), pp. 279-89.

29. V, 92, 14-5.

30. Herodotus does not mention the positioning of the *kupsele*, this rural object from the rural – if not wild – space, introduced into the domestic precinct. Georges Roux reasonably enough supposes that it must have been in the courtyard of Eëtiōn's house, where the ten Bacchiads first presented themselves to Labda. Until Roux produced his study, the term *kupsele* had been interpreted in the light of a remark made by Pausanias, at V, 17, 5. In the temple of Hera at Olympia he had seen a wooden chest (*larnax*) said to be the very one in which Cypselus had been hidden. But a *larnax* is not a *kupsele*, as Pausanias very well knew, so he was obliged to say that a wooden chest called a *larnax* in Greek was known, in Corinth (alone) and (only) at the time of Cypselus, as a *kupsele*. The *kupsele* was actually a terra cotta receptacle often used as a hive but that could also serve as a storage container for wheat (cf. Aristophanes, *Peace*, 631). It is worth noting that wooden chests (*larnax*) and earthenware pots (*chutra, astrakon*) were the two types of receptacles in which, in heroic legend, parents deposited the children whom they decided to expose. By depositing her baby in the earthenware hive, to hide him, Labda, in a sense, "exposed" him at home, within the house. Of course, it was only a simulated exposure, the reversal of a real one, but in Plutarch's summary of Herodotus' account, the point comes over clearly. At 164a, Plutarch recounts how the Bacchiads sought, but did not find, the newborn infant whom his mother had "deposited" (ἀποτεθέντα) in a hive (κυψέλη). The verb *apotithemi* and the noun *apothesis* are, together with *ektithemi* and *ekthesis*, the technical terms used to denote exposure (cf. J.-P. Vernant, *Myth and Thought in Ancient Greece*, Boston 1983, p. 173, n.153).

31. V, 92, 2-3.

32. V, 92, 4-5.

33. Diogenes Laertius, I, 96.

34. Herodotus, V, 92, 6-7.

35. V, 92, 8-9.

36. III, 50-4.

37. On the contrast between the two sons, cf. Diogenes Laertius, I, 94: "he had two sons, Cypselus and Lycophron, the younger a man of intelligence [σύνητος], the elder weak in mind."

38. III, 51, 4.

39. III, 50, 13-4.

40. The opposition is emphasized by the repetition of the same wording three lines farther on: The elder son does not understand [οὐ νοοῖ λάβον], but Periander does understand [νοοῖ λάβον]; III, 51, 4 and III, 51, 7.

41. III, 51, 14-52.

42. III, 52, 6: ἐν τῇσι στοιῇσι ἐκαλινδέετο. The verb kalindeomai, to roll, probably results from alindeomai being crossed with kulindeomai, to roll (Chantraine, *Dictionnaire étymologique de la langue grecque*, II, p. 485). On the use of kulindo, in the active sense, meaning to make a stone roll, spinning, down a hill, cf. Xenophon, *Anabasis*, IV, 2-3: ἐκυλίνδουν ὁλοιτρόχους and Theocritus, XXII, 49-50: πέτροι ὁλοίτροχοι, οὔστε κυλίνδων . . . ποταμός . . . περιέξεσε.

43. III, 52, 9-20.

44. III, 52, 24-5.

45. III, 53.

46. III, 53, 6.

47. III, 53, 16-8. On the affinities between "unstable" and "lame," cf. the old expression used in execration of those who set out on a hunting expedition without performing the rites due to Pan and Artemis: for them "the horses go lame [χωλεύονται] and men stumble [σφάλλονται]," Arrian, *Cyneg.*, 35, 3.

48. To settle the fundamental misunderstanding that set them against each other, Oedipus' sons Polynices and Eteocles had also considered a solution similar to Periander's. Oedipus' children had confined him under lock and key so as to "forget" his fate; but Oedipus cursed them both, expressing the wish that they should share the palace with the stroke of a sword. Then the two boys "were afraid that if they lived together the gods might grant his prayers. So they agreed that Polynices should go, a willing exile, while Eteocles stayed in this land and held the scepter, to change though, year by year" (Euripides, *Phoenician Women*, 69-74). But in this case too the projected swap-over never took place. Once in harness, Eteocles refused to hand over the throne and made sure that Polynices remained in exile. The two brothers were not to meet again until they came face to face, sword in hand, to kill each other.

49. *Anthropologie de la Grèce antique*, Paris 1968, p. 344.

50. *Ibid.*, p. 350.

51. Cf. *supra*, pp. 131-8. In "Histoire de tyran ou comment la cité grecque construit ses marges," Pauline Schmitt-Pantel writes: "The tryant, who is at once, or in some cases successively, effeminate and excessively masculine, fails to keep

sexuality at bay as he should and this makes him an impossible citizen" (*Les marginaux et les exclus dans l'Histoire*, Cahiers Jussieu 15, p. 299). "Effeminate and excessively masculine" is certainly what the sexually lame hermaphrodite Kaineus is. And it is one of his descendents who, through his marriage to the lame Labda, founds the dynasty of the Cypselid tyrants.

52. Plato, *Republic*, 571c-d and 619b-c.

53. On tyranny, *isotheos*, being like a god, cf. Euripides, *The Trojan Women*, 1168; Plato, *Republic*, 360c and 568b.

54. Cristea Sandra Timoc, *Songs of the Past and Cantilenas* (in Rumanian), Bucharest EPL 1967.

55. These are the three fairies who preside over births. They can be either beneficent or malevolent.

CHAPTER XI

*An early version of this text appeared in *Belfagor* 6 (1979), pp. 636-42.

1. Karl Marx, *Critique of Political Economy*, "Introduction," tr. N.I. Stone, pp. 265-312, Chicago 1904.

2. *Op. cit.*, pp. 311-2.

3. *Ibid.*, p. 309.

4. *Ibid.*, p. 312.

5. Karl Marx, *Economic and Philosophic Manuscripts of 1844*, ed. D.J. Struick, tr. M. Milligan, London 1970.

6. *Op. cit.*, p. 141.

7. *Ibid.*, p. 139.

8. *Ibid.*

9. *Ibid.*, p. 141.

10. *Ibid.*

11. "Introduction to a Critique of Political Economy," p. 280.

12. *Ibid.*

13. See *supra*, Ch. 1 and *passim*.

14. Cf. J.-P. Vernant, *Religions, histoires, raisons*, Paris 1979, pp. 106 ff.

15. Herodotus, VI, 21.

16. Aristotle, *Poetics*, 1451a 36-b 32.

17. *Ibid.*, 6, 1449b 28. On the problems of Aristotelian *katharsis* and the meaning of this purification of "purging" of emotions such as pity and terror,

through tragic representation, cf. Roselyne Dupont-Roc and Jean Lallot, *Aristote, La Poétique*, text, translation and notes, Paris 1980, pp. 188-93.

18. *Poetics*, 1449b 24.

CHAPTER XII

*Preface to Eschyle, tr. Paul Mazon, *Tragédies*, Gallimard, coll. Folio, Paris 1982, pp. 7-39.

1. Pseudo-Plutarch, *Life of Lycurgus*, 15. Cf. *infra*, p. 362.

2. Aristophanes, *Wasps*, 219-20.

3. See the recent study by Thomas G. Rosenmeyer, in *The Legacy of Greece*, ed. Moses I. Finley, Oxford 1981, pp. 120-54. Some idea of the immensity and complexity of the Aeschylean tradition can be gained by leafing through the *Bibliographie historique et critique d'Eschyle et de la tragédie grecque, 1518-1974* compiled by André Wartelle, Paris 1978.

4. *Thucydides Mythistoricus*, London 1907 (repr. New York 1969).

5. Bernard M.W. Knox, "The Lion in the House," *CPh* 47 (1957), pp. 17-25, reprinted in *Word and Action: Essays on the Ancient Theater*, Baltimore-London 1979, pp. 27-38.

6. Cf. *infra*, Ch. 13.

7. Victor Hugo, *William Shakespeare*, tr. A. Baillot, London 1864, pp. 37, 68.

8. Arnaldo Momigliano, *Essays in Ancient and Modern Historiography*, Oxford 1977, p. 9.

9. *Life of Aeschylus*, 10.

10. *Pap. Ox.*, XX, 2256, fr. 3.

11. See N. Loraux, *The Invention of Athens*, Cambridge, Mass. 1987.

12. See Diego Lanza, *Il Tiranno e il suo pubblico*, Turin 1977.

13. This torrent of crimes may be compared with what Richard Marienstras has to say of the Shakespearean world: "Social violence mechanically pursues its devastating course: a first murder (or offense) is followed by a second murder to avenge the first, and then a third to avenge the second. It is an ever-expanding spiral...." *New Perspectives on the Shakespearean World*, Cambridge 1985, p. 5.

14. Cf. George Thomson, *Aeschylus and Athens*, London 1941 (repr. many times).

15. See R.G.A. Buxton, *Persuasion in Greek Tragedy: A Study of Peitho*, Cambridge 1982.

16. Cf. Froma Zeitlin, "The Motif of the Corrupted Sacrifice in Aeschylus' *Oresteia*," *TAPhA* 96 (1965), pp. 463-508; see also, in general, Zoe Petre, "La représentation de la mort dans la tragédie grecque," *Stud. Clas.* XXIII (1985), pp. 21-35.

17. Cf. *supra*, Ch. 6.

18. Cf. J.-P. Vernant, *Myth and Thought in Ancient Greece*, London 1983, pp. 133-5 from whom I have also borrowed the quotation below.

19. On these matters, see the works of N. Loraux, in particular *Les Enfants d'Athéna*, Paris 1981 (to be published in English by Harvard University Press), and those of F.I. Zeitlin, esp. "The Dynamics of Misogyny: Myth and Mythmaking in the *Oresteia*," *Arethusa* 11, 1-2 (1978), pp. 149-89.

20. See N. Loraux, "Le lit, la guerre," *L'Homme* XXI, 1 (1981), pp. 37-67.

21. Cf. *supra*, pp. 154-5, and also "The Black Hunter Revisited," *PCPhS* (1986).

22. Charles W. Fornara, "The Hoplite Achievement at Psyttaleia," *JHS* 86 (1966), pp. 51-4; Georges Roux, "Eschyle, Hérodote, Diodore, Plutarch racontent la bataille de Salamine," *BCH* 98 (1974), pp. 51-94, interprets the text in a completely opposite fashion: To his mind, the bowmen are the Persians (p. 91).

23. Cf. Nathalie Daladier, "Les mères aveugles," *Nouvelle Revue de psychanalyse* XIX (1979), pp. 229-44.

24. Cf. Katerina Synodinou, *On the Concept of Slavery in Euripides*, Jannina 1977, p. 92.

25. Jesper Svenbro, *La parole et le marbre. Aux origines de la poétique grecque*, Lund 1976.

26. See Suzanne Saïd, "Sophiste et tyran ou le problème du 'Prométhée enchainé,'" Paris 1985, esp. pp. 131-54.

CHAPTER XIII

1. The first draft of this study was delivered, toward the end of 1976, in a provisional English version, in Bergen (Norway), Bristol, Cambridge, Liverpool, Oxford, and London. The questions tackled here were also the subject of seminars in France and Italy, and then of a paper given to the "Association pour l'encouragement des études grecques" on 9 January 1978. I should like to thank all those who took part for their remarks but, once again, my most fruitful discussions have been those with Nicole Loraux. Over a number of years we have many times exchanged views on Aeschylus' text. I had already completed this

study when I came across two extremely important unpublished studies: D. Pralon, "Eschyle: *Les Sept contre Thèbes*" and P. Judet de la Combe, "Histoire des interprétations des *Sept contre Thèbes* d'Eschyle (fin XVIIIe-XXe siecles)." Of the second article, which is to appear in *Actes de la Recherche en Science sociale*, I have been able to read only the part concerning the debate up to Wilamowitz, which is precisely my own point of departure. The notes will indicate where I am indebted to Dr. Pralon's study.

Of the second article, I have been able to read only the part concerning the debate up to Wilamowitz, which expresses precisely my own point of view. The notes indicate where I am indebted to D. Pralon's study. Unfortunately, neither of these two papers have yet been published.

I finished writing this text in August 1978. Since then, in the course of a discussion on the *Seven* organized at Princeton University, I was fortunate enough to learn of the unpublished work of F.I. Zeitlin and W.G. Thalmann's dissertation, *Dramatic Art in Aeschylus' Seven against Thebes*, New Haven 1978. I was delighted to find these works to be entirely in agreement with my own. Since this text was published, the problems that it tackles have been discussed in particular by Liana Lupas and Zoe Petre, *Commentaire aux* Sept contre Thèbes *d'Eschyle*, Bucharest and Paris 1981, and F.I. Zeitlin, *Under the Sign of the Shield*, Rome 1982; see also P. Judet de La Combe's synthesis in Lallot and Haussmann (Eds.), *Etudes de littératures anciennes* III, Paris 1987, pp. 57-79.

2. G. Murray, *Aeschylus: The Creator of Tragedy*, Oxford 1940, p. 140.

3. The English translations are, in the main, taken from C. Dawson's translation of the *Seven*, although they are sometimes slightly adapted. The translation by H. Bacon and A. Hecht, Oxford 1974, has also sometimes been used. In some cases the English follows the author's translations.

4. "Drei Schlusszenen griechischer Drama," *S.B. Berlin* (1903), p. 436 ff.; I quote from p. 438.

5. Wilamowitz, *Aischylos Interpretationen*, Berlin 1914, pp. 641-3; see also *Griechische Versekunst*, Berlin 1921, p. 199.

6. F. Solmsen, "The Erinyes in Aeschylus' *Septem*," *TAPhA* 69 (1937), pp. 197-211.

7. The most important articles in the recent debate are to be found in the review article by R.P. Winnington-Ingram, "Septem contra Thebas," *YCS* XXV (1977), pp. 1-45. Long after I had finished and even sent this article to press, I

came across first, an important chapter in F.I. Zeitlin's book on women in Greek tragedy, still in preparation, and then William G. Thalmanns' *Dramatic Art in Aeschylus' Seven against Thebes*, New Haven and London 1978. On many points I found myself in agreement with these two authors, especially with Zeitlin. Thalmann's book gives excellent analyses of many problems.

8. R.D. Dawe, "Inconsistency of Plot and Character in Aeschylus," *PCPhS* 189 (1963), pp. 21-62, cf. p. 32. A.J. Podlecki's interpretation, "The Character of Eteocles in Aeschylus' *Septem*," *TAPhA* 95 (1964), pp. 283-99, is very close to that of R. Dawe.

9. W. Schadewaldt, "Die Waffnung des Eteokles," *Festschrift H. Hommel*, Tübingen 1961, pp. 105-16, but see the objections raised by O. Taplin, *op. cit., infra*, n.19, pp. 158-61.

10. Cf. G. Kirkwood, "Eteokles Oiakostrophos," *Phoenix* 23 (1969), pp. 9-25; see also, on the maritime and political imagery, Z. Petre, "Thèmes dominants et attitudes politiques dans les *Sept contre Thèbes* d'Eschyle," *Studii Classici*, XIII (1971), pp. 15-28. This article played a considerable part in stimulating my interest in the *Seven*.

11. I will limit myself here to referring the reader to a number of articles that represent the debate between different points of view: E. Wolff, "Die Entscheidung des Eteokles in den *Sieben gegen Theben*," *HSPh* 63 (1958), pp. 89-95; H. Patzer, "Die dramatische Handlung den *Sieben gegen Theben*," *ibid.*, pp. 97-119; B. Otis, "The Unity of the *Seven against Thebes*," *GRBS* 3 (1963), pp. 153-74; K. Von Fritz, "Die Gestalt des Eteokles in Aeschylus' *Sieben gegen Theben*," in *Antike und moderne Tragödie*, Berlin 1962, pp. 193-222; A. Lesky, "Eteokles in den *Sieben gegen Theben*," *WS* 74 (1961), pp. 5-17.

12. R. Dawe, *loc. cit. supra*, n.8, p. 21: "We are not so much learning about Aeschylus as witnessing the transactions of a private club."

13. As well as E. Wolff's article cited above, n.11, see, for example, F. Ferrari, "La Scelta dei difensori nei *Sette contra Tebe* di Eschilo," *SCO* 19-20 (1970-1), pp. 140-55.

14. L. Golden, "The Character of Eteocles and the Meaning of the *Septem*," *CPh* 59 (1964), pp. 78-89 (I quote from p. 80). L. Golden's Eteocles is a skilled statesman who does not believe in fatality.

15. Cf. *supra*, pp. 35-7.

16. See however, R.S. Caldwell, "The Misogyny of Eteocles," *Arethusa* 6

(1973), pp. 197-231; R.P. Winnington-Ingram, "Aeschylus, *Septem* 187-90, 750-71" *BICS* 13 (1966), pp. 83-93; H. Bacon, "The Shield of Eteocles," *Arion* III, 3 (1964), pp. 27-38 (an essential article); *eadem*, "Woman's Two Faces: Sophocles' View of the Tragedy of Oedipus and his Family," *Science and Psychoanalysis* X (1966), pp. 13-23; S. Benardete, "Two Notes on Aeschylus' *Septem*," *WS, n.f.* 1 (1967), pp. 22-30 and n.f. 2 (1968), pp. 15-7, especially pp. 26-30 with its illuminating remarks; U. Albini, "Aspetti dei *Sette a Tebe*," *Parola del Passato* 27 (1962), pp. 289-300; on the much more studied problem of the women in the *Oresteia*, F.I. Zeitlin's article, "The Dynamics of Misogyny: Myth and Mythmaking in the *Oresteia*," *Arethusa* 11, 1-2 (1978) pp. 7-21 and 149-89 is of fundamental importance and refers the reader to an extensive bibliography.

17. U. Albini, *loc. cit.*, p. 290.

18. See, for example, H.J. Rose, *A Commentary on the Surviving Plays of Aeschylus*, I, Amsterdam 1957, *ad. loc.*; Rose is followed by C. Dawson in his translation with commentary of the *Seven*, Prentice-Hall, Englewood Cliffs, N.J., p. 29; see also D. Lanza "Lo spettatore sulla scena," in D. Lanza, M. Vegetti, G.Caiani, F. Sircana, *L'Ideologia della Città*, Naples 1977, p. 61. In their recent translation of the play (London and New York 1974), H. Bacon and A. Hecht note the presence on stage of "male citizens of Thebes," without however producing any substantiating evidence.

19. *The Stagecraft of Aeschylus*, Oxford 1977, pp. 129-36; Taplin's demonstration seems to me quite conclusive. He shows clearly that, unlike comedy, tragedy includes no speeches addressed to the spectators and that in any production of the play the characters involved are actually present on stage.

20. *Loc. cit. supra*, n.16, pp. 27-38.

21. See the article by Nicole Loraux, "Sur la race des femmes et quelques-unes de ses tribus," *Arethusa* 11, 1-2 (1978), pp. 43-87; the article focuses upon the poem Semonides of Amorgos directed against the various tribes of women, but it has much wider implications.

22. M. Shaw correctly remarks in connection with the female characters in Greek tragedy: "Indeed, by the very act of being in a drama, which always occurs outside the house, they are doing what women should not do" ("The Female Intruder: Women in Fifth-Century Drama," *CPh* 70 (1975), pp. 255-66 (v. p. 256)). But does this remark apply exclusively to figures in tragedy? The question is, at the very least, one that requires investigation.

23. See D. Lanza, *Il tiranno e il suo pubblico*, Turin 1977. It is a pity that this book takes so little account of Aeschylus' Eteocles.

24. Cf. C. Lévi-Strauss, *Structural Anthropology*, New York 1963, pp. 213-8 and, in general, F. Vian, *Les origines de Thèbes. Cadmos et les Spartes*, Paris 1963; on the myths of autochthony see especially N. Loraux, "L'autochtonie: une topique athénienne, Le mythe dans l'espace civique," *Annales E.S.C.* 34 (1979), pp. 3-26.

25. In the *parodos*, 110-65, in contrast, the Chorus addresses four female deities (Athena, Aphrodite, Artemis, and Hera) and four male deities (Zeus, Poseidon, Ares, and Apollo); cf. S. Benardete, *loc. cit. supra*, n.16, p. 27.

26. This text has been the subject of a detailed study by L. Deubner, "Ololyge und Verwandtes," *Abhandl. Preuss. Ak.* (1947), I, pp. 22-3.

27. L. Deubner, *ibid.*, and p. 4, referring to Pollux I, 28.

28. As in line 825. As S. Benardete notes, *loc. cit. supra* n.16, the chorus does not respond to Eteocles' appeal immediately.

29. I have elsewhere referred to a similar perverse use of the terminology connected with sacrifice: cf. *supra*, Ch. 6.

30. πειρωμένους is what seems to be an excellent correction made by H. Weil. The manuscripts hesitate between πειρωμένοις and πειρωμένων.

31. Cf. N. Loraux, "L'intérference tragique," *Critique* 317 (1973), pp. 908-25. In emphasizing the "transgressive" aspect of Eteocles' demand I am going beyond the interpretation of J.-P. Vernant who writes, "The only contribution Eteocles will allow the women to make toward a public and political religion that knows how to respect the distant character of the gods without trying to mix the divine with the human, is the *ololugē*, the wail, which is described as *hieros* because the city has integrated it into its own religion, recognizing it as the ritual cry to accompany the fall of the victim in the great blood sacrifice," *supra*, pp. 40-1.

32. μεταίχμιον in line 197 means "what is intermediary." Is Eteocles "too angry to speak completely coherently" (C. Dawson, translation cited *supra*, p. 50) or does he on the contrary overstep the male-female polarity by reason of his *hubris*? Note the importance of the political terminology (C. Dawson, *ibid.*). In line 199 ψῆφος is the stone used for stoning to death but it is also the object used to cast a vote. It is a fine example of tragic ambiguity.

33. On the significance of this phenomenon in mythical thought, cf. P. Vidal-

Naquet, "Esclavage et gynécocratie dans la tradition, le mythe, l'utopie" in C. Nicolet ed., *Recherches sur les structures sociales dans l'Antiquité classique*, Paris 1970, pp. 63-80; on the theme of gynocracy in the *Oresteia*, cf. F.I. Zeitlin, *loc. cit. supra*, n.16, pp. 153-6, who refers to the earlier literature on the subject, in particular to the review article by M.B. Arthur, on women in the classical world, *Signs: Journal of Women in Culture and Society* 2 (1976), pp. 382-403. I should like to thank F.I. Zeitlin for having sent me this article. I have also found most useful an unpublished paper by Nicole Loraux (delivered at the conference on the imaginary at Cérisy in July, 1978): "Le nom athénien. Structures imaginaires de la parenté athénienne."

34. I do not intend to tackle this problem directly here and so will not cite the huge bibiography connected with it.

35. See lines 1065-75; I am in agreement here with S. Benardete who writes, *loc. cit.*, p. 29: "Antigone survives Eteocles to split the city exactly where he boldly assumed that it was whole."

36. F. Ritschl, "Der Parallelismus der Sieben Redenpaare in den *Sieben gegen Theben* des Aischylos," *Jahrb. f. Class. Phil.*, 77 (1858), pp. 761-84, reprinted in *Kleine Philologische Schriften*, I, Leipzig 1866, pp. 300-64 (appendix, pp. 362-4).

37. *Aischylos Interpretationen*, cited *supra*, n.5, p. 74.

38. J. Larsen, "Federation for Peace in Ancient Greece," *CPh* 39 (1944), pp. 145-62; my quotation is taken from page 145 and is a reference for which I am indebted to A. Aymard, "Report" to the *IXth International Congress of Historical Sciences*, I, Paris 1950, p. 516.

39. E. Fraenkel, "Die Sieben Redenpaare in Thebaner Drama des Aischylos," *SBR* (1957) Heft 5. Fraenkel's article naturally contains much useful information of a detailed nature.

40. Apart from the above mentioned article (n.16) by H. Bacon, the studies that have been most useful to me are S. Benardete, cited *supra* n.16; A. Moreau, "Fonction du personnage d'Amphiaraos dans les *Sept contre Thèbes*: le 'Blason en abyme,' " *BAGB* (1976), pp. 158-81 (a study that owes much to the unpublished study of D. Pralon); and H.D. Cameron's book, *Studies on the Seven against Thebes of Aeschylus*, The Hague and Paris 1971.

41. H.D. Cameron speaks, precisely, of "two intimately connecting systems, one of plot and theme and one of imagery," *op. cit.*, p. 15.

42. Archaeology has taught us much on the subject of devices, either through

the direct study of shields or, even more, through their representation in vase paintings. Anne Jacquemin, at present a member of the French School at Athens, has under the guidance of P. Devambez and F. Robert produced an M.A. dissertation on this subject (1973). She shows that we cannot hope to interpret Aeschylus' devices through archaeology.

43. See, apart from the above-mentioned articles of S. Benardete, H.D. Cameron, "The Power of Words in the *Seven against Thebes*," *TAPhA* CI (1970), pp. 95-108.

44. Only D. Pralon has been so bold as to attempt it, which is why I so very much regret that he has not published his study.

45. Although our methods are very different, I cannot but refer the reader to J. Myres' attempt to interpret the text of Herodotus in this way: See his *Herodotus, Father of History*, Oxford 1948. The diagram illustrating my hypothesis was drawn by Annie Schnapp whom I should like to thank. It has, needless to say, no archaeological pretensions whatsoever.

46. Cf. S. Benardete, *loc. cit. supra*, n.16, p. 5.

47. Cf. in general the study by Claire Préaux, *La Lune dans la Pensée grecque*, Brussels 1973, *passim*.

48. H. Weir Smyth, in the Loeb Classical Library translation, has "armourless."

49. See *The Black Hunter*, Baltimore 1986 pp. 106-128 and "Les Jeunes: Le Cru, l'enfant grec et le cuit" in J. le Goff and P. Nora, ed., *Faire de l'histoire*, III, Paris 1974, pp. 137-68; F.I. Zeitlin has shown in detail, *loc. cit. supra*, n.16, pp. 160-2, how these oppositions operate in the *Oresteia* and how they help to define the character of Orestes.

50. It is hardly necessary to point out that, in Greek literature, the burning of a town always takes place by night.

51. I do not count the Cadmeian pinioned by the Sphinx in line 543 as a man. At any rate he is not the central character in the scene. He can — for obvious reasons — neither speak nor write.

52. Hesiod, *Theogony*, 820 ff.; on this text see M. Detienne and J.-P. Vernant, *Cunning Intelligence in Greek Culture and Society* (tr. J. Lloyd), Hassocks 1977, pp. 117-120.

53. Dindorf and, following him, Mazon were quite wrong to athetize lines 515-20.

54. In the notes in his edition of the *Seven* (London 1887), A. Verrall tried,

quite unsuccessfully, to show that, in lines 473 and 622, Megareus, the strength of whose arm is renowned (473), bears an arm on his shield and that Lasthenes bears an escutcheon showing a leg. Nor do I think that Helen Bacon has any valid arguments to support her hypothesis (*loc. cit.*, n.16) that Eteocles bears on his shield the symbol of the Erinys.

55. I need do no more here than refer the reader to E. Lapalus, *Le Fronton sculpté en Grèce*, Paris 1947, pp. 284 ff.

56. In the text of the manuscripts, the name of the bearer of the shield is given in line 547 after his description and that of his shield and I think this order should be retained.

57. I am not in agreement with H. Bacon and A. Hecht who translate προβλήματι by "riddle," seeing it as an allusion to the Sphinx's riddle; but a play on words cannot be totally ruled out.

58. S. Benardete, *loc. cit.*, p. 12, writes, not without a degree of litotes: "Parthenopaeus now carries an image which, though inimical to the Thebans, is not alien, as Typhon was, to them."

59. As A. Moreau, *loc. cit. supra*, n.40, has correctly pointed out, Amphiaraos is "the author's mouthpiece" (p. 164). This is the normal role for a diviner in a tragedy; cf. *supra*, pp. 261-2.

60. On this point, cf. S. Benardete, *loc. cit.*, pp. 16-7.

61. S. Benardete speaks with reason of "this absorption, as it were, of Eteocles into his image" *loc. cit.*, p. 8.

62. The same is true of Capaneus who, precisely, is a *gigas* (424).

63. Sophocles glosses Aeschylus as follows: "Parthenopaeus, the loyal son of Atalanta owes his name to his mother who remained for so long a virgin before giving him birth [ἐπώνυμος τῆς πρόσθεν ἀδμήτης χρόνῳ/μητρὸς λοχευθείς, πιστὸς Ἀταλάντης γόνος]" *Oedipus at Colonus*, 1321-2, following Mazon's French translation ("Il doit son nom à sa mère, qui demeura si longtemps vierge avant de lui donner le jour, Parthenopée, loyal fils d'Atalante").

64. As D. Pralon correctly saw. Since we cannot prove that Aeschylus really did have them in mind, I will not dwell here on those aspects of the legend of Amphiaraos and his wife Eriphyle that could easily account for the diviner's position in the "gynocratic" half of the schema. And yet it is impossible not to remember Homer's line: "But he perished at Thebes on account of gifts from women [ἀλλ᾽ ὄλετ᾽ ἐν Θήβῃσι γυναίων εἵνεκα δώρων]" (*Odyssey*, XV, 247). On this

point see A. Moreau, *loc. cit. supra*, n.40, p. 169. Amphiaraos himself, in line 578, plays on the name of Polynices, *the man of a thousand quarrels*.

65. κλητήρ is close to the Homeric καλήτωρ, and the Mycenaean *ko-re-te* which refers to a civic officer; on these last two words, cf. J. Taillardat, "Notules mycéniennes," I, *REG* LXXIII (1960), pp. 1-5.

66. To be precise: earth-fatherland.

67. The spring is mentioned by the chorus in line 307.

68. The comparison is made by C. Dawson in the Introduction to his translation cited n.18, p. 21.

69. Apollodorus III, 6, 8.

70. There are many translations for this expression: in English, "Dikē, his blood sister" (H. Bacon and A. Hecht); "Justice his true kin in blood" (H. Weir Smyth); "Justice, Goddess of Kindred's duty" (P. Vellacott, in the Penguin collection); "True Duty to his Kin" (C. Dawson). K. Wilkins has an original interpretation, *ΔΙΚΗ ΟΜΑΙΜΩΝ*, "Zu Aischylos *Sieben* 415," *Hermes* (1969), pp. 117-21. She makes ὁμαιμών into a genitive plural dependent on the πρός of προστέλλεται. *Dikē* places Melanippus before her blood-brothers. But against this interpretation is the existence in Aeschylus of a Zeus ὁμαίμων (*Suppliants*, 402) and the scholium of M: "the right of kinship [τὸ τῆς συγγενείας δίκαιον]."

71. "Eteocles beyond the walls" (H. Bacon and A. Hecht, preface to the translation *loc. cit. supra*, n.18, p. 11). D. Pralon, independently, makes the same remark. This character is unknown before Aeschylus and appears in later lists given by tragedians (for example, Sophocles' *Oedipus at Colonus*, 1316) only when Adrastus does not. There was nevertheless a statue to him on the monument to the Seven, at Delphi (Pausanias X, 10, 3). Despite the importance I attach to the character of Eteocles, I cannot agree with A. Moreau when he writes: "The moment when Eteocles mentions the name of Eteoclos' adversary is the moment when we understand that he has fallen into the trap laid by *Atē* (*loc. cit.*, p. 181, n.1).

72. The force of the γέ cannot be minimized here, cf. R. Dawe, *loc. cit. supra*, n.8, p. 27.

73. *Loc. cit. supra*, n.16, p. 35.

74. Cf. also "kings of the same root [βασιλέες ὁμόσποροι]" (804), an expression that is repeated in line 820.

75. *Op. cit. supra*, n.40, p. 89: "The story of Thebes has come full circle, as the two brothers recapitulate the tale of the Sown men."

76. Cf. in general, F. Vian, *Les origines de Thèbes. Cadmos et les Spartes*, Paris 1963.

77. Cf. the study cited *supra*, n.24, by Nicole Loraux.

78. Pherecydes, *F Gr Hist*, 3, F 22a-b; cf. F. Vian, *op. cit.*, p. 23. Αὐτοκτόνως, having themselves killed each other, is the adverb used in connection with Eteocles and Polynices (734).

79. F. Vian, *op. cit.*, pp. 169 and 185; cf. *Iliad*, IV, 395 ff.

80. F. Vian, *op. cit.*, p. 169, thinks that Hyperbios and his brother Aktor may be Spartoi: "the name of the former is borne by a Giant and is reminiscent of that of the Spartos Hyperenor."

81. Cf. line 69 again.

82. Cf. *supra*, p. 142.

83. N. Loraux is quite right to compare *Eumenides*, 665, where Athena is described as "not having been nourished in the darkness of the womb [οὐδ' ἐν σκότοισι νηδύος τεθραμμένη]"; this is what qualifies Athena to preside over autochthonous births. To say that Polynices has escaped from the maternal shadows is to annihilate any claim to autochthony on his part – and hence also on his brother's.

84. At this point I am doing no more than very briefly indicating a subject for research. If properly done it would call for a systematic study of the *Phoenician Women* and the *Suppliants* of Euripides, not to mention lines 1309-30 of Sophocles' *Oedipus at Colonus*.

85. Amphiaraos comes second in the order given by Euripides.

86. The text is very obscure and I will not venture to interpret it here.

CHAPTER XIV

*Preface to Sophocles, *Tragédies*, tr. Paul Mazon, Gallimard, coll. Folio, Paris 1973, pp. 9-37.

1. *Apud*, Athenaeus, XIII, 604d.

2. See R. Goossens, *Euripide et Athènes*, Brussels 1960.

3. As F. Robert suggests, "Sophocle, Pericles, Hérodote et la date d'*Ajax*," *RPh* XXXVIII (1964), pp. 213-27.

4. The tragedies were produced in groups of three (trilogies) to which a satyr play was added, in which the chorus was composed of actors disguised as satyrs. No complete trilogy by Sophocles has come down to us. A trilogy together with a satyr play made up a tetralogy.

5. Plutarch, *Moralia* ("On progress in virtue"), 79b.

6. *Odyssey*, XI, 275-6.

7. The voting is depicted on fifth-century red-figure vases, some time before Sophocles. It does not appear on vases of the archaic period.

8. Herodotus, VII, 220.

9. See Leo Schrade, *La Représentation d'Edipo-Tiranno au Teatro Olimpico*, CNRS, Paris 1960, and *infra*, pp. 364-71.

10. Cf. *supra*, Ch. 5.

11. *Politics*, I, 1253a.

12. See *supra*, Ch. 7.

CHAPTER XV

*Also published in *Metis* I (1986).

1. The following pages stem from a series of seminars that began in the early seventies, in which Pierre Ellinger played a particularly constructive part. Since then, I spoke on this material on April 9th, 1984 at Delphi where, thanks to Yangos Andreadis, I was the guest of the Centre européen de Culture, and in that May at Padua, at the Greek Institute, where I was the guest of O. Longo and G. Serra. More recently I have had the opportunity to discuss these problems in seminars held in Brussels, Holland (in several universities), Naples, Catania, Tel Aviv, and Lille. I should like to offer my warmest thanks to those who took part, whether or not they agreed with me, and in particular to J. Bollack, J. Bremmer, B. Cohen, and P. Judet de La Combe. I should also like to thank my old friend B. Bravo who made a close, critical study of my text. I shall not attempt to provide even a sketchy summary of the huge bibliography of *Oedipus at Colonus*. I was delighted to find myself on familiar ground in the chapter devoted to this tragedy in Charles Segal's *Tragedy and Civilization: An Interpretation of Sophocles*, Cambridge, Mass. 1981, pp. 362-408. I owe much to J. Jones, *On Aristotle and Greek Tragedy*, London 1962, pp. 214-35, to B. Knox, *The Heroic Temper: Studies in Sophoclean Tragedy*, Cambridge 1964; "Sophocles and the Polis," *Entretiens de la Fondation Hardt*, Vandoeuvres-Geneva 1983, *Sophocle*, pp. 1-32; Introduction to *Oedipus at Colonus* in *Sophocles, The Three Theban Plays*, 1984, pp. 255-77. I have also consulted J. Kamerbeek's commentary, *The Plays of Sophocles* VII, Leyden 1984, but did not find it particularly helpful. Of the recently produced works of synthesis on Sophocles that I have consulted, I would in particular draw atten-

tion to R.P. Winnington-Ingram, *Sophocles: An Interpretation*, Cambridge 1980, pp. 248-79 and 335-40; A. Machin, *Cohérence et continuité dans le théâtre de Sophocle*, Quebec 1981, pp. 105-49 and 405-35; V. Di Benedetto, *Sofocle*, Florence 1983, pp. 217-47 and, last but not least, the illuminating remarks on p. 30 in R.G.A. Buxton, *Sophocles*, published as no. 16 in *New Surveys in the Classics of Greece and Rome*, Oxford 1984. The Greek texts used are those of R.D. Dawe (Teubner and Leipzig 1979) and in the Loeb Classics series except where otherwise indicated and apart from a few spelling variations. The translations (occasionally modified) are those published by the University of Chicago Press. I should like to thank Denise Fourgous for all her help in preparing this study and Maud Sissung for the friendly support that she has, once again, given me.

2. See M.I. Finley, *Politics in the Ancient World*, Cambridge 1983; and C. Ampolo, *La politica in Grecia*, Bari 1981.

3. Cf. M.I. Finley, *Politics*, pp. 64-5.

4. Thucydides, II, 65, 2-4; the translation, by Charles Forster Smith (Loeb Classical Library), has been slightly modified.

5. *Pericles*, 35, 4-6, 37.

6. I am not suggesting this as a general rule where Plutarch is concerned, but we should note the skepticism expressed by Finley, *Politics*, pp. 50-1.

7. "All levels of intensity were embraced by the splendid Greek portmanteauword *stasis*," writes Finley, *Politics*, p. 105.

8. N. Loraux, "L'Oubli dans la cité," *Le temps de la réflexion* 1 (1980), pp. 213-42.

9. Cf. Finley, *Politics*, pp. 54-5.

10. In my opinion, this has been conclusively demonstrated by N. Loraux, *The Invention of Athens*, Cambridge, Mass. 1987. C. Ampolo has, for his part, devoted a chapter in his *La politica in Grecia, op. cit. supra*, n.2, to this negation of politics (pp. 40-55), but his argument does not go far enough. The negation of politics did not concern the philosophers alone.

11. S.G. Benardete's translation, slightly adapted.

12. Cf. R.G.A. Buxton, *Persuasion in Greek Tragedy: A Study of Peitho*, Cambridge 1982, esp. p.79: "For the moment, political *peitho* is supreme."

13. For a discussion of their number and role, cf. O. Taplin, *The Stagecraft of Aeschylus: The Dramatic Use of Exits and Entrances in Greek Tragedy*, Oxford 1977, pp. 392-5.

14. I have borrowed this idea from the seminars of F.I. Zeitlin, who is soon to publish on this subject an essay the substance of which was familiar to me when I wrote the present paper; meanwhile, see *Under the Sign of the Shield*, Rome 1982, p. 199 n.5.

15. It describes an assembly held "on the hill, the same place where they say old Danaus held the first public meeting in Argos" (871-3), in other words on the spot where democracy was founded.

16. "At a moment of profound skepticism about democratic life and the function of the *ekklesia* in Athens," comments V. Di Benedetto in his edition of the play, Florence 1965, p. 171.

17. Cf. R. Goossens, *Euripide et Athènes*, Brussels 1962, pp. 556-9, and C. Mossé, *La fin de la démocratie athenienne*, Paris 1962, pp. 251-3.

18. See P. Lévêque and P. Vidal-Naquet, *Clisthène l'Athenien*, Besançon and Paris 1964, pp. 112-3.

19. That is why I am not in agreement with B. Knox who, in his well-known book *Oedipus at Thebes*, (New Haven 1957), suggests that Oedipus (in ·*Oedipus Rex*) represents the imperial ambition of Athens; I do not believe that there is any such conscious representation, at any rate. Nor do I agree with J. Dalfon, "*Philoktet* und *Oedipus auf Kolonos*," *Festschrift E. Grassi*, Munich 1973, pp. 43-63, who regards the conflict between the two brothers at Thebes as a transposition of Athenian *stasis* (pp. 56-7).

20. The presence of ἔρις κακή in line 372 implies that in line 367, we should retain the word eris that Tyrwhitt, followed by Jebb, corrected to ἔρος. Jebb believed that the influence of Hesiod's text was detectable here, requiring that the text be altered; see his note in his own edition with commentary (Cambridge 1899, repr. Hakkert, Amsterdam 1965), pp. 65-6.

21. See Jebb's note, *loc. cit.*, p. 67. In Euripides' *Phoenician Women* (71), Eteocles draws attention to his rights as elder brother. Polynices refers to *his* in *Oedipus at Colonus*, at lines 1294 and 1422. Mazon, in his edition of the play, notes in connection with line 1354 that "in fact, Polynices had never reigned over Thebes." But what does "fact" have to do with the past in a tragic action? In the new Lille fragment (*P. Lille*, 73), the two brothers are placed on a footing of equality by their mother, and there is no mention of the rights of seniority: The political power goes to Eteocles, the wealth to Polynices.

22. "Tyrant," not simply "lords it" as Robert Fitzgerald translates it in line

1338. Many translators have a deplorable habit of translating *turannos* as "king."

23. See also lines 540-1 where Oedipus speaks of the "reward" that his city granted him.

24. Cf. Buxton, *Persuasion*, pp. 140-1.

25. Following Jebb and Dawe, I have retained the reading ἀστῶν given by one group of manuscripts, whereas others (including the Laurentianus) give ἄνδρον, which seems to have been prompted by the ἄνδρα of line 735.

26. See B. Bravo, "*Sulân*. Représailles et justice privée contre des étrangers dans les cités grecques," ASNP, Ser. III, 10 (1980), pp. 675-987; as regards the interpretation of line 858 of *Oedipus at Colonus* and the word ῥύσιον, I do not believe, as Bravo does, that the use of the word *rhusion* is neutral. Creon uses it specifically in the sense of "reprisal," but the Athenian spectator understood it as violence pure and simple.

27. *Apud* Tycho von Wilamowitz-Möllendorf, "Die dramatische Technik des Sophokles," Berlin 1917, pp. 368-9. This interpretation infuriated K. Reinhardt, *Sophocle*, 1933 (Fr. tr. E. Martineau, Paris 1971, p. 274).

28. *Die griechische Tragödie*, Leipzig 1939, II, p. 245 n. *ad* Vol. I, p. 368, cited by Karl Reinhardt, *op. cit.*, p. 274 n.18.

29. Xenophon, *Hell.*, III, 5, 8: Diodorus, XII, 6, 3.

30. Cf. Segal, *op. cit. supra*, n.1, p. 362: "The contrast between the two cities and the two images of society that they embody is essential to an understanding of the play."

31. A Greek etymology with a military slant is defended by A. Heubeck, "κοίρανος, κόρραγος und Verwandtes," *Würzburger Jahrbücher für die Altertumswissenschaft*, NF 4 (1970), pp. 91-8.

32. On the disagreements surrounding the freedom of citizens in Athens at the end of the fifth century, see K.A. Raaflaub, "Democracy, Oligarchy and the Concept of the *Free Citizen* in Late Fifty-Century Athens," *Political Theory* 11, 4 (Nov. 1983), pp. 517-44.

33. Cf. lines 58-61: "All men of this land claim descent from him/Whose statue stands nearby: Colonus the horseman,/And bear his name in common with their own. That is this country...." Aeschylus, from the deme of Eleusis entitles one of his tragedies, now lost, *The Eleusinians*. One of those who heard me speak in Utrect, H. Teitler, has pointed out to me that Colonus was also the location for the extraordinary meeting of the popular assembly

that introduced the constitution of 411 (Thucydides, VIII, 67, 3).

34. See lines 638-40; Theseus leaves the choice to Oedipus: he can either remain at Colonus or accompany him to the center of the city.

35. See J.-P. Vernant, "La Tragédie grecque selon Louis Gernet," *Hommage à Louis Gernet*, Paris 1966, pp. 31-5.

36. P. Gauthier, *Symbola, Les étrangers et la justice dans les cités grecques*, Nancy 1972, p. 53.

37. Gauthier maintains that it is a matter of traditional proxeny, *op. cit.*, p. 53-4 and he cites (p. 54, n.126) Wilamowitz's contrary opinion.

38. For a meticulous study of the right of seizure, see B. Bravo, *op. cit. supra*, n.26.

39. See the classic study by D. Musti, "Sull' idea di συγγένεια in iscrizioni greche," *ASNP* 32 (1963), pp. 225-39.

40. I am leaving aside the connected question of the human sacrifice demanded by the oracle for the salvation of the Heracleidae.

41. Cf. A.-J. Festugière, "Tragédie et tomes sacrées," *RHR* (1973), pp. 3-24, reprinted in *Études d'histoire et de philologie*, Paris 1975, pp. 47-68, esp. pp. 67-8.

42. "Sophocles and the *polis*" (*supra*, n.1), p. 21.

43. I am here provisionally translating ἔμπολις as citizen, as Knox does. Most interpreters understand it exactly as he does.

44. It has recently been accepted by Dawe but not by Dain (1960), nor by M. Gigante in his translation (Syracuse 1976), nor by Colonna (1983), nor yet by Kamerbeek who, in his commentary, is loath to come to a decision, although he admits that ἔμπαλιν is not impossible (p. 101). In connection with the remarks that follow, I owe much to B. Bravo, J. Bollack, and M. Casevitz. All three have communicated to me a series of extremely detailed observations from which I learned a great deal – enough to persuade me to make a number of radical modifications to my initial hypothesis.

45. One would expect τοὔμπαλιν here, as in Euripides' *Hippolytus*, 390, but cf. *The Women of Trachis*, 358.

46. "Expel" is the precise meaning of the verb *ekballo*.

47. *The Libation Bearers*, 76; the *Seven*, 501.

48. Fr. 137, Kock, cited by Pollux, *Onomasticon*, IX, 27 (ed. Bethe, II, p. 153).

49. *Oedipus at Colonus*, 1372 and the note on p. 134 of Mazon's edition.

50. Robert Fitzgerald translates: "though not of Thebes." Mazon has "qui

ne serait pas ton concitoyen" (who would not be your fellow-citizen), but a more neutral translation is preferable. The scholiast interprets it as follows: ἐν τῇ αὐτῇ πόλει οἰκοῦντα (resident in the same city).

51. M. Casevitz categorically confirms this derivation: ἐμπολιτεύω is derived from ἔμπολις not from ἐμπολίτης (which would be absurd).

52. See the points made by J. De Romilly, pp. XX-XXI in her edition of Books IV and V (Belles-Lettres, 1967).

53. The problem should have been examined by F.G. Schnitzer, *Abhängige Orte im griechischen Altertum*, Munich 1958, pp. 91-2, but was not; for a study in depth, see D. Asheri, "Studio sulla storia della colonizzazione di Anfipoli sino alla conquista macedone," *RFIC* 3rd Series, 95 (1967), pp. 5-30; he concludes that all the groups of *empoliteuontes* were citizens; A.J. Graham, *Colony and Mother-city in Ancient Greece*, Manchester 1964, pp. 245-9, has the merit of posing the question of double citizenship squarely. While he rejects the notion that the Athenians of Amphipolis might have remained citizens of Athens, he nevertheless concludes that they eventually regained their former citizenship automatically, which is a clear indication of the fragility of the status of citizenship in Amphipolis.

54. On the facts, see E. Will, *Histoire politique du monde hellénistique*, I², Nancy 1978, pp. 374-98.

55. *IG* V, 2, 263, and *IG* V, 2, 19. The first text is noted by E.J. Bickerman, *RPh* 53 (1927), p. 365 and n.2; the comparison with the second text and the interpretation are due to Ivana Savalli, *Recherches sur les procédures relatives à l'octroi du droit de cité dans la Grèce antique d'après les inscriptions*, 3ᵉ cycle (thesis, Paris-I) 1983, 2 vols., I, pp. 112-3.

56. This is Bickerman's interpretation of the decree of Antigoneia.

57. There was no city comparable to Athens in the vicinity, in the fifty century, and so there were few contacts with neighboring cities so far as individuals were concerned, except in times of major crises. The situation was not the same in the case of two cities in Arcadia such as Tegaea and Magalopolis.

58. R. Fitzgerald translates simply as: "O Athens!"

59. B. Knox, "Sophocles and the *polis*," p. 24.

60. The Greek that I am translating here is δορύξενος, literally "guest by the lance"; on this subject see Plutarch, *Quaestiones* No. 17 together with the commentary by Halliday (Oxford 1928), p. 98. The word appears to have oscillated

between an individual who was *inside* the city and one who was *outside* it, as in this case. On these questions, see G. Herman's *Ritualised Friendship and the Greek City*, Cambridge 1985, pp. 160-75, although the occurrence of *doruxenos* on which I am commenting here is not mentioned.

61. See for example lines 1637, 1705, 1713-4, which I have deliberately selected from the end of the play.

62. In this instance, it is a matter of a hearth that is common to Theseus and Oedipus, but it would be difficult not to make the connection with the *prytaneum*; on this, see L. Gernet's classic study, "Sur le symbolisme politique: le foyer commun," in *Anthropologie de la Grèce antique*, Paris 1968, pp. 382-402.

63. I am repeating it here for the benefit of V. Di Benedetto, (not that I entertain much hope of convincing him), for whom tragic ambiguity is no more than an expression of the *mal du siècle* of the disorientated intellectuals of today; see his article, "La tragedia greca di Jean-Pierre Vernant," *Belfagor* 32, 4 (1977), and *Filologia e marxismo. Contra le mistificazioni*, Naples 1981, pp. 107-14.

64. See *supra*, Ch. 5.

65. Lysias, *Against Andocides*, 108.

66. Cf. N. Loraux, "L'Interférence tragique," *Critique* 317 (1973), pp. 908-25.

67. See *Oedipus Rex*, lines 1436-9, 1450-4 and 1516-21.

68. J. Gould, "Hiketeia," *JHS* 93 (1973), pp. 74-103; on the theme of the suppliant and the savior, see P. Burian, "Suppliant and Saviour: Oedipus at Colonus," *Phoenix* 28 (1974), pp. 408-29; D. Pralon has written a stimulating study on Greek supplication, which he has unfortunately not published.

69. The two classic studies on the subject are without doubt A.-J. Festugière's *op. cit. supra*, n.41; and Ch. VIII, pp. 307-55 of C.M. Bowra's *Sophoclean Tragedy*, Oxford 1944; it is possible to trace the historiography of this discussion further back thanks to D.A. Hester, "To Help One's Friends and Harm One's Enemies. A Study on the *Oedipus at Colonus*," *Antichthon* 11 (1977), pp. 22-41; Hester opposes what he calls the "orthodox" vision of the play, which interprets it as a triumph for heroic humanism and insists on Oedipus' moral rehabilitation.

70. It is a temptation to which those studying heroic cults have, to put it mildly, frequently succumbed; cf. the very title of L.R. Farnell's *Greek Hero Cults and Ideas of Immortality*, Oxford 1921; characteristically enough, in his *Sofocle* (*supra*, n.1), V. Di Benedetto entitles the chapter on *Oedipus at Colonus* "La buona

morte," pp. 217-47, although he does express reservations about the "orthodox" interpretation; *contra* the latter, the necessary antidotes can be found in the article by D.A. Hester (*supra* n.69), and in the pamphlet (*supra*, n.1) by R.G.A. Buxton, p. 30; even better is H. Dietz's study, "Sophokles, *Oed. Col.* 1583 ff.," *Gymnasium* 79 (1972), pp. 239-42; he shows that the idea of Oedipus' personal immortality, even more than his Athenian citizenship, rests upon a correction to the text of the manuscripts made by Z. Mudge in 1769. Where the manuscripts have at 1583-1584: ὡς λελοιπότα/κεῖνον τὸν αἰεὶ βίοτον ἐξεπίστασο [know that he has abandoned the kind of life that he has always lived], the text has been corrected to λελογχότα and translated — by Mazon, for example, into French, as: "Sache qu'il a conquis une vie qui ne finit pas" (know that he has won a life that will never end).

71. See the work edited by G. Gnoli and J.-P. Vernant, *La mort, les morts dans les sociétés anciennes*, Maison des sciences de l'homme, Cambridge and Paris 1982, esp. the introduction by J.-P. Vernant, pp. 5-15, and the studies by N. Loraux, pp. 27-43, C. Bérard, pp. 89-105, and A. Snodgrass, pp. 107-19; for *Oedipus at Colonus*, N.D. Wallace notes a number of further points in "*Oedipus at Colonus*: The Hero in his Collective Context," *QUCC* 32 (1979), pp. 39-52.

72. Let me cite, in chronological order, J. Pecirka, *The Formula for the Grant of Enktesis in Attic Inscriptions*, Acta Universitatis Carolina, Prague 1969; P. Gauthier, *Symbola* (*supra*, n.36); B. Bravo, "Sulân" (*supra*, n.26), together with P. Gauthier's review, *RD* 60 (1982), pp. 553-76; M.J. Osborne, *Naturalization in Athens*, 2 vols. (as of this writing); *Verhand. Konink. Aacad. Letteren*, nos. 98 (1981) and 101 (1982); I. Savalli, *Recherches sur...l'octroi du droit de cité* (*supra*, n.55); M.-F. Baslez, *L'étranger dans la Grèce antique*, Paris 1984. But one should, naturally, always return to A. Wilhelm's famous study, "Proxenie und Evergesie," Attische Urkunden, V, *SAWW* 220 (1942), pp. 11-86. In connection with one particular case, in Thasos (?), J. Pouilloux and F. Salviat, "Lichos, Lacédémonien, archonte à Thasos et le livre VIII de Thucydide," *CRAI* (April-June 1983), pp. 376-403, have also reflected upon the integration of foreigners. P. Gauthier has quite recently published *Les cités grecs et leurs bienfaiteurs*, Athens and Paris 1985. I. Savalli has produced a summary of his work in an article published in *Historia* XXXIV (1985), pp. 387-431.

73. M.J. Osborne, *Naturalization*, I, p.5.

74. The epigraphic documents are numbers 3 and 6, in Osborne's collec-

tion (*Naturalization*, I, pp. 31-33 and 37-41, and for the commentary, II, pp. 21-4 and 26-43).

75. As is well known, Wilamowitz, in a famous study, "Demotika der attischen Metoeken," *Hermes* XXII (1887), pp. 107-28 and 211-59, repr. in *Kleine Schriften*, V, I, Berlin 1937, pp. 272-342, called metics — somewhat exaggeratedly — "Quasi-bürger"; this expression is adopted for the *proxenos*, by M.-F. Baslez, *op. cit.*, p. 120. The expression will not do for ordinary metics but it is a useful label for the position of distinguished figures such as those mentioned by J. Pouilloux and F. Salviat, *op. cit. supra*, n.72, pp. 385-6.

76. It is easy to form some idea of this common area by comparing the evidence collected by Osborne and the tables published by Pecirka, *The Formula*, pp. 152-9.

77. I. Savalli, *Recherches ... sur l'octroi du droit de cité*, I, p. 19.

78. Aristotle, *Rhetoric* I, 136la, notes that honors go to "those who have done good but also to those who have the power to do so"; I am indebted to I. Savalli, who drew this text to my attention.

79. I. Savalli, *op. cit.*, II, pp. 17-8, gives two definite examples, from the fourth century, of the connection between a "supplication" and a "request": IG II², 218 and IG II², 337 (= Tod, *Greek Hist. inscr.* II, no. 189). The first text is particularly interesting here: It grants two natives of Abdera the protection of the council and the *strategoi* and, in an amendment, also the right to reside in Athens until they return home.

80. See Wilamowitz's study cited *supra*, n.75, and P. Gauthier, *Symbola*, p. 112.

81. Cf. Osborne, *Naturalization*, II, p. 33, on the subject of metics who proved themselves to be saviors of democracy.

82. In line 583, Theseus speaks of Oedipus' request: "your request concerns your last moments [τὰ λοίσθι' αἰτῆ τοῦ βίου])."

83. J. Jones, *op. cit. supra* n.1, p. 219, and more recently, R.P. Winnington-Ingram, *Sophocles*, pp. 339-40; Charles Segal, in his chapter devoted to *Oedipus at Colonus*, is also very conscious of this problem.

84. Cf. C. Segal, *Tragedy and Civilization*, p. 369; R.G.A. Buxton, *Sophocles*, p. 30, for his part comments: "It [*Oedipus at Colonus*] charts the crossing of a series of boundaries: from sacred grove to lawful ground, from outside a *polis* to inside it, from life to death."

492

85. The scholiast on line 1248 is clearly mistaken in situating them far to the west. On the Rhipaea, whose situation oscillates between the north and the northeast, see J. Desautels, "Les monts Rhipées et les Hyperboréens dans le traité hippocratique *Des Airs, des Eaux et des Lieux*," *REG* LXXXIV (1971), pp. 289-96; See also A. Ballabriga, *Le Soleil et le Tartare. L'image mythique du monde en Grèce archaïque*, Paris 1986, pp. 243-5.

86. Cf. B. Knox, in *The Three Theban Plays*, p. 264: "They will bury him just at the frontier, where he can be of no use to any other city."

87. As is usually explained, ὁδός here is certainly an alternative spelling for οὐδός, the threshold, introduced for reasons of meter. Οὐδός is also to be found in an oracle cited by the scholiast to line 57. According to other explanations, we should read ὁδός, road or path, and assume it to be an allusion to the path that leads to Hades. A play on words is certainly a possibility; cf. also *infra*, n.89.

88. For the exact location of this deme and what little we know of it, cf. D.M. Lewis, "The Deme Kolonos," *ABSA* (1955), pp. 12-7; Lewis writes: "We can now say with security that there was only one deme Kolonos, that it was a city-deme of Aigeis, and that it was the deme of Sophocles" (p. 16); cf. also P. Siewert, *Die Trittyn Attikas und die Heeresreform des Kleisthenes*, Munich 1982, pp. 88-9; on the exact form of the demotic, a vexed question for many years, see most recently J. Fairweather in F. Cairns (ed.), *Papers of the Liverpool Latin Seminar IV* (Liverpool 1984), pp. 343-4.

89. Cf. the scholium to line 1590, which refers to the descent to Hades and the rape there of Korē, the daughter of Demeter. Modern scholars have often followed a similar line of reasoning: cf. A.-J. Festugière, *op. cit. supra*, n.41, p.55, and R.P. Winnington-Ingram, *Sophocles*, p. 340. Neither cite their distant predecessor. Festugière points out that Hades is normally made of bronze and rightly considers as absurd the following explanation given in a note to line 1590 in the Dain-Mazon edition: "The entire hill was known as 'the threshold of bronze.' It was the mining threshold of Attica." That explanation may also stem from a scholium to line 57. To all these suggestions I should like to add one proposed by my Norwegian colleague, Vigdis Soleim: In Hesiod's *Theogony*, 749-50 and 811, we find a great bronze threshold, μέγαν οὐδὸν χάλκεον, at the foot of the door that separates day from night.

90. V. Di Benedetto writes (*Sofocle*, p. 234), that "it would be wrong to interpret this stasimon as a sign of Sophocles' commitment to the strictly politi-

cal values of the Athenian State. What Sophocles is exalting is not the *polis* as an urban center, but the countryside of Attica." His interpretation seems utterly mistaken to me. It ignores the fact that Colonus was a deme of the town and that sailors represent the spirit of the town better than that of the countryside.

91. Pausanias, I, 28, 7; cf. Valerius Maximus, V, 3, 3. Sophocles is the source of the Pseudo-Apollodorus, III, 5, 9. Pausanias (I, 30, 4) situated a *heroon* to Theseus and Pirithoos and one to Oedipus and Adrastus at Colonus. On this question of the Eumenides in reality and in tragedy, see the article by A.L. Brown, "Eumenides in Greek Tragedy," *CQ* 34 (1984), pp. 260-81. It provides so perfect an example of confusion that it seems worth mentioning. The "demonstration" that sets out to show that Sophocles' Eumenides have nothing to do with those of Aeschylus is a model of its kind.

92. A crater is also mentioned at line 159, which proves its importance.

93. He abstains from wine, and is sober (νέφον), as befits a companion of goddesses who receive offerings without wine (νεφάλια) and so are ἄοινοι (100); on the different meanings of line 100, cf. A. Henrichs, "The 'sobriety' of Oedipus; Sophocles *Oedipus at Colonus* 100 misunderstood," *HSPh* 87 (1983), pp. 87-100.

94. There is clearly a play on words here, between the accusative form of Oedipus' name, 'Οἰδίποδα, and ἐκ ὁδοῦ πόδα (113): "a foot off the road."

95. This expression remains mysterious. The scholium to line 192 provides a whole series of explanations: for instance, this step is compared to the "threshold of bronze" of line 57. Another explanation is that it is not really stone, but bronze. Two other remarks certainly make more sense: one is that this is "the equivalent of a rock," in other words a piece of stage scenery; the other, that it represents "the limit of the accessible zone": *horion*; the text of the manuscripts gives ἀντιπέτρου. Musgrave suggested correcting this to αὐτοπέτρου, that is to say, I suppose, a stone in the strict sense of the word, a correction that is followed by Dawe and mentioned, somewhat hesitantly, by Segal, p. 372. To me, it seems unacceptable: I believe that a hewn stone here stands in contrast to the unhewn stone on which Oedipus first sat down.

96. Cf. D. Seale, *Vision and Stagecraft in Sophocles*, London and Canberra 1982, p. 122: "Oedipus is now in a position to come to the necessary understanding and accommodation with the people of Colonus. He is also literally on the threshold between sacred and common ground."

97. See Charles Segal's attempt, *op. cit.*, p. 369, which is certainly the most

494

detailed. He points out that, according to a scholium of Lycophron, 766, and another of Pindar, *Pythian* IV, 246, the rock of Thoricus was connected with the creation of the horse from the semen of Poseidon.

98. A recent summary of the relevant discussions may be found in N.C. Hourmouziades, *Production and Imagination in Euripides: Form and Function of the Scenic Space*, Greek Soc. for Hum. Stud., Athens 1965, pp. 58-74, and O. Taplin, *op. cit. supra*, n.13, pp. 441-2. D. Seale's book cited above, n.96, does not really tackle the question in relation to Sophocles.

99. Cf. J. Jouanna, "Texte et espace théâtral dans les *Phéniciennes* d'Euripide," *Ktema* I (1976), pp. 81-97.

100. O. Taplin, who is somewhat hesitant over this question but does not dismiss the possibility of a relatively low platform, calls lines 192 ff. of *Oedipus at Colonus* "perhaps the strongest evidence in tragedy" of the existence of such platforms (*op. cit.*), p. 441.

101. P. Arnott, *Greek Scenic Conventions in the Fifth Century B.C.*, Oxford 1962, p. 35.

102. Cf. at 196, ὀκλάσας, "having crouched down."

CHAPTER XVI

*This study first appeared in *Quaderni di Storia* 14 (July-December 1981), pp. 3-29.

1. Apart from a few details, this study is substantially the same as the paper that I delivered in Bologna, at the Montenari Palace on May 17th, 1980, on the occasion of a round-table conference devoted to *Oedipus Rex* organized by ATER (Associazione teatrale di Emilia-Romagna) of Modena. I should like to thank the organizers most warmly for inviting me and the participants for their comments. In February 1981, I presented the same paper at Namur, at the conference of the Federation of Greek and Latin professors.

2. Plutarch, *Lycurgus*, 15; and *supra*, p. 249.

3. The works of E. Havelock drew my attention to this transformation.

4. At the Bologna Colloquium, the problem of Freud and *Oedipus Rex* was tackled by Sergio Molinari; see his book *Notazioni sulla Scienza dei Sogni in Freud*, Bologna 1979.

5. See *supra*, Ch. 4.

6. D. Anzieu, "Oedipe avant le complexe ou de l'interpretation pyschana-

lytique des mythes," *Les Temps modernes* 245 (October 1966), pp. 675-715.

7. See *supra*, p. 103.

8. J. Starobinski, Preface to E. Jones, *Hamlet et Oedipe*, tr. A.-M. Le Gall, Paris 1967, p. xix.

9. L. Constans, *La Légende d'Oedipe*, Paris 1881, pp. 93-103.

10. L. Schrade, *La Représentation d'Edipo Tiranno au Teatro Olimpico (Vicence 1585)*, a study followed by a critical edition of Sophocles' tragedy by Orsatto Giustiniani and of the music for the choruses by Angelo Gabrieli, *CNRS*, Paris 1960; A. Gallo, *La Prima Rappresentazione al teatro Olimpico con i progetti e le relazioni dei contemporanei*, preface by L. Puppi, Milan 1973. Henceforward I shall refer to these two works respectively as *Représentation* and *Prima Rappresentazione*. A second performance took place on March 5th, 1585.

11. The text is given in *Prima Rappresentazione*, pp. 53-8; cf. *Représentation*, pp. 47-51.

12. *Le Pain et le Cirque*, Paris 1976.

13. Count G. Montenari, *Del Teatro Olimpico di Andrea Palladio*, Padua 1749[2], p. 3. Montenari bases his information on a plea addressed "*a' Deputati al governo di essa Citta*," requesting them to grant "*Cittadinanza*" to twelve individuals; this was done in 1581.

14. In the long work by A. Visconti, *L'Italia nell'epoca della Contro-riforma dal 1516 al 1713*, Milan 1958, I found only two references to Vicenza, the one mentioning that Palladio had worked there (p. 128), the other noting the existence of workers in wool there (p. 229).

15. *La Historia di Vicenza*, Venice 1591, p. 160.

16. In the Venetian area, the fifteenth century saw a sharp increase in the influence of the aristocracy; cf. A. Ventura, *Nobiltà e popolo nella società veneta del '400 e '500*, Bari 1964, pp. 275-374; on Vicenza, cf. pp. 279-80 and 362-3; the information provided by this work nevertheless indicates that *cittadinanza* was still considered a privilege. My thanks go to my colleague A. Tenenti, who brought this work to my attention.

17. *Prima Rappresentazione*, p. 56.

18. *Ibid.*, pp. 39-51; cf. A. Gallo, *ibid.*, pp. xxii and xxviii, who cites a document from the archives of the Academy: "The *podestà* refuses to attend the performance." A. Gallo considers this behavior "difficult to interpret" but thinks that it represented a personal decision rather than official policy.

19. *Ibid.*, p. 55.

20. J.S. Ackerman, *Palladio*, Harmondsworth 1966, p. 180; of course there might be more to be said about that precise "moment." On the subject of Palladio and his theater, I have also consulted the following works and articles: L. Magagnato, "The Genesis of the Teatro Olimpico," *JWI* XIV (1951), pp. 209-20; L. Puppi, *Palladio*, London 1975; R. Schiavo, *Guida al Teatro Olimpico*, Vicenza 1980; H. Spelmann, *Andrea Palladio und die Antike*, Munich and Berlin 1964; the essential documentation is to be found in G. Zorzi's *Le Ville e i Teatri di A. Palladio*, Vicenza 1969.

21. J.S. Ackerman, *Palladio*, p. 40.

22. In the article cited *supra*, n.20.

23. *De Architectura*, V, 6, 8: "*secundum autem spatio ad ornatus comparato*"; *secundum* was for a long time understood as meaning "behind" rather than "beside."

24. There are constant references to Aristotle, in Pigafetta as well as in Riccoboni; cf. *Prima Rappresentazione*, pp. 39-42 and 54. On the choice of a Greek tragedy rather than a pastoral drama or an Italian tragedy, cf. *Prima Rappresentazione*, pp. 53-4, and A. Gallo, *ibid.*, pp. xix, xxi.

25. *Ibid.*, p. 59; besides, Pinelli was not present on March 3rd, 1585; cf. A. Gallo, *ibid.*, p. xxiii; contemporaries sometimes overestimated the capacity of the theater. G. Marzari (*Historia di Vicenza*, p. 117) declared that it could hold 5,000 spectators — a gross exaggeration: cf. *Représentation*, p. 48.

26. Little is known of the details; the main relevant document is a cameo by Antiodeo representing a performance of, as it happens, *Edipo Tiranno*; cf. R. Schiavo, *Guida*, pp. 127-32.

27. It is reproduced in *Prima Rappresentazione*, pp. 3-25; on the stage set, see in particular L. Schrade, *Représentation,*, pp. 51-6.

28. *Prima Rappresentazione*, p. 56; the curtain that concealed the stage set was lowered, not raised, cf. *ibid.*, and *Représentation*, p. 49.

29. Cf. L. Schrade, *Représentation*, pp. 65-77; I say "not deliberately" since the director, Ingegneri, certainly regarded the chorus as embodying the presence of the people on stage: "The chorus represents the country (*terra*)," *op. cit. infra*, n.40, pp. 18-9; *terra* here has the meaning of city, then.

30. *Prima Rappresentazione*, p. 49; L. Schrade notes (p. 76) that "of all these — mostly obtuse — observations put forward by Riccoboni...," this one,

at least, makes some sense since Gabrieli's music may well have been inspired by a number of polyphonic versions of the Lamentations.

31. *Prima Rappresentazione*, p. 9.

32. *Ibid.*, p. 10.

33. These are the figures recorded by A. Gallo, *ibid.*, p. xlv, and L. Schrade, *op. cit.*, p. 53; the documentation is somewhat contradictory and in some cases the figures given are lower.

34. *Prima Rappresentazione*, pp. 13-5; the priests' costumes appear to have been inspired by the traditional costumes of Jewish priests in Renaissance art.

35. Respectively, *Prima Rappresentazione*, p. 15 and p. 56.

36. *Ibid.*, p. 12.

37. A solemn mass was celebrated by the academicians on March 4th, 1585.

38. "For the king and the people as a whole, it was a time for supplication, not for pomp" (*ibid.*, p. 31).

39. *Ibid.*

40. Ingegneri was an important theoretician of stage management, a subject on which he wrote several specialist works (cf. L. Schrade, *Représentation*, pp. 51-2); his most important work, published in Ferrara in 1598 was entitled: *Della poesia rappresentativa a del modo di rappresentare le favole sceniche*; it includes some general remarks on the subject of the staging of *Edipo Tiranno*, see in particular p. 18.

41. *Prima Rappresentazione*, p. 8. This dichotomy comes from Aristotle, *Rhetoric*, III, 1403b 20-1404a 8, and *Poetics* 26, 1461b 26-1462a 4; on these texts, see A. Lienhard-Lukinovitch, *La voce e il gesto nella retorica di Aristotele*, in Societa di linguistica italiana, *Retorica e scienze del linguaggio*, Rome 1979, pp. 75-92.

42. *Ibid.*, p. 18.

43. *Ibid.*, p. 8.

44. A. Dacier, *L'Oedipe et L'Electre de Sophocle, tragédies grecques traduites en Français, avec des remarques*, Paris 1692.

45. By Boivin (together with Aristophanes' *Birds*), Paris 1729; by Father Brumoy, in *Théâtre des Grecs*, Paris 1730, itself produced in a new edition by Rochefort and Laporte du Theil in 1785); and by Rochefort as part of the complete works of Sophocles, I, Paris 1788, pp. 3-133.

46. Marie Delcourt, *Etudes sur les traductions grecs et latins en France depuis la Renaissance*, Brussels 1925, p. 5.

47. By M.L. Coupe, a translation in the *Théâtre de Sénèque*, Paris 1795, I, pp. 309-400; the commentary is interesting in that it suggests an amalgam of "tragic novels" (p. 398).

48. The edition by Brunck, with a preface by J. Schweighaüser, was published in Strasburg in 1779, and one by F.A. Wolf in Halle in 1787.

49. R. Bray, cited by R. Zuber, *Perrot d'Ablancourt et ses 'belles infidéles'. Traduction et critique de Balzac à Boileau*, thesis, Paris 1968, p. 19; many references could be given here; for example, G. De Rochefort in his "Observations sur les difficultés qui se rencontrent dans la traduction des Poètes tragiques grecs," published as an Introduction to *Théâtre de Sophocle*, I, Paris 1788, pp. xxi-xliii, explained that the readers who are most to be feared "are the half-scholars. They raise their voices in society; they are to be found all over the place; they are believed without question; they are regarded as profound by superficial people; they are not afraid to make rash pronouncements, on the basis of no more than a cursory glance, on works upon which the authors have meditated at length"; now the enemy to be feared was the "educated gentleman."

50. Just about the only work that can be cited is a dissertation from Bochum (1933): W. Jordens, *Die französischen Oidipusdramen. Ein Beitrag zum Fortleben der Antike und zur Geschichte der französischen Tragödie*. Even W. Jordens traced only five adaptations in the eighteenth century.

51. C. Biet, *Les transcriptions théâtrales d'Oedipe-Roi au XVIIIe siècle*, 3e cycle (thesis, supervised by J. Chouillet, Paris-III, Paris), 1980; I was privileged to be one of the examiners and have since enjoyed discussing the author's conclusions with him on a number of occasions.

52. I shall be mentioning a number of these adaptations; but we must hope that C. Biet will himself publish the documentation that he has collected.

53. See Noemi Hepp, *Homère en France au XVIIe siècle*, Paris 1969.

54. P. Coustel, *Règles de l'Education des Enfants où il est parlé de la manière dont il faut se conduire, pour leur inspirer les sentiments d'un solide piété et pour leur apprendre parfaitement les Belles Lettres*, 2 vols., Paris 1687, pp. 193-4; I am indebted to C. Biet for this reference and for many others too; on the problems of translating the Bible, see M. de Certeau, "L'idée de traduction de la Bible au XVIIe siècle: Sacy et Simon," *Recherches de science religieuse* 66 (1978), pp. 73-92; I have borrowed the following important statistics from him (p. 80): between 1695 and 1700, fifty-five out of the sixty Parisian editions of the Bible were in the

French language. Half a century earlier the proportions were reversed. The two authors studied held different, even opposed, views about translation; see also M. Delcourt, *op. cit. supra*, n.46, who stresses the importance of the role played by Pierre-Daniel Huet.

55. Voltaire's *Oeuvres complètes*, Edition Besterman 86, Geneva 1969, p. 49 (for the date, see p. 50).

56. "De l'Iphigénie de Racine à celle de Goethe," in *Pour un esthétique de la reception*, tr. C. Maillard, preface by J. Starobinski, Paris 1978, pp. 210-62.

57. *Lettres écrites par l'auteur qui contiennent la critique de l'Oedipe de Sophocle, de celui de Corneille et du sien*, Paris 1719, reprinted in Voltaire, *Oeuvres*, II, Paris 1877, pp. 11-46. For the year 1719 alone, Biet mentions no less than six pamphlets discussing the new Oedipus; cf. R. Pomeau, *La Religion de Voltaire*, Paris 1969, pp. 85-91, and J. Moureaux, *L'Oedipe de Voltaire. Introduction à une psychocritique*, Paris 1973.

58. Vol. III, published under the direction of MM. de Rochefort and Du Theil of the Académie royale des Inscriptions et Belles Lettres.

59. In the catalogue of the Bibliothèque nationale, and in Cioranescu's *Bibliographie de la Littérature française*, n.53638, this dissertation is attributed to G. de Rochefort, upon what grounds I do not know, but the text is certainly presented as being the work of the author of *Jocaste*; on Lauraguais, the study by P. Fromageot, "Les fantaisies littéraires, galantes, politiques et autres d'un grand seigneur. Le comte de Lauraguais (1733-1824)," *Revue des Etudes historiques*, 80 (1914), pp. 15-46, does not mention this *Jocaste*.

60. They are to be found in Vol. IV, pp. 3-68, and VIII, pp. 459-519 of *Oeuvres* by A. Houdar de la Motte, Paris 1754; see also in VIII, pp. 377-458, the "Quatrième discours à l'occasion de la tragédie d'Oedipe."

61. His reflections on the relationship between Oedipus and his adoptive father Polybus strike me as virtually unique.

62. S. Dubrovsky, *Corneille et la dialectique du héros*, Paris 1963, pp. 337-9; A. Stegmann, *L'Héroisme cornelien. Genèse et signification*, I, Paris 1968, pp. 618-9; A. Viala, *Naissance de l'écrivain*, Paris 1985, pp. 225-8.

63. A. Dacier, *op. cit.*, pp. 149, 169, 198.

64. These quotations are taken from his letter VI on *Oedipus* (1729), "which comprises a dissertation on the choruses," in *Oeuvres complètes*, II, Gernier, Paris 1877, pp. 42-4.

65. N.-G. Leonard, *Oedipe ou la Fatalité*, in *Oeuvres*, I, Paris 1798, pp. 51-91.

66. The only exceptions among the plays that have come down to us are Sophocles' *Ajax* and *Philoctetes* and the *Rhesus* that is attributed to Euripides: In these three plays, the chorus is composed of adult soldiers or sailors.

67. Brumoy, *Théâtre des Grecs*, Paris 1785, I, pp. 186-7.

68. IV, Ch. 71, p. 32.

69. The two characters are quite distinct in the plays by Voltaire; de Buffardin D'Aix, *Oedipe à Thèbes ou le fatalisme*, Paris 1784; Marie-Joseph Chénier, Bernard D'Héry, *Oedipe-Roi*, London and Paris 1786, Duprat De La Touloubre, *Oedipe à Thèbes* (an opera), Paris 1791; and N.G. Léonard, *Oedipe ou la Fatalité*.

70. P.F. Biancolelli (alias Dominique) and A.F. Riccoboni, *Oedipe travesti, comédie par M. Dominique*, Paris 1719.

71. M.A. Legrand, *Le Chevalier Errant. Parodie de l'Oedipe de Monsieur de la Motte*, Paris (N.D.; 1726?).

72. *Oedipe-Roi*, 707-10; 857-8; 946-7; on Voltaire's struggle against the "terrible god" and the "cruel priest," at the time he was writing *Oedipe*, cf. the pages already mentioned, by R. Pomeau, *La Religion de Voltaire*[2], pp. 85-91.

73. *Oedipe-Roi*, a lyrical tragedy in five acts, London and Paris 1786.

CHAPTER XVII

*An earlier version of this study appeared in *L'Homme* 93, XXV (1) (January–March 1985), pp. 31-58.

1. The play was written during Euripides' stay with King Archelaus, in Macedon where the poet, already over seventy, visited in 408 and where he later died in 406. It was produced for the first time in Athens in 405, directed by Euripides the Younger, who was either his son or his nephew, as part of a trilogy that also comprised *Iphigenia at Aulis* and *Alcmeon* and that won Euripides a posthumous first prize.

2. E. Sandys, *The* Bacchae *of Euripides*, Cambridge 1980 (4th ed.); E.R. Dodds, Euripides, *Bacchae*, Oxford 1960 (2nd ed.); R.P. Winnington-Ingram, *Euripides and Dionysus: An Interpretation of the* Bacchae, Cambridge 1948; G.S. Kirk, *The* Bacchae *of Euripides*, Cambridge 1979 (1st ed. 1970); Jeanne Roux, *Les* Bacchantes, Vol. I: *Introduction, texte, traduction*, Paris 1970, Vol. II: *Commentaire*, 1972; Charles Segal, *Dionysiac Poetics and Euripides'* Bacchae, Princeton 1982. The following may also be consulted: M. Lacroix, *Les* Bacchantes *d'Euripide*, Paris

1976; E. Coche De La Ferté, "Penthée et Dionysos. Nouvel essai d'interprétation des *Bacchantes* d'Euripide" in Raymond Bloch (ed.), *Recherches sur les religions de l'Antiquité classique*, Geneva 1980, pp. 105-258; H. Foley, *Ritual Irony: Poetry and Sacrifice in Euripides*, Ithaca 1985, pp. 205-58.

3. On this point, cf. the fine study by H. Foley, "The Masque of Dionysus," *TAPhA* 110 (1980), pp. 107-33.

4. On a whole series of vases that archaeologists are in the habit of calling the "Lenaea vases," the idol of Dionysus is represented as a post or pillar draped in some clothing and bearing a bearded mask, often seen full face, fixing the onlooker with wide-open eyes. On this series, cf. J.-L. Durand and F. Frontisi-Ducroux, "Idoles, figures, images," *RA* I (1982), pp. 81-108.

5. Cf. Park McGinty, *Interpretation and Dionysus: Method in the Study of the God*, The Hague, Paris and New York 1978; and in the collective work, *Studies in Nietzsche and the Classical Tradition*, James L. O'Flaherty, Timothy F. Sellner, and Robert M. Helm (eds.), Chapel Hill 1976, and the following study: Hugh Lloyd-Jones, "Nietzsche and the Tradition of the Dionysian," pp. 165-89. Finally, attention should also be drawn to the important study by Albert Henrichs, "Loss of Self, Suffering, Violence: The Modern View of Dionysus from Nietzsche to Girard," *HSPh* 88 (1984), pp. 205-40.

6. D. Sabatucci, *Saggio sul misticismo greco*, Rome 1965.

7. Cf. Plato, *Symposium*, 210a; *Phaedo*, 69c; and IG 1⁶6, 49.

8. Cf. Aristotle, fr. 115, Rose.

9. Any study of the "interferences" that may have arisen at particular times, in particular places, between Dionysism, Eleusianism, and Orphism should consider the terms: τελετή, ὄργια, ὀργιασμός, ὀργιάζειν, βάκχος, βακχεύς, βακχεύειν, βάκχειος; cf. Giovanni Casadio, "Per un' indagine storico-religiosa sul culto di Dioniso in relazione alla fenomenologia dei Misteri," I and II, *Studie e Materiali di Storia delle Religioni* VI, 1-2 (1982), pp. 209-34, and VII,.1 (1983), pp. 123-49.

10. Cf., most recently, Gilbert Rouget, *La musique et la transe. Esquisse d'une théorie générale des relations de la musique et de la possession*, Paris 1980 (preface by Michel Leiris).

11. On the affinities between "magi" such as Abaris, Aristeas, Hermotimus, Epimenides, Pherecydes, Zalmoxis as well as Pythagoras and the Hyperborean Apollo, cf. E. Rohde, *Psyche: The Cult of Souls and Belief in Immortality among the Greeks*, tr. W.B. Hillis, New York 1966, pp. 88 ff.; E.R. Dodds, *The Greeks*

and the Irrational, Berkeley 1959; M. Detienne, *La notion de Daimon dans le pythagorisme ancien*, Paris 1963, pp. 69 ff.

12. Cf. on this point, the important article by A. Henrichs, "Changing Dionysiac Identities," pp. 143-7 of which are devoted to maenad rituals, *Jewish and Christian Self-Definition*, vol. III, *Self Definition in the Graeco-Roman World*, ed. Ben E. Meyer and E.P. Sanders, London 1982, pp. 137-60.

13. δείκνυμι: 47, 50; φαίνομαι: 42, 182, 528, 646, 1031.

14. γιγνώσκω: 859, 1088; μανθάνω: 1113, 1296, 1345.

15. φανερὸς ὄμμασιν.

16. μορφή: 4, 54; εἶδος: 53; φύσις: 54.

17. At 810 ff., the stranger asks Pentheus if he wishes to see the bacchants on the mountain. "I would pay a great sum to see that sight," exclaims the young man, confessing to his ardent desire to see a spectacle that he at the same time claims he would be sorry to behold. "But for all your sorrow, you'd like very much to see this bitter [πικρά] spectacle," says the stranger ironically (815). And a bitter spectacle is exactly what Pentheus had planned for the young bacchant (357) by casting him into chains, chains that the palace miracle turned into the most bitter of spectacles for Pentheus himself (634). On his desire to behold the bacchants indulging in their shameful behavior, see also 957-8 and 1058-62.

18. φύλαξ: 959; κατάσκοπος: 916, 956, 981.

19. ἐμφανῶς: 818; cf. the irony, for Dionysus, of a comparison with line 22.

20. ἀναφαίνει: 538; cf. again, the irony, for Dionysus, of a comparison with line 528.

21. τὸν θεὸν ὁρᾶν γὰρ φῇς σαφῶς, ποῖός τις ἦν.

22. ὅστις ἔστι: 220, 247, 769, cf. 894.

23. παρὼν ὁρᾶ.

24. οὐ γὰρ φανερὸς ὄμμασίν γ᾽ ἐμοῖς./... οὐκ εἰσορᾷς, 501-2.

25. φάνηθι... ἰδεῖν/... ὁρᾶσθαι, 1017-8.

26. γελῶντι προσώπῳ, 1021.

27. F. Frontisi and J.-P. Vernant, "Features of the Mask in Ancient Greece," *supra*, Ch. 9.

28. οὐκέτ᾽ εἰσορᾶν παρῆν, 1077.

29. ἐκ δ᾽ αἰθέρος φωνή τις, 1078; αἰθήρ, 1084.

30. At 971, Dionysus tells Pentheus: "You are an extraordinary young man, and you go to an extraordinary experience." Cf. also 856. On Dionysus

deinos and the *deina* that he provokes, cf. 667, 716, 760, 861, 1260, 1352.

31. στηρίζον...κλέος, 972.

32. πεσόντι, 1022-3.

33. ὀρθὴ δ' ἐς ὀρθὸν αἰθέρ' ἐστηρίζετο, 1073.

34. ὑψοῦ δὲ θάσσων ὑψόθεν χαμαιπετὴς/ πίπτει πρὸς οὖδας, 1111-2.

35. εἰς αἰθέρα, 150; cf. 240.

36. πέσῃ πεδόσε, 136.

37. χωροῦσι δ' ὥστ' ὄρνιθες ἀρθεῖσαι, 748. "Breaking loose like startled doves, ...they flew...," πελείας ὠκύτητ' οὐκ ἥσσονες, 1090.

38. πρὸς οὐρανὸν/ καὶ γαῖαν ἐστήριζε φῶς σεμνοῦ πυρός, 1082-3.

39. δεινὰ δρῶσι θαυμάτων τ' ἐπάξια, 716, cf. 667.

40. Eubulus, the fourth-century comic poet has Dionysus speak of the tenth crater of wine, which no longer brings health or pleasure or love or sleep, but only *mania*: "That is the one that makes men stumble [σφάλλειν]," 11 fr. 94 Koch = Athenaeus, II, 36. Together with Iacobs' correction at line 10. On Dionysus *sphaleotas*, cf. G. Roux, *Delphes, son oracle et ses dieux*, Paris 1976, pp. 181-4, and M. Detienne, *Dionysos à ciel ouvert*, Paris 1986.

41. δεινότατος, ἠπιώτατος, 861.

42. τελετὰς εἰδώς, 73.

43. βιοτὰν ἁγιστεύει, 74; θιασεύεται ψυχάν, 75, which may also be translated "make oneself, in one's soul, a member of the *thiasos*" or "is made, in one's soul, a member of the *thiasos*."

44. Cf. J. Roux, *Les Bacchantes*, I, *op. cit.*, pp. 43-71, and also, although in a rather different form, H. Rohdich, *Die euripideische Tragödie*, Heidelberg 1968, pp. 131-68.

45. Cf. 491, where it is Dionysus that Pentheus describes as θρασύς and οὐκ ἀγύμναστος λόγων, "not lacking in training in replying."

46. In particular, E.R. Dodds, *Euripides' Bacchae, op. cit.*, pp. 103-5; cf. also J. Roux, *op. cit.*, p. 337, and C. Segal, *Dionysiac Poetics...*, *op. cit.*, p. 294.

47. Cf. C. Segal, *op. cit.*, p. 27 ff.

48. ἐπτόπται, 214; πτοηθέν, 1268.

49. μαίνῃ, 326; μέμηνας, 359.

50. τὸ φρονεῖν, 390; cf. 427: σοφὸν...πραπίδα φρένα τε.

51. εὖ φρονοῦμεν, 196; σωφρονεῖς, 329; σοφὸν...φρένα, 427; φρένας...ὑγιεῖς, 947-8; σωφρονεῖν, 1341. Similarly, cf. the words addressed to Dionysus by the

comic poet Diphilus (Fr. 86 Kock = Athenaeus, II, 35d): "O you, the most dear to all sensible men [τοῖς φρονοῦσι] and the most wise [σοφώτατε], Dionysus." Wine itself possesses intellectual virtues to be celebrated: to those who use it properly, it brings "laughter, wisdom [σοφία], good understanding [εὐμαθία], and good advice [εὐβουλία]." *Chairemon*, fr. 15 N² = Athenaeus, II, 2, 35d.

52. οὐδὲν φρονεῖς, 332; cf. also 312; ἀφροσύνη, 387, 1301.

53. ἐμάνητε, 1295; cf. G.S. Kirk, *The* Bacchae *of Euripides*, *op. cit.*, p. 129, the commentary on line 1295.

54. ἐμμανεῖς, 1094; cf. also ἀφροσύνης, 1301.

55. οὐ φρονοῦσ' ἃ χρὴ φρονεῖν, 1123.

56. ἡδύ... ἐν οὔρεσιν, 135; χάριν, 139, which balances the χαίρει at 134.

57. Cf. 680-713; 1050-3. In the course of the marvels that they cause to happen, armed with their wands (*thursoi*), the mountain itself, with all its beasts, was swept up in the same spirit, joining in the bacchanale (726-7).

58. On this abrupt change of attitude and behavior, this sudden switch from *mania* to *lussa*, cf. 731 ff., and 1093 ff.

59. φάνηθι, 1018; φανερός, 992, 1012.

60. δεικνὺς ἐμαυτόν, 50.

61. δεῖξον, 1200.

62. Cf. 1296: "now, I understand [ἄρτι μανθάνω]"; similarly, at 1113, Pentheus, dashed to the ground and delivered into the hands of the frenzied bacchants, on the point of death, "understood [ἐμάνθανεν]."

63. Cf. 1345, where Dionysus declares: "You have understood me too late. When there was time, you did not know me." So, earlier, when Agave and the Theban women "clearly recognized" the call of Bacchus which launched them against Pentheus, that did not mean that they knew Dionysus. To recognize the call of the god, κελευσμὸν Βακχίου, that is, to give way to his impulsion, is one thing; to know the god, that is, to experience the revelation of his epiphany, is quite another.

64. J. De Romilly, "Le thème du bonheur dans les *Bacchantes* d'Euripide," *REG* LXXVI (1963), p. 367.

65. εὐδαίμων, 902, 904, 911; μακαρίζω, 911.

66. βίοτος εὐδαίμων, 911; cf. 426: εὐαίωνα διαζῆν, "he devotes his life to happiness," and 74: βιοτὰν ἁγιστεύει, "he hallows his life."

67. In particular in Ch. VII: "Metatragedy: Art, Illusion, Imitation," *op. cit.*

68. *Translator's Note.* The translation of the classical texts I have used, some-times slightly adapting them, are as follows:

The Loeb Classical Library, London and Cambridge, Mass.
AESCHYLUS: *Agamemnon*, transl. Herbert Weir Smyth, 1926; *The Eumenides*, transl. Herbert Weir Smyth, 1926; *The Libation Bearers*, transl. Herbert Weir Smyth, 1926; *Seven against Thebes*, transl. Herbert Weir Smyth, 1930. ARISTOPHANES: *Frogs*, transl. Benjamin Bickley Rogers, 1968; *Wasps*, transl. Benjamin Bickley Rogers, 1967. ATHENAEUS: transl. Charles Burton Gulick, 1957. DIOGENES LAERTIUS: transl. R.D. Hicks, 1966. HERODOTUS: transl. A.D. Godley, 1940. PAUSANIAS: transl. W.H.S. Jones, 1969. PLUTARCH: *Agesilaus*, transl. Bernadotte Perrin, 1961; *Lysander*, transl. Bernadotte Perrin, 1968; *Pericles*, transl. Bernadotte Perrin, 1951. THUCYDIDES: transl. Charles Forster Smith, 1969; XENOPHON: *Hellenica*, transl. Carleton L. Brown, 1968.

The University of Chicago Press, Chicago and London.
AESCHYLUS: *The Suppliant Maidens*, transl. S.G. Bernardete, 1956. EURIPIDES: *The Bacchae*, transl. William Arrowsmith, 1958; *The Heraclidae*, transl. Ralph Gladstone, 1955; *Orestes*, transl. William Arrowsmith, 1958; *The Phoenician Women*, transl. Elizabeth Wyckoff, 1959. SOPHOCLES: *Ajax*, transl. John Moore, 1957; *Antigone*, transl. Elizabeth Wyckoff, 1954; *Electra*, transl. David Grene, 1957; *Oedipus at Colonus*, transl. Robert FitzGerald, 1954; *Oedipus Rex*, transl. David Grene, 1957; *The Women of Trachis*, transl. Michael Jameson, 1957.

The Penguin Classics, Harmondsworth.
HOMER: *The Odyssey*, transl. E.V. Rieu, 1948.

Subject Index

ABARIS, 502 n.11.
aboulia, 66.
Absence/presence, 187, 190, 205, 243-5, 383, 395-6.
Accademie Olimpica (Olympic Academy), Academicians, 361, 365-8.
Acculturation, 385.
Acheloos, 320.
Achaemenides, 308.
Achilles, 146, 307.
Ackerman, J., 368.
Act, action, 26-7, 32-3, 57-64, 66, 72, 77-8, 89-92, 121; see also Agent.
Actor(s), 24, 34, 305, 308, 310-1, 359.
adikein, adikēma, adikia, 64, 121.
Adonis, 402.
Adrastus, 300, 305, 494 n.91.
Aegis, 192.
Aegisthus, 74-7, 150, 153-6, 321.
Aeschines, 332.
Aeschylus, 33, 181, 249-272 passim; and agent, 51-4; and responsibility, 70-1, 74-7; Agamemnon, 92-3, 114-5, 135-53 passim, 334; Choephori, 153-7, 334; The Eleusinians, n. 33; Eumenides, 154-9 passim; Oresteia, 141-59 passim, 252-3; The Persians, 244, 251-2, 255, 257, 303; Philoctetes, 163; Prometheus; 256-7; Seven Against Thebes, 35-8, 40, 251, 253,

256, 273-300 passim, 305, 334, 375; The Suppliants, 26, 39, 256-7, 334, 339, 341.
Aegyptus, 340.
Aethra, 141.
Agamemnon, 47-8, 71-7, 115, 141-159 passim, 253, 257, 263, 266, 270, 272.
Agathon, 28, 305, 324.
Agave, 152, 398, 403-9.
Age groups, 161-179 passim, 198-9, 267.
Agent, 32, 36, 44-7, 49-54, 60-71, 77-83, 88-92.
Agesilaus, 211.
Agis, 211.
agnoia, 64; see Ignorance.
agōn, 179, 249.
Agora, 306, 419.
agos, 122, 128, 131-3, 137, 435 n.101.
Agriculture, 159,166.
agrios, 167; see Wild, wildness.
agronomos, 161.
agros, 166.
aitēsis, 352.
aitia, aitios, 67-8, 75, 81; see Guilt; Responsibility.
aix, 185.
Ajax, 18, 312, 319, 343, 351.
akōn, akousios, 46, 56, 60-1, 63-4, 78.
Aktor, 297, 483 n.80.

alastōr, 74.
Alberti, L.B., 324.
Alcibiades, 211, 252-3, 436 n.121, 460 n.98.
Alcmeonids, 128, 313.
alektroi, 314.
Amazon, 99.
Ambiguity, 17-9, 29-48 *passim*, 319-21.
Ambivalence, 201-2, 209.
Ambush, 320.
Amphiaraos, 262, 284, 290, 299.
Amphipolis, 345.
amphiptolis, 344.
amumōn, 132.
Amynus, 303.
anagnōrisis, 117.
anaitios, 74.
anankē, 52, 59, 70, 72; see Necessity.
anaphainein, 503 n.20.
Anarchy/despotism, 265, 336, 419.
Ancients and moderns, 272.
andreia, 199.
Androgynous, 217.
Animal, animality, 135-7, 143, 152, 167, 183, 193-4, 197, 199, 204, 227, 390, 393.
anomia, 138.
Anthesteria, 383.
Antigone, 16, 26, 40-2, 101-2, 113, 258, 266, 306-7, 314-5, 334.
Antigonus Doson, 346.
Antigoneia, 346.
Anzieu, D., 93-109 *passim*, 363.
Apate, 161-2, 170-1, 463 n.138; *see* Cunning.
Apatouria, 161, 170.
aphoria, 130; *see* Sterility.
Aphrodite, 39, 55, 97-9, 421 n.11.
apodiopompeisthai, 434 n.96.
apoikiai, 346.
apolis, 122, 135, 137, 172, 223, 316, 342.
Apollo, 39; and Dionysus, 384, 388; in *Eumenides*, 333, 418 n.4; and masculine heredity, 267; Hyperbo-

rean, 502 n.11; oracular, 262-3; and responsibility, 79, 316; savior, 123; at the Thargelia, 129.
apopempein, 434 n.96.
apoptolis, 342.
aporia, 51.
Apotropaic, 192.
apparato, 371.
ara, 35; *see* Curse.
archē, 67-8.
archegos, 400.
Archelaus, 501 n.1.
Archon(s), 33, 185, 341.
Areopagus, 255-6, 333-4, 338, 419-20.
Ares, 288, 293.
aretē, 171.
Argos, 35, 333-5, 339-41, 356.
Aristeas, 245 n.11.
Aristides, 269, 350.
Aristophanes, 383; *Frogs*, 249, 252-3, 324, 362.
Aristotle, 241; and action, 37-66; and *mimesis*, 44, 242-3; and ostracism, 135-6; and *philia*, 100; *Poetics*, 15, 29, 89, 250; and responsibility, will, 55-60, 66-9; in Vicenza, 368, 371.
Arnaud D'Andily, 372.
Art, 237-40, 321-4; *see techné*.
Artemis, 39, 145; in *Agamemnon*, 47, 145-7, 261; and mask, 190, 195-201; and virginity, 99.
artipous, 211.
Artisans, 264-272.
Ascetic, 385, 387, 390, 411.
Asclepius, 303.
asphaleia, 340.
Assembly of the People, 334, 376.
astos, 344.
astu, 356.
Atalanta, 294, 299.
atē, Atē, 35, 62, 74, 76, 81, 253, 293, 297, 308.
Athamas, 132.
Athena, 123; at Colonus, 357; in *Eumenides*, 39, 159, 259, 265, 333,

336, 418-20; and Gorgon, 192-3;
and incest, 99; in the *Oresteia*, 267;
and Philoctetes, 176-8.
atimastēr, 295.
atimos, 168.
Atreidae, 48, 73-4, 147, 257, 260-1.
Attis, 402.
atuchēma, 65.
autezousion, 424 n.22.
Autochthonous, autochthony, 207,
280-1, 298, 483 n.83.; *see also*
Spartoi.
Autonoe, 405.
Autophonos, 298.
Authority, 26, 39.
autourgoi, 335.
azux, 135.

BACCHANTS, 158, 381-412 *passim*.
baccheios, baccheuein, baccheus, bacchos,
502 n.9.
Bacchiads, 217-21.
Bacchylides, 252.
Bacon, H., 279, 297, 481 n.54.
Barbarians, 265, 292, 399, 403.
Barrel, 228, 230, 232, 235.
Barthelemy, Abbé, *Le voyage du jeune
Anacharsis*, 378.
basileus (*vs*. tyrant), 338.
Bastard, bastardy, 219, 303; *see nothos*.
Battiads, Battus, 209.
Baubo, 195.
Bear, 198.
Beard, 194.
bebaios, 211.
bēma, 310, 357-9.
Bendis, 402.
Bestial, bestiality; *see* Animal,
animality.
Beyond, 397, 399, 411.
bia, Bia, 39, 55, 260.
Biancolelli, P.F., 378.
Biet, C., 375, 379, 499 n.51.
bios, 168.
Bisexuality, 218.

Black: *see* White.
Blind, blindness, 32, 91, 106, 119,
409.
Blood, 159, 296.
Boar, 193, 299.
Body, 271.
Boivin, 375.
Bollack, J., 19-21, 343, 362, 484 n.1.
bomos, 153.
bora, 150-2, 457 n.46, 457 n.52.
Boulē, 255.
*boule, boulema, boulesis, boulesthai,
bouleuein/esthai, bouleusis*, 57-8,
65-6, 76.
Bouphonia, 144.
Bouzuges, 313.
Bow, 155, 164-5, 167, 170-6, 307,
317-8, 321; *see also* Bowman.
Bowman/hoplite, 155, 161-79 *passim*,
264, 267-9.
Brasidas, 345.
Brauronia, 197.
Bravo, B., 343, 484 n.1, 487 n.26.
Brumoy, Abbé, 374, 378.
Bull, 152.
Bulgakov, V., 398.
Burkert, W., 142.

CADMUS, 298.
Calchas, 146-7, 362.
Callimachus, 270, 309.
Callisto, 198.
Cambyses, 308.
Cannibalism, 150.
Capaneus, 286, 289, 293, 298-9.
Carnival, 132, 200.
Casevitz, M., 343, 346.
Cassandra, 148, 150, 263, 271-2.
Castration, 95-8.
Catalepsy, 388.
Chance, *see Tuche*.
Change of state, 388-9.
Chaos, 95-6, 400, 402.
Character (and responsibility), 36,
67-70, 75-80, 83.

Charis, charis, 98-9, 397.
Chenier, M.-J., 361, 377, 379.
Chersonese, 309.
choleuein, 467 n.18.
cholos, 211.
chōra, 162-167.
Chorus, *vs.* actor, 23-4, 33-4, 257; in *Agamemnon,* 74-7, 115; and city, citizens, 258, 311-2, 377, 418 n.3; and decision, 258, 312; in the eighteenth century, 376-9; *vs.* hero, 18, 43, 186, 258, 305, 310-2; in *Oedipus at Colonus,* 338-9; in *Oedipus Rex,* 77-9; and people, 258; in *Seven against Thebes,* 279-82; in Vicenza, 369-70.
chrestoi, 335.
Christ, 17.
Christus patiens, 17.
Chrysaor, 194.
Chrysothemis, 307.
Chthonians, 40, 306.
Cimon, 255, 350.
Circularity (and lameness), 210.
Citizens (in *Seven against Thebes*) 278-82; *see* Chorus.
Citizenship, 342-54; double, 345.
City, 301-8 *passim;* divided, 344-5; *vs.* mythical hero, tragic hero, 7, 25, 27, 33-5, 43, 305-8; in Herodotus, 308-9; institutions, 30-3; and justice, 438 n.131; and law, 61; and the mean, 133-5; and *oikos,* 19, 291, 336; and religion, 40; and responsibility, 46, 60; in *Seven against Thebes,* 278-81; and legitimate violence, 419 n.4; and wildness, 156-9; *see* Chorus.
Classicism, "classics," 251, 324, 362.
Cleisthenes, 10, 255, 302, 326, 330.
Cleisthenes of Sicyon, 305.
Cleomenes, 346.
Cleophon, 335.
Clytemnestra, 48, 73-7, 93, 115-6, 141-59 *passim,* 266, 271, 314.

Colonus, 302-3, 338-9, 353-8.
Communication, 114, 208, 223, 226, 317, 319.
Communion, 406-7.
Contraries, union of, 97.
Cooking, 144.
Corcyra, 222.
Corinth, *see* Bacchiads and Cypselids.
Corneille, P., 374-6, 380.
Cornford, F.M., 95, 252.
Corrupt (sacrifice), 16, 141, 153, 263.
Corybantic, 388.
Cosmic, cosmos, 286, 289, 292.
Cottyto, 402.
Coup d'État of 411, 256-302.
Court, *see* Tribunal.
Coustel, P., 373.
Cowardice, 443 n.50.
Cratinus, 133.
Creon, 41-2, 101-2, 105-6, 109-10, 172, 306-7, 311-2, 317, 329, 335-7, 348, 370, 378.
Crime(s), 31, 36, 72, 81, 419 n.4; *see* Fault.
Croesus, 308.
Curse; *see* Erinyes.
Custom (and responsibility), 68.
Cybele, 402.
Cypselids, Cypselus, 209, 216-226, 472 n.51.
Cyrene, 209.
Cyrus, 308.

DACIER, A., 361, 371-4, 376.
daimon, 36-7, 45, 76-8, 81, 122.
daimonan, 36.
dais, 457 n.52.
Damnation, damned, 21.
Danaids, 39-40, 258, 267, 333, 420-1 n.11.
Danaus, 486 n.15.
Darius, 245, 263, 269.
Dead, cult of the, 41-2.
Death, and Gorgo, 193-4, 205-6; and night, 286; of Oedipus, 358.

Defilement, 35, 45, 62-3, 74, 80, 91, 100, 106-7, 122, 125, 128, 130, 132, 157, 299, 326, 329, 335, 349-50, 353.
deina, deinon, deinos, 32, 42, 91, 397, 418-9 n.4, 428 n.6, 504 n.41.
Dejanira, 313, 322.
Delcourt, M., 111, 372, 433 n.80, 433 n.87.
Delirium, 204, 404-9.
Delos, 129.
Delphi, 156.
Delphinion, 61.
Demagogue, 176.
Deme, 338, 347, 352.
Demeter, 309, 320, 357, 399.
Democracy, 256-8, 265, 305-8, 315, 334, 375, 418-9 n.4; *see also* City.
Demon; *see daimon*.
Demophon, 341.
dēmos, 258, 376.
Demosthenes, 332.
Descartes, 50.
Despot(s), enlightened, 379; Eastern, 308; *see* Anarchy.
Destiny, 45, 77-9, 81, 86, 89.
Detienne, M., 209, 444 n.55, 454 n.15.
dianoia, 66.
diapompein, 434 n.96.
Di Benedetto, V., 18, 486 n.16, 490 n.63, 490 n.70, 493 n.90.
dikaios, 46, 61, 81.
Dikē, dikē, 26, 40, 73, 76-7, 102, 155, 284, 290-1, 294-5, 306, 418 n.4, 429 n.6.
Diogenes, 137.
Diomedes, 164, 176.
Dionysia, Great, 181, 184, 189, 324.
Dionysism, *vs.* city, 383-9, 401.
Dionysus, 14, 181-7 *passim*, 259, 305, 381-411 *passim*; altar of, 310-1; in *Antigone*, 41-2, 102; hunter, 152, 157; and mask, 189-90, 192, 201-6; and wildness, 145, 320, 322; and

transgression, 264.
Dirke, 294.
Disguise, 24, 183, 200, 202, 391, 402.
dissoi logoi, 319, 418 n.2.
Dithyramb, 182, 305.
Diviner, 261-3, 323; *see* Calchas, Tiresias.
Dodds, E.R., 381, 384.
Dog, bitch, 152, 157, 270, 429 n.10.
Donkey, 204.
doruxenos, 489 n.60.
Double, 297, 382, 395, 407.
Draco, 61,63, 306.
dran, 44, 78-9.
Dreams, 86-7, 89, 93, 260-1, 392.
Dumézil, G., 98, 164.
Duprat de la Touloubre, 379.
Du Theil, 378.

Eagle(s), 73, 142-50, 156, 261, 268.
Earth, 96; mother, 298; *see* Gaia, Gē.
Ecclesia, 340; *see* Assembly of the People.
Ecstasy, 182, 202, 206, 384, 387, 408, 410, 412.
Eētiōn, 216, 218, 222, 469 n.25.
Egypt, 265.
eidenai, eidotes, eidōs, 64, 393, 400.
eiresiōnē, 129-30, 133.
Elections, 330-2.
Electra, 153-6, 266, 307, 314, 318.
Eleusis, 386.
emphanes, emphanos, 393.
Empedocles, 252.
Empire, Athenian, 245-6.
empolis, 343-6.
empoliteuein, 345.
enchorios, 344.
enktēsis, 352.
entopios, 344.
Ephebe, ephebeia, 10, 143, 148, 161-79 *passim*, 264, 327; Orestes, 154, 267, 449 n.116.
Ephialtes, 255-6, 303.

ephiesthai, 66.
epiboulē, 66.
Epic, 91, 237, 243.
Epiclerate, 100.
Epimenides, 133, 418-9 n.4, 502 n.11.
Epiphany, 381, 390-8.
Episeme(s), *see* Shield, devices/
emblems.
epithumein, epithumia, 56-7, 75.
epoptia, 387, 391.
Eretria, 305.
erēmos, 166.
Erinye(s), Erinus, 35, 39, 62, 74, 76,
97, 142, 150, 153, 156-9, 260, 263,
265, 267, 276, 280, 284, 289,
293-5, 333, 336, 420 n.4, 481 n.54.
Eriphyle, 481 n.64.
eris, 335.
Eros, *ēros*, 41-2, 55, 95, 100; *vs. philia*,
102.
erēmos, 166.
eschatia, 162, 165.
Eteocles, 292-319, 34-7, 40, 212, 215,
258, 260, 266, 273-300 *passim*,
335-7, 471 n.48.
Eteoclos, 292, 296, 298.
ethelein, 65.
ēthos, 35-7, 45, 103, 67, 70, 103, 121.
Euclid, 241.
eudaimonia, 409; *see* Happiness.
eumeneia, 353.
euergetai, 250, 352-3.
Eumenides, 159, 260, 265, 329, 353,
256-7, 419-20 n.4.
Eupolis, 344.
Euripides, and agent, 83; *vs.* Aeschylus, 36, 250, 299-300; and politics,
256; *vs.* Sophocles, 250, 303-4;
Alcmeon, 501 n.1.; *Bacchae*, 17, 145,
182, 202-4, 259, 334, 381-412 *pas-*
sim; *Electra*, 250, 334; *Iphigenia*
at Aulis, 501 n.1.; *Heracles*, 334;
Heracleidae, 333, 341-2; *Orestes*,
334; *The Phoenician Women*, 250,
334, 359, 364, 375; *Philoctetes*,

163-4; *Rhesus*, 312, 501 n.66; *The*
Suppliants, 333-4.
Eurystheus, 341-2.
eusebēs, 122.
euthus, 211.
Evagores of Cyprus, 351.
Exekias, 253.
Exposure, 127, 166, 169, 212, 219,
470 n.30.

FAMILY, *vs.* city, 41-2, 278, 282; and
philia, 41-2, 100-2.
Fascination, 202-4, 206, 382, 392,
396.
Fault, 61-2, 74, 80, 121, 168, 249-57.
Fawn, 157.
Fecundity, 128, 132, 159.
Feet, 123-4, 207, 210-6, 225, 469
n.27.
Fiction, 181-8 *passim*, 242-7.
Filiation and lameness, 211, 217-27
passim.
Fire, cooking, 167; sacrificial, 144.
Flute, 29.
Folard, 377.
Forgetfulness, 208, 223.
Fraenkel, E., 95, 142, 443 n.49, 444
n.62, 444-5 n.64.
Free associations, 103.
Free will, 50, 59.
Freud, S., 15, 85-111 *passim*, 325,
363-4.
Fright, 418-20 n.4.
Frontier, 162, 196-7, 206, 264, 320,
354-6, 359.
Full face, 192, 202.
Funeral speech, 257.

GABRIELI, A., 369.
Gaia, 95-7.
ganos, 410, 412.
Gardener, 159.
Gate, of Hades, 115.
Gauthier, P., 424 n.18, 424 n.19, 488
n.37, 491 n.72.

Gaze, 192, 203.
Gē, 280.
Gelos, 206.
genē, genos, 26, 35, 101, 313, 418 n.4.
gunaikon, 280.
Genre, literary, 9, 18, 20, 23, 31, 71, 79, 88, 113, 185-6, 205, 237, 240, 305.
Geometry, 241.
Gernet, L., 7, 14, 25, 60, 62, 128, 217, 226, 339, 116 n.82, 436 n.116, 436-7 n.121.
Giant, 97, 289, 293, 300.
Girard, R., 16-7, 184.
Giustiniani, O., 361, 366, 374.
gnēsios, 212-4.
gnōmē, 46, 82, 105, 116, 119.
Goat, 158, 204; and origin of tragedy, 184-5, 305; scapegoat, 16-7, 184, 326, 349; see pharmakos.
Gods, 11, 18, 32, 44-5, 116; in conflict, 40-91; language of, 117, 120 and responsibility, 44, 48, 52-5, 64-5, 70-83, 89-93, 116.
Goethe, 374.
Golden age, 397.
Goldschmidt, V., 417 n.2.
Goossens, R., 415 n.2.
Gorgias, 403.
Gorgo, Gorgon, gorgoneion, 190-5, 199, 205-6, 396.
Graiae, 194, 199.
Grotesque, 195, 199, 204.
Guilt (culpability): 32, 45, 54, 77, 81, 86, 91, 111, 154, 442 n.46.
gumnos, 287.
Gynocracy, 282, 292, 294.

HADES, 42, 115, 493 n.89.
Haemon, 306, 315, 319.
Hair, 154, 161.
hamartanein, hamartema, hamartia, 45, 62, 64.
Happiness, 397, 400, 409-11.
Harrison, J., 384.

Hare, 146, 157.
Hare, female, 142, 146-7, 150, 261-2.
Hawk, 268.
Healer, god, 262-3.
Heaven, 96.
hedus, 397.
Hegel, 251, 275, 314.
hēgemōn, 329, 338-9.
hekōn, 56-7, 60-1, 63, 75-6, 78.
hekousion, 56, 60-1, 64.
Helenus, 163.
Hephaestus, 98-9, 210, 272, 454 n.15.
Hera, 98-9; temple of, 222.
Heracles, 341.
Heracleidae, 341-2.
Heraclitus, 37, 252, 304.
Herald, 294, 334, 340.
Hermaphrodite, 217.
Hermes, 272.
Hermotimus, 504 n.11.
Herodotus, 216, 221, 226, 245, 252, 305, 308.
Hero, religious, 24, 305.
Hero, tragic, 7, 11, 24-5, 34-7, 42, 79, 310-2; and city, 350-4.
Heroic (legend, tradition), 7, 24, 26-8, 33-4, 88-91, 182, 186, 242-5, 305-6.
Héry, B. d', 379.
Hesiod, 24, 95-8, 143, 252, 288, 335.
hestia, Hestia, 99, 313, 347.
Hexameter, 420 n.6.
hexeis, 67.
hieros, 122.
hiketeia, 352; see Suppliants.
hiketēriai, 130, 435 n.103.
Hippias, 111.
Hippomedon, 288, 293, 297, 299.
Hipponax, 435 n.101.
History, and tragedy, 245, 303-4, 308-10.
hodos, 356.
Homer, 24, 26; and Dionysism, 384; and Aeschylus, 252; and responsibility, 51, 53.
homōnumia, 113.

homos, 136.
Homosexuality, 212.
homosporon, 136.
Hoplite, in Aeschylus, 277, 282; *vs.*
   ephebe, young, 143, 150, 320;
   Eteocles, 277, 282; *vs.* sailor, 256;
   on shields, 287-8; *vs.* woman, 334;
   see Bowman.
horan, 393.
Horror, 195-206.
Horse, 194, 204.
Houdar de la Motte, 375, 378.
hubris, 28, 35, 47, 73, 106, 109, 265,
   267, 282, 293, 308, 435 n.100,
   438 n.131, 478 n.32.
hugieia, 434-5 n.100.
Hugo, V., 254, 286.
Human condition, 120, 131, 139, 164,
   215, 247, 386, 388, 411.
Hunting, 10, 122, 141-59 *passim*, 162,
   167-8, 170, 176, 265, 321, 407-8.
hupsipolis, 172.
Hyperbius, 284, 289, 297, 483 n.80.
Hyperbolos, 437 n.121.

IAMBIC, 184, 420 n.6.
Iambulus, 211.
idea, 393, 400.
Ignorance, 62-5, 164.
Illegality, 339.
Illusion, 187-8, 205-6, 244, 382, 390,
   392, 394, 397, 411.
Immoderation, 309, 311, 314, 327;
   see hubris.
Immortality, 350, 385, 388, 411.
Impiety, 48.
Incest, 15, 85-111 *passim*, 121, 124,
   136-7, 152, 213, 221, 227-36, 306,
   315, 322, 376, 379, 433 n.82,
   439 n.134.
Individual, 54, 63, 65, 68-9, 82-3,
   275, 311.
Ingegneri, 369-71.
Initiation, initiatory (rituals), 195,
   199, 267, 386.

Ino, 405.
Intention, 49-84 *passim*, 63-6, 69-70,
   79-81.
Interpretation, 18-21, 275, 284-5,
   324-6, 362-3, 383.
Interpreter (of dreams and omens),
   261-2.
Io, 39, 263.
Iocasta, 107-8, 136-7, 212, 294, 317,
   322, 363-4, 370, 375, 379.
Iolaus, 341.
Iole, 313.
Iphigenia, 47, 71-3, 76, 142, 145-50,
   152-3, 257, 261.
Ismene, 258, 266, 282, 307, 314-5,
   335, 356.
isos, 136.
isotheos, 135, 137, 472 n.53.

JAUSS, H.R., 374.
Jeanmaire, H., 169, 384.
Jeremiah, 369.
Jesuits, 378.
Job, 254.
Judas, 364.
Judet de la Combe, P., 474 n.1, 484
   n.1.
Juridical, categories, 21, 348; vocabu-
   lary, 21, 32, 39, 42-3, 75, 91-2,
   295.
Justice, justice, 32, 38-9, 91, 155,
   255, 291, 438 n.132; *see* Zeus.

KAINEUS, 217.
kagourgoi, 128.
Kant, 52.
katharmos, 129, 133.
katharsios, 133.
katharsis, 130, 472 n.17; *see*
   Purification.
kerde, kerdos, 42, 353, 428 n.6.
Kilissa, 270-1.
King, 7, 34, 131-3, 351, 378; *see*
   basileus.
Knowledge/power, 321-4.

Knox, B.M.W., 122, 127, 169, 342-3, 347, 442 n.44, 460 n.95, 473 n.5, 486 n.19.
koiranos, 338.
komos, 392, 402, 407.
kōpō, 129.
Kore, n.89.
kourotrophē, 197.
kratein, kratos, 26, 41, 258, 260.
Kronos, 97, 137, 260.
kruptēs, 161.
kupselē: 220.
kurios, 39, 67-8.

LABDA, 209, 217-21, 226, 230, 472 n.51.
Labdacid(s), 35-6, 207, 209, 212-5, 218-9, 222, 225-6, 260, 266, 284, 314, 329.
Labdacus, 207, 212, 225.
Laius, 105, 118, 121, 136-7, 207, 212-5, 218, 221-2, 258, 326, 469 n.27.
Lameness, lame, 98, 207-236 *passim*.
Laodamas, 307.
Lapith, 217.
larnax, 228, 470 n.30.
Lasthenes, 481 n.54, 470 n.30.
Lauraguais, Cte. de, 374.
Laughter, 195, 206.
Laval, P., 314.
Law, 14, 25-6, 30, 38-9, 79, 88, 91, 339, 418-9 n.4; and individual, 82; and responsibility, 46-7, 60-1, 63, 81.
Lebeck, A., 153.
Lefthander, 207, 212, 215.
Legrand, M.A., 378.
Lemnos, 163, 175.
Lenaea, 502 n.4.
Léonard, N.G., 377, 379.
Leonidas, 308.
Leotychidas, 211.
Lesky, A., 53, 72.
Leukas, 129.
Lévi-Strauss, C., 207-8, 214, 280, 325.

Libations, 158, 445 n.69.
limos, 129, 132, 435 n.101.
Linear B., 386.
Lion, lion cub, 144, 147, 150, 156-7, 174, 193, 252-3, 265, 299, 469 n.25.
Lioness, 150, 450 n.121.
logos, 66, 137, 438 n.132, 439 n.134.
loimos, 128-30, 132-3, 435 n.100.
Look, 392.
Loraux, N., 16, 18, 332, 469 n.25, 473 n.11, 474 n.1, 477 n.21, 478 n.31, 483 n.83.
Lussa, lussa, 35, 405.
Lycophron (son of Periander), 223-5.
Lycurgus, 132.
Lycurgus of Athens, 249, 324, 362.
Lydian, Lydians, 386, 405, 408.
Lyric (poets, poetry), 24, 51, 91.
Lysias, 19, 129.

MADNESS, 35; divine, 182, 204; *vs.* wisdom, 400, 403-9; *see atē, lussa, mania.*
Maenads, 204, 392, 399.
Magi, 388.
Magician, 397.
mainades, 405; *see* Maenads.
mainomai, 405.
Maistre, J., 17.
makarismos, 410; *see* Happiness.
mania, 35, 78, 202, 385, 388, 404, 406, 409; *see* Madness.
Marathon, 255-6, 270, 309.
Marble (of Paros), 250.
Marriage, 97, 99, 197, 258, 299, 314-5.
Marshes, 196.
Marseilles, 129.
Marx, marxism, 19, 237-40.
Marzari, G., 365, 367.
Masculine/feminine, 178, 194, 267, 278-83, 292, 293-4, 298-9, 398, 402.
Mask, 14, 23-4, 34, 183, 189-206 *passim*, 311, 371, 381-412 *passim*.

Masquerade, 23, 189, 196, 198, 206.
Matriarchy, 260.
Matricide, 306, 418 n.4; see also
    Orestes.
maza, 133.
Meat (eating), 143.
mechanēma, 154.
Medical (vocabulary), 123.
Medusa, 191-2, 194.
Megalopolis, 346.
Megareus, 296, 298, 481 n.54.
Melanion, 162.
Melanippus, 295, 298.
Melanthus, 162.
melathron, 461 n.128.
Melissa, 222-3.
Menander, 19, 304.
Mercenary, 163.
Merope, 108, 363.
mesogaia, 356.
metaitios, 75.
Metaphor, 261.
Metics, 265, 293, 333-4, 340, 342,
    345, 351-4.
mētis, 293.
metoikōs, 349; see Metic.
Meuli, K., 143.
Meyerson, I., 18, 50.
miasma, 35, 128, 131; see Defilement.
Miltiades, 270, 309-10.
mimēsis, 44, 187, 198, 242-3, 247, 250.
Mimetism, 204.
Miracle(s), 398, 410.
moira, 78.
Momigliano, A., 433 n.8.
Monster, monstrosity, 189-95, 208,
    288-9.
Montenari, G., 365.
Moral, 26, 38, 60, 62.
mormolukeia, 195.
morphē, 393.
Moschopoulos, M., 362.
Mudge, Z., 491 n.70.
muein, muēsis, 386-7.
Murray, G., 273.

Musgrave, S., 343-4.
mustērion, mustikos, 386-7.
Mysticism, 385.

NAKED; see gumnos.
Naturalization, 351.
Nature, human, 46, 50, 81, 92.
Necessity, 52, 59, 70.
nemein, 428 n.7.
Neoptolemus, 161-79 passim, 312,
    317, 327.
nephalia, -os, 158, 494 n.93.
Nestle, W., 33, 305.
Net, 116, 154-5, 429 n.10, 446 n.69.
Neuroses, 85.
Nicias, 302, 436 n.121.
Nietzsche, 283, 383.
Night, 150, 158-9, 136; see also Black,
    Nocturnal.
Nocturnal (combat), 320, 327.
nomos, -oi, 26, 41-2, 113, 139, 428 n.8,
    439 n.135.
nothos, 211-2, 214.
nous, intellect, 58; praktikos, 423 n.17.
numen, 35.
Nurse, 270.

OATH, of Ephebes, 161-2, 170.
Obedience 282.
Oblivion, 44.
Obscenity, 199-200.
Odysseus, 163-79 passim, 193, 307,
    317-8.
Oedipus, 16-7, 21, 45, 77-80, 207-30
    passim, 258, 290, 292, 294, 301-80
    passim, 447 n.74.
Oedipus complex, 77-111 passim, 363.
oida, 123.
oidos, 123.
oikēsis, 352.
oikos, see City, Family, War.
Oinoclos, 132.
Old Men, in the chorus, 312.
ololugē, ololugmos, 40, 141, 281, 478
    n.31.

Olympians, *vs.* Chthonians, 40.
Omens, 260-1, 286.
Omophagy, 115, 397, 406.
Oracle, 104-7, 115, 218, 225, 259, 309, 317-8.
orchestra, 339, 356, 359.
orektikos, -on, 51, 425 n.37.
Orestes, 44, 48, 81, 142, 153-8, 263, 265, 267, 271, 318, 321, 334.
orexis, 58, 425 n.37.
orgē, orgia, orgy, *orgiasmos, orgiazein*, 42, 75, 392, 400.
oribasic, 409.
Origins of tragedy, 23, 183, 305.
Osborne, M.J., 351.
Oschophoria, 434 n.99.
Ostracism, 10, 133-5, 326, 330, 349-50.
Other, 197, 389, 394, 398, 400, 402, 411.
Otherness, 193, 199-206, 384-5, 388-9, 398, 402.
Ouranidae, Ouranos, 95-7, 141, 260.
oureia, 162.
Oxen, 144.

PACE, B., 463 n.138.
Paean, 130, 281.
Palamedes, 463 n.138.
Palladio, 324-5, 361, 365, 368.
Palladion, 61.
Pallene, 342.
Pandora, 144.
panspermia, 434 n.99.
Papyrus, literary, 250.
paraitias, 75.
parakopa, 76.
paralia, 356.
paraulos, 354.
Paris, 253, 442 n.44.
Parmenides, 252.
parousia, 390.
Parricide, 15, 85-111 *passim*, 121, 124, 136-8, 213, 221, 227-36, 306, 376.
Parthenopaea, 289-93, 297-8.

parthenos, -oi, 99, 197; *see* Virginity.
Pastoral, 175, 368.
patris, 299.
Pediment, 285, 289-90, 293, 297.
Pegasus, 194.
peitharchia, peithō, Peithō, 39-40, 163, 260, 333, 336, 359, 418-9 n.4, 463 n.138.
pelanos, 158.
Pelasgus, 39-40, 44, 258, 265, 340.
Peloponnesian War, 162, 304, 331, 401.
Pelops, 212.
Pentheus, 145, 152, 202, 334, 391, 393-8, 400, 402-5, 407-9.
Periander, 221-5.
Pericles, 244, 255-6, 302-3, 313, 331.
peripeteia, 117, 130, 318.
peripolos, 161.
Perrot D'Ablancourt, 372.
Perseus, 190.
Personality, 20, 36, 49-51, 55.
Persuasion, 39-40, 170, 418-9 n.4; *see peithō*.
Petrification, 192-3.
People, *vs.* king, 376-80; *see* Chorus.
phainein, 392, 393, 505 n.59.
Phallus, 194-5.
phaneros, 391, 393, 505 n.59.
pharmakon, 400, 404.
pharmakos, 10, 17, 106, 125, 128-35, 139, 224, 326, 349-50.
phaulos, -oi, 128, 135.
Pherecydes, 502 n.11.
philia, philos, 41-2, 100-2, 314, 418-9 n.4, 428 n.6; *see eros*, Family.
Philoctetes, 161-79 *passim*, 307, 317, 327, 343, 379.
Philosophy, 29, 241.
phitupoimēn, 159.
Phobos, phobos, 159, 206, 418-20 n.4.
phonos, 46, 60-1, 81.
Phorbas, 370, 372.
Phratry, 161.
phronēsis, 46, 82, 423 n.17.

Phrynicus (tragic poet), 181, 244, 251, 255.
Phrynicus (comic poet), 301.
Phthonos, 106, 110, 134.
Pigafetta, F., 365, 367, 370.
Pillar with mask, 383.
Pindar, 19, 25, 252, 164.
Pinelli, G.V., 369.
Pirithoos, 356, 358, 494 n.91.
Pisistratus, 27.
Pity, 244, 246, 412.
Plague, 9, 303, 318; see loimos.
Plataea, Plataeans, 269, 351.
Plato, 57, 62, 241, 243, 305, 323, 417 n.2.
Pleiades, 444-5 n.64.
Plotinus, 387.
poiēsis, 82.
polis (interplay), 423 n.123.
polis; see City.
politēs, 345; see Citizen.
Politics, 33, 42, 82-3, 272, 294.
Polybus, 108.
Polycrates, 308.
Polynices, 35, 101, 212, 215, 262, 266, 273-300 passim, 329, 335-8, 344-5, 356, 375, 471 n.48.
Polyphontes, 298.
Poseidon, 194, 356.
Possession, 183, 194, 205, 383-90, 409-10.
Potnia thērōn, 196.
Pralon, D., 474 n.1, 480 n.44, 481 n.64, 482 n.71.
prattein, praxis, 44, 82.
Presence, 390-4, 409; see Absence.
Priest, high, 376, 378.
proairesis, 56-8, 68, 70, 425 n.37.
proboulē, 66.
probouloi, 302.
Prodigies, 398.
Prometheus, 39, 144, 254, 263, 272, 299.
pronoia, 64.
prostatēs, 340.

Protagoras, 304, 323.
proteleia, 141.
proxenos, 339-40, 352.
psēphos, 418 n.4, 478 n.32.
psuche, 384; see Soul.
Psychoanalysis, 9, 85-111 passim, 277, 325, 363.
Psychology, historical, 87-8.
Psychological (interpretation), 35-6, 47, 71, 121, 165, 273-8, 364.
Puanepsion, puanion, 434 n.99.
Public; see Spectator.
Punishment, 62-3, 74, 77, 80.
Purification, 130-1, 133-4, 184-5, 246, 385, 387, 389, 391, 412.
Pyrrhus, 171.
Pythagoras, 502 n.11.
Pythia, 156, 262, 309.
Python, 156.

Rabbi, 378.
Racine, 241, 257.
Rampart, 288, 294.
Rationality, 57-8.
Raw, 158-9, 292.
Recognition, 117, 318.
Redemption, 16.
Religion, 30-1, 38-42, 62-3, 91, 101, 105, 134, 186-7, 189, 387.
Renouncement, 387, 390.
Responsibility, 23, 27, 32, 38, 46, 49-55, 59-60, 69-71, 75, 78-9, 88-93, 116.
Reversal, 23, 27, 113-140 passim, 282, 329.
Rhea, 97.
Rhodes, 129.
rhusios, 39.
Riccoboni, A., 367, 369.
Riddle, 45, 208, 214-5, 242, 318.
Ritschl, F., 283.
Rivier, A., 51-4, 69-72, 75-6.
Rochefort, G. De, 378, 499 n.49.
Rohde, E., 384.
Romilly, J. De, 71, 83.

Rolling, 218, 222, 224, 227-8, 230.
Rousseau, 19.
Roux, G., 469 n.28, 470 n.30.
Roux, J., 381.

SABATUCCI, D., 385-7.
Sabazios, 402.
Sacrifice, 10, 16-7, 41, 141-159 passim, 263-4, 272, 281, 305, 320-1, 488 n.40.
Saïd, S., 16, 474 n.26.
Salamis, 255, 268-9, 303.
Samos, 129, 332.
Satyrs, 183, 195, 204.
Satyr play, 252, 304.
Saviour, 17, 123, 125, 326, 342.
Savalli, I., 489 n.55, 492 n.79.
Scamozzi, V., 368-9.
Schadewaldt, W., 277.
Schrade, L., 364.
Seale, D., 494 n.96.
sebas, 42, 159, 420 n.4.
Secret, 387, 400.
See, 391-5, 407-8.
Segal, C., 16, 42, 381, 403, 412, 447 n.74, 484 n.1, 487 n.30, 494 n.97.
Seneca, 370, 372, 374.
Setti, S., 463 n.138.
Sexual organs/face, 195.
Sexuality, and culture, 196-7; and tyranny, 207-236 passim.
Shakespeare, 175, 241, 254.
Shaw, M., 477 n.22.
Shields, 192-3; of Seven against Thebes, 260, 273-300 passim.
Signs, 260-1.
Simonides, 25.
skēnē, 311, 359.
Skepticism, 383.
Slavery, slave, 264, 270-1, 280.
Snake(s), 144, 155-6, 193, 300, 399.
Snell, B., 51-2, 424 n.24.
Socrates, 41, 55, 57.
Solmsen, F., 276.

Solon, 27, 306, 330.
sophia, 404, 407.
sophismata, 397.
Sophists, 171, 321, 384, 403.
Sophocles, 19, 161-84 passim, 420 n.9; Ajax, 259, 501 n.66; Antigone, 26, 374; Electra, 334, 354, 371, 374; Ichneutai, 304; Oedipus at Colonus, 21, 101, 106, 168, 265, 329-59 passim; Oedipus Rex, 9-10, 15, 21, 77-9, 85-111 passim; Philoctetes, 10, 161-79 passim, 259, 354, 501 n.66; Skyrioi, 460 n.100.
Sophocles the Younger, 302.
sophon, -to, 404, 411.
sōphrosunē, sōphrōn, 40, 198, 283, 399.
Soul, 384, 387, 411.
Space, sacred vs. profane, 357-8; scenic vs. represented, 356-9.
Sparta, 198-9, 211, 269, 308, 313, 327.
Spartoi, 280, 295-9, 466 n.2.
Spectators, 18, 34, 114-5, 117, 121, 390, 395.
Sperone Speroni, 370.
sphagia, 159.
sphaleotas, 398.
Sphinx, 313-4, 288, 290, 292, 299, 318, 326.
Spring, 129-31.
Staging, 356-9, 368-71.
Stanford, W.B., 113.
Starobinski, J., 363.
stasis, 332, 334, 338, 354.
Sterility, 208, 212; see Fecundity.
stratēgos, strategy, 302, 304, 309, 313, 331-2.
Structural, structuralism, 7-8, 14, 283.
Stuttering, 208.
Subconscious, 363.
sullēptōr, 74.
Sun, island of, 210.
sungeneia, 341.
Suppliant, supplication, 130, 350, 352.
Swelling, 123-4.

TANTALUS, 76.
Taplin, O., 278, 495 n.100.
technē, technology, 82, 144, 172, 272; *vs. aretē*, 171; *vs.* power, 321-4.
Tecmessa, 303.
Tegaea, 346.
telētē, 387.
Teresa of Avila, 387.
Terror, 192-5, 206.
Tetrameter, 183.
Text, 19-21.
Thalmann, W.G., 475 n.1.
Thanatos, 206.
Thargelia, *thargelōs*, 17, 128-31, 133, 135.
thaumata, 397.
theates, 393; *see* Spectators.
Theater (building), 310-1, 365, 367-8.
Thebes, 35, 273-300 *passim*; *vs.* Athens, 329-38, 355; *Roman de Thèbes*, 364; in Vincenza, 370.
thelein, 65.
thelumorphos, 398.
Themistocles, 255, 268.
Thermopylae, 269, 308.
Theseus, 324, 329-59 *passim*.
Thespis, 183, 250-1.
thiasos, 389, 392, 397, 400-2, 404-6.
Thirty tyrants, 338.
Thoricus, 358.
Thrace, 385.
Thenody, 131.
threpterion, 154.
Thucydides, 37, 47, 245, 253.
thumos, 57.
thusiai, 159.
Thysestes, 74, 150, 261, 263.
thymelē, 182, 184, 189, 310.
Time, 83; divine *vs.* human, 43-4, 47, 260, 316-19.
timē, 42, 267, 295, 419, 428 n.6.
Tiresias, 262, 323, 376, 378, 399, 403.
tolma, 42.
Torch, 287, 289, 299.

Tournelle, 375.
Tradition (literary, philosophic, scientific), 241.
Tragic competitions, 9, 32-3, 185, 308.
Tragic consciousness, 9, 27, 31, 33, 43, 92, 186, 240-1.
tragos, 184-5, 305; *see* He-goat.
Transe, 392, 405; *see* Possession.
Translation, 371-3.
Transgression, 264, 282, 306.
Trap, 115, 153, 446 n.70.
Tribunals (courts), 25, 31, 33, 46, 61, 63, 80-1, 88, 186, 418-20 n.4.
Trick, 154-5, 161-5, 170-1, 178, 268-9, 307, 321, 397.
Trissino, G.G., 365, 367.
Tuchē, 45, 47-8, 106, 124-6, 318; *see* Chance.
turannos, 127, 132, 139, 338, 366; *see* Tyrant.
Turner, T., 208.
Tydeus, 262, 284-5, 293-5, 298-9.
Typhoeus (Typhon), 288-9, 293.
Tyrant, 7, 15, 28, 127, 134, 137, 185, 216-27 *passim*, 253, 257, 265, 272, 280, 306-10, 313, 315-6, 319, 326-7, 329, 336, 349, 379, 403.

UNANIMITY, 333.
Unconscious, 103, 363.

VASE, Françoise, 202.
Vengeance, 61, 147.
Venice, 367.
Veyne, P., 365.
Vicenza, 324, 361, 364-71, 374.
Violence, 39, 197, 199.
Viper, 156.
Virginity, 99, 198, 266.
Vitruvius, 368.
Vlastos, 95.
Voltaire, 361, 373-9.
Vote, 333-4, 418-20 n.4.
Vultures, 148, 156, 261.

WAR, 97, 99, 320; and culture, 143; foreign *vs.* civil or private, 159, 292-5, 297, 331; *vs. oikos*, 166, 173.
Webster, T.B.L., 462 n.135.
Wheat, 399.
White (*vs.* black), 16, 145-147, 158, 443 n.50.
Wilamowitz, T. Von, 165, 173, 276.
Wilamowitz, U. Von, 34, 275, 283, 337, 475 n.1.
Wild, wildness, 144, 147, 156-9, 197, 199-200, 204, 206, 265, 293.
Will, 9, 46, 49-84 *passim*, 89, 121.
Wine, 144, 158, 203, 385, 399, 402, 410.
Winnington-Ingram, R.P., 37, 71, 77, 381.
Wisman, N.H., 416 n.15.
Wolf, 144, 150, 265.
Woman, women; on shields, 291; in choruses, 311-2, 418 n.3; and *kratos*, 39; and politics, 40, 266-7, 418 n.3; and religion, 35, 40; and sacrifice, 344; in *Seven against Thebes*, 35, 278-84.
Word play, 262, 293, 319, 494 n.94.
Written, writing, 288, 291, 362.

XANTHOS, 161-2.
xenoi, xenos, 341, 349.
Xerxes, 265, 268, 308.
xunaitia, 75.

YOUNG: *vs.* adult, 315, 320; *vs.* hoplite, 327; *vs.* old, 224-5, 263, 307, 398.

ZALMOXIS, 502 n.11.
Zeitlin, F.I., 16, 142, 445 n.69, 475 n.1, 477 n.16, 479 n.33, 480 n.49, 486 n.14.
zētein, 122.
Zeus, 298; *agoraios*, 419; on shields, 288-90, 292; and Kronos, 137; in Aeschylus, 259-60; justice of, 26, 38, 73-4, 77; and *kratos*, 39; in *Oedipus Rex*, 123; *vs.* Prometheus, 39-40, 263; Teleios, 479 n.10; tyrant, 272.

Index of Textual References

AELIAN, *N.A.*, 12, 34: 441 n.21; *Var. Hist.*, 8, 3: 441 n.22; *Var. Hist.*, 5, 14: 441 n.21.

Aeschylus, *Agamemnon*, 141-53 *passim*; *38-9*: 428 n.9; *47-54*: 261; *49-54*: 443 n.51; *105-59*: 441 n.26; *114-20*: 261; *120*: 146; *136*: 146, 428 n.9; *141*: 442 n.46; *150*: 146; *167-75*: 260; *169*: 426 n.58; *184-7*: 425 n.50; *187*: 422 n.30; *213*: 422 n.29; *214-7*: 425 n.59; *224-7*: 425 n.49; *537*: 148; *604*: 429 n.10; *606-7*: 429 n.10; *645*: 435 n. 105; *694-5*: 148; *717-28*: 252; *717-36*: 442 n.44; *735-6*: 253; *822*: 442 n.62; *824-8*: 268; *825*: 444 n.63; *827-8*: 442 n.44, 445 n.66; *868*: 429 n.10; *910*: 429 n.11; *911*: 429 n.10; *921*: 429 n.11; *936*: 429 n.11; *946*: 429 n.11; *949*: 429 n.11; *960-1*: 429; *973-4*: 429 n.10; *1036-7*: 271; *1046*: 271; *1110*: 429 n.10; *1115*: 429 n.10; *1126-8*: 147; *1223*: 450 n.121; *1259*: 442 n.44; *1275-6*: 263; *1291*: 429 n.10; *1309-12*: 148; *1337-8*: 422 n.28; *1370-1*: 258; *1372*: 426 n.57; *1377*: 426 n.58; *1382*: 429 n.10; *1383*: 429 n.11; *1390*: 429 n.11; *1395*: 445 n.69; *1401*: 426 n.58; *1424-30*: 426 n.61; *1431*: 426 n.60, 445 n.69; *1468 ff.*: 426 n.63; *1487-8*: 426 n.65; *1497-1504*: 426 n.53; *1502-3*: 147; *1505-6*: 426 n.54; *1564*: 446 n.72; *1580 and 1609*: 426 n.64; *1615-6*: 426 n.66; *Choephori (Libation Bearers)*: 153-4, 157; *32-4*: 261; *76*: 488 n.47; *150-1*: 435 n.105; *313*: 446 n.72; *899*: 422 n.25; *980-1*: 443 n.49; *1010-23*: 429 n.11; *Eumenides*: 156; *264-6*: 158; *451-2*: 267; *460*: 448 n.96; *476, 511, 514, 539, 550, 554, 564*: 418 n.4; *516-25*: 419; *525-6*: 336; *627-8*: 448 n.96; *665*: 483 n.83; *690-9*: 419; *696*: 336; *705-6*: 420 n.4; *734-53*: 259; *737, 751-2, 754*: 418 n.4; *737-8*: 267; *sch. to 746*: 418 n.4; *752*: 333; *795-6*: 267; *796, 807, 833, 868, 884, 891, 894, 917, 930-1, 950-2, 954-5, 974, 989-91, 1029*: 418-20 n.4; *886*: 992-4: 265; *1011*: 353; *The Persians*: 146-8: 268; *205-6*: 268; *345-6*: 270; *353-4*: 270; *424*: 269; *459-61*: 269; *490*: 447 n.74; *719 ff.*: 263; *742*: 426 n.56; *816-7*: 269; *Prometheus*: 450: 439 n.135; *583*: 445 n.65; *966-7*: 272; *Seven against Thebes*: 273-300 *passim*: 1-2: 258; *186*: 421 n.17; *191-2, 236-8*: 421 n.15; *224*: 421 n.18; *268*: 421 n.19; *280*: 421 n.16; *501*: 488 n.47;

Aeschylus (continued)
  558: 445 n.65; 712: 257; 868,
  915 ff.: 435 n.105; The Suppliants:
  16: 339; 154-61: 421 n.13; 226: 431
  n.226; 231: 421 n.13; 238-9: 339;
  274: 339; 315: 39; 365-75: 258;
  379-80: 422 n.26; 387, 392-3, 820,
  831, 863, 940-1, 943, 951, 1041,
  1056, 1069: 420-1 n.11; 418-9: 340;
  491-2: 340; 603-5, 607, 613-4,
  622-3: 333; 605-24: 340; 610-1:
  340; 957: 341; 963-4: 341.
Alcman, fr. 56 D 137 Ed.: 436 n.106.
Apollodorus (Pseudo), I, 4, 2: 465
  n.6; II, 3, 4: 465 n.12; III, 5, 9:
  494 n.91; III, 6, 8: 482 n.69.
Aristophanes, Frogs: 730-34: 93;
  1189-95: 467 n.18; Knights: 728:
  435 n.101; Lysistrata: 783-92: 162;
  Peace: 631: 470 n.30; Plutus:
  1053-4: 435 n.101; Wasps: 219-20:
  435 n.101.
Aristophanes of Byzantium, Epitome:
  I, 11 (Lambros): 446 n.71.
Aristotle, De anima: 432b 27-8: 423
  n.11; Eudemian Ethics: 1228a: 423
  n.7; Nicomachean Ethics: 1103a
  6-10: 425 n.44; 1103a 19-b 22:
  423 n.12; 1103b 24-5: 425 n.46;
  1111a 25-7, 1111b 7-8: 425 n.10;
  1111b 5-6: 423 n.7; 1111b 20-3:
  423 n.11; 1111b 26: 423 n.16; 1112a
  15-7: 425 n.38; 1113b 3-5: 423
  n.16; 1113b 17-9: 425 n.41; 1114a
  3-8, 13-21: 425 n.45; 1114a 7-8:
  425 n.43; 1135b ff.: 425 n.34; 1139a
  17-20: 423 n.14; 1139a 31: 423
  n.17; 1139a 34-5: 425 n.44; 1139b
  2-3: 423 n.15; 1140b 16-7: 425
  n.40; 1145a 15 ff.: 437 n.122; 1145a
  25: 438 n.129; 1147 a 29-31: 424
  n.18; 1179b 31 ff.: 425 n.46; Historia animalum: I, 1, 488b: 446
  n.71, 450 n.125; IX, 1, 609a: 450
  n.125; IX, 32, 2: 441 n.33; Metaphysics: 1046b 5-10: 423 n.12; Poetics: 1449a 11: 183; 1449a 15, 1449a
  20-5: 183; 1449a 24-8: 420 n.6;
  1449b 24, 31, 36: 420 n.8; 1449b
  24: 473 n.18; 1449b 28: 472 n.17;
  1450a 15-23, 1450 23-5, 1450a
  38-9, 1450b 2-3: 420 n.8; 1451a
  36-b 32: 472 n.16; 1452a 32-3:
  430 n.14; 1452a 29 ff.: 318; 1458a
  26: 431 n.39; 1461b 26, 1462a 4:
  498 n.41; Politics: I, 1253a: 327; I,
  1253a 2-29: 437 n.122, n.123; I,
  1253a 10-18: 438 n.132; I, 1256b
  23: 440 n.14; 1284a 3-b 13: 436
  n.120; 1342b ff.: 465 n.6; Problemata: 19, 48: 420 n.5; 29, 13:
  418 n.4; De sophisticus elenchis: I,
  165a 11: 428 n.4; Rhetoric: I, 1361a:
  492 n.78; III, 1430b, 20, 1404a 8:
  498 n.41; fr. 115 Rose: 502 n.8.
Aristoxenes of Tarentum, fr. 117
  Wherli: 435 n.106.
Arnobius, Adversus notiones: V, 25,
  p.196, 3 Reiff (Kern, fr. 52, 53):
  465 n.14.
Arrian, Cynegetica: 35, 3: 471 n.47.
Artemidorus, I, 77 (84, 2-4, Pack):
  429 n.11.
Anthenaeus, 114a: 434 n.97; X, 456b:
  468 n.20; XIII, 558d: 468 n.20;
  602c-d: 436 n.115; XIV, 616e-f: 465
  n.6; 648b: 434 n.99.

Chairemon, fr. 15 N² = Athenaeus,
  II, 2, 35d: 505 n.51.
Clement of Alexandria, Protrepica: II,
  21: 465 n.14.
Columella, 6, praef.: 441 n.21.

Diodurus Siculus, II, 18: 467 n.13;
  IV, 64: 468 n.20; XII, 6, 3: 487
  n.29; XIX, 105, 4: 424 n.22.
Diogenes Laertius, I, 94: 470 n.37; I,
  96: 470 n.33; I, 110: 436 n.115; II,
  44: 433 n.90.

Dio Chrysostomus, *10, 29*: 438 n.133; *52 and 59*: 453 n.11, n.13.
Diphilus, *fr. 86 Kock* = Athenaeus, *II, 2, 53d*: 505 n.51.

EPICTETUS, *Dissertationes: I, 2, 3, IV, 1, 56, 62, 68, 100*: 424 n.22.
Etymologicum magnum, *s.v. eiresiōnē*: 434 n.98; *s.v. exostrakismos*: 436 n.117.
Eubulus, *11 fr. 94 Kock* = Athenaeus, *II, 4, 36c*: 504 n.40.
Eupolis, *fr. 137 Kock*, cited by Pollux, *Onomasticon: IX, 27* (ed. by Bethe, p.153): 488 n.48.
Euripides, *Andromache: 1135*: 460 n.92; *Bacchae: 381-412 passim; 142*: 451 n.152; *470*; 466 n.23; *686-7*: 451 n.152; *1108, 1114, 1142, 1146*: 448 n.81; *1188, 1192*: 448 n.82, n.83; *Heracleidae: 15-6, 36-7, 184-6, 340-3*: 341; *335, 1032*: 342; *Heracles: 153-64*: 449 n.116; *931 ff.*: 465 n.13; *Hyppolitus: 390*: 488 n.45; *952*: 447 n.74; *Iphigenia at Aulis: 1469*: 418 n.4; *Orestes: 189*: 447 n.74; *871-3*: 486 n.15; *901-30, 335; The Phoenician Women, argument*: 468 n.20, 439 n.136; *13-20*: 468 n.25; *37, 40, 42*: 469 n.27; *69-74*: 471 n.48; *71*: 486 n.21; *751*: 299; *499 ff.*: 428 n.5; *754-60*: 299; *888*: 420 n.7; *1110-38*: 299; *1505-6*: 432 n.66; *The Trojan Women: 1168*: 472 n.53; *1169*: 433 n.83; *The Women of Trachis: 358*: 488 n.45.
Eustatius, *Commentary on the Iliad: 1283, 6*: 435 n.103; *1283, 7*: 434 n.98, n.99; *530*: 129; *Commentary on the Odyssey: 22, 481*: 434 n.96.

HERACLITUS, *fr. 48 Diels*: 458 n.56; *fr. 88*: 431 n.39.
Herodotus, *I, 119, 15*: 447 n.74; *II,* *65, 15*: 447 n.74; *III, 16, 15*: 447 n.74; *III, 50-4*: 222-6; *III, 108*: 441 n.32; *IV, 147-62*: 466 n.6; *V, 67*: 305; *V, 70-1*: 433 n.88; *V, 92*: 216-22; *VI, 21*: 244; *VI, 109*: 270, 309; *VI, 132-6*: 309; *VIII, 52, 10*: 469 n.26; *VIII, 95*: 270.
Hesiod, *Theogony: 280-1*: 465 n.11; *535-6*: 440 n.18; *591*: 280, 440 n.19; *820 ff.*: 480 n.52; *Works: 225 ff.*: 436 n.111; *238 ff.*: 436 n.112.
Hesychius, *s.v. kradiēs nomos*: 433 n.91; *s.v. koruthalia*: 434 n.98; *s.v. pharmakoi*: 433 n.89; *s.v. thargēlia*: 434 n.97, 435 n.103.
Hopponax, *fr. 4 and 5 Bergk*: 433 n.91; *fr. 7 Bergk*: 436 n.114.

IAMBLICHUS, *Mysteries: 3, 9*: 465 n.7; *Life of Pythagoras: 110, Deubner*: 435 n.106.
I.G., I, 3-4: Hecatompedon Decree: 425 n.30.
I.G., I, 6, 49: 502 n.7.
I.G., II, 218, 337: 492 n.7.
I.G., V, 19: 489 n.55.
I.G., V, 263: 489 n.55.
Iliad: II, 301-29: 442 n.40; *II, 718-25*: 163; *V, 738*: 465 n.3, n.4; *VIII, 349*: 465 n.3; *XII, 200-9*: 450 n.125; *XIII, 136 ff.*: 469 n.26; *XVII, 657-60*: 445 n.64; *XVII, 674-7*: 441 n.33; *XVIII, 372*: 466 n.9; *XVIII, 375-8*: 467 n.12; *XVIII, 411, 417, 421*: 467 n.18; *XIX, 252-3*: 441 n.33; *XXII, 310*: 441 n.33; *XXIII, 679*: 364; *XXIV, 315-6*: 441 n.33.
Ion of Chios, *apud, Athenaeus, XIII, 604d*: 302-3.
Isocrates, *Philip: V*: 345.

LACTANTIUS PLACIDUS, *Commentary on Statius' Thebais: 10, 793*: 434 n.95, 436 n.114.

Leonidas of Alexandria, *Palatine
Anthology: 6, 323*: 468 n.21.
Life of Aeschylus: 10: 251, 473 n.9.
Lucian, *De saltatione: 11*: 459 n.92.
Lycurgas, *Against Leocrates: 76*: 452
n.6.
Lysias, *Against Andocides: 108*: 349;
108, 4: 129.

NICHOLAS OF DAMASCUS, *fr. 103
Jacoby*: 441 n.21.

ODYSSEY: *X, 521, 536*: 465 n.9; *XI,
29, 49*: 465 n.9; *XI, 271*: 364; *XI,
275-6*: L 484 n.6; *XI, 633-5*: 465;
XII, 356-96: 144; *XV, 247*: 481
n.64; *XIX, 109 ff.*: 436 n.111.
Ovid, *Metamorphoses: IV, 795 ff.*: 465
n.12; *VII, 386-7, X. 324-31*: 438
n.133.

PALATINE ANTHOLOGY: *14, 64*: 468
n.20.
Pausanius, *I, 14, 5*: 255; *I, 28, 5-6*:
418-20 n.4; *I, 28, 7*: 494 n.91; *I,
28, 10*: 441 n.22; *I, 30, 4*: 494
n.91; *III, 8-10*: 467 n.17; *V, 17, 5*:
470 n.30; *IX, 26, 3-5*: 467 n.19.
Pherecydes, *FGr Hist. 3, F. 22 a-b*:
483 n.78.
Photius, *s.v. leukatēs*: 434 n.95; *s.v.
ostrakismos*: 436 n.117; *Library
(Bekker, p.534)*: 433 n.89, n.91.
Pindar, *Pythian I, 1-53*: 164; *Pythian
IV, 57-123*: 466 n.6; *Pythian IV,
452-66*: 466 n.6; *Pythian XII,
12-42*: 465 n.5.
Plato, *Cratylus: 420c-d*: 425 n.39;
Crito: 51a-c: 421 n.21; *Laws: VII,
790c-91b*: 465 n.7; *IX, 863c*: 425
n.32; *Phaedo: 69c*: 502 n.7; *265a*:
388; *Protagoras: 322b*: 143, 440
n.13; *Republic: 360b-d*: 433 n.85;
360c: 438 n.131, 472 n.53; *535d ff.*:
467 n.14; *586b*: 433 n.85, 472

n.53; *569b*: 438 n.130; *571c-d,
619b-c*: 472 n.52; *Symposium:
188a-b*: 434 n.100; *189e*: 467 n.10:
210a: 502 n.7.
Pliny, *Natural History: VIII, 180*: 441
n.21.
Plutarch, *Agesilaus: III, 1-9*: 211; *De
curiositate: 522c*: 432 n.53; *Lycurgus:
15*: 495 n.2; *Lysander: 22, 12*: 467
n.17; *Moralia: 79b*: 484 n.5; *164a*:
470 n.30; *456b ff.*: 465 n.6; *Pericles:
35, 4-6, 37*: 485 n.5; *Quaestiones
conviviales: 717d*: 434 n.97; *Quaestiones grecae: 17*: 489 n.60; *Theseus:
15, 1*: 435 n.102; *18, 1 and 2*: 434
n.99, 435 n.103; *22*: 434 n.98; *22,
5-7*: 434 n.99; *22, 6-7*: 435 n.102,
n.103.
Pseudo-Plutarch, 473 n.1.
Pollux, *I, 28*: 478 n.27; *8, 105 s.v.
peripoloi*: 452 n.6; *9, 98*: 437 n.123.
Polybius, *V, 9, 9*: 346.
Porphyry, *On Abstinence: 2, 28*: 441
n.22.

SAPPHO *fr. 52 Bergk*: 445 n.64.
Schol. ad Aristophanes, Frogs: 703: 433
n.94; *Knights: 728*: 434 n.99,
n.100; *729*: 434 n.97; *1133*: 433
n.94; *Plutus: 1055*: 434 n.97, n.98,
n.99.
*Scholia ad Euripedes, The Phoenician
Women: 45*: 432 n.64.
Scholia ad Exeg. in Iliadem: A 122:
468 n.24.
*Scholia ad Lycophron, Alexandra: 7,
I.22 (Scheer, II, p.11)*: 468 n.20.
Scholia Vict. ad Iliadem: X, 391: 435
n.105.
Scholia ad Odyssey: XII, 353: 441 n.21.
Servius, *Commentary on the Aeneid:
III, 57*: 434 n.95, 436 n.114; *III,
402*: 458 n.58.
Solon, *fr. 9-10 Edmonds*: 134.
Sophocles, *Antigone: 23 ff.*: 421 n.14;

370: 172; *451*: 421 n.14; *481*: 428
n.8; *538-42*: 421 n.14; *853 ff.*: 421
n.14; *872-5*: 421 n.20; *1113*: 428
n.8; *Oedipus at Colonus*: 329-59
passim; *56*: 355; *265 ff.*: 431 n.42;
287: 431 n.44; *521, 525, 539-41*:
431 n.41; *636-7*: 343; *1156*: 344;
1309-30: 483 n.84; *1316*: 482 n.71;
1321-2: 481 n.63; *1590-1*: 356;
Oedipus Rex: 85-111 *passim*; *5*: 435
n.104; *124*: 429 n.13; *132*: 118;
137-41: 430 n.13; *186*: 435 n.104;
258-65: 430 n.13; *383-4*: 427
n.11; *451-3*: 348, 427 n.12; *551-2,
572-3*: 430 n.13; *816, 828-9*: 426
n.68; *842-7*: 429 n.13; *863-911*:
438 n.131; *928, 955-6*: 430 n.13;
999: 427 n.13; *1183*: 430 n.13;
1189 ff.: 431 n.37; *1193-6*: 426
n.69; *1196-7*: 431 n.36; *1213*: 426
n.70; *1230-1*: 426 n.71; *1297-1302*:
426 n.72; *1463-4*: 447 n.74; *1529-
30*: 301; *Philoctetes*: 161-79 *passim*;
146-7: 456 n.37; *274*: 447 n.74;
308: 447 n.74; *708-15*: 166; *The
Women of Trachis*: *1-3*: 301.
Stesichorus, *fr. 37 Bergk, 14 Diehl*:
435 n.106.
Strabo, *X, 9*: 434 n.95.
Suda, *s.v. diakonion*: 434 n.98; *s.v.
pharmakous*: 436 n.114.
Suetonius, *Peri paidōn, I, 16*: 437
n.123.

THEOCRITUS, *XXIII, 49-50*: 471 n.42.
Theognis, *39*, 469 n.25.
Thucydides, *I, 126-7*: 433 n.88; *I,
142*: 321; *II, 60-5*: 331; *IV, 103,
106*: 345; *VIII, 67, 3*: 488 n.33.
Tzetzes, *Chiliades: V, 729*: 433 n.91,
n.94.

VALERIUS MAXIMUS, *V, 3, 3*: 494
n.91.
Varro, *De re rustica: II, 5, 4*: 441 n.21.

Vitruvius, *De architectura: V, 6, 8*: 497
n.23.

XENOPHON, *Anabasis: IV, 2, 3*: 469
n.26, 471 n.42; *Cynegetics: V, 14,
IX, 10*: 146; *Cyropedia: III, 1, 38*:
425 n.31; *Hellenica: III, 1-3*: 211;
III, 5, 8: 487 n.29; *Constitution of
the Lacedaemonians: III, 5*: 465 n.19.

This edition designed by Bruce Mau
Type composed by Archie at Canadian Composition
Printed and bound Smythe-sewn by Arcata Graphics/Halliday
using Sebago acid-free paper